TAKING THE STAND

ALSO BY ALAN DERSHOWITZ

The Trials of Zion

The Case for Moral Clarity: Israel, Hamas and Gaza

The Case Against Israel's Enemies: Exposing Jimmy Carter and Others Who Stand in the Way of Peace

Is There a Right to Remain Silent? Coercive Interrogation and the Fifth Amendment after 9/11

Finding Jefferson: A Lost Letter, a Remarkable Discovery, and the First Amendment in an Age of Terrorism

Blasphemy: How the Religious Right Is Hijacking Our Declaration of Independence

Preemption: A Knife That Cuts Both Ways

What Israel Means to Me: By 80 Prominent Writers, Performers, Scholars, Politicians, and Journalists

Rights from Wrongs: A Secular Theory of the Origins of Rights

America on Trial: Inside the Legal Battles That Transformed Our Nation

The Case for Peace: How the Arab-Israeli Conflict Can Be Resolved

The Case for Israel

America Declares Independence

Why Terrorism Works: Understanding the Threat, Responding to the Challenge

Shouting Fire: Civil Liberties in a Turbulent Age

Letters to a Young Lawyer

Supreme Injustice: How the High Court Hijacked Election 2000

Genesis of Justice: Ten Stories of Biblical Injustice That Led to the Ten Commandments and Modern Law

Just Revenge

Sexual McCarthyism: Clinton, Starr, and the Emerging Constitutional Crisis

The Vanishing American Jew: In Search of Jewish Identity for the Next Century

Reasonable Doubts: The Criminal Justice System and the O.J. Simpson Case

The Abuse Excuse: And Other Cop-Outs, Sob Stories, and Evasions of Responsibility

The Advocate's Devil

Contrary to Popular Opinion

Chutzpah

Taking Liberties: A Decade of Hard Cases, Bad Laws, and Bum Raps

Reversal of Fortune: Inside the von Bülow Case

The Best Defense

Criminal Law: Theory and Process (with Joseph Goldstein and Richard Schwartz)

Psychoanalysis, Psychiatry and Law (with Joseph Goldstein and Jay Katz)

TAKING THE STAND

MY LIFE IN THE LAW

ALAN DERSHOWITZ

CROWN PUBLISHERS / NEW YORK

Published in the United States by Crown Publishers,
an imprint of the Crown Publishing Group,
a division of Random House LLC,
a Penguin Random House Company, New York.
www.crownpublishing.com

Library of Congress Cataloging-in-Publication Data
Dershowitz, Alan M.
Taking the stand : an autobiography / by Alan Dershowitz.—First edition.
pages cm.
1. Dershowitz, Alan M. 2. Lawyers—United States—Biography. 3. Jewish lawyers—United States—Biography. 4. Law teachers—United States—Biography. 5. Freedom of speech—United States—Cases. 6. Capital punishment—United States—Cases. I. Title.
KF373.D46A3 2013
340.092—dc23
[B] 2013022762

ISBN 978-0-307-71927-0
eISBN 978-0-307-71929-4

Printed in the United States of America

Book design by Ralph Fowler, rlf design
Jacket design by Eric White
Jacket photography: Michael Weschler

10 9 8 7 6 5 4 3 2 1

First Edition

This book is lovingly dedicated to my family—

past, present, and future.

L'dor v'dor.

CONTENTS

PART IV

THE NEVER-ENDING QUEST FOR EQUALITY AND JUSTICE

INTRODUCTION

A Life of Continuous Change

An autobiographer is like a defendant who takes the stand. We all have the right to remain silent, in life and in law. But if one elects to bear witness, he must tell the truth, the whole truth, and nothing but the truth, subject only to limited privileges, such as between a lawyer and a client, or a husband and a wife.

What Tocqueville observed two centuries ago—that in our country, great issues find their way into courts[1]—is even truer today. Accordingly, my autobiography will be a history of the last half century as seen through the eyes of a lawyer privileged to have participated in some of the most intriguing and important cases and controversies of our era. It is also an account of one man's intellectual and ideological development during a dramatic period of world, American, and Jewish history, enriched with anecdotes and behind-the-scenes stories from my life and the lives of those I have encountered.

The law has changed considerably over the past half century. I have not only observed and written about these changes, I have helped to bring some about through litigation, writing, and teaching. This book presents an account of these changes and of my participation in the cases that precipitated them. My commitment to full disclosure requires that I not hide behind the distorting shield of feigned humility—calculated to preempt criticism—that denies the reader an accurate picture of the impact the author has had on events.[2] (One of my favorite jokes is about feigned humility: The pompous rabbi prostrates himself on Yom Kippur, shouting to God, "I am nothing before you." The equally pompous cantor emulates the rabbi, shouting even louder, "I am less than nothing before you." The lowly sexton ("shammes"), seeing the rabbi and the cantor engaging in such self-flagellation, also gets down on his knees and screams, "I too am nothing." The rabbi looks contemptuously at the sexton and whispers to the cantor, "Look who's claiming to be nothing.") Nor will I rewrite my past to conform to present notions of political correctness. Instead, I will try to offer an honest assessment of the roles I have played—for better or worse—in legal developments.

You may have witnessed my public persona—confrontational, unapologetic, brash, tough, argumentative, and uncompromising. These characteristics have provoked strong reactions, both positive and negative, rarely neutral. Yet those who know me—family, friends, and colleagues—hardly recognize the "character" I come across as on TV. In my personal life, I shy away from confrontation and am something of a pushover. My son Elon says that when people bring me up in conversation, he can instantly tell whether they know me from TV or from personal interactions—whether they know what he calls "the Dersh Character" or "the real Alan."

This sharp dichotomy between my public and private persona was brought home to me vividly when a motion picture, *Reversal of Fortune*,[3] was made about the Claus von Bülow case. I was played by Tony Award–winning actor Ron Silver.

The opening scene had my character playing an energetic basketball game with himself—true enough. When he's interrupted by a phone call giving him the news that he has lost a case involving two brothers on death row,[4] he smashes the phone on the pavement. When I complained to my son, who had coproduced the film, that I don't throw phones, my son responded: "Dad, the person on the screen isn't you; it's 'the Dersh Character.'" He explained that characters have to "establish themselves" early in a film, and that this establishing was intended to convey my passion for the rights of criminal defendants. "If we had several hours, we could have recounted your involvement in many other cases, but we had about a minute; hence the smashed phone."

"That scene doesn't show passion," I said. "It shows a temper tantrum." My son explained that a character has to have faults, so that he can "overcome" them. "The viewing audience has to see you grow."

In the film, I'm portrayed as a person whose passions are reserved exclusively for his professional life. I hope that's not me, although I have to acknowledge that people who know me only professionally assume that I have nothing left for those I love. They see me busily at work in different jobs—professor, author, litigator, lecturer, and television commentator—

and they assume that either I never sleep or that there are several of me. But the fact is that I reserve a lot of love, loyalty, and friendship for family and people close to me. I even make time for having fun—ball games, concerts, walks on the beach, parties, jokes, and schmoozing.

In this book, I intend to explore both sides of my life, the interaction between them, and how they are both the products of my early upbringing and lifelong experiences. So if you think you know me from my public appearances, you may be in for a surprise.

Although this autobiography is my first attempt to explore my life in full, I have written books that touch on earlier aspects of my public life. *The Best Defense*[5] dealt with my first cases. *Reversal of Fortune*[6] and *Reasonable Doubts*[7] each dealt with one specific case (von Bülow and O. J. Simpson). *Chutzpah*[8] covered my Jewish causes. I will try not to repeat what I wrote in those books.[9] This more ambitious effort seeks to place my entire professional life into the broader context of how the law has changed over the past half century and how my private life prepared me to play a role in these changes.

I bring to this task a strong and dynamic worldview, shaped by my experiences. In looking back, I am inevitably peering through the prism of the ideology that has provided a compass for my actions.

I believe that ideology *is* biography. Where we stand (and who and what we can't stand) is the result of where we sat, whom we sat next to, what we sat through, and how we reacted to our experiences. The philosopher Descartes, who famously said, "I think therefore I am,"[10] got it backwards. I am—I was, I will be—therefore I think what I think.[11] It is our interactions—with other human beings, with nature, with nurture, with love, with hate, with pleasure, with pain, with our own limitations and mortality—that shape our worldviews. It is also our genetic endowment—our temperament, our energy, our intelligence.

And our luck! An old Yiddish saying puts it succinctly: "Man plans, God laughs."

Many of the most important decisions that impact a person's life are made by others and are beyond his control. Probably the most significant decisions affecting my life were made by my great-grandparents and grandparents: the decision to leave the shtetels of Poland and move to New York. Had they remained in Europe, as some of my relatives did, I would probably not have survived the Holocaust, since I was three years old when the systematic genocide began.[12] Nearly all my relatives who remained in Poland were murdered by the Nazis. That may be why Jews of my generation are so influenced by the Holocaust. There but for the grace of God, and the forethought of our grandparents, go we.[13]

My life has been very different from the lives of my grandparents and parents, who lived insular lives in the Jewish shtetels of Galicia, Poland, the Lower East Side of Manhattan, and the Williamsburg, Crown Heights, and Boro Park Orthodox Jewish neighborhoods of Brooklyn. They had little formal education and rarely traveled beyond their routes to and from work.[14] My grandparents never flew on airplanes despite living into the 1970s and '80s. My parents rarely attended concerts, the Broadway theater, or dance recitals. They owned no art, few books, and no classical records. They didn't visit museums or galleries. Their exposure to culture was limited to things Jewish—cantorial recitations, Yiddish theater, lectures by Orthodox rabbis, Jewish museums, Catskill Mountain and Miami Beach entertainment.

My adult life has been different. I travel the globe, meet with world leaders, own art, am involved in music, theater, and other forms of culture, and lead a secular life (though I too enjoy cantorial music, "borscht belt" humor, Miami Beach, and a good pastrami sandwich—which you can't get in Miami Beach).

Yet I am their son and grandson. Although my life has taken a different course, I could not begin to explain who I am and where I am heading without exploring my background and heritage. It is this history that helped to form me, caused me to react against parts of it, and—most important—gave me the tools necessary to choose which aspects of my traditions to accept and which to reject.

I was born to a family with strong views on religion, morality, politics, and community service. Our neighborhood was tightly knit. Everyone knew his place. Status was important, as was *yichus* (the Yiddish term for ancestry). But I grew up at a time of change, growth, excitement, and opportunity.

Despite the reality of anti-Jewish discrimination—in college admission, employment, residency, and social clubs—my generation believed there were no limits to what we could accomplish. If Jackie Robinson could play second base for the Brooklyn Dodgers, we could do anything. Maybe that was the reason so many successful people grew up in Brooklyn in the postwar period. (In 1971, I was selected from among forty young scholars for a distinguished fellowship. When the fellows met in Palo Alto, California, we discovered close to half the group had Brooklyn roots!) We were the breakout generation, standing on the broad shoulders and backbreaking work of our immigrant grandparents and working-class parents.[15] We are not smarter than our forebears, only luckier to have been born at a time of greater opportunities to be educated, to choose careers, and to thrive in an expanding economy. As a bumper sticker I saw near the Harvard Business School put it: DON'T CONFUSE BRAINS WITH A BULL MARKET. My parents came of age during the Depression. I came of age during a bull market.

I cannot explain my worldview without describing those on whose shoulders I stand. So I will begin at the beginning, with my earliest memories.

But formative experiences do not, of course, end at childhood or adolescence. Learning never stops, at least for those with open minds and hearts. A quip attributed to Winston Churchill put it this way: "Show me a young conservative and I'll show you someone with no heart. Show me an old liberal and I'll show you someone with no brain."[16] It is true that some young liberals become less idealistic with age, economic security, and family responsibilities. But it is also true that some young conservatives become more liberal as they seek common ground with their children. Others remain true to their earlier worldviews, depending on the lives they have lived.

I have been fortunate to live an ever-changing life. Although my views on particular issues have been modified, my basic commitment to liberal values has remained constant, because of my strong upbringing and because I have spent my life among students, who bring to the classroom the views of their contemporaries. An ancient Chinese curse says, "May you live in interesting times." I have been blessed with living an interesting, if often controversial, life.

As an adolescent, I was involved in causes such as justice for the Rosenbergs, abolition of the death penalty, and the end of McCarthyism. In college and law school I became passionate about civil rights, civil liberties, and politics.

As a law clerk, during one of the most dramatic periods of our judicial history, I worked on some of the most important constitutional cases of the Warren court, heard the "I Have a Dream" speech of Martin Luther King, was close to the Cuban Missile Crisis, and partook of events following the assassination of John F. Kennedy.

As a young lawyer, I played a role in the Pentagon Papers case, the forced resignation of Richard Nixon, and the antiwar prosecutions of Dr. Spock, the Chicago Seven, the Weather Underground, and Patricia Hearst. I litigated the *I Am Curious (Yellow)* censorship prosecution, the

Deep Throat case, and the *Hair* case. I consulted on the Chappaquiddick investigation of Ted Kennedy, the attempted deportation of John Lennon, and the draft case against Muhammad Ali. I helped to formulate the strategy designed to strike down the death penalty as unconstitutional, and I litigated all types of cases that broadened freedom of expression under the First Amendment and the right to a zealous defense under the Sixth Amendment.

Later in my career, I was a lawyer in the Bill Clinton impeachment, the *Bush v. Gore* election case, and the efforts to free Nelson Mandela, Natan Sharansky, and other political prisoners. I participated in the Senate censure of California senator Alan Cranston, the Frank Snepp CIA censorship case, prosecutions in The Hague involving the former Yugoslavia, the defense of Israel against international war crime prosecution, and the investigation of WikiLeaks and Julian Assange. I worked on the appeal of Jonathan Pollard and was an observer at the trial of accused Nazi war criminal John Demjanjuk and subsequently consulted with the Israeli government about that case. I worked on the defense of director John Landis, the O. J. Simpson double murder case, and the Bakke "affirmative action" litigation. I challenged the tenure denial of Maoist Bruce Franklin at Stanford and Harvard's investigation of Dr. John Mack, who wrote about human contact with extraterrestrials. I appealed the Claus von Bülow attempted murder conviction, the Leona Helmsley tax case, the Mike Tyson rape prosecution, the Conrad Black fraud conviction, the David Crosby drug rap, and the Tison brothers multiple murder case. I participated in the Woody Allen–Mia Farrow child custody litigation, the defense of Michael Milken, the litigation against the cigarette industry, and the wrongful death suit on behalf of Stephen J. Gould.

I have litigated or consulted on cases and causes throughout the world, including the Ukraine, the Soviet Union, the Russian Federation, the Republic of Georgia, Italy, Israel, China, New Zealand, Australia, Great Britain, Poland, the Vatican, France, Libya, The Hague, Norway, Sweden, Switzerland, Germany, South Africa, Pakistan, and Macedonia.

I have won more than one hundred cases and have been called—with a bit of hyperbole—"the winningest appellate criminal defense lawyer in history." Of the more than three dozen murder and attempted murder cases in which I have participated, I lost only a handful. None of my capital punishment clients has been executed.

I will describe and analyze some of these cases and reveal the unique tactics I have developed over the years that helped win so many of them.

Among the people I have advised in legal, political, and other matters are President Barack Obama; President Bill Clinton; Israeli prime minister Benjamin Netanyahu; Canadian prime minister Pierre Trudeau; Assistant Secretary General of the United Nations Luis Maria Gomez; Senator Ted Kennedy; Marlon Brando; Frank Sinatra; Woody Harrelson; Michael Jackson; Natalie Portman; Ben and Casey Affleck; David Merrick; Bill Belichick; Isabella Rossellini; Adnan Khashoggi; Carly Simon; Hakeem Olajuwon; Kevin Youkilis; Stan Getz; Peter Max; Yo-Yo Ma; Steven Wright; Robert Downey, Jr.; several billionaires, such as Sheldon Adelson and Mark Rich; authors such as Saul Bellow, David Mamet, and Elie Wiesel; and judges, senators, congressmen, governors, and other public officials.

In addition I have played a role in some of the most interesting litigations involving people who are not well known but whose cases raised intriguing and fascinating issues, such as whether a man can be prosecuted for attempted murder for shooting a dead body that he thought was alive,[17] whether a husband can be prosecuted on charges of slavery for not doing anything about his wife's alleged abuse of domestic employees,[18] whether a husband can be forced to adopt a child,[19] whether a law firm can discriminate on ethnic grounds in its decision to promote an associate to partner,[20] and whether a tenured professor of psychiatry should be investigated for publishing a book suggesting that some of his patients may actually have been abducted by space aliens.[21]

Among the broad constitutional and legal questions I have confronted in my practice and teaching are the following:

- Should governments be empowered to censor speech that endangers national security, defames or offends individuals, falsifies history, or provokes violence?

- Should the death penalty be imposed on a nontriggerman who did not intend to cause the death of a victim?

- Should governments, universities, or employers be allowed to consider race in order to achieve positive goals such as diversity, reparation, or representation?

- Should evidence that conclusively proves the guilt of a criminal defendant—even one charged with multiple murders—be admissible against him if it was obtained in violation of his constitutional rights?

- Should a president be impeached for lying about his sex life?
- Should the courts order a recount of a hotly disputed presidential election?
- Should the President be allowed to secure a warrant to authorize the use of nonlethal torture in an effort to prevent an imminent mass-casualty terrorist attack?
- Should governments be permitted to target and kill suspected terrorists whom they cannot arrest?
- Should the Palestinian Authority be authorized to bring criminal charges against Israeli officials in the International Criminal Court?

An Italian magazine, after reviewing my cases, described my legal practice—also with some hyperbole—as "the most fascinating on the planet," and a biographer of Clarence Darrow, when asked by National Public Radio whether there was "any attorney in this country today with the stature of a Clarence Darrow," responded by mentioning me and saying that my cases "equaled some of the trials that Darrow had."[22]

My cases have been more interesting because I have brought the classroom into the courtroom, and my classes have been interesting because I bring the courtroom into the classroom. I have learned a great deal from my students, as I hope they have from me. I have always been skeptical of the distinction between "theory" and "practice" when it comes to a real-world discipline such as law. Theory has helped me to win cases, and practice has helped me to teach students. Both have been a major source of my writing. My primary job has been that of a professor and writer. I have taught thousands of students during the one hundred semesters of my career at Harvard. Some have gone on to become world, national, and local leaders, in politics, in the judiciary, in education, in business, and in the arts. I remain in touch with many of them.

In the first phase of my academic career, I focused my writing on scholarly articles for law reviews, publishing more than two dozen on law and psychiatry and the prediction and prevention of violence.

In the next phase, I turned to writing articles for the general public about the law, becoming the first law professor regularly to write about legal issues for the Week in Review, Book Review, and op-ed sections of the *New York Times*;[23] to appear frequently on television shows, such as *Nightline*, the *MacNeil-Lehrer Report*, *Larry King Live*, *The Today Show*, and

Good Morning America; and to write about the law in popular magazines, ranging from the *New York Review* to *Penthouse*.[24]

In the third phase, I began to write books for the general public, including six national bestsellers and one—*Chutzpah*—that became the number one bestseller in the United States. I have written thirty books, including three novels, and continue to write every day about a wide range of subjects, including sports, art, politics, literature, and even delicatessens.[25]

I write everything by hand, and one of my secretaries, who types my scribbles, has estimated that she types a million of my words each year. I venture to guess that I've probably published more words (not necessarily wiser or better) than any professor in the law school's history.

I've probably also taught more different courses than most other professors. These include Criminal Law; Constitutional Litigation; Family Law; Psychiatry and the Law; Prediction and Prevention of Harmful Conduct; Comparative Criminal Law Theory; Race and Violence; Scriptural Sources of Justice; Law of Sports; Legal, Moral, and Psychological Implications of Shakespeare's Tragedies; Ethics and Tactics in the Trial of Criminal Cases; Human Rights; Terrorism and the Law; Probabilities and the Law; Comparative Analysis of Talmud and Common Law; WikiLeaks and the First Amendment; the Arab-Israeli Conflict Through Literature; Black Power and Its Legal Implications; Writings of Thomas Jefferson; and Constraining Prosecutorial Misconduct.

In addition to my classes at the law school, I have taught numerous classes at Harvard College, including a large course that I created with Professors Robert Nozick and Stephen J. Gould, entitled Thinking About Thinking; a seminar with Professor Stephen Kosslyn on Neurobiology and the Law; a large class with Professor Steve Pinker on Taboos; and a series of freshman seminars entitled Where Does Your Morality Come From?

I have engaged in public debates and controversies with some of the most contentious figures of the age, including William F. Buckley, Noam Chomsky, Rabbi Meir Kahane, Rabbi Adin Steinsaltz, Justice Antonin Scalia, Ken Starr, Elie Wiesel, Václav Havel, Golda Meir, Red Auerbach, William Kunstler, Roy Cohn, Norman Mailer, Patrick Buchanan, Norman Podhoretz, Bill O'Reilly, Sean Hannity, Skip Gates, Alan Keyes, Dennis Prager, Jeremy Ben-Ami, Peter Beinart, Mike Huckabee, William Bulger, Hannah Arendt, Wayne La Pierre, James Zogby, Jimmy Carter, Richard Goldstone, Norman Finkelstein, and others.

I was part of an American team selected to confront Soviet debaters on a nationally televised show, during the height of the Soviet oppression of refuseniks, for which William Buckley suggested that the U.S. team be given Medals of Freedom. I was a regular "advocate" on the nationally televised Peabody Award–winning show *The Advocates*. I have been interviewed by nearly every major television and radio talk and news show.

In recent years, I have devoted considerable energy to the defense of Israel, while remaining critical of some of its policies. The *Forward* has called me "America's most public Jewish defender"[26] and "Israel's single most visible defender—the Jewish state's lead attorney in the court of public opinion."[27] In 2010, the *Jerusalem Post* surveyed its readers and editors as to who were the fifty most influential Jews in the world. The readers ranked me fifth, while the editors placed me ninth.[28] In 2010, the prime minister of Israel asked me to become Israel's ambassador to the United Nations—an offer I respectfully declined because I am an American, not an Israeli, citizen.

I keep fairly complete records of my cases and controversies. My archives are in the Brooklyn College Library. My professional life has been an open book, and the accessibility of my archives—containing letters, drafts, and other unpublished material—opens the book even further.

But beyond the written record lies a trove of memories, ideas, dreams, conversations, actions, inactions, passions, joys, and feelings. Fortunately, I have a very good memory, and I am prepared to open much of my memory bank in this autobiography, because I believe that the biography that informs my ideology and life choices cannot be limited to the externalities of my career. It must dig deeper into the thought processes that motivate actions, inactions, and choices. I don't know how much I will be able to retrieve, but I will try. Nor can I be absolutely certain that all of my memories are photographically precise, since my children chide me that my stories get "better" with each retelling.

The law has changed in the half century I have been practicing and teaching it. If the past is the best predictor of the future, then it will change even more during the next half century. I will risk making some predictions about the changes we might anticipate.

Oliver Wendell Holmes once admonished his young colleagues that "it is required [that you] share the passion and action of [your] time at peril of being judged not to have lived."[29]

I have lived the passion and action of my times. I now wish to share these experiences with my readers.

PART I

FROM BROOKLYN TO CAMBRIDGE

With Stops in New Haven and Washington

I

BORN AND RELIGIOUSLY EDUCATED IN BROOKLYN

Williamsburg and Boro Park

I was born on September 1, 1938, in a hospital—the first in my family not delivered at home. My parents lived in the Williamsburg neighborhood of Brooklyn, having moved as youngsters from the Lower East Side of Manhattan. Their parents were Orthodox Jews who had emigrated from Poland at the end of the nineteenth and the beginning of the twentieth century.[1] When my mother was pregnant with my brother, Nathan, who is four years younger than me, we moved to the Boro Park neighborhood of Brooklyn, where I grew up and where my parents remained until their deaths. The Boro Park of my youth was a Modern Orthodox community of second-generation Jews. Following the end of World War II, some displaced persons who had survived the Holocaust moved into the neighborhood. The current occupants of Boro Park are Chasidic Jews who have moved from Williamsburg seeking to re-create the shtetels of Eastern Europe. (My daughter Ella and her contemporaries now see Williamsburg as a cool neighborhood—a far cry from the "old country" where grandparents with Yiddish accents lived when I was growing up.)

My parents grew up in Williamsburg during the peak of the Depression. My mother, Claire, had been a very good student at Eastern District High School, graduating with honors at fifteen and a half. She then enrolled at City College in the fall of 1929—the first of her family to attend college. She was forced by her father's deteriorating economic situation to leave before the end of the semester. She worked as a bookkeeper, earning $12 a week.

My father, who was not a good student, attended Torah V'Daas—translated as "Bible and Knowledge"—Yeshiva in Williamsburg. He began to work during high school and never attended college.

My grandparents knew each other from the neighborhood. My grandfathers were both *chazanim*, cantors, who sang the Jewish liturgy in small synagogues, called *shteebles*. They were involved in the founding of several Jewish institutions, including a free loan society, a burial society, the Young Israel synagogue, and the Torah V'Daas Yeshiva.[2] Their day jobs were typical for their generation of immigrants. Louis Dershowitz sold corrugated boxes. Naphtali Ringel was a jeweler. My grandmothers, Ida and Blima, took care of their children. Each had eight, but two of Blima's died of diphtheria during an epidemic. My mother, Blima's second surviving child, nearly died during the influenza outbreak of 1917, but according to family lore, she was saved by being "bleeded."

Born toward the end of the Depression and exactly a year to the day before the outbreak of the Second World War, I was the first of more than thirty grandchildren on both sides of my family.

My maternal grandfather had been married to my grandmother's older sister, who died during childbirth, leaving two children. Pursuant to Jewish tradition, he then married the younger sister, my grandmother Blima, who was fifteen. In the 1930s, he traveled to Palestine by boat. Having little money, he worked as a *mashkeach*—the person whose job it was to make sure the Kosher food was ritually acceptable—to earn his fare. Once in Palestine, he purchased a small parcel of land on which he someday hoped to build a home, but he quickly realized that he couldn't earn a living there and returned to Brooklyn. Several years later, he suddenly died. Since I was a toddler, I knew him only through family memories and sepia photographs. My grandmother, who still had three unmarried daughters at home, one son in the army, and another in California,[3] could not afford to maintain her apartment, so my family moved in and my father paid the rent. We took in a border to help with the expenses, and I shared a room with her. After about a year, we moved to our own small apartment and then to the two-and-a-half-family house in which I grew up.

My paternal great-grandfather, Zecharja, who was the first of us to arrive in America in 1888, died in 1921 at age sixty-two. His wife, Lea, died in 1941, at age eighty-two, and I vaguely remember her.

My family has now been in the United States for more than half of our nation's existence. Most of Zecharja's numerous descendants have been very religious and relatively poor, giving rise to the family quip that the Dershowitzes have the lowest rate of wealth to time in America of any Jewish family.[4] My grandfather Louis Dershowitz died when I was fifteen (he was seventy-one), so I knew him as a child. Though poor, he was respected for having saved many relatives from the Holocaust, by creating "jobs" for them as rabbis, cantors, ritual slaughterers, and other religious functionaries. The questionable affidavits he had concocted to "make up" these jobs helped to secure visas for twenty-eight of his European relatives, who arrived in America just before the outbreak of the war. A twenty-ninth relative, a young girl who was studying the violin in Poland, was trapped. My grandfather refused to give up on her, sending his oldest, unmarried son—my uncle Menash—into the belly of the beast to find and "marry" her, so she could come to America. Although the marriage was supposed to be a sham, it lasted for more than fifty years, ending with their deaths less than a year apart.

Both of my grandmothers, Blima and Ida, lived to ripe old ages (Blima into her nineties, Ida into her eighties), and I knew them well. Blima played a significant role in my upbringing, since my mother worked and "Gramma Ringel" was always there to serve me milk and her homemade cookies when I came home from school.

Among my earliest memories were vignettes from the Second World War, which ended when I was nearly seven. I can see my father pasting on the Frigidaire door newspaper maps depicting the progress of Allied troops. I remember hearing radio accounts, in deep, stentorian voices, from WOR (which I thought spelled "war"), announcing military victories. I can still sing a ditty (sung to the tune of the Disney song from *Snow White*):

Whistle while you work
Hitler is a jerk
Mussolini is a meanie
And the Japs are worse[5]

The comic books we read during the war always pitted the superheroes against the Nazis and the "Japs," and I wanted to help. I decided that if Billy Batson could turn into Captain Marvel by simply shouting "Shazam!," so could I. And so, after making a cape out of a red towel, I jumped out of the window yelling "Shazam!" Fortunately, I lived on the first floor and I only sustained a scraped knee and a bad case of disillusionment.[6]

When I was four years old, German spies landed on Long Island in a submarine. Although they were quickly captured, there were rumors of other planned landings. If I couldn't help our war effort by turning myself into a superhero, at least I could look out for German spies. Over the next few summers, which my family spent in a rented room near Rockaway Beach, a police officer paid us kids a penny a day to be on the lookout for "Kraut subs." We took our job seriously and spotted a few suspicious objects that turned out to be birds, or flotsam and jetsam.

I remember both VE (Victory in Europe) and VJ (Victory over Japan) days. There was dancing in the streets, block parties, and prayers. Our soldiers, including several of my uncles, were coming home. (My father received a medical deferment because he had an ulcer, which my mother said was caused by my bad behavior.)[7]

We weren't told of the Holocaust or Shoah, just that we had lost many relatives in Europe to Hitler (*Yemach Sh'mo*—"May his name be erased"). We cheered Hitler's death, which, according to a Jewish joke, we knew would occur on a Jewish holiday—because whatever day he died would *be* a Jewish holiday![8]

The "greenies" (recent immigrants, "greenhorns") who moved to Boro Park from the displaced persons camps never talked about what had happened "over there." The tattooed numbers on their arms remained unexplained, though we knew they were dark reminders of terrible events. Even my grandfather rarely talked about the noble role he had played in saving family members, because he knew how many friends had lost relatives in Europe. My maternal grandparents lost nearly all their families, except for one couple who had managed to emigrate to Palestine before the war.

I grew up in a home entirely free of any racial prejudice. My parents admired black leaders (we called them "Negro" or "colored"). My father, who sold men's work clothing and underwear, had several black customers, whom he treated as equals. My favorite college professor was black. Once every two weeks my mother hired a "cleaning woman" to dust and help her with the house. Some were black. Some were white. A few were Jewish immigrants. The only bigotry I remember was directed against Hungarian Jews by my maternal grandmother. She had obviously brought her prejudice with her from Poland. Following the end of World War II, several Hungarian Jewish families moved into the neighborhood. My grandmother immediately expressed a dislike. I recall her joking about the recipe for a Hungarian omelet: "First steal two eggs!"

Among my other memories was Israel's struggle for statehood. My family members were religious Zionists. We had blue-and-white Jewish

National Fund *pushkas* ("charity boxes") in our homes, and every time we made a phone call, we were supposed to deposit a penny. We sang the "Jewish National Anthem" ("Hatikvah") in school assemblies. I still remember its original words, before Israel became a state: *"lashuv l'eretz avosainv"* ("to return to the land of our ancestors").

One particular incident remains a painful memory. My mother had a friend named Mrs. Perlestein, whose son Moshe went off to fight in Israel's War of Independence. There was a party to celebrate his leaving. Several months later, I saw my mother crying. Moshe had been killed, along with thirty-four other Jewish soldiers and civilians, trying to bring supplies to a Jewish outpost near Jerusalem. My mother kept sobbing, "She was in the movies, when her son was killed." Israel's war had come home. Everyone in the neighborhood knew Moshe. He had attended my elementary school, played stickball on my block, and was a hero. It was a shared tragedy, and Moshe's death—combined with my mother's reaction to it—had a profound and lasting effect on me.

My friends and I formed a "club"—really just a group of kids who played ball together. We named it "the Palmach"—after the Israeli strike force that was helping to win the war. We memorized the Palmach anthem, *"Rishonim, tamid anachnu tamid, anu, anu Hapalmach."* ("We are always the first, we are the Palmach.")

VIGNETTE

Vidal Sassoon

Several years ago, I spoke to a Jewish group in Los Angeles, and among the guests were David Steinberg (the comedian) and the late Vidal Sassoon (the style master). Steinberg mentioned to me that when Sassoon was young, he fought for the Palmach. (If you think that seems unlikely, consider that "Dr. Ruth" Westheimer served as a sniper in the same war.) I challenged Sassoon to sing the Palmach anthem, and before you knew it, Sassoon and I were loudly belting out the Hebrew words to the amusement of the other surprised guests.

Israel declared statehood in May 1948, when I was nine years old. Following its bold declaration that after two thousand years of exile, there has arisen a Jewish state in the Land of Israel (supported by the United Nations, the United States, the Soviet Union, and most Western nations), the nascent state was attacked by the armies of the surrounding Arab countries. One out of every hundred Israeli men, women, and children were killed while defending their new state—some in cold blood, after surrendering. Many of those killed had managed to survive the Holocaust. That summer I went to a Hebrew-speaking Zionist summer camp called Massad (where the counselor in an adjoining bunk was Noam Chomsky, then a fervent left-wing Zionist). We heard daily announcements regarding the War of Independence. We sang Israeli songs, danced the hora, and played sports using Hebrew words (a strike was a *shkeya*, a ball a *kadur*).

Shortly after Israel defended itself against the Arab attacks, we learned of a new threat to the Jewish people: Stalin's campaign against Jewish writers, politicians, and Zionists. Stalin became the new Hitler as we read about show trials, pogroms, and executions of Jews. We hated Communism almost as much as we hated fascism. We were also frightened of the threat posed by the Soviet Union, with its atomic arsenal. Our school made us practice running to the "shelter" in the event of a nuclear attack. During my latter years in elementary school, I wrote the following poem:

Engines all around us roaring with steam
Powerfull [sic, *powerful*] *bombers and jets that gleam*
Sources [sic, *saucers*] *in the skyline, vechels* [sic, *vehicles*] *on earth*
Atomic energy surrounding us from birth
Medical wonders, and scientific news
Wonderfull [sic, *wonderful*] *progress, we hope to never loose* [sic, *lose*]
But someday, in the future when energy turns to bombs
Atoms spliting [sic, *splitting*] *all around us recking* [sic, *wrecking*] *homes and farms.*
Someday in the future we shall be in the past.
Without electric bulbs to warm us—and without the funsets [sic, *furnace's*] *blast.*

These early memories contributed significantly to my emerging ideology and worldview. My family's politics were liberal, Zionist, and anti-Communist. Presidents Roosevelt and Truman and Mayor La Guardia were our heroes.

Although there were plenty of discussions about current events, politics, and religion, our home had few books, little music, no art, no secular culture. My parents were smart but had no time or patience for these "luxuries." Our apartment was modest—the ground floor of a two-and-a-half-family house. The upstairs was rented to my uncle, aunt, and their two children, while the finished basement was rented to my cousin and her husband, who had recently been discharged from the army. We lived in two small bedrooms, the smaller of which I shared with my brother. We ate in the kitchen. My mother's dream, never realized, was to have "a real dining room." The living room, which had the mandatory couch covered with plastic, was reserved for guests (who were rare). The tiny bathroom was shared by the four of us. The foyer doubled as a dining area for Shabbos meals. The total area was about one thousand square feet. But we had an outside—and what an outside it was! In the front there was a small garden and a stoop. In the rear we had a tiny back porch, a yard, and a garage. Since we had no car, we rented the garage to another cousin, who used it to store the toys he sold wholesale.

We were not poor. We always had food. But we couldn't afford luxuries, such as restaurants. We passed down clothing from generation to generation and ate a lot of "leftovers." (Remember the comedian who said, "We always ate leftovers—nobody has ever found the 'original' meal.") My mother has always said we were "comfortable." (The same comedian told about the Jewish man who was hit by a car and was lying on the ground when the ambulance attendant asked him, "Are you comfortable?" He replied, "I make a living.") I worked at part-time jobs beginning in elementary school and throughout high school and college—delivery boy, deli slicer, babysitter, Bar Mitzvah tutor, camp waiter and counselor.

VIGNETTE

Deli Guy

My first job was as a deli guy in a kosher delicatessen on the Lower East Side of New York. I tied the strings on the hot dogs and took pickles out of the barrels. One day I was locked in the freezer with an elderly worker, who figured out, fortunately for both of us, how to open the door from the inside. I also made deliveries on my bike. I couldn't drive, because I was only fourteen. One of my teachers, to whom I made a delivery, had suggested I become a deli guy.

Nearly half a century later, I opened a kosher deli in Harvard Square, in partnership with several friends. We called it Mavin's Kosher Court. The reviews were great, there were always lines to get in, but we were losing about two bucks a sandwich. With the high price of importing good pastrami and corned beef from New York, and with the need to close on Friday night and Saturday, we simply couldn't turn a profit. And so in less than a year, we paid off all our debts and closed shop. It turns out I wasn't suited to be a deli guy after all.

The social heart of our home was the front stoop. We conversed on it, played stoop ball on it, jumped from it, and slid down the sides. It was like a personal playground. On nice days, the family was on the stoop. We listened to the radio—Brooklyn Dodger baseball games, *The Lone Ranger, Can You Top This?, The Shadow, Captain Midnight*, and *The Arthur Godfrey Show* (we hadn't yet learned of his anti-Semitism)—with the radio connected to an inside socket by a long, frayed extension cord. We ate lunch on the stoop, had our milk and cookies on the stoop when we got back from school, traded jokes and even did our homework on the stoop. Mostly, we just sat on the stoop and talked among ourselves and to passing neighbors, who knew where to find us. In those days, nobody called ahead—phone calls were expensive. They just dropped by.

In front of the stoop was what we called "the gutter." (Today it is referred to as "the street.") The gutter was part of our playground, since cars were rare. We played punch ball in the gutter, stickball in the driveway, and basketball in front of the garage—shooting at a rim screwed to an old Ping-Pong table secured to the roof of the garage by two-by-fours.

Our house became the magnet for my friends because we had a stoop, a hoop, and a gutter in front of our stoop with few trees to hinder the punched ball. (A ball that hit a tree was called a "hindoo"—probably a corruption of "hinder.")

The stereotype of the Brooklyn Jewish home during the post–World War II era was one filled with books, music, art prints, and intellectual parents forcing knowledge into their upwardly mobile male children aspiring to become doctors, professors, lawyers, and businessmen.[9] (The daughters were also taught to be upwardly mobile by marrying the doctors, lawyers, et cetera.)

My home could not have been more different. My musical training was limited to a year of accordion lessons (we couldn't afford a piano), which ended unceremoniously when my cousin who lived upstairs threw my accordion (which cost $20) out the window because he hated "the noise"

I was making. The living room bookshelves were filled with inexpensive tchotchkes. The only books were a faux leather yellow dictionary that my parents got for free by subscribing to *Coronet* magazine. When I was in college, they briefly subscribed to the *Reader's Digest* Condensed Books. There was, of course, a *Chumash* (Hebrew Bible) and half a dozen prayer books. I do not recall seeing my parents read anything but newspapers (the *New York Post*) until I went to college. They were just too busy making a living and keeping house.

There were no bookstores in Boro Park, except for a small used bookshop that seemed to specialize in subversive books. The owner, who smelled like his mildewed books, looked like Trotsky, who he was said to admire. We were warned to stay away, lest we be put on some "list" of subversives.

My parents, especially my mother, were terrified about "lists" and "records." This was, after all, the age of "blacklists," "Red Channels," and other colored compilations that kept anyone on them from getting a job. "They will put you on a list," my mother would warn. Or "It will go on your permanent record." When I was fourteen, I actually did something that may have gotten me on a list

It was during the height of the McCarthy period, shortly after Julius and Ethel Rosenberg had been sentenced to death. A Rosenberg relative was asking people to sign a petition to save the Rosenbergs' lives. I read the petition and it made sense to me, so I signed it. A neighbor observed the transaction and duly reported it to my mother. She was convinced that my life was over, my career ruined, and my willingness to sign a Communist-inspired petition part of my permanent record. My mother decided that I had to be taught a lesson. She told my father the story. I could see that my father was proud of what I had done, but my mother told him to slap me. Ever obedient, he did, causing him, I suspect, more pain than me.[10]

In addition to the "subversive" bookstore, our neighborhood had a library that was tiny and decrepit. When I was nearing the end of high school, a spacious library opened. We went there every Friday afternoon because that's where the girls were and because we could take out up to four books. The two reasons merged when Artie Edelman realized that we could impress the girls by taking out serious books. Up until that time my reading of literature had been limited to Classic Comics.

Don't laugh! Classic Comics were marvelous. Not only could we read about the adventures of Ivanhoe, we could see what he looked like! My first erotic desires were aroused by the illustration of the dark-haired

"Jewess" Rebecca. (I have searched for a copy of this Classic Comic at flea markets to relive my unrequited adolescent lust.)

I recently came across the Classic Comic of *Crime and Punishment*. Having now read three translations of this great work, I was amazed at how faithful the comic was to the tone, atmosphere, and even words of the original. I tried to give it to my granddaughter, who was reading the book for class, but she politely turned down the offer, with an air of condescension that one accepts only from a grandchild.

Among the first real books I read were several to which I had been introduced by the Classic Comics: *The Count of Monte Cristo, The Red Badge of Courage, Moby Dick*, and *A Connecticut Yankee in King Arthur's Court*. (The first three were better than the Classic Comic; the fourth, not as good!)

During my senior year in high school, I became a voracious reader, to the disdain of some family members. My uncle Hedgie (a nickname for Harry) would berate me for sitting around the house reading when I could be working or playing sports. "Be a man," he would demand. "Get off your ass." But I would stay in my tiny room, with my tape recorder playing classical music I had recorded off WQXR, the *New York Times* classical music station, or off a record I borrowed from the library and recorded from my friend Artie's turntable. I also saved enough money from my jobs to buy a used copy of the *Encyclopedia Americana*. My friend Norman Sohn had found an old bookstore on Fourth Avenue in Manhattan that sold used encyclopedias, and the *Americana* cost only $75, as contrasted with the *Britannica*, which was $200.

During my early years, all we had was a small plastic radio that lived in the kitchen, unless it was moved near the stoop. When I was ten years old, we bought a ten-inch TV "console" that included a 78-rpm phonograph player that opened at the top. But my mother had situated her "good" lamp on top of the console, so I couldn't get access to the turntable. With my Bar Mitzvah money, I bought a humongous Webcor reel-to-reel tape recorder, which must have been a foot cubed. I could barely lift it, and the tape often tangled or split, but it was better than the wire recorder technology that it replaced.

I loved classical music, especially opera. As an adolescent I had sung alto in the local synagogue choir, and I had a fairly good voice. My passion for music took me to the Metropolitan Opera House, where for 50 cents, a student could get a seat with a table and a lamp if he came with a score of the opera. We would borrow the score from the library, take a train to Times Square, and listen to Richard Tucker, Robert Merrill, Jan Peerce,

Risë Stevens, and Roberta Peters sing *Carmen*, *La Bohème*, and *La Traviata*. (We were forbidden to listen to Wagner, because he was an anti-Semite whom Hitler admired.)

I also became passionate about art. All kinds of art, from Egyptian and Roman sculpture to Picasso's *Guernica* and Rodin's *The Thinker*. There were no art posters or prints in our home. The walls had mirrors (to make the apartment seem bigger). But there were free museums all around us, and the library had art books—with pictures of naked women! I loved Goya's *Nude Maja*, especially when contrasted with the clothed version, who I imagined was undressing just for me!

The girls loved to be asked on a museum date, and we loved to ask because it was free and it showed them that we had "culture" (pronounced "culchah").

To this day I have no idea how I fell in love with literature, music, and art. I was never exposed to classical music or art, even in school, where our music teacher taught us "exotic" songs like "Finiculi, Funicula," American songs by Stephen Foster, and an assortment of religious and Zionist Hebrew songs ("*Zum Gali, Gali, Gali*," "*Tsena, Tsena*," "*Hayveynu Shalom Alechem*"). Our art teachers tried to teach us to draw "useful" objects, like cars, trains, and horses.

My friends' homes were as barren of culture as mine, with the exception of Artie Edelman and Bernie Beck, whose parents were better educated and more cultured than mine. I must have picked up some appreciation of music and art from them. When I went to sleepaway camp as a junior counselor, I came in contact with music and art through the "rich" Manhattan kids who had attended the expensive camp as paying campers and were now also junior counselors.

None of these peripheral contacts with culture fully explains my transition from a home barren of books, records, and art to my home as an adult, which is filled with books, music, paintings, sculpture, and historical objects.[11]

Nor can I explain why none of my three children has any real passion for the classical arts. They are by no means uncultured. They love popular music, films, current fiction, theater, and gourmet food. But they don't have the same passion for classical music or fine art that my wife and I have. For someone who strongly believes in the power of nurture, exposure, and experience, this generational skip poses a dilemma. My passion may well have been a reaction to my parents, as my children's lack of passion for what moves me so deeply may be a reaction to me. So be it.

The family values that shaped my upbringing focused on Modern Orthodox Judaism, religious Zionism, political liberalism of the sort represented by FDR, anti-Nazism, anti-Communism, opposition to all kinds of discrimination, support for freedom of speech, a hatred of McCarthyism, opposition to the death penalty, a commitment to self-defense and defense of family and community, a strong sense of patriotism, and a desire to be as truly American as was consistent with not assimilating and losing our traditions and heritage.

My father, who was physically strong but rather meek, wanted me to be "a tough Jew" who always "fought back." He urged me to never let "them" get away with "it." By "them" he meant anti-Semites, and by "it" he meant pushing Jews around. He taught me to box and wrestle and insisted that I never "tattle" on my friends, regardless of the consequences to me.

One of my father's brothers was a man named Yitzchak, whom we called Itchie. One day my uncle took me to a Brooklyn Dodgers baseball game that got rained out halfway through. We ran to the train station, only to find no one tending the token booth. My uncle had one token, and so the two of us squeezed through the turnstile on his token. As soon as we got home, he took a dime, put it in an envelope, and sent it to the transit authority, apologizing for temporarily cheating them out of their ten cents. A year later he did the same thing, but on a larger scale. My uncle stowed away on a ship headed for Palestine in order to participate in Israel's struggle for statehood. He did not have enough money for passage, so he hid during the nearly monthlong trip, getting food from a friend who was paying his own way over. My uncle then swam from the ship to shore, evading British authorities. After working for several months, he then sent the full fare for the lowest class of service to the shipping company. Those were the values with which I was brought up. You do what you have to do, but then you pay.

Religion in my home was not a matter of faith or an accepted theology. To this day, I have no idea what my parents believed about the nature of God, the literal truth of the Bible, heaven and hell, or other issues so central to most religions. We never talked about such theological matters. Ours was a religion of rules—of required acts and omissions. A cartoon I once saw perfectly represented my parents' approach to religion. It showed a father dragging his young son in the direction of the synagogue and saying: "Atheist, Shmatheist, I don't care—as long as you come to shul."

Our Judaism was rule-bound. Before every activity, there was a required *brucha*—a formulistic blessing appropriate to the activity. "*Baruch ata*

Adonoy — Blessed be you our God —followed by a reference to His creation: "who brings forth bread from the earth" or "wine from the grapes" or "fruit from the trees" or "produce from the ground." Then there was a generic *brucha* that covered everything not included among the specific blessings: "*Sheh-hakol Nihiye B'Dvaroh.*" My grandmother Ringel, who was the religious enforcer in the family, if she saw me drinking a glass of water would ask demandingly, "Did you make a *shakel*?"—referring to the previously mentioned generic blessing. My grandmother, who spoke no Hebrew, probably had no idea of the literal meaning of the blessing, but she knew—and insisted that I know—you had to recite it (even just mumble it) before you drank the water.

There were rules for everything. If you accidentally used a *milichdika* (dairy) fork on a *flayshidika* (meat) item, the offending item had to be buried in the earth for exactly seven days, which restored its kosher quality. After eating meat, we had to wait precisely six hours before eating dairy. After eating dairy, however, you had to wait only half an hour to eat meat, but a full hour if the "dairy" meal contained fish. When my parents told me the rules of swimming after eating—wait two hours after a heavy meal, one hour after a light meal, half an hour after a piece of fruit, and fifteen minutes after a Hershey bar—I thought these too were religious rules.

From my earliest days, I accepted these highly technical, rule-oriented religious obligations. It was a lot easier for me to obey rules—even if I didn't understand the reasons behind them—than to accept a theology that was always somewhat alien to my rational mind-set. (And I suspect, to my parents', if they even bothered to think about it.) Everyone in the Modern Orthodox community followed the rules. Few, I suspect, accepted the entire theological framework that included the literal truth of the Bible, the resurrection of the dead, heaven and hell (which were not in the Jewish Bible), and the incorporeal nature of a single God. What we cared about was the precise ingredients in a candy bar (no lard or gelatin), the number of steps you could take if your yarmulke fell off, whether you could wear your house key as a tiepin to avoid the prohibition against carrying on the Sabbath, whether it was permissible to use an automatic timer—a "Shabbos clock"—to turn on the TV for a Saturday afternoon World Series game, and whether you could ride in an elevator on Shabbos if it automatically stopped on every floor. The rabbis answered these questions, but they didn't always agree. My mother had little patience with most of the local rabbis because her late father, who was not a rabbi, "knew so much more than they did" and always resolved religious disputes by accepting the approach that was "easiest" and most adaptive to the modern lifestyle. Even my grandmother knew more than these "phony rabbis," my mother would insist contemptuously. My mother always said, "Respect people, not titles." Then she was appalled when I showed disrespect for my frequently incompetent teachers!

Most of the rules we were required to obey were negative ones: Don't—eat unkosher, drive or work on Shabbos, eat anything on fast days, marry a non-Jew, eat ice cream after a hot dog, wear leather on Yom Kippur, talk after washing your hands but before making a "motzie" and eating the challah.

My grandmother—the enforcer—had a favorite Yiddish word: *meturnished*—"it is forbidden to do!" She would shout it out in anticipation of any potential violation. If she saw you about to eat a Nabisco cookie (it bore no magic U that certified the item as kosher), she would intone the M word. If she saw you putting a handkerchief in your pocket on Shabbos, the word would ring in your ear. If you even thought about putting your yarmulke in your pocket, you would hear the word. Once I began to whistle a tune. My musical effort was greeted with a loud "*Meturnished*." "Why?" I implored her. There's nothing in the Torah about whistling. "It is un-Jewish," my grandmother insisted. "The Goyim whistle, we don't." It's now more than thirty years since Grandma Ringel died, but the M word still rings in my ears every time I indulge in a prohibited food or contemplate an un-Jewish activity (such as enjoying a Wagnerian opera). Freud called it the "superego." He too had a Jewish grandmother.

Of course we tried to figure out ways around these prohibitions—half of Jewish law seems to be creating technical prohibitions, while the other half seems to be creating ways around them. Much like the Internal Revenue Code. No wonder so many Jews become lawyers and accountants. It's not in our DNA; it's in our religious training.

A story from my earliest childhood illustrates the extraordinary hold that religion—really observance of religious obligations—held over all of us.

A few months before my brother was born, my father was holding my hand on a busy street, while my mother was shopping. She had just bought me a new pair of high leather shoes—they went above my ankles. For some reason, I bolted away from my father and ran into the street. My foot was run over by an eighteen-wheeler truck. It would have been much worse had my father not pulled me out from under the large vehicle. Fortunately, the new shoes saved my foot from being crushed, but several bones were broken and I was rushed to the nearest hospital, which was Catholic.

My parents left me there. At about 8 P.M. one of the nurses called my mother and said that I was refusing to eat and demanding to go to Florida. My mother said, "He's never even heard of Florida." She was told to come to the hospital. She saw me sitting in front of my tray of food refusing to eat and screaming, "Miami, Miami!" To the nurses, that referred to a city in Florida. My mother understood that I was referring to my "yami"—which was short for yarmulke, the religious skullcap that every Jewish male must wear while eating. I refused to eat without my yami, even though I was only three years old. As soon as my mother made a yarmulke for me out of a handkerchief and placed it on my head, I ate all the food (the Catholic hospital provided kosher food for Jewish patients). I'm sure I mumbled the appropriate *bruchas* for each item of food.

We learned these rules first at home and then in the yeshiva—Jewish day school—which nearly everyone in the neighborhood attended. As is typical in Orthodox Jewish neighborhoods, there were two competing yeshivas: One taught Yiddish, the other Hebrew.

I started out in the Yiddish-speaking, more traditional school, named Torahs Emes (the Truthful Bible), where my grandma Ringel wanted me to go to learn the *mamma loshen*—"the mother tongue." But after two years, my parents switched me to the Hebrew-speaking, more modern yeshiva named Etz Chaim (the Tree of Life), which I attended through eighth grade, when I shifted to a yeshiva high school, where I stayed until I finished twelfth grade.

My yeshiva education was a decidedly mixed blessing. The hours were long: elementary school went from 8:30 A.M. to 4:30 P.M.; high school from 9 A.M. to 6:10 P.M. We had only one full day off, Saturday, but it really wasn't a day off, since we spent much of it in the synagogue—9 A.M. to noon and then afternoon and evening services, which varied in time depending on when it got dark (two stars had to be visible to the naked eye). On Friday, school ended at 1 P.M. to allow us to prepare for the Sabbath, which included Friday evening, when we also had to go to shul, before enjoying a home-cooked Shabbos feast. And Sunday was also a half day, though this compromise with secularism engendered grumbling from some of the old-fashioned rabbis, who wanted us to spend the entire Christian day of rest in class, as the more religious Jewish schools required.

Mornings in school were generally devoted to religious subjects—

Bible, Talmud, Ritual Rules, and Ethics. Afternoons were devoted to the usual secular subjects—Math, Science, History, English, French (for the smart kids who wanted to become doctors) or Spanish (for the rest of us) (no German or Latin), Civics, Gym, Art, Music Appreciation—as well as "Jewish secular" subjects, such as Hebrew, Jewish History, Zionism, and Jewish Literature. Then there was debate, student government, basketball, and other "extracurricular" activities. Lunch "hour" separated the religious from the secular classes and was the only time we ever discussed the conflict between what we were taught in the morning, such as the creation story, and what we were taught in the afternoon, such as evolution and genetics. No attempt was made to reconcile *Torah* (scripture) and *Madah* (secular knowledge). They were simply distinct and entirely separate worldviews (or as my late colleague Stephen Jay Gould put it in his always elegant choice of words, "separate magisteria").[12] We lived by the rule of separation between church and state, and for most of the students it raised no issue of cognitive dissonance. In the morning, they thought like rabbis; in the afternoon like scientists; and there was no need to reconcile. It was like being immersed in a good science fiction novel or film: One simply accepted the premises and everything else followed quite logically.

For a few of us, that wasn't good enough. I recall vividly our efforts to find—or contrive—common ground. For some, this quest took them to wonder whether the God of Genesis could have created evolution. For them there was an abiding faith that *both* religion and science could be right. For me, the common ground was an abiding conviction that both could be wrong—or at least incomplete as explanations of how we came to be. I was skeptical of both religion and science. Genesis, though elegant and poetic, seemed too simple. But so did evolution—at least the way we were taught it.

The apparent conflict between religion and science moved me to search for doubts, for holes, for inconsistencies not *between* religion and science—that was too easy—but rather *within* religious doctrine and *within* scientific "truth." I loved hard questions. I hated the easy answers often given, with a smirk of self-satisfaction, by my religious and secular teachers.

I recall one day inventing a new *bracha* for skeptics. It began with the traditional "*Baruch atta*" ("blessed are thou"), but then substituted doubt for God. Here is how I recall it sixty years later:

Barch ata i don't know
Barach ata i deny

Barach ata im not sure
Barach ata show me why
Barach ata maybe so
Barach ata why not try
Barach ata still not sure

I didn't show my blessing to my teachers, just mumbled it under my breath in lieu of the traditional *bracha*.

The mission of our Modern Orthodox yeshiva was to integrate us into the mainstream of American life while preserving our commitment to Judaism. *Torah* and *Madah* were the themes. *Torah*, which means "Bible," represented the religious component. *Madah*, which literally means "knowledge," represented the secular. They were thought to be reconcilable, though little explicit effort was directed at reconciling the very different worldviews implicit in the relatively closed system of Orthodox Judaism and the openness that was required to obtain real secular knowledge.

When it came to culture, however, there was little conflict, because becoming good Americans—including immersing ourselves in mainstream culture—was part of the mission of our schools. We were taught to be patriotic to the *goldena madena*, the nation that was "so good to the Jews." We were also taught to hate America's Communist enemies, who were "bad for the Jews." As a teenager, I sometimes delivered the *dvar Torah*—the commentary on the Bible portion of the week in our local synagogue. My mother saved one of them in which I contrasted three distinct biblical words for "law" in an effort to show why American democracy was superior to Soviet Communism:

> *Three words—*chok *("divine decree"),* mishpat *("a rule based on justice"), and* g'zaira *("a despotic human decree")—have played a major role in the political evolution of many nations. The concept of* g'zaira *has been the basis of the absolute monarchy of the past and the totalitarianism of the present, while* mishpat *has been the essence of democracy. But* g'zaira*, the despotic decree, could not exist for long without help. The people as far back as the fifteenth century realized that the proclaiming of decrees without apparent reason is the sole privilege of G-d and not of mortal kings, and so in order to rationalize their despotic actions the monarchs utilize the concept of* chok*, the G-dly decree, and so there came to be the divine rights theory of monarchies, which claim that the law of the land was actually the* chok *of the Almighty, but that the king as the direct messenger of G-d could execute his desires without*

> *question as* chok *rather than* g'zaira*. Communism sought also to rationalize its totalitarianistic principles by* chok *rather than* g'zaira*, and so they invented their own pseudo-gods, their Lenin or Stalin, who then acting as G-d of the Russian people could execute his own* chukim.
>
> *In our own United States, however, with the help of G-d, political evolution has always been based on the concept of* mishpat*, justice or, as we prefer to call it, democracy. We . . . demand that all law be opened to the checks and balances of* mishpat.

My teachers and rabbis didn't even approve of my using the Bible to make the case for American democracy, because I went beyond the traditional sources and demanded a reason for everything, rather than an unquestioning acceptance of God's decrees, as interpreted by the rabbis.

I hated anything the rabbis tried to imbue us with, because with a few exceptions, they taught by rote and memorization. Although I was good at memorization, I rebelled against the authoritarianism implicit in religious teaching.

As much as I hated my teachers, they hated me even more. I loved conflict, doubt, questions, debates, and uncertainty. I expressed these attitudes openly, often without being called on.[13] I was repeatedly disciplined for my "poor attitude." My sixth grade report card, which I still have, graded me "unsatisfactory" in "deportment" and "getting along with others." I received grades of D in "effort," D in "conduct," D in "achievement," C in spelling, D in "respects the rights of others," D in "comprehension," C+ in geography, and A in "speaks clearly." One teacher even gave me an "unsatisfactory" in "personal hygiene." My mother, who was meticulous about cleanliness and scrubbed me clean every day before school, complained. The teacher replied, "His body is clean, but his mind is dirty; he refuses to show respect to his rabbis."

To be sure, I was a mediocre yeshiva student—actually I exaggerate: I was *worse* than mediocre, once having received a grade of *bayn ani minus*, which literally means "mediocre minus." I couldn't even quite make it to mediocrity. At least I had something to which to aspire!

When I was in sixth grade, the school decided to administer IQ tests to all the students. The school called my mother and said that I had gotten one of the highest scores. At first the principal thought I had cheated, but when he was persuaded that in fact I had a high IQ, he decided to put me in the A class. We had a track system that divided students into the A, B, and C classes. I had always been in the C class. My mother was worried about my having to compete with all those smart kids, so she persuaded the principal to compromise and put me in the B class, where I remained throughout elementary school, getting C's until I graduated.

I wanted to go to Flatbush Yeshiva High School, which was the elite Jewish school, but I was turned down and went instead to Yeshiva University High School, a few blocks from Ebbets Field. I spent my four high school years in what was called "the garbage class," which focused more on discipline than learning.

I had a well-deserved reputation in both elementary and high school as a "bad kid"—a *bon-dit*. My grades were low (except on statewide standardized tests called "the Regents," on which I generally did well). My conduct, called "deportment," was terrible. I was always getting into trouble because of my pranks, because I "talked back" and was "fresh" to teachers, because I questioned everything, because I didn't show "respect," and because I was a "wise guy."

One day I asked Rabbi Oretsky a particularly provocative question. Instead of trying to answer, he called me a *shtik drek*. I had no idea what that Yiddish phrase meant, so I asked my grandmother. She smacked me for talking dirty. It meant "piece of shit." From then on my friends and I referred to our teacher as Rabbi "Or-drek-sky."

My parents were shocked to learn how disrespectful I was in school, because I was always on good behavior with them and with my grandparents, whom I deeply respected, despite their lack of formal education. I had little respect for my teachers, especially the rabbis, because they showed no respect for, or interest in, me or in the questions I was always asking.

This was the greatest gift—OK, I will even say "blessing"—of my yeshiva education: learning to question everything and everyone. It may have been merely an unintended consequence of the yeshiva method, but I was certainly not its only beneficiary or (according to the rabbis) its only "failure." The Jewish characteristic of questioning is not a coincidence. It is a product of experiences, and surely the yeshiva education—which juxtaposes religion and science with little explicit effort to reconcile these distinct approaches to the search for truth—is an element of these experiences for at least some young Jews. It certainly was for me, and for that I will be eternally grateful.

What then was my take-away from yeshiva? For me it has been a lifelong belief in the certainty of doubt. For most of my classmates, the take-away has been a lifelong belief in the certainty of certainty. Why the difference? Surely minor genetic disparities do not explain such a profound difference in worldviews. Nor does mere intelligence, since many of my "certain" classmates were brilliant. I think it was the environment underneath the roof of our homes. I *came* to yeshiva ready to doubt. Although my parents were both strictly observant, Modern Orthodox Jews, they too were skeptics, especially my mother. Despite her lack of formal education and culture, she was a cynic, always doubting, always questioning, though this became less apparent as she grew older and observed—to her chagrin—what she had actually transmitted to her children. She doubted while continuing to observe all the rituals. That was the traditional Jewish approach to learning and ritual. My brother and I started that way, but ultimately our doubts carried over into action—or, more precisely, inaction. We stopped observing all the religious prohibitions and obligations in our mid-twenties. My mother couldn't accept that. "I don't care what you believe or don't believe," she would insist, "as long as you go to shul, keep kosher and don't work [broadly defined to include driving, watching television, or going to a ball game] on Shabbos. Is that so much to ask!"

When we started to break the rules, my mother began to doubt her doubting. Doubting was good as long as it didn't lead to breaking with the rituals—and it didn't in her case. She believed in doubt until she saw, with her own eyes, the wages of it in her own children. This led her to embrace certainty. She would never completely abandon her doubting nature, but she no longer believed that doubt was cost-free. It had cost her the loss of her own children to "excessive doubt" and the real sin of *acting* on one's doubt. I certainly don't mean to suggest that our mother "lost" us in any sense other than the observance of ritual, but that was important to her. Although my brother and I maintained an extremely close relationship with her until her death at age ninety-five—we spoke to her every day—it was never the same once we left the "club" and followed our own rules as they pertained to Jewish practices.

My mother may not have been happy with the way I used the doubt she instilled in me, but for me it has become the most important quality in my life—and the most significant ingredient in whatever success I may have achieved. It certainly played an important role in my decision to become a lawyer defending freedom of speech, accused criminals, and other unpopular causes. So thank you, Mom! And even thank you, Yeshiva Etz Chaim and Yeshiva University High School, for provoking me to be a skeptic, a doubter, and an agnostic about life.

My mother influenced me in many ways with her skepticism, not the least of which was when she repeatedly had to defend me for my conduct at school. I remember one incident in particular. I was playing "Ring a Levio" in the schoolyard on any icy day and chasing a classmate named Victor Botnick. He slipped and his leg got stuck under the gate, and he broke it while trying to stand up. I was accused of breaking his leg and called into the principal's office. My mother came to school. I told her the story and assured her that I would never break my friend Victor's leg purposely. My mother served as my defense attorney, making charts and diagrams that proved that I could not have possibly broken his leg deliberately and that he caused it to break while trying to stand up with his foot stuck under the gate. I was acquitted, though the principal still had his suspicions. This was my first experience with the adversarial process and with a defense attorney. My mother, of course, was not a lawyer. But she was an important inspiration for why I decided to become a defense lawyer. For me the presumption of innocence was not a theory. I knew I was innocent, yet the principal presumed me guilty. Only my mother's advocacy kept me from being suspended.

My decision to become a criminal lawyer was certainly not influenced by any exposure to real crime. I lived in a neighborhood where we never locked our doors and where violent crime was unheard of. There were of course fights, in which I sometimes participated, but the Boro Park section of Brooklyn was a safe neighborhood.

Several years after I moved out of the house, my parents' apartment was burglarized. The burglars took Jewish ritual items, such as the Chanukah menorah, the Sabbath candles, and so on. When my mother called to tell me about the burglary, I responded, "See, Jews can be burglars too." My mother rebuked me. "They weren't Jews, they were Israelis." For my mother, real Jews, who in her world were all Orthodox, and Israelis, who tended to be secular, were different breeds.

My father, though rarely at home, influenced me as well. He had a small store on the Lower East Side where he sold men's underwear, socks, and work clothes wholesale during the week and retail on Sunday (he was closed on Saturday). I would sometimes help him on Sunday after my school finished at 1 P.M. It was really the only time I ever got to spend with him, because he worked six days a week and we spent Friday night and Saturday in shul, where we were always being shushed—*meturnished redin* ("not allowed to talk"). One Sunday my father got a ticket for violating the local Sunday closing law. I went to court with him a few days later, and the presiding judge was a man named Hyman Barshay. It was my first experience in a real court. The judge asked my father why he was open on

Sunday, and my father responded that he had to stay closed on Saturday because he was an Orthodox Jew and he couldn't afford to be closed for two days. "Did you go to shul on Saturday?" the judge asked. My father replied, "Of course." The judge challenged him, asking, "Then what was the Torah portion of the week?" When my father responded correctly, the judge tore up the ticket. If he had gotten the answer wrong, the judge would've doubled the fine. So much for separation between church and state.

This was not my only experience with the First Amendment. My friends and I formed a social athletic club—a euphemism for a Jewish gang, but without the rough stuff. We named our club the Shields, and we designed our own jackets, which we got wholesale, since the father of one of our members owned an athletic store. His name was "Snot" Chaitman. I leave the source of that nickname to your imagination. Whitey, the leader of our club, decided that we should have something sexy and not at all Jewish-looking (whatever that meant). The colors we selected were chartreuse and black. We really wanted to look like hoods, despite our wimpy nature. Our yeshiva immediately banned the jackets as too tough-looking and not consistent with the Jewish values of the school. Fortunately one of our club members lived across the street from the school, and so we would go to school wearing approved clothes, then, upon leaving school, go to our friend's house and change into our costumes. We felt like superheroes, but I was no longer jumping out of windows.

Boro Park in the 1940s and '50s was not only a religious neighborhood; it was a funny neighborhood. Two houses away from me lived Jackie Mason. Around the corner was Elliott Gould (née Goldstein). A few blocks away, in my uncle's building, lived Buddy Hackett. Woody Allen grew up in a nearby neighborhood, as did Larry David and Mel Brooks.

Joke telling among my friends was a competitive sport. We didn't know anybody who actually made up a joke. Every rendition would begin with "I heard a good joke" or "Have you heard the one about—the rabbi and the farmer's daughter? . . . or the rabbi, the priest, and the minister?" (The rabbi was always the butt of the joke!)

The first joke I remember hearing involved a put-down of Russia. It was about the time the Russians wanted to one-up the Americans by ordering a large number of condoms fourteen inches long. The Americans sent them the fourteen-inch condoms—marked "medium." The jokes improved as we got older!

Our favorite radio show was *Can You Top This?*, which involved professional comics who would try to top one another and listeners who submitted jokes. A "laugh meter" determined whose joke was funniest. There were cash prizes for listeners who topped the pros. The jokes told by the panelists, such as Harry Hershfield and Joe Laurie, Jr., had to be spontaneous and related to the subject of the original joke. The panelists boasted that they knew fifteen thousand jokes among them.

We would sit around the radio and try to top the pros. We would also send in our own jokes, which were never chosen.[14]

Living in a funny neighborhood served me well. I use humor in the courtroom, in the classroom, and in every other aspect of my life. A highlight of my current summers is sitting on the porch of the Chilmark Store on Martha's Vineyard and playing a contemporary version of *Can You Top This?* with my friend Harold Ramis, who easily knows more than fifteen thousand Jewish jokes! Sometimes Larry David, Ted Danson, Clyde Phillips, Gary Foster, Nick Stevens, Seth Meyers, or Tony Shalhoub will drop by. I never "top" Harold, but I hold my own.

I learned many of my jokes in the Catskill Mountains, where I worked as a busboy over the Jewish holidays. The only hotel that would hire me was the King David. It was a run-down place that conveniently burned to the ground right after the Jewish holidays. (We called it "Jewish lightning"!) It was across the road from the posh Brown's, made famous by Jerry Lewis, who frequently performed there. Nearby were Grossinger's, Concord, Kutsher's, President, Nevele, Tamarack, Pine View, and Pioneer. I played and watched basketball, played Simon Says with Lou Goldstein, who claimed to have invented the adult version of the game. My mother was the champ at Simon Says, because she figured out a way to beat Goldstein, who always fooled the participants by giving an oral direction—"Simon Says, raise your right arm"—while at the same time doing the opposite: raising his left arm. My mother's secret: Play with your eyes closed, so as to avoid confusion between the verbal and the visual! I snuck into the shows that featured Alan King, Freddie Roman, Shecky Greene, and Red Buttons. It was *Can You Top This?* on steroids. Plus, there were girls.

I need to thank my local synagogue for helping me discover sex. I am convinced that some higher authority built the benches at precisely the right height to introduce sexual feelings at precisely the right time. When Orthodox Jews pray, they shake back and forth while standing. When I reached a certain height, the top of the bench in front of me, which had a curve, was exactly parallel to my genitals. It was while shuckling back and forth in the synagogue that I experienced my first arousal.

Although we were Orthodox, none of us abided by the rules regulating sexuality. We were as anxious to make out as anyone; the problem was we had no one to make out with, because the girls all had to be beyond reproach. In our senior year we discovered that a bus ride to Union City would get us to the burlesque house, where at least we could see what we could not touch. One day we took along one particularly Orthodox classmate who insisted on wearing his yarmulke. The rest of us had tucked ours into our pockets. Of course we sat in the front row, to get the best view. When a guy in the back started screaming, "Take it off! Take it off!," Irving was sure he was referring to his yarmulke. He stood and confronted the guy, shouting, "I will not take it off!" To this day, whenever I see Irving, I always yell, "Take it off! Take it off!" He'll never live it down.

The yeshiva I went to was strongly Zionist, supporting Israel's struggle for independence, but some of the rabbis hated David Ben-Gurion, Israel's first leader, who believed that Israel should be a secular socialist democracy. These rabbis wanted it to be an Orthodox Jewish theocracy. Thank God Ben-Gurion won. (Recently, I acquired a letter he wrote in 1963, stating that the religious and secular elements of Israeli society must be sensitive to each other's beliefs:

> *There is no doubt that the feelings of a religious man are to be respected, but religious people must respect the freedom of choice of a fellow man, and no coercion is to be exercised for or against religious conduct.*[15]

Words that could have been spoken by Jefferson or Madison!)

One day, Ben-Gurion was giving a speech in Manhattan to a vast audience of supporters. My friend Tsvi Groner, who subsequently made *aliya* to Israel, and I decided to cut school to listen to Ben-Gurion. When we were caught being out of school, we told the rabbis that we'd gone to a Brooklyn Dodgers baseball game. For *that* we received less of a punishment than we would have if we had admitted going to hear the atheist Ben-Gurion.

My mother was summoned to my high school so often that some of the students thought she worked in the principal's office. One day, after I had done something egregious—I threw a dummy dressed like me off of the building, after threatening to jump off the roof when my teacher threw me out of class[16]—the principal demanded of my mother, "What are we going to do with your son?" Without any hesitation my mother responded, "I don't know what you're going to do, but as for me, I'm going to keep him." Ultimately I was suspended for a few weeks on the ground of "lack of respect" and spent them at the local library and museum, where I learned considerably more than I was learning in my classes.

It was not my last encounter with my principal, Rabbi Zuroff, who in my senior year called me to his office for some career advice: "You have a good mouth, but not much of a *Yiddisher kop*," which means "Jewish head (or brain)," as distinguished from a *Goyisher* ("non-Jewish") *kop*—a slightly bigoted concept suggesting that Jews are endowed with special mental qualities or capacities.[17] He continued: "You should do something where you use your mouth, not your brains." I asked him what he would suggest. He replied: "You should become either a lawyer or a Conservative rabbi." (He was an Orthodox rabbi who held his Conservative colleagues in utter contempt.) To make sure the latter part of his advice was followed, he urged Yeshiva University, which trained Orthodox rabbis, to reject me, which it did.

My classmates as well valued my verbal over my intellectual skills. The first draft of my high school yearbook description said that I have "a mouth of Webster, but a head of Clay." (My mother made them change it!)

Rabbi Zuroff's career advice was better than the choices given to me by the New York City Department of Employment, to which my mother turned in desperation. After reviewing my high school record and administering an aptitude test, the counselor told my mother that because of my verbal skills I could aspire to work in an advertising firm or a funeral parlor. My mother asked whether I could be a lawyer, to which the counselor replied, "Mrs. Dershowitz, I'm afraid you have to go to college to be a lawyer, and your boy just isn't college material."

Many years later, following a talk I gave at a temple in Los Angeles, a man about my age asked whether I was related to a guy he went to high school with named Avi Dershowitz. "Avi" was the Hebrew nickname by which I was known all through high school. I began to use my "real" name, Alan, when I started Brooklyn College, though my old friends and family still call me Avi.

I decided to put the questioner on, so I said, "Yeah, yeah, we are related."

"Whatever happened to Avi?" he asked.

I continued the put-on: "We don't talk about him in our family. He came to no good."

Showing no surprise, my questioner replied: "I knew he would come to no good. He was such a bad kid in high school."

I'm sure some of my critics would agree that I came to "no good," but at least by objective standards I've exceeded the expectations my high school teachers and principal had for me. None of them thought I was "college material."

The only successful part of my high school career, other than my debating, was making the varsity basketball team in my junior year. Though I was never a starter (except when the starters were sick), I did manage to accompany my team to Madison Square Garden for the inter-yeshiva finals. I shared a locker with Dolph Schayes, whose team, the Syracuse Nationals, was playing against the New York Knicks in the main event, to which our game was a preliminary. One of the people on the opposing team was a kid shorter than me named Ralph Lifshitz. He eventually decided that to make it in the fashion business he would have to change his name. So Lifshitz became Lauren.

I was expected to become a starting guard in my senior year, but I was disqualified from playing on academic grounds. My grade average was below the 75 required to qualify for a varsity sport.

All of the teams we played against in our league were Jewish high schools, but some were more Orthodox than we were. We did not wear yarmulkes when we played, but some of our opponents did. They believed that it was improper to walk more than four steps without wearing a yarmulke. In one game, an opponent stole the ball and had an open lane to the basket. I grabbed the yarmulke off the top of his head and threw it on the floor and yelled, "You can't go more than four steps." He stopped, shot the ball, and missed. I got a technical foul, which was well deserved.

Basketball was not our only passion. We all loved baseball, especially since Ebbets Field was located just a short walk from our high school. The morning recess generally coincided with the time when several of the players walked past our school to the stadium. These players were working stiffs being paid low salaries and generally taking public transportation to and from the games. We would wait for them to pass school and walk with them to Ebbets Field. I got to know several, including Carl Furillo, Pee Wee Reese, Gene Hermanski, Gil Hodges, and Ralph Branca (whose mother, it now turns out, was Jewish!).[18] Jackie Robinson, who was our hero, generally was driven to the stadium for safety reasons.

I will never forget Jackie Robinson's first game with the Dodgers. We persuaded our European-born rabbi to make a blessing for him, without his knowing whom he was blessing, since he never would have approved blessing a baseball player. We made up a Hebrew name for Jackie Robinson, calling him Yakov (Jacob) Gnov (Rob) buh (in) Ben (son). When he got his first hit, we were convinced the blessing had worked. I had a spiral notebook in which I had collected autographs of every single Brooklyn Dodger who played during my high school years. As soon as I moved out of the house, my mother tossed it in the garbage pail, along with my signed baseball cards and my comic book collection.

One of the autographs I didn't get—until years later—was Sandy Koufax's, who moved into our neighborhood shortly before he signed with the Dodgers. His father, Irving, had a small law practice out of his house down the block from where we lived. Sandy was the closest thing to a real celebrity in Boro Park. Many years later, my wife, Carolyn, arranged for Koufax's, now long retired, to come to our house in Cambridge as a surprise birthday gift for me. I reminisced with him about his days in Boro Park, but he didn't remember several of the classic stories we had been recounting for years about his youthful exploits. Memories seem to improve with time and retelling.

It's not surprising that my high school memories are long on sports and short on academics, because my academic performance was abysmal. In my senior semester my first half grades were as follows (I still have the report card): English, 80; Math, 60 (F); Hebrew, 65; History, 65; Physics, 60 (F). With two failing grades, I couldn't graduate, and so by the end of the last semester, I had raised my Physics grade to the minimum passing number of 65 (by scoring an 89 on the Regents exam); my Math grade to 75; and my History grade to 70 (the others remained the same).

Yet despite my poor grades, I still remember much of what the teachers taught, however poorly they taught it. Half a century after finishing my religious education, I wrote a book entitled *The Genesis of Justice*,[19] in which I analyzed the first book of the Bible from a secular lawyer's perspective. When I showed the galley proofs to my uncle Zacky, an Orthodox rabbi, he said he admired the book's intellectual content but not its heretical views. He pleaded with me to "change just one word." I asked him, "Which word?" He responded, "The word 'Dershowitz' on the cover."

In my family, directness was more of a virtue than politeness, and interrupting someone was a sign of respect. It meant, "I get it, so you don't have to finish your thought." The interrupter fully expected to be interrupted in turn, and so on. Nobody ever got to finish what he was saying.[20]

My mother regarded people who were "too polite" with suspicion: "You never know what Muriel is really thinking," she would say about my extremely polite aunt (by marriage, of course) Muriel, who lived upstairs from us and was married to my somewhat rude (in the best sense of that word, at least to my family) uncle Hedgie, who never left any doubt about what he was thinking.

When I began teaching, some of my more "proper" students objected to my constant interruptions, until I persuaded them that being interrupted was a compliment, signifying that their point had been made and understood. Some television viewers have also written to me about my penchant for interrupting opposing "talking heads." It's simply a matter of style, not rudeness, though some mistake the former for the latter.

Another blessing of my early religious training relates to memory and my use of it in my professional life. My mother was blessed with a near perfect memory. (Probably more nature than nurture.) She could recall virtually everything from her youth. When she was in her eighties, she would spot someone on the train and go over to her and ask, "Aren't you Mildred Cohen and weren't you in my sixth grade class?" She was invariably right. She remembered, word for word, what she had been taught in the third or fourth grade. She remembered every melody she had ever learned, even though she never went to concerts and didn't listen to recordings as an adult. She could recite from memory long poems she learned in elementary school. Most surprising of all, she had committed to memory an entire Latin Mass, which a Catholic public school teacher, in an effort to Americanize the children of immigrants, had made them memorize. My mother had no idea what it meant, but it was one of her favorite parlor tricks to repeat its Latin words, accompanied by the church melody she had learned. She never forgot anything she had heard, read, or smelled. Growing up with a mother who never forgot was a curse for me, because I did a good many things I wished she could forget.

Beyond her great memory, my mother was brilliant in other ways. Her insights into people were remarkable. Had she lived a generation or two later, she might have been a superb lawyer or businesswoman. Instead, her brilliance, coupled with her lack of opportunity, left her frustrated. It also led her to live her life vicariously through her children, who had the opportunities she was denied.

VIGNETTE

Does Colin Powell Speak Yiddish?

My mother accompanied me to a ceremony at which then general Colin Powell and I were being honored. She approached the general and said, "There is a rumor that you speak Yiddish." Powell responded quite formally, "No ma'am, I'm sorry to say, I do not speak Yiddish." Then he put his arm around my mother and whispered in her ear, "*Epis a bissle*," which in Yiddish means, "maybe a little." He then explained that he worked in a Jewish-owned furniture store in Harlem and his boss taught him a few words of Yiddish so that he could converse with the Yiddish-speaking clientele. My mother was thrilled and declared him to be "a real mensch."

Despite my mother's lack of opportunities, she—like many Jewish mothers of her time—was the dominant figure in our family. The old borscht belt joke has a son telling his Jewish mother that he got a part in the school drama, playing a Jewish father. The disappointed mother says: "Too bad they didn't give you a speaking role." The women in my neighborhood were more outspoken and self-confident, and often better educated, than their struggling male counterparts. In my family, my mother was also smarter, although my father had a more positive disposition. My mother's photographic and phonographic memory was legendary.

Although I knew I had a good memory, I discovered that I had inherited my mother's extraordinary gift while participating in intercollegiate debates. The debate tournaments always took place on Saturday. I pleaded with my parents to let me go, promising that I would say my prayers. My parents agreed on the condition that I not write during the Sabbath. ("*Meturnished*.") My mother told me it wasn't necessary for me to write because I could remember things that others had to write down. ("Our family has good memories.") I was doubtful, but it proved to be true. I became a champion debater, and my teammates marveled at the fact that I didn't bring a pencil or pad but could recite word for word what my opponent had said before responding to it. I then realized what a blessing this memory was. I went through the rest of college and law school without taking notes. This enabled me to listen to what was being taught and to have a better understanding of it than the student "stenographers" who were busy taking down every word the teacher said, as if putting it in writing was a substitute for understanding it. To this day, I rarely take notes, even in court, though my memory for new information is not nearly as good as it used to be.

VIGNETTE

Memory

Recently, after watching the film *Invictus,* my wife asked me if I had any idea who wrote the poem by that name. She thought it must be a well-known poet, such as Byron or Shelley. Without thinking, I blurted out, "Henley." She replied, "Who the hell is Henley?" I said, "I don't have the slightest idea, but I think 'Invictus' was written by some English poet named Henley." She checked Google and sure enough the poem was written by a relatively obscure Victorian poet named William Ernest Henley (1849–1903). His name popped into my head as a sixty-year-old memory association from a high school English class in which we had to memorize the authors of works that we read and memorized.

A few years earlier, I impressed my children at Steve's ice cream shop in Cambridge, which offered free ice cream to anyone who could answer obscure Trivial Pursuit questions. The question that no one had answered was "What was the Lone Ranger's family name?" I immediately blurted out, "Reed." I added that Reed was also the Green Hornet's family name, because, according to the "origin story" in a comic book that I had read more than half a century earlier, they were cousins.

During my junior year in high school, my memory for obscure facts and the "parlor tricks" I played with it got me an interview with the producers of a television game show called *The $64,000 Question,* but I failed the personality part of the test and was rejected. That was fortunate, since the show was rigged.[21] My "mother's memory" has served me well as a lawyer, teacher—and joke teller. (The downside of remembering every joke I ever heard is that I rarely get to hear a "new" joke.) I also remember nearly every case I ever read, nearly every fact in the records of cases, and nearly every principle of law I ever learned. I try to teach my students to develop and rely on their memories rather than on their stenographic skills, urging them to learn how to listen and remember, because this ability will be very important in court and other professional settings.

My good memory went mostly to waste in my early years, because there was so little worth remembering. We would be given a quarter to memorize passages from holy texts and a dollar if we could recite "by heart" (what does that mean?) an entire chapter from the Bible. Only once did my memory serve me well during my adolescence, and that was at my Bar Mitzvah. Prior to "becoming a man," I had never really excelled at anything. I was good, but not great, at athletics; good, but not great, with my social life; and god-awful in academics and behavior. But my Bar Mitzvah performance was perfect. I had read the Torah portion—"Judges and Magistrates"[22]—flawlessly, because I was able to memorize the entire reading, melody and all. My performance was the talk of the neighborhood. But a month later, my friend Jerry (now a prominent rabbi) read his Torah portion in the same synagogue. He was awful, making mistake after mistake, and singing off-key. The rabbi then got up to give the sermon. He recognized that Jerry had not done well, and in order to console him, he referred to "another Bar Mitzvah boy" who had done a better job reading from the Torah but who wasn't nearly as good a student or person as Jerry. "We judge boys not by the quality of their voices or their ability to memorize, but by their understanding of what they were reciting and by the lives they lead based on their understanding." It was a direct put-down of me, and so understood by the congregation. It stung me and led me to conclude that I could do nothing right in the eyes of the religious authority figures. Even when I did something perfectly, they would find some way to turn my success against me.

A few years later, I had a similar experience in high school. The one subject that interested me was History, and the teacher was young and dynamic. I studied hard—a rarity—for a statewide exam and got an 88. When the teacher, who knew my reputation as a mediocre student, told me my score, he said: "Don't let it go to your head. You're a 75 student. You've always been a 75 student and you'll always be a 75 student." (He gave me a 70 despite my 88 grade on the Regents exam.) It became a self-fulfilling prophecy for two reasons. First, all my teachers believed it. Second, I believed it and stopped studying, because I could get 70s without much work, and if that's who I was anyway, why take time away from activities I enjoyed, such as sports, jokes, girls, and messing around?

I also enjoyed debating and public speaking. In my junior year I entered the Journal American Tournament of Orators, a citywide public speaking contest. My topic was Abraham Lincoln, whose life I researched in the public library. I wrote and memorized a ten-minute oration. My mother took me to a neighbor who was a paraplegic from war injuries and who made his living running a small recording studio. He recorded my oration as a 78-rpm record, which I recently found among my mother's things. When I played it, I realized that despite the heavy Brooklyn accent, it came across as relatively thoughtful and well researched for a fifteen-year-old high school junior. Some excerpts:

> *As we gaze in retrospect through the annals of American history, we find many men who helped us achieve democratic rule and world power. But overshadowing even the greatest of them was a soft-spoken gentleman, who gave us, and upheld, the very principles which today mark the creed of the free world, and which today are the obstacles to world Communist domination. It was Abraham Lincoln who displayed to the world that the life of no man should be controlled by the whim of another, regardless of race, color, or creed.*
>
> *Lincoln's love for his fellow man . . . was displayed at best on his trip to Gettysburg. Carl Sandburg relates how, while engaged in political business with a high-ranking officer, Lincoln was politely approached by an elderly man who informed the President that he had recently lost his only son at Gettysburg. Abraham Lincoln then excused himself from the officer and spent many minutes endeavoring to convince this skeptical father that his son's great sacrifice was not a vain one. He told this common man of the lives yet to be sacrificed and the homes yet to be made desolate before the termination of this horrible internal struggle. And Abraham Lincoln put his head in his hand and wept, wept for the lives of his beloved fellow men and wept for the sacrifice of this elderly man and his son. Abraham Lincoln, President of the U.S. and the most influential political figure of his day, wept in bitter sorrow over the death of a common soldier whom he had never met.*
>
> *. . . Finally, his laborious task was achieved. The Confederacy had crumbled. But then, seven days later, and he was no more. . . . Yes, Abraham Lincoln was gone, but in the hearts of his people for whom he had preserved the union, the memory of Abraham Lincoln is enshrined forever.*

Not a single teacher ever complimented me on this talk, even when I finished second among the students in Jewish high schools in New York City. To them I was still "a 75 student" with a big mouth.

It was in the summer of my junior year in high school when an authority figure—the camp dramatics counselor, Yitz Greenberg (now a prominent rabbi)—finally told me that I wasn't "a 75 student." He had cast me in the difficult role of Cyrano de Bergerac in the camp play. I memorized the lines and did a good job (my prominent nose helped). After the performance, Yitz put his arm around me and said, "You know, you're very smart." I replied, "No, I just have a good memory." He insisted that my smarts went beyond memorization. He told me I could be a good lawyer. I respected and believed him. It was an important moment in my life, for which I will be forever grateful. My parents loved me but never told me I was smart, because they believed my teachers and saw my report cards. My eighth-grade teacher, Mr. Kien, had told me I was smart, but he had also been my father's teacher thirty years earlier, and I didn't quite believe he was being straight with me. I needed to hear it from an authority figure with no connection to my family, and Yitz was that figure. He encouraged me to read on my own and to broaden my interests, which I began to do in my senior year.

Despite my inglorious high school career, Yitz's faith in me led me to consider college. My father thought I should go to work and take some classes at night, but my mother wanted me to graduate from college—as she couldn't do. She wanted me to attend Yeshiva University, as most of my high school classmates were planning to do, but I was denied admission because of my poor grades and bad attitude. My mother filled out my application to Brooklyn College, though she later regretted allowing me to go to a secular school, which she believed was the beginning of the end of my remaining a strictly observant Jew. I wanted to go to City College in Manhattan, because my best friend, Norman Sohn, was going there, but my parents wouldn't let me go to an "out-of-town college."

Brooklyn College was part of the New York City College system, which had an excellent academic program, but little by way of any social or athletic life. It was free to any New York City resident, and anyone who had a sufficiently high grade average in high school was automatically admitted. Remarkably, the required grade score was different for boys and girls. Boys needed an 82 or 83 average (depending on the year) while girls needed an 86 or 87. Imagine the lawsuit today! The reason for this differential was that the school wanted "gender balance," and if the same score were required, the college would be predominantly female.[23]

I did not come close to having an 82 average, but fortunately there was also a test that an applicant with nonqualifying grades could take. I did well on the test and was admitted.

I also won a New York State Regents Scholarship, which paid me $1,400 to go to college. (I put the money in an interest-bearing account that paid for my first year at law school.) The state scholarship was based entirely on a single, highly competitive exam. High schools took great pride in how many state scholarships their students won. The relevant statistic that helped rank the schools was the percentage of those who won based on the number of students who took the exam. My high school was obsessed with doing well, so it limited those who could take the exam to students with grade points over 80. I did not qualify, but I knew I could do well on a statewide competitive exam that was graded by outsiders, not by my teachers, who were predisposed against me. So I pleaded with Rabbi Zuroff to take the exam. He refused, telling me I would never win and that my taking it would just bring down the percentage. Not satisfied with his answer, I filed a petition with the New York Regents—my first of many petitions. To everyone's surprise, the Regents ruled in my favor and the school was ordered to let me, and everyone else, take the exam. Two of us who had averages below 80, along with four or five others, won the scholarship. My principal's first reaction was that I must have cheated, but a check of the seating chart showed that I was not sitting near anyone else who won. So off I went to Brooklyn College, with money in my bank account. It was a turning point for me academically, professionally, religiously, and existentially.

Several years ago, the *New York Times Magazine* asked me to reflect back on my teen years for a column entitled About Men.[24] I wrote about my nostalgia for the 1950s:

> *. . . chintzy replicas of vintage Chevys and Thunderbirds, overpriced miniature jukeboxes that play "Rock Around the Clock," anything reminiscent of the 1955 world champion Brooklyn Dodgers, reruns of television sitcoms and revivals of shows I hated in their original incarnations.*

Then I noted the irony, because my early teen years were miserable, filled with self-doubt and humbling experiences, such as this:

> *It was prom time, and the girls had established a committee of three to which the boys had to apply for dates. I had my eye on a pretty blonde from an adjoining neighborhood (her distance, I hoped, might have kept her from learning of my questionable reputation among the local parents). As I approached the committee and shyly uttered "Karen," all three arbiters laughed. "Don't you know," the cruelest admonished me, "that Karen is on the A list and*

you're on the C list? You can only pick from the C or D lists." It was a relief to learn there was a list lower than mine, but a shock to be confronted with my official ranking.

The early 1950s—my high school years—were not my finest hours. Yet they were as formative as any other period, though the dynamic was mostly reactive. I think about them often. My wife, who is a psychologist, says I am obsessed with nostalgia for my troubled adolescent past because I would like to relive that time—both to regain my vigorous youth and to use it in a more productive manner. Or maybe it's because I can now relive those years without the pain and uncertainty I felt back then. I'm not sure. But I am sure that my early teens laid a firm foundation for my successful late teens—my college years at Brooklyn between the ages of sixteen and twenty.

I had something to prove, and I went about proving it with a vengeance.

My parents were hoping I would make a B average in college, which was very respectable in those days before grade inflation. They didn't want me to get As because A students became schoolteachers, and they didn't want me to get Cs, as I had in high school. I could never satisfy them. I went straight from Cs to As, almost never getting a B in anything. I blossomed in college, though I didn't do anything very different from what I had done in high school. I was a "smart aleck" and a "wise guy," but these qualities were appreciated and rewarded at Brooklyn College, while at Yeshiva High School they were punished. Whenever I came up with anything original in my high school religious classes, my rabbis would say: "If your idea is so good, then the ancient rabbis, who were so much smarter than you, would have come up with it first. If those rabbis, who were so much smarter than you, didn't come up with the idea first, then it can't be any good." End of discussion. College was very different.

2

MY SECULAR EDUCATION

Brooklyn and Yale

A recent biographical vignette described the beginning of my college career in somewhat dramatic terms: "Then—like an earthquake—suddenly, without warning and with great force, Alan Dershowitz happened . . . when he scrambled to barely gain admission to Brooklyn College. It seems like the man we know as one of the most respected lawyers in the land was born the day he first crossed the threshold of that institution."[1] There is some truth to that. I loved everything about Brooklyn College. The inner-city campus was a green and lush oasis amid the grit of Flatbush. Though it was only an hour walk from Boro Park, it was as far away—intellectually and emotionally—as Cambridge, New Haven, or Palo Alto. The professors were phenomenal teachers—many of them en route to more elite universities. The students, though mostly Jewish, seemed diverse to me because so few were Orthodox. Debate filled the classrooms, the lunchrooms, and the quad. No one said "*Meturnished*." Every idea was acceptable (except Communism; the stench of McCarthyism still hung in the air).

I felt free to experiment with my thoughts and words. Yet I remained an Orthodox Jew in practice, and I did not try drugs or alcohol.

My friends and I founded a "house plan"—an urban fraternity for students who lived at home with their parents. We called it Knight House, and our boastful Latin slogan was *Semil equis satis*—"Once a knight is enough." Since we were Orthodox, we could not attend the Friday night parties, so our house plan had its parties on Saturday night. We were desperate to defy the stereotype of Orthodox wimps, so we worked hard on our athletic skills, ultimately winning the house plan championship in several sports. (I still have news clippings attesting to our accomplishments: KNIGHT SOCCER CHAMPS—AL DERSHOWITZ LED THE KNIGHTERS TO VICTORY, SCORING TWO LARGE GOALS.

During my first year at Brooklyn College, a group of Knight Housers took a trip to Washington, D.C. The king of Saudi Arabia was a state visitor, and green Saudi flags draped the important monuments. When I saw the flag of that slave-owning dictator on the Lincoln Memorial, I tore it down and was immediately taken into custody by a park policeman. His superior was sympathetic, however, and let me go with a warning: "Next time, make sure no one sees you when you tear down the rest of those damn flags."

In my senior year, a group of us decided it was time to lose our virginity. We heard that there was a special deal over Christmas to travel to Havana. We drove to Florida and bought round-trip tickets to Havana for $59. We had the name of a house that specialized in transitioning young boys into men. We were scheduled to make the flight the day before the 1959 New Year, but a bearded guy named Fidel got there first and we couldn't make it.[2]

Mostly, I worked hard, achieving an A average and Phi Beta Kappa, winning debate tournaments and being elected president of the student council and captain of the debate team. Reading became a passion: literature (Dostoevsky, Shakespeare, Bellow); philosophy (Kant, Aristotle, Plato, Nietzsche); history (Churchill, C. Vann Woodward, Schlesinger). I loved arguing with professors. One of my favorites was John Hope Franklin, the first African-American appointed to the chairmanship of a department in a college that was not historically black. We remained friends and colleagues until his death.

Another favorite was a philosopher named John Hospers, who excelled at the Socratic method. He was a libertarian whose favorite author was Ayn Rand. After leaving Brooklyn College for a West Coast professorship, Hospers helped to found the Libertarian Party and became its candidate for President of the United States.

My presidency of the student council brought me into conflict with Harry Gideonse, the president of the college, a midwestern conservative who was brought to Brooklyn to "clean out" what had become "the little red schoolhouse." Several professors had been fired because of their "red" affiliations, and I fought against this post-McCarthy purge. Leading the other side was a professor of Romance languages named Eugene Scalia, an elegant and brilliant reactionary whose son Antonin has followed in his ideological footsteps.

Despite my conflict with President Gideonse, the school nominated me for a Rhodes Scholarship.[3] But in those days Jewish boys (only males were eligible) from Brooklyn were not selected, and despite my academic, political, and athletic accomplishments, I did not even get an interview. It took more than thirty years for a Brooklyn College student to be awarded a Rhodes Scholarship.[4]

Since I had done very well in college, I got into all the law schools to which I applied. I chose Yale, much to my mother's regret.[5] When people asked her where I went to law school, she replied, "He got into Harvard, but he went to Yale."

Immediately after graduating from Brooklyn, I married my girlfriend, whom I had met at the Jewish summer camp that boasted of the many *shidachs* ("meetings that resulted in marriages") for which it was responsible. I was not yet twenty-one. (My parents had to sign my marriage application.) Sue was nineteen. My mother wouldn't let me go to an out-of-town law school unless I was married, for fear that I would meet "the wrong kind of girl." Even though I was married, my parents picked my apartment, which they made sure was across the street from the Orthodox shul so the rabbi "could keep an eye" on me. A year after we were married, Sue became pregnant with our first child, Elon.

Because I was married and had a child, I did not participate fully in the social life of Yale. I ate lunch with other married students; our wives prepared sandwiches for us. (One of my classmates was married to Martha Stewart. She made one hell of a sandwich.) Nevertheless, I loved Yale Law School because of its academic excellence. During my first semester, I had Professor Guido Calabresi. It was his first year of teaching, and he looked more like a student than a professor, but he was a fantastic teacher. My first written assignment earned me a D from the teaching fellow and a suggestion that I might not be suited to the study of law. I was devastated. But that night Calabresi called and told me that my paper, though the worst written, was the most brilliant in the class. "You write like you're having a conversation with your friends in Brooklyn." He worked with me all semester to improve my writing.

When I told my mother that my most brilliant professor was named Guido Calabresi, she immediately asked, "Is he an Italian Jew?" I replied,

"Ma, non-Jews can be smart too." She looked at me as if to say, "Wait, you'll see." When I later learned that he was in fact a descendant of the famous Finzi-Contini family of Italian Jews,[6] I refused to give my mother the satisfaction of telling her she was right—at least about Calabresi.

VIGNETTE

How a Frozen Tongue Saved Me

I was coming from my parents' house in Brooklyn and heading back to school in New Haven. My mother, as usual, had given me some food to take back. It was a solidly frozen tongue. As I got off the subway and approached the railroad station, a guy grabbed my briefcase and started to kick me. I swung my tongue at his knee, knocked him to the ground, grabbed my briefcase, and escaped. Had the tongue not been frozen solid, who knows what would have happened?

I was reminded of this event while watching an episode of *Alfred Hitchcock Presents,* in which a wife kills her husband by hitting him over the head with a frozen leg of lamb. When a policeman comes looking for the weapon, the murderer serves him the lamb, and he eats the evidence. I too ate my weapon.

One of my teachers was Abe Goldstein, who had grown up in Williamsburg, near my family. My class contained lots of students with famous names—William Brennan, Jr. (son of the justice); a grandson of Chief Justice Warren; a descendant of President Taft; a descendant of John Marshall; and others. When Abe Goldstein called on each of these men, he did it without mentioning their heritage. But when he came to me, he said, "Dershowitz, from *the* well-known Dershowitz family?" The class burst out laughing. For a moment I thought he was mocking me, but he explained that in Williamsburg, the Dershowitz name was highly regarded.

It was not the only time I would be laughed at by my fellow Yale students. The first time I was called on to recite a case, there were chuckles at my thick Brooklyn accent, as there had been at my non-preppy garb, which included Bermuda shorts with a Phi Beta Kappa key ostentatiously dangling from a pocket.

My lack of sophistication cost me my first teaching job. During my first semester at Yale, I applied for a job as a teaching assistant for a political science course at New Haven State Teachers College, where the president made the hiring decisions. The day I went to meet him was rainy, and as soon as he saw my muddy shoes, he told me I wasn't suitable for the job. It would be the last time I was ever turned down for a teaching job.

All first year law students at Yale were required to participate in a moot court competition. My opponent was named Taft, one of the most prominent names in America. My mother was convinced that I couldn't possibly compete with a Taft. To provide support, she and my father came to watch me argue. When my mother told my grandmother that I had beaten a Taft, she replied, "Taft? That's a funny name. I wonder what he changed it from." In my neighborhood, many short names, like many short noses, had once been longer.

In my second year, I was elected editor in chief of the *Yale Law Journal*. I was the first Orthodox Jew to serve in that capacity, so some doubted that this seven-day-a-week job could be done by a six-day-a-week worker. At the end of the year a few of my associate editors presented me with a mock copy of the law journal in which every seventh page was blank.

Yale Law School was an institution of meritocracy, where one could rise to the top, regardless of name or heritage. I was first in my class. But that wasn't enough for the Wall Street firms. During my second year, I applied to about thirty such firms for a summer job, and was turned down by every one. The hiring partner of Sullivan & Cromwell looked at my transcript and saw all As, except for one C in Contracts. (I was so angry with my Contracts professor that I immediately enrolled in Advanced Contracts with the same teacher and got an A.) The hiring partner brushed me away and said, "We don't take C students." Years later he approached me at a Yale reunion and told me that he had saved me from a bad experience. He disclosed that he was a closet Jew and realized that I would never fit into the culture of that firm. Within several years, however, that firm along with most other Wall Street firms, had significant numbers of Jewish associates and partners.[7] (In the late 1970s, I sued one of the firms that hadn't hired me, for refusing to promote an Italian-American to partnership, and won a ruling that discrimination in promotion was prohibited by the law.)[8]

After being turned down for a summer job by the Wall Street firms, I went to see the dean of Yale Law School, Eugene Rostow. Rostow was Jewish but had managed to get a job at a Wall Street firm, and so he was called "Dean Gene, the white-shoe Jew." He explained that it was not impossible for an Eastern European Jew to break into Wall Street and that an important consideration was "appearance." He told me to "think Yiddish, but dress British," and he gave me $100 from the dean's fund to buy an appropriate "interview suit" at J. Press, the local preppy store. I bought a blue blazer with brass buttons, a striped tie, and a pair of loafers. As my grandmother would have put it: *S'gurnished helfen*—"It didn't help." No Wall Street firm wanted me, blazer or not.

I got two offers, both with Jewish firms, but even one of them discriminated against me on account of my religion. Paul, Weiss, Rifkin, Wharton, and Garrison offered me a summer job at $100 a week. (I still have the letter!) I accepted and wrote to them that I could not work on Saturday. I was told to come and meet some of the partners when I was next in New York. I was introduced to the firm's major "rainmaker," Simon Rifkin, a prominent Jew who was active in numerous Jewish organizations. He told me how pleased he was that I would be working with the firm, but asked me why I would not be available on Saturdays. When I told him it was because I was Sabbath observant, he replied, "Oh no, we can't have that here. I thought it was just a restriction on your availability this summer. I need associates who are available seven days a week." So I took a job with the other Jewish firm, Kaye, Scholer, Fierman, Hays, and Handler. They were perfectly comfortable with my being Sabbath observant. The big rainmaker at that firm was Milton Handler, who was so busy seeing clients that he would ask associates to drive home with him or to go with him to Columbia when he was going to teach. One day his secretary called and said Mr. Handler wanted me to meet him at a particular address. When I got there, his private barber was cutting his hair. I was seated next to him, and he dictated to me while he got his haircut. It wasn't as bad as what Lyndon Johnson would do, requiring aides to join him in the bathroom.

While working at Kay, Scholer, I was asked to join two partners for lunch at an elegant private club. Though I was twenty-two years old, I had never before eaten out other than at delis. When the waiter put a napkin in my lap, I didn't know what to do with it. So I tucked it under my neck to protect my new tie. One of the partners pulled it off and said, "Young man, this is not a barbershop."

During my years at law school, I developed an interest in writing academic articles. At Brooklyn College, I had written a paper about the Fifth Amendment privilege against self-incrimination. In it, I explored the history, policies, and applications of the privilege, especially in the context of legislative investigations, where many of the battles over the scope of the

Fifth Amendment were then being fought, as witnesses were forced to name names or be branded "Fifth Amendment Communists." I pointed out that the privilege had been "adapted to changing times and needs," and concluded that though we "are considering the very same constitutional phrase, we are dealing with a completely new and hitherto unknown privilege."[9] (I would repeat the theme of a changing Constitution in many of my writings over the years and would eventually write a book about the Fifth Amendment.)[10]

At Yale, I wrote two articles for the law journal—one about attempted murder,[11] the other about corporate crime[12]—that brought me to the attention of the faculty not only at Yale but at Harvard as well. Both schools had their eyes out for me as a potential faculty recruit.

The professor who most influenced my legal thinking was Joseph Goldstein, who taught Criminal Law, but he really didn't teach much about the actual law; his role was to get the students to question everything and to rethink every principle of law. Some students hated his course, because they learned no law. Goldstein had failed the bar and had never practiced. I loved his course and was deeply influenced by his approach to law, which was the opposite of my rabbinical teachers who had demanded acceptance of what previous rabbis had decreed.

Another professor who influenced my approach to law was Alex Bickel, who taught me Constitutional Law. He looked at our Constitution politically and structurally and had a coherent, if imperfect, theory of how it should be interpreted. Both of these mentors defied conventional labels such as liberal or conservative.

The professor who had the most influence on my career choice was Telford Taylor, who combined an active constitutional law practice with teaching and writing. Although we could not have been more different in background and bearing—he was a tall, elegant WASP, had served as a general in the army, was the chief prosecutor at the Nuremberg trials, always wore a suit and tie, and was polite to a fault—we had much in common and became close friends and colleagues. I consciously tried to model my career (except for the army part) after his.

Shortly after John F. Kennedy was elected president, rumors began to circulate that Taylor was being considered to head the CIA. He took me aside one day and asked me, in confidence, whether I would consider coming with him to Washington, if he were to get the appointment, and serving as his executive assistant. I told him I would certainly consider such an offer. Eventually President Kennedy appointed someone else, deeming Taylor too liberal. Years later, Telford and I discussed how different our lives would have been if we had both joined the CIA.

Telford Taylor made me another offer, during my second year in law school. He had been hired to go to Jerusalem to broadcast the trial of Adolf Eichmann. He asked me to serve as his research assistant and translator. But I had just been elected editor in chief of the *Yale Law Journal* and didn't feel comfortable being away. I declined, and have always regretted missing that important historical event. (Years later, I observed the trial of accused Nazi war criminal John Demjanjuk in Jerusalem.)[13]

During law school I developed an interest in the relationship between law and other disciplines, such as economics and science—both physical and social. I worked as a research assistant on Professor Calabresi's groundbreaking article on law and economics[14] and as a research assistant to Professors Goldstein and Katz on their writing on law and psychiatry.[15] I eventually collaborated with them on a book entitled *Psychoanalysis, Psychiatry and the Law.*[16] Later I collaborated with Telford Taylor on a book and several human rights projects,[17] and with Alex Bickel on some constitutional cases.

During law school I also increased my interest in civil rights. Several of my professors were active in litigating cases challenging Jim Crow. In college I had joined the NAACP and had participated in a bus protest to Washington. In my second summer at law school, Professor Louis Pollak arranged for me to go to Howard University in Washington and train to become a civil rights observer in the South. My family was frightened by my trips to the South. I returned unscathed but forever sensitized to the evils of segregation.

The speaker at my law school graduation was President John F. Kennedy. He used the occasion to make the statement about having the best of both worlds, a Harvard education and a Yale degree.[18] My son Elon was a year old and I brought him along. During Kennedy's speech, he started crying. A local New Haven television station caught him in the act, and the voice-over said that Yale was always a Republican school. (I don't think Elon has ever voted for a Republican in his life.)

Having completed Yale Law School with flying colors, I was now ready for the next stage in my life—a clerkship in the nation's capital.

3

MY CLERKSHIPS

Judge Bazelon and Justice Goldberg

Appellate court clerkships, especially with a Supreme Court justice, are the most coveted positions following graduation from law school. Today, many law firms pay huge signing bonuses—some as high as $280,000—to attract Supreme Court clerks.[1] In my day, the value of such clerkships was prestige. In 1962, there were eighteen clerks serving the nine justices; the chief justice had three, the associate justices were entitled to two, but Justice Douglas—who rarely used his clerk—opted for only one. Today, each justice has four law clerks, and the chief justice is allowed five.

The competition for these coveted positions has always been fierce. Although any law school graduate can apply, most of the clerkships go to a handful of elite schools. (Probably because so many of the justices attended elite schools: The current Supreme Court has five justices who graduated Harvard, three Yale, and one who attended Harvard for two years but graduated Columbia.) Some clerkships were reserved for those who met certain criteria. Justices Brennan and Frankfurter picked only from Harvard. Justice Harlan generally limited his selections to Harvard and Columbia. Justice Douglas usually picked from the West Coast. Justice Black favored Southerners, tennis players, and "kissin' cousins" but was open to accepting recommendations from certain Yale Law School professors. Chief Justice Warren favored hail-fellows-well-met and athletes! Justice Clark preferred Texans. Justice Goldberg (who replaced Justice Frankfurter shortly after I graduated) liked to have one clerk with Chicago connections.

I fit none of the pigeonholes, except that I was male and white—as were all the law clerks. This meant that I was competing for three or four slots. My best shot was with Justice Black, because Guido Calabresi had been his recent clerk, and he recommended me. But there was a problem. I had alienated another Yale law professor, who was also close to Black. Fred Rodell was something of an iconoclast. (It was rumored that he had once filed a lawsuit seeking the court's permission to have extramarital sex, since his wife was disabled.) He insisted on teaching his seminar on the Supreme Court at Mory's, a private club near the law school (whose "tables" had been made famous by "The Whiffenpoof Song": "From the tables down at Mory's to the place where Louie dwells"). Mory's was a men's club,[2] so Rodell, who fancied himself a left-wing radical, effectively excluded women. When I learned of this, I quit the seminar. To add insult to injury, I substituted a seminar by Professor Alex Bickel, whom Rodell despised because Bickel took a "Frankfurtiarian" approach to constitutional law, rather than a "Blackian" approach. Though I myself favored Justice Black's "absolutist" view of the Bill of Rights, I admired Professor Bickel's writings and loved his class.[3] This was enough to make me unkosher for Rodell.

Professor Bickel gave me an important piece of advice: "Alan, I'm going to recommend you for clerkships, but you have to promise me you're going to turn off at least one of your barrels when you clerk. Judges aren't used to being confronted, and you have to be respectful and polite. If you want to say anything critical, put it in writing. Don't criticize them in front of them, and certainly not in front of another clerk." So he taught me the etiquette of being a clerk, because in law school, I was doing to my law professors what I had done to my rabbis. At Yale, this confrontational approach was generally admired. It had not been acceptable to the rabbis, nor would it be to justices and judges.

Professor Bickel himself was a confrontational teacher. He would walk right up to students in his seminar on advanced constitutional law, stare them down, and begin a relentless cross-examination. I loved it, and he loved my equally provocative challenges to his theories.

Even at Yale, my chutzpah was not welcomed by all. Professor Friedrich Kessler was an older European-trained academic who taught Jurisprudence. One day, he was lecturing on Freud's influence on German jurisprudence and he misunderstood one of Freud's theories. I raised my hand and corrected him. After class, an older student, who had been a marine and was married to another student, grabbed me and said, "You embarrassed someone I love. If you ever do that again, I'll deck you." I was startled and replied, "How did I embarrass your wife?" He said, "Not my wife, stupid. Professor Kessler. Don't ever correct him publicly." So much for academic freedom! Professor Bickel was wise to caution me about toning down my aggressiveness if I wanted to succeed as a clerk.

Professor Rodell was so concerned that I might contaminate the elderly Justice Black that he took the train to Washington to persuade him to reject the recommendation of his former law clerk. In the end, Black told Calabresi that he had to defer to his friend's veto for that year but that he would consider me for the following year. This was the best possible news because it allowed me to accept a clerkship with Judge David Bazelon on the United States Court of Appeals for the District of Columbia.

Judge Bazelon was my first choice for a clerkship, but I wanted—indeed I felt I needed—the status that came along with a Supreme Court clerkship, in order to obtain the kind of job offers I would be seeking. Two of my other mentors at law school, Professors Joseph Goldstein and Abraham Goldstein (not related), had both clerked for Judge Bazelon. One of my primary interests in law school was the relationship between law and psychiatry. Another was criminal law. Those were also Judge Bazelon's specialties.

MY YEAR OF CLERKING FOR JUDGE BAZELON

I arrived in Washington during the summer of 1962, in the midst of the Kennedy administration. It was a heady time for a young liberal lawyer to be in the nation's capital. Judge David Bazelon was at the center of Washington life, both socially and politically. He fraternized with senators, congressmen, cabinet members, White House staffers, Supreme Court justices, diplomats, and other movers and shakers.

At the center of his social life were the weekly lunches at the office restaurant of a local liquor distributor named Milton Kronheim, whose personal chef would prepare simple but superb lunches for "Milton's boys." Kronheim himself was in his mid-seventies when I met him. (He would live to ninety-seven, pitching in his weekly company softball game until his late eighties.) His frequent guests, in addition to Judge Bazelon, included Chief Justice Earl Warren; Associate Justices William Brennan, William Douglas, and later Thurgood Marshall; Judges J. Skelly Wright and Simon Soboloff; Senators Abe Ribicoff and Jacob Javits; and many other judicial and political notables from the liberal side. The small lunchroom where

Milton entertained had photographs of Kronheim with every president since Harding. Hundreds of other wall-to-wall photographs showed him with just about every important political, business, and sports figure of the twentieth century. (When Woody Allen's film *Zelig*—which portrayed a character who seemed to be involved with every historical figure of his age—was released in 1983, Judge Bazelon joked that Kronheim was the real-life Zelig.)

VIGNETTE

Bazelon on Kronheim

Judge Bazelon once told me a joke about Kronheim, which, with a change of name, from Kronheim to Katz, became a standard part of the Jewish joke cannon.

"There was a guy named Kronheim who bragged he was so famous he could be photographed with 'anyone in the world.' A skeptical friend challenged him: 'You can't be photographed with the President!' Within days, Kronheim was standing on the White House balcony with JFK, as photographers snapped pictures.

"OK," the friend conceded, "maybe in the United States, but not in other parts of the world! You could never be photographed with Israel's Prime Minister Ben-Gurion." The next day they were on a plane to Israel, and that afternoon Kronheim was standing on the balcony of the prime minister's house being photographed with Ben-Gurion.

"OK, maybe among Jews and Americans you're famous, but you'll never get a picture with the pope." Next day, they're off to Rome, and by afternoon, Kronheim is standing on the balcony of St. Peters next to the holy father. A nun standing in the crowd turns to the skeptical friend and asks, "Who's that guy standing next to Kronheim?"

I was privileged to participate in many of their lunches—mostly as a quiet observer—during my clerkship. (When I became a professor, Judge Bazelon invited me whenever I visited—then as a full participant.)

The first time I went to Kronheim's for lunch, we picked up two justices: William O. Douglas and William Brennan. Justice Brennan was just about the nicest, sweetest, most modest important person I had ever met. Justice Douglas was entirely different. Nobody ever accused him of being nice or friendly. He was surly, arrogant, and condescending. He mistreated his law clerks, referring to them as the "lowest form of life."[4] He was also a hypocrite. I learned this several weeks after the lunch, when Judge Bazelon buzzed me into his office and pointed to the extension phone, signaling me to pick it up. I heard a familiar voice berating Judge Bazelon for canceling a speaking engagement. Bazelon turned to me and silently mouthed the words "Bill Douglas," pointing to the phone. Bazelon kept trying to reply, saying, "I just can't do it, Bill. It's a matter of principle." Douglas responded, "We're not asking you to join, just to speak." Bazelon replied, "That's the point, Bill. They wouldn't let me join. They don't accept Jews or blacks."

It soon became evident that the two liberal judges were arguing about a private club that excluded Jews and blacks. Douglas was a member and had invited Bazelon to give a luncheon talk. Bazelon had agreed, but when he learned of the club's "restricted" nature, he withdrew his acceptance. Douglas was furious, Bazelon adamant. I couldn't believe that the great liberal justice not only belonged to a restricted club, but that he was utterly insensitive to Bazelon's principled refusal to speak at such a club. This was at the height of the civil rights movement, and Justice Douglas was writing decision after decision decrying public segregation. Yet he himself was participating in private segregation and condemning Bazelon's refusal to become complicit in it.

This phone call had a profound effect on my own subsequent actions and my refusal to speak at, or remain silent about, private clubs that discriminated, whether it was the Harvard Club of New York, which refused to accept women for many years,[5] or Jewish clubs, which limited their memberships to my own coreligionists.

Judge Bazelon played hard and worked even harder. For his law clerks it was all work. We had to be in before he arrived and had to stay until after he left, and he often worked late. He did not believe in vacation for the clerks—"It's only a one-year job, and that means 365 days." There was no personal time off (except in my case for Saturdays). When I first came to work over the summer, I asked him for a few days off to take a prep course for the D.C. bar exam. He assured me that I didn't need time off to prepare! "I hired you because you were first in your law school class. You don't have to study for this test." I told him I had been first *because* I always prepared, but he was dismissive of my request. I tried to prepare late at night, but the material was so dry and boring that I always fell asleep. "I'm going to fail the bar," I told him worriedly, "and it may embarrass you." Finally, he relented when I told him that I was really having trouble focusing on the ridiculous bar exam questions, and he allowed me to leave a bit early for a week to take a crash course that met from seven to nine in the evening.

A few weeks after the exam, Bazelon came storming out of his office holding a paper and not smiling. I knew that he got advance notice of the bar results, and I thought that he was coming to tell me I had flunked. Instead he shouted, "You didn't need time off. You got the goddamn highest grade in the city. You're a faker," he complained, not bothering even to congratulate me.

Several months later, when my second son, Jamin, was about to be born, I asked the judge for the day off to accompany my wife to the hospital. He asked, "Isn't Sue's mother here?" She was. "You did your part of the job already. You can visit after the baby is born. It isn't your first child. You don't have to be there for the birth."

Fortunately, he was traveling on the day of the birth and I made it to the hospital in time.

In light of Judge Bazelon's attitudes toward his clerks' workday, one can only imagine how shocked I was when Judge Bazelon came back to the office from a lunch at the White House in mid-October and told his entire staff to "go home and be with your families." He was grim-faced and pale. "Why?" we asked. "There may be a nuclear attack," he said solemnly. "I've just been briefed on the presence of Soviet nuclear rockets in Cuba. Neither side is backing down. Nobody wants war, but each side is calling the other's bluff. No one knows how this will turn out. Be with your families."

We all left in a panic. Bazelon called me later that evening at home. "I have no faith in those Kennedy brothers. They're a bunch of spoiled brats—their father's children," he said contemptuously of Joseph Kennedy. "I don't trust them. Look at the way they screwed up the Bay of Pigs. A bunch of arrogant amateurs."

Early the next morning, he called me back. "I've spoken to Abe Chayes," he said, referring to a Harvard Law professor who was then serving as legal advisor in the State Department. "He's more optimistic that cooler heads will prevail. Come into work."

So off I went to the courthouse, where Bazelon gave us hourly updates on the Cuban Missile Crisis until it was resolved by a deal. "I misjudged those Kennedy boys," he told me when the crisis was over. "Abe tells me they did good. Much better than the Bay of Pigs. They were actually quite mature. They're quick learners. They did good."

A few weeks into my clerkship, Justice Felix Frankfurter resigned from the Supreme Court, leaving the so-called "Jewish seat" vacant. Judge Bazelon was on the short list, along with Senator Abraham Ribicoff and labor secretary Arthur Goldberg. Ribicoff and Goldberg were close friends of Bazelon. All three wanted the job, but Bazelon was regarded as too liberal, especially on criminal justice matters, and was strongly opposed by Justice Department officials. I vividly remember the day Goldberg was nominated. "Arthur will be a great justice, if he has the *sitzfleish* [literally, "enough meat on his rear end to sit for long periods of time"] to stay on the bench," Bazelon told me. "He's used to the active life of the labor lawyer. Always in the middle of the action. He's going to have to get used to the isolation, but he's smart as hell, and he's always wanted to be on the Supreme Court."

Bazelon was disappointed, but he knew it would have taken a miracle to overcome the objections of the Justice Department, and he didn't have close connections to the Kennedys.

"Good for you. Not so good for me. And good for the country" is how he summarized the appointment to me. Good for me, because the new justice would certainly consider a recommendation from his old Chicago friend when picking his next year's clerks.

Judge Bazelon became chief judge of the U.S. Court of Appeals soon after I began working for him and dominated that important court—second only to the Supreme Court—during his long tenure. His rival was Judge (later Chief Justice) Warren Burger. Bazelon was deeply committed to equality in the criminal justice system—between rich and poor, white and black, mentally sound and mentally ill.

These passions brought him into constant conflict with the executive and legislative branches of government, and especially with prosecutors. He knew he could never win his battles by relying on public opinion, which showed little compassion for accused criminals. His weapons were education and elite academic opinion. His goal was to change minds through his opinion writing, speeches, and articles. He chose his law clerks based on their ability to assist him in these tasks. "Every case presents an opportunity to change minds, to teach, to influence," he would say. "The court is a bully pulpit, and we must make the most of it." His favorite story was about the New York judge who complained, "Why does Cardozo always get the interesting cases?," referring to the great New York Court of Appeals chief judge (later justice) who transformed tort law and other parts of the legal landscape with his elegant opinions. The point, of course, was that the cases weren't interesting until Benjamin Cardozo got his hand—or pen—on them. He turned mundane legal controversies, such as a railroad accident or a conventional contract dispute, into monumental legal decisions.

Judge Bazelon did the same with regard to criminal cases, especially those involving defendants who could not afford an adequate defense and those with mental illnesses. He would ask me to scour the records of cases—even those not assigned him—for evidence of injustice. He told me that most indigent defendants—and most defendants in D.C. were indeed indigent—did not have adequate lawyers: "You're their lawyer of last resort," he would tell me. "Search the record. Tell me if you find any injustices."

"But the case isn't even before you," I would protest, or "There were no objections and so the issues aren't properly preserved for appeal."

"No matter. We will find a way to secure justice. Your job is to find injustices. My job is to figure out a way to bring about justice."

He told me about a conversation between the great Justice Oliver Wendell Holmes and one of the justice's clerks. After the justice rendered an opinion denying relief to a morally deserving litigant, the clerk complained, "But Mr. Justice, the result is unjust." To which Holmes responded: "We're in the law business, young man, not the justice business."[6]

David Bazelon was in the justice business, though he used the law—sometimes stretching it beyond existing precedent—to bring about what he regarded as a just result. He was a "judicial activist," at least when it came to doing justice to the poor, the disadvantaged, and the sick—and he was proud of it. That catchphrase had not yet become a term of opprobrium, as it has to so many today.

I recall telling Bazelon, who was Jewish but not well educated in Jewish religious tradition, that the Torah commands not merely that we *be* just, or even that we *do* justice, but rather that we *actively* pursue justice, as if injustice never rests. The exact words of Deuteronomy—which I recalled because I recited them in my Bar Mitzvah portion—were "Justice, justice, you must actively chase after."[7]

Bazelon asked me to make a sign for his office with these words. He quoted them frequently in defense of his activism. They became his mantra, as they have become mine. The sign now hangs in my office. Another example of the good that has come from my not-so-good Jewish education!

The other good lesson—this one taught by Bazelon to me by example—

was that justice requires some degree of compassion. When I told Bazelon about the justice quote from the Torah, he asked me why the word "justice" was repeated. Wouldn't it have been enough to say, "Justice you must actively chase after." Why "justice, justice"? No word, or even syllable, of the Torah is supposed to be redundant. I told Judge Bazelon that the rabbis had a field day providing interpretation to the repeat of justice. My favorite, the one I had proposed in my Bar Mitzvah speech, was that the first *tzedek* meant legal justice, while the second meant compassionate justice.[8] Judge Bazelon corrected me: "Compassion must come before law." Whichever came first in Judge Bazelon's court, every decision that he wrote or joined combined both. His compassion wasn't always appreciated, even by its objects. Judge Bazelon once showed me a letter he received from his most famous defendant, a man named Monte Durham. Durham was the defendant in the case in which Bazelon announced his innovative approach to the insanity defense in the form of a new rule called the "Durham Rule," which declared a person to be not guilty by reason of insanity if his crime was "the product" of a mental disease or defect.[9] This controversial rule revolutionized the relationship between law and psychiatry. The letter from Monte Durham complained about the rule bearing his name. "Now everyone calls me 'Durham the Nut.'" He noted that when doctors discover a new disease, they name it after themselves. He wondered why the new rule wasn't called "the Bazelon Rule" instead of "the Durham Rule"! Bazelon apologized, noting that if judges could name new rules after themselves, there would be too many new rules.

Judge Bazelon and I were a match made, if not in heaven, at least in legal nirvana. I learned a lot from him and even taught him a little. We remained lifelong friends, though the year of clerking was more like hell than heaven, at least as regards working conditions.

Bazelon was never satisfied. He never told me that a draft was good. It always needed to be "made better." "It's getting there" or "It's close" was the highest compliment he ever paid.[10] But when it was published, and colleagues complimented him, he would always give me credit. But never to my face. He knew his opinions would be read by generations of law students, professors, lower court judges, and assorted critics. He was on a never-ending mission, and nothing was ever good enough. Even if it was good enough to publish or deliver because of deadlines, it was never quite good enough for him. But the long hours, demanding boss, and difficult working conditions were well worth it. Law clerks who endured this trial by fire went on to great careers. Former Bazelon clerks include the deans of Harvard and Yale Law Schools, the president of New York University, the former chancellor of the New York City school system, a prominent reform rabbi, and numerous law professors, lawyers, and business and political leaders. He influenced us all, and his influence persists. As Peter Strauss, a law professor at Columbia, once aptly characterized the relationship between Bazelon and his clerks: "He the pebble, we the ripples."[11]

The primary job of the law clerk related to the cases that came before the United States Court of Appeals for the District of Columbia. In the years I was a clerk, that court served not only as a federal appellate court, but also as the Supreme Court of the District of Columbia, a reasonably sized city with a racially mixed population and a relatively high violent crime rate.[12] Many of our cases involved appeals relating to federal administrative agencies—the so-called "alphabet agencies"—such as the FCC, FPC, SEC, and FDA. The rest were run-of-the-mill criminal cases—murder, robbery, rape, assault, and other street crimes. It was a perfect combination for a budding law professor who was interested in constitutional and criminal law.

Our task began with a record, consisting of the appellate briefs filed by the lawyers and an "appendix," which included excerpts from the trial transcript. Some records were relatively short, perhaps three hundred pages in total if the trial took only one day. Others were humongous, as many as five thousand pages. Then there was the complete trial transcript—a verbatim account of every word spoken during the trial, as well as during the pretrial and posttrial proceedings. Judge Bazelon would often ask me to read the entire transcript in search of errors or particular issues that were of interest to him.

When we completed the review, we would discuss the case with the judge, who had read the briefs and perused the appendix in preparation for the oral argument. Occasionally, we were permitted to listen to the argument, especially when leading lawyers were arguing, or when issues close to the judge's heart were being considered. But generally, we were required to remain in the chambers working while the judge presided over the argument.

Since Bazelon was the chief judge, he got to assign the opinion to one of the three judges on a panel (or nine when on rare occasions the entire court heard the case "en banc"). Following the oral argument, there was a conference among the judges, during which a tentative result was reached and the case assigned. Bazelon always assigned the most interesting cases to himself, or to a judge whose decisions he wanted to influence. We would then meet with Bazelon, and he would tell us which clerk was to work on the opinion. I always got the interesting cases (at least the ones that interested the judge).

After many drafts, and some pressure from the other judges on the panel, the opinion was released to the public. Generally, they were majority opinions, often unanimous, but frequently there were dissenting or concurring opinions. This was a deeply divided court and the dissenting opinions pulled no punches in criticizing the majority, and vice versa.

At the end of the year, the clerks would prepare bound volumes of all the opinions we'd worked on during our clerkship. As I write these words, I have in front of me the maroon volume engraved with the following words:

Chief Judge David L. Bazelon
Opinions 1962–1963
Alan M. Dershowitz, Law Clerk

It is a treasured possession.

My first case involved a man named "Daniel Jackson Oliver Wendell Holmes Morgan."[13] Any lawyer would be proud to have been named after Daniel Webster, Andrew Jackson, and Oliver Wendell Holmes. The problem was he wasn't a lawyer and that wasn't his name! He was an uneducated, but slick, African-American man whose parents were sharecroppers and who had made his way to the District of Columbia, where he bought a dead lawyer's bar certificate in a junk shop. He started to practice, and he did extremely well, beating real prosecutors in cases involving street crimes. His reputation spread in the downtown area, as he kept winning difficult cases. Ultimately the feds checked him out, discovered he wasn't a lawyer, and charged him with multiple counts of fraud, forgery, impersonating an officer of the court, and false pretenses. He represented himself at trial and was convicted and sentenced to three to ten years in prison.

The court appointed a lawyer named Monroe Freedman to argue his appeal. Judge Bazelon invited me to watch the oral argument. I was blown away by Freedman's eloquence, erudition, command of the record, and ability to further his argument while responding to hard questions. I had participated in moot court appeals as a law student, and I had done very well—even earning a job offer from one of the judges who was a partner at a Jewish law firm. But this was a different league. I remember thinking, "I want to be like this guy," and wondering whether I could ever be that good. The lawyer for the prosecution was also quite good, though not up to Freedman's high standards. He was an African-American named Charles Duncan, who, I later was told, was the son of the singer Todd Duncan, who had played Porgy in the original Broadway run of the Gershwin opera *Porgy and Bess*.

Following the argument, the judges decided to affirm the conviction. I was upset, because Freedman had clearly "won" the argument and had certainly convinced me that his client deserved a new trial. I pleaded with Bazelon to let me try to draft an opinion reversing the conviction. He said, "Go ahead," because he too was somewhat sympathetic to the defendant. "But you must find a valid *legal* basis for reversal. It's not enough that the defendant's lawyer was better than the government's lawyer. Nor is it enough that *we* think the defendant should get relief. There has to be a legal basis, even if you need to stretch the law a bit. Go ahead and look for one."

I searched and searched, but Freedman had mined every possible nugget. There was no plausible legal basis for reversal. I learned several important lessons from this exercise in futility: There's an enormous difference between winning an appellate argument and reversing a conviction; there's an equally significant difference between wanting to see a conviction reversed and finding a valid basis for reversal; all the hard work in the world cannot bring about a result if the facts and the law don't justify it.

Subsequently, I learned a series of related lessons that paralleled the above: Even when there is a basis for reversal, a bad job of lawyering will not bring it about; a court that is determined to affirm a conviction—because they don't like the defendant or for some ideological reason—will not be convinced even by the most compelling arguments; without hard work, many of the most persuasive reasons for reversal are never uncovered. I learned these lessons because in Judge Bazelon's court, the judge and the law clerks often did the jobs that the lawyers were supposed to do. But not in the case of Daniel Jackson Oliver Wendell Holmes Morgan, because his lawyer, Monroe Freedman, had done all the hard work and made all the plausible arguments.

Eventually Freedman and I became friends and colleagues, and he went on to become dean of Hofstra Law School and one of the nation's leading experts in legal ethics. I tried to follow in his large footsteps, but I'm not sure I ever made as good an oral argument as he did that day back in 1962.

The remaining cases during my year were in many ways representative of the Supreme Court's future docket during the heyday of the Warren court. Many dealt with the rights of indigent defendants—an issue that came to the fore in the Supreme Court's decision in *Gideon v. Wainright,*[14] decided toward the end of the year of my Bazelon clerkship. That decision ruled that every indigent criminal defendant in a serious case had the right to counsel.

The opinions of Judge Bazelon over the years had laid the foundation for this decision, and several of them were cited in the briefs filed by his friends Abe Fortas and Abe Krash, who had been appointed to represent Gideon. (My friend John Hart Ely was working for the Fortas firm, Arnold & Porter, during the summer the briefs were being prepared,[15] and I reviewed and edited several drafts with John.) Bazelon's opinions—more often dissenting than majority—had established the conceptual framework for a broad-based claim of equality in the criminal justice system. He had gone considerably further than the Supreme Court would ever go in seeking to ensure that indigent defendants were treated no differently from wealthy ones. Many of the cases my year dealt with this issue.

One of the most intriguing cases began as an ordinary pickpocketing of a wallet containing $14.[16] Based on the sparse evidence, "the jury could have inferred either that the wallet was picked from [the alleged victim's] pocket, or that it was accidentally dropped . . . and was picked up by someone who ran off with it."[17] The judge instructed the jury that there was a legal presumption that a defendant's "flight may be considered by jurors as evidence of guilt."[18]

There was no dispute that the defendant did flee when confronted by the alleged victim shouting, "Hey, that's my wallet. Give it back to me." But of course the defendant might well have fled even if he'd simply picked up a dropped wallet and didn't want to return it. Such an action would be immoral but not felonious. The jury convicted him of robbery and the judge sentenced him to prison for two to six years.

When the case came across my desk, I saw it as an opportunity to use my law school background in psychiatry and law—I was working on a casebook with two of my law school professors on *Psychoanalysis, Psychiatry and the Law*[19]—to reverse what appeared to be an unjust conviction. The great legal commentator Wigmore had written the following about evidence of guilty feelings:

> *The commission of a crime leaves usually upon the consciousness a moral impression which is characteristic. The innocent man is without it; the guilty man usually has it. Its evidential value has never been doubted.*[20]

This view had become the accepted wisdom of lawyers, judges, and professors and was the basis for the trial judge's instructions to the jury. I found it questionable, especially in the context of the facts of the case.

In an effort to support my conclusion that the defendant's flight in this case was equally consistent with the legally innocent explanation that he was fleeing to avoid returning a dropped wallet and the guilty explanation that he was fleeing from a pickpocketing crime, I introduced a quote from Sigmund Freud:

> *You may be lead astray . . . by a neurotic who reacts as though he were guilty even though he is innocent—because a lurking sense of guilt already in him assimilates the accusation made against him on this particular occasion. . . . People of this kind are often to be met, and it is indeed a question whether your technique will succeed in distinguishing such self-accused persons from those who are really guilty.*[21]

In addition to citing Freud and dozens of other psychological sources, I also invoked my favorite novelist, Dostoyevsky, noting that in *The Brothers Karamazov*

> *the author describes how Ivan—the brother who had desired death of the father but had not perpetrated the act—manifests all the traditional symptoms of guilt described by Wigmore, whereas the actual murderer reacts in a cool dispassionate way, consistent—according to Wigmore—with innocence.*[22]

Judge Bazelon approved of my somewhat sophomoric display of erudition, and the conviction was reversed for a new trial with proper instructions. Judge Warren Burger wrote a scathing dissent—arguing that our proposed instructions "may be appropriate to a philosophical interchange between judges, lawyers and experts in psychology . . . but are unnecessary to a jury."[23] Judge Bazelon assured me that Burger's dissent "proves we're right."

Other cases dealt with the pervasive problem of police perjury—today it's called "testilying."[24] If a search or interrogation is found to be unconstitutional, its fruits are generally excluded, even if they would prove the defendant's guilt.[25] Not surprisingly, many police officers (as well as prosecutors) hate these "exclusionary rules" and do whatever they can to circumvent them. Some policemen resort to perjury, occasionally assisted by prosecutors in making their "testilies" fit the law. I was shocked when Judge Bazelon first told me about this phenomenon. We didn't learn about this dark side of the law at Yale, and at first I was skeptical. But then I read case after case in which police officers—often the same ones, from the same drug unit—would give essentially the same scripted testimony. Somehow, the suspect always "dropped" the drugs before the police officer arrested him. Bazelon called this "dropsie testimony." Or the suspect would "blurt out" a confession before being interrogated. Bazelon called this a "blurtsie confession."

Bazelon had no patience for testilyiers, for the prosecutors who coached them, or for trial judges who pretended to believe their obvious lies. He would call them out on it, much to the chagrin of some of his fellow judges, especially Warren Burger. Sparks would fly and Bazelon generally ended up in dissent, but he had made his point.

Years later, in my first popular book, *The Best Defense*, I summarized what I had seen in Judge Bazelon's chambers and had then experienced in several cases I had litigated. I called my summary "The Rules of the Justice Game."[26] Slightly amended by subsequent experience, here are "the rules":

Rule I: Most criminal defendants are, in fact, guilty.

Rule II: All criminal defense lawyers, prosecutors, and judges understand and believe Rule I.

Rule III: It is generally easier to convict guilty defendants by violating the Constitution than by complying with it, and in some cases it is impossible to convict guilty defendants without violating the Constitution.

Rule IV: In order to convict guilty defendants, many police witnesses lie about whether they violated the Constitution.

Rule V: All prosecutors, judges, and defense attorneys are aware of Rule IV.

Rule VI: In order to convict guilty defendants, many prosecutors implicitly encourage the police to lie about whether they violated the Constitution.

Rule VII: All judges are aware of Rule VI.

Rule VIII: Many trial judges pretend to believe police officers who they know are lying.

Rule IX: All appellate judges are aware of Rule VIII, yet many pretend to believe the trial judges who pretend to believe the lying police officers.

Rule X: Many judges claim to disbelieve defendants about whether their constitutional rights have been violated, even if they are telling the truth.

Rule XI: Most judges and prosecutors would not knowingly convict a defendant they believe to be innocent of the crime charged (or a closely related crime).

Rule XII: Rule XI does not apply to members of organized crime, drug dealers, career criminals, terrorists, or potential informers.

Rule XIII: Almost nobody really wants justice.

All in all the Bazelon clerkship proved to be a turning point. He helped shape me into the person I have become. He influenced me as a lawyer, teacher, writer, public intellectual, and as a liberal Jew. His highest praise for any person was that he or she was "a mensch." I have aspired to that accolade. When Judge Bazelon retired in 1985, I wrote the following about his contributions to our nation:

> *David Bazelon is certainly not a household name to most Americans. Yet Judge Bazelon—who just retired after thirty-six years of distinguished service on the U.S. Court of Appeals—has been your conscience in Washington since 1949.*
>
> *No single judge—whether on the Supreme Court, the lower federal courts or the state courts—has had a more profound impact on the law's sensitivity to human needs. . . .*
>
> *As a judge, he saw the enormous disparities between how the wealthy are treated in court and how the poor are mistreated. Although he provided few final answers, he pricked the conscience of a nation, and he goaded the U.S. Supreme Court into action in several cases.*[27]

No student can go through a three-year course at any major law school without studying the life work of David Bazelon. The reason for Bazelon's continuing impact is that his primary role—as he saw it—was to raise enduring questions, not to provide transient, trendy solutions. He saw the intermediate appellate courts, such as the one he served on, as uniquely capable of raising questions and directing them at the Supreme Court, the lower district courts, the legislatures, and the executives.

Over my own career, I have certainly not been known for effusively praising the judiciary. Indeed, part of the reason I have been so critical of so many judges is that I learned at the feet of one who set a tone and provided a model that few can meet. Perhaps in that respect Bazelon has made me too tough a critic of others. I know he would be proud of having provoked hard questions, even about the judiciary that he loved.

Several years after retiring, David Bazelon called to inform me that he had early stage Alzheimer's, a disease that also afflicted my father. I visited with Bazelon all through his illness, often with his closest friend, Bill Brennan. We would take Bazelon on walks, reminisce with him, and tell him stories. I remained his law clerk until he died at age eighty-three.

Halfway through my year with David Bazelon I was offered a clerkship with Justice Arthur Goldberg. I was also offered a clerkship with Justice Hugo Black, but I strongly preferred to clerk for a new justice, whose views were not as firmly formed. I asked to see Justice Goldberg before I formally accepted his offer. I told him that I would not be able to work on Saturday or Friday night and asked him if he still wanted to extend the offer. He angrily replied, "I should withdraw the offer just because you asked me that ridiculous question. What do you think I am? How could I possibly turn down somebody because he is an Orthodox Jew?" I apologized for asking the question, but told him that I had previously been turned down by the firm of Paul, Weiss, Rifkind, Wharton, and Garrison. He said, "Paul, Weiss turned you down because you were Orthodox? I'm going to call my friend Si Rifkind. He won't let them get away with that." I sheepishly replied that it was Simon Rifkind who turned me down. (Years later, Arthur Goldberg was offered a partnership at Paul, Weiss, and before accepting he insisted on being assured that what had happened to his law clerk would never happen to another Orthodox Jew. Paul, Weiss now has many Orthodox Jews.) Goldberg told me that my co-clerk was Christian and didn't work on Sunday, so he would have assistance available to him seven days a week.[28] It worked very well, except that on one Saturday an emergency death penalty petition came to Justice Goldberg, and I was the death penalty specialist. So Justice Goldberg had his driver take him to my house in Hyattsville, Maryland, where he knew I would be, and we conferred on the case and he made his decision.

A few months before I started my Supreme Court clerkship, my grandmother came to town, and I took her and my son Elon, who was then two years old, to see the Supreme Court. We got permission to go to Justice Goldberg's chambers, but he was not there. His secretary, Fran Gilbert, invited me to take my grandmother and my son into the justice's private office to look at the paintings, which were done by his artistic wife, Dorothy. The new decorations in his office had just been finished, and his secretary told me that Goldberg was proud of how nice they looked. My son, however, had no appreciation for the new rug and proceeded to leave a large yellow stain in front of Justice Goldberg's desk. When the justice came in, I was on my hands and knees scrubbing the rug with soap. This time, he almost did fire me, but with my grandmother there he would have had a hard time. My grandmother did have an argument with him. She told him that she noticed that morning that I had *davened* (prayed) for only twenty minutes. "It takes at least a half hour," she said. "He's skipping. Tell him to take the full half hour." Justice Goldberg shook his finger at me and said, "Listen to your grandmother."

Before I knew I was to be selected by Justice Goldberg, I interviewed with several of the other justices, including John Harlan, an elegant aristocrat whose grandfather had also served on the Supreme Court. He was impressed with my grades, but he gently asked me why I hadn't worked during the summer for one of the "great Wall Street firms." I couldn't believe that he didn't know that the "great Wall Street firms" were not hiring Jewish kids from Brooklyn. Harlan had himself been a senior partner in one of those firms, and I assumed that he was familiar with their hiring policies. I later learned from one of his Jewish law clerks—he hired many Jews to work for him when he was a judge—that Justice Harlan was probably oblivious to his firm's hiring practices, or at least never really thought about them. Maybe!

I began working for Justice Goldberg on August 1, 1963, just a month before Martin Luther King delivered his "I Have a Dream" speech from the steps of the Lincoln Memorial. A large rally was planned and I wanted to attend. But Justice Goldberg told me that Chief Justice Earl Warren did not want members of the judiciary—which included clerks—to be on the mall that day, because there might be violence, and cases growing out of the violence might come before the courts. I asked Judge Bazelon what I should do. "Come with me," he proposed. He and another judge were going to the mall to listen from the rear and off to the side, in relative anonymity. I went with them and so was able to hear that remarkable speech (following several long-winded speakers representing the groups that had organized the event). I never told Justice Goldberg.

My clerkship with Justice Arthur Goldberg was, in many ways, more exciting than my clerkship with Judge Bazelon. It was, after all, on the Supreme Court, where nearly every case made headlines. During my Goldberg clerkship, President Kennedy was assassinated, Lee Harvey Oswald was killed, and Lyndon Johnson ascended to the Oval Office. Many transforming decisions were rendered in areas as wide-ranging and important as desegregation, freedom of the press, the rights of criminal defendants, reapportionment, the law of obscenity, the death penalty, and trial by jury. Yet, in a more personal way, my second clerkship was anticlimactic. I learned more during my year on the court of appeals than during my year on the high court, in part because Judge Bazelon was such a remarkable teacher and in part because it was my first exposure to the judiciary. This is not to diminish the impact Justice Goldberg had on my life. It too was profound and enduring. The major difference was that Justice Goldberg, who saw me as a protégé, had a specific life plan for me: He wanted me to follow in his footsteps. He saw my professional life unfolding parallel to his. He wanted me to work in the Kennedy administration. Indeed he arranged for me to become an assistant to then attorney general Robert Kennedy—without even asking me! It was well intentioned, and it might even have been the right choice of job following the clerkships, but it was *his* choice, not mine. He wanted me to aspire to a judgeship, perhaps even justice of the Supreme Court, but I never wanted to be a judge. (Neither, it turned out, did he, since he resigned from the Supreme Court after only three years.)

Judge Bazelon, on the other hand, encouraged me to create my own unique career path and avoid the "cookie cutter" paths for which most elite young lawyers opt. "Don't follow in anyone's footsteps," he urged me. "Your feet are too big to fit anyone else's print. Create your own life. You are unique. Live a unique life. Take risks. Live boldly." It was scary, but it fit my personality to a T.

MY YEAR OF CLERKING FOR JUSTICE GOLDBERG

Justice Arthur Goldberg was a man of action. Before being nominated at age fifty-four to the Supreme Court by President John F. Kennedy, Goldberg had accomplished an enormous amount. Unlike most of the current justices, he would have been in the history books even had he never served on the high court.

Arthur Goldberg helped establish the profession of labor law. He represented the most important labor unions; he helped merge the American Federation of Labor (AFL) with the Congress of Industrial Organizations (CIO); he helped rid unions of Communist influence; and he argued some of the most significant labor cases before the Supreme Court, including the steel seizure case of 1952,[29] which challenged the authority of the President to take control over an entire industry in response to a strike. He was perhaps the most successful secretary of labor in history, settling one strike after another and being recognized as a legendary mediator.[30]

The Supreme Court is not a place of action, it is an institution of reaction—to cases and controversies generated by others. It is a place of thoughtful, often solitary, meditation and research. Justice Goldberg was used to working with many people. He was accustomed to crises. When he arrived at the Supreme Court, he once summarized the situation this way: "My phone never rings." The high court is the loneliest of institutions. As Justice Brandeis once put it, "Here we do our own work."[31] The justices only occasionally interact: on the bench; in the weekly, somewhat formal, conference; and in informal one-on-one meetings, which were rare then and even rarer today.[32] In the 1960s the justices almost never appeared on television or gave interviews. (Today, several do.) It is fair to say that Justice Goldberg was lonely and restless and craved the active life he had left behind.

This is not to say that Justice Goldberg was not a serious intellectual. He was. He was also one of the smartest justices in history. He loved the Supreme Court. He loved the law. He loved having intense discussions with his law clerks about jurisprudence. But he needed more than contemplation, deliberation, and discussion. The "passive virtues," as Professor Alexander Bickel once characterized the Supreme Court's role in *not* making decisions, were vices to Arthur Goldberg.[33] He wanted to get things done. He too was an unapologetic judicial activist. He came to the high court with an agenda—a list of changes he wanted to engender.

I will never forget my first meeting with my new boss when I came to work in the Supreme Court during the summer of 1963. He tossed a certiorari petition—an application by a prisoner for review by the high court—at me from across his desk and asked me to read it in his presence. He then asked me, "What do you see in it?" I said, "It's a pro se cert petition in a capital case." He said, "No, what you're holding is the vehicle by which we can end capital punishment in the United States." Abolishing the death penalty was the first item on his "to do" list as a justice.

My major responsibility during the first part of my clerkship was to draft a memorandum supporting Justice Goldberg's view that the death penalty was cruel and unusual punishment. He knew we had no chance of getting the majority to support that view—at least not yet—but he wanted to start a dialogue that would ultimately lead to the judicial abolition of the death penalty. He decided to focus first on an interracial rape case involving a black defendant and a white victim, since almost no whites had been executed for raping blacks, but many blacks had been executed for raping white women. He knew that the key justice would be William Brennan, since if the liberal Brennan would not go along with him, he had no chance of beginning any meaningful dialogue. Because I had done all the research, he assigned me the delicate task of trying to get Justice Brennan to join our opinion. It was a daunting task for a twenty-four-year-old law clerk to persuade a justice of anything, but I went in to see Justice Brennan and he listened to me politely without committing himself. Eventually he did join Justice Goldberg's dissenting opinion and the dialogue was begun. Within less than a decade, it resulted in the judicial abolition of capital punishment, but soon thereafter it was resurrected. The "game" of two steps forward, one step backwards is ongoing.

Justice Goldberg always tried to find a legal basis to save the life of every condemned inmate. Mostly he succeeded. In one such case, he was petitioned to stay an execution and he needed the approval of one more justice to obtain a majority. He called Justice Harlan and secured his oral consent. He then asked me to drive to Justice Harlan's home to have him sign off on the stay. He told me to wait until the justice and Mrs. Harlan finished dinner. And so, at about 9 P.M., I arrived and was shown in by a butler. The justice was sitting at one end of a rather long table, Mrs. Harlan at the other end. Both were wearing formal dinner attire. It was a scene right out of the nineteenth century. Justice Harlan asked me to wait in the library. When he joined me, the butler brought me a coffee, and the justice and I had a brief, polite discussion about the news and then went about the business at hand. It was an evening I will never forget. Not only did we save a life, but I was introduced to a world that I'd thought no longer existed.

Justice Goldberg regarded his "one year clerks" as "law clerks for life." After I completed my clerkship, Justice Goldberg continued to give me assignments, ranging from helping him pick future clerks (such as current Justice Stephen Breyer), to editing his speeches and articles, to helping him draft resolutions at the United Nations (most notably Security Council Resolution 242, following Israel's victory in the Six Day War of 1967),[34] to assisting in his political aspirations. He called me for help, advice, and just to "schmooze" about the state of the world, until his death at the age of eighty-one.

Even while he served on the Supreme Court he took an interest in his law clerks, including us in his weekly Friday afternoon lunches or teas with noteworthy people. Knowing that I was interested in Israel, he invited me to meet the Israeli ambassador to the United States, Avraham Harman, as well as visiting Israeli public officials. When I went to Israel in 1970, he asked me to smuggle a carton of Lucky Strike cigarettes to Israel's prime minister, Golda Meir, whom he had known from their earliest Zionist days in the Midwest.

Three months after I started working for Justice Goldberg I was in his secretary's office while she was talking on the phone to her husband, who was an officer in the U.S. armed forces. He had something to do with communications, because he told her that shots had been fired in Dallas. We turned on a small television set that had been in my cubicle ever since I had brought it from home to watch the World Series a couple of months earlier. Nothing was yet on the news. A few minutes later everyone in the world knew that President Kennedy had been shot. It was a Friday and the justices were in their weekly conference, which no one else was allowed to attend. I had been given strict instructions never to interrupt Justice Goldberg during one of these conferences, but I knew this was an exception. I went to the door of the conference room and knocked. Justice Goldberg, being the junior justice, answered and gave me a dirty look, saying, "I told you not to interrupt me." I said, "Mr. Justice, you are going to want to know that the President has been shot." Several of the justices immediately gathered around my TV, which, it turned out, was the only one in the entire Supreme Court building. We watched as the news got progressively worse, finally leading to the announcement that the President was dead. The chief justice asked the justices to disperse for fear that there might be a conspiracy involving attacks on other institutions, such as occurred following the Lincoln assassination. The clerks stayed behind.

The following night, right after the Sabbath was over, Justice Goldberg asked me to drive him to the White House. He was closely connected both to the Kennedy family and to Lyndon Johnson, and the new president wanted his advice. I picked up the justice in my old Peugeot, which was filled with children's toys, and I drove him to the White House gate. Goldberg asked me to wait for him, since the meeting would be relatively brief, and drive him home. When the White House guard looked into the car, he immediately flung the back door open and grabbed a toy gun.

Nerves were tense. Later, I also drove the justice to the funeral and was with him when the news came over the radio that Lee Harvey Oswald had been shot. Goldberg exclaimed angrily, "What kind of a country are we living in!"

Shortly thereafter, Chief Justice Earl Warren told the Supreme Court staff that he was being appointed chairman of the newly formed Warren Commission. Goldberg told me that the President had asked the chief justice to perform a patriotic duty and to convince the American public that the act was that of a lone gunman, and not the result of a conspiracy by the Communists. Warren agreed because he did not want to allow any excuses either for the return of McCarthyism or military hostilities between the Soviet Union and the United States. I later learned that Lyndon Johnson personally believed that there was a conspiracy behind the Kennedy assassination, but he handpicked the Warren Commission to ensure that even if the evidence pointed in that direction, it would be covered up in the interest of national security.

A controversial issue during my clerkship was obscenity. I recall Justice Goldberg coming back from a screening of an allegedly obscene movie called *The Lovers*[35] and saying, "That damn movie ought to be banned, not for obscenity, but for fraud. There were no good dirty parts." Another case involved an erotic memoir called *Fanny Hill*.[36] The book was not included in the record, but Justice Goldberg wanted to read it. He was embarrassed to go to a bookstore and buy it himself, so he asked me to buy a copy of the book, but not to read it. Ha!

A man once knocked at the door of Justice Goldberg's chambers (in those days, anybody could walk into the chambers; today, that is impossible). He told me that he had met the justice and that he was making a financial sacrifice to serve on the Supreme Court. He was starting a foundation to help people make the transition from lucrative private life to low-paying government jobs, and he wanted to offer the justice the opportunity to have his salary supplemented. When I told the justice the story, he told me to "throw the bum out." The "bum" turned out to be Louis Wolfson, a man facing stock fraud charges. He later made a similar offer to Justice Fortas, who accepted it and lost his seat on the Supreme Court as a result.[37] Justice Goldberg was far more scrupulous. One day he received a basket of fruit for his birthday. He looked at the card and saw that it was from Katherine Graham, the publisher of the *Washington Post*. The important case of *New York Times v. Sullivan* was pending,[38] and Goldberg insisted that we send the basket back. I told him that I had eaten a banana from it. He insisted that I go to the fruit store and replace it before having the basket returned.

Justice Goldberg was a deeply ethical but only marginally religious man. He did not attend synagogue regularly, though he was very active in numerous aspects of Jewish life. Every year he had a Passover Seder, to which he invited Washington luminaries. When I was his law clerk, he invited me, and I gladly accepted. Knowing that I was kosher, he arranged to have the entire Seder dinner provided by an expensive kosher caterer. At the last minute, my mother forbade me from attending a Seder other than hers, and I had to decide whose views trumped, a justice of the Supreme Court or a Jewish mother. I don't have to tell you who won, and Justice Goldberg remained angry with me for months, saying, "All those people had to eat catered kosher food because of you, while you ate your mother's home-cooked food."

One day, while he was hearing arguments, I received a note asking me whether it was required under Jewish law that an Orthodox woman always wear a hat, even while arguing a case in the Supreme Court. The Supreme Court had a rule prohibiting wearing any head covering.[39] But Goldberg was willing to insist that there be an exception if there was a religious obligation. I wrote back saying that there was such a rule for strictly Orthodox women.[40] He wrote back asking me to come into the courtroom, which I did. I looked at the offending hat. Just as I did so, I got another note from Justice Goldberg, asking if there was anything in Jewish law that required a woman to wear such a big ugly hat. I assured him that there was not. They made an exception, but Justice Goldberg told me to discreetly inform the woman that the next time she argued, she should wear a smaller hat.

Justice Goldberg also asked my advice about whether he should sit on the opening day of court, which fell on Yom Kippur,[41] the holiest day of the Jewish calendar, on which work is prohibited. I looked at the calendar of cases and noted that there was a capital case. I told the justice that Jewish law permitted violation of nearly all religious precepts if human life was at stake.[42] He sat and helped save the life of the condemned man.

A few weeks after I began to work in the Supreme Court, I was walking through the hall and needed to use the bathroom. I went to the nearest bathroom. Suddenly an arm was gently on my shoulder. It was one of the justices' messengers. "That bathroom is for us," he said. "Yours is over there." He pointed. I quickly understood what was going on. *All* the guards, secretaries, clerks, and justices were white. *All* the messengers were black. The bathrooms in the Supreme Court were, as a matter of practice, segregated. This was nearly a decade after *Brown v. Board of Education*. I rushed to tell Justice Goldberg.

He was appalled not only at what I had told him, but at the fact that he hadn't figured it out himself. He summoned his messenger, who confirmed the practice and assured the justice that his fellow black messengers liked having their own bathroom, where they could hang out during breaks. But Goldberg would have none of it. He asked me to check on whether there were, in fact, any nonwhite employees, other than messengers, on the Supreme Court payroll. I reported back that there was one: The court's barber was a black man (who, it later turned out, refused to cut the hair of any black person, because, as he proudly claimed, he was trained to be a "white man's barber" and didn't know how to cut the "kinky" hair of black customers).

Justice Goldberg immediately hired the Supreme Court's first black secretary. He advised Chief Justice Earl Warren of the court's de facto segregation and got him to put an end to it. His actions produced some grumbling among the white guards and the black messengers, but everyone soon got used to the new regime. (It took the appointment of Thurgood Marshall to get the barber to begin to cut the hair of a black man, but only after Goldberg told him that his own hair was kinkier than Marshall's.)

The Supreme Court had a small basketball court on the top floor. The clerks called it "the Highest Court in the Land," since it was directly above the courtroom itself. The games were in early evening, and occasionally Justice White, who was a former professional football player, participated. As a basketball player, White was a great football player—not much finesse, but lots of elbows. I played only occasionally, but once he boxed me out for a rebound and, in the process of grabbing the ball, hit me in the face with his elbow. I instinctively yelled, "That's a foul, damn it!" to which I quickly added, "Mr. Justice." I was overruled by His Honor.

According to historians of the Supreme Court, the 1963–1964 term was among the most significant and innovative in the history of the American judiciary, and Justice Goldberg was at the center of the action.[43] He assigned me to draft the famous *Escobedo* opinion,[44] which changed the law of confessions and led to the even more famous *Miranda* decision,[45] which set out the well known "Miranda warnings" ("You have the right to remain silent . . ."). Escobedo was suspected of killing a relative, and he was interrogated without his lawyer being present, even though his lawyer was in the police station, trying to advise him on his right to remain silent. I drafted the following words, which became an important part of my legal philosophy throughout my career:

> *We have . . . learned the . . . lesson of history that no system of criminal justice can, or should, survive if it comes to depend for its continued effectiveness on the citizens' abdication through unawareness of their constitutional rights. No system worth preserving should have to* fear *that if an accused is permitted to consult with a lawyer, he will become aware of, and exercise, these rights. If the exercise of constitutional rights will thwart the effectiveness of a system of law enforcement, then there is something very wrong with that system.*[46]

The theme of this paragraph—the right to know of one's rights—has pervaded my thinking and teaching ever since.[47]

During that term, I also drafted opinions—some majority, some concurring, some dissenting—on trial by jury, freedom of speech, desegregation, reapportionment, immunity, and other important and changing areas of the law. There could be no better foundation for the next phase of my career—teaching law students at the nation's largest and most prestigious law school, Harvard.

One of the great villains of the day to all liberals was J. Edgar Hoover, the head of the FBI. On several occasions, I let my negative views about Hoover be known to Goldberg, but he never said a word. I didn't understand why. A few years later, I asked Judge Bazelon, who smiled and said, "I probably shouldn't tell you, but it's important for you to know that there are no perfect heroes." He continued, "Hoover and Goldberg got along well, because when Goldberg was the lawyer for the labor movement, he worked hard to rid the CIO of Communist influence." I asked whether that meant he informed on Communists within the union. Bazelon replied, "I wouldn't use the word 'informed,' but he worked closely with Hoover on a common goal: to rid the CIO of Communist influence."[48]

Bazelon told me that Thurgood Marshall had played a similar role with regard to the NAACP—trying to cleanse it of Communist influences.

"That's how Thurgood and Arthur made it to the court. If Hoover had opposed them, they might not have been appointed."

I was shocked. "But there have been other liberals appointed as well," I insisted.

"Yes, Douglas, but he was Joe Kennedy's boy, and Hoover liked Joe Kennedy, at least back in the day when Douglas was appointed. With Hoover, it wasn't so much what you believed as were you with Hoover or against him. It was also whether he had anything on you that he could use as leverage."

"What about Justice Brennan?" I asked.

"Bill was an accident, an Eisenhower mistake. They didn't know he would be so liberal. Eisenhower regarded Warren and Brennan as his worst mistakes."[49]

About a year after I finished my clerkship with Justice Goldberg, I received a phone call from Dorothy Goldberg, Arthur's wife. She was sobbing. "Alan, make him change his mind." Justice Goldberg had decided to leave the Supreme Court after three terms in order to become the U.S. ambassador to the UN. Mrs. Goldberg was very upset with her husband's decision, but there was nothing I could say that would make him change his mind. He talked about patriotism and the need to end the war in Vietnam and insisted that he was doing the right thing.

When I reminded him that his was the swing vote on many important issues and that he might be replaced by someone more conservative who might swing the court the other way, he assured me that President Johnson would select his friend and former lawyer Abe Fortas to fill the vacancy. "Abe will vote the same way I did," Goldberg assured me. "I won't be missed on the court," he said, "but I can make a difference in ending the Vietnam War."

Neither of us realized at the time that President Johnson wanted Goldberg off the court precisely so that he could appoint his loyal friend Abe Fortas, whom he could count on to support him if the corruption investigation—involving Bobby Baker and Lady Bird Johnson's ownership of radio and television stations—that was still swirling around him were ever to reach the Supreme Court. Fortas did become Johnson's "man" on the court when it came to issues relating to the Vietnam War and soon found himself embroiled in a corruption scandal that cost him his seat.

Five years after he retired from the Supreme Court, Justice Goldberg decided to run for governor of New York. He asked his former law clerks, including current Supreme Court justice Stephen Breyer and me, to help him in his campaign. Goldberg was a stiff campaigner, and not particularly knowledgeable about New York. Once while eating a knish at Yonah Schimmel's on Houston Street on the Lower East Side of Manhattan, he told the assembled press how pleased he was to be in Brooklyn. A few days later an acquaintance who was a reporter with the *Daily News* called to have me comment on a story he was writing concerning how stiff and formal Justice Goldberg was. He said he had heard reports that he required his former law clerks still to call him "Mr. Justice." It was true. I went in to see the justice and told him about the upcoming story. He replied, "Well it's true, so why don't you just confirm it?" I said, "Mr. Justice, can't we just change it?" He said, "No, I want you to continue to call me Mr. Justice." I replied with a compromise: "How about if we continue to call you Mr. Justice in private but we call you Arthur or Art or Artie in public?" He reluctantly agreed to be called "Arthur" in public, so long as we still continued to call him "Mr. Justice" in private. I called him "Mr. Justice" till the day he died. Needless to say, he lost the election to Nelson Rockefeller.

Justice Goldberg always wanted me to become a judge, perhaps even a justice. I never had any interest in wearing a robe, since judging requires the kind of passivity that is not suitable to my temperament. I was surprised that Justice Goldberg was so insistent, since he himself had left the bench after only three years. I don't think I would have lasted three months. In any event, I never lived my life so as to make it possible to be nominated for anything that required confirmation. I was once flattered by an article that listed some of the most talented people in America who were unconfirmable for any office. I was included on that honor roll. My friend Steve Breyer, on the other hand, was always the perfect judge, and I worked hard behind the scenes to do everything I could to help his chances of serving on the bench. I helped him get confirmed for the court of appeals and lobbied President Clinton to appoint him to the Supreme Court. On the night of his nomination, he and his wife came to our home for an intimate celebration of his assuming the Goldberg seat on the court. He has proved to be an extraordinary judge and is one of the fairest people I know.

Justice Goldberg would have been so proud that one of his law clerks had followed in his footsteps.

Some lawyers describe their clerkships as career-enhancing "jobs." My clerkships were life-changing experiences, which continue to influence me to this day. There could have been no better preparation for my life as a professor at Harvard Law School—a job offered to me during my clerkship.

Having completed my two years of clerking, I was now on my way to begin my career as an assistant professor of law. I was also completing the most transformative decade of my young life—past and probably future. In the spring of 1955 I had been a C student in a not very good high school. By the fall of 1964, I had become the youngest assistant professor in the history of the law school of the greatest university in the world. I reflected on this transformation—and the reasons underlying it—on the drive from D.C. to Cambridge.

4

BEGINNING MY LIFE AS AN ACADEMIC

Harvard Law School

I arrived in the Boston area during the summer of 1964 with my wife and two sons, first renting an apartment in Brookline and then moving to Cambridge a year later.

I began my teaching career at Harvard at the age of twenty-five, having been hired while still a law clerk, on the basis of my law school record and several articles I had published as a student. Some of my students were older than I was, and more experienced. I was called the "Boy Professor."[1] It was intimidating. It was also exhilarating to stand in front of 175 brilliant recent graduates of the colleges I couldn't even have dreamed of attending—and teaching *them*. Here I could unload both barrels and not worry that I was offending a teacher or judge. I *was* the teacher. My students were worried about offending me!

Preparing for classes that I had never before taught was a full-time job. When I began teaching, the two "best" teachers were reputed to be Clark Byse and Ben Kaplan. I wanted to learn from the best, so I asked if I could sit in on some of their classes. Both refused. Professor Kaplan asked me, rhetorically, whether I "allowed people to watch while you make love with your wife?" I replied, "Of course not." He smiled and said, "Well, I make love with my students and don't want anyone watching." I was tempted to respond that if I had 175 wives and made love to them all at once, I wouldn't notice if people watched. I had to figure out how to teach based on trial and error. For the first several years I did nothing but teach and write. It was a full-time job, and I had no time for cases or other outside activities.

My first assignment was to teach the required first year course in criminal law.[2] The men were dressed in shirts and ties; the handful of women wore skirts. The teaching style of the day was Socratic, with the teacher posing hypothetical questions based on real cases. The Socratic method came naturally to me because of my Talmudic background and argumentative nature. From the beginning I sensed that the traditional casebooks did not give the students an appropriate balance between the theory of law and its real-world practice. I decided to write my own book, along with my criminal law mentor at Yale, Joseph Goldstein.[3] I also decided to supplement my book weekly with materials about current developments. My goal was to keep the students up-to-date while also preparing them to practice, teach, judge, or legislate until the end of their careers a half century hence. I also wanted to introduce my students to other disciplines—psychology, sociology, economics, biology, literature—that would enrich their lives as lawyers. I rejected any sharp distinction between "theoretical" and "practical" approaches to teaching, believing that theory must be tested by practice, and that practice should be informed by theory.

From the first day, I loved the Socratic exchange with students. But I noticed that even though several of my students were older than me (William Bennett, who even back then was a brilliant, articulate, and unembarrassed conservative, was among them, as was David Gergen), many were intimidated by the fact that I was the professor. The professors depicted in the movie *The Paper Chase* were still the rule at Harvard, and students were terrified of making a mistake. I wanted to loosen them up, so I decided on a ploy. About a week into the class I deliberately made a mistake about a case, asking what the jury instruction had been. A student sheepishly raised his hand and said, "Professor, there was no jury instruction—the case was tried before a judge." I said, "Woops—I made a mistake. You're right," and I moved on. After that "mistake" the students loosened up and were prepared to take more risks.

Sometimes my mistakes in class were unintentional and embarrassing.[4]

I offended some of my Jewish students while discussing affirmative action in Canada, where only "visible minorities" are eligible for preference. A student asked me whether Jews were a visible minority. I responded, "No, we're an audible minority." I got flack from a number of students who thought I was reaffirming a stereotype. I quickly learned that humor was important to my teaching, but that humor based on racial, gender, or religious stereotyping could raise sensitivities.

I was sympathetic, therefore, when I asked a first year student how he would have responded to a particular plea bargain offer. His response: "I would have tried to Jew him down a bit." The class was appalled at his ethnic slur. But I understood that he was probably just regurgitating what he had heard at his dinner table. I spoke to him after class. He was genuinely mortified. I'm sure he never repeated that slur.

One day in Criminal Law I had a particularly obnoxious student who kept trying to one-up other students by referring to his background in philosophy. He would always begin his statements by saying, "Kant would say . . . " or "Hegel would say. . . ." We were going to be studying an essay by the great contemporary philosopher Robert Nozick. This was shortly after the release of *Annie Hall*, in which Woody Allen is standing in line for a movie and overhears a pretentious man regaling his date with information about Marshall McLuhan. Woody then pulls McLuhan from behind a sign and has him confront the man, saying, "You know nothing of my work."[5] I told Bob Nozick, who was a close friend, about the student, and on the day in question, Bob sat in the back of the room with a hat over his head. As soon as the student began, "As Professor Nozick would say . . . ," Bob took his hat off, strutted to the front, and declared, "You know nothing of my philosophy." He then turned to me and said, "And neither do you." We all had a good laugh, and Bob co-taught the rest of the class with me.

Because I was a rookie, I tended to spend an enormous number of hours preparing for each class. I stayed up the night before planning my questions and strategies and got to the law school at 7 A.M., parking in the first available slot. Several days into the semester Professor Clark Byse mentioned at lunch that Dean Griswold was sizzling mad because someone was taking his parking spot. Nobody had told me that the first spot was traditionally reserved for the dean.

Dean Griswold was quite concerned about my lack of sophistication. I had never been outside the United States, barely out of the Northeast. I still spoke with a Brooklyn accent and, occasionally, allowed Yiddishisms to creep into my conversation. Griswold decided to take me on as a project. In the spring of my first year, he told me that he wanted me to go to England and France to look into criminology institutes. The school would pay for the trip, and various alumni would show me around. I was a bit surprised when I got to Paris and discovered that there was no criminology institute to speak of. In London, I was invited to represent Harvard Law School at the 750th anniversary of the Magna Carta, at Westminster Abbey, where I sat several rows behind the Queen. It was only years later that Griswold acknowledged to me that the criminology institutes were just an excuse to have me travel and acquire a bit of culture. It worked. I bought my first piece of art in Paris on that trip—a Kandinsky lithograph for which I paid $25.[6] While in Paris, I was offered the opportunity one night either to attend a Paris opera or to hear a new group of British pop singers. Because I was trying to acquire culture, I chose the opera, and missed an opportunity to hear the Beatles in person. My children still kid me about that one.[7]

Shortly after I began teaching, the *Harvard Law Record* wrote an article, headlined "The Psyche and the Law,"[8] describing my somewhat unusual approach to teaching.

> *His course in criminal law seems to some not to be a law course at all. For in place of abstracted appellate decisions, the would-be lawyers read pages by Margaret Mead. Where one would expect a capsule treatment of criminal procedure, he is apt to find a papal lecture on medical research and morality. Instead of listing categories of offences, the students skim Alfred Kinsey's report on the sex life of American males.*[9]

The article described me as "probably the youngest man ever named to the Harvard Law School faculty, [who] got his appointment at age 24."[10] It quoted me saying that "there's no such thing as The Law. . . . Law is one of our many processes for ordering society. You can't view this process as a neatly compartmentalized entity. It must be viewed in its full perspective as an ongoing system."[11]

The article said that I saw my job not as teaching "the specifics of law in any jurisdiction; anyone can find that on his own," but as teaching my students how "to ask the right questions and bring to bear the right information for the right purpose."[12] In other words, how to think critically and teach themselves.

Some traditionalists were appalled. One alumnus wrote to the school newspaper:

> *Professor Dershowitz seems to epitomize some of the lack of reality at the law school. . . . Until such time as our whole penological system is changed, the law student is going to have to know his "law" [to] do a lawyer's job. One cannot deny the credentials of Professor Dershowitz's genius, but I question*

> *whether the application of his genius as apparently applied, is of any help making good lawyers out of Harvard law students.*[13]

Justice Arthur Goldberg wrote a letter defending my approach, assuring my critics that "Mr. Dershowitz's students will be the beneficiaries of his engaging personality and extraordinary insight into the subjects he will teach, just as I was."[14]

The *Harvard Law Record* also editorialized that

> *it is good to know that many of these subjects are being injected into the Harvard Law curriculum by young Professor Alan M. Dershowitz; no doubt, even with our liberal arts backgrounds, we could stand and benefit from more such learning.*

Shortly thereafter, an article in the *New York Times Magazine*, comparing Harvard and Yale Law Schools, described me as "a fresh wind blowing through Harvard" and an extremely popular teacher.[15] That article accorded me legitimacy even among some skeptics. At the end of my first year, I was given the highest teaching rating among the faculty. A subsequent article said that "his students have praised him as 'the master of the hypothetical—answer one correctly, and he's got one in his arsenal that's guaranteed to tie your tongue in knots.'" Soon, younger teachers were asking to sit in on my classes. I said yes.

I had the same goal for every class, and when I think back on it, it was far too ambitious: I had to say something original, teach something that had never been written before. That was my aspiration, and I worked hard to achieve it. Law, of course, is based on precedent: You got points for showing that someone, particularly a judge, had said earlier what you were saying now. I hated that approach. It reminded me of my yeshiva education. I wanted to be original. I knew the students wouldn't appreciate it, because they wouldn't know that what I was saying had never been said by anybody, but that was my way of satisfying myself. I would rip up my notes at the end of the year and start from scratch. I was an energetic teacher, trying to put everything I had into each class.

Because I was teaching Criminal Law, I had a lot of freedom: No one really cared about Criminal Law at Harvard. Our students were unlikely to become criminal lawyers. In fact, I started out one of my classes by saying, "Statistically, more of you are going to be criminal defendants than criminal lawyers, so pay attention." My first year "Crim" class was not a bread-and-butter course like those concerning corporations or tax.

I don't think I would have had the same freedom had I been assigned to teach contracts or property.

From the very beginning of my career at Harvard, I taught the widest assortment of classes. If I wanted to learn a new subject, the best way was to offer a seminar in that subject and learn it along with my students. I measured the success of a class not only by what I had taught my students but also by what I had learned from them. My standard courses were Criminal Law and Criminal Procedure, as well as Law and Psychiatry. I taught those every year, though I varied the content. I also offered a course or seminar in a new subject that I had never previously taught. Often it reflected the passion of the times, such as the Vietnam War, racial violence, Watergate, and the like. It was a challenge to learn a new subject every year, but it kept me fresh and made me avoid the problem some teachers have of simply regurgitating the same ideas.

One reason why so many teachers become stale is that their students spend the class time taking notes. Many students are quite adept at verbatim transcription, using various forms of shorthand. (Today, of course, computers are the note-taking tool of choice.) I hated to see my students behaving like courtroom stenographers, looking down at their notebooks while I or one of their classmates talked. To counteract this phenomenon, I would walk up and down the aisle, confronting students and asking them questions face-to-face, emulating the approach that had been used by Professor Bickel in his seminar. I loved Bickel's style because I never took notes, but it had made some of my note-taking classmates nervous to miss getting down even a few of the professor's pearls. It also upset some of my students. So I developed another approach.

In my first year Criminal Law class, I prohibited (*meturnished*) any note-taking during the first two weeks, banning pens, pencils, and notebooks. I insisted that the students learn to listen, remember, and respond without any crutches. In exchange for denying them the right to take notes, I promised that none of the introductory material covered during this note-free period would be on the exam. This helped to loosen them up. By the beginning of the third week, when note-taking was permitted, many fewer students behaved like stenographers. More of them looked directly at me and their fellow students when we were speaking, and more of them participated in the class discussion.

Although I came to Harvard Law School as an avowed liberal, I have tried hard not to use the classroom to propagandize my captive audience. My goal is not to turn conservatives into liberals, but to make conservatives more thoughtful conservatives, better able to articulate and defend nuanced positions. The same is true of liberals and everyone else. I always play the devil's advocate, challenging every view and questioning every idea.

VIGNETTE

Malcolm X at Harvard

Shortly after I began teaching, students from the Harvard Law Forum asked me if I would introduce the controversial Malcolm X. He had been invited to speak, but no senior faculty member would agree to introduce him, and the rules required that a faculty member perform this function. I agreed, despite my disagreement with many of Malcolm X's views. He had just returned from a trip to Mecca, where he embraced Islam and began to say some awful things about Israel, Zionists, and Jews. But, believing in free speech, I agreed to facilitate his appearance.

As I introduced him, I noticed that he was wearing what appeared to be a large camera case slung over his shoulder. I later learned that it contained a gun, and that the reason no other faculty member would agree to share the stage with him was as much because his life was under constant threat as because of his controversial views.

The event went smoothly. Archie Epps—a distinguished African-American Harvard dean—made introductory comments in which he sharply distanced himself from the views of Malcolm X. Then I made my somewhat more critical introduction. Malcolm X then proceeded to regale the crowd with his controversial views on black liberation.

Following the speech, we went to dinner. I was seated next to Malcolm X, and we spent most of the dinner arguing about the Middle East. I asked if he would be willing to travel to Israel. He said no, because he regarded it as occupied Muslim land, but he added, "I would be much safer in Israel than in the Arab countries I visited, and safer than I am here in the United States." Within months of making that comment, Malcolm X was gunned down in Harlem.

Several years later, Dean Epps edited a book entitled *Malcolm X: Speeches at Harvard*.[16] He included the speech as well as my critical introduction. But he excluded his own critical introduction. By this time,

Malcolm X had become a martyr, and my critical views seemed out of place, so I called Epps and asked him why he decided to include my critical comments but not his own. He responded, "That's the advantage of being the editor. You decide what stays in and what goes out."

Students who don't read my outside articles are often unaware of my political views. For example, in class I generally make the case *for* capital punishment, because that is an unpopular view among the students. I espouse other "devil's advocate" positions as well. I also assign readings with which I fundamentally disagree, so long as they are well reasoned and present a perspective that the students are likely to encounter in the real world.

A few years after I became a full professor, Derek Bok, then dean of the law school, called me into his office and told me that I was a very expensive professor. Since salaries are fairly standard at Harvard, I didn't know what he was talking about. He pulled out a letter from a Harvard alum saying that he would make a very considerable donation to Harvard Law School on condition that I was fired. Many of the old-fashioned alumni were upset that I was teaching subjects like Psychiatry and Law, but this alum had a more personal grievance. I had successfully represented, on a pro bono basis, a young man I had grown up with in Brooklyn, who had been accused of making a bomb for the Jewish Defense League that had caused the death of a young woman employee of Sol Hurok's.[17] The young woman was the sister-in-law of this wealthy alumnus. If I were fired, he would donate a large building worth millions of dollars. I suggested to Derek Bok that maybe we could make a deal for a significant severance package. We both laughed, knowing that a great (and rich) university like Harvard could never, by the threat of withholding any amount of money, be intimidated into firing a tenured professor.

In my second semester of teaching, I was assigned to teach Family Law, which was an elective popular with women—women lawyers were thought suitable to practice in such "soft" areas of law as divorce and child custody. My class included some of the most prominent women graduates of that era, including Liddy Dole, who became a United States senator; Elizabeth Holtzman, who became a member of Congress and the district attorney of Brooklyn; Elizabeth Bartholet, who is a professor at Harvard Law School; and several other prominent figures.

When I began teaching, Harvard Law School had been admitting women for only a decade, and some of the professors still didn't believe that women could make good lawyers.[18] I encountered this prejudice at the end of my first year.

The star student in my class was a woman from New York who eventually became a distinguished judge. She received an A grade on the final exam. Three of her other first year teachers also gave her A grades, but her Contracts teacher gave her a D. She asked me to read her exam. It was clearly of A quality. I was sure that her Contracts professor had simply made a transcription error, and so I went to his office to discuss it. He glanced at the exam and said, "Oh yes, I remember her. She doesn't think like a lawyer. That's why I gave her a D." I later learned that this professor has been opposed to admitting women to Harvard Law School.

This episode persuaded me that something had to be done about the lingering prejudices of some of the faculty. Accordingly, I proposed "blind grading" of all exams, so that professors could not know the gender of the student until *after* the grades were submitted.

Decades later, my wife and I, and my son Elon, had dinner with then president Clinton and the First Lady. We had invited them to our synagogue on Martha's Vineyard for Rosh Hashanah services, and they asked us to join them for dinner after the services. I asked Hillary why she had chosen Yale Law School over Harvard. She laughed and said, "Harvard didn't want me." I said I was sorry that Harvard had turned her down. She replied, "No, I received letters of acceptance from both schools." She explained that a boyfriend had then invited her to the Harvard Law School Christmas dance, at which several Harvard Law School professors were in attendance. She asked one for advice about which law school to attend. The professor looked at her and said, "We have about as many women as we need here. You should go to Yale. The teaching there is more suited to women." I asked who the professor was, and she told me she couldn't remember his name but that she thought it started with a B. A few days later, we met the Clintons at a party. I came prepared with yearbook photos of all the professors from that year whose name began with B. She immediately identified the culprit. He was the same professor who had given my A student a D, because she didn't "think like a lawyer." It turned out, of course, that it was this professor—and not the two (and no doubt more) brilliant women he was prejudiced against—who didn't think like a lawyer. Lawyers are supposed to act on the evidence, rather than on their prejudgments. The sexist professor ultimately became a judge on the International Court of Justice.

I told Hillary that it was too bad I wasn't at that Christmas dance, because I would have urged her to come to Harvard. She laughed, turned to her husband, and said, "But then I wouldn't have met him . . . and he wouldn't have become President."

Professor "B" was not alone in his negative views of women as lawyers. One teacher refused to call on women, except on one day of the year, which he called "ladies' day." On that day, he picked on them and verbally abused them to the point that some deliberately stayed away. Erwin Griswold, the dean of the law school and a great defender of civil liberties and civil rights, was a misogynist. Near the beginning of my teaching career, he invited me and all the entering women students—a small number—to his home for dinner. He warned the women that if they'd come to law school to find husbands, they would be disappointed: "Harvard Law School men don't date Harvard Law School girls. They date girls from Lesley." (Lesley was a neighboring women's college.) He then went around the table asking each female student why she was taking up the place of a man who would actually practice law, while they got married and raised children.

Dean Griswold wasn't particularly comfortable with Jews either. At the same dinner, he noticed that I didn't eat the meat, and he asked why. I told him I was kosher, to which he responded: "Even the Catholics have eliminated the prohibition against eating meat on Friday. Don't you think it's time for your people to eat what everyone else eats?" I thought he was kidding, so I said: "I'll check with my people." He wasn't kidding. The next time I saw him, I said: "I've checked with my people, and they said that they've been keeping kosher for thousands of years, so a few more centuries couldn't hurt." He didn't laugh. I think this exchange kept me kosher for an extra few years!

For more than a year, Griswold called me "Shapiro," which was the name of another assistant professor with a Jewish-sounding name. Griswold demanded that I teach classes on Saturday. I refused. He said he couldn't make a special exception for me because I was a practicing Jew. I still refused. So he abolished Saturday classes.

Shortly after I was appointed to the Harvard Law School faculty, I had received a call from Judge Bailey Aldrich inviting me to present a talk to the members of his private club, called the "Club of Odd Volumes." He assured me that its members included some of the best and most important lawyers in Boston, including several justices of the Supreme Court and other judges. "We invite all the new dons to tell us about their work," he advised me.

Remembering Judge Bazelon's refusal to speak at Justice Douglas's restricted club, I politely told Judge Aldrich that I would get back to him. I then called the head of the Anti-Defamation League and inquired about the club. "They don't accept Jews, Catholics, blacks, or women," he responded. I called Judge Aldrich and told him that I had a strict policy against speaking at any "restricted" club and so I would respectfully have to decline his kind invitation. (I adopted that "policy" that day, having never before been invited to speak at a restricted, or any other, club.) He thanked me for considering the invitation. Within an hour, I was abruptly summoned into the dean's office.

Dean Griswold informed me that I had offended one of the law school's most important alumni, that I was the only assistant professor ever to turn down an invitation to speak at that club, and that it was important for untenured faculty to present their work there, because several of the members served on the Harvard Board of Overseers, which approved all tenure decisions. He chided me: "You've hurt your chances. Why did you decline their invitation? Will you reconsider it if I can get them to invite you again?"

I said no and explained my reasons. Griswold, who despite his Midwest origins considered himself an honorary Brahmin, was a cautious advocate of civil rights and civil liberties, so I thought he would understand. He paused, looked directly at me, and said, "While I don't agree with you, considering your background I can understand why you would feel uncomfortable at that club. I'll call Bailey and try to explain. I hope you haven't hurt your chances." That was the last I heard, until a few years later, when Dean Griswold informed me that the chairman of the overseers subcommittee being asked to review and approve the faculty decision recommending me for tenure was an active member of "the club." I was ready for a fight. But I was approved, the dean later told me, by a unanimous vote.

Several years after I began teaching, I was invited to deliver a named lectureship at a major university. Following my talk, there was a dinner at the local university club. When I got to the club, several women were picketing because it was a men's-only club. I refused to cross the picket line, and the dinner had to be moved to a different venue, over the strong objections of the chief justice of the state, who had sponsored the dinner. I had a similar experience in Columbus, Ohio, after I argued an important case on behalf of a law firm in the city. They invited my female associate and me to have dinner with them at the local university club. When we got there, they asked my associate if she wouldn't mind walking in through the side door since the main entrance was for men only. Since she was a young associate, she reluctantly agreed, but I refused to let her demean herself. We had dinner at a local restaurant. Several years later, I was invited to Australia to give a series of lectures, and the Harvard Club of Sydney asked me to give a luncheon talk. I agreed. When I mentioned to a friend that I was going to be speaking at the Australia club, he advised me that it was closed to Jews, women, and blacks. I gave the club two options: I would keep my commitment, but I would speak about why it was wrong for Harvard to hold events at segregated clubs, or they could move the speech and I would give a talk about life at Harvard. They chose the second alternative. When I returned to Harvard, I wrote to the dean, and a memo was circulated mandating that henceforth no Harvard professors, speaking on behalf of Harvard, should appear in a segregated venue. When a Jewish country club in Boston asked me to talk, I declined the invitation. They explained that the club had been established in reaction to the unwillingness of other country clubs in the area to accept Jewish members. I told them that this did not justify further discrimination. The membership chairman called and told me that, in fact, the club had six non-Jewish members. I made the speech. A young member approached me and told me I had been conned: "Sure, we have six non-Jewish members, but they're all sons-in-law of Jewish members."

When I joined the Harvard Law School faculty, it was quite small—perhaps three dozen full-time professors. (Today there are more than one hundred, with a student body that hasn't increased in size.) The entire faculty would meet for lunch in a small dining room, around a large table presided over by the dean. The discussions would revolve around legal issues. The criterion for judging an argument was its "soundness." That word still rings in my ear, like my grandmother's "*meturnished*." All faculty nominees had to have "sound" judgment. Their writing had to be "sound," rather than creative, speculative, quirky, or provocative. I was concerned because my views were anything but "sound"—at least as judged by some of the more traditional faculty members.

When I was choosing between teaching at Harvard and teaching at Yale, my Yale mentor, Professor Alex Bickel, who had been turned down for a professorship at Harvard because his views of constitutional law weren't "sound" and who subsequently became one of the most distinguished law professors at Yale, advised me against going to Harvard. "You won't fit in there," he warned me. When I recounted this story recently to a Harvard colleague of fifty years, he replied: "Alex was right. You don't fit in here." I never tried to.

In order to obtain tenure, each assistant professor had to publish a "tenure piece." I wrote an article on the relationship between law and psychiatry that was critical of the law's overreliance on psychiatry in judging whether mentally ill criminals could be held responsible for their crimes and whether people thought to be dangerously mentally ill should be preventively detained in asylums.[19] Because the article insisted that these decisions should be based on clearly articulated legal rather than on vague and subjective psychiatric criteria, and because it was somewhat critical of certain views espoused by Judge Bazelon—who was regarded as the epitome of unsoundness by the Harvard Law School establishment—it was deemed sound.

While I was being considered for tenure, I began to get offers from the other elite law schools—Columbia, Chicago, Stanford, Yale, NYU. I was earning $12,000 a year at Harvard and would be offered a raise to $14,000 when I received tenure. Stanford offered me $20,000, which at the time was the highest offer any assistant professor had ever received in the history of law teaching. It was well above what many full professors at Harvard were then making. I went to Dean Griswold and told him I couldn't afford to turn down an additional $6,000 since I had two kids in private school and no money in the bank. He told me sternly that he could not pay me more than older professors. So he raised *everyone's* salary, starting with mine, to $21,000. I became the most popular professor among my young colleagues, who all benefited from what became known as "the Dershowitz bump."

In my early years of teaching, I was the only young faculty member who was clearly identified with civil liberties, teaching seminars and writing law review articles in that area. The faculty was largely conservative, though a few older members were active in liberal causes, the major one being racial equality. But freedom of speech and the rights of criminal defendants were not high on the agenda of most professors. So my active membership in the American Civil Liberties Union was viewed with suspicion, because some of the positions taken by that organization were not deemed "sound." One faculty member—an old Brahmin named Mark DeWolf Howe—strongly encouraged me to become even more active, and he nominated me for membership on the national board of the American Civil Liberties Union, which I accepted. At the beginning of my tenure, the board was populated by genuine civil libertarians with no political or ideological agenda beyond the protection of everyone's freedom of speech and due process right. My own approach to civil liberties was well represented by the final sentence of Thomas Paine's essay on "First Principles of Government" (I own an original pamphlet):

> *He that would make his own liberty secure, must guard even his enemy from oppression; for if he violates this duty, he establishes a precedent that will reach to himself.*[20]

It was for that reason, among others, that I supported the ACLU when it defended the rights of Nazis, Klansmen, and Communists to express obnoxious, even dangerous, views.

This neutral approach to civil liberties was challenged when efforts were made to impeach President Nixon in 1974. Nixon was indeed an enemy of civil liberties, and of the ACLU. (He apparently regarded me as an enemy as well, since I was repeatedly audited by the IRS during his tenure; I never had to pay a penny.) But when Nixon was named as an "unindicted co-conspirator" by a grand jury under the direction of the special prosecutor, I yelled foul. This caused some discomfort among my faculty colleagues, because the Special Prosecutor's Office, originally headed by Harvard professor Archibald Cox, who was eventually fired, still had several Harvard people in important roles. But I thought it was unfair to designate the President as an unindicted co-conspirator, since a person in that status has no right to defend himself, because he is never brought to trial. I urged the ACLU to challenge this misuse of the grand jury and to protect our enemy's civil liberties. The ACLU refused. Instead, it broke with its long-standing policy of not taking positions on political matters and officially called for Nixon's impeachment. I dissented. I did not regard it as proper for the ACLU to take a position on so political a matter. It should have, in my view, defended Nixon's civil liberties against unfair legal tactics.

Though I personally favored Nixon's impeachment, the ACLU's decision in the Nixon matter marked the beginning of a movement by the ACLU away from its longtime neutral commitment to free speech and due process and toward a more political, partisan, and ideological approach. The organization began to elect board members based on race, gender, and sexual orientation, rather than on commitment to neutral civil liberties. Board members so elected naturally regarded themselves as "representatives" of their constituencies and pushed the organization toward an agenda that emphasized the political goals of these groups, such as abortion rights and affirmative action—both worthy causes that I personally supported but did not regard as core civil liberties concerns. Before long, I left the board of the ACLU, though I continued to support its actions on behalf of civil liberties. I continued to teach and write in the area of civil liberties, using the Nixon situation as an example of the complexity of defending the civil liberties of those who would deny civil liberties to others.

In addition to teaching, my main job as a professor was to publish scholarship. During my first decade at Harvard, nearly all of my articles were published in law reviews. They focused on the role of prevention in our legal system. I wrote several long articles on preventive detention of persons believed to be dangerous, exploring the historical, empirical, and jurisprudential aspects of what I called the emerging preventive state.[21] This was not only an important theoretical issue, it also had practical consequences, since more people were being confined based on predictions of what they *might do* in the future than on determinations of what they *had done* in the past.[22] These "predictive prisoners" included hundreds of thousands of psychiatric patients, pretrial detainees, sexual predators, "persons in need of supervision," individuals with communicable diseases, material witnesses, and other deemed too dangerous to be left at liberty. I had become sensitized to the plight of these detainees without rights—this "black hole" in our legal system—through my work on psychiatry and the law, first at Yale and then during my clerkship with Judge Bazelon. I saw an opportunity both to do good on a practical level and to contribute to legal theory.

In one of my articles, I explored the history of prevention from the earliest biblical laws, through the British common law, to current American law. In another, I analyzed the claims of those who believed they could accurately predict future misconduct. I proposed a new jurisprudence designed to balance the need for preventive governmental action against the dangers posed by the preventive state. In my book-length article entitled "The Origins of Preventive Confinement in Anglo-American Law,"[23] I issued a challenge to my fellow academics to help construct a new jurisprudence for the emerging preventive state:

> *Although preventive confinement has always been and will always be practiced, no jurisprudence of preventive intervention has ever emerged. It may sound surprising, even arrogant, to say this, but it appears to be true. No philosopher, legal writer, or political theorist has ever, to this writer's knowl-*

edge, attempted to construct a systematic theory of when it is appropriate for the state to confine preventively.[24]

I then gave several reasons why there was no jurisprudence regulating prevention:

The mechanisms of prevention have been, for the most part, informal; accordingly, they have not required articulate defense or justification. Moreover, there are many scholars who simply deny that preventive intervention, especially preventive confinement, really exists; or if they acknowledge the existence of these mechanisms, they deny their legitimacy, thus obviating the need for a theory of jurisprudence. Finally, it is extremely difficult to construct a theory of preventive confinement that neatly fits into existing theories of criminal law and democracy.[25]

Whatever the reasons, the upshot is that

there has always existed a widespread series of practices, involving significant restraints on human liberty, without an articulated jurisprudence circumscribing and limiting its application. People are confined to prevent predicted harms without any systematic effort to decide what kinds *of harms warrant preventive confinement; or what* degree *of likelihood should be required; or what* duration *of preventive confinement should be permitted; or what* relationship *should exist between the harm, the likelihood, or the duration.*[26]

Finally, I contrasted the absence of a jurisprudence regulating the prevention of *future* misconduct to the existing jurisprudence regulating the punishment of *past* misconduct.

This is not to say that there currently exists a completely satisfactory jurisprudence or theory justifying the imposition of punishment for past acts. But at least many of the right questions have been asked and some interesting answers have been attempted. Even Blackstone's primitive statement "that it is better that ten guilty persons escape, than that one innocent suffer" tells us something important about how to devise rules of evidence and procedure. There is no comparable aphorism for preventive confinement: is it better for X number of "false positives" to be erroneously confined (and for how long?) than for Y number of preventable harms (and of what kind?) to occur? What relationship between X and Y does justice require? We have not even begun to ask these kinds of questions, or to develop modes of analysis for answering them.[27]

Since the time I wrote these words, "the preventive state" has expanded in scope, especially with regard to the prevention of terrorism. Many constitutionally and morally dubious measures—from Guantanamo, to waterboarding, to massive electronic snooping—have been justified in the name of preventing terrorist attacks. Yet we have still not come up with a satisfactory jurisprudence that appropriately balances the legitimate concerns of government in preventing terrorism against the compelling need to preserve the rule of law.

Between 1968 and 1976, I wrote more than two dozen scholarly articles on these issues, becoming the first academic to focus in a systematic way on the preventive aspect of law. My work earned me a distinguished fellowship at the Center for Advanced Study of the Behavioral Sciences at Stanford University, a Guggenheim Fellowship, Ford Foundation and Fulbright travel grants, and several other scholarly recognitions. More important, it helped to change the laws governing the civil commitment of the mentally ill and the pretrial detention of defendants believed to be dangerous.

My law review articles tended to be quite technical and written in legalese. But about a decade into my teaching career, I began to write for a more general audience. The *New York Times* asked me to contribute columns to the Week in Review section. In these columns, I analyzed Supreme Court decisions and other legal developments. I soon discovered that I had a knack for legal writing that was accessible to the general public. I recalled Professor Calabresi's criticism of my earliest and unsuccessful efforts at writing: "You write like you're having a conversation with your friends in Brooklyn." I decided to turn that disadvantage as a law student into an advantage as a law professor: I would write for the general public the way I talked to my Brooklyn friends, who were smart as hell but not legally educated. It worked. I quickly became the "go to" professor when it came to explaining technical legal issues in ways that were understandable to the general public.

Soon I was writing book reviews and articles for popular magazines, as well as law review articles. I loved writing, and wrote every single day. In that respect, I was emulating one of my mentors, Professor Alexander Bickel, who had told me that he never left his home until he had filled his daily quota of "three thousand good words." I set myself a similar goal. I wrote everything by hand on legal pads, since I never learned to type. ("Typing is for girls," my mother told me, as she typed all my term papers.)

Within a few years of beginning to teach at Harvard, I had become one of the best known law professors in the country. My classes were over-subscribed, my scholarly articles were highly regarded, and my role as a public intellectual, though controversial among some faculty members, was gratifying. But there was something missing from my professional life. I was not yet a "real lawyer."

When I was offered the job at Harvard at age twenty-four, I knew that I was qualified to teach theoretical subjects, but I worried about my lack of real-world experience, since I had never practiced law. (One summer at a law firm between the second and third year at Yale does not a practitioner make.) My Brooklyn upbringing gave me a practical bent of mind—"street smarts"—but I craved some actual experience. I looked for opportunities to become involved in cases that would provide a smooth transition from theory to practice. I wanted to become a lawyer in addition to being a law professor.

Deciding to become a real lawyer was not without controversy within the Harvard Law School faculty. One of my colleagues approached me, upon hearing that I had taken on a case, and said, "At Harvard Law School, we don't have clients." His voice dripped with contempt as he uttered the word "clients." Most elite law schools prided themselves on teaching theory. To be sure, some of my colleagues came from a background of practice, but they had not begun to practice while teaching at the law school, although the school rules explicitly permitted it within certain limitations. Since I came to teaching directly from clerkships, I desperately felt the need for courtroom experience. But it would be untrue for me to suggest that this was my only reason for taking cases. I was dissatisfied with being only a teacher and a writer of articles. I wanted to make legal history, rather than just write about others who did. Like Justice Goldberg, I too was a man of action who could never be a complete person sitting behind a desk or standing in front of a classroom. I needed to be in the courtroom. I needed to be a real lawyer. I needed to know what it felt like to have flesh and blood clients whose lives would be affected by the law, rather than merely reading about abstract cases with faceless names. I needed to know what it felt like to win a case—and to lose one.

I didn't quite feel as Oliver Wendell Holmes did after a brief career as a Harvard law professor, that "academic life is but half life . . . a withdrawal from the fight in order to utter smart things that cost you nothing except for thinking of them from a cloister." But I did feel that my life would be more complete and fulfilling if it included some cutting-edge litigation.

In the beginning nearly all my cases were pro bono—without fee—and many were in association with the American Civil Liberties Union. They involved First Amendment challenges to censorship and Eighth Amendment challenges to the death penalty. Because these issues were within my area of academic expertise, the cases provided a smooth transition from theory to practice. In the next chapters I recount some of these cases and others that followed.

PART II

THE CHANGING SOUND OF FREEDOM OF SPEECH

From the Pentagon Papers to WikiLeaks

5

THE EVOLUTION OF THE FIRST AMENDMENT

New Meanings for Cherished Words

I always wanted to be a First Amendment lawyer. Everything in my upbringing led me to the defense of freedom of speech. I was always a dissident—though the authorities when I was growing up used the less polite terms "troublemaker" and "*bon-dit.*" I argued with everyone. I defended other troublemakers. I questioned everything and everybody. I rarely exercised my Fifth Amendment right to "remain silent." For me, the freedom to speak, to write, to dissent, to seek a redress of grievances, to assemble, to doubt, to challenge, has always been central not only to democratic governance but to life itself. It is both a means and an end.

The First Amendment has always been my favorite part of the Constitution, not because it is first—in its original, proposed form, it was the Third Amendment[1]—but because without its protection, all other rights are in danger.

Not everyone agrees. Actor Charlton Heston once claimed that

> *the Second Amendment is, in order of importance, the first amendment. It is America's First Freedom, the one right that protects all the others. Among freedom of speech, of the press, of religion, of assembly, of redress of grievances, it is the first among equals. It alone offers the absolute capacity to live without fear. The right to keep and bear arms is the one right that allows "rights" to exist at all.*[2]

Both history and geography have proved Heston dead wrong: Nearly every other freedom-loving country has restrictions on gun ownership;

while none has severe restrictions on expression. Experience has shown that liberty can thrive without the right to bear arms, but not without freedom of speech. The movement from weapons to words has marked the progress of civilization. As Sigmund Freud once put it: "The first human who hurled an insult instead of a stone was the founder of civilization." That's why hurling insults, not stones, is protected by our First Amendment.

The stirring words of the First Amendment—"Congress shall make no law . . . abridging the freedom of speech or of the press"—haven't been altered between my first case defending freedom of expression in the 1960s and my most recent ones, but the meaning of these iconic words has undergone dramatic transformation over the past half century. The major reason has been the rapid change in the manner by which speech is transmitted. Technology has altered the sound and look of freedom of expression.

When I was a law clerk, carbon paper was the means by which a written message could be sent to a handful of readers. We were required to circulate memoranda to all the justices, and we did so by typing them and using carbon paper to produce nine "flimsies," as we referred to the carbon copies. Even in the 1970s, when I first traveled to the Soviet Union, the dissidents and refuseniks asked me to bring carbon paper so they could make multiple copies of their banned samizdat literature. The Pentagon Papers were reproduced by hand on primitive copying machines. Today, with faxes and the Internet, the click of a button sends WikiLeak disclosures around the globe in an instant.

Over the past fifty years I have defended every means, manner, and mode of expression—films, plays, books, magazines, newspapers, graffiti, photographs, leaflets, pamphlets, megaphones, wall postings, websites, Internet postings, speeches, heckling, cartoons, faxes, composites, noises, threats, incitements, videos, ads, prayers, classes, live and filmed nudity (frontal, sideal, backal), defamation, blasphemy, and digital communication (by which I mean a raised middle finger).

I have defended neo-Nazi and racist speech, Stalinist rhetoric, anti-Israel hate speech, soft-core erotica, hard-core pornography, nude photographs of children, and disgusting videos of bestiality. I have defended the rights of major newspapers and book publishers, as well as of anonymous and not-so-anonymous bloggers, tweeters, website operators, and whistleblowers, to disclose classified information, state secrets, and other material the government would prefer to keep under wraps.

I have represented people I love, people I hate, and people I don't give a damn about—good guys, bad guys, and everything in between. H. L. Mencken used to bemoan the reality that

> *the trouble about fighting for human freedom is that you have to spend much of your life defending sons of bitches: for oppressive laws are always aimed at them originally, and oppression must be stopped in the beginning if it is to be stopped at all.*[3]

I have criticized nations I admire—such as the United States, Canada, Israel, Great Britain, Italy, and France—for censoring people I despise. And I have defended people I despise for attacking nations, institutions, and individuals I admire.

In each instance, I've stood up for an important principle: the right of the individual, rather than the government, to decide what to say, what to show, what to hear, what to see, what to teach, what to learn. I have opposed the power of the state (and other state-like institutions) to censor, punish, chill, or impose costs on the exercise of the freedom of expression—even, perhaps especially, expression with which I disagree and despise or believe may be hateful, hurtful, or even dangerous.

I have myself been the victim of outrageously false defamations,[4] and I have been falsely accused of defaming others. I have been informally charged with inciting war crimes[5] and formally charged with criminally defaming a judge[6]—to which I plead not guilty! I have defended the right of my enemies to lie about me, to heckle me, to boycott me, and even to try to get me fired. While defending the *right* of my opponents to say nearly anything they want, I have insisted on my own right to criticize, condemn, and vilify them for the *wrongness* of what they have chosen to say. Freedom of expression includes the right to be wrong, but it does not include the right to be immune from verbal counterattack.

I am not a free speech absolutist when it comes to the First Amendment—at least not in theory. But in practice I nearly always side with the freedom to speak, rather than the power to censor.

It's not that I always trust the citizenry; it's that I never trust the government. It's not that I believe the exercise of the freedom of speech will always bring about good results; it's that I believe that the exercise of the power to censor will almost always bring about bad results. It's not that I believe the free marketplace of ideas will always produce truth; it's that I believe that the shutting down of that marketplace by government will prevent the possibility of truth.[7]

My family and educational background—especially my constant arguments with rabbis, teachers, neighbors, and friends—made me into a skeptic about everything. I am certain that certainty is the enemy of truth, freedom, and progress. Hobbes has been proved wrong by the verdict of history in his inclusion among the "rights of sovereigns" the power to censor "all books before they are published" that are "averse" to "the truth" or not conducive to peace.[8]

I realize that I will never know "the truth." Neither will anyone else. All I can do is doubt, challenge, question, and keep open the channels of knowledge, the flow of information, and the right to change my mind and the minds of others. To me, truth is not a noun; it is an active verb, as in "truthing" (or knowing, learning, or experiencing).[9]

My favorite characters in the Bible and in literature are those who challenge authority: Adam and Eve defying God and eating the forbidden fruit of knowledge; Abraham chastising God for threatening to sweep away the innocent along with the guilty; Moses imploring God to change his mind about destroying the "stiff-necked" Jewish people; Jesus for arguing with the Pharisees and defying Roman authority; Don Quixote tilting at windmills; Ivan Karamazov challenging conventional wisdom; and the child who shouted "The Emperor has no clothes."

My favorite justices of the Supreme Court are the dissenters. My favorite historical figures are political and religious dissidents. My closest friends are iconoclasts. Some of my best teachers were fired.

The First Amendment would have been nothing more than a parchment promise had it not been given life by brave political dissidents and bold judicial dissenters. Because of these provocateurs, the First Amendment has not become ossified with age. It has changed with the times, sometimes for the better, sometimes for the worse.

Although the literal words have remained the same for more than two centuries, two of the most important ones have been changed beyond recognition. These words are "Congress" and "no." ("*Congress* shall make *no* law. . . .") The controversial role of these words can best be illustrated by a story, perhaps apocryphal but reflecting reality, about two great and contentious justices, Hugo Black, who claimed to be an absolutist and literalist when it came to the words of the First Amendment, and Felix Frankfurter, who advocated a more functional balancing approach (a "sound" view) despite the seemingly clear words of that amendment. In a case involving censorship by a state, Black pulled out his ragged copy of the Constitution and read the First Amendment out loud to the lawyer representing the state. "It says Congress shall make *no* law abridging the freedom of speech." He banged the table as he shouted and repeated the word "no." "What don't you understand about the word 'no'?" he asked rhetorically. Justice Frankfurter interrupted and said, "You're reading the words wrong." The lawyer looked startled as the justice explained. "It doesn't say 'Congress shall make *no* law.' It says, '*Congress* shall make no law.'" And he banged the table as he shouted and repeated the word "Congress." He then continued, "This law wasn't passed by Congress, it was passed by a state legislature. What don't you understand about the word 'Congress'?" he asked, mocking his fellow justice.

By emphasizing different words, the justices were giving different meanings to the same language of the First Amendment.

The reality is that both these words—"Congress" and "no"—have been excised over time. The first—"Congress"—was central to the history of the Bill of Rights, which was seen by its framers largely as a bill of *restrictions* on the power of the *national* legislature—namely "Congress." There was considerable concern that the Constitution, which replaced the Articles of Confederation, bestowed too much power on the national legislature, thus reducing the rights (really the powers) of the states to legislate for their citizens.[10] The First Amendment was not intended by its framers to impose restrictions on *the states*. In fact when the Bill of Rights was enacted, and for years thereafter, several states had laws severely abridging freedom of speech and the press.[11] (Some states also had officially established churches and legally discriminated against Catholics, Jews, Turks, and "other" heathens.)[12] If the framers had wanted to impose restriction on the states, they could have written a more general declaration protecting the right of free speech from abridgment by *any* government. For example: "The freedom of speech shall not be abridged by Congress *or by the states*." Indeed, many scholars[13] and judges believe that this was accomplished three-quarters of a century later by the Fourteenth Amendment, which provides in relevant part:

> *Nor shall any State deprive any person of life, liberty, or property, without due process of law; nor deny to any person within its jurisdiction the equal protection of the laws.*[14]

The current judicial view is that the phrase "Nor shall any State" in the Fourteenth Amendment "incorporated" the First Amendment (along with most but not all of the others)[15] and applied it to the states.[16] According to this view, the First Amendment now reads, in effect, as follows:

> *Congress and the state legislatures shall make no law abridging the freedom of speech*

Actually, it now reads even more broadly, since the courts have not limited the prohibitions of the First Amendment to the *legislative* branches, but have extended them to the *executive* and *judicial* branches—to any governmental action. So the First Amendment now reads, in effect, as follows:

> *Congress* and the state legislatures, *as well as* the executive, judicial, and administrative branches of the federal and state governments, *shall make no law and shall take no executive or judicial action abridging the freedom of speech.*

Thus the first major change—from "Congress" to "government"—has expanded the meaning of the First Amendment and broadened the right to free speech. The second change has narrowed the right, at least as literally written, by excising the word "no," as in "no law."

The words "no law"—an absolute prohibition on all legislation abridging any speech—are somewhat understandable if limited to Congress. A democracy can survive if the *national* legislature has no power to abridge speech of any kind, regardless of how dangerous or harmful, so long as the *state* legislatures can pick up the slack and enact what reasonable people would agree are essential limitations on some forms of expression, such as disclosing the names of spies, the locations or warships, the plans for battle, the nature of secret weapons, and other matters that must be kept from enemies. But the words "no law"—read literally—make little sense when applied both to the federal and state legislatures, indeed to all governmental bodies, because there really is no rational case for a total and absolute prohibition by any and all governmental institutions on any and all abridgment of any and all possible utterances, especially those directly endangering national security, such as the names of spies and the location of satellites.

The irony is that it is precisely the *national* legislature—Congress—and not the states that has the most legitimate interest in protecting the national security against unwarranted disclosures. It would have made more sense, absent the fear of excessive federal power, for the First Amendment to have declared that "the states shall make no law abridging the freedom of speech," but that Congress may enact narrowly drawn laws essential to the protection of national security. In effect, this is the way some courts have interpreted the combined words of the First and Fourteenth Amendments, granting Congress the power to make *some* laws narrowly abridging the freedom of speech when absolutely necessary to preserve legitimate state secrets, while curtailing the power of the state to censor pornography, defamation, and blasphemy (which were within the powers of the states to regulate at the time the First Amendment was ratified). The courts have recognized that in the modern world, the power to protect the national security from real threats is far more important than the power to protect individuals from being offended by offensive speech. This process of redefining old words to meet new realities demonstrates the interrelatedness of the various provisions of the Constitution. When one "moving part" is changed, the other parts, as well as the whole, are affected.

Even those, such as Justice Hugo Black, who purport to be absolutist for the protection of all speech, have figured out ways to finesse the problem. Consider the case of *Cohen v. California,*[17] in which an opponent of the Vietnam War wore to court a jacket displaying the words FUCK THE DRAFT. Justice Black, the absolutist, joined a dissenting opinion that would have affirmed Cohen's conviction on the ground that "Cohen's absurd and immature antic" was "mainly conduct and little speech."[18] Black insisted to his law clerks that no one should "have to see this word" and that displaying it on a jacket was conduct, not speech. His clerks could not persuade him otherwise.[19] Under this hypocritical approach, "all" speech remains constitutionally protected, but if you don't like the content of a particular speech—"Fuck the draft" worn on a jacket—simply call it "conduct" and by sleight of hand (or abuse of language), the constitutional protection vanishes. In other words, First Amendment absolutists—those who claim to read literally and apply absolutely the words "no law . . . abridging the freedom of speech"—simply declare a genre of expression that they do not wish to protect to be "not speech."[20] Justice Black essentially admitted employing this charade when he reportedly told his law clerk (in the context of the Pentagon Papers case), "Somehow I'll find a way to call this conduct rather than speech."[21] This word game reminds me of the story of the Theodore White banquet in China that was hosted by Zhou Enlai. The main dish was suckling pig. White, a somewhat traditional Jew, told the Communist leader that he could not eat pig. Without missing a beat, the leader said that in China he had the power to declare what a food item actually was. "It looks to you like a pig. But in China this is not a pig—this is a duck," he said. So White ate the "duck."[22]

According to the absolutist view, obscenity[23]—including a dirty word used in the context of a political protest[24]—is not speech. (Perhaps it's "duck.") The same is true for other categories of expression that do not—in the view of at least some absolutists—warrant the protection of the First Amendment. I know of no absolutist who would argue that all expression—including words of extortion, falsely shouting fire in a crowded theater, and disclosure of all secrets—is protected by the First Amendment.

Nonabsolutists recognize that these forms of verbal expression are indeed "speech," but argue that the words of the First Amendment should not be read literally. Some argue that they must be understood in the context of the times when they were written, and they point to restrictions on speech that were widely recognized in 1793. Under this approach, much of what we take for granted today as protected speech—such as blasphemy, truthful criticism of judges, and serious art and literature of a sexual nature—would not fall within the protection of the First Amendment.

Other nonabsolutists reject this "originalist" approach, preferring instead to argue for a "living," "evolving," and "adapting" view of the First Amendment (and the Constitution in general), which explicitly acknowledges that courts must have the power to redefine old words to meet the needs of changing times.[25]

Whichever approach is taken, it is clear that not all verbal and other forms of expression are protected by the First Amendment. There is widespread disagreement over what are appropriate exceptions, as reflected by the divided votes of the justices and the lack of consensus among scholars. All seem to agree with Justice Oliver Wendell Holmes that even "the most stringent protection of free speech would not protect a man in falsely shouting fire in a theatre."[26]

From this "shouting fire" paradigm, there flow several general categories of speech that are arguably unprotected because they may result in harms. They include the following:

1. *Offensiveness:* Expressions that either directly or vicariously offend others, such as sexist, scatological, racist, anti-Semitic, anti-Muslim, anti-Christian, homophobic, and other demeaning or repulsive speech.

2. *Fighting words:* Speech that is so offensively provocative that it may cause some who hear it to react violently. This includes racial or religious epithets hurled at minorities.

3. *Criminogenic speech:* Violent sexualized images that may cause, directly or indirectly, such harms as rape or sexual harassment.

4. *Disclosure* of information that may harm the nation or individuals, including military and diplomatic secrets and other information that the government or individuals may have a right to keep from the public. This may also include disclosure of personal information that may embarrass individuals.

5. *Defamation:* Expressions that libel, slander, or harass others, by conveying false or ridiculing information about them.

6. *Incitements:* Expressions that are calculated to incite others to commit violent or other illegal actions.

7. *Disruptions:* Expressions that are designed to disrupt speakers or otherwise prevent opposing views from being expressed or heard.

8. *Speech that supports terrorism:* Speeches or writings that provide "material support" to a designated foreign terrorist organization.[27]

These alleged harms sometimes overlap, as with obscenity, which may offend and also cause violence against women, or racist speech, which may both offend and provoke violence.

The First Amendment has changed dramatically over the last half century, and I have played a role in bringing about some of those changes. In some instances, exceptions to the First Amendment have been narrowed, while in others they have been expanded. I will begin by exploring the roots and rationality of the "mother" of all exceptions to the First Amendment: "falsely shouting fire in a theater." This metaphor has been invoked to justify censorship in nearly all of my cases: pornography, revealing state secrets, defamation, ridicule, incitement, fighting words, disrupting speakers, and supporting terrorism. Those advocating censorship generally argue that these exceptions "are just like shouting fire in a theater." It is important, therefore, to consider whether this paradigm has a strong enough foundation to support the many exceptions to freedom of expression that purport to rest on it.

SHOUTING FIRE: THE MOTHER OF ALL EXCEPTIONS TO THE FIRST AMENDMENT

Justice Oliver Wendell Holmes's statement that freedom of speech does not protect someone who falsely shouts fire in a theater has been invoked so often, by so many people, in such diverse contexts, that it has become part of our national folk language. It has even appeared — most appropriately — in the theater: In Tom Stoppard's play *Rosencrantz and Guildenstern Are Dead*, a character shouts at the audience, "Fire!" He then quickly explains, "I'm demonstrating the misuse of free speech."[28]

Shouting fire in the theater may well be the only jurisprudential analogy that has assumed the status of a folk argument. A prominent historian characterized it as "the most brilliantly persuasive expression that ever came from Holmes' pen."[29] But in spite of its hallowed position in both the jurisprudence of the First Amendment and the arsenal of political discourse, it is an inapt analogy, even in the context in which it was originally offered. It has lately become little more than a caricature of logical argumentation. From the beginning of my career, both in my writings and in my cases, I have taken aim at this analogy as one of the least persuasive, though most influential, arguments for censorship that ever came from anyone's pen!

I recently learned that Holmes's most famous phrase was borrowed, without any attribution, from an obscure and second-rate lawyer, the prosecutor in the case that gave rise to the "shouting fire" analogy. That prosecutor had made the following argument to the jury:

> *A man in a crowded auditorium, or any theatre, who yells "fire" and there is no fire, and a panic ensues and someone is trampled to death, may be rightfully indicted and charged with murder.*

Holmes simply changed a few words and appropriated to himself the prosecutor's vivid example—an intellectual theft all too commonly engaged in by judges.[30]

The case *Schenck v. United States*[31] involved the prosecution of Charles Schenck, who was the general secretary of the Socialist Party in Philadelphia. In 1917 a jury found Schenck guilty of attempting to cause insubordination among soldiers drafted in the First World War. He had circulated leaflets urging draftees not to "submit to intimidation" by fighting in a war being conducted on behalf of "Wall Street's chosen few." Schenck admitted that his intent was to "influence" draftees to resist the draft, but nothing in the pamphlet suggested that the draftees should use unlawful means to oppose conscription. As Justice Holmes found: "In form at least [the pamphlet] confined itself to peaceful measures, such as a petition for the repeal of the act" and an exhortation to exercise "your right to assert your opposition to the draft." Many of the pamphlet's words were quoted directly from the Constitution. It would be hard to imagine a clearer case of petitioning one's government for a redress of grievances, which is protected by the words of the First Amendment.

Holmes acknowledged that "in many places and in ordinary times the defendants, in saying all that was said in the circular, would have been within their constitutional rights. But," he added, "the character of every act depends upon the circumstances in which it is done." To illustrate that truism he went on to say, "The most stringent protection of free speech would not protect a man in falsely shouting fire in a theater, and causing a panic."

He upheld the convictions, finding that the pamphlet created "a clear and present danger" of hindering the war effort—an absurd and counterfactual conclusion that had no support in the trial record.

The example of shouting fire obviously bore little relationship to the facts of the case. The Schenck pamphlet contained a political message—a series of ideas and arguments. It urged its draftee readers to *think* about the message and then—if they so chose—to act on it in a lawful way. The man who shouts fire in a theater is neither sending a political message nor inviting his listener to think and decide what to do in a rational manner. On the contrary, the message is designed to force action *without* contemplation. The shout of "Fire!" is directed not to the mind and the conscience of the listener but, rather, to his adrenaline and his feet. It is a stimulus to immediate *action*, not to thoughtful reflection or debate.

Indeed, in that respect the shout of "Fire!" is not even speech, in any meaningful sense of that term. It is a *clang* sound—the equivalent of setting off a nonverbal alarm.[32] Had Justice Holmes been more honest about his example, he would have said that freedom of speech does not protect a person who pulls a fire alarm in a theater when there is no fire, and thereby causes a panic. But that obviously would have been irrelevant to the case at hand because pulling an alarm is clearly action rather than speech—and it is action with no substantive political message. The proposition that pulling an alarm is not protected speech certainly leads to the conclusion that shouting the word "fire" is also not protected, but it does not support the very different conclusion that circulating a thoughtful pamphlet is also not protected.

The analogy is thus not only inapt but also insulting. Most Americans do not respond to written political advocacy with the same kind of automatic acceptance expected of schoolchildren responding to a fire drill. Not a single recipient of the Schenck pamphlet is known to have changed his mind after reading it. Indeed, one draftee was asked whether reading a pamphlet asserting that the draft law was unjust would make him "immediately decide that you must erase that law." Not surprisingly, he testified, "I do my own thinking." A theatergoer would probably not respond similarly if asked how he would react to a shout of "Fire!"

Another important reason the analogy is inapt is that Holmes emphasizes the factual falsity of the shout "Fire!" The Schenck pamphlet, however, was not factually false. It contained political opinions about the causes of war and about appropriate and lawful responses to the draft. As the Supreme Court has repeatedly stated, "The First Amendment recognizes no such thing as a 'false' idea."[33] Nor does it recognize false opinions about the causes of war.

A closer analogy to the facts of the Schenck case might have been a person standing outside a theater, offering patrons a leaflet advising them that in his opinion the theater was a fire hazard, and urging them not to enter but to complain to the building inspectors. That analogy, however, would not have served Holmes's argument for punishing Schenck, because such leafleting is plainly within the protective ambit of the First Amendment. Holmes needed an analogy that would appear relevant to Schenck's political speech but that would invite the conclusion that censorship was appropriate. His invocation of "shouting fire" constituted intellectual cheating, designed to reach a result that Holmes could not justify honestly.

The fire analogy is all that survives from the Schenck case; the ruling itself is no longer good law. Pamphlets of the kind that resulted in Schenck's imprisonment have been circulated with impunity during subsequent wars. It remains to be seen whether Holmes's flawed "reasoning" will be resurrected in our current war against terrorism, to uphold a statute that has been interpreted to criminalize political speech that is deemed to lend "material support" to terrorist organizations.[34]

Over the years I have assembled a collection of instances—including my own cases, speeches I have heard, articles I have read—in which proponents of censorship have maintained that the expression at issue is "just like" falsely shouting fire in a theater. The analogy is generally invoked, often with self-satisfaction, as an absolute argument stopper. It does, after all, claim the high authority of the great Justice Holmes. I have rarely heard it invoked in a convincing, or even particularly relevant, way. But that too can claim lineage from the great Holmes.

In the coming pages I will describe a series of pornography cases I have litigated. In several of them, those advocating censorship have cited a state supreme court that held that "Holmes's aphorism . . . applies with equal force to pornography." Another court analogized "picketing . . . in support of a secondary boycott" to shouting fire because in both instances "speech and conduct are brigaded." A civil rights lawyer, in a *New York Times* op-ed piece, analogized a baseball player's bigoted statements about blacks, gays, and foreigners to shouting fire.[35] I wrote an op-ed, disputing the analogy.[36] The Reverend Jerry Falwell, in arguing that the First Amendment doesn't protect a parody of him having drunken sex with his mother, invoked the Holmes example: "Just as no person may scream 'Fire!' in a crowded theater . . . likewise, no sleaze merchant like Larry Flynt should be able to use the First Amendment as an excuse for maliciously and dishonestly attacking public figures, as he has so often done." In the famous Skokie case, in which I supported the right of neo-Nazis to march through a heavily Jewish Chicago suburb, one of the judges argued that allowing Nazis to march through a city where a large number of Holocaust survivors live "just might fall into the same category as one's 'right' to cry fire in a crowded theater."[37] And some Palestinian students seeking to silence an Israeli speaker at a university offered the false analogy that "defending Israeli war crimes is like shouting fire."

Some close analogies to shouting "Fire!" or setting off an alarm are, of course, available: calling in a false bomb threat; dialing 911 and falsely describing an emergency; making a loud, gun-like sound in the presence of the President; setting off a voice-activated sprinkler system by falsely shouting "Fire!" (or any other word or sound); or shouting "Bomb!" on an airplane in flight.[38]

Analogies are, by their nature, matters of degree. Some are closer to the core example than others. But any attempt to analogize political ideas in a pamphlet, an ugly parody in a magazine, offensive movies in a theater, controversial newspaper articles, or any of the other expressions and actions catalogued above, to the very different act of shouting "Fire!" in a crowded theater, is either self-deceptive or self-serving.

Abbie Hoffman, on whose Chicago conspiracy case I worked, once described an occasion when he was standing near a fire with a crowd of people and got in trouble for yelling "Theater, theater!"[39] That, I think, is about as clever a use as anyone has ever made of Holmes's deeply flawed analogy. And it is about the right level of logical response Holmes's silly argument deserves.

As I wrote in a 1989 article criticizing the Holmes analogy:

> *Let us hear no more nonsensical analogies to shouting fire in a crowded theater. Those who seek to censor speech will just have to come up with a somewhat more cogent illustration—one that bears at least some relationship to real speech.*[40]

In the next several chapters, we will explore whether other arguments, analogies, or illustrations that purport to justify censorship are more cogent than Holmes's deeply flawed effort.

6

DIRECT AND VICARIOUS "OFFENSIVENESS" OF OBSCENITY

I Am Curious (Yellow) and Deep Throat

Freedom of speech is not free. It often carries a heavy price tag. As kids, we recited the ditty "Sticks and stones may break my bones, but names will never harm me." Before long we learned, often from painful experiences, how wrong this was. Names—such as "kike," "fag," "wop," "nigger," "retard," "sissy," "fatso"—could harm more than sticks and stones. Lies, rumors, gossip, slurs, insults, and caricatures could be painful. Bullying and verbal taunting can drive vulnerable people to desperate measures, including suicide. The truth can hurt.[1] That's why we learn to be "polite"—to self-censor. That's why families, schools, groups, and other institutions have rules, sometimes explicit, more often implicit, regulating speech. "We just don't say that kind of thing around here" is a common, if informal, limitation on freedom of expression.

Informal family understanding, however, is a far cry from formal government legislation and legally enforceable restrictions on expression. I would never use the kind of epithets listed above, but nor would I want the government to prohibit, under threat of criminal punishment, the use of those words in the open marketplace of ideas.[2]

You may remember that in the 1970s, the comedian George Carlin listed the seven words that could never be uttered on radio or television. The list included such innocent words as "piss" and "tits." (Use your imagination for the other five!)

Although the list was never officially promulgated by the Federal Communications Commission, the uttering of the prohibited words on a Pacifica radio station that broadcast Carlin's routine led to a Supreme Court decision setting out standards for what could and could not be said during certain hours of the day and night.[3]

Carlin's routine also became fodder for other comedians and led to the widespread mocking of any attempt to create lists of approved and unapproved words.

Nonetheless, governments have understandably sought to protect some adult citizens[4] from being "offended" by the words or expressions of other citizens. Nudists are not free to bare their privates in public, since most people are (or claim to be) offended by the sight of other people's naked bodies, though the nudists may be free to do their thing in special areas set aside for those who are not so offended. I defended the right of skinny-dippers to sunbathe in an isolated section of the Cape Cod National Seashore.[5] The federal judge in that case recognized a limited right to nude sunbathing in areas that present no conflicts with the rights of others.[6] The decision was characterized as a "Magna Carta for nudism." I refused to defend the right of a radical feminist to parade naked in areas not set aside for nudity.[7]

Pornography, like nudity, offends many Americans, but there are those who would ban not only public displays of pornography, but private use as well. They argue that three distinct types of harm are caused by pornography. The first, as with nudity, is that it is offensive to many people who are involuntarily exposed to it. No empirical evidence is required to prove this kind of harm: If people say they are offended, that is the end of the matter. The second is that some people are offended by the *mere knowledge* that other people, who are not offended by pornography, are looking at it in private. This alleged harm was mocked by H. L. Mencken's definition of puritanism as "the haunting fear that someone, somewhere, may be happy." Whether this type of what I call "vicarious offensiveness" warrants an exception to the First Amendment raises complex legal issues. The third, very different, kind of harm is that pornography is alleged to cause rape and other physical violence against women. This empirical claim, which if true would warrant legal protection, is hotly disputed and unproven, if not unprovable.[8]

I AM CURIOUS (YELLOW): VICARIOUS OFFENSIVENESS

My initial professional encounter with the First Amendment involved a direct challenge to the concept of "vicarious offensiveness"—a term I coined, building on Mencken's quip about puritanism—in the context of a Swedish antiwar film called *I Am Curious (Yellow)*. The story involved a young girl coming of age both politically and sexually during the Vietnam War. It included scenes in which she engaged in sexual activities. By today's standards, it could be shown on cable television and in art theaters with an R rating—indeed, it can now be downloaded by anyone on YouTube—but in the late 1960s, it was scandalous.[9]

The film was seized by U.S. Customs and banned throughout the country. Grove Press, a radical publishing house in New York, owned the film and retained me to argue for its protection under the First Amendment. I don't recall whether I charged a small fee or whether I took the case pro bono, but I put everything I had into my newfound role as part-time litigator on behalf of my beloved First Amendment.

I decided on a bold challenge to the traditional power of government to censor obscene material—indeed to censor *any* "offensive" material shown only to people who aren't offended by it. Instead of arguing that the film itself was not obscene, I decided to argue that it was none of the government's constitutional business to act as censors—to tell its adult citizens what they could and could not watch in the privacy of a movie theater that was off-limits to children and that did not advertise in a pandering manner that would reasonably offend people outside the theater. There was no legally binding precedent for such a challenge to the concept of "vicarious offensiveness" as a basis for censorship. Indeed the Supreme Court had recently reaffirmed the power of the government to prosecute obscenity, as an exception to the freedom of speech. In this respect, my unprecedented challenge was much like the one I helped Justice Goldberg devise against the death penalty, with the difference being that he was a justice of the Supreme Court, while I was a novice lawyer litigating my first constitutional case. What both challenges shared was a large dose of chutzpah.

The leading case affirming the power of government to censor porn was *Roth v. United States*.[10] But in a more recent case, *Stanley v. Georgia*,[11] the court had carved out a narrow exception to the exception. A divided court ruled, in an opinion by Justice Thurgood Marshall, that the state had no power to prosecute an adult for merely possessing obscene material—

in this case some old stag films—in the privacy of his home. The ruling was a combination of Fourth Amendment (the right of privacy in one's home) and First Amendment principles and was somewhat unclear as to its reach, because it went out of its way to reaffirm the holding in *Roth* that obscenity was not protected by the First Amendment.

I decided to use the Stanley case as a battering ram against the very idea that government had the power to tell adults what films they could watch in a theater. The mechanism I chose for this attack was to challenge the constitutionality of the Massachusetts obscenity statute under which the owner of an art theater located across the street from the famous Boston Symphony Hall was being prosecuted for showing *I Am Curious (Yellow)*.[12]

In those days, a challenge to the constitutionality of a state statute could be brought in front of a three-judge district court with the right to appeal its ruling directly to the Supreme Court.[13] The three judges we drew were not a promising crew.

When I learned that Judge Bailey Aldrich would preside, I was concerned that he would remember the incident we'd had when I turned down his invitation to speak at a restricted club. I didn't know the other two judges, both of whom were Italian-American. One of them, Judge Anthony Julian, had anglicized his original Italian name, but his strict Catholic upbringing and worldview became evident throughout the hearing. The third judge, Raymond Pettine, was from Providence, Rhode Island, and he surprised me with his apparent liberalism.

I argued the case for several hours over three separate days. I began by presenting my broad challenge to the power of the state to regulate the content of films shown in adult-only theaters, on the basis of a fear that it might vicariously offend those who chose not to view it:

> *If the First Amendment means anything, it means that a state has no business telling a man, sitting alone in his own house, what books he may read or what films he may watch. Our constitutional heritage rebels at the thought of giving government the power to control men's minds.*

I argued that the ruling in the Stanley case was analogous to what was occurring in our case:

> *There is no distinction in law, in logic, in common sense between the individual [watching a film at home or] deciding to go to a movie theater [and] pay his $2.50.*

I could see skepticism in the faces of the judges—they did not seem to see any connection between the Stanley case and this one—as I acknowledged that "the Supreme Court ruled only on [home] possession in the Stanley case." I argued, however, that there was no real difference between home possession and limited, controlled exhibition:

> *Surely Stanley could not have been prosecuted under Justice Marshall's decision if he were caught putting the film in the 8mm projector and showing the film to himself or his friends in the privacy of his basement.*

Judge Aldrich expressed skepticism about the reach of my argument, suggesting that the *Stanley* decision wasn't relevant to a movie theater. He told me about his grandmother, who "once went to a movie entitled *Sur Les Troits de Paris*. She thought it was a travelogue. She didn't after she got there of course. . . . I heard about it." I assured him that we had dealt with that problem by providing a "prologue" that advised the audience, who were admitted only before the film began, what they were about to see.[14]

As Judge Aldrich continued to press me about his grandmother's sensibilities, I was reminded of the old Jewish joke about the man with a broken clock who goes into a store with clocks in the window and asks the man behind the counter to fix his clock. "I don't fix clocks. I perform circumcisions," the man replied. "Then why do you have clocks in your window?" the customer wondered. The store owner responded: "What do you want me to put in my window?"

I had that joke in my head when I offered the following argument to Judge Aldrich:

> *If a store were to open in Boston which was simply marked* PORNOGRAPHY SHOP, *it had nothing in the window, it had no advertising, it was a place where people like Stanley could come and quietly and discreetly purchase their 8mm films, [I submit] that* Stanley vs. Georgia *would proscribe prosecution of that seller. I submit that necessarily if there is this right to exercise one's freedom to read and see a film, there is necessarily the concomitant right to purchase it.*

The judges pressed me on whether obscene films, even when viewed in a restricted theater, could cause viewers to go out and commit crimes such as rape. I responded that if that were true, it would be just as likely—perhaps even more so—that a person watching such films *alone* in his basement would be influenced in that manner. I argued that *Stanley* had implicitly rejected that theory.

The questioning persisted, with Judge Julian wondering whether Judge Aldrich's grandmother was typical:

> JUDGE JULIAN: As a matter of common sense though, unless we are to be so gullible as to be incredibly gullible, don't the great vast majority of the people who go to a theater to see a film like this know what they're going to see?
>
> MR. DERSHOWITZ: Precisely.
>
> JUDGE JULIAN: So this prologue is a lot of nonsense, just a gesture to try to wipe out—
>
> JUDGE ALDRICH: He's looking after my grandmother who went to see *Sur Les Toits de Paris*.
>
> MR. DERSHOWITZ: The only valid basis for punishing obscenity . . . is to protect people [like Judge Aldrich's grandmother] from being offended, from having something thrust on them in an unwilling manner and also to protect youngsters.

When I then advised the court that under my theory, the judges would not have to view the film, Judge Aldrich immediately interjected with a broad smile: "Are you trying to bribe us to decide the case so we don't have to see the film? . . . I will admit that's the best bribe I have ever been offered."

Judge Julian did not seem to understand my argument. He kept asking me whether I wanted the court to assume that *I Am Curious (Yellow)* was not "pornographic."

I tried to explain:

> *It's exactly the opposite. We do not ask you to decide whether or not the film is pornographic. We are asking you to decide that the film shown in a nonobtrusive way, advertised in the way that it's been advertised right from the beginning, with no hint, no suggestion of obscenity or prurience, played, if you wish, with the warning being given—exhibited in that manner, the film is protected by the First Amendment without regard to its contents.*

Judge Julian then questioned me about whether this case was really about money, rather than freedom of speech, because Grove Press was a commercial distributor of films for profit. I replied that the *New York Times* also makes a profit and that if the First Amendment were limited to nonprofit media, it would become a "dead letter" in our profit-driven economy.

I then returned to my distinction between an enclosed theater and an open display:

MR. DERSHOWITZ: If Grove Press were to put up a billboard . . . above a large area where people congregate and there were to be an alleged obscene picture on the billboard, and the state were to try to enjoin that, I would have to [concede that there might be some harm to people who didn't want to be exposed to obscenity].

JUDGE JULIAN: That's a very generous concession.

MR. DERSHOWITZ: But in this case . . . nobody is being exposed to anything that he doesn't want to be exposed to at all. The only thing that people are being exposed to is the fact that they know that a film is being played in Boston . . . and that fact, if it offends people [vicariously], is not entitled to constitutional protection so long as they can avoid being exposed directly to the contents of the film.

Judge Aldrich was intrigued by this last point and said that he wished to pursue it. I knew I was in for tough questioning:

I wish to pursue that point. I happen to be very straightlaced. Every time I walk down through Harvard Square and I see there is a movie going on there that I know is obscene, of course, I don't have to go in. I can protect myself. But I'm offended by the fact that I see all these students who are age twenty-one and a half going in and that we are maintaining in my hometown, in which I have such great pride, we are maintaining this house—I use the word "house" advisedly—filthy pictures are being shown. Do I have any interests or rights?

Judge Aldrich had put his finger directly on the vicarious offensiveness rationale for censorship. I needed to come up with an answer that didn't devalue his concerns (and his grandmother's):

It seems to me you have an interest but no right. . . . I can understand how you would be offended by that. But one of the prices of living in a complex society, with freedom, is for you to have to simply tolerate the fact that you know that certain people are engaging in conduct that you don't approve of. That was precisely the argument made by the State of Connecticut in the birth control [clinic] case.[15] *They said that people of the State of Connecticut are offended by knowing that this kind of immoral conduct is being engaged in by people, married people, all over the state. And the Supreme Court did say that this is something that members of the society must tolerate in a pluralistic society. There are a great many things which offend me, to know that they're going on in people's homes—I have an interest in that, but I don't think I have a protected constitutional right [to be] disturbed about what's going on.*

Judge Julian asked whether "that interest [should] be legally protected." I responded:

Now, there may be ways of protecting it, perhaps through zoning regulations. . . .

But if the issue is total banning on the one hand as against being vicariously offended by knowing people are doing this kind of thing, I would submit that the Constitution has a clear answer to that. It must permit the film to be shown in a way to minimize your exposure to it and to permit you both fully to see and to avoid being exposed to the contents of the film.

So I do submit that Your Honor does have an interest and I can understand it. But I think you will realize that on balance this interest could be used to upset almost every kind of freedom that Americans ought to be at liberty to engage in.

Judge Aldrich seemed intrigued by our argument, while continuing to press me hard on its implications. He clearly understood my distinction between *direct* offensiveness, in which an unwilling viewer is immediately confronted with material that is offensive to him or her (as his grandmother was), and *vicarious* offensiveness, in which a person is offended by the mere knowledge that others, who are not offended, are choosing to watch material that would be offensive to him *if* he viewed it. The distinction was new to him, but it seemed to resonate. At one point Judge Aldrich asked me what I would do if the Supreme Court ruled against my novel theory. "Will that be the end of the road . . . ?"

I responded: "Well, I, as an attorney, will continue to urge the court to accept this principle because I think it's the correct approach to the regulation of obscenity."

Following three days of intensive argument and questioning, the judges issued a decision written by Judge Aldrich. He bought my argument—and my distinction between direct and vicarious offensiveness—totally. He began by accepting my assumption about the nature of the film:

For purposes of this case we assume that the film is obscene by standards currently applied by the Massachusetts courts.[16]

He then went on to discuss the implications of the *Stanley* decision, which the prosecutor had argued was "irrelevant" to this case and which, at the beginning of my argument, Judge Aldrich too had thought was not relevant to movie theaters:

> *In* Stanley *[the] Court held that in certain circumstances possession of a moving picture film is constitutionally protected even though by contemporary standards the film is obscene. We do not consider this irrelevant.*[17]

The question, as he colorfully put it, was whether the *Stanley* decision is "the high watermark of a past flood, or the precursor of a new one."[18] In seeking to answer that question, the court went on to consider the state's argument that an obscene film, even viewed in a restricted theater, can induce the viewer to commit rape.

> *Of necessity the* Stanley *court held that obscenity presented no clear and present danger to the adult viewer, or to the public as a result of his exposure. Obscenity may be offensive; it is not per se harmful. Had the Court considered obscenity harmful as such, the fact that the defendant possessed it privately in his home would have been of no consequence.*

In the end, the court decided that obscenity laws were constitutional only as applied to "public distribution in the full sense, and that restricted distribution, adequately controlled, is no longer to be condemned."[19]

This is how the court summarized its conclusion:

> *If a rich Stanley can view a film, or read a book, in his home, a poorer Stanley should be free to visit a protected theater or library. We see no reason for saying he must go alone.*[20]

It was the first time in history that a court—any court—had ruled that the government had no power to ban or prosecute an "obscene" film that was shown to the public in a theater on the ground that it might vicariously offend people who had a choice not to enter that theater. I had won a victory not only for my client, but for my novel approach to offensiveness under the First Amendment. Not a bad way to begin my career as a thirty-year-old lawyer. The victory would, however, be short-lived, at least in theory, if not in practice.

The district attorney appealed our victory to the Supreme Court, which accepted the case. I was asked to argue for Grove Press. And so, at the age of thirty-one, I argued my first case before the high court.

I prepared extensively for my oral argument, expecting to be questioned aggressively by the recently appointed chief justice, Warren Burger. Burger and Bazelon were archenemies, both ideologically and personally.

Burger knew I was close to Bazelon, and so I expected some tension. But I could not have anticipated what awaited me. I had hardly reached the lectern when Burger asked if he could "interrupt" to inquire whether I thought a state had the power to prohibit a "bear-baiting contest." Though I didn't know exactly what a bear-baiting contest was, I guessed that it must involve cruelty. I responded that torturing bears was not protected by the Constitution, since the states have the power to protect animals from suffering.

I tried to get the argument back to my case: "I think the example would be better if it were a film of bear-baiting." But the chief justice would have none of it: "Let's stay on the live." I drew a distinction between an act that harmed another creature and a film of consensual lovemaking that did not intrude upon the sensibilities of those who chose to view it. The chief justice shot back:

> *You are saying that it's all right to kill one bear and five dogs in the filming process, but it isn't right to kill many more of them in live showings, is that a distinction?*

I had no idea what he was getting at with his obviously scripted questions, so I tried again:

> *No, I would say a state would have the right to prohibit the actual killing of dogs and bears whether for film or other purposes.*

The chief justice persisted in his obsession with bears!

> *Let's say fourteen states didn't have any statutes against bear-baiting, and 4.5 million had watched bear-baiting or the filming of bear-baiting. Would that have the slightest relevance in your judgment on whether the showing of bear-baiting in Boston, Massachusetts, could or could not be stopped?*

I tried to direct my answer away from bear-baiting and to the issue of whether the Constitution permitted a consenting adult to view an obscene film in the privacy of a restricted movie theater:

> *No, the First Amendment protects the individual's right to receive information necessary to satisfy his emotional and intellectual needs. The thrust of our [position would take prosecutors] from [inside] the theater—that is only attended by people who want to go—and would put them outside the theater to protect you and me from the intrusion on our sensibilities that would occur if movies . . . thrust [explicit] pictures on unwilling viewers.*

But the chief justice would still not be diverted from his bears. Though I had never mentioned a bear in my answer, he challenged me:

> *Are you suggesting that it is a universal rule that everybody is offended by bear-baiting?*

That, of course, was precisely my point: Those who were not offended should be free to watch a film in which no one was hurt.

With less than a minute before my time would expire, the chief justice asked whether I thought the analogy to the bear-baiting contest was "valid." I politely told him what I thought:

> *I think the analogy of bear-baiting is not valid [because it] is an illegal act which hurts animals. It is different from [lovemaking] presented on a screen to a public which has chosen to view it.*

By this point my time was nearly up. I quickly summarized my argument that under a functional definition of privacy,

> *a theater with its curtains drawn deserves [at least as much constitutional protection as] a home with its shades drawn up.*

The chief justice had monopolized the entire argument with his bear-baiting analogy. He or his law clerks had apparently prepared a series of questions for me about bear-baiting, and Burger had simply gone down the list, ignoring my answers. The other eight justices were unable to ask questions, though several of them seemed anxious to probe certain points. Some of them seemed embarrassed by their chief's performance. By the end of the argument, I finally understood what a bear-baiting contest must feel like—at least to the bear. It was the dumbest series of questions I have ever been asked during an oral argument, and it was probably the stupidest conversation I've ever had with anyone about the First Amendment. It was particularly unintelligent compared to the argument in the lower court, where Judge Aldrich had asked thoughtful and probing questions, and had been persuaded to change his mind by my answers. But no one ever said that intelligence was a criterion for being a chief justice. What mattered to Warren Burger, with his shock of white hair and handsome face, was that he *looked* like what a chief justice was supposed to look like! His deep, stentorian voice even made him sound like a chief justice, as long as one didn't consider the content of what he was saying.

A few months later the Supreme Court rendered a 5–3 decision in the *I Am Curious (Yellow)* case that did not reach the broad issue decided by the district court (nor did it mention bear-baiting); instead, it decided the case on a narrow procedural ground.[21] We eventually settled the case to the advantage of the defendants. The film was shown throughout the country, and no one went to prison. Judge Aldrich's opinion, suggesting that all censorship of the content of movies exhibited to adults in discreet settings was unconstitutional, remained the only court decision on that issue until June 1973, when the Supreme Court changed the definition of obscenity in *Miller v. California*[22] and a series of companion decisions[23] (in which I played no role).

In these cases Chief Justice Burger, writing for the majority, emphatically rejected the approach I had argued in the *I Am Curious (Yellow)* case. Instead he accepted, whole hog, the vicarious offensiveness rationale that Judge Aldrich had rejected:

> *We categorically disapprove the theory . . . that obscene, pornographic films acquire constitutional immunity from state regulation simply because they are exhibited for consenting adults only.*[24] *. . . The States have a long-recognized legitimate interest in the quality of life and the total community environment, the tone of commerce in the great city centers, and, possibly, the public safety itself.*[25]

But as I promised Judge Aldrich, I continued to press my principle in the court of public opinion and in a series of other obscenity cases over the next several decades. Ultimately my view would prevail, if not in law then certainly in practice. Chief Justice Burger may have won in the courthouse, but we won in theaters and on television sets throughout the nation, as sexually explicit films—far more explicit than *I Am Curious (Yellow)*—became pervasive and "legal" in fact if not in law.[26] This disparity between the law as set down in theory by the Supreme Court and the law as implemented in practice throughout the country is an interesting story in itself.[27]

DEEP THROAT: WHY I CHOSE NOT TO WATCH IT

My initial victory in the *I Am Curious (Yellow)* case—getting a three-judge court to declare unconstitutional all obscenity laws that applied to adults-only theaters—made me something of a hero in the "adult film" industry, and something of a pariah among radical feminists who regarded such films as dangerously sexist. Many "obscenity" clients came my way, including the producers of the musical *Hair*, which was "banned in Boston," and several "soft-core" films, such as the very forgettable *Belinda*[28] and the unforgettable hard-core film *Deep Throat*.[29]

I'm told that *Deep Throat* is a very hard-core and very bad movie. I can't personally attest to these claims because, to this day, I have not seen it.[30] I avoided seeing the film not because I'm a prude—I enjoy a good erotic movie as much as the next person—but rather because I wanted to make a point about the law of obscenity: The decision to watch or not to watch a particular film should be a matter of choice for every adult citizen. Just as I'd told the judges in the *I Am Curious (Yellow)* case that they didn't have to view the film in order to rule that an adult had the constitutional right to view it in an adults-only theater, so too I had the right to argue that position without myself viewing *Deep Throat*. I also believed that my not viewing the film was a good tactic that helped to dramatize my point that vicarious offensiveness is not a proper basis for censoring a film or prosecuting an actor who starred in it.

I used that tactic in two separate cases involving *Deep Throat*. The first was the prosecution of Harry Reems for his role as an actor in the film. Reems was the first actor in history ever to be prosecuted for obscenity. He was charged with participating in a nationwide conspiracy to transport an obscene film in interstate commerce. The United States government charged him with conspiracy because Reems had nothing to do with the actual distribution of the film. As the prosecutor acknowledged:

> *[Reems] made the film, got his money, and got out back in 1972, that is, he didn't do anything else as a part of the conspiracy, he didn't do any more overt acts, he didn't participate any further, and the question arises why in the thunder does he wind up being charged [with acts that took place] four years later?*

His answer was that "once a person joins a conspiracy, he is liable for everything that happens in that conspiracy until it is ended." (Reems asked me whether he could have been charged with murder, if strong-arm methods used by the distributors had resulted in a death years after the film had been completed. I told him that under the prosecutor's theory that was possible.)

In order to get out of the conspiracy, according to the government, Reems was obliged "to take up affirmative actions to defeat and destroy the conspiracy." But what could Reems have done? He could not have "exposed" the crime, as one might expose a secret conspiracy, since everyone knew who had participated in the film's production and distribution. Nor could he have prevented the distribution and exhibition of the film, since he retained no rights to it.

The jury, selected from residents of Memphis, a city called "the buckle of the Bible Belt," convicted Reems and his coconspirators, and Harry was left to search for an appellate lawyer. Because of my involvement in the *I Am Curious (Yellow)* case, he called me.

When we met, Reems described himself to me as "a nice Jewish boy earning his livelihood by doing what lots of people would pay to do." He was born in Scarsdale, New York, with the name Herbert Streicher, dropped out of college, joined the marines, and later set out to become a stage actor, performing with the La Mama troupe, the New York Theater Ensemble, and the National Shakespeare Company in New York City. During Christmas of 1969, "when things got rough and there was no work around . . . a fellow said he knew where I could make $75 doing a stag film." His two female costars, both students in sociology at NYU, put him at ease, and he completed several "loops." Streicher was successful, not so much because of his looks or size, but rather because of his extraordinary ability to perform repeatedly on cue.

Streicher had been hired as a sound and lighting technician for a sex film being shot near Miami, Florida, in January 1972. When the original male lead failed to appear, the director, Gerard Damiano, asked Streicher to fill in. Since it took only one day to shoot the film's sex shots, he earned $100 for his performance. He received no royalties. He did not participate in the editing or distribution of the film. Even his stage name, "Harry Reems," was picked by the director. He retained his stage name and performed in several other sex films. But his role in *Deep Throat* was over, or so he thought, until he was arrested two years later in New York City and taken to Memphis, a city that Streicher had never even visited.

The prosecuting attorney was a Bible Belt fundamentalist appropriately named Larry Parrish, who was dubbed by the press as "Mr. Clean," "the Memphis Heat," and "the Memphis Smut Raker." A born-again Christian, Parrish believed that pornography was the bane of modern America. He told a reporter that he would "rather see dope on the streets than these movies," explaining that drugs could be cleansed from the body, but pornography's damage was "permanent." As a prosecutor of pornography, he had already secured forty convictions.

The decision to bring Reems to trial was an instance of Parrish's creativity. As a Memphis lawyer put it: "Parrish figured that putting an actor on trial was the way to get publicity [and] a man is less likely to pick up public sympathy than a woman." Parrish acknowledged that his purpose in prosecuting Reems was to make it clear that no one involved with a porno film was immune from criminal liability.

Having been convicted, Reems faced years in prison. He had no money and asked me to take his appeal on a pro bono basis. I agreed. I told him I preferred not to watch the film and explained to him my theory of vicarious offensiveness, "choice," and "externalities," but I assured him that I would make every argument that had any chance of freeing him.

There's an old saying: "If you have the law on your side, bang on the law. If you have the facts on your side, bang on the facts. If you have neither, bang on the table." I have never believed that, but I do believe in a variation on that theme: If you don't have the law or legal facts on your side, argue your case in the court of public opinion. In the Reems case, the Memphis jury had rejected Reems's factual defense, and the judge had rejected his legal defense. The Supreme Court had rejected my "choice" and "externality" approach. I continued to believe, however, that the broader general public, or at least its most influential segment, would be sympathetic to my libertarian approach to obscenity, especially in the context of an actor being prosecuted. Reems, to be sure, was no Helen Hayes, but to make the point that the principle was the same, we adopted the following slogan: "Harry Reems today, Helen Hayes tomorrow." We elicited support from the mainstream entertainment industry and received the backing of several eminent figures, such as Mike Nichols, Gregory Peck, Stephen Sondheim, Jack Nicholson, and Colleen Dewhurst.

We succeeded in getting the *New York Times* to cover the case. Its initial story told how the Reems prosecution was first seen "as a joke," but was now being understood "as a very serious issue":

> *As Mr. Dershowitz interprets the Deep Throat case, "Any person who participates in any way in the creation, production, editing or distribution of a sexually explicit film, newspaper, book, painting or magazine can be hauled into a Federal court anywhere in the United States and charged with participating in a national conspiracy.*[31]

Shortly thereafter, Nat Hentoff wrote a long front-page analysis in the *Village Voice*, explaining

> *that the implications of the Reems prosecution go well beyond obscenity. If a conspiracy charge like this one was to be upheld on appeal, the government*

could make dangerous use of that precedent in political cases involving, for example, antiwar activists.

Here was an actor who, on the one day he worked on Deep Throat, *had no idea what the ultimate film was going to look like. He knew it was a sex film, but he had not seen any script in advance. There was no way he could know whether it was going to be soft core or hard core. And, in fact, Harry never even saw the film before it was released. Yet he's convicted of a conspiracy to move the film, in the form it finally took, across state lines.*[32]

Following the publication of the Hentoff article, hundreds of readers came forward and volunteered their assistance.[33]

Reems and I crisscrossed the country, speaking at universities, town halls, and other venues. Our appearances were widely covered by the media.[34]

Not all the stories were flattering. Mike Royko complained in a syndicated article how depressing it was that after two hundred years of men like Jefferson, Paine, Debs, and Darrow, "we are now asked to fight for the right of Harry Reems to be a public creep. . . . Anybody who contributes to his defense fund," Royko concluded, "is a mental moonbeam."[35]

But people contributed, and Reems and I persisted in making our case in the court of public opinion. In time, the publicity had its intended effect on the public, on the Justice Department, and on the courts. We began to get the message that the Reems conviction was an embarrassment.

In the end, the Justice Department decided to drop the case. Reems's conviction was vacated and his indictment was dismissed, over the strong objections of the Memphis prosecutor and judge. We did not have the law on our side, but we did have public opinion. We might have lost our case in the court of law (or won it on grounds other than my "choice," "externality" approach), but we had clearly won in the court of public opinion.[36] Harry Reems went free, retired from the porn business, became a born-again Christian, and moved to Utah, where he sold real estate. As my legal "fee" for winning his freedom, he sent me a photograph of him with the following inscription: "To Alan Dershowitz, who taught me everything I know." The First Amendment was safe from the likes of Larry Parrish—at least for a time. Herb Streiker died in March 2013 of pancreatic cancer at the age of sixty-five.[37]

My second encounter with *Deep Throat* presented a more daunting challenge to my legal theory of choice. It took place on my home turf of Harvard, and the people urging criminal prosecution were not Bible Belt fundamentalists but Harvard students. The people whom these students wanted to see prosecuted were *other students*, one of whom eventually became a founder of Microsoft.

It all began with some drunken Harvard College students viewing the film *Animal House* and throwing beer cans at the screen, damaging it. The Quincy House Film Society was responsible for the screen. In order to raise the several hundred dollars needed for repair, they decided to show *Deep Throat*.

Some women students who lived in Quincy House protested. "This is our home," one complained. "We shouldn't have to be subjected to abuse and degradation right in our own living room."

The uproar caught the film society by surprise. The showing of *Deep Throat* had become a preexam tradition at many colleges. My own nephew sponsored a showing at MIT.[38] It was seen as a lark, an escape from the tensions of the tests. But feminists were beginning to take pornographic movies, especially *Deep Throat*, quite seriously.

Shortly before the scheduled showing, Gloria Steinem wrote an article in *Ms.* magazine about *Deep Throat* and its impact on women: "Literally millions seem to have been taken to *Deep Throat* by their boyfriends or husbands (not to mention prostitutes by pimps) so that each one might learn what a woman could do to please a man if she really wanted to."[39]

Moreover, Linda Lovelace was now claiming that her innocent face had been a mask covering up a battered wife who had been imprisoned by her husband-pimp. Several years after the completion of *Deep Throat*, Lovelace wrote an autobiography entitled *Ordeal*,[40] in which she told a sordid story of how she had been compelled to perform her "sexual sword-swallower trick" at gunpoint.

I called Reems and asked him whether his recollections of the filming of *Deep Throat* corroborated her claim that she had been forced into performing. Harry, who was then working off-Broadway in a stage play, replied, "Are you kidding? Sure her husband, Chuck, was an asshole, but he was hardly around during the filming. Damiano sent him away because he would get jealous of how much she was enjoying the sex. She was really into it. We had a good relationship before and during the filming."

I asked Reems whether it was possible that Lovelace was only acting when she "enjoyed" the sex.

"Linda Lovelace acting?" Harry exclaimed. "Have you seen her in a film? She couldn't even pretend to be acting."

Lovelace's account, whether true or false, struck a responsive chord among feminists. (A film based on her story was premiered at Sundance in 2013).[41] Steinem's article presented a sympathetic portrait of Lovelace as the victim of everything the "sleazy pornocrats" had come to represent. The movie *Deep Throat* came to symbolize the antiwomen evils of the sex industry. And I became the symbol of the "pornocrat lawyer," getting rich off the suffering of exploited women (even though I charged nothing for most of these cases).

The organization through which Gloria Steinem spoke—Women Against Pornography—advocated boycotts directed not only at theaters and bookstores, but at lawyers who represented them on First Amendment grounds. When I and several friends opened a kosher deli in Harvard Square, it was picketed with signs saying HOW CAN A PORN PIG SERVE KOSHER FOOD? A headline in the local newspaper read, NOTED LAW PROFESSOR ALAN DERSHOWITZ UPHOLDS FEMINISTS' RIGHT TO CALL HIM A "PIG." It described how I put a sign up in the window of our deli that read: IF ANYONE TRIES TO STOP YOU FROM PICKETING ME, I WILL DEFEND YOUR RIGHT OF FREE SPEECH TOO.

Some radical feminists went beyond boycotts, shooting bullets through a bookstore window in Harvard Square to protest its sale of *Playboy* magazine. Some theaters showing *Deep Throat* received threats of violence, and at least one was firebombed after the patrons left.

Some of the women of Quincy House who were opposed to *Deep Throat* were not content to protest. They tried to cancel the showing by calling for a vote of the students. They lost by a margin of three to one. Women too were divided. Next the Quincy House women tried to get the university administration to forbid the showing. The dean of students wrote a letter to the Quincy House Film Society urging it not to show *Deep Throat*, but he would not ban it. The members of the film society, caught up in the challenge, voted to go forward with the event.

The Quincy House women decided to picket the performances and to use the occasion to sensitize students to the evils of pornography. I defended their right to picket the film.

The First Amendment seemed to be in full bloom at Harvard. No one was being prevented from expressing any views. The Quincy House Film Society was going to show *Deep Throat;* the Harvard administration was expressing but not imposing its view; the feminists were preparing pamphlets, slide shows, and speakers to present theirs; and everyone was free to see and listen to all or none of these expressions.

The feminists seemed to be making their point quite effectively: More students were expected on the picket lines than at the movie. Many in the Harvard community, while supporting the right of the Quincy House Film Society to show *Deep Throat*, now believed that the society had been insensitive to the feelings of their feminist housemates by exhibiting an offensive film in the dormitory that was home to them all. I shared that view.

Then everything changed. Days before the scheduled showing, two women residents of Quincy House, not satisfied to protest and picket, called the local district attorney's office and asked the police to prevent the showing of *Deep Throat* and to arrest the students who were planning to show it.

The local district attorney was an elderly political hack named John Droney. When he learned that the twin evils of obscenity and Harvard might merge on that fateful night, he dispatched an assistant to court in an effort to secure an injunction.

Only hours before the scheduled performance, Carl Stork and Nathan J. Hagen—the copresidents of the Quincy House Film Society—received telephone calls from the DA's office directing them to be in court at two o'clock for a hearing. They tried to call me, but I was at lunch. I returned from lunch at two-fifteen, to learn that I was expected in court—fifteen minutes earlier!

I quickly borrowed a colleague's ill-fitting jacket, dug an old brown tie out of my desk drawer, and drove to the courthouse in downtown Cambridge.

Within minutes, I found myself arguing against the injunction. With no books, cases, or statutes in my possession, I had to wing it.

I argued that the judge need not view the film: No matter what its content, I said, it would be unconstitutional for him to enjoin the showing of any film. The judge insisted on having *Deep Throat* screened for him. I informed him that I had no intention of watching.

I was preserving an important point for any jury trial that the students might have in the future. I would tell the jurors that I had never seen *Deep Throat* because I had chosen not to, and that they had never seen *Deep Throat* because they had chosen not to. I would argue that the right to choose not to see a film is just as important as the right to choose to see a film. Indeed, most countries that *prevent* their citizens from seeing certain films also *require* their citizens to see other films. I would remind the jurors that it was the district attorney who was making them see a film they had chosen not to see, in order to have them decide whether other people, who have also chosen not to see the film, would be offended if they were to see it. I hoped, by this argument, to point out the absurd nature of the jurors' task in an obscenity prosecution based on vicarious offensiveness, and to get them to focus on the important issue—namely, whether the outside of the movie theater, the only thing that the unwilling public might have to endure, was offensive to those who could not avoid it.

The judge excused me from watching *Deep Throat*, while he, half a dozen assistant DAs, and a few courthouse personnel watched Linda Lovelace and Harry Reems on a small video machine.

After about forty minutes the judge stopped the videotape and summoned us back into court. "I've seen enough," he declared with a disgusted look on his face. Then, turning to me, he said, "You're the lucky one. I had to sit through that trash." The judge declined to issue an injunction against the scheduled showing of *Deep Throat*, ruling that it was not obscene under Massachusetts law.

When I arrived at Quincy House shortly before eight o'clock, a circus atmosphere prevailed. Hundreds of pickets marched outside urging viewers to stay away.[42] There was some pushing. Slogans were shouted: "Freedom of the press is not freedom to molest!" "Pornography is an incitement to violence!"

I walked past the pickets and spoke to the assembled viewers and protesters:

> *Whether you folks like it or not, you are part of a rather important political event. . . . I am not here to either encourage or discourage the students who decided to see this film. . . . Were I not involved in this lawsuit, I would be out there defending the rights of those picketers to . . . persuade you not to see this film.*

Notwithstanding the judge's ruling that the film was not obscene, the district attorney decided to arrest Stork and Hagen.[43]

Amid shouts of "Free the Quincy House Two!," Stork and Hagen were taken to police headquarters and booked on charges of disseminating matter they knew to be obscene, despite the reality that they knew it *not* to be obscene, because the judge had so ruled. A band of students marched behind them and protested the arrest on the steps of the police station. Among the protesting students were some of the same women who earlier had organized the feminist demonstration. They were furious at the students who were trying to put two of their fellow students in prison for exercising their freedom of expression. To complicate matters, one of the arrested students wasn't a U.S. citizen—he was German—and faced deportation if convicted. As I later described this reversal:

> *The minute the kids were arrested . . . everything changed—the women [who had called the cops] became the goats, the kids [who were arrested] became the heroes. One lesson that we all learned was that the least effective way of delegitimizing this kind of speech is to invoke the law; it has the opposite effect.*

Several days after the arrest, we filed a civil rights action in federal court charging District Attorney Droney with violating the rights of Stork and Hagen, as well as those of the audience members who were denied the right to attend the three scheduled showings that had to be canceled after the film was seized.

Eventually all the charges against Stork and Hagen were dismissed, after the lawsuit forced the district attorney to admit, under oath, that he had willfully defied the judicial determination that *Deep Throat* was not obscene, and that his goal was to serve as a "censor," regardless of the law. The "Quincy House Two" were free and life returned to normal at Harvard.

My encounters with fundamentalists, feminists, and pornographers made clear to me the important, and often underestimated, relationship between the court of law and the court of public opinion.

I once had a European student who wanted to study why there was so much censorship of erotic material in the United States. He had come to his erroneous conclusion from reading United States Supreme Court decisions. I told him that before he undertook his study, he should visit some video stores (this was several years ago) and adult-only movie theaters. He did and came back to me in shock. "They don't follow the Supreme Court in the United States," he exclaimed. "Now, that's a subject worthy of study," I replied.

It is important to remember that in a democracy, even a democracy in which the Supreme Court plays so central a role, in the end the people decide. This is especially true in an area, like obscenity, where "community standards" help define the law.[44] Such values are ever-shifting and subject to influence. While the Supreme Court has insisted that the government has the *power* to punish the showing of "obscene" films in adult-only theaters (and on cable and "on demand" television), the people have voted the other way with their feet (and their remotes). The law in action today bears little resemblance to Chief Justice Burger's "categorical . . . disapprov[al] of [my] theory that obscene, pornographic films acquire constitutional immunity from state regulation simply because they are exhibited for consenting adults only."[45] The law in action more closely resembles the approach I advocated in my first encounter with the law of obscenity back in 1969. I promised Judge Aldrich that if we lost in the Supreme Court, I would continue to urge acceptance of the argument that the government has no business telling a consenting adult what he may or may not watch in a theater (or on video or TV) from which children are excluded, so long as the "externalities"—the images that appear in public view outside the theater—are not obscene.

I have kept my promise, and despite the Supreme Court's continued insistence—most recently in the violent video games case[46]—that "obscenity" is not protected by the First Amendment, porn is widely available to consenting adults who choose to watch it without thrusting it upon unwilling viewers. That's the law in action. Inevitably, the law, as articulated by the courts, will follow the law in action, lest it become irrelevantly anachronistic or patently hypocritical. Hypocrisy, it has been said, is the homage paid by vice to virtue.[47] In the area of obscenity, hypocrisy functions to allow the courts to maintain a pretense of puritanism in a world of prurience. T. B. Macaulay once observed that "the Puritan hated bear-baiting, not because it gave pain to the bear, but because it gave pleasure to the spectators."[48] Perhaps that's why our "puritan" former chief justice insisted on comparing adult films to bear-baiting. Some adults enjoy watching obscene films. Although some puritans and feminists hate this, there is no evidence that this activity causes the type of harm (or pleasure) that government should be empowered to prevent by censorship.[49]

Most Americans seem to understand that pornography, while offensive to some, is not provably harmful to others. That's why obscenity prosecutions have a relatively low rate of success. I have been involved in dozens of obscenity cases over the years and do not recall ever losing one.[50]

In addition to litigating many obscenity cases, I have written extensively on the subject. My article "Why Pornography?"[51] set out to determine whether there is any actual relationship between "hard-core pornography" and violence against women.[52]

The available evidence strongly suggests that there is no correlation (to say nothing of causation) between the sexual explicitness of a film and the likelihood that it will induce violence by its viewer.[53] Indeed it is possible that there may well be a negative correlation, since rape has gone down considerably in those societies in which sexually explicit films are pervasive, while rape has certainly not gone down in those societies that persist in censoring films with explicit sex.

I argued therefore that "pornography is a red herring" and that in the absence of compelling evidence—of which there is none—that it causes actual harm beyond vicariously offending those who can choose not to see it, the government should get out of the business of censoring films and other media.[54]

Other types of speech pose far greater potential dangers. These communications include the divulgence of state secrets, the dissemination of classified information, and the publication of news stories that compromise the national interest and endanger citizens. The problem is that the censorship of such expression may also pose far greater risks to democracy and liberty than the censorship of obscenity. Put another way, democracy could survive the censorship of hard-core pornography, despite the "slippery slope" from porn to politics and art (or from Harry Reems to Helen Hayes). A society that banned pornography would, perhaps, be less vibrant, less tolerant, less pluralistic, less committed to choice, than one that did not. It might also be more subject to sliding down the slope toward other forms of artistic censorship at the margins. But so long as core political discourse remained free and open, democracy could survive. The same could not confidently be said about the widespread censorship of expression regarded by the government as state secrets, classified information, and "dangerous" news stories. These go to the very heart of our democratic system of checks and balances, in which the ultimate check is an informed public. As James Madison cautioned nearly two centuries ago: "A popular Government, without popular information, or the means of acquiring it, is but a Prologue to a Farce or a Tragedy; or, perhaps both."[55]

7

DISCLOSURE OF SECRETS

The Pentagon Papers and Julian Assange

The conflict between national security and free expression is real. It must be confronted and resolved by every society committed to civil liberties yet concerned for its safety. It is different from the alleged conflicts that motivate the censorship of obscene material, because there is ample room in a diverse society for accommodating the desires of those who get pleasure from porn and those who want to be protected from offensive material. The guiding principle that "your right to swing your fist ends at the tip of my nose"[1] suggests a workable approach to the regulation of offensive material. But there is no simple rule for the accommodation of free expression and national security, where the expression may expose our security to real danger.

No reasonable person can dispute the reality that there are "necessary secrets," like the names of spies, the movement of troops, the content of codes, the location of satellites, and the nature of secret weapons. Nor can any student of history doubt that there are unnecessary secrets, like old information that remains classified by bureaucratic inertia. There is also information kept secret under the pretext of national security but really in order to protect the reputation or electability of government officials. And then there is the most interesting category of secrets—those that are genuinely designed to protect national security in the short run, but whose disclosure may well serve the national interest in the long run. The most controversial genre are secrets the disclosure of which would, in the reasonable view of the government, endanger national security, but whose disclosure, in the equally reasonable view of the press, might ultimately serve the national interest.

The real issue is not *whether* such secrets should be published, since that question will often be a close one about which well-intentioned people will disagree. The real issue, as it often is in a democracy, is *who* should be entrusted to make this real-time decision.

The other difficult issue is not *whether*, but *when* to publish. In a democracy, there should be no permanent secrets, since history and accountability are paramount. The public must ultimately know everything its government has done in its name. But it is sometimes necessary to postpone publication until an immediate danger has passed, since in the modern world, there is no way of disclosing secrets to friends without also disclosing them to foes.

There is no "one size fits all" solution to this daunting conflict, but there are some useful guidelines in striking the proper balance. In the first place, the vast majority of *claims* that national security will be endangered by free expression are simply not true; most such claims are not even believed by the government officials who assert them. The talismanic phrase "national security" is invoked as a cover for convenience, for political advantage, and for protection from personal or political embarrassment. Every claim of "national security"—or "corporate security" or "university security" or the security of any institution—should be subject to rigorous challenge, in an effort to separate the contrived from the authentic. But this will not eliminate all disputes. There will be some cases of real and intractable conflict between security and freedom. Our Constitution purports to resolve doubts in favor of freedom, but there are cases where even that presumption will not resolve the problem: where the authentic claims of national security will seem to outweigh the powerful presumption in favor of free expression.

In those cases we need to develop mechanisms for resolving the dispute. Resolution cannot be left entirely in the hands of those responsible for security, such as the executive or the military. Our experience in delegating decision-making authority to these institutions in times of crisis is discouraging.

It has indeed been fortunate for the survival of our liberties that there have always been some Americans willing to challenge governmental high-handedness, even during periods of crisis.[2] Under our constitutional system, it takes only a single person challenging the government to create a case or controversy suitable for judicial resolution.

This is not to suggest that justice should remain blind to the existence of a real emergency endangering the survival of the nation. As Justice

Arthur Goldberg once wrote: "While the Constitution protects against the invasion of individual rights, it is not a suicide pact."[3] But it is precisely during times of crisis—when the balance between momentary expediency and enduring safeguards often goes askew—that courts can perform their most critical function: to preserve or restore a sense of perspective.

In the eternal struggle between liberty and security, we have come to expect the executive and legislative branches to champion the latter. The judiciary—with its lifetime tenure, its tradition of independence, and its unique stewardship over our rights—is the institution most able to resist the passing fears of a dangerous moment.

But liberty is not a commodity that can be obtained once and for all and then passively held on to. The battle for civil liberties, as Roger Baldwin, the late founder of the ACLU, liked to say, never "stays won."[4] (A variation on the biblical admonition that justice must be actively pursued, because it too never stays won.)[5] The struggle must be endured by every new generation and in each new crisis. What Thomas Paine taught us on the eve of our own revolution remains true today: "Those who expect to reap the blessings of freedom must . . . undergo the fatigue of supporting it."[6]

The stakes on both sides are much higher when the government seeks to censor dangerous "leaks" than when it seeks to censor merely offensive or disturbing speech. The danger of publication is greater and the danger of repression is also greater. There are serious risks in *not* censoring, and there are serious risks *in* censoring. Striking the proper constitutional balance is a daunting challenge. Unfortunately too few democracies—including our own—have confronted it wisely.[7]

I was asked to help confront this challenge early in my career in several important cases pitting national security against the First Amendment. These early cases grew out of our disastrous experience in Vietnam, and I observed at close range the ravages of war on our freedoms.

The first major Vietnam case was the conspiracy prosecution against Dr. Benjamin Spock, the Reverend William Sloane Coffin, and several other antiwar leaders. I played a consulting role in the defense of Dr. Spock and in the appeal of Reverend Coffin and eventually wrote an article for the *New York Times* about the case after the convictions were reversed on appeal.[8]

The most publicized and notorious of the Vietnam protest cases was the conspiracy prosecution against the "Chicago Seven," growing out of demonstrations during the 1968 Democratic National Convention. After the trial of that case, the lead defense lawyer—William Kunstler—was held in contempt of court and sentenced to four years' imprisonment. I was part of the legal team assembled to prepare the appeal of that contempt order. We won.

Another major prosecution took place against the Berrigan brothers and other radical leaders of the draft resistance movement. I was asked to work on the defense of that case, but was "fired" by one of the more militant defendants when he learned that I was a Zionist.

The bitterness of the Vietnam War spread rapidly over college and university campuses. What began as peaceful teach-ins and protests soon turned into confrontations and violence. In 1969, there was an antiwar protest at Harvard that led to violence and several years of continuous turmoil on that venerable campus. These events led Harvard to attempt to dismiss numerous students. I represented several of them against the university. One was accused of "giving the finger" to a speaker. Another was accused of shouting "No silence in the face of death!" when a speaker requested a moment of silence for soldiers killed in combat. We won both cases.

As the war was winding down and the United States was deciding to withdraw from Vietnam, the CIA was given a major role in overseeing the American evacuation. One of the CIA agents in charge of the operation was Frank Snepp, who wrote an uncensored account of his experiences—taking care, however, not to disclose any classified material. He refused to submit his manuscript for prior "approval" by the CIA, as required in his employment contract. When his book, entitled *Decent Interval*,[9] was published, the CIA sued him, and the case eventually was decided against him by the Supreme Court.[10] I was one of his pro bono lawyers throughout the litigation.[11]

The release and publication of the Pentagon Papers in 1971 was perhaps the single most important event in turning American public opinion against the Vietnam War. While the *New York Times* and the *Washington Post* were fighting in court to continue publishing portions of the papers, Senator Mike Gravel of Alaska was taking more direct action: He convened an emergency nighttime meeting of his Subcommittee on Buildings and Grounds—hard to imagine a committee less relevant to the Pentagon Papers—and placed the papers in the public record. The "Gravel edition" of the Pentagon Papers was then published by Beacon Press of Boston.[12] I represented Beacon Press and, subsequently, Senator Gravel in litigation that eventually went to the United States Supreme Court.[13]

I also conferred with my teacher and dear friend Alexander Bickel, who was lead counsel for the *Times* in the Pentagon Papers case.[14] Since our cases shared a common constitutional approach, we exchanged ideas and drafts.

The difficulty of defending an absolutist view of the First Amendment was well illustrated by an exchange during the Supreme Court argument between Justice Potter Stewart and Professor Bickel. Stewart asked Bickel about "a hypothetical case":

> *Let us assume that when the members of the Court go back and open up this sealed record we find something there that absolutely convinces us that its disclosure would result in the sentencing to death of a hundred young men whose only offense had been that they were nineteen years old and had low draft numbers. What should we do?*

Bickel fumbled: "I wish there were a statute that covered it."

Justice Stewart persisted: "You would say the Constitution requires that it be published, and that these men die, is that it?"

Finally, Bickel answered his hypothetical directly: "No, I'm afraid that my inclinations to humanity overcome the somewhat more abstract devotion to the First Amendment in a case of that sort."

The lawyer for the government, Solicitor General Erwin Griswold (former dean of Harvard Law School) did not regard Justice Stewart's case as hypothetical.

"I haven't the slightest doubt myself that the material which has already been published and the publication of the other materials affects American lives and is a thoroughly serious matter."[15]

The court ruled that the publication of the Pentagon Papers could not be stopped by the government.

Several years after the argument, Griswold expressed a rather different view:

> *I have never seen any trace of a threat to national security from the publication. Indeed, I have never seen it even suggested that there was such an actual threat. [He, of course, had suggested just that in his oral argument.] . . . It quickly becomes apparent to any person who has considerable experience with classified material that there is massive overclassification and that the principal concern of the classifiers is not with national security, but rather with governmental embarrassment of one sort or another. There may be some basis for short-term classification while plans are being made, or negotiations are going on, but apart from details of weapons systems, there is very rarely*

> *any real risk to current national security from the publication of facts relating to transactions in the past, even the fairly recent past. This is the lesson of the Pentagon Papers experience.*[16]

The First Amendment emerged victorious in the Pentagon Papers case, as it did in most of the antiwar cases of the 1970s. But this was before the age of the Internet, which changed the sounds and sights of expression—as well as raising the stakes involved in the debate by disseminating massive amounts of classified material throughout the world in the blink of an eye.

JULIAN ASSANGE AND WIKILEAKS

Important as it was as a First Amendment precedent, the Pentagon Papers case was First Amendment "child's play" compared with the WikiLeaks case and other current threats to national security posed by modern computer technology. The Pentagon Papers, after all, were to be published by "mainstream," "responsible," and "patriotic" media,[17] such as the *New York Times*, the *Washington Post*, and Beacon Press, which would be "sensible" in what they exposed to public view. They would never publish the names of spies, informers, or other people whose lives might be endangered by disclosure. (They don't even publish the names of alleged rape victims, though in some cases there are good arguments for doing so.)[18]

These "established" media have permanent "addresses." They can be found and held legally accountable if they violate the law, as the Supreme Court reminded them in the Pentagon Papers case. They are also "businesses" that need public support and are therefore unlikely to take actions that would alienate their paying readership, their advertisers, and their stockholders. These constraints provide some assurance that such established members of "the Fourth Estate" will not pose the worst kind of dangers to our national security, and they serve as an informal "check and balance" on the excesses of journalistic freedom.[19]

None of these assurances or checks are in place when it comes to the "hackers," "cyber-thieves," "anarchists," and other "outsiders"—many of whom are "anonymous"—who currently threaten to expose our deepest, most dangerous, and most valuable "secrets."

There are, of course, some historical low-tech antecedents to the current high-tech dangers. During our prerevolutionary, revolutionary, and immediate postrevolutionary eras, there were many "radical," "irresponsible," "anarchistic," and "anonymous" "rabble-rousers" and even "whistle-blowers," "eavesdroppers," and "leakers" who were believed to be endangering the "security" of the government. "Secret presses" published "anonymous" or pseudonymous screeds, some of which disclosed "secrets" or other "dangerous" information.

The language of the First Amendment would seem to protect these dissidents against abridgement of their freedom of expression—at least from the United States government. But our history in this regard has been checkered at best, especially in the context of fear of war.

Less than a decade after the ratification of the First Amendment, Congress (the very Congress that was directed to "make no law" abridging the freedom of speech) enacted the Alien and Sedition Laws, which abridged the freedom of speech of critics of the Adams administration. The justification for this legislation was the fear of war with France.[20] During every war or threatened war since, there have been efforts to abridge the speech of "disloyal," "unpatriotic," and "irresponsible" dissenters,[21] such as those who, in Justice Holmes's benighted view, "shouted fire" by protesting World War I.

These "retail" dangers posed by individual troublemakers (or even by groups) were, of course, rather meager compared to the "wholesale" dangers currently posed by "cyber-troublemakers," such as Julian Assange and WikiLeaks. Indeed, even Assange and WikiLeaks are somewhat closer to established media than are others whom we know little about. After all, WikiLeaks worked closely with the *New York Times* and other mainstream media. There are generally several levels of vetting before anything is published. It can be argued that WikiLeaks has served as a "filter" for material that might otherwise have been published directly on the Internet, without names or other such material having been removed.

There are hackers out there who regard Assange as a "sellout" for "tampering with the truth" by excising *anything*. They would—and do if they can—publish *everything* they manage to hack. That is why the first line of defense against the disclosure of secrets is to *protect* the most important secrets from hacking or other means of accessing them by preventive steps. As Assange once told me, "The best way to keep a secret is not to know it." The United States does a terrible job of protecting its secrets, often giving access to some of the most unstable, irresponsible, or risky individuals (such as Bradley Manning and Edward Snowden), while denying security clearance to loyal and cautious people. Inevitably some secrets will become known to those who have no stake in keeping them secret and a stake in making them public. That's why the rule of law, rather than the whim of government officials, is needed to strike the appropriate balance.

In 2011, Julian Assange asked me to become involved in a case that threatened to skew that balance. He invited me to consult with him regarding a possible indictment by the United States against him and others.

I went to London in March of that year to meet with Assange and the British lawyers who were representing him. He was facing the immediate prospect of extradition to Sweden on sexual assault charges, but he also faced the possibility of being extradited to the United States to face charges that carried far more serious consequences. It was the possible American prosecution that he wished to discuss with me.

Before traveling to London, I spent several hours with Assange and his legal team over the phone and by e-mail. We worried about the security of our lawyer-client communications, which some might think ironic in light of Assange's penchant for disclosure of secret communications, but he had little choice but to communicate about the legal issues. We decided that a face-to-face meeting was required, and we met in his lawyer's office.

I found Assange to be earnest and deeply devoted to the principle of maximal transparency of governmental actions. He was, however, sensitive to the need to keep some secrets—if not from him, at least from the general public, which inevitably includes some bad people determined to do bad things to innocent and perhaps not so innocent people.

Assange insisted[22] that he was a journalist, in every relevant sense of that term. He published, and turned over to others to publish, important and relevant material that had been provided to him anonymously. He and his colleagues had devised a technology for allowing "whistle-blowers" to "drop" material to WikiLeaks anonymously and with little possibility of it being traced to its source by WikiLeaks or anyone else. This "drop box" technology was the cyber manifestation of the notion that the best way to keep a secret is not to know it in the first place.

His job as a journalist was to authenticate the raw material, vet it for names and other life-threatening information that in his journalistic judgment should not be published (for example, the location of safe houses), and arrange for it to receive maximal reach by having it published by mainstream media outlets around the world, which would do further vetting to meet their own journalistic standards.

When he finished explaining his journalistic modus operandi, two names immediately popped into my head: Seymour Hersh of the *New Yorker* and Bob Woodward of the *Washington Post*. Both are pillars of the journalistic establishment and both have made their reputations by publishing secrets the government—or at least *some* in the government—did not want to see in print.

Hersh specializes in publishing classified information about national security that has been provided to him by whistle-blowers inside the government who disagree with particular governmental policies and want to see them exposed by someone who is believed to be sympathetic to their dissenting views. Some of these whistle-blowers are breaking the law by disclosing classified material. Hersh and his publishers know that they are publishing classified information before they publish it. Yet neither he nor his publishers have been prosecuted.

It is likely, moreover, that Hersh has encouraged at least some of his more reluctant sources to become whistle-blowers, or if they came to him without any prior encouragement, he's encouraged them to continue to provide him with classified material. I do not know this to be a fact, but I have been told by several experienced investigative reporters that this is how it is done—that without encouragement and promises of confidentiality and positive portrayal of the source, the leaks "dry up." When I read books by these authors, I can often surmise who at least some of the sources are: They're usually the ones who are portrayed positively in other parts of the book—quid pro quo!

In other words, authors like Seymour Hersh not only *report* the classified information given to them by sources, they *develop*, *encourage*, and in other ways *facilitate* the continuing flow of information—information that they know is classified and hence being illegally turned over to them—from their "criminal" sources. An important difference is that Hersh has a political agenda: He tends to publish information that serves that agenda. Assange, on the other hand, seems willing to publish material equally critical of all governments. For engaging in such journalism, Hersh wins Pulitzer Prizes and gets invited to White House dinners and to lecture at schools of journalism that teach these methods.

Woodward is different in some respects and similar in others. Whereas Hersh's sources tend to be beauracratic dissidents, Woodward relies on high-ranking members of the administration who want their "spin" to be heard on the story he is publishing to a very wide audience. Some of those politicians may be authorized to disclose the material, but certainly some are not, and some of the material is almost certainly classified (though it probably shouldn't be).

Both authors recognize the reality that many, if not most, "state" secrets

Above: *My paternal grandparents, Ida and Louis Dershowitz. (From the author's collection)*

Right: *My maternal grandparents, Blima and Naftuli Ringel, and one of their sons, Morris. (From the author's collection)*

Below: *My mother, Claire, then Clara, graduating from high school at age fifteen. (From the author's collection)*

Below: *Me before the age of three, when according to Jewish tradition, a boy receives his first haircut. (From the author's collection)*

My younger brother, Nathan (Tully), and me at Coney Island. (From the author's collection)

Above: *My Bar Mitzvah picture. (From the author's collection)*

Below, left: *My senior term high school report card, with two flunking grades for the first half. (From the author's collection)*. Below, center: *Me as a seventeen-year-old assistant counselor at Camp Maple Lake, between my unsuccessful high school years and my successful college years.* Below, right: *Me as a crew-cut freshman at Brooklyn College, wearing my high school varsity jacket. (From the author's collection)*

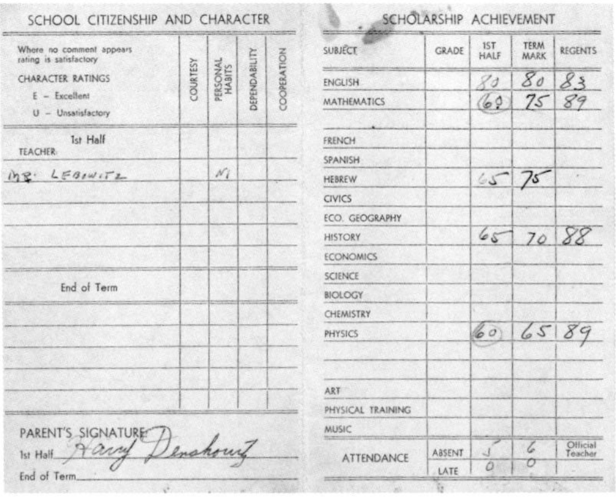

SCHOOL CITIZENSHIP AND CHARACTER

Where no comment appears rating is satisfactory CHARACTER RATINGS E – Excellent U – Unsatisfactory	COURTESY	PERSONAL HABITS	DEPENDABILITY	COOPERATION
1st Half TEACHER				
MR. LEBOWITZ		N		
End of Term				

PARENT'S SIGNATURE
1st Half Harry Dershowitz
End of Term

SCHOLARSHIP ACHIEVEMENT

SUBJECT	GRADE	1ST HALF	TERM MARK	REGENTS
ENGLISH		80	80	83
MATHEMATICS		60	75	89
FRENCH				
SPANISH				
HEBREW		65	75	
CIVICS				
ECO. GEOGRAPHY				
HISTORY		65	70	88
ECONOMICS				
SCIENCE				
BIOLOGY				
CHEMISTRY				
PHYSICS		60	65	89
ART				
PHYSICAL TRAINING				
MUSIC				
ATTENDANCE	ABSENT	5	6	Official Teacher
	LATE	0	0	

Above, left: *Judge David Bazelon. (From the author's collection)*

Above, right: *Me as editor in chief of the* Yale Law Journal. *(From the author's collection)*

Below: *Me with Justice Arthur Goldberg, shortly after he left the Supreme Court. (From the author's collection)*

Above: *Interviewing Prime Minister Golda Meir for the TV show* The Advocates. *(From the author's collection)*

Below: *Giving a standing-room-only lecture at Harvard Law School. (From the author's collection)*

Above: *At graduation, with three of my research assistants: Jim Cramer, Eliot Spitzer, and Cliff Sloan. (From the author's collection)*

Below: *A* New York Post *write-up of a fund-raiser for Harry Reems, in which I am misidentified. (Courtesy of the* New York Post*)*

N.Y. POST 6/30/76

Funds for Throat Star

Ramsey Clark, who hopes to win the Democratic nomination for U. S. Senate, and his wife, Georgia, stand with actor Harry Reems (second from right) during a fund-raising dinner last night for the porno sta r, who faces up to five years in jail for the part he played in "Deep Throat." At right is Bruce S. Kramer, Reems' defense lawyer. Clark, a former U. S. Attorney General, has been associated with many controversial civil liberties causes. A number of celebrities were at the invitation-only party at Ted Hook's Backstage, 318 W. 45th St.

Associated Press Photo

Top: *With Jeremy Irons, who won the Academy Award for Best Actor portraying Claus von Bülow in the film version of* Reversal of Fortune, *and Elon Dershowitz, who co-produced the film. (From the author's collection)*

Above: *The real Claus von Bülow in his Fifth Avenue, New York, apartment. (Courtesy of the* New York Times*)*

Right: *A* New York Times *cartoon of me and my clients, Jim and Tammy Bakker. (Courtesy of the* New York Times*)*

Above: *With Leona Helmsley. (Getty Images)*

Left: *The Tison brothers, in T-shirts, with Randy Greenawalt in foreground. (Courtesy of the Pinal County Sheriff's office)*

Below: *With my client and friend Natan Sharansky. (From the author's collection)*

are designed not to protect the security of the nation, but rather to protect (and enhance) the reputations of the incumbent officials. In this regard, I recall a joke that made the rounds of the Soviet dissident community when I represented several of them in the 1970s. It is set during the period of the Stalin show trials, when a dissident was arrested for calling Stalin "a fool." He wanted to defend himself by showing that Stalin was indeed a fool, but he was cut off by the judge, who said: "If you were being charged with defamation, truth might be a defense. But it is not a defense to what you are being charged with." The dissident was taken aback and asked the judge, "If I am not being charged with defaming Stalin for calling him a fool, what *am* I being charged with?"

The judge responded solemnly: "You are being charged with revealing a state secret!"

Many current state secrets are really secrets whose disclosure would embarrass officeholders. Even the solicitor general who argued for the Nixon administration to prevent publication of the Pentagon Papers later acknowledged this reality.[23] That's why *selective* leaking and *selective* withholding of classified material is so damaging to truth, accountability, and historical accuracy. And that's also why it is so prevalent in every administration.

For example, the May 13, 2013, edition of *Time* magazine openly boasted that it was publishing information that "is still classified" but that was "made available to *Time*," presumably by someone inside the government who had an interest in seeing it published.

WikiLeaks is different precisely because Assange is not publishing selectively in order to tell a story favorable to one group or another. He has no apparent political agenda. His goal is transparency for the sake of accountability. With the exception of some names and addresses, WikiLeaks has let the leaked documents speak for themselves. Assange allowed the chips to fall where they may, and they often fall on the heads of the current officeholders around the world.

On February 28, 2013, PFC Bradley Manning confessed to providing the vast archive of military and diplomatic files to WikiLeaks, but in doing so, he put Assange in a position comparable to mainstream journalists, and he put WikiLeaks in a position comparable to mainstream newspapers. Manning said that he had simply uploaded the data to WikiLeaks, without any prompting from Assange: "No one associated with [WikiLeaks] pressured me into sending more information." He used a broadband connection at a Barnes & Noble store because a snowstorm had disabled the Internet connection at his aunt's house, where he was staying.[24] He sent the material first to the WikiLeaks website and subsequently to a "cloud drop-box server." He said he engaged in "online conversations" with someone from WikiLeaks who he assumed was a senior figure like Assange[25] and with whom he had what he characterized as an "artificial" relationship. He did not explain what he meant, but his statement provided no evidence that Assange pressured him into providing the data or told him how to download it. To the contrary, Manning's statement supports the claim that Assange and WikiLeaks were the *passive* recipients of unsolicited data which they then vetted and published, much like the *New York Times* and the *Washington Post* did with the Pentagon Papers.

Prosecuting WikiLeaks or its founder for "the crime" of publishing classified information, while at the same time rewarding—with prizes, access, interviews, and status—"reputable" journalists and newspapers for doing essentially the same thing, would constitute selective prosecution. American law, as distinguished, for example, from German law, generally permits selective prosecution of criminals, on the ground that resources are limited and prosecutors must have some discretion in deciding how to expend their limited resources.[26] In order to "get the most bang for the buck," prosecutors are generally free to pick and choose among the many who violate open-ended and often vague criminal statutes, such as tax, regulatory, and criminal negligence laws. They are not free to exercise this discretion in a partisan manner, such as going after members of the opposing political party, as President Nixon did with his "enemies list." Nor can they properly do so on the basis of race, religion, or other protected categories. But they may select for prosecution the most visible or notorious offenders, since such prosecutions are likely to have the greatest deterrent effect on other potential law violators.[27] For example, Leona Helmsley, one of the most famous women in America, was indicted for tax evasion—on April 15!

One area in which it is dangerous and wrong to permit selective prosecution is the publication of classified information by the media. If the government can pick and choose the few it decides to prosecute among the many who publish classified information, it will have too much power over the content of what the media reports.[28] The First Amendment recognizes no distinction between patriotic and unpatriotic, responsible and irresponsible, favorable and unfavorable media. It was precisely these improper distinctions that were employed by the John Adams administration when it selectively enforced the Alien and Sedition Laws against

"Jeffersonians," "Jacobins," and other perceived enemies of the Federalists. It took more than a century and a half for the Supreme Court to declare that although "the Sedition Act was never tested in this court, the attack upon its validity has carried the day in the court of history," citing "a broad consensus that the act was inconsistent with the First Amendment."[29] (I was a law clerk when that opinion was issued in 1964.)

Not only has the verdict of history condemned the *words* of the Sedition Act, it has also condemned the *selective manner* in which it was enforced against certain journalists and newspapers but not others. If there are to be any restrictions of freedom in the press, they should be applied uniformly. If the publication of classified material is to be prosecuted, then *all* who publish it should be prosecuted, not only the marginal, the powerless, the "irresponsible," and the unpatriotic—in the eyes of the government. If all are prosecuted, there is the possibility of the self-correcting mechanism of democracy operating to change the law, by narrowing it to criminalize only those categories of currently classified information that truly endangers national security. If untrammeled prosecutorial discretion is permitted, then the law can be kept as broad and overinclusive as it currently is, without fear that the *New York Times* will be caught in its web. If only the weak and the unpopular are selected for prosecution, there will be little pressures for change.

Moreover, selective prosecution of only certain journalists who violate broad statutes will encourage some in the media to curry favor with the government, and the government to curry favor with certain media. This is an unhealthy and dangerous relationship in a democracy in which the press is supposed to check the government and be independent of its control.

The exercise of some discretion may be necessary under the statutory scheme that currently criminalizes the publication of classified material. If *all* journalists who publish *any* classified material were to be prosecuted, there would be few left. The *New York Times* and its publishers, editors, and national security reporters would be convicted felons, since the current statutes are written in the broadest of terms that invite the exercise of discretion, which has generally been employed to immunize the mainstream media.

Some scholars trust the exercise of prosecutorial discretion and the common sense of juries to prevent unfair application of overbroad laws.[30] History has not vindicated this trust, especially in times of national turmoil and fear. For me, a better democratic answer is for the courts to demand that legislatures enact clear, precise, and limited prohibitions on the real-time disclosure of only the most necessary of secrets. These statutes must neither be overinclusive or underinclusive (as are current laws). They should be capable of uniform application that constrains the power of the government to pick and choose. Precise codification is not a perfect solution to an intractable dilemma, but it would be a significant improvement over the unacceptable current situation.

As I write these words, the United States government is seeking to apprehend and try Edward Snowden, the former technical contractor for the National Security Agency, who disclosed classified information to *The Guardian*, which published it. The public is closely divided over whether Snowden, who was indicted for espionage and theft, is a heroic whistleblower or a criminal traitor.

In vibrant democracies there will always be tensions between the government's need to keep secrets and the news media's need to reveal them. This is as it should be. Constant tension between the government and the press is an essential requisite of our informal system of checks and balances.

SPEECH CODES

I have always been close to being an absolutist against censorship. In my book *Finding Jefferson* I argued that "all speech should be presumed to be protected by the Constitution, and a heavy burden should be placed on those who would censor to demonstrate with relative certainty that the speech at issue, if not censored, would lead to irremediable and immediate serious harm."[31]

I am particularly critical of the censorship of speech on university campuses in the name of "political correctness."[32] Universities should be the paradigms of open discourse, where students learn to debate and counter disagreeable opinions, rather than to censor them.

Yet despite my strong opposition to censorship, I have surprised both my supporters and detractors by calling for precise and narrow "speech codes" on campuses. My reasoning is simple: Censorship is inevitable on all university campuses in extreme situations; if a professor were to use the "N" word to call on an African-American student in class—or comparable taboo words to call on a woman, a Jew, a gay man or lesbian, a Latino, or an Asian-American—that teacher would be fired (or at least disciplined). There are other forms of expression as well that would simply not be tolerated in any university, public or private. Precisely what those are we don't know (recall Carlin's seven dirty words), but we will probably know them when we see them (recall Justice Stewart on hard-core pornography). Accordingly, there already exists a censorship *common law* at every university.

The issue, therefore, is not *whether* there is or should be any censorship of expression by universities. We already know the answer to that question: There is, and there should be in those kinds of extreme cases. I know of no responsible person or organization that would defend the right of a teacher to use the "N" word in calling on or routinely discussing African-American students. The remaining question is whether it is better to leave the decision as to *which* words in which contexts are prohibited to the *after-the-fact* discretion of an administrator, or to decide *in advance* on a list or category of prohibited expressions. In other words, is it more protective of freedom of expression to have a "censorship *common law*" to be applied on an ad hoc basis by a dean, or to have a "censorship *code*" debated and agreed upon in advance by the equivalent of the legislative branch of the university—a student or faculty senate or some other representative body.

I favor a narrow code over a potentially broad common law, because it provides advanced fair warning and an opportunity to challenge its provisions before they are enforced. (That's why I also favor a narrow code criminalizing the publication of only the most dangerous state secrets.)

This controversial view regarding speech is paralleled, in some respect, by my equally controversial view regarding "torture warrants." I am opposed to both censorship and torture, but I realize that both will be employed in extreme cases (in response to the use of the "N" word in the speech context, or in response to ticking-bomb terrorism with regard to torture). I prefer explicit and narrow limitations, with advance notice, visibility in both contexts, because they promote clarity and democratic accountability.[33]

Several years ago, there was an ugly racial incident at Harvard Law School that led to a campaign by some student groups for censorship of offensive speech. The dean appointed a committee to recommend an approach to this delicate problem. He put me on it because of my support for freedom of speech. My fellow committee members were surprised therefore when I proposed that we try to draft a speech code.

"I thought you were against censorship," one of the libertarian student members said in frustration.

"I am," I replied. "That's why I want a code. I don't trust the dean—or anyone else—to decide which speech should be prohibited."

"No speech should be prohibited," the student replied.

I then gave my examples of the professor and the "N" word.

"That's different," the student insisted.

"Then let's try to codify exactly what else may be 'different,'" I responded.

The committee spent more than a year trying to design a code of prohibited expressions. But we could not agree. The "N" word itself could not be prohibited because a black professor had written a brilliant book entitled *Nigger: The Strange Career of a Troublesome Word*.[34] We tried to define the circumstances under which the "N" word could and could not be used. One person suggested that the "N" word could be used by blacks but not whites. Another suggested it could be used in a book but not in oral discussion. A third said it could be used as part of an academic discussion, but not directed at a particular individual. We couldn't agree on this or other disputed expressions, such as opinions regarding negative characteristics associated with particular groups.

At the end, we could not agree on a code. It was a useful experiment in democracy and accountability. I would have preferred us to adopt a code limited to those instances of expression—such as a teacher calling a minority student by a negative racial or other term—which everyone agrees is unacceptable in a classroom setting. This would have sent a powerful message that *no other* type of speech, regardless of how offensive it might be to some, can be prohibited. If a particularly inappropriate expression that had not been included in the codification was then used, the committee could consider including it for the *future*, but that could not be the basis for imposing discipline on speech that took place *prior* to the expression's inclusion in the code.

The virtue of a code is that it leaves no room for "common law crimes" or broad discretion. The vice of a code is that it is often underinclusive—it excludes conduct (or, in this case, speech) that is novel or that was not considered by the codifiers. In the area of freedom of expression, that virtue trumps its vice: It is better to have rules regulating speech that are underinclusive than to have rules that are overinclusive.[35]

There will never be a perfect balance struck between the need for open discourse and the demand to censor deeply offensive and arguably dangerous speech. The struggle to strike this delicate balance never does stay won. What history seems to teach us is generally to err on the side of more disclosure rather than more censorship, even when it comes to national security. This certainly should be true when it comes to speech deemed offensive to some on a university campus.

8

EXPRESSIONS THAT INCITE VIOLENCE AND DISRUPT SPEAKERS

Bruce Franklin and the Muslim Student Association

Expressions that incite violence or disrupt speakers also require a difficult balance among the rights of the disruptive speaker, the rights of the potential victims of the incited violence, and the rights of the disrupted speaker.

There are at least two types of expression that incite violence. The first is *reactive*—that is, the speaker so deeply upsets or offends the person to whom he is speaking that the listener reacts to the speech by physically attacking the speaker. This comes under the legal rubric of "fighting words"—words that cause the listener to fight back.[1] The second is *proactive*—that is, the speaker urges his listeners to commit violence and the listeners comply by hurting a third person or institution. This comes under the legal rubric of "clear and present danger."[2]

Early in my career I was involved in both types of cases.

FIGHTING WORDS

In the famous neo-Nazi march through Skokie, Illinois, the Nazi thugs decided to march—with anti-Semitic chants, signs, and uniforms—through a Jewish community with a large number of Holocaust survivors. The city banned the march on the ground that it would provoke a violent reaction from survivors. The Nazis sued. To the surprise of many, and to the dismay of my mother, I urged the ACLU to defend the right of the Nazis to march through Skokie, and I urged the Jews to ignore them, in order not to give the Nazis the publicity they craved. I don't believe in the "fighting words" exception to the First Amendment. The law should not legitimate or justify violence by recognizing this exception. Experience demonstrates that when victims respond to such offensive provocations by violence or censorship, the provocateurs win in the court of public opinion. That's what happened in Skokie. The Nazi thugs became the focus of attention as a result of being censored by Skokie. They were interviewed by the media, their numbers and influence grew, and they received a degree of legitimacy they had previously been denied.

I understood why the Holocaust survivors would be deeply offended, even possibly traumatized, by being forced to reexperience the spectacle of brown-shirted Nazis wearing swastikas, but I worried about the implications of a judicial decision authorizing censorship. It could be used to justify the censorship of a march by the likes of Martin Luther King through a segregated community in the South, whose residents would be deeply offended by an integrated group marching through their streets. It's no answer to say that King was good or right and the Nazis are bad and wrong, because the First Amendment must always be content-neutral and not prefer good and right speech over bad and wrong speech. That's for the public to decide, only after being presented with both sides without government interference. That's how the marketplace of ideas is supposed to operate in a democracy. The government must *protect* bad, wrong, and offensive speakers from those who would react violently. Speech, not violence, is protected by the First Amendment, even if the violence is a predictable and understandable reaction to the speech.[3]

Moreover, if a violent reaction to speech is deemed to justify censorship, then the threat to commit violence empowers "the victims" of provocative speech to serve as censors. It thus incentivizes and encourages violent reactions to bad speech. (It may also encourage, perhaps unconsciously, some victims to exaggerate the outrage they feel, because the law rewards such exaggerated feelings with the power of censorship.) This "violence veto" should not be encouraged by the law. Hard as it may be to arrest the good "victims" rather than the bad provokers, the First Amendment requires that the government side with the "bad" speakers, rather than the "good" violence-threateners.

In the end, the Nazis "won" the encounter in Skokie because good and decent people in that community decided to try to censor rather than ridicule them.

CLEAR AND PRESENT DANGER

My experience with "clear and present danger" incitement to violence also took place in a small community—the campus of Stanford University. Shortly after arriving at Stanford in the fall of 1971 for what I expected would be a year of scholarly research as a fellow of the Center for Advanced Studies in the Behavioral Sciences, I was asked to represent a tenured English professor named Bruce Franklin, who was being fired for inciting students. Franklin, who was born in Brooklyn, had become a follower of Mao Zedong and Ho Chi Minh—and had edited a book on the writings of Stalin. Students renamed his course on Melville and Hawthorne "Mao-ville and Ho-thorne." He was a believer in a "people's war" against Stanford and other institutions that aided the Vietnam War. Franklin had spoken at an antiwar rally directed against the Stanford Computation Center, which was involved in war-related research. His speech included the following: "What we're asking is for people to make that little tiny gesture to show that we're willing to inconvenience ourselves a little bit and to begin to shut down the most obvious machinery of war, such as—and I think it is a good target—that Computation Center." Following shouts of "Right on," a group of listeners marched on the Computation Center and physically shut it down, causing some damage. Franklin watched from a safe distance. The police ordered the demonstrators to disperse. At this point, Franklin joined the crowd and protested the order. He walked up to the police, argued with them that the dispersal order was illegal, and urged the crowd to remain. Many did, and the police used force to implement their order. Minor injuries were sustained by some demonstrators.

Later that night a rally was held on the campus, at which Franklin gave the closing speech. In it he advocated "the methods of people's war." There was some dispute about whether he explained what he meant by this term. He claimed that he told the demonstrators that "people's war meant that they should go back to the dormitories, organize people into small groups, and talk with them, or play football, or whatever, as late into the night as possible." Whatever his intent, his speech resulted in more violence and this time several people were seriously hurt.

The next day President Richard Lyman announced that Professor

Franklin would be fired from his tenured position on the charge of "substantial and manifest neglect of duty and a substantial impairment of his appropriate functions within the University community." (Imagine a speech code using such vague and general language!)

Franklin demanded a hearing, and a faculty committee was convened. It was difficult to find seven professors who did not despise Franklin—and with good cause. Franklin was an unrepentant Stalinist who had no tolerance for the free speech of others. He was also believed to have been responsible for other violence on the campus. As my "fee" for representing him, he gave me a little red volume of the speeches of Lin Biao, then one of the leading theoreticians of Communist China. Shortly thereafter, Lin Biao was killed—probably assassinated—in a plane crash and discredited by the Chinese authorities. Franklin came to my home and demanded that I return the book, since he was under orders from "the Party" to have all copies destroyed. I refused and he threatened to use physical violence, if necessary, to retrieve the book. So much for the freedom of speech that he was demanding for himself!

I persuaded the local ACLU chapter to become involved in Franklin's defense, but I, and my research assistant Joel Klein, took the lead in defending Franklin.

Word quickly spread around the Stanford campus that I had gotten the ACLU into the case. I was criticized for my intrusion into the affairs of my host university. President Lyman went on the radio to attack me:

> *It is a myth that all speech is constitutionally protected. No constitutional lawyer in the land—no, not even Mr. Dershowitz, the Harvard law professor come to Stanford to save us all from sin—not even Mr. Dershowitz could make such a sweeping claim.*

I responded with my own statement in the *Stanford Daily*:

> *There are important civil liberties issues at stake in the Franklin firing. If Dr. Lyman wants to challenge my view of the Constitution or civil liberties—and those of the ACLU—I invite that challenge, on its merits.*

Lyman rejected my invitation to debate and continued to attack me—both personally and through his surrogates—in highly personal terms. The hostility toward me and toward the ACLU spread quickly among the established faculty.

We filed a brief on behalf of the ACLU urging Stanford, which is a private university, to apply the spirit of the First Amendment to Franklin's case. The faculty committee agreed and said they were applying First Amendment standards, but they ruled, in a divided vote, that Franklin's speeches violated those standards. They found that he "did intentionally write and urge" students and others to "occupy the computation center illegally," to "disobey the order to disperse," and to "engage in conduct which would disrupt activities of the university and threaten injury to individuals and property."

Following the Franklin firing, I gave a lecture on the implications of the case, predicting that Franklin would soon be forgotten because his message would be rejected in the free marketplace of ideas. But the committee's decision would be long remembered as a leading precedent in the jurisprudence of universities, because of the broad definition of "incitement" employed by Stanford against a tenured faculty member who made provocative speeches to students.

I concluded by pointing an accusing finger at some of the faculty who pretended that the Franklin case raised no important civil liberties issues:

> *How often have I heard the absurd remark that Franklin is being fired for what he "did," not for what he "said," without a recognition that this quibble doesn't hide the fact what he "did" was to make speeches. How often I have heard the statement that this case does not involve "academic freedom," it is simply an employer firing an employee for disloyalty—as if a requirement of loyalty and academic freedom were compatible. The true test of a genuine civil libertarian is how he responds to a crisis close at hand.*

Franklin moved on to Rutgers University, where he essentially disappeared from public view, though he continued to praise Stalin and other suppressors of free speech.

DELIBERATELY DISRUPTING A SPEAKER WITH WHOM ONE DISAGREES

The Bruce Franklin case involved a second asserted exception to the First Amendment: that although there is a constitutional right to heckle speakers (at least in some context), there is no right to silence a speaker by shouting him down.[4]

When Henry Cabot Lodge came to speak at Stanford in January 1971, he was shouted down with cries of "pig" and "war criminal" and then drowned out by continuous chanting and clapping. Eventually, the program had to be canceled. Professor Franklin participated in the shouting but denied complicity in the chanting and clapping that brought the program to an untimely end.

Our brief disagreed with Franklin's contention that there is a "right" to silence a speaker who is deemed to be a "war criminal":

> *If the Board concludes that Professor Franklin intentionally engaged in concerted activity designed to silence Ambassador Lodge—that is, to prevent him from speaking at all—then it is the Civil Liberties Union's position that some discipline would be appropriate.*

It defended, however, Franklin's right to heckle, boo, and express substantive disagreement with the speaker or his views. If members of the audience may cheer and applaud approval, they must also have a coextensive right to demonstrate disapproval:

> *The rule of thumb [is] that the speaker's entire address must be allowed to be heard, but it may be frequently interrupted, so long as he is permitted to continue a short time after each interruption. This rule does not make for the most comfortable or effective oratory, but the American Civil Liberties Union believes it to be the constitutionally required balance.*

We won that aspect of the case. The Stanford committee followed the ACLU guidelines and concluded that Franklin had not tried to prevent Lodge from speaking.

Forty years later, I tried to get the Southern California branch of the ACLU to apply these same guidelines to another case involving the disruption of a speaker who had been invited by a university—this time the University of California at Irvine, a public university. But by this point, various chapters of the ACLU had become so politicized that radical politics prevailed over free speech principles.

Michael Oren—a distinguished scholar and writer, a moderate supporter of the two-state solution, and then Israel's ambassador to the United States—was invited to speak. The Muslim Student Union set out to prevent him from delivering his talk. Here is the way Erwin Chemerinksy, dean of the law school, described what the students did:

> *The Muslim Student Union orchestrated a concerted effort to disrupt the speech. One student after another stood and shouted so that the ambassador could not be heard. Each student was taken away only to be replaced by another doing the same thing.*[5]

Chemerinsky understates what happened, as anyone can see by watching a video of the event.[6] This was more than a "concerted effort to disrupt the speech." It was a concerted effort to stop it completely—to censor Oren's right to speak and his audience's right to hear him. There is undisputed evidence that a *well-planned conspiracy* was organized to prevent Oren from speaking. The efforts to disrupt succeeded; the effort to stop the speech completely ultimately failed, but only because the disruptors were arrested and removed after they shouted down the speaker.

The students were disciplined by the university for their actions, though the nature and degree of the discipline has been kept confidential. Campus sources have characterized it as "a slap on the wrist." Since the students had to be arrested to prevent the speech from being drowned out, the district attorney, quite understandably, commenced a criminal investigation. After learning of the careful planning that went into the concerted effort to prevent Oren from speaking, the DA filed misdemeanor charges against those involved.

This decision resulted in an outcry by those who favor censorship of pro-Israel speakers. In a letter to the DA signed by many well-known anti-Israel zealots, as well as by the two leaders of the local ACLU, the incident was mendaciously described as merely a protest: "The students non-violently and verbally protested a university-invited speaker. The students left the event peacefully."[7]

Then, in an effort to blame the victims, the letter pointed the finger at pro-Israel students who wanted to listen to Oren speak, claiming—falsely—that the Muslim Student Union censors "conducted themselves in less of a disruptive manner than some of the counter-protestors."[8]

The Muslim students themselves have been more honest about their intentions than the ACLU leaders. One student leader refused to acknowledge that Mr. Oren had First Amendment rights of his own by interrupting him and shouting, "Propagating murder is not an expression of free speech!" (Shades of Bruce Franklin!) Another student was caught on video telling a crowd assembled outside the event that "we pretty much shut them down."[9]

The fact that radical anti-Israel zealots would support censorship of a pro-Israel speaker comes as no surprise. But the fact that the letter of support was signed by two ACLU leaders, in their capacities as ACLU officers, was shocking. (One was the president, the other the executive director of local ACLU chapters.) I have been a supporter of the ACLU for half a century and was a national board member. In addition to supporting the right of Nazis to march through Skokie, I have defended the right of the most virulent anti-Israel speakers to participate in the marketplace of ideas. The ACLU policy has always been to oppose concerted efforts to prevent speakers from delivering their remarks, as evidenced by the brief filed in its name in the Franklin case. While supporting sporadic heckling and jeering that merely demonstrates opposition to the content of the remarks, the ACLU has always condemned the kind of concerted efforts to silence an invited speaker that occurred at Irvine. In the Franklin case, the ACLU argued that if Franklin had participated in the effort to shut down the speaker, it would be appropriate to discipline him.

Yet the ACLU *letter* never once criticizes the censoring Muslim Union students, while it condemns those who simply wanted to hear the speaker.

Dean Chemerinsky, while opposing criminal prosecution, made a point to condemn the censoring students:

> *The students' behavior was wrong and deserves punishment. There is no basis for the claim that the disruptive students were just exercising their First Amendment rights. There is no constitutional right to disrupt an event and keep a speaker from being heard. Otherwise, any speaker could be silenced by a heckler's veto. The Muslim students could have expressed their message in many other ways: picketing or handing out leaflets outside the auditorium where Ambassador Oren was speaking, making statements during the question and answer period, holding their own events on campus.*[10]

After being criticized for supporting censorship, the executive director of the ACLU sought to justify his signing the letter by the following "logic":

> *The district attorney's action will undoubtedly intimidate students in Orange County and across the state and discourage them from engaging in any controversial speech or protest for fear of criminal charges.*[11]

The opposite is true. If these students had been let off with a slap on the wrist from the university, that would have encouraged other students around the nation and the world to continue with the efforts to prevent pro-Israel and other "politically incorrect" speakers from delivering their speeches. Indeed, even after these students were disciplined, other students tried to shut down several invited visiting students who had served in the Israeli army and were recounting their experiences.[12]

The prosecutors in the case asked me to testify on their behalf as an expert witness on the issues relating to freedom of expression in the campus context. I was tempted but ultimately decided it would be better for them to use a witness with less personal involvement in the matter: I too had been shouted down by anti-Israel groups—on that very campus and on others. The jury convicted the students, and they were sentenced to probation and a fine.[13]

There were some who criticized the prosecutor for bringing these charges, but I defended him on the ground that prosecuting these student censors was his duty in protecting the First Amendment:

> *It was imperative . . . that a public prosecutor apply the law to these students, because to do otherwise would be to tolerate, if not encourage, conduct that would undercut the constitutional rights of an invited speaker. Moreover, these students must be made to understand that their conduct is not only morally indefensible; it is criminal.*[14]

The same would be true if Jewish students were to try to prevent an anti-Israel speaker from presenting the case against Israel.

The successful prosecution of the Irvine Ten did not "chill" the free speech rights of hecklers. No one should be prosecuted for simply booing the content of a speech, leafleting a speaker, holding up signs in the back of the auditorium, conducting a counterevent or demonstration. These young criminals were trying to chill, indeed freeze, the constitutional rights of the speaker and those who came to hear him. They should not be treated as heroes by anyone who loves freedom and supports the First Amendment, and especially not by officials of the ACLU.

It was a good day for the First Amendment when the prosecutor decided to apply the law to their censorial conduct. It was another good day when the jury appropriately convicted them. Sometimes it takes tough measures to enforce the First Amendment against those who believe that only they own the "truth" and who seek to silence opposing views by shouting and shutting them down.

9

THE RIGHT TO FALSIFY HISTORY AND SCIENCE

Holocaust Denial, Space Aliens, and Academic Freedom

The American First Amendment is not emulated by all freedom-loving nations. In some European countries (particularly Germany,[1] Austria,[2] and France[3]), it is a crime to deny the Holocaust. In France, legislation was proposed to make it a crime to deny the Armenian Genocide. In Turkey it is a crime to claim that the Turks engaged in genocide against the Armenians,[4] even though it is a historical fact recognized by scholars around the world.

Under our First Amendment, no one can be punished either for denying a historical event or for proclaiming that it occurred.

Several years ago I became embroiled in a heated controversy with Professor Noam Chomsky over the issue of Holocaust denial and the proper role of a civil libertarian in defending the *right* of Holocaust deniers, without defending the *substance* of their claims.

In the 1970s a Frenchman named Robert Faurisson, who was an obscure lecturer on French literature at the University of Lyon, began to traffic in Holocaust denial. He wrote a book—and gave talks—in which he mocked Holocaust victims and survivors as perpetrators of a hoax. The Holocaust, according to Faurisson, "never took place." The "Hitler gas chambers" never existed. "The Jews" bear "responsibility" for World War II. Hitler acted reasonably and in self-defense when he rounded up the Jews and put them in "labor camps," not death camps. The "massive lie" about genocide was a deliberate concoction begun by "American Zionists"—and in context he obviously means Jews. The principal beneficiary of this hoax is "Israel," which has encouraged this "enormous political and financial fraud." The principal victims of this "fraud" have been "the German people" and "the Palestinian people." Faurisson also called the diary of Anne Frank a "forgery."[5]

Following the publication of Faurisson's book, the lecturer received threats from irate survivors. The University of Lyon, claiming that it could not guarantee his safety, suspended him for a semester.

Chomsky sprang to Faurisson's defense, not only on the issue of free speech, but on the *merits* of his "scholarship" and of his "character." Chomsky signed a petition that characterized Faurisson's falsifications of history as "findings" and said that they were based on "extensive historical research."

I too defended Faurisson's *right* to express his views. But I also took the time to check his "historical research" and found it to be entirely faked. He made up phony diary entries, omitted others that disproved his "research," and distorted the historical record.[6] Faurisson's writing was not based on "extensive historical research." It was not research at all. It was the fraudulent manufacturing of false antihistory. It was the kind of deception for which professors are rightly fired—not because their views are controversial, but because they are violating the most basic canons of historical scholarship. I exposed Faurisson's deceptions in my own writings, while continuing to defend his *right* to rewrite history.

Chomsky wrote an essay in defense of Faurisson that he allowed to be used as a foreword to Faurisson's next book, about his career as a Holocaust denier![7] In this book, Faurisson again calls the gas chambers a lie and repeats his claims about the "hoax" of the Holocaust.

A few years later, after it became unmistakably clear that Faurisson was consciously lending his name to all sorts of anti-Semitic and neo-Nazi groups, Chomsky repeated his character reference, this time going even further and defending Faurisson against the charge that his writings and speeches were anti-Semitic:

> *I see no anti-Semitic implications in denial of the existence of gas chambers, or even denial of the Holocaust. Nor would there be anti-Semitic implications, per se, in the claim that the Holocaust (whether one believes it took place or not) is being exploited, viciously so, by apologists for Israeli repression and violence. I see no hint of anti-Semitic implications in Faurisson's work.*[8]

When this statement was quoted in a *Boston Globe* article praising Chomsky for his defense of "underdogs" like Faurisson, I wrote a letter to the editor:

> *While some may regard Chomsky as an eminent linguist, he does not understand the most obvious meaning of words in context. To fail to see any "hint of anti-Semitic implications" in Faurisson's collective condemnation of the Jewish people as liars, is to be either a fool or a knave. . . . Chomsky's actions in defending the* substance *of Faurisson's bigoted remarks against valid charges of anti-Semitism—as distinguished from defending Faurisson's right to publish such pernicious drivel—disqualify Chomsky from being considered an honorable defender of the "underdog." The victims of the Holocaust, not its defenders or deniers, are the underdogs.*[9]

Following this exchange, I challenged Chomsky to a public debate on the issue of whether it is anti-Semitic or anti-Jewish to deny the Holocaust. This was his answer: "It is so obvious that there is no point in debating it because *nobody* believes there is an anti-Semitic connotation to the denial of the Holocaust" (emphasis added).

Well, I believe there is, and so do most other reasonable people who understand the meaning of words in context. I also believe that civil libertarians who defend the free speech rights of neo-Nazis should not get into bed with them by legitimating their false "findings" as having been based on "extensive historical research" and by defending them—on the merits—against well-documented charges of anti-Semitism. Moreover, providing a foreword for a book is joining with the author and publisher in an effort to sell the book. It is intended not merely to leave the marketplace of ideas open. It is intended to influence the marketplace substantively in favor of the author's ideas. This is not the defense of free speech. It is the promotion of Holocaust denial.

Several years after my encounters with Chomsky, I was asked to defend a neo-Nazi Holocaust denier named Matthew Hale, who was the head of an anti-Semitic group that called itself "the Church of the Creation." He had been denied admission to the Illinois bar because of his neo-Nazi views.

Hale was invited to appear on *The Today Show* to be interviewed by Katie Couric. I was asked to explain why I would even consider representing such a horrible racist and anti-Semite. Couric began by asking Hale to describe his views "in a nutshell." He went on about how non-Europeans—by which he meant blacks and Jews—were destroying the "white race" and how he was going to change all that if he was admitted to the bar.

Couric then asked me why I believed a man with Hale's views should be allowed to become a lawyer.

ALAN DERSHOWITZ: Well, first of all I am not a supporter of Mr. Hale. You asked about his views in a nutshell. That's where his views belong, in a nutshell. They are despicable, revolting views. But what I'm concerned about is the precedential effect of giving character committees the right to determine who shall and who shall not have the right to practice law on the basis of ideology and belief. Remember character committees were invented to originally keep out blacks, Jews, gays, women, leftists. . . . I just don't want to see a resurrection of character committees probing into the ideology of people like Mr. Hale. If I take his case, and he's asked me to represent him, I told him this and he knows this. All the fees will be contributed to anti-racist organizations which will fight the ideology of bigots like him. I hope the American public listening to him would reject his ideas in the marketplace but not through censorship of the kind that the character committee is trying to practice.

KATIE COURIC: But simply espousing these views, couldn't that lead to violence, by other individuals?

AD: Well, there is no question how our Constitution strikes that balance. Reading the work of Marx can lead to incitement. Reading the Bible can lead to incitement. But we don't draw the line at the espousal of views. We draw it at incitement or violence itself and we don't want to have a different standard for racists than we do for other people.

Couric then turned back to Hale:

KC: Do you see the irony that you hate Jews and yet you are calling on Mr. Dershowitz to help you?

MATTHEW HALE: Having a "Dershowitz" in this equation has brought our church an incredible amount of publicity.

AD: I have faith in the American people that they will reject your ideas in the marketplace of ideas and you should not have the benefit of censorship so that you can stand up and proclaim your views. You know, if the character committee hadn't kept him out, nobody would have

> heard of this despicable person. Censorship creates publicity. What we are doing is hoping to give you the worst and most negative kind of publicity so people will reject your ideas.[10]

Ultimately, I did not represent Hale, because he refused to allow me to donate his legal fee to the ADL, the NAACP, and other organizations that seek to combat his racist views in the marketplace of ideas. He lost his case[11] and is now in prison for trying to arrange a "hit" on the judge who ruled against him.[12]

Following Hale's imprisonment, I received a call from the FBI advising me that Hale might have put out a hit on me as well. For several weeks, FBI agents monitored and protected me. So much for Matthew Hale merely believing in freedom of speech! This was neither the first nor the last time I was physically threatened for what I believe. Free speech is anything but free in the real world of high passions and violent tempers.

It is imperative that those of us who defend the rights of bigots and others to express horrible views go out of our way to challenge these bad views in the marketplace of ideas. Unlike Chomsky, I have always taken this obligation seriously. The appropriate answer to bad speech is good speech, not censorship. We must provide that good speech as we defend the bad speech.

I had the opportunity to do just that in 1982 when the Boston Symphony Orchestra hired Vanessa Redgrave to narrate several performances of Stravinsky's opera-oratorio *Oedipus Rex*. There is some dispute over whether she was hired entirely because of her unquestionable acting ability or also because of her political "courage." As soon as the decision was announced, there was outrage among some of the orchestra's musicians, subscribers, and board members. Some musicians suggested that they would exercise their own freedom of association by refusing to perform with a terrorist collaborator who justified assassination of artists.

I defended her right to perform but challenged her to a debate about her outrageous political views. She declined because she was on the Central Committee of the Workers Revolutionary Party—a British Communist group—and the Party had to approve in advance everything she said in public. I then explained the hypocrisy of *her* complaints about being "blacklisted" for her political views and activities, while she herself, and her Party, demanded that the British Actors Union blacklist Israeli artists and boycott Israeli audiences. Several years later, she justified as "entirely correct" the blacklisting of Zionist speakers at British universities. And she has praised the ultimate form of censorship: the political assassination of Israeli artists, because they "may well have been enlisted . . . to do the work" of the Zionists.

In 1977, Redgrave made a film calling for the destruction of the Jewish state by armed struggle. She has personally received training in terrorism at camps from which terrorist raids were staged. She advocated the assassination of Nobel Peace Prize winner Anwar Sadat. After playing her controversial role as concentration camp survivor in Arthur Miller's 1980 television drama *Playing for Time*, she traveled around the world arguing that her selection for the role constituted a propaganda victory against Israel.

In the end, the BSO decided—wrongly, in my view—to cancel the performances of *Oedipus Rex*. They offered to pay Redgrave the money she would have received if the show had gone on. Redgrave declined the offer and sued the orchestra for breach of contract, seeking $5 million in damages.

When Redgrave's supporters threw a fund-raiser for her, I distributed a leaflet that provided the facts regarding her own support for blacklisting Israeli artists. Several of her erstwhile supporters, who had not been aware of her hypocrisy, refused to support her lawsuit.

In the end, the case was settled. I was comfortable in my role defending Redgrave's rights while exposing her wrongs.

Not everyone, of course, understands this distinction. Chomsky certainly doesn't. Neither did my mother, who insisted that I was "helping" Nazis and terrorists when I supported their right to speak, even while condemning what they were saying. Far better educated people than my mother also claimed not to understand.[13]

But a group of Harvard Palestinian students did understand.

When Yasser Arafat died in 2004, I was asked by Palestinian students to represent them in their failed efforts to fly the Palestinian flag from a flagpole in the Harvard Yard. They knew my negative views of their hero—I had called Arafat's death "untimely," because if he had only died five years earlier, the Palestinian Authority might well have accepted the Clinton-Barak peace offer[14]—but they also knew my views on freedom of speech. I agreed to represent them, as long as they understood that I would continue to criticize both Arafat and those who considered him a martyr. They agreed and we got Harvard to allow them to fly their flag.[15] It was a great day for freedom of speech at Harvard, as all sides were able to express their very different views.

Academic freedom is an important aspect of the First Amendment. It applies to students and faculty alike, outside and inside the classroom. But inside the classroom, no professor has the right to propagandize his captive classroom audience or to grade them down if they disagree with his political opinions. It is sometimes difficult to distinguish between acceptable teaching and unacceptable proselytizing. This too is an area where rights may be in conflict, and a delicate balance, always skewed in favor of speech, is required.

DOES ACADEMIC FREEDOM INCLUDE A PROFESSOR'S RIGHT TO PUBLISH A BOOK ABOUT THE POSSIBILITY THAT "ALIEN ABDUCTIONS" MAY BE REAL?

Over the years several Holocaust deniers have challenged me to debate them on whether the Holocaust occurred. I have a standard answer:

> *I will debate whether the Holocaust occurred but only as a part of a series of debates on the following subjects: Elvis Presley is alive and well; the space shuttle never landed on the moon; the earth is flat; and space aliens have made contact with lots of Americans.*

I regard the debatability of the Holocaust as akin to the debatability of these other absurd fantasies. But in 1995, I actually became involved in a case that tested the limits of academic freedom in the context of claims that space aliens may actually have visited the patients of a well-known Harvard medical researcher.

The case centered on a book written by a distinguished Harvard Medical School professor named Dr. John Mack, a psychiatrist and Pulitzer Prize–winning author. The book that became the subject of the case was called *Abduction: Human Encounters with Aliens.*[16] It recounted Dr. Mack's treatment of numerous psychiatric patients who had been referred to him after claiming that they had been abducted by space aliens. After examining them, he concluded that many of them exhibited none of the classic symptoms of the kind of mental illness that would produce delusions of abduction. Instead, they exhibited symptoms similar to those of classic trauma victims who had actually been abducted. These findings left open several possible explanations, including that the diagnostic categories were flawed or incomplete. Nothing controversial there! But it also did not preclude the possibility, according to Dr. Mack, that these patients were not delusional—that they had actually experienced alien abductions! Although Dr. Mack was careful to hedge his own conclusion by acknowledging that "we do not know if any of [these] phenomena exist literally on the purely material plane of reality,"[17] he refused to dismiss the possibility that his patients were accurately reporting what had happened to them.

Dr. Mack's book became an instant bestseller and he became a talk show celebrity. Harvard was not amused. The dean of Harvard Medical School called Dr. Mack on the carpet and appointed a faculty committee to investigate his "astounding" claims about the possible reality of alien abductions.

Dr. Mack called and asked, "Would you like to represent a modern day Galileo?" I told him that he needed a lawyer outside of Harvard and recommended Eric MacLeish, a superb lawyer with whom I had worked on other cases involving academic discipline. I decided to limit my role to advocating academic freedom at Harvard and critiquing the appointment of an investigatory committee.

Because it is a private university, Harvard is not legally bound by the First Amendment, but over the years—and through many cases involving students and faculty—I have helped persuade Harvard to accept the principles of the First Amendment and to impose its restrictions on Harvard's actions.

Harvard took the position that it was investigating only Dr. Mack's "methods of study" and the "quality of his scholarship," rather than his "astounding" conclusions. But the reality was that they never would have considered questioning a tenured professor's methodology or scholarship if he had concluded that his patients were hallucinating about space aliens. It was his astounding conclusions that had motivated the investigation.

I posed the following questions in the *Harvard Crimson*:

> *Should a distinguished Harvard professor of psychiatry be subject to formal investigation and potential discipline for doing research on the possibility that people who claim that they were abducted by space aliens may not all be crazy after all?*
>
> *. . . Will the next professor who is thinking about an unconventional research project be deterred by the prospect of having to hire a lawyer to defend his ideas?*[18]

These questions bitterly divided the academic community, not only at Harvard but throughout the world. Some academics argued that a

Harvard Medical School professor should not be lending his credibility to stories of space alien abductions. Others believed that great universities should not second-guess the research or publications of their tenured faculty, except for allegations of fraud, plagiarism, or violations of patients' or students' rights—none of which were alleged against Dr. Mack.

I pointed out that New York City College had never investigated the "research" of Professor Leonard Jeffries, who claimed that melanin had an influence on racial characteristics and made blacks better than whites, or of a white professor who argued that blacks had lower IQs than whites.

If Dr. Mack had taught at the divinity school, it is unlikely that any investigation would have been tolerated, since divinity schools are not governed by the laws of science. Indeed, it is at least as likely that space aliens exist as it is that God exists. The former is, however, a scientifically testable hypothesis (at least in theory); whereas the latter—for at least most theologians—is not. It is a matter of faith, not proof, and faith is not subject to the scientific method. But the paradigm of the scientific method—testable propositions subjected to double-blind and replicable experimentation—is not the only criterion for evaluating academic undertakings. This is certainly true in the formative, exploratory phases in the development of an idea. If Sigmund Freud, Karl Marx, or Martin Buber had been required to satisfy a committee before he could continue his research, the world might have been deprived of significant insights.

What was troubling was the *principle* behind a dean convening an investigative committee, at least in the absence of clear guidelines or criteria. Unless challenged, the precedent-setting effect of the appointment of an investigatory committee would act as a sword of Damocles hanging over the head of every professor who drifted outside the mainstream, especially in politically sensitive areas. It is noteworthy that the issue of space aliens is not a politically, racially, or sexually divisive one. Imagine if a committee were to be convened to examine controversial research that touched on any of these hot-button issues. There would be student demonstrations, alumni threatening to withhold contributions, and perhaps even governmental pressure. I urged the dean to reverse his decision to appoint an investigating committee and to undo the damage before it established a dangerous precedent. No great university should be in the business of investigating the ideas of its tenured faculty.

I then responded to those who argued that Harvard was interested only in Dr. Mack's "methodology":

> *To be sure, it is legitimate for a university to be concerned about the integrity of its faculty's research. There are widely accepted criteria by which such integrity is judged: research must be reported honestly; sources must be attributed properly; informed consent must be obtained; biases must be disclosed. But these are not the criticisms directed against Dr. Mack's research. What is on trial in his case are his ideas—his willingness to consider the possibility that the numerous accounts of alien abductions may not all be products of insane delusions. He has certainly not convinced me, but surely that cannot be the criteria.*[19]

Finally, I issued a challenge to those who disagreed with Dr. Mack's research: Respond to it *on the merits*—by reviews, rebuttals, debates, and books of their own. The marketplace of academic ideas is wide open. Dr. Mack's idea "shop" in the marketplace should not be shut down; nor should it be subjected to extraordinary "inspections." Critics should open their own idea "shops" and try to compete. Eventually the truth will out. That is what a university is all about.

After more than a year of "investigation" and thirty closed-door meetings and hearings, costing Dr. Mack close to $100,000 in legal expenses, the Harvard Committee decided to do nothing.[20]

Dr. Mack called me to thank me for my involvement in his case, saying that until my article appeared, no one had seen this as an issue of academic freedom, and that my support had changed the dynamics. "When it was Harvard against just me, I had no chance, but when you came in, everything changed." I told him that I became involved to defend academic freedom, but that I was utterly unpersuaded by his book or by the possibility that actual "alien abductions" explained his patients' symptoms. He replied, "That's the safe approach."

10

DEFAMATION AND PRIVACY

"He That Filches from Me My Good Name"[1]

Whenever a Holocaust denier or defamer of the Jews—whether it be Chomsky, Hale, Redgrave, or Faurisson—spews out his poison, I get calls and e-mails demanding that I sue him for defaming the Jewish people or committing "a blood libel." But under the First Amendment only an individual can be defamed. There is no such thing as group libel.[2] In other words you can say all you want about "the Jews," "the Democratic Party," "the blacks," "the gays," and "the women"—obnoxious as such generalizations might be. An anti-Semite is constitutionally free to spread libels against the Jewish people or the Jewish religion, so long as he is careful not to accuse a specific individual of, say, killing Christian children for their blood. This is not true in other countries that do have group libel laws.

Under our laws, defamatory statements must be directed against a specific individual, casting him in a negative light. That used to be easier to define than it is today. For example, when a newspaper in the segregated Deep South made a typographical error and described a white man as a "colored gentleman," instead of a "cultured gentleman," that error was deemed defamatory, since describing a white person as colored clearly could damage his career and hurt his position. Today, no court would consider it defamatory to mistakenly report on someone's race. It's a little more complicated when it comes to sexual preference. If a newspaper were to characterize a heterosexual politician as gay, that might well hurt his electoral chances, but courts would be reluctant today to rule that being called gay is an insult.[3] The same is true of other former words of opprobrium that have lost or decreased their negative connotations over the years.

In addition to being damaging, a defamation must also be untrue. This wasn't always the case. Thomas Jefferson fought to limit defamations to untruthful statements about an individual.[4]

If the individual defamed is a public figure, such as a politician, celebrity, or anyone else who sought the limelight, yet another hurdle must now be overcome. Since the Supreme Court's 1964 decision in *New York Times v. Sullivan*, a defamation action can be brought by a public figure only if the false statement was made with "actual malice—that is knowledge that it was false or with reckless disregard of whether it was false or not."[5]

I was Justice Goldberg's law clerk when the Supreme Court rendered that precedent-shattering decision. Goldberg told me that he was concerned that the daunting requirements of the case would make it open season on public figures and would lower the standards of journalistic ethics. He himself, as a public figure, had been defamed on several occasions, and it had stung him. Nonetheless, he concurred in the decision and wrote the following stirring words about the freedom to criticize:

> *The theory of our Constitution is that every citizen may speak his mind and every newspaper express its view on matters of public concern, and may not be barred from speaking or publishing because those in control of government think that what is said or written is unwise, unfair, false, or malicious. In a democratic society, one who assumes to act for the citizens in an executive, legislative, or judicial capacity must expect that his official acts will be commented upon and criticized. Such criticism cannot, in my opinion, be muzzled or deterred by the courts at the instance of public officials under the label of libel.*[6]

Since I am a public figure under the law, I have been defamed on numerous occasions, especially on the Internet. The libels and slanders have been both personal and political. Although these defamations were published with actual malice, I have not sued, though I have often been tempted. (I once threatened to sue when a journalist made up a false racist and sexist quotation and attributed it to me; the newspaper investigated, agreed with me, and made a contribution to my favorite charity.)[7]

Many years after *New York Times v. Sullivan*, I was charged with criminal defamation for exercising my freedom of speech to criticize a judge for an opinion she wrote.[8]

One day in my office I opened an envelope and saw a notice that an Italian prosecutor had initiated a criminal investigation against me. I had no idea what she could be referring to. The letter stated that I had committed the alleged act in the city of Turin on January 27, 2005. I checked my calendar and discovered that I had been teaching students at Harvard Law School on that day and then attended a lecture by a prominent federal judge. Pretty good alibi (which literally means "somewhere else" in Latin!). I could not possibly have been in Turin or engaged in any criminal act there. Yet I soon discovered that I was being charged with criminal libel for statements I had made in an interview with an Italian journalist over the telephone. The journalist was in New York. I was in Cambridge. But the interview was published by the newspaper *La Stampa* in Turin on January 27, 2005.[9] Accordingly, the alleged criminal act had taken place in Turin, even though I had never set foot in that city. Nor had I engaged in any act other than responding to questions and expressing my heartfelt views about a judge who had written a foolish and dangerous judicial opinion that ruled that three men suspected of recruiting suicide bombers were "guerrillas" and not terrorists, and therefore not guilty.

I characterized her opinion as a "Magna Carta for terrorism,"[10] and instead of answering (or ignoring) me, she filed criminal charges with the Turin prosecutor, who decided to open an investigation.

As far as I know, the charges against me are still pending in Italy. I have every intention of fighting them if it comes to that. The Turin prosecution made me appreciate our First Amendment all the more.

One age-old form of defamation is ridicule. Cartoons and drawings have long been used to ridicule the high and mighty. More recently, Photoshopped pictures have superimposed the heads of public figures on the bodies of others to demean or insult them. In 1988, the Supreme Court ruled that the Reverend Jerry Falwell could not sue *Hustler* magazine for publishing a parody of the well-known Campari aperitif ads in which a celebrity described his "first time." The ad relies on the obvious double-entendre between one's first sexual and first drinking experience. In the parody, Falwell is shown drinking and having sex with his mother—pretty disgusting! But as the Supreme Court rightly observed:

> *Despite their sometimes caustic nature, from the early cartoon portraying George Washington as an ass down to the present day, graphic depictions and satirical cartoons have played a prominent role in public and political debate. Nast's castigation of the Tweed Ring, Walt McDougall's*

> *characterization of presidential candidate James G. Blaine's banquet with the millionaires at Delmonico's as "The Royal Feast of Belshazzar," and numerous other efforts have undoubtedly had an effect on the course and outcome of contemporaneous debate. Lincoln's tall, gangling posture, Teddy Roosevelt's glasses and teeth, and Franklin D. Roosevelt's jutting jaw and cigarette holder have been memorialized by political cartoons with an effect that could not have been obtained by the photographer or the portrait artist. From the viewpoint of history it is clear that our political discourse would have been considerably poorer without them.*[11]

The court ruled that parodies and caricatures, even revolting ones, were protected by the First Amendment, especially if the person being parodied is a public figure.

Several years after the Falwell decision, a young man named David Heller called me. He had been sued by a sixty-year-old fellow employee, Sylvia Smith Bowman, who was running for the presidency of their local union. Here is how the court described what Heller had done:

> *While the plaintiff was on an approved leave to campaign in the union election, the defendant, David Heller, an employee in the plaintiff's office who supported the incumbent president, created two distinct photocopied representations of the plaintiff by superimposing a photograph of her face and name on two different photographs of women striking lewd or masturbatory poses. The photograph of the plaintiff's face was taken from a campaign card she had distributed to union members. The photographs on which the defendant superimposed the plaintiff's face were taken by the defendant from pornographic magazines. In one of the photographs, the model is nude from the waist down, except for garters, and is posed toward the camera with her legs wide apart as she holds a banana next to her exposed breast. In the other photograph, the model is entirely naked, and appears to be engaged in masturbation. The representations were crafted by the defendant during regular office hours and reproduced on photocopiers owned by the department. The defendant then distributed his handiwork to five coworkers in the Worcester office. Subsequently, the representations were reproduced by employees other than the defendant and distributed to a wider office audience.*[12]

Heller claimed that he had decided to create these parodies after Bowman had made what he regarded as crude and sexist statements against men, including calling them "dickheads."

The Supreme Judicial Court of Massachusetts eventually ruled, over a strong dissent, that Bowman was not "a public figure" because the union election was not "a public controversy." The dissenting judges disagreed, arguing that "an election is the absolute paradigm of a public controversy."[13] I believe that the majority, especially the woman who wrote the decision, was so deeply offended by the image at issue that it blinded them to the obvious public nature of a contentious union election in which both sides sling dirt in the tradition of American elections. It was a hard case that made bad law. Fortunately the bad law it made has not been followed in other cases involving less disturbing images or more public personalities.

I understood how Bowman must have felt when several years later I was victimized by a cartoon that was similar to the one at issue in her case. It was commissioned by the notorious Israel-basher Norman Finkelstein[14] and used to illustrate an article he wrote calling for my assassination.[15] It was a full-color cartoon by a South American neo-Nazi Holocaust denier portraying me as watching the Israeli army kill Lebanese civilians. It had me sitting in front of the television and masturbating in ecstasy over the civilian bodies strewn on the ground.[16] Since I am clearly a public figure, and since this was plainly a parody, it was protected speech under the First Amendment. Sometimes being a First Amendment lawyer requires thick skin.

THE RIGHT TO BE LEFT ALONE

The right of the media to publish purely private though truthful information was the subject, more than one hundred years ago, of a classic law review article coauthored by Louis Brandeis, who eventually became one of the "founding fathers" of the twentieth-century rebirth of the First Amendment. As a young lawyer, Brandeis was concerned about how local tabloids were publishing gossip about prominent people, including members of his own partner's family. He and his partner wrote "The Right to Privacy"[17] in the *Harvard Law Review* (1890), in which they set out this new right to "be let alone,"[18] which they analogized, at least superficially, to the law of defamation. Remarkably, especially in light of subsequent developments, Brandeis did not seem particularly sensitive to how his new right of privacy might conflict with the established right of the press to publish scandalous material.

The conflict between privacy and publication becomes particularly sensitive when the privacy at issue relates to minors. I have been involved in several such cases. One of them pitted the right of Brooke Shields to prevent the publication of nude photographs taken of her when she was ten years old against the right of the man who "owned" the photos to publish them.

When Brooke was ten, her ambitious mother, Teri, signed a contract with an equally ambitious photographer to photograph Brooke naked, taking a bath. Brooke was paid $450 for the photo sessions by Playboy Press, and her mother signed a release giving the photographer the unlimited right to publish the photographs anywhere and at any time.

Seven years later, as Brooke was about the enter Princeton as a freshman, the photographer decided to exploit her fame by producing a calendar featuring naked pictures of the ten-year-old. Brooke was upset that any such calendar would circulate among her fellow students at Princeton and would cause her great embarrassment.

She hired a former student of mine to try to negotiate with the photographer to buy back the rights, and if that failed, to try to prevent publication of the photographs. My former student sought my advice on the matter. I told him it would be an uphill fight to try to enjoin the publication of the pictures, because they were not obscene and because prior restraint is always disfavored by the law.

The only theory on which I thought she could possibly succeed was that Brooke's mother had no right to surrender her daughter's privacy and that Brooke, now approaching adulthood, should have control over her own image.

Ultimately the court ruled, in a bizarre opinion, that Brooke had essentially waived her right to privacy by pursuing a career in which she has relied on her sexuality for her success. The court put it this way:

> *Much of plaintiff's recent commercial activity upon which her fame is based has been far more sexually suggestive than the photographs which have been shown to the court. These photographs are not sexually suggestive, provocative or pornographic; they do not suggest promiscuity. They are photos of a prepubescent girl in innocent poses at her bath. In contrast, defense counsel have submitted numerous samples of sex-oriented publicity concerning plaintiff. Particularly notable is her widely televised sexually suggestive advertisement for blue jeans. Recent film appearances have been sexually provocative (e.g.,* The Blue Lagoon, Endless Love*). Plaintiff's claim of harm is thus undermined to a substantial extent by the development of her career projecting a sexually provocative image.*[19]

This reasoning fails to distinguish between the rights of a seventeen-year-old and a ten-year-old. The earlier photographs were taken of a ten-year-old kid, whose mother controlled what she would do. Her decisions to appear later were made by a near-adult and were far more within her own control. The court simply ignored the argument that the seventeen-year-old should not be bound by foolish decisions made by an ambitious mother when Brooke was too young to say no.

I believe that if this case were to come before a court today, in light of the new sensitivity toward child exploitation, the case would be decided in favor of Brooke Shields. I had mixed feelings at the time about the result because it was a victory for the First Amendment, but at a heavy cost to a young woman about to enter college. Eventually the case was settled and the calendar wasn't distributed to Brooke's Princeton classmates. Brooke Shields went on to a successful career as a multidimensional actress.

Another conflict arose when a blogger posted a naked photograph of a famous athlete's two-year-old son. The caption focused the viewer's attention on the size of the boy's penis. The issue I was asked to address was whether the blog met the criteria for child pornography, which is not protected by the First Amendment. This was an unusual request, since in most of my prior cases invoking charges of child pornography, I had defended the person charged. In one such case, a medical student who had worked as a camp counselor had taken thousands of photographs of his campers, including several of them "skinny-dipping." The focus of the photographs was not on the genitals, and we argued that they were no different, as a matter of law, from nude photographs taken by recognized artists such as Robert Mapplethorpe, Sally Mann, and David Hamilton that were exhibited in museums. We won that case and several others like it.

This situation was different, because the only purpose of publishing the child's photograph was to call attention to his penis. Moreover, his parents had not consented to their child being photographed by a paparazzi on an isolated beach, and so the family's privacy rights had been violated. Eventually, the matter was resolved by the court of public opinion and the marketplace of ideas. Viewers of the blog were so outraged, and the person who posted it so roundly condemned, that the post was removed.

Another area of conflict between the First Amendment and other provisions of the Bill of Rights arises in the context of criminal trials, when the media seeks to publish information—such as an excluded confession—that may prejudice a defendant's right to a fair trial. A variation on this theme is the media's refusal to publish the names of alleged rape victims, while publishing the names and mug shots of the defendants. This practice does not directly impinge on the First Amendment because the decision not to publish is made by the media, rather than the government. Indeed, the Supreme Court has struck down a statute that precluded the media from publishing the names of alleged crime victims.[20]

I have been involved in several cases that pitted the rights of the media under the free speech rights of the First Amendment against the fair trial rights of criminal defendants under the Sixth Amendment. I have generally been on the side of the First Amendment, while sympathizing with the situation faced by defendants who would prefer to see the press muzzled when it came to their cases.

One case in which I sided with the privacy rights of a public figure over the publication rights of the media was Chappaquiddick. (More of this in the chapter on homicide.) I was part of the defense team organized by Senator Kennedy's staff. Part of my job was to assure the confidentiality of the testimony given at the inquest concerning the death of Mary Jo Kopechne. The witnesses who were subpoenaed to testify at this secret inquest—especially the young women who shared the house with Kopechne for the weekend—were not offered the right to counsel or other rights available at an open proceeding. We argued, with some success, that because the inquest was secret and lacked the usual legal safeguards of public hearings, the right of the witnesses to confidentiality trumped the right of the media to immediate disclosure.

The First Amendment requires that the media and dissenters need breathing room, and that presumption should always be in favor of free speech. But this presumption is not without significant risks to deservedly good reputations that can be damaged by defamatory or ridiculing speech. As with other potentially harmful types of expression, defamation and ridicule come with a heavy price—one we must be prepared to pay to keep the First Amendment vibrant. Not everyone is prepared to pay that price.

11

SPEECH THAT "SUPPORTS" TERRORIST GROUPS

The MEK Case

We are currently involved in an ongoing war against terrorism. We live in fear of another terrorist attack, such as the one that killed nearly three thousand people on 9/11, or the one that killed three and injured more than two hundred spectators and participants in the 2013 Boston Marathon. The first victim of fear has often been freedom of speech. Even before the 9/11 attacks, the understandable fear of terrorism had begun to endanger our First Amendment. Here too there is the need to strike a delicate balance, and here too we appear to be striking it improperly.

Congress has passed laws punishing anyone who knowingly provided "material support or resources" to any foreign terrorist organization.[1] Such "support" could, in the view of the government, take the form of otherwise constitutionally protected speeches, writings, and other forms of expression. A "blacklist" of terrorist organizations has been compiled by the State Department. It included such obvious terrorist organizations as Al Qaeda and Hamas, but it also included some questionable groups, such as the MEK (People's Mujahedin of Iran). The MEK is an Iranian dissident group that strongly opposes the current Iranian regime. Early in its history, it allegedly engaged in some terrorist activities, which got the group listed by the State Department, but in 2001, it renounced terrorism and surrendered its arms to the United States military in exchange for a promise of protection against Iranian violence. Its remaining members in Iraq—some 3,400 men, women, and children—were allowed to construct a small town in a place called Camp Ashraf, where they were protected by the U.S. military. But when the United States left Iraq and turned over Camp Ashraf to the Iraqi government in 2009, the protection of this vulnerable group was left in the hands of a government that was becoming more beholden to the Iranian mullahs. The result was several attacks against the residents of Camp Ashraf in which dozens of people were killed and hundreds injured. More attacks were threatened, and the Iraqi government demanded the closure of Camp Ashraf and the movement of its residents to a far smaller and more vulnerable camp, euphemistically called Camp Liberty. A humanitarian crisis loomed, and the leaders of the MEK reached out to human rights advocates around the world, including Elie Wiesel, Irwin Cotler, John Bolton, Wesley Clark, and others. They also sought the help of public figures in the United States, including Rudy Giuliani, Ed Rendell, Howard Dean, Patrick Kennedy, Louis Freeh, Michael Mukasey, Bob Torcelli, and Tom Ridge. Among those lending support were former generals who had been stationed in Iraq and had worked with the MEK.

Conferences were convened in the Capitol Building, in Paris, and in other locations, where these and other public figures spoke in support of the human rights of the residents of Camp Ashraf. They also advocated the delisting of the MEK from the State Department's anachronistic blacklist of terrorist organizations, so that the unarmed and peaceful residents of Camp Ashraf could be resettled in other countries that had policies against accepting "terrorists."

In 2012, I was asked to address one of these conferences. I had never heard of the MEK at the time, but was told that Elie Wiesel had spoken at an earlier conference. I checked and found Elie's speech on the Internet. Because I agreed with what he said, I decided to accept the invitation. Over the next year, I delivered several speeches with the following theme:

I'm here today on behalf of our Constitution:

- *to petition Congress for a redress of grievances*
- *to exercise my freedom of speech, which our government is trying to abridge*

- *to appeal to the press to exercise its freedom to publicize a humanitarian crisis*
- *to peaceably assemble to assure that our government keeps its promise.*

Our government made a sacred contract—in our name—with the residents of Camp Ashraf, who have completely fulfilled their contractual obligations.

Now it's time for our government to fulfill its contractual obligation.

My speech continued:

I have been in contact with representatives of our State Department and high officials in the White House, who have asked our assistance in helping to transition the residents of Ashraf to safe havens outside of Iraq. We have done our part, now the government and the United Nations must do its part. This must be a joint effort.

We cannot fail. If we do, there will be a humanitarian disaster, which is easily preventable. Lives are at stake. So is the honor of the United States. The world will hold our nation responsible if we fail.

Normally, we who have devoted our lives to human rights can act only after rights have been violated. Here we have the privilege of saving lives, not only holding responsible those who have taken lives.[2]

It would be difficult to imagine words that fit more closely into the paradigm of First Amendment protected political speech than petitions of government for a redress of grievances.

Yet after delivering these words, I was informed that a subpoena had been issued against my speaker agency, and those of other speakers, seeking records of all speeches delivered "in support" of the MEK. I had to retain a lawyer to defend my constitutional right to deliver a speech "on behalf of the Constitution." I was also retained as a lawyer on behalf of former mayor Giuliani, former attorney general Mukasey, former FBI head Freeh, and several generals who wanted to file an amicus curie (friend of the court) brief seeking the delisting of the MEK on humanitarian grounds.

In September 2012, Secretary of State Hillary Clinton removed the MEK from the State Department's list of organized terrorist organizations.[3] So now anyone can speak in support of this group without risking prosecution for lending "material support" to a terrorist organization.

But the statute making it a crime to provide "material support" to a listed terrorist organization remains on the books, and there are some in the government who interpret that statute to include speeches that would otherwise be protected by the First Amendment. It remains to be seen whether the courts will strike the balance in favor of freedom of speech when the thumb of terrorism weighs heavily on the scale.

CONCLUSION: THE DANGER OF SELF-CENSORSHIP

The First Amendment has undergone more change in the past fifty years than it did in the first 170 years of its existence. Most of the changes have been for the better, such as the virtual elimination of offensiveness—especially vicarious offensiveness—as a justification for censorship, and the severe limitations placed on defamation actions involving public figures. I'm proud of the role I have played in helping bring about these positive changes.

It is never easy to strengthen the First Amendment, because most Americans support freedom of speech in the abstract but far fewer support speech that hurts, endangers, or deeply offends *them*. Echoing Justice Black, many Americans characterize speech of which they disapprove as "not really speech," or as speech that fits into the category of "shouting fire."

Nearly two hundred years ago, the French philosopher Voltaire articulated the fundamental premise underlying true support for freedom of speech: "I disapprove of what you say, but I will defend to the death your right to say it."[4] Defending "to the death" may be a bit strong and "disapprove" a bit weak, but the core of Voltaire's point is crucial. It is easy, and rather self-serving, to rally round the flag of the First Amendment on behalf of those whose speech you admire or enjoy. But unless you are prepared to defend the freedom to speak of those who make your blood boil, you cannot count yourself as a member of that rather select club of true believers in freedom of expression.

I call it a select club because most people, even most who claim adherence to the First Amendment, favor some censorship.

The current war against radical Islamic terrorism may become the new test for membership in the First Amendment Club. It is quickly becoming the battleground, not only because of governmental efforts to censor speech that is deemed supportive of terrorism, but also because of self-censorship that results from fear of violent responses from radical Muslims who are offended by constitutionally protected speech. Although the "fighting words" doctrine has always imposed a limitation on freedom of speech, it had been considerably weakened both in theory and in practice until the recent advent of radical Islam, with its threats to kill anyone who insults the religion or its prophet. These threats have been accompanied by murders in several parts of the world, thus escalating the concept of "fighting words" into the more lethal concept of "killing words." As a result, publishing houses have been reluctant to include material that might give rise to threatened violence. Following the publication by several Scandinavian newspapers of cartoons that depicted Muhammad, there were death threats and acts of violence. This led Yale University Press to decide not to include these cartoons in an academic book about the controversy. This act of censorship was not brought about by any governmental pressure, since the First Amendment would clearly have protected the publication of the cartoons. It was brought about by the self-censorship of the publishing house, growing out of the understandable fear that publication would result in violence. This phenomenon gives those who threaten violence an effective veto over what can be published in the United States.[5]

In recent years, there have been efforts to internationalize the censorship of material deemed offensive to Islam and other religions. Various agencies of the United Nations have proposed, in the name of "multiculturalism," severe restrictions on the right to criticize controversial cultural and religious practices deemed sacred by some and offensive by others.[6] The motivation behind some of these proposals is to limit the rights of those who would blaspheme Islam or its prophet and to legitimate those governments that still insist on criminalizing such blasphemy. But criticizing religion and religious practices—whether of Islam, Judaism, or Christianity—lies at the core of freedom of expression. Indeed, throughout history, religious dissenters have been crucified, beheaded, hanged, burned, and killed in other gruesome ways. The fatwa issued against Salman Rushdie and those who published cartoons of Muhammed show that this problem persists. Unless freedom to criticize religion—to commit blasphemy—is fully protected, freedom of expression will be severely compromised.

Historically, most censorship efforts have come from the authoritarian right—tyrannical governments, intolerant churches, fascist movements. Although right-wing censorship persists, today much of the pressure to censor comes from the hard left: multiculturalists who reject the superiority of the open marketplace of ideas as Western bias, radical feminists who seek to purge images and attitudes that reflect sexism, academics who insist on imposing their notions of political correctness on their students, other radicals who "know" the "truth" and see no reason to tolerate the untruths of their opponents.

Eternal vigilance—against censors of the right and left alike—is essential to the preservation of liberties that many Americans take for granted. The struggle for freedom of expression—like the struggle for other rights—never stays won.

On balance, the First Amendment remains relatively healthy and vibrant in America and continues to serve as a model for many, but not all, emerging democracies. The same cannot be said about our criminal justice system, the other area of law I have been teaching and practicing for so many years.

12

LIFE INTRUDES ON LAW

Illness and Other Close Calls

By the early 1970s I had become well established as a young academic, as a budding First Amendment lawyer, and as a father. Life was good. Suddenly everything changed.

My older son, Elon, fell while playing hockey, hit his head on the ice, and was taken, unconscious, to St. Elizabeth's Hospital. Nobody was sure whether he had fainted before he hit his head or whether the impact with the ice had caused his unconsciousness. The initial diagnosis was adolescent epilepsy, which was treated pharmaceutically.

In the summer of 1971, the family traveled by car to Palo Alto, California, where I was to take up residency for a year at the Center for Advanced Study in Behavioral Sciences. My project was to complete a long, scholarly book titled *Predictive Justice: Toward a Jurisprudence of Harm Prevention*. It was an ambitious project for a thirty-three-year-old academic, but I felt up to the task of formulating a new legal framework for what I saw as the emerging "preventive state."

The center, located adjacent to the Stanford University Campus, was a unique institution. It would invite approximately forty scholars from around the world, each from different disciplines that touched on behavioral sciences. I was the only law professor that year, among a group that included the philosopher Robert Nozick, the political theorist Michael Walzer, the linguists Robin and George Lakoff, the psychologists Philip Zimbardo and Amos Tversky, the sociologist Nathan Glazer, the psychiatrist Albert Stunkard, the Romanian economist Michael Cernea, and the psychoanalyst Bruno Bettelheim.

We were each assigned a small cabin in which to write our own books, but we were expected to join the others for luncheon talks and seminar presentations. Collaborations were encouraged, and many fine books emerged from the serene hills of Palo Alto.

Mine, however, was not among them. In early December, after I had completed my historical research and writing, my son Elon was diagnosed with a malignant brain tumor—a diagnosis missed by the Boston doctors in the days before CT scans. The first person to suggest the dreaded diagnosis was Bruno Bettelheim, who worked in the adjoining cabin and invited me for "high tea," which his Viennese-born wife would bring him every afternoon. Although Bruno was not a physician—indeed he had never been able to complete college because of the emergence of Nazism in Germany and Austria—he had studied with Sigmund Freud and was regarded as one of the most distinguished, though controversial, psychoanalytic thinkers in the world.

When I told him about my son's recurring headaches and seizures, his first comment was "Remember George Gershwin?" I was a great fan of Gershwin's music, and family lore suggested we might even be related, since his original name was Gershowitz, and the *G*s, *D*s, and *H*s sometimes got mixed up at Ellis Island. But I didn't know what Bruno was referring to. He explained: "Gershwin had headaches for years and underwent lengthy psychoanalysis by analysts who believed that every pain was caused by early childhood experiences, and could be treated by the talking cure. Eventually, it was discovered, he had a brain tumor from which he died at age thirty-eight."

Following this morbid conversation, I took Elon to Stanford Hospital, where a brain scan disclosed a tumor. We rushed him to Boston's Children's Hospital, where a remarkable neurosurgeon, John Shilito, removed it. We then returned to Stanford, where another remarkable doctor, Henry Kaplan, performed radiation therapy over several months.

I did not have enough money to afford this extraordinary medical care, and Judge David Bazelon—who was Elon's godfather—loaned me what I needed. He also loaned me money to invest in a real estate venture with a friend of his in Washington, Charles E. Smith. The return on that venture allowed me to pay off my loan to Bazelon over several years, but I vowed never again to require help from others to take care of my family's medical needs. From then on, I began to charge clients who could afford my legal services. Within a few years, I had saved enough to be able to pay for any medical or other family emergency.

When I returned to the center at Stanford, nothing was the same. I couldn't concentrate on my book. My marriage, which had been suffering for several years even before our trip to California, was now in deep trouble. All I could think about and work on was my son's condition. The clock was always ticking. The doctors told me that if he made it past a year, the odds of his survival would go up, and if he made it past two years, they would go up even more. These years went by very slowly, with several scares but thankfully no recurrence.

During this time I spent hours in the medical library, learning all I could about Elon's condition. The doctors were encouraging but the research was not. (Research has no bedside manner!)

Although I did not turn to religion as a source of solace, I did read and reread the book of Job, a remarkable story about how human beings confront tragedy. When God decided to test Job's faith, his first action was to afflict his children. The author of Job understood, as anyone who has experienced the serious illness of a child understands, that there is no greater test a parent confronts than when a child faces death.

Everything changes. Life is put on hold. Samuel Johnson once observed that nothing focuses the mind quite as clearly as an appointment with the hangman.[1] Johnson obviously didn't have a child with cancer. Nothing can make a parent focus more single-mindedly on any issue than a child with a life-threatening illness and the steps that must be taken to maximize the chances of survival, both physical and psychological.

I have discussed this issue with friends who have lived through life-threatening illnesses suffered by their children. Some, like me, try to become super-scientists, reading everything they can get their hands on, conferring with every expert they can reach, and micromanaging every medical decision. Others leave these matters to the doctors and devote themselves to showering their child with love and support. Still others find it difficult to engage either scientifically or emotionally. Every parent is different, as are the needs of every child. Illness among children does not come with a one-size-fits-all instruction manual. The first priority, of course, is the life of the child, but not far behind is the psychological welfare, both short- and long-term, of the child who survives the illness.

One common reaction among parents of seriously ill children who have made it through the initial treatment phase is to try to bury the difficult memories by not thinking or talking about the traumatic past. With cancer survivors this is especially problematic, since the threat of recurrence is ever present, and past may become prologue. Healthy vigilance must be balanced against unhealthy obsession with every possible symptom. The struggle never ends. The scars, though sometimes invisible, remain.

A seriously ill child tests the strength of every individual and every relationship. Some endure, even thrive, while others weaken or even shatter. There is no way to prepare for the challenge, because a family's journey to the valley of the shadow of death almost always comes on without warning.

There are several stages a parent goes through during and following the diagnosis. The first involves immediate panic, overwhelming frustration, and a sense of helplessness. This may be followed by intense involvement in the treatment process. Then there is the treatment itself—often surgery followed by radiation and chemotherapy. Finally, there is waiting—a year, five years, ten years—before one can be relatively confident that the treatment has worked. During this waiting period, it becomes difficult to concentrate on anything else, as your child seems cured, but you know there is the lingering fear of recurrence. I could not focus on long-term projects. I needed short deadlines that did not allow my mind to wander. But wander it did, to my child's future, to whether I was subtly treating him differently because of his encounter with illness, to every minor symptom that might signal a recurrence.

Elon is the hero in this saga. The doctors told him that the surgery might affect his manual dexterity. His hobby was close-up magic, which requires extraordinary dexterity. He was determined to prove the doctors wrong, so he worked endlessly on his moves. Before the surgery, he had a magic act that he performed to friends and some Stanford fraternities. He had billed himself "Elon the Pretty Good." Following the surgery he quickly became, at least to me, "Elon the Great," performing at Boston Celtics Christmas parties, Patrick Kennedy's birthday party, and at the Legal Sea Foods Restaurant.

More importantly, he performed for kids with brain tumors and other neurological problems at hospitals and radiation centers, even when he himself was undergoing radiation therapy. It was a difficult time for all of us, but Elon's determination lifted our spirits.

Nor did Elon's friends (and their parents) make it easier on Elon. His closest friend in California was told by his parents to keep his distance from Elon. When I raised the issue with them, they said they did not want their son to become too close to a boy who might die. Schoolmates taunted Elon about his wig and called him "tumor boy." But Elon persisted, even playing football within a year of the surgery.

VIGNETTE

My Only "Crime"

I can think of only one crime that I may have committed in my life, and I know that if I had been tried for it, I would not only have been acquitted, but the jurors would have cheered me.

Shortly after my son Elon's surgery, he went back to work selling newspapers in the subway station at Harvard Square. One day two young hoodlums from Somerville beat him up, broke his tooth, and stole the few dollars he had earned. A local policeman, Frank Burns, who knew Harvard Square like the back of his hand, immediately recognized the MO of the thugs and arrested them.

Several days later, the thugs came back to Harvard Square, robbed my son again, and told him that unless he withdrew his complaint, they would throw him in front of a moving train. He called me and I ran to the square, where I saw the two thugs taking a victory lap. I approached them and I said, "I have only two words to say to you." I then mentioned the name of a man on whose case I was then consulting. Although the charge against him involved marijuana trafficking, the man himself was known to be a notorious hit man for one of Boston's most violent gangs. I told the two youths that if they ever came near my son again, I would tell my client, who would do anything for me. The two thugs got down on their hands and knees and pleaded with me not to tell my client what they had done. They never came back. I never told my client; indeed I had never met my client, and still haven't. I was just consulting with another lawyer on a constitutional issue related to the case. But simply mentioning his name terrorized the thugs. I'm not sure whether what I did was a crime. But I would do it again if anyone ever threatened any of my children. Forty years later, Elon was again hospitalized for possible damage to his field of vision caused by the earlier radiation. A few days after he left the hospital, we hailed a taxi in New York. Elon opened the door and a bottle of wine that a female passenger was holding fell to the ground and broke. Elon apologized and offered to pay for it, but the other passenger—a man in his forties—started to attack Elon with his fist. Without thinking, I reared back and punched him square in his jaw, causing his glasses to fall from his face. It was the first time

I had punched anyone in sixty years. I would do it again if anyone physically attacked one of my children.

My wife and I separated briefly during our stay in Palo Alto, but we decided to try to remain together, in order to see whether a return to our more usual life in Cambridge could salvage the marriage.

On the road trip back east, during the summer of 1973, I received a call that would change the direction of my life, both professionally and personally. It came from an old Boro Park neighbor, who grew up two doors away from me. He had the unlikely name of Elefant, which had given rise to much youthful teasing, but now he too was a lawyer. Among his clients was the Jewish Defense League, a controversial organization headed by the fiery and charismatic Rabbi Meir Kahane.

The JDL case would thrust me back into a world I thought I had left. The major events of the case had taken place in Boro Park, literally a few blocks away from where I had lived. Elefant asked me if I would be willing to represent a young man named Sheldon Siegel, who was facing the death penalty for having constructed a smoke bomb that others had planted in the office of Sol Hurok, a world famous impresario who brought Soviet musicians to the United States. The bomb had killed a young Jewish woman named Iris Kones, who worked as a receptionist in the office. Hurok's office had been targeted because the JDL opposed any cultural exchanges with the Soviet Union so long as Jews were not allowed to emigrate and were imprisoned for trying.

I had been acquainted with Shelley Siegel growing up. His older sister was part of my social circle, and I had taken dancing lessons in her basement. Elefant told me that I was not their first choice as a lawyer, since I had no experience in trying murder cases at that time, but no other lawyers were willing to take this case, especially on a pro bono basis. Despite my need for money, I quickly agreed to put together a team to try to save Shelley's life.

The JDL case, which would be tried in the New York Federal Courthouse at Foley Square, would take me away from Cambridge for several days each week. Fortunately, all my classes were on three mornings, so I could come into New York on Wednesday afternoon and remain there through the weekend. My marriage, which was hanging on by a thread, began to unravel as I discovered that I enjoyed being away from home more than being at home, though I missed my children during my time away.

I have written about the JDL case, with its twists and turns, at considerable length in my first book, *The Best Defense.*[2] I also allude to it in the forthcoming chapter on homicide cases. For present purposes, it is enough to say that the case changed my attitude toward the law and shook my faith in our judicial system, despite the fact that we eventually won a total victory.

My client, as it turned out, was not only the expert bomb maker for the JDL; he was also a secret government informer who was providing information to the police about the activities of his organization. The government intended to grant him immunity and use him as the star witness against the other defendants. I did not learn this crucial fact until well into the case, and when I did, I thought seriously about getting out, because my client had not been straight with me. But I soon realized that he had been pressured into becoming an informer by threats against his life made by a New York City policeman, who himself had grown up in my old neighborhood. I was able to use my familiarity with guys like him to trap him with my cross-examination. Siegel had surreptitiously recorded these threats, and I used those recordings to expose the policeman's improper conduct and to prove that he had promised never to use Siegel as a witness. The court of appeals ultimately ruled that Siegel could not be called as a witness. Without his testimony, the case against the others crumbled and everyone went free.

I sat in court for a full hour after everyone else had left. I wanted no part of any victory celebration. I was thinking of Iris Kones. This was the first time I had used my legal talents to help free guilty murderers. It would not be the last.

I worked on the case with my former student Harvey Silverglate, and a young associate at his firm, Jeanne Baker. Working together with these two extraordinary young lawyers—both of whom became close personal friends—made it clear to me how unhappy I was in my marriage, which soon ended formally with a separation and then a divorce. I had failed in my marriage, and I was beginning to experience doubts about my commitment to producing scholarly writings. My blood pressure went up, and for the first time in my adult life, I felt vulnerable and lacked self-confidence.

I was also feeling ambivalence concerning my connections to my Jewish heritage. My involvement with the JDL, and my return to Boro Park to investigate the case, forced me to confront my own complicated feelings regarding my Orthodox Jewish past. I hated the violent means selected by the JDL to achieve their ends, but I felt an increasing sympathy for their goal of freeing Soviet Jewry. I had been introduced to the plight of Soviet Jews by Elie Wiesel several years earlier, but Rabbi Kahane and his followers forced me to confront the depth of my emotional attachment to my brothers and sisters in the Soviet Union. There, but for the grace of God, and the willingness of my grandparents to leave Eastern Europe, go I. I became determined to show the JDL that there were other and better ways to help Soviet Jews than by killing and endangering American Jews and others.

My encounter with the JDL also made it clear to me that my Jewishness was very much a part of my being, but that I had to define it on my own terms and live it my own way. I was not a theological Jew, or any longer a fully practicing one. Neither could I be a radical or violent Jew. I decided to become a Jewish lawyer. But what exactly does that mean? Sandy Koufax, my neighbor in Boro Park, was a Jewish baseball player, but there was nothing about his playing that reflected his Jewish heritage. Indeed his most famous Jewish act was not an act at all. It was a refusal to act—his decision *not to play* on Yom Kippur. I too do not play or work on Yom Kippur, and probably for much the same cultural and emotional reasons that influenced Sandy's decision. I did not fully understand my emotional attachment to a religious culture whose theological underpinning I could not accept, but I decided that a substantial part of my legal career would be devoted to defending Jewish values and Jews in trouble around the world. Shortly after the JDL case, I traveled to the Soviet Union to defend, on a pro bono basis, numerous Jewish refuseniks and prisoners of Zion.[3]

My surprising victory in the JDL case brought me dozens of requests to represent others—Jews and non-Jews, paying and pro bono clients—charged with serious crimes, especially homicide.

By the time the JDL case was over, I was divorced, and my two sons, then in their early teen years, were living with me. For the next several years, I devoted much of my time to trying my best to be a good father. We moved into a large, rented house in Cambridge, which my kids called "Camp Dershowitz." It had a basketball hoop in the backyard, a pinball machine in the basement, a Ping-Pong table, and lots of other sports equipment. It became a gathering place for my children's friends and classmates. It also became a crash pad for my friends. At one point, a Soviet Jew I had helped emigrate lived with us for several months, followed by a Romanian Jew whose family I had helped. (The Romanian Jew was the daughter of Michael Cernea, the economist I had met at the Center for Advanced Study of Behavioral Sciences.) By the end of the 1970s, my children were well settled. Elon had been accepted at the University of Colorado and Jamin was nearing the end of his high school career. Both were doing very well.

In the beginning of September 1979, I took Elon to the University of Colorado to begin college. It was the happiest day of my life. He had made it through the critical five-year benchmark and was nearing the ten-year mark. I spent a nice day with Elon helping him move into his freshman dorm and buying him the usual stuff for school. I then returned to Stapleton Airport, intending to fly to New York for dinner with my brother and sister-in-law.

The plane took off routinely, but when it got to about ten thousand feet, it began to rattle and shake. The pilot came on the loudspeaker and spoke the words everybody dreads: "We have a serious problem." He explained that the flaps were locked in the takeoff position and that neither automatic nor manual efforts to reposition them were working. We would have to make an emergency landing with the flaps in the takeoff position. He assured us that he was trained for this maneuver, but a man sitting next to me who had been in the air force told me that this was quite dangerous. That view was confirmed when the pilot soon asked if there was anybody on the plane who was experienced in situations of this kind. A few volunteers came forward, and they were seated near the exits and given special instructions on how to help the passengers off the plane in the event of a crash landing. The crew then made some of us, including me, change our seats. I was placed next to a pregnant woman and asked if I would be responsible for helping her leave the plane. I agreed. The pilot then told us that he would be dumping fuel over the farmlands and that once we were near empty, he would try to land the plane on a runway filled with foam and adjacent to firefighting equipment. He told us we had about an hour before he would be attempting the landing.

People all around me were praying. Nobody panicked. The crew asked us all to remove our eyeglasses and taught us the brace position for a crash landing. Women were required to remove their high-heeled shoes. Passengers were told to take sharp items out of their pockets. We were also told to retrieve soft items—underwear, shirts, and such—from our overhead baggage and use them as pillows to blunt any anticipated impact.

We then had about a half an hour before we would either land or crash. I was nervous but remarkably calm, focusing on exit routes and ways of improving the odds of surviving. I learned at that time, for an absolute certainty, that I did not believe in an intervening God, since I did not spend one second praying or trying to make a deal with God. It simply never occurred to me. It was not true, at least in my case, that there are no agnostics in a foxhole. Instead, I decided to write a long letter about my children, who were the focus of my thoughts. I've never showed them the letter but here are some excerpts from it, which summarize my feelings at what I thought might be the end of my life but which has turned out to be closer to its midpoint.

> *At about 11:50, pilot told us that we were having a flap problem; that he was trying to get in touch with S.F. (about what he didn't say) and that we might have to go back to Denver. . . . Haven't heard anything now for 15 or so minutes. . . . Captain just told us emergency landing at high speed. They're telling us about precautions and evacuation.*
>
> *Heck of a way to end a trip putting my firstborn in college.*
>
> *I'm nervous and feel a bit shaky.*
>
> *I find my thoughts turning to my kids. Are they really ready to cope with the world without me? I think so. But I wish there had been more time. I'm very proud of them both. Elon has been incredible in the way he has overcome his hardships. His ability to teach himself magic has been phenomenal. Sometimes I haven't shown the kind of appreciation I should have, because I have been somewhat ambivalent about encouraging him to spend too much time on it. But I can't get over how he has managed to become a great—really great—magician in such a short period of time. His individualism—his ability to remain himself even when it has been painful to do so—has been very admirable.*
>
> *Jamin has been a joy in every way. I know he will do well in everything he does.*
>
> *Nobody should grieve for me. It's been a wonderful life. I have done more in my 41 years than most people do in more. I have no complaints.*
>
> *I hope that my family will continue the work and ideas that have been important to me. But don't let me rule you from the past. You're all your own people.*

I put the letter in the plastic case that held my shaver, as the pilot maneuvered the plane for the emergency landing. It was the longest five minutes of my life. The plane landed at a sharp angle and with a heavy thud on the left side. Several people on the plane were shaken up and bruised, but there were no serious injuries. When the pilot came out of the cockpit, greeted by thunderous applause and cheers, he was dripping wet. He announced, "We all just dodged a bullet. Now you can start your lives again."

I really did regard this as the beginning of a new phase of my life. I was not quite an empty nester, but neither was I the kind of hands-on parent

I had been over the past several years. I was ready to resume my life and my career.

Early in the next decade, shortly after Jamin went off to college at the University of Pennsylvania, I met my second wife, Carolyn Cohen, and we moved together into a smaller house in Cambridge, where we began our life as a couple.

My relationship and eventual marriage to Carolyn—followed by the birth of our daughter, Ella—marked another important transition in my attitude toward life. Before I met Carolyn (which in our family we refer to as "BC"), I had never owned a home, always living in rented apartments, with few personal possessions, such as a half dozen small lithographs. My home life lacked the sort of stability to warrant the permanence of home owning or significant art collecting. My children called it my "Holocaust mentality," which Elon explained as "You've got to be able to move away at a moment's notice, so don't burden yourself with immovable objects."

Once I met Carolyn, I began to imagine a future secure enough to justify purchasing a home and filling it—really filling it—with paintings, sculptures, antiquities, Judaica, and tchotchkes. Our large new home, which we purchased shortly after Ella was born, became a kind of museum, in which we entertained students and held charitable and political fund-raisers. We were there to stay.

Beyond the material manifestations of this change in attitude, there were also the psychological. In the decade after I met Carolyn, I became more self-confident—writing books, litigating more cases, and generally achieving a better balance among the different aspects of my life and career.

When I first met Carolyn, she noticed that I often worked through the weekends. When she asked me why, I said: "Weekend, weekday, it's all the same. They're just days of the week." She changed that, urging me to set aside specific "no work" time over the weekend. I've been doing that and enjoying my new secular "Sabbath" ever since. We also bought a vacation home on Martha's Vineyard, where we spend our summers. I do much of my writing in my office there, overlooking the Atlantic Ocean. We have a community of Vineyard friends, and my family spends time there with us as well. Carolyn brought love, confidence, structure, and stability into my life just when I needed it. The decade to come included some of the most challenging, controversial, and high-profile cases and causes of my career, focusing heavily on issues of life and death. My own encounter with my son's life-and-death crisis, and the loving support provided by Carolyn, prepared me for this emerging phase of my life and career.

PART III

CRIMINAL JUSTICE

From Sherlock Holmes to CSI

13

"DEATH IS DIFFERENT"[1]

Challenging Capital Punishment

From the beginning of my academic career, I taught classes involving criminal justice, but I had little practical experience as a criminal lawyer. Nor had I grown up with a passion for criminal law, as I had with respect to freedom of expression. Like most kids growing up in Brooklyn, I always rooted for the good guys—the United States Army, the local police (whom we met at events sponsored by the Police Athletic League, or PAL), the cowboys with white hats on the screen of the local movie theater, and our beloved Brooklyn Dodgers.

When I thought of becoming a lawyer, I imagined myself defending only the innocent and winning their justly deserved freedom. I didn't know any real criminals, and so the issue for me was abstract, with a simple—indeed simpleminded—solution: The guilty should all be convicted and punished; the innocent should all be acquitted and freed. It was black-and-white. No moral or emotional ambiguity or conflict.

I was aware that some innocent people—particularly from groups discriminated against, such as Communists or blacks—had been wrongfully convicted. I wanted to become one of those heroic defense lawyers who helped secure justice for the wrongly convicted, like the Rosenbergs and the Scottsboro Boys.

It never occurred to me that someday I would also be helping guilty murderers go free. That was not a narrative with which I was familiar, either from real life, the movies, or television, where the acquitted were always innocent and the convicted always guilty. Indeed, the Hays Code—which used to determine what could be shown on the big screen—explicitly required that the guilty be punished. And Perry Mason always represented innocent clients, and was able to secure justice by discovering who the real killer was.

That's the kind of criminal lawyer I wanted to be!

The only problem, as I soon learned, was that Perry Mason is a fictional lawyer. In real life, there are no lawyers who represent only the innocent, though there are some who mendaciously claim they do. Moreover, as I also learned, there are no criminal defense lawyers who win all of their cases. And finally, I learned that guilt and innocence are often not black-and-white extremes, but rather matters of degree.

My primary exposure to the criminal justice system had come during my clerkships, which focused on the death penalty and cases involving the interface of law and science. Not surprisingly, when I decided to obtain some practical experience, I was most comfortable beginning with such cases and causes. I was drawn immediately to cases involving death, because such cases are the most challenging.

Cases involving death really are different.[2]

Whenever a defendant is at risk of losing his liberty, the stakes are high, but when he is at risk of losing life—when the death penalty is on the table—the stakes are the highest. Even in murder or attempted murder cases in which the death penalty is off the table, the life-and-death nature of the case makes it different.

Usually, though not always, I am called after the defendant has been convicted and is seeking an appeal or habeas corpus, where the prospects for success are quite low. Yet I have won the vast majority of the death cases in which I played a significant role. In no case has one of my clients been executed.

The reason I have won so many death cases has more to do with science than law. Most of my death cases were centered on forensics. Even before the popularity of such television shows as *CSI*, *Bones*, and *Dexter*, I had developed an expertise in the scientific aspects of homicide cases. My academic focus has been on the interface of law and science, and so it was natural for me to employ my expertise in the courtroom. Many of my death cases have become the basis for films, television shows, and books.[3] Death is not only different—it is the stuff of drama.

In addition to the individual cases involving death that I have litigated, I have also played a significant role in the campaign to abolish or limit the death penalty. This began more than a half century ago, when I was a law clerk responsible for drafting the first judicial opinion challenging the constitutionality of the death penalty.[4]

MY ROLE IN CHALLENGING THE CONSTITUTIONALITY OF CAPITAL PUNISHMENT

As recounted earlier, my initial assignment as Justice Goldberg's law clerk was to write a memorandum on the unconstitutionality of the death penalty. Justice Goldberg told me of his plan to use the Eighth Amendment—which prohibits "cruel and unusual punishment"—to abolish the death penalty.[5] "What could be more cruel than the deliberate decision by the state to take a human life?" he asked rhetorically.

I agreed that the death penalty was cruel, but I reminded the justice that for a punishment to be unconstitutional under the Eighth Amendment, it must be *both* cruel *and* unusual, and the death penalty was anything but unusual—either at the time the Eighth Amendment was ratified or now. "The Colonists were executing people all over the place," I said, and "even today states such as Texas, Alabama, and Florida are executing not only murderers but rapists and armed robbers."

Justice Goldberg looked at me somberly and spoke: "Therein lies the beauty of our Bill of Rights. It's an evolving document. It means something different today than it meant in 1792."[6] He continued: "It's true that the death penalty is not *yet* unusual, but we can help make it so. I don't expect to be able to abolish capital punishment in one fell swoop, but we must begin a process that will lead to its *becoming* unusual and eventually anachronistic."

He assigned me to search among the death penalty petitions that were then pending before the court and to try to find a few compelling cases that would allow him to write an opinion raising questions about the constitutionality of the death penalty as applied to the facts of those cases. He had already selected a rape case from Alabama in which a black man had been sentenced to death for raping a white woman. I found several others in which armed robbers and murderers who were mentally ill were sentenced to death.

I was enthusiastic about my assignment because I had long opposed capital punishment. As a high school debater, I argued against it. I still have a handwritten note card from my first debate, in which I advocated the "abolision [*sic*] of C.P." because "most murderers are products of invirnment [*sic*]."[7] In law school I wrote to the prime minister of Israel arguing that even Adolf Eichmann should be spared the noose. As Evan Mandery, whose book *A Wild Justice* details the history of the campaign to declare the death penalty unconstitutional, put it:

> *Goldberg's choice of Dershowitz to write his capital punishment opinion was no coincidence. Goldberg passed on the issue during his first year on the bench in part because he did not feel that he had the right clerks. He inherited his first set of clerks from Felix Frankfurter. Though he had high regard for the retiring justice's selections, he didn't feel they were right for the job. . . . In Alan Dershowitz, Goldberg found a kindred spirit and a life story that was in many ways the New York parallel of his own Chicago childhood. . . . Also like Goldberg, Dershowitz had an aversion to capital punishment, which traced back to his childhood.*[8]

Justice Goldberg said that he saw me as his "perfect" collaborator on this "uphill battle."[9]

I set to work on the capital punishment project but found no suggestion in the case law that any court had ever considered the death penalty to be of questionable constitutionality. Not even the American Civil Liberties Union challenged the constitutionality of capital punishment. Just five years earlier, Chief Justice Earl Warren had written in *Trop v. Dulles* that "whatever the arguments may be against capital punishment, both on moral grounds and in terms of accomplishing the purposes of punishment—and they are forceful—the death penalty has been employed throughout our history, and, in a day when it is still widely accepted it cannot be said to violate the constitutional concept of cruelty."[10]

I duly reported this to Justice Goldberg, suggesting that if even the liberal chief justice believed that the death penalty was constitutional, what chance did he have of getting a serious hearing for his view that the cruel and unusual punishment clause should now be construed to prohibit the imposition of capital punishment? Justice Goldberg asked me to talk to Justice Brennan and see what his views were. Unless Justice Brennan agreed to join, the entire project would be scuttled, because Justice Goldberg, the court's rookie, did not want to "be out there alone," against the chief justice and the rest of the court.

I had previously met Justice Brennan several times over the preceding few years, since his son Bill was my classmate and moot-court partner at Yale Law School. I had also had lunch several times with the justice and his friend Judge David Bazelon. But none of our discussions had been substantive, and I nervously anticipated the task of discussing an important issue with one of my judicial heroes.

VIGNETTE

Justice Brennan

My conversation with Justice Brennan marked the beginning of what developed into a lifelong friendship and mutual admiration society. One of my great treasures is a handwritten letter from the justice in 1982 that includes the following:

> *There are winds swirling these days that too few resist—it's a comfort to know that outside there are steadfast champions who are putting up a gallant fight. You are first among them and that's a matter of special pride for those of us who have followed your career with increasing satisfaction.*

I brought to the meeting a rough draft of the memorandum[11] I was working on, but Justice Brennan did not want to look at it. He asked me to describe the results of my research, promising to read the memorandum later. I stated the nascent constitutional case against the death penalty as best I could. I told him that *Weems v. United States*,[12] an old case from 1910, could be read as recognizing the following tests for whether punishment was "cruel and unusual": (1) if a less severe one can as effectively achieve the permissible ends of punishment (that is, deterrence, isolation, rehabilitation); (2) if it offends the contemporary sense of decency (for example, torture); (3) if the evil it produces is disproportionally higher than the harm it seeks to prevent (the death penalty for economic crimes).

In addition to these abstract formulations, I also told Justice Brennan that my research had disclosed a pattern of unequal application of the death penalty on racial grounds. I cited national prison statistics showing that over a fifteen-year period, 233 blacks were executed for rape in the United States, while only 26 whites were executed for that crime, though whites committed many more rapes than blacks.

Justice Brennan encouraged me to continue my research, without making any promises. Several weeks later, Justice Goldberg told me that Justice Brennan had agreed to join a short dissent from the denial of certiorari in *Rudolph v. Alabama* (1963)[13]—the case involving imposition of the death penalty on a black man who was convicted of raping a white woman. Justice William O. Douglas signed on as well. The dissenters invited the bar to address the following questions, which they deemed "relevant and worthy of argument and consideration":

1. In light of the trend both in the country and throughout the world against punishing rape by death, does the imposition of the death penalty by those States which retain it for rape violate "evolving standards of decency that mark the progress of [our] maturing society," or "standards of decency more or less universally accepted"?

2. Is the taking of human life to protect a value other than human life consistent with the constitutional proscription against "punishments which by their excessive . . . severity are greatly disproportional to the offenses charged"?

3. Can the permissible aims of punishment (e.g., deterrence, isolation, rehabilitation) be achieved as effectively by punishing rape less severely than by death . . . ; if so, does the imposition of the death penalty for rape constitute "unnecessary cruelty"?[14]

I had drafted these questions based on my research and conversations with Justices Goldberg and Brennan.

As soon as the dissent was published, there was an immediate reaction. Conservative journalists had a field day lambasting the very notion that a court could strike down a long-standing punishment that is explicitly referred to in the Constitution.

One extreme criticism appeared in the *New Hampshire Union Leader* under the banner headline U.S. SUPREME COURT TRIO ENCOURAGES RAPE:

> *The three U.S. Supreme Court justices, Goldberg, Brennan, Douglas, raised the question of whether it was proper to condemn a man to death for the crime of rape if there has been no endangering of the life of the victim. This incredible opinion, of course, can serve only to encourage would-be rapists. These fiends, freed from the fear of the death penalty for their foul deed, . . . will be inclined to take a chance.*
>
> *Thus, not content with forbidding our schoolchildren to pray in school, not content with banishing Bible reading from our schools, and not content letting every type of filthy book be published, at least three members of the Supreme Court are now out to encourage rape.*[15]

The editorial neglected to mention that New Hampshire had abolished the death penalty for rape generations ago and had one of the lowest rates of rape in the country—far lower than states that still executed convicted rapists.

Several state courts went out of their way to announce their disagreement with the dissent. The Georgia Supreme Court questioned

> *the judicial right of any American judge to construe the American Constitution contrary to its apparent meaning, the American history of the clause, and its construction by American courts, simply because the numerous nations and States have abandoned capital punishment for rape. First we believe the history of no nation will show the high values of woman's virtue and purity that America has shown. We would regret to see the day when this freedom loving country would lower our respect for womanhood or lessen her legal protection for no better reason than that many or even all other countries have done so. She is entitled to every legal protection of her body, her decency, her purity and good name.*[16]

The court went on to reject this attempt to reduce the protection of the

> *mothers of mankind, the cornerstone of civilized society, and the zenith of God's creation, against a crime more horrible than death, which is the forcible sexual invasion of her body, the temple of her soul, thereby soiling for life her purity, the most precious attribute of all mankind.*[17]

Georgia, at that time, had one of the worst records in the nation with regard to women's rights.

There was scholarly criticism as well. In the *Harvard Law Review*, Professor Herbert Packer of Stanford correctly identified Justice Goldberg's ultimate goal and then criticized the means he had selected to implement it:

> *What Justice Goldberg may really be troubled about is not the death penalty for rape but the death penalty. The problem may not be one of proportionality but of mode of punishment, the problem that concerned the framers of the eighth amendment and to which its provisions still seem most relevant. The Supreme Court is obviously not about to declare that the death penalty simpliciter is so cruel and unusual as to be constitutionally intolerable. Other social forces will have to work us closer than we are now to the point at which a judicial coup de grace becomes more than mere fiat. Meanwhile, there may well be legitimate devices for judicial control of the administration of the death penalty . . . [but] the device proposed by Justice Goldberg is not one of them.*[18]

These were the short-term reactions. Far more important, however, was the long-term reaction of the bar, especially the American Civil Liberties Union and the NAACP, which combined forces to establish a death penalty litigation project designed to take up the challenge of the dissenting opinion in *Rudolph*. The history of this project has been recounted brilliantly by Professor Michael Meltsner in his book *Cruel and Unusual*,[19] and I could not possibly improve upon it here. But the results achieved were dramatic. Meltsner and the other members of the Legal Defense Fund, a group that included a number of talented and committed lawyers, litigated hundreds of cases on behalf of defendants sentenced to death, and in many of these cases, they succeeded in holding the executioner at bay until the Supreme Court was ready to consider the constitutionality of the death penalty. I consulted on a number of these cases, lending insights from my experience as the law clerk who had drafted the *Rudolph* dissent.

The strategy was simple in outline: The Supreme Court should not be allowed the luxury of deciding the issue of capital punishment as an abstraction; instead, it must be confronted with the concrete responsibility of determining the immediate fates of many hundreds of condemned persons at the same time. In this way, the court could not evade the issue, or lightly refuse to decide it if the court's refusal would result in the specter of mass executions of hundreds of convicts. The court could decline to decide the ultimate issue— the constitutionality of capital punishment—if in doing so it could find some other way of keeping alive those on death row. And the legal team always provided the court with this other way—a narrower issue, usually in the form of an irregularity in the procedure by which the death penalty was imposed or administered.

Pursuant to this strategy, the Supreme Court decided a number of cases involving the administration of the death penalty; in each of these cases the court declined to consider the ultimate issue, but it always ruled in favor of the doomed, thereby sparing their lives. With the passage of each year, the number of those on death row increased and the stakes grew higher.

Then in 1971 the court took its first turn backwards: It held that a condemned person's constitutional rights were not violated "by permitting the jury to impose the death penalty without any governing standards"[20] It looked like the string might have been played out: There were no more "narrow" procedural grounds. The court would have to confront the ultimate issue. But it was not the same court that had been sitting when the strategy was devised; there were four new Nixon appointees, and it was clear that some of them believed the death penalty to be constitutional. The umpires had changed after the strategy of the game had been implemented.

The drama intensified. The court let it be known that it was ready to decide the ultimate issue. Knowledgeable lawyers—counting noses—were predicting that the death penalty would be sustained by a narrow majority. Some thought that it might be struck down for rape but sustained for murder. Some predicted that the court would once again find—or contrive—a reason for avoiding the ultimate issue. A few, of optimistic bent, kept the faith and expressed the belief that the court—even this court—would simply not send hundreds to their death.

And then came a major and unanticipated break. The California Supreme Court—perhaps the most influential state court in the nation—ruled that its constitution (which had similar wording to the federal Constitution) forbade the death penalty.[21] On the last day of the United States Supreme Court's 1971 term, the decision was rendered in a case called *Furman v. Georgia*.[22] The court ruled that the death penalty, as administered in this country, was unconstitutional. The argument proposed by Justice Goldberg on my first day as his law clerk had now been accepted by a majority of the justices. Goldberg called me in joy, offering mutual congratulations and crediting me with implementing his idea. I was thrilled.

But this would not be the high court's last word on the subject. Chief Justice Burger, in his dissenting opinion, provided the states with a road map as to how to draft death penalty statutes that might pass constitutional muster.[23] What ensued was a constitutional Ping-Pong match between proponents of capital punishment and abolitionists; the proponents would draft new statutes, and the abolitionists would challenge them in court. Justice Goldberg, now in private practice, and I continued to play a role in this life-and-death conflict by writing joint articles for newspapers and law reviews.[24]

In one article I wrote after observing the trial and sentencing of John Demjanjuk—a Ukrainian death camp guard who was responsible for brutalizing and murdering numerous Jews—I made "the case against executing" him, regardless of whether he was Ivan the Terrible of Treblinka, or merely Ivan the Very Bad of Sobibor. I began by acknowledging that

> *if ever there was a case that cried out for the death penalty, it would be that of John Demjanjuk. There can be no doubt whatever that he was an SS-trained death camp guard who was complicitous in the mass murder of Jews. He repeatedly lied about his past and he shows no remorse.*[25]

I then argued that there

> *is a corollary to the proposition that if anybody deserves capital punishment, it is John Demjanjuk. The corollary is that if John Demjanjuk is not executed, then no one should ever be. Sparing Demjanjuk's life may thus save the lives of many others by strengthening the case against capital punishment throughout the world. Israel could be a beacon to the world if it withheld the noose from the neck of one on whom it would seem to fit so justifiably.*[26]

In 2013, I made a similar argument against imposing the death penalty on the surviving accused Boston Marathon bomber.[27]

In the end, the Supreme Court of Israel reversed Demjanjuk's conviction based on new evidence that cast some doubt on whether he was Ivan the Terrible of Treblinka.[28] He was subsequently convicted by a German court of being Ivan the Very Bad of Sobibor.[29] He died at age ninety-one while free on bail during the appeal of his conviction.[30]

At about the same time of the Demanjuk trial, I was given an opportunity to participate directly in the court battle against capital punishment, in a dramatic and controversial case called *Tison v. Arizona*.

14

THE DEATH PENALTY FOR THOSE WHO DON'T KILL

Ricky and Raymond Tison

The story of the Tison case was the stuff of films and television dramas.[1] It involved two families. The family of the killers consisted of the father, mother, and three sons. The family of the victims consisted of a father, mother, baby, and niece. They would meet—with horrendous consequences—on a dark, isolated road in Arizona.

Beyond the tragic facts of the case was the important legal issue they presented, since neither Ricky nor his brother Raymond Tison actually killed anyone. Nor did they intend anyone to die when they helped their father, Gary, and his cellmate Randy Greenawalt escape from prison. But at least four innocent people—including a baby and a fifteen-year-old girl—were brutally murdered by the prisoners whom the Tison brothers helped escape. And for playing that role Ricky and Raymond Tison, who were teenagers, were sentenced to die in the Arizona gas chamber.

As part of the overall challenge to the death penalty, abolitionists were focusing on the significant number of death row inmates who had not themselves killed anyone. Most of these nontriggermen had been convicted of murder on the basis of two legal fictions. The first was the law of conspiracy, under which each member of a conspiracy is deemed to have committed every crime actually committed by any coconspirator in furtherance of the conspiracy.[2] (Remember Harry Reems.) The second legal fiction was the felony-murder rule, under which anyone who intentionally commits a serious felony, such as breaking someone out of prison, is deemed to have "intended" any death that results from the felony, even if he actually intended that no one should die.[3] The combined effect of these fictions was to deem Ricky and Raymond as guilty of intentional murder as Gary Tison and Randy Greenawalt—the men who actually pulled the trigger with intent to kill the victims.

The Tison case thus starkly presented an issue that had not clearly been resolved by the Supreme Court since the Furman case:[4] Can conspirators who helped murderers escape from prison be sentenced to death for intentional murders committed by their coconspirators, if the conspirators themselves neither killed nor intended to kill?

I was approached to help the Tison brothers in 1979 by a journalist who was working on a book project about the case (eventually a movie, called *A Killer in the Family*, was made starring Robert Mitchum as the father and James Spader—in his first major film role—as one of the brothers).[5] I was asked to appeal the brothers' death sentence. Since they had no money, I agreed to prepare and argue the appeal without a fee.

I knew the appeal would be tough because the facts of the murders were horrible and the personnel on the Supreme Court was changing in a rightward direction. The strongest point in our favor was the factual situation as it related directly to the brothers Tison. Their story was compelling.

The Tison brothers—there were three originally—grew up without a father who was there for them. They referred to Gary as their "prison father," since he had spent most of his adult life behind bars, having been convicted of armed robbery and other predatory crimes. On the way back to prison from a court appearance, Gary had killed the guard, taken his gun, and run away. He was recaptured and sentenced to life imprisonment. He began to plan his next escape—this time across the border to Mexico, which was only a two-hour drive from the prison.

Gary had to first get himself removed from the "escape risk" list and maximum security. When some young prisoners acted up, Gary helped to control them. He served on various prison committees, earning the right to have visits with his family in an outdoor recreation area. During these visits, Gary persuaded his children that it was their duty to help him escape. They were reluctant at first, but Gary persuaded them that no one would be hurt.

"We told Dad," Raymond later said, "we'll do this on one condition—that no one gets hurt."

"The more firepower you have, the less likely you'll have to use it,"

Gary assured the boys. "We'll make it out without firing a shot or being fired at. And once outside, it will be clear sailing. I know how it works. I've been there before." He had been there before, but it hadn't worked.

To the three boys, their father wasn't a killer. A guard had been accidentally shot in a scuffle. They believed their father was incapable of cold-blooded murder. Gary told them that his criminal conduct had been a result of secret training he had received in the "Service," claiming it was "top secret." They believed this fantasy like they believed everything else their father told them. "Nobody is going to get shot," their father promised.

In July 1978, the three Tison brothers arrived at the Florence State Prison with their picnic basket. Beneath the fried chicken were pistols and shotguns.

While Raymond went to meet his father in the picnic area, his brothers Ricky and Donny went into the waiting room with their basket. A friend of Gary's, Randy Greenawalt—also a convicted murderer—was in an adjoining control room. When the other visitors had left, the boys pulled out their shotguns and held the guards at bay. Raymond and Gary quickly joined them, arming themselves.

The power was turned off. And the five simply walked out the front door without a shot being fired. Gary Tison had been right—at least about the initial breakout.

Within minutes, the alarm was sounded and the manhunt was on. The escapees, who had arranged for a getaway car to be parked at a nearby hospital lot, kept to back roads. Their getaway car, an old white Lincoln, had been supplied by the boys' uncle Joe, a marijuana dealer. A tire went flat the next day, and was replaced with a spare. Later that night, another went flat. They didn't have another spare.

At about the same time, a young marine named John Lyons was driving his family on a vacation. John saw a young man standing at the side of the road next to a white Lincoln, waving his arms for assistance. At first John passed by the man seeking help, but then he changed his mind and backed his Mazda up to the Lincoln. Suddenly four more men appeared with guns drawn. They ordered the Lyons family out of the Mazda and directed them into the backseat of the Lincoln. Two of the men got into the Lincoln with them, and the others got into the Mazda.

The two cars bumped along the rocky dirt road until they reached an isolated stretch of desert. The men cleaned out the Mazda, put their guns in it, and loaded the family's suitcases into the Lincoln.

Then Gary and Randy drove the Lincoln farther into the desert. They shot holes into the engine to disable it. Gary turned to Ricky and said, "You boys go back to the Mazda and get the water jug." The brothers expressed relief that the Lyons family would be left with enough water to survive until help arrived.

As Donny, Ricky, and Ray walked toward the Mazda to get the water, Gary and Randy discussed what to do with the Lyons family. After some back-and-forth, they made their fateful decision: They would not risk the chance that the family might make it back to the main road and notify the authorities. The Lyonses pleaded for their lives, promising to remain silent. As the Tison brothers were on their way back to the Lincoln with the water jug, they heard the shotguns fire. They could see flashes of light through the darkness. Then it was quiet.

As the boys came closer they could see the devastation their father and Randy had wrought.

The two escapees had murdered an entire family—father, mother, baby, and niece—in cold blood. The brothers sat immobilized by horror as Randy Greenawalt drove them away in the Mazda.

The Arizona police soon found the Lyons family. John and his wife and baby were dead. The niece was missing, raising the fear that the Tisons had kidnapped her. Several days later she was found: She had been shot in the hip and had managed to drag herself toward the main road before bleeding to death. The family dog lay dead from dehydration a few feet away.

The disclosure of this mass murder shocked the public, who had initially followed the news of the manhunt with a mixture of fear and admiration for the daring prison escape. Now revulsion replaced admiration. The crimes were characterized by the media as "a mad-dog murder spree" and "a death orgy." The killers were described as "crazed" and "desperate." Some people refused to drive at night until the Tisons and Greenawalt were caught. Among the mothers who feared for their families was Sandra Day O'Connor, who was then serving as a Maricopa County trial judge.

The largest manhunt in Arizona history got under way, involving patrol cars, helicopters, search dogs, roadblocks, and a sophisticated communications system.

The Tisons were exhausted and low on cash. They hadn't planned for the detour caused by the flat tires and the murder of the Lyons family. Gary decided that they had to make a run for the Mexican border, risky as that was in light of the extensive manhunt.

At 2:58 in the morning of August 11, 1978, the Tison vehicle approached a police roadblock and crashed through it. The police gave chase, traveling at close to a hundred miles an hour, and called in helicopters. For a moment, Gary, who was manning the gun out the rear window, thought they had made it. Then Donny, the oldest brother, who was driving, saw a second roadblock. He crashed through it, but not before several shots from the waiting police cars struck him in the head, causing the car to crash. Gary yelled, "Every man for himself," and ran. Ricky, Ray, and Randy threw themselves to the ground.

The police found Donny, slumped in the driver's seat, unconscious from his head wounds. They handcuffed him, called an ambulance, and left him there after removing the guns from the van. At 3:40 A.M., the ambulance arrived at the scene of the roadblock. But the medics were made to wait there for more than five hours, while the life drained out of Donny's body.

The police shoved a shotgun against the back of Ricky's head and a pistol barrel into his mouth. They cut his clothes off his body. He was pulled by his hair into a police car surrounded by three officers and interrogated—naked and shivering—for five hours. When he expressed reluctance to talk, he was asked, "Do you want to see your dying brother?"

The police told Ricky and Raymond that Donny, bleeding and unconscious, would receive no medical attention until his brothers confessed. Finally, the two brothers confessed to their roles in the events surrounding the breakout. When the medics were finally allowed to go to Donny, he had bled to death.

For over a week no trace was found of Gary Tison. Police combed the desert. A SWAT team was lowered into abandoned mines and caves. Dogs were used. Rumors circulated about the fugitive's whereabouts. He was reported in dozens of locations, ranging from the Grand Canyon to southern Mexico.

Several days later, a local Native American smelled something in the underbrush. It was the decomposing body of Gary Tison. He had been hiding out in the desert, just a mile north of the roadblock. He died of dehydration on an Indian reservation, lying among the brush with a sock full of cactus berries squeezed dry near his head. Underneath him was John Lyons's pistol.

With two of the culprits now dead, public outrage focused on those who were still alive. The media zeroed in on the murdered toddler, expressing the view that "if [the brothers] hadn't gotten Gary Tison and Greenawalt out, none of this would have happened." Politicians demanded the gas chamber.

The two surviving brothers were tried and convicted of the murders. Under the laws of felony murder and conspiracy, they were as guilty of murdering the Lyons family as were the men who pulled the triggers. The judge employed the same legal fictions in sentencing them both to die in Arizona's gas chamber. My job was to try to save their lives. Other lawyers would be arguing that their confessions were involuntary.

After several unsuccessful appeals in the Arizona state courts, we decided to seek review in the Supreme Court. This decision was itself controversial within the anti–capital punishment community. The legal landscape had changed since the Supreme Court decided *Furman* and several other cases imposing restrictions on the use of the death penalty. In 1982, the justices decided the case of *Enmund v. Florida*,[6] reversing the death penalty of a defendant who had driven the "getaway" car in the armed robbery of a home in which Enmund's accomplices killed the elderly couple they had robbed. Enmund himself had not pulled the trigger, though he probably provided the gun to the man who did. That was not enough to justify the death penalty, the court ruled. The 5–4 majority went on to say that

> *it would be very different if the likelihood of a killing in the course of a robbery were so substantial that one should share the blame for the killing if he somehow participated in the felony.*[7]

The facts of the Tison case presented this question directly: Was the likelihood of the killings substantial enough that the brothers should share the blame and the death penalty? We believed the answer was no. But there had been an important change of personnel in the high court between the time Enmund was decided and the filing of our petition for review. Justice Antonin Scalia had joined the court, and he soon became its most outspoken critic of the campaign to abolish the death penalty. William Rehnquist, also a strong supporter of capital punishment and an Arizona resident who was aware of the Tison rampage, was now the chief justice. Justice Sandra Day O'Connor, who had lived in that state during the murder spree, had dissented in *Enmund* and might now be in a position to turn her dissent into a majority decision, because Justice Byron White, who had written the majority opinion in *Enmund*, had seemed to be backtracking a bit in subsequent cases.

Before we decided to file our petition for a writ of certiorari—an application requesting the justices to exercise their discretion to review the case—I had received several phone calls from anti–capital punishment lawyers with whom I had previously worked, imploring me not to seek Supreme Court review in the Tison case. "Count the noses," one of them warned. "You may not have five anymore." He urged me to leave well enough alone: "We have *Enmund*. Most courts will follow *Enmund* and reverse felony-murder death sentences. But if the Supremes take your case and reverse or limit *Enmund*, people will die because of you. You have to go by the numbers."[8]

I understood his reference to "the numbers" as meaning two different things: First, the numbers on the Supreme Court, which now might be 5–4 against us. And second, the large number of condemned inmates who faced execution on a theory similar to that which had led the judge in Arizona to sentence the Tison brothers to die even though they had not killed the Lyons family or intended their death.

I respected the insights and judgments of the callers, but I had two actual clients on death row. I was *their* lawyer, not the lawyer for the many other death row inmates whose fates could be adversely affected by a negative ruling in our case. I cared deeply about every inmate facing the death penalty, as I did about the issue itself. But I could not allow these strong feelings to influence my decision regarding my clients. I was the only person between them and the canisters of death that stood ready to end their young lives. At that moment in time, I was not a "capital punishment" lawyer or a "cause" lawyer. I was Ricky and Raymond's lawyer. They desperately wanted to live, as they told me, tearfully, when we met on death row. Following our meeting, I had nightmares in which I visualized the two boys being pulled out of my arms and strapped into the chairs as the lethal gas ended their lives. I also had nightmares about the Lyons family desperately but futily begging for their lives, as Gary and Randy aimed shotguns at them. But I could not, even in my dreams, save the lives of the Lyons family. I could, in reality, try to save the lives of Ricky and Raymond Tison.

I had to put case before cause, client before campaign, the Tison brothers before the others on death row. It was an excruciating emotional conflict, but not a difficult legal or ethical decision.

I decided to file a petition for certiorari to the Supreme Court. Our hope was that the justices would not want to hear full argument on an issue they had so recently considered: namely, the constitutionality of the death penalty for defendants who had not been the triggermen in a crime that had resulted in the death of the victim. We hoped the justices would simply "remand the case for reconsideration in light of *Enmund*." In other words, that they would send the case back to the Arizona courts so that those judges could apply the *Enmund* precedent to the facts of the Tison case. That would have been the best of all possible worlds. The court would have reaffirmed *Enmund* as the binding precedent and sent a strong message to the state courts to be sure to follow that precedent, thus saving the lives of the dozens of similarly situated defendants on death row. And it would have saved the lives of Ricky and Raymond. But it was not to be. To our disappointment and worry, the justices granted review and set the case down for briefing and argument.

Generally, lawyers are ecstatic when the high court grants review of one of their cases. It means that they will have the privilege of arguing before the Supreme Court—a rare honor that few lawyers experience. It also means they will have an opportunity to influence the development of constitutional law—a knife that cuts both ways, since the influence may be positive or negative.

In this case, I was far from ecstatic, since the granting of review so soon after the divided decision in *Enmund* signaled a desire on the part of at least some of the justices to reconsider and perhaps reverse or limit *Enmund*. Justice Scalia had already made it clear that he had little respect for past precedents, especially recent ones. His oath, he insisted, was to uphold the Constitution, not the erroneous precedents of the Supreme Court. The next to last thing I wanted to be was the vehicle by which the justices would shift the existing trend in favor of contracting the death penalty to a trend in favor of expanding it. The last thing I wanted to be was the lawyer who not only expanded the reach of the death penalty but also caused the execution of my own clients. The stakes were enormous, both for the Tison brothers and for the many other death row inmates who had not been triggermen—as well as for the campaign against capital punishment.

In preparing for the oral argument, I read the trial and sentencing transcripts not only of the Tison case, but also of the Enmund case, which I knew would be the basis of questions from the justices.[9]

I began my argument with a simple statement that I thought would be beyond dispute: "The State of Arizona seeks to execute two young men who it acknowledges lacked the specific intent to kill, and did not, in fact, kill."

I was immediately interrupted by Justice White, the author of the

Enmund majority opinion, on which I was relying: "Did you say the state concedes what?"

I repeated my point: "The state concedes that there was no specific intent to kill, and that there was no killing."

Justice White pressed me: "What do you mean by that?"

I explained that no one had ever suggested that the brothers specifically intended to kill the Lyons family. Indeed, it was clear from the record that they specifically intended *not* to kill and that Gary and Randy had to trick the brothers into going for water before opening fire. I also pointed to a finding by the Arizona Supreme Court that the murder of the Lyons family was not part of the original plan and was utterly "unnecessary" to the escape. I told the court, "There is no evidence to support a finding for specific intent."

The justice immediately shot back, "Well, if that's true, of course, that's the end of the case."

I was pleased by his assessment and immediately agreed with it: "That's the end of the case. Your Honor, we think that's the end of the case."

But it was far from the end of the case, at least in the minds of some of the justices. The recently appointed Antonin Scalia came after me with a hypothetical case, an exercise I was thoroughly familiar with, since it is the weapon of choice for law professors, which Scalia had been before ascending the bench.

Scalia asked me what my position would be if one bank robber had a gun and the other one didn't, and the one with the gun "throw[s] the gun to the triggerman, as the policeman's approaching him."

I had prepared for every likely question I might be asked by the justices, but the idea of a gun being thrown by one robber to another had never occurred to me. In the classroom, a poor answer to a professor's bizarre "hypo" might reduce a grade, but in the courtroom it could be a matter of life and death. I quickly recalled the facts of the Enmund case and reminded the justices that Enmund too had provided a gun to his co-conspirators, who then killed the couple, and that there was no difference between "throwing" a gun, as in Scalia's hypothetical, and "providing" a gun, as in the real facts of *Enmund*.

Scalia repeated his hypothetical: "Please, please. I don't understand your response to the . . . hypothetical I put to you. Never mind the triggerman. The person who tosses the gun to the triggerman. There is no way in which he has an intent to kill within the constitutional rule; is that right? . . . He doesn't care whether the policeman lives or dies."

Scalia persisted: "But the triggerman asks for a gun. 'Toss me a gun.' He tosses him the gun. . . . That wouldn't be enough?"

I was reminded of Chief Justice Burger's bear-baiting hypothetical in the *I Am Curious (Yellow)* case, but this time the stakes were much higher. I answered the justice's question: "No. That wouldn't be enough. And that is not this case in any event. This case is handing guns over, under an agreement that no shooting would take place. In *Enmund* the guns were also provided. What Your Honor, Justice Scalia, is asking for, in a sense, is a return to the felony-murder rule where guns are provided."

Justice Scalia didn't seem satisfied with my answer, so I threw a hypothetical back to him—law professor to law professor: "And to throw a hypothetical back, which I'm not entitled to do, but I'll throw it back to myself. . . . What if there were a statute saying anyone who provides guns to an armed robber in the course of an armed robbery whereby death results is guilty of first-degree capital murder? That would be clearly within *Enmund*. That's what *Enmund* decided. Because the facts of *Enmund* were exactly that."

The dialogue continued, with Justice Scalia asking me whether Enmund himself had "provided the gun" to the actual triggerman.

I was prepared for this question because I had read the transcript of the Enmund case in anticipation of being asked about it. The only advantage a lawyer has over the judges in arguing on appeal is superior knowledge of the facts of the case. That's why I always immerse myself in these facts before arguing. I was ready to respond to Justice Scalia's challenge: "The state certainly argued that [Mr. Enmund] had provided the gun in [the Enmund case]. The gun had belonged to his common law wife. He then disposed of the gun. Certainly, a reasonable judge and jury could conclude that he had provided the gun."

I then compared the facts in *Enmund* to those in *Tison*: "[Enmund] was the one who planned the robbery. In this case, these young boys were brought in . . . at the last minute. One of the codefendants, Greenawalt, directed what went on in the penitentiary. Their father directed what went on thereafter. There was never a time when they could have left their father's side, when the father left any of them alone, the three of them, so that they could leave. These are young kids under the control of their father."

I concluded my opening argument by acknowledging the responsibility of the brothers for the prison escape, but insisting that they could not be executed for the unanticipated murders: "Nobody is denying their responsibility for these serious crimes of kidnapping, breakout of prison. But then after the crime was completed, after the car was taken, the father then, without any necessity . . . as the courts found—no necessity at all—could have easily have left them there . . . the father and the other defendant, on their own, after sending the boys away, made a shocking and surprising decision to kill this family in cold blood. This is just like *Enmund*. In *Enmund* there was spontaneity. It was not part of the original plan. After the co-defendants left Enmund and went into the house, something unexpected happened. In this case it was the father who did something unexpected. In the [Enmund] case it was the gunman. A family was tragically killed in both cases. This Arizona case is an attempt to relitigate *Enmund*."

I then made a final pragmatic appeal to the court's own overcrowded docket, about which several of the justices had frequently complained: "And we will hear relitigation after relitigation in every state if this court allows every state to redefine intent the way it chooses to redefine it."

I sat down, satisfied that I had made the best possible argument for my clients. Now it was the State of Arizona's time to argue. The attorney general was hardly interrupted as he delivered his argument. After a while, he too was asked a hypothetical, but one much closer to the facts of this case: "Supposing right after they stopped the car with the family in it, the two boys, instead of following along as they did, had just gone on a hike, walked away half a mile, and then the father . . . killed the family?"

The attorney general seemed unprepared for this question and made an important concession, acknowledging that this "would be different" and that the brothers' "presence at the scene" was "essential." He insisted, however, that they *were* "present," even if not right next to the car in which the shootings occurred. He also conceded that "I can't stand here today and tell you that [the brothers] knew . . . at that time that the trigger would be pulled."

I had just a few minutes for my rebuttal. In light of the attorney general's concessions, I decided to point the court to the record evidence that the brothers were not at the scene of the crime and did not foresee that their father and Randy would kill the Lyons family: "First, there is a specific finding [by the lower court] on page 336 that it was not essential to the defendants' continued evasion of arrest that these persons be murdered. Second . . . there is not a single statement in this record [that] does not consistently say that the boys, all three of them, were sent away to get water."

I then pointed out that the evidence in this case led overwhelmingly to the conclusion that they were not present and that they had deliberately been sent away to get water—been tricked into believing the family would be kept alive—precisely because their father knew that they did not want anyone to die. Picking up on the attorney general's surprising concession, I pointed out that "the state concedes that it is essential to this case that they be present at the scene of the crime. Why is presence essential? [Because it is] relevant to the intent of the defendants [, and the defendants' intent was to ensure that the Lyons remain alive]."

I was satisfied that I had done the best I could with the facts and the law. If the court were to reaffirm the principles of *Enmund*, and apply them fairly to the facts of our case, we would win. The justices seemed to acknowledge that if there was no evidence that Ricky and Raymond had the "specific intent" to kill the Lyons family, "that's the end of the case." I was confident that when the justices reviewed the entire record, which clearly they had not done prior to the argument, they would find that there was no such evidence.

And I was right—at least about that!

Several months after the argument, I received a midmorning phone call from the ABC News legal reporter.

"They just decided the Tison case," he told me.

"Did we win or lose?" I asked nervously.

"I can't tell. It's quite confusing. It's five to four. Let me fax you the opinion. And you tell me."

I read each page as it came out of the fax machine.

The majority opinion began its analysis with the following acknowledgment:

> *Petitioners argue strenuously that they did not "intend to kill" as that concept has been generally understood in the common law.* We accept this as true. . . . *As petitioners point out, there is no evidence that either Ricky or Raymond Tison took any act which he desired to, or was substantially certain would, cause death.*[10]

When I read these words, I thought that we had surely won a complete victory. That was precisely what I had argued. The court had accepted my argument in full. It should have followed from this acceptance that, in the words of one of the justices, "that's the end of the case." But it was only the beginning.

I suspected we might be in trouble when I saw that Justice Sandra Day O'Connor, who had dissented in *Enmund*, was now writing the majority opinion in the Tison case. After acknowledging that I was right about the Tison brothers not having intended to kill, as intent had been traditionally understood by the law, Justice O'Connor proceeded to move the goal line, by expressing dissatisfaction with the traditional rule that had been established in *Enmund*:

> *A narrow focus on the question of whether or not a given defendant "intended to kill," however, is a highly unsatisfactory means of definitively distinguishing the most culpable and dangerous of murderers. Many who intend to, and do, kill are not criminally liable at all—those who act in self-defense or with other justification or excuse. Other intentional homicides, though criminal, are often felt undeserving of the death penalty—those that are the result of provocation. On the other hand, some nonintentional murderers may be among the most dangerous and inhumane of all—the person who tortures another not caring whether the victim lives or dies, or the robber who shoots someone in the course of the robbery, utterly indifferent to the fact that the desire to rob may have the unintended consequence of killing the victim as well as taking the victim's property. This reckless indifference to the value of human life may be every bit as shocking to the moral sense as an "intent to kill."*[11]

She then went on to create an entirely new category of crime that warranted execution even in the absence of a specific intent to kill:

> *We hold that the reckless disregard for human life implicit in knowingly engaging in criminal activities known to carry a grave risk of death represents a highly culpable mental state, a mental state that may be taken into account in making a capital sentencing judgment when that conduct causes its natural, though also not inevitable, lethal result.*[12]

This new category—a killing by a triggerman that reflected "a reckless disregard" for life by the nontriggerman—had not been the basis for the Arizona court's decision. Nor had it been argued by the Arizona attorney general. Neither had we been given an opportunity to argue against it, because the justices seemed to agree that if there was no intent to kill—which they had now ruled there was *not*—that would be "the end of the case." The majority had simply concocted a new rule out of whole cloth and applied it in ex post facto fashion to our case. They seemed determined to overrule *Enmund*, without appearing to be doing so. It was judicial activism to the extreme.

But the Supreme Court could not simply apply this new rule to the old facts of the Tison case. The Arizona courts had never found that the condemned brothers had shown "a reckless disregard for human life,"[13] since that was not the governing criterion prior to the Supreme Court announcing its brand-new rule. As I read the last words of the majority opinion, I saw that they had "vacated" the death penalty against my clients and remanded the case back to the Arizona courts "for determination" whether the Tison brothers met this new criterion. Had they simply "affirmed" the judgment—the death sentence—the case would have been over, and the Tison brothers would have been gassed to death, but by "vacating" the death sentence, the justices gave us a new beginning.

We were still alive. More important, so were Ricky and Raymond. Their fates would now be in the hands of the Arizona courts, which could not order them executed unless they could make a finding that these boys had shown "reckless indifference" or "disregard" for human life. The concessions made by the attorney general in response to the justices' questions would help us demonstrate that the Tison brothers did not fit this new criterion. It was a bad day for the campaign against capital punishment, but a hopeful one for my clients Ricky and Raymond, who were no longer under sentence of death—at least for the moment.

The State of Arizona continued to seek the death penalty and asked the trial court to find that the Tison brothers possessed "a reckless indifference to human life." Without even conducting an evidentiary hearing, the trial court reimposed death sentences, concluding that the trial record itself demonstrated reckless indifference. The judge refused to allow us to introduce any evidence that might contradict his "finding." A new execution date was set.

We appealed to the Arizona Supreme Court, which had affirmed the original death sentence. This time the court unanimously reversed the trial judge, vacated the death sentences, and remanded the case back to the trial judge, ordering him to give us an opportunity to introduce "additional evidence" relating to whether the boys were recklessly indifferent to human life. We relished the opportunity, confident that a full exploration of the facts would lead to the inescapable conclusion that Ricky and Raymond were anything but indifferent to the fate of the Lyons family. They desperately wanted them to live.

Eventually, after a long and torturous road through the Arizona courts, the death penalties against Ricky and Raymond Tison were reversed. They would not be executed, despite the Supreme Court's green light. Once again, as with the issue of obscenity, the high court did not get the last word. We refused to give up, and in the end we prevailed. Ricky and Raymond will be eligible for parole and may eventually go free after serving long prison terms. Greenawalt, the actual triggerman, who was represented by other lawyers, was executed.

Following the reversal of their death penalties, one of the brothers wrote me a letter from prison saying that his minister had told him that Jews can't go to heaven. My client pleaded with me to convert to Christianity so that we could spend eternity in the same place. I wrote him a nice letter back saying that Jews believe that they can go to heaven. He wrote back telling me that he had decided to become a Jew, because he wanted to be sure he would be in the same heaven alongside the man who had saved his life. I replied, assuring him that Jews and Christians go to the same heaven, so that he didn't have to convert.[14]

15

USING SCIENCE, LAW, LOGIC, AND EXPERIENCE TO DISPROVE MURDER

Von Bülow, Simpson, Sybers, Murphy, and MacDonald

INTRODUCTION

In 1881, Oliver Wendell Holmes, Jr., taught us that the life of the law has not been logic—it has been experience.[1] Recent experience has dramatically changed the way murders are prosecuted and defended.

The crime of murder is as old as human nature. Virtually every important work of fiction and nonfiction includes accounts of murder, or murder trials, and of unsolved homicides. The Bible recounts the murder of Abel by Cain.[2] That crime was solved by God questioning Cain: "Where is your brother Abel?" Cain's evasive answer—"Am I my brother's keeper?"—convinced God, and the reader, of Cain's guilt.[3] Shakespeare's "perfect" murder is committed by Hamlet's uncle pouring poison into the ear of the king.[4] That crime too is solved by provoking the killer into demonstrating his guilty conscience. Both the Bible and Shakespeare also recount cases in which innocent people are framed by planted evidence: Potaphor's wife frames Joseph;[5] and Iago frames Desdemona.[6] Dostoevsky creates an interrogator so subtle that Raskolnikov needs to confess.[7] Sherlock Holmes solves murders through observation, deduction, and primitive science. Then came the lie detector, ballistics testing, fingerprint matching, voice analysis, and other techniques that purported to be based on science.[8]

Throughout history, we have relied on eyewitnesses, informers, and accessories. Now we have DNA.

DNA and other recent scientific developments have cast doubt upon the previous techniques of solving homicide cases. Defendants who had been convicted on the basis of confessions, eyewitness testimony, ballistics, fiber, hair, fingerprints, voice analysis, accomplice testimony, and other "reliable" indicia of guilt have been exonerated by DNA and other scientific breakthroughs. Some who were not suspected have now been convicted on the basis of this new science.

The pervasiveness of surveillance cameras, social media, and other means of recording events has also contributed to the increasing accuracy of detecting homicides and other serious crimes, as have more sophisticated forensic testing and better crime laboratories. Without these new technologies it is unlikely that the Boston Marathon bombers would have been so quickly identified.

Every technique for solving homicides can also be used to defend against false charges of homicide. Every prosecutorial sword can become a shield in the hands of an astute criminal defense lawyer.

Most of my murder and attempted murder cases have been appeals from convictions. I've handled a few trials, and I wish I could have done more—I love developing evidence and arguing to juries. But my teaching commitments are more conducive to arguing hour-long appeals than month-long trials.

In many of my cases, I use science not only as a shield to protect my client, but also as a sword to prove misconduct on the part of the prosecution, police, or laboratory technicians.

My emphasis on scientific evidence led me early in my career to realize that the traditional way of arguing appeals did not maximize the chances of success. The rules for an appeal provide that only errors made at trial may be raised and argued on appeal. All other issues, such as newly discovered evidence, ineffective assistance of counsel, and prosecutorial misconduct discovered after trial, must be raised on what is called "collateral attack"—by a writ of habeas corpus or other procedures that are disfavored by courts. I came to realize that appellate judges, like all human beings, care more about whether a defendant is guilty or innocent than about whether there was a technical mistake at the trial. This perception was solidified by the approach many judges, such as the respected Henry Friendly, espoused: that innocence or guilt should play a greater role in reviewing convictions than what they called "technicalities."[9] This approach has led to a dramatic expansion of the concept of "harmless error," which means that no matter how serious the errors made at the trial, the conviction will still be affirmed if the errors did not influence the jury's verdict—that is, if the evidence of guilt is overwhelming.[10] The upshot of this expansion is that in order to win an appeal in a criminal case, the appellate lawyer must cast doubt on his client's guilt.

Accordingly, I developed a technique, which has now been adopted by other lawyers, under which I tried to combine the appeal and habeas corpus aspects of the case into one challenge to the conviction. As soon as I am retained to do an appeal, I gather together a legal team that includes investigators, law students, and experts in other disciplines, such as medicine and forensics. (My students call this my *Mission: Impossible* team, based on the television show and movies in which the leader assembles a team of specialists to undertake "impossible" national security missions.) I direct my team to investigate the case from scratch. If the investigation then turns up new information suggestive of innocence, I quickly file a habeas corpus petition and do not wait for the outcome of the appeal. If the petition is denied, as petitions often are by the trial judge, I then try to combine it with the appeal so that the appellate court has a fuller view of the actual situation. I did this in the Claus von Bülow case. The court reversed that conviction not only because of errors made at trial, but because of new evidence of innocence that we had discovered after the trial. I have used this approach, often quite successfully, in many of my appeals, especially those involving homicides, where new evidence frequently emerges.

I suspect that some of my clients, including some whose cases I have won, have been guilty. I know that some have been innocent. As to the majority, I am not certain. There is a myth that criminal defense lawyers always know whether their clients are guilty, because guilty clients confess in confidence. This has certainly not been my experience. Of the three dozen or so homicide cases in which I have been involved, only one client has confessed his guilt to me. I won that case on the basis of constitutional issues.[11] I have never had a case in which I have helped to free a guilty client who then killed again. I tell my clients that under no circumstances will I represent them a second time.[12]

The question I am asked most often—by students, friends, family, and strangers—is, Why do you or how can you represent such awful people who you know or suspect are guilty of committing horrible crimes, especially murder? (Nearly everyone seems to understand why, as a lifelong opponent of capital punishment, I would represent guilty defendants who were sentenced to death, in an effort to save their lives.)

My initial answer—and not a particularly satisfying one—is "That's my job." All criminal defense lawyers represent some guilty defendants, for the obvious reason that most criminal defendants are guilty. And that's a good thing. Would anyone want to live in a country in which most criminal defendants were innocent? That may have been true of Stalin's Soviet Union, when the head of the secret police, Laurenty Beria, told Stalin, "Point me to the man, and I will find the crime." It may still be true in today's Iran, where dissidents are killed without any semblance of justice, or in other countries were defense attorneys are forbidden to defend clients with zeal. It is not true in the United States, which has a long tradition—dating back to John Adams, who defended the British soldiers accused of committing the Boston Massacre—of lawyers zealously defending even the most despised of accused criminals.

A zealous American defense attorney has the opportunity to challenge the government's case against his client at different points in the process, because the evidence of guilt must pass through several gatekeepers before a defendant can be imprisoned or executed. These include the arresting police officers; the assistant prosecutor, who makes the initial charging decision; the senior prosecutor, who approves that decision; the grand jury (in those jurisdictions that require a grand jury indictment),[13] the initial judge, who must decide whether to dismiss the case; the petit jury, which must decide whether to convict the defendant; the trial judge, who must decide whether to grant a motion to acquit; and the various appellate courts that must review the conviction.

It should come as no surprise therefore that, according to the Supreme Court, approximately 97 percent of federal convictions and 94 percent of state convictions are the result of guilty pleas,[14] and that of those defendants who go to trial 93 percent are convicted.[15] Think about that for a moment. It means that only a tiny fraction of Americans who are indicted or otherwise formally charged with crimes are acquitted. This is very different from the media perception, fueled by fictional accounts of Perry Mason–type lawyers who always get their clients off, and by real-life criticism of lawyers who do occasionally win cases for defendants who the public believe are guilty. One reason for this disparity between perception and reality is that a high percentage of Americans who are charged with crime are guilty. But another reason is that the current system—which rewards pleading guilty and punishes pleading innocent—places enormous pressure on defendants and their lawyers to cop a plea. I know of at least some arguably innocent defendants who have "chosen" to plead guilty in order to assure a relatively low sentence, rather than risk a much greater one if convicted. I even recommended such a tactic to one client, who rejected my advice, was convicted, and was sentenced to eleven years in prison instead of the one-year suspended sentence he could have received had he pleaded guilty to a "crime" he did not commit.

Since I am primarily an appellate lawyer, by the time a case comes to me, it has passed through all but the appellate gatekeepers. The most obviously innocent defendants rarely make it past these gatekeepers, so the ones who get to me are—as a statistical matter—very likely to be guilty. Nevertheless, I fight hard to try to get their convictions reversed. This is always an uphill struggle, since only a tiny fraction of criminal convictions are reversed on appeal. In the federal system, that number is in the 5 to 6 percent range.[16] In the state system, it is even lower.[17] In some state appellate courts, the rate of reversal in criminal cases is as low as 1 or 2 percent.

A good lawyer can change these daunting odds, not because good lawyers are more likely to represent innocent defendants, but because having a good lawyer increases the chances of winning, whether the client is innocent or guilty. By challenging the prosecution at every turn, and winning close cases more often than bad lawyers, the zealous defense lawyer puts considerable pressure on prosecutors to bring charges only against those defendants who are likely to be convicted, even if defended zealously. This check on prosecutorial power would diminish if defense attorneys were willing to defend only obviously innocent defendants. So one important reason I zealously defend the probably guilty is to protect the possibly innocent from being falsely charged.

It is also true, however, that in a system under which zealous lawyers are willing to defend the guilty as well as the innocent—and all the gray cases in between—the end result will be the acquittal of some guilty and bad defendants. I know, because I have helped bring about such results. But I have also helped to free some innocent defendants whom nearly everyone believed to be guilty.

Although there have been cases throughout our history in which innocent people have been wrongly convicted, some even executed, our system still boasts of very high percentage of just outcomes—that is, cases where the guilty are convicted and the innocent acquitted. Obviously no one can reliably calculate the number or percentage of mistakes our system makes, but there are probably more cases where the guilty are acquitted than where the innocent are convicted. That is as it should be in a system that boasts "better ten guilty be wrongfully acquitted than even one innocent wrongly convicted." Yet the public complaints seem to be louder and angrier when defendants who are perceived to be guilty are freed than when the possibly innocent are wrongly imprisoned.

There have been periods during our history when lawyers were afraid to defend certain kinds of people—blacks in the South during Jim Crow, accused Communists during McCarthyism, suspected terrorists in the post-9/11 age. These were not our finest hours, and it would not be surprising if during these periods, the percentage of innocent defendants who were convicted increased (particularly among those in the despised groups).

No lawyer can accept every client who seeks representation. We are entitled to pick and choose, within certain limits, among the cases offered us. We are also entitled to decide which cases to handle on a pro bono basis and for which to charge fees, although there is now a movement in some states to require lawyers to accept some pro bono cases. Over my own career, I have sought to strike a balance by charging fees in about half my cases and charging no fees in the other half. I do not treat paying and nonpaying clients differently, and my win-loss percentage is about the same in both categories.

In a Massachusetts case a feminist attorney who specializes in representing women in divorce cases refused to represent a male nurse's aide who was seeking financial support from his wealthy wife, who was a doctor. The lawyer told the man that she simply did not accept male clients in divorce cases, even if winning for the man would help the cause of women.[18] A panel of the Massachusetts Commission Against Discrimination ruled "that an attorney [holding herself] out as open to the public may not reject a potential client solely on the basis of gender or some other protected class."[19] In other words, a lawyer may be a *feminist*, but not a *sexist*. The distinction may be subtle, but it is real.

In the end, I hope lawyers will not need laws to tell them that they should represent those most in need of zealous advocacy, without regard to gender, race, ideology, economic situation, or popularity. Such an approach will make for a better legal system and a freer America.

The one thing a lawyer is never free to do is accept a case and pursue it without zeal or adequate preparation. Although there are no specific criteria for measuring these qualities, there certainly are general guidelines. Being someone's lawyer is different from being their friend. For a friend or relative, you may be willing to sacrifice your life, your liberty, or your fortune. You need not—and should not—do that for a client. Zealous advocacy has limits imposed by law, ethics, and common sense. We know what unzealous representation means. Just look at some of the capital case lawyers in Texas! Several fell asleep during trial..(In one capital case that I appealed, the lawyer fell asleep during the trial, but *that* was his finest hour, because when he was awake he hurt his client by telling the jury that he didn't believe his own client's testimony!)[20] (The same lawyer—a former Klansman representing a black defendant accused of killing a white state trooper—refused to conduct any investigation in black neighborhoods.) Many judges prefer underzealous to overzealous lawyers. That's why they appoint the former—who make their job easier, if they define their job as sentencing as many defendants as possible to death. Overzealous lawyers are a pain in the ass to some judges. I know. I am one. We make their job harder by contesting every issue, demanding every right, and disputing every prosecutorial allegation, so long as it is in the best interest of the client. That is the key to defining appropriately zealous advocacy: It must always be in the legitimate interest of the client. Its purpose is not to make you feel good or virtuous, but to help the client—whether innocent or guilty—win (or get the best result) by any ethical and lawful means.

I'm proud to be a criminal defense lawyer who stands up to the government and defends people without regard to their possible guilt or innocence, though it sometimes pains me to win cases on behalf of awful people who have done terrible things. I don't celebrate such victories, though I understand—as an intellectual matter—that the occasional wrongful acquittal of the guilty is the price we pay for preserving the important principle that it is better for the guilty to be acquitted than for the innocent to be convicted. The occasional conviction of the innocent is the price we pay for having a necessarily imperfect justice system, run by fallible human beings, but it is a very high price that we should do everything to avoid, or at least minimize.[21]

"Don't you ask your clients whether they're innocent or guilty?" is another common question. I don't, at least not directly, because the guilty ones would simply lie, and I wouldn't know enough to believe the innocent ones. The nature of my initial conversation with a client will depend on the stage of the case. If a client seeks my help before trial, it is essential that I know whether he is guilty or innocent (or somewhere in between). Without knowing what actually happened, I would not be able to advise my client whether to cooperate with law enforcement, consent to a search, testify, or try to make a plea bargain. If a client retains me after he has been convicted, it is less important for me to know whether he is innocent or guilty, because the appeal will be based on the trial record, which cannot be changed. I would still like to know, because the facts may influence my decision whether to conduct further investigation and file additional motions and petitions for habeas corpus.

The way I generally approach the issue of innocence or guilt is to ask my client what his worst enemy would say about him or what the most damning evidence against him might be. In this way, the client can, in effect, tell me what probably happened, without acknowledging his own guilt.

One reason why defendants so often lie to their lawyers is that they think a lawyer will work harder for a client he believes is innocent than for one he knows is guilty. That may well be true—at least for some lawyers. I don't think it is true of me, but I can't be absolutely sure. Even so, most lawyers are experienced enough to regard a self-serving claim of innocence with suspicion.

In an abundance of caution, I initially presume that *all* clients are probably guilty. I know this violates the spirit of "the presumption of innocence," but it is essential to protecting the rights of the client. If a lawyer too quickly presumes his client innocent, he is more likely to make a mistake, such as allowing the police or prosecutor to speak to the client or search his house or office. Just as a cautious doctor should initially presume his patient sick—treating a chest pain in an elderly patient as a possible coronary event rather than indigestion—so too a cautious lawyer should presume that his client "did it," rather than that he was "framed." It follows from this presumption of guilt that the defendant should not speak to law enforcement officials or allow them to conduct searches unless and until that presumption has been overcome by hard evidence of innocence and clear indications that there is more to gain than to lose by such cooperation.

I see my job as trying to reverse the presumption of guilt—the realistic presumption shared by prosecutors, judges, and jurors despite the theoretical presumption of innocence mandated by the Constitution. Once a defendant has been indicted, the burden of proof rests on him, in practice, even though the judge will instruct the jury that the prosecution always bears a heavy burden of proving guilt beyond a reasonable doubt. The common view is that if the defendant were actually innocent, he never would have been arrested, indicted, and put on trial. "Where there's smoke . . ."

This perception is even more powerful after a defendant has been found guilty by a jury and is appealing the conviction or challenging it by a writ of habeas corpus. At that point he has lost the constitutional presumption of innocence, and everyone in the system presumes him guilty both as a matter of law and of fact. That's when I generally come into a case.

The odds against reversing a criminal conviction have always been daunting, because the vast majority of those convicted are factually guilty, and appellate courts are reluctant to free guilty defendants on the basis of "legal technicalities," even when such technicalities are rooted in the Constitution.

For example, when I signed on to handle the appeal of Claus von Bülow in 1982, the media was understandably skeptical. *New York* magazine quoted "one of the country's leading criminal lawyers" predicting that I would lose the appeal: "He'll add something useful and do a brilliant analysis of the record. He isn't going to make it. Of some guys you can say 'That's a patient he isn't going to save. He can only make him more comfortable.'"[22] *Esquire* magazine commented that the von Bülow appeal "looked like another ritualistic exercise in civil libertarian dogma" that "would churn through the courts simply because there was money available and a set of arguments that could be made, rather than because [I] had any real sense that justice had in some way gone astray."[23] And one commentator snidely observed that von Bülow's "recruitment of Harvard Law Professor Alan Dershowitz shortly after his conviction would tend to reinforce" the view that Claus von Bülow "was no longer protesting his innocence, merely the methods used to catch him. . . . Dershowitz enjoys a wide reputation as a last resort for convicted criminals, being especially keen at finding legal loopholes that render his clients' convictions unconstitutional."[24]

It is precisely because this perception is so widespread that I always try to find an "innocence" argument to present to the appellate court, along with the constitutional and other legalistic arguments. Often the court will use the "hook" of the legal argument on which to hang its decision to reverse, but it will be more motivated to "find" that hook if the judges have doubts about the defendant's factual guilt. It is my job to find and plant those seeds of doubt, based, whenever possible, on scientific or forensic evidence.

O. J. SIMPSON AND CLAUS VON BÜLOW

My two most famous—infamous?—cases involved homicide: the O. J. Simpson double murder prosecution and the Claus von Bülow assault with intent to kill (or attempted murder) prosecution. I have written books about both these cases,[25] and I will not repeat what I wrote, except to highlight how important it is for lawyers, especially those involved in complex homicide cases, to master the science, to be able to question the other side's scientific conclusions, and to accept nothing on face value.

I agreed to join the O. J. Simpson defense team, despite my earlier public statements that the evidence pointed to him as the likely killer,[26] because Simpson was facing the death penalty, and I have a policy of generally accepting capital cases.

Eventually the district attorney decided not to seek the death penalty. This was surprising, because if Simpson did, in fact, murder his wife and the man she was with, the death penalty would seem appropriate under the usual criteria for imposing it. The killings seemed to be in cold blood, especially brutal, and there were two victims, one of whom may have been killed because he was a witness. The fact that the district attorney opted against it, demonstrated, once again, the entirely arbitrary nature of decision making as it relates to who is and who is not subjected to capital punishment. The decision not to ask for the death penalty against O. J. Simpson was especially surprising since prosecutors often seek capital punishment in order to gain a tactical advantage at the guilt or innocence phase of the trial. This advantage derives from the fact that in death penalty cases, the prosecutor is entitled to a "death qualified" jury consisting of twelve people who have no conscientious objection to capital punishment and would be willing to sentence someone to death. Such jurors, according to jury experts, tend to be proprosecution in general and more likely to vote guilty. Prosecutors know this and ask for the death penalty even in cases not warranting it, simply to improve the chances of securing a conviction. Once they get their proprosecution jury, they sometimes decline to seek the death penalty. Early in my career, I was retained by F. Lee Bailey to prepare a petition for certiorari to the Supreme Court challenging this practice. The Supreme Court granted my petition for review, but then after oral argument by Bailey, the justices denied the review over a strong dissent.[27]

In any event, having agreed to join the Simpson defense team, I couldn't abandon my client, even though the death penalty was now off the table.

Simpson still faced life imprisonment without the possibility of parole—for some a fate worse than death.

My role in the case was to prepare and argue complex legal motions and to help formulate the scientific, or forensic, defense. I would also argue the appeal in the event of a conviction. Simpson called me his "God forbid" lawyer. I recommended that Barry Scheck and Peter Neufeld, who were experts in the relatively new science of DNA, be added to the team.

VIGNETTE

O.J.'s Glove

I happened to be on the way to Australia to deliver a talk. There was a stopover in Los Angeles and I decided to pay a visit to the O.J. trial. My usual role was to provide legal briefs from my office in Cambridge. On two or three occasions I appeared in court to argue motions, but these appearances were rare and episodic. On this day, I had no real business to conduct in the courtroom, but when my son picked me up at the airport, I suggested that we drop by and say hello and join the legal team for lunch. My son turned on the radio, which was carrying the trial live. The man on the witness stand was an expert in gloves. He was testifying in the most tedious manner, about the stitching in gloves. We practically fell asleep listening. Elon begged me not to go to the courthouse, but I insisted. Upon entering the courthouse, I sat down next to the lawyers, and my son sat in the spectator section. Within five minutes of our appearance in court, Prosecutor Darden got up and asked to have O.J. try on the glove. It was about the dumbest ploy any prosecutor could have attempted, since under California law, he could have insisted that O.J. try on the glove outside the presence of the jury, before he decided to conduct this experiment in front of the jury. But Darden was not one for legal subtlety. O.J. walked right next to me, tried on the glove, and in the most dramatic moment of the long trial, stood in front of the jury, and showed them that it didn't fit. He even testified, "It's too small."

Shortly after this dramatic moment, the lunch recess was called, and I went to O.J.'s holding cell behind the courtroom and told him that they might ask him to try on the glove without the latex underglove he wore during the courtroom experiment. He assured me that it still wouldn't fit.

My grandmother would have said, "It was *bashert*"—ordained—that I would be in the courtroom just at the moment that led to the famous closing argument "If it doesn't fit, you must acquit."[28]

After extensive investigation, we were able to demonstrate, by means of sophisticated scientific evidence, that the police had planted O.J. Simpson's blood, along with the blood of his alleged victims, on a sock found in Simpson's bedroom after the crime. The blood on the sock had high levels of a chemical that is not found in human blood, but that is added to vials of blood to prevent it from coagulating. The bloodstains on the sock also proved that the blood had been dripped on it from test tubes while the sock was lying flat, rather than splattered on it while it was being worn at the crime scene. There were mirror-image stains on all four surfaces, which meant that the blood had flowed through the flattened sock, establishing that it was not being worn at the time the blood made contact with it. Had it been splattered while being worn, there would have been mirror-image stains only on two surfaces—the outside and the inside of the sock part that was splattered—but not on the two other surfaces, which would have been blocked by the wearer's leg. (We discovered this before the popular television show *Dexter* made the public familiar with "blood splatter analysis.") The jurors were convinced by this and other evidence that the police had dripped the blood onto the sock from vials, to make it appear that the sock Simpson was wearing during the murders had been splattered with blood at the crime scene. This led the jurors to believe that the police were trying to frame Simpson for a murder they believed he had committed, and that the veracity of their testimony and other evidence could not be trusted. They acquitted Simpson of killings for which a subsequent civil jury (with different lawyers and different evidence) found him financially liable.

VIGNETTE

Marsha Clark Without Underwear

Marsha Clark may not have been the most sophisticated prosecutor I ever encountered, but she certainly was among the most resourceful, employing everything she had to her advantage. As Johnnie Cochran was about to make his closing argument, Marsha Clark went over to him and whispered, "When you're up there, I want you think of only one thing: I'm not wearing any underwear." When Johnnie Cochran told me this story, I was skeptical. So I called Marsha Clark and asked her. She told me, "Absolutely true." I asked, "Which part of it was true: that you told him you weren't wearing any underwear or that you weren't, in fact, wearing any underwear?" She replied, "That's one thing you'll never know."

My expertise in the science of disproving murder had been at the center of my earlier famous case involving Claus von Bülow. Von Bülow's original trial lawyers were not able effectively to challenge the prosecution's evidence that Sunny von Bülow's coma was caused by an injection of insulin, that high levels of insulin were found in Sunny's blood, that traces of insulin were found on a needle in a bag that belonged to her husband, Claus, and that a vial of injectable insulin had been found in Claus's bag by Sunny's maid. On appeal, and in a motion for a new trial based on newly discovered evidence, we disproved each of these pillars of the prosecution case. We demonstrated through our own experts that Sunny's coma was caused by the oral ingestion of barbiturates, rather than by an injection of insulin; that there were no high levels of insulin in Sunny's blood; that the alleged traces of insulin on the needle were the result of a false positive reading; and that the maid could not have seen a vial of insulin in Claus's bag. The Rhode Island Supreme Court reversed the conviction and ordered a new trial,[29] at which the jury, after hearing the new scientific evidence, quickly acquitted von Bülow.

VIGNETTE

Claus von Bülow

After we won the case, Claus decided to host a dinner party. I told him I would not come if it was a victory party, since I have a policy of not going to victory parties of criminal defendants. He assured me that it was merely a dinner for several interesting people, and that among his guests would be the novelist Norman Mailer. When the dinner began, Claus regaled everybody with stories from the trial, and I explained why the evidence pointed to his innocence. About halfway through the dinner, Mailer grabbed his wife's arm and said, "Let's get out of here. I think this guy is innocent. I thought we were going to be having dinner with a man who actually tried to kill his wife. This is boring."

In fact, many of my most exciting cases involved very boring people, though Claus was not one of them. When the movie *Reversal of Fortune* came out, Claus refused to go to see it, insisting that he would never watch Jeremy Irons play him. Several months later I was having lunch with Claus and a woman friend. After about an hour of conversation with me, his friend turned to him and said, "Now that I've met Alan, I believe that Ron Silver really didn't do him justice. He overplayed him." Claus immediately shook his head in agreement, saying, "You're right, my dear, I too think he overplayed him."

The book and film *Reversal of Fortune* brought the issue of scientific defense to a wide public audience, and I became the go-to lawyer in several subsequent cases.

These cases included some involving clients whose celebrity brought me a considerable amount of fame and notoriety. During the 1980s and 1990s, I had so many high-profile cases, several of them at the same time, that my son Elon commented, "Every time I see a case in the newspaper, I know you are going to get a call." This was not far from the truth, though I had to turn down the vast majority of clients I was asked to defend, including some very wealthy and prominent men and women. I also appeared on TV and radio more frequently, sometimes defending my clients in the court of public opinion, other times commenting on high-profile cases in which I was not involved.

People began to recognize me on the street. I received an enormous volume of mail, some praising, some damning me, my clients, and my approach to defending the accused. Journalists began to write about me—I became newsworthy (and gossip-worthy). My name began to appear in novels,[30] TV shows, *New Yorker* cartoons, *New York Times* crossword puzzles, Trivial Pursuit games, and other forms of popular culture. I was offered a "shoe contract" to pay me to wear to court a brand that the company claimed looked formal but felt comfortable. I declined. I was even included on *Boston* magazine's list of "Best Dressed Bostonians," despite my penchant for buying clothing at Filene's Basement. I had mixed feelings about my celebrity, enjoying the positive aspects of it, such as getting invited to cultural and sports events, and bemoaning the lack of privacy that follows from becoming recognizable.

My first negative experience with fame came in the form of a bill I received from a furniture company for office equipment rented by a law firm called Cramer and Dershowitz. I was curious whether there was such a firm, so I drove to the address in Somerville. Sure enough there was a big sign that said CRAMER AND DERSHOWITZ—ACCIDENTS, TRAFFIC TICKETS, DIVORCES, INSURANCE CLAIMS, TAX PROBLEMS AND NOTARY PUBLIC. I went up to the second-floor office and asked to see Mr. Dershowitz. The woman behind the desk said, "Nobody gets to see the professor. He works at Harvard. Mr. Cramer will see you, and then he will send the case over to Professor Dershowitz to write the briefs and other legal documents." She told me that Cramer was "in court" and should be back soon. I waited. When Cramer walked into the office and saw me, he turned white. I immediately recognized him. About a year earlier, I had bought a Volvo from him at a showroom a few blocks from the office. He quickly ushered me into his office, which had a large cropped photograph of him and me standing next to the Volvo I had bought. He began to sob and pleaded with me not to send him to prison. He promised he would close up the office and go back to selling cars. I told him I would have to think about it.

Concerned that he might have made representations about me to some court, I immediately notified the bar association about the scam, but they told me they couldn't do anything about him "because he's not a lawyer." Nor, technically, was he practicing law, as I soon learned. His "practice" was limited to settling automobile accidents with insurance companies and other matters that did not actually require him to appear in a courtroom, despite his secretary's cover story. But he was clearly holding himself out to be a lawyer and my partner. This constituted fraud, both on his "clients" and on me.

Being soft-hearted, I decided not to press charges, on the condition that Cramer notify all of his "clients," past and current, that he was not a lawyer and that he had no association whatsoever with me. When I checked back several weeks later, the office was closed, the sign had been taken down, and he was back to selling cars, this time on Long Island.

Another manifestation of my growing name (but apparently not face) recognition came in the form of a romantic letter from a woman whom I had "picked up" in a bar the previous week and taken away for a weekend in Maine at my ski lodge, where we made love in front of a roaring fire.

She described the wonderful time we had had and asked if we could do it again sometime. The only problem was that I have no ski lodge in Maine and I had been in New York with my wife and daughter that entire weekend. Putting two and two together, my wife and I figured out that someone had impersonated me in his, apparently successful, effort to woo and seduce a woman. I'm happy that the experience was a good one for her, because I can only imagine the consequences if the "Alan Dershowitz" she'd gone to Maine with had treated her poorly.

Another example of name recognition occurred when a judge in Arizona allowed a man who claimed to be the object of a mafia murder contract to change his name. That sounds reasonable enough, but he wanted to change it to Alan Dershowitz. Without notifying me and giving me an opportunity to object, the judge allowed the man to take my name. I wrote to the judge advising him that the next time one of my clients had to go into the "witness protection program" and assume a new identity, I would recommend he take the judge's name.

All of these mixed experiences with fame were more than made up for by a positive experience I had when I was invited to address a singles breakfast, sponsored by the Combined Jewish Philanthropies of Boston, on the subject of "the changing nature of human rights." I was single at the time, and as soon as I got up to speak, I spotted a beautiful woman near the back of the audience. Whenever I speak, I try to focus on one or two audience members in order to gauge their reaction. This time I focused only on her. As soon as the event was over, I bolted to the back of the auditorium to get her name and phone number. All I managed to get was her name. Immediately upon returning home, I looked up "Carolyn Cohen" in the phone book and found five of them. I called the first one and asked if she would be interested in having dinner with me. She said she would but that she had to be back to the nursing home by 9 P.M. The second Carolyn Cohen also said she'd be happy to have dinner with me, but she wondered if she could bring her husband along. I finally reached my future wife on the third phone call. During dinner I mentioned that this was the first time I had actually obtained an advantage from being well known. Carolyn quickly responded, "I had never heard of you when I decided to go to what sounded like a talk on an interesting subject."

Carolyn never allows my recognition to go to my head. Once, after we dropped off our daughter at summer camp in rural Maine, we stopped at a local antiques store on the way home. The owner looked at me and said: "It's a pleasure having you in our shop, Mr. Dershowitz." I whispered to

Carolyn, "They even know me in Maine," to which she quickly responded, "That's because you didn't take off the name tag they gave you in camp," as she removed the HELLO, I'M ALAN DERSHOWITZ tag from my lapel

VIGNETTE

Israel Philharmonic

Shortly after the O. J. Simpson case, my wife and I were attending a concert at Boston Symphony Hall featuring the Israel Philharmonic and the violinist Midori. When the concert was over, a woman raced down the aisle. My wife was sitting on the aisle; I was one seat in. We were giving Midori a standing ovation. We thought the woman was heading toward the stage to give flowers to Midori. She wasn't. She pushed passed my wife and starting hitting me, screaming, "Murderer, you shouldn't be allowed to listen to music! You are responsible for the deaths of Nicole Simpson and Ron Goldman!" My wife, who is taller, younger, and stronger than me, shielded me from the woman's blows, blocking her from getting to me. We quickly left the hall, but later learned that the woman asked the people sitting near us to be witnesses to the fact that I attacked her. They all told her they would be witnesses to her attack on me. I bring Carolyn with me everywhere. She is my protector.

Being well known and recognized from television frequently results in people thinking they know you and that you know them. This often creates an awkward situation. Someone once came up to me at an airport and said, "I know who you are!" I extended my hand and said, "Hi, I'm Alan Dershowitz." She pulled her hand away quickly and said, "No, I know who you are." Clearly she had confused me with someone else she had seen on television. People who know you from the media sometimes think they know what your ideas are and what you stand for. They become "disappointed" when you depart from the image they have of you. I receive many letters expressing disappointment in my views or in my decision to take on a particular case. My standard answer is that my wife, my children, my late mother—all have the right to be disappointed in me, but a stranger has no such right. "You can hate me, despise my views, or disagree with me, but you do not have sufficient claim on me to express disappointment." Nonetheless, many do, and they express it with passion and deep feelings of personal affront. And when they turn against you, they do so with a fury more typical of family arguments than disagreements between strangers.

Following the jury acquittal of O. J. Simpson, in particular, I received a barrage of hate mail from Jewish people who said they had admired me for having written my book *Chutzpah* but had become "disappointed" in me for representing Simpson "against the Jewish man he had murdered." "Whose side are you on?" asked one writer. Another threatened to "do to your mother what your client did to Ron Goldman." One disappointed fan sent me his copy of *Chutzpah* defaced with a swastika.

VIGNETTE

Hate and Love Mail

One disturbing aspect of fame is hate mail, which I make a point of exhibiting on my office door, so students will understand what they face if they become public figures. Much of my recent hate mail has been anti-Semitic, because I am identified with support for Israel. Among them:

> Dear Dirtyshits,
>
> Why don't you go spill your filthy Jew guts for Israel instead of demanding that real American men and women spill theirs? Oh, I forgot—kikes are the Chosen People and all others should give it up for them. Never forget—MILLIONS of us hate you kike bastards and would love to see all of you herded into gas chambers. Hitler's crime was leaving the job half done.
>
> Alan Dershowitz, you sir are a zionist dick sucking FASCIST, you pig!!!!!!!
>
> Alan,
>
> You're a money-grubbing piece of shit Zionist who should've been taken out during the Third Reich. On behalf of the silent majority, LEAVE AMERICA!
>
> The letter was signed with a large swastika.

Some of the hate mail I receive regarding Israel comes from right-wing Jewish extremists who believe my support for a two-state solution constitutes disloyalty to the Jewish people:

> Professor, any Jew who voted for Obama is asking for a second holocaust & the destruction of Israel and Jews. I hope you are satisfied with your complete & utter sellout of the Jewish people. You, sir, are a Judas.

Another:

> You remind me of the Jews that worked for the Nazi's in the death camps. DROP DEAD YOU PIECE OF SHIT!!!

When I was publicly more identified with the defense of O. J. Simpson, much of my hate mail came from Jews. Several of them reflected anti-Semitic tropes:

> As a Holocaust survivor, I am ashamed you are a Jew. You never met a $ you did not like. You fulfill the stereotype of a Jew and I declare you: not Jewish.

Another:

> Dear lying Jew (remember, I'm Jewish):
>
> Congratulations—a murdering butcher is on the street. If the nigger is so innocent, then he should have no problem speaking. May you catch cancer.

That charming note was from a practicing dentist and was written on his prescription pad. Another of this genre:

> I hope I can still be alive when I hear someday that you have terminal cancer or even better, that you are a victim of a vicious crime which would be so appropriate for "dreck" like you.

My support for civil liberties and for Israel has also brought me positive responses, such as a letter from Kirk Douglas saying, "I'm a fan of yours," a call from Herman Wouk telling me how much he supports my positions on Israel, several supportive calls from Barbra Streisand, a letter from Justice William Brennan, and admiring notes from President Clinton, President Obama, and several prime ministers and presidents of Israel.

Because I am a controversial lawyer who is both admired and detested, I feel obligated to caution my clients before they retain me. Accordingly, I often begin my discussion with a new client with "the warning":

> *You should think hard before deciding to retain me as your lawyer. I come with baggage, some positive, some negative. People tend to either love me or hate me. Almost no one is neutral. When I become involved in a case, it tends to raise its profile in the media. Sometimes that's an advantage, sometimes a disadvantage. Prosecutors sometimes work harder when I am their opponent, because they think that beating me in court will be a kind of trophy.*

As a result of this speech some clients wisely choose to retain other lawyers. Those who pick me generally fall into several categories: clients who need more attention brought to their case; clients who have lost hope in more conventional legalistic approaches to the law; clients whose cases have already achieved maximum notoriety; and clients who have heard, quite erroneously, that I never lose.

I am also quick to point out to clients that no lawyer can promise them success, that all I can promise them is my best effort; and that—to paraphrase the offering pamphlets of money managers—past performance is no guarantee of future success.

I have also lost some clients because I told them what they did not want to hear—that the likelihood of success with their appeal is very low, that certain legal arguments will not work, or that their best hope is to try to make a deal. A good lawyer must always be ready to be fired by his clients for telling them the truth rather than acting as a cheerleader to a lost cause. But a good lawyer can sometimes turn what looks like a lost cause into a winning case, especially if there is new evidence or if the old evidence has not been correctly analyzed.

Because the death cases that brought me fame involved science and technology, many of the cases that followed also involved these disciplines. Defendants wanted me to use science in their cases to secure reversals of their conviction. One such case bore such an eerie resemblance to the von Bülow case that at first I thought it might have been a "copycat crime."

"MY FATHER DIDN'T KILL MY MOTHER": THE CASE OF DR. WILLIAM SYBERS

The call came from a young woman pleading with me to take her father's appeal. He had been convicted of killing her mother by injecting her with a drug that stops the heart from working. "It's just like the von Bülow case," the daughter insisted. "My father didn't kill my mother. He didn't inject anything into her. She died of natural causes." (No one seeking my help ever tells me their case is "just like" O. J. Simpson's!)

When the daughter of an alleged murder victim is so certain the defendant is innocent, even when the defendant is her father, the case is certainly worthy of a hard second look. I agreed to provide that look.

My initial review was not encouraging. There was a needle mark on the victim's arm that was consistent with an injection. Moreover, a subsequent lab test had revealed traces of the metabolite of a drug called succinylcholine—a paralytic agent capable of stopping the heart. Finally, the defendant was having an affair, and he was a medical doctor—indeed the medical examiner of his Florida county—and thus had the motive and knowledge necessary to stop his wife's heart. All the classic components for homicide—motive, opportunity, means, and scientific evidence—were present, and they pointed in the direction of guilt. I could easily understand why a jury would convict. And it did convict by a unanimous vote, coming very close to imposing a death sentence on Dr. William Sybers. Instead, he was sentenced to life imprisonment.

The Sybers case had begun more than a decade before I was called. Kay Sybers had died in her sleep on May 30, 1991. She was fifty-two years old and in good health, though she had suffered from allergies for which she took medication. An autopsy was performed, but no cause of death could be determined. One of the investigators did, however, think she saw a needle mark. The original death certificate read: "sudden unexpected death due to undetermined natural causes."

Rumors immediately began to circulate that Dr. Sybers was having an affair with a lab technician, and an investigation was begun. An officer was dispatched to the Sybers home, and the grieving husband was asked to describe his wife's final night. He told the investigator that at about 4 A.M. his wife awoke with chest pains. She had taken some medication, so Dr. Sybers decided to draw some blood to give to her doctor the next day. He did not succeed in drawing the blood, and he threw the syringe into the garbage. The syringe could not be found because the trash had already been collected. This all seemed suspicious and the investigation continued. After more than a year, the state attorney reported that he had found no physical evidence that Dr. Sybers had killed his wife. The case was closed.

But a year later the Sybers' twenty-seven-year-old son killed himself on his mother's birthday. Shortly before he shot himself, Tim was talking on the phone with a friend about his mother's death and the suspicion that his father might have killed her. Tim's suicide resulted in a reopening of the investigation. The case was now on "the front burner." It was also on the front pages of local newspapers.[31]

Investigators began to focus on the drug potassium, which in large enough doses can kill and which is difficult to detect in a body. It was a perfect murder weapon, especially for a sophisticated medical examiner with extensive experience in causes of death.

Bowing to pressure from the media, the governor of Florida appointed a "special prosecutor" from a different county to investigate the case. He had only one job: to prove that Dr. William Sybers had murdered his wife. With the single-minded determination of an Inspector Javert, the special prosecutor set out to get Dr. Sybers.

On February 18, 1997, he had Sybers indicted for capital murder. The indictment alleged that he had murdered his wife with an "unknown substance." There was no hard evidence of any substance, but the prosecutor was confident he could find it. It was an example of indict first—and then search for the evidence later.

The prosecutor was convinced that Dr. Sybers had injected his wife with potassium and that a thorough analysis of her tissues, preserved from the autopsy, would prove that theory. The problem was this theory was based on "junk" science. A "test" that purported to show high concentrations of potassium in the preserved tissues was not scientifically valid. It could not be replicated by other scientists, and the methodology had never been peer-approved. Accordingly, one court denied the petition for exhumation of Kay's body, and another court ruled that the potassium evidence could not be presented to the jury. The theory that Dr. Sybers had used potassium as the murder weapon was now dead.

The special prosecutor was left with a capital indictment, but no theory, no evidence, and no weapon. So he set out to find a new murder weapon. He turned his attention to the drug succinylcholine. The paralytic drug itself quickly disappears from the human body, but a scientist assured him that a by-product of the drug—succinyl*mono*choline, or SMC—could be detected in tissues even years later by a sophisticated test. That test was then conducted, and it purportedly found traces of SMC in Kay's tissues. This time the test results could be replicated by the famous FBI lab, although with slight variations. The prosecutor had his smoking gun—his murder weapon. And it had been certified by no less an authority than the Federal Bureau of Investigation.

The same judge who had excluded the potassium theory as "junk science" now concluded, after an extensive hearing, that the succinylcholine theory was based on real science and could be presented to the jury.

The prosecutor not only now had science on his side, he also had a sex motive that would surely grab the jury's attention, even if it were to become bored by the highly technical scientific evidence.

The state's scientific case gave rise to the usual clash of experts. The two primary witnesses for the prosecution were the scientist who had conducted the test and the FBI chemist who had replicated it. The defense introduced experts who opined that since the body had been embalmed before autopsy, any chemical analysis could have been contaminated by the embalming fluid.

The jury, after only a few minutes of deliberation, convicted Dr. Sybers of first-degree murder. He was sentenced to life. His only hope of experiencing freedom was an appeal, or a new trial motion, which my brother and I were retained to prepare and argue.

My brother, Nathan, four years my junior, has long been my secret weapon. After graduating from NYU Law School, he served as an appeals lawyer in the New York Legal Aid Society, where he argued hundreds of criminal appeals. Then he worked in a large law firm and at the American Jewish Congress, before starting his own boutique appellate law firm. His firm includes two other excellent appellate lawyers who are his partners, as well as several associates. I work on many of my most difficult cases with the firm—Dershowitz, Eiger and Adelson. Their work proved invaluable in the Sybers case, as it did in many others.

We began by reviewing the scientific evidence, as we had in the von Bülow and Simpson cases. We discovered massive incompetence and sloppiness on the part of the private lab that had "found" traces of SMC, and serious problems in the FBI lab as well.

We were fortunate that among the judges assigned to hear our appeal, one—Judge Peter D. Webster—had a background in chemistry. I had learned of this when inquiring—as I always do, with any appeal in which I'm involved—about the judges who would be hearing the appeal. I decided to direct my argument to this judge. I wasn't sure whether his background would make him more or less skeptical regarding scientific evidence, but I knew he would be interested in the issue, and it was my job to persuade him to apply the principle, articulated by the courts over the years, that "novel scientific evidence" can be admitted at a criminal trial only if it is "sufficiently established to have gained general acceptance" by the scientific community.[32] He immediately glommed on to that principle. As he was later to put it: "A courtroom is not a laboratory, and as such is not the place to conduct scientific experiments,"[33] and "doubts as to admissibility" of such evidence should be resolved "in a manner that minimizes the chance of a wrongful conviction."[34]

With these salutary principles in mind, we set out to convince the appellate court that the "science" on which Sybers had been convicted was not science at all, but was the result of an unscientific effort by an overzealous prosecutor to discover, or if necessary concoct, "evidence" that would confirm his vendetta against Dr. Sybers. We were convinced, based on our research, that the "finding" of SMC in Kay's tissues was the result of a classic *false positive*, based on contamination. We presented our new evidence of massive contamination, along with our legal issues, to the appellate court.

The appellate argument turned into a seminar on the scientific method. I began as the "teacher" but soon became the "student" when I realized that Judge Webster knew at least as much about the science as I did. He quickly made the argument we had laid out in our brief his own, asking questions that appeared calculated to persuade the other judges. Realizing that it is always better to let a judge make your argument for you, I deferred to his expertise and agreed with the thrust of his questions.

A few months after the argument, the court published its decision reversing Sybers's conviction, on the ground that the prosecution had failed to prove the scientific validity of its theory.[35]

We later learned that the special prosecutor had information that should have led him to know or at least suspect that the test results were at best highly questionable and at worst flat-out false.[36] Yet he did not disclose this information to the court or to the defense. We also learned that a fellow prisoner (who had murdered a prosecutor) was trying to secure his freedom by claiming that Dr. Sybers had "confessed" to him that he had murdered his wife. The prosecutor was trying to use that "confession" against Dr. Sybers, despite his knowledge that the prisoner had made several similar claims—all proved to be false—against other fellow prisoners in an effort to buy his way out of prison. We filed a complaint with the appropriate authorities, since such conduct on the part of the prosecutor raises grave ethical issues. The prosecutor then filed a countercomplaint alleging—quite absurdly—that the very act of filing a complaint against *him* constituted misconduct. This tactic is only one of the ways overly aggressive prosecutors discourage lawyers from complaining about their ethical violations. Nothing came of either complaint,[37] but when President Obama was considering appointing this prosecutor to become a United States attorney in Florida, we notified the White House and the Senate Judiciary Committee of his ethical lapses and he was passed over for the job.[38] (The White House reportedly claimed he was rejected for other reasons.)

Dr. Sybers married the lab technician with whom he had been having an affair.[39] Every Christmas, the couple sends me, my brother, and the lawyers in his firm a card thanking us for saving Dr. Sybers.

THE BINION CASE: MURDER OR DRUG OVERDOSE?

The classic thriller case is a whodunit. The fact of a murder is clear, as it was in the O. J. Simpson case. The only question is *who* committed it. "Who Killed Cock Robin?," as the old ditty asks.

Many of my homicide cases have not been whodunits, but rather wasitduns—was anything criminal done at all? Was the dead (or comatose) body the result of a criminal act, or the result of natural causes, self-induced harm, or accident?

That was the issue in the von Bülow and Sybers cases. It was also the question presented when Ted Binion, the owner of the Binion Horseshoe Casino in Las Vegas—the home of the World Series of Poker—was found dead in his home on September 17, 1998.

Binion's live-in fiancée, Sandra Murphy—a young sometime exotic dancer—and her equally young lover, Richard Tabish, were accused of murdering Binion, by an unusual means harking back to the days of Sherlock Holmes. Dr. Michael Baden, one of the world's leading forensic pathologists (and a friend), concluded that Binion had been "burked" to death.

The term "burke" derives from two notorious nineteenth-century Scottish murderers, who killed their victims in order to provide fresh cadavers to medical students for research. The case was so notorious that it became the subject of a short story, "The Body Snatchers," by Robert Louis Stevenson,[40] and of several films, including one that starred Boris Karloff and

Bela Lugosi[41] and "Burke and Hare"[42] directed by my client John Landis. Burke and Hare compressed the chest of their victims, smothering them to death, without leaving bruises.

Dr. Baden opined that Sandra Murphy and her lover had done this to Binion.[43] And their diabolical plan—if there was such a plan—worked, at least for a while. Since it was well known that the high-living Ted Binion was a heroin addict, and since there was evidence that his drug supplier had delivered black tar heroin just hours before his body was found, the police concluded that this was just another Las Vegas drug overdose, albeit by one of the city's most famous celebrities.[44] Since no crime (other than charges relating to the drugs) was suspected, the home was not declared a "crime scene," but an autopsy the next day noted various marks on the body and the examiner photographed them. It was these marks that led Dr. Baden to conclude that Binion had been burked to death. Other medical experts also concluded that Binion had been murdered, but not by "burking." Their theory was that he had been forced to swallow a deadly mixture of heroin, Xanax, and Valium—a cocktail of death.[45]

In addition to the scientific evidence, Binion's estate lawyer testified that on the day before his death, Binion had said to him: "Take Sandy [Sandra Murphy] out of the will if she doesn't kill me tonight. If I'm dead, you'll know what happened."[46] It was the stuff of soap operas, and several television shows treated it as such. But it was a real case, the outcome of which would determine whether Sandy Murphy would spend the rest of her life in prison.

The prosecution had evidence of motive, means, and opportunity, and they charged Murphy and her lover with "murder by suffocation and/or poisoning." At trial, they presented what I later characterized as a "multiple choice" prosecution:[47] The jury could choose either burking or poisoning; they did not have to agree on the *means* used to murder Binion, as long as they all agreed that "his death was caused by a criminal agency." Nor did they have to tell anyone which theory they had chosen if they found the defendant guilty.

The jury deliberated for eight days and found the defendants guilty.[48] My brother and I were retained to prepare and argue Sandy Murphy's appeal and to file a motion for a new trial based on newly discovered evidence.

We began our investigation by focusing on the burking theory. Since the jury could have convicted based on that theory alone, if we could undercut it, Murphy would have to be given a new trial,[49] since the jury might have convicted on that false theory. We would turn the prosecution's "multiple choice" offense into an appellate defense.

One important pillar of the burking theory was a "bruise" on Binion's chest that had been photographed. Since Dr. Baden hadn't examined Binion's body, he had to rely on the photograph alone. Dr. Baden concluded that the bruise—which appeared consistent with the shape of Binion's shirt button—had been caused by Binion being burked. We had the photograph enlarged and enhanced by the most sophisticated technology. We showed it to one of the world's most distinguished dermatologists, who examined it "at high magnification." His conclusion dealt a powerful blow to the burking theory: The mark on Binion's body was *not* a bruise; instead, the structure of the blood vessels proved that it was a benign skin tumor he had for years *before* his death.[50] It had not been produced by "an external cause." Our expert, who had examined thousands of lesions, wrote that he had "never in my experience seen lesions such as this caused by pressure."

Additional field research further discredited both the burking and the cocktail theories.[51] We were now confident that if Murphy were to receive a new trial, a jury would acquit her. The prosecution's "multiple choice" theory had become a "no choice" near certainty.

Now all we needed was an opportunity to obtain a new trial. Our best chance was to win the appeal, and the best issue on appeal—the safest and neatest—was the judge's decision to allow Binion's lawyer to testify that Binion had told him the day before his death that if he were found dead, Murphy would be his killer. This was a smoking gun that must have influenced the jury, since it was, in effect, testimony from the grave. The ghost of the dead man, as in Shakespeare's *Hamlet*,[52] was pointing to his killer.

We did not believe that the conversation had occurred. Murphy told us that the lawyer, who hated her, had made it up after the fact to assure her conviction. But the jury had believed the lawyer, and we could not challenge his credibility on appeal, since credibility issues—whether in-court witnesses are telling the truth or lying—are for the jury to decide. But we could try to raise doubts about the credibility of *the dead man*, who had *not* testified in court—the man whose words were quoted by the lawyer. How could the jurors assess Binion's credibility, since he could not be cross-examined? His "testimony" from the grave was classic hearsay,[53] and his unavailability denied Murphy the constitutional right to confront her accuser.[54]

The prosecution responded that the only reason Binion wasn't in court was that my client had murdered him. Our argument, they claimed, paralleled the classic definition of "chutzpah": the young man who murders his parents and demands mercy from the court on the ground that he is an orphan. Murphy had murdered Binion and was now demanding that his last words be excluded. What chutzpah! But the conclusion that Murphy had, in fact, murdered Binion begged the very question to be decided by the jury: Did Murphy, in fact, murder him?

Although hearsay statements—that is, in-court testimony by one person as to out-of-court statements made by another—are generally not admitted at trial, there are exceptions to this rule of exclusion. One of them is the "chutzpah exception": A defendant can't kill a witness and then seek to exclude testimony about what he would have said if he were alive.[55] This exception was created to discourage defendants from murdering witnesses. But to invoke that exception, it has to be clear that the defendant did, in fact, kill the witness. This presented a chicken-egg problem: The jury had concluded Murphy killed Binion, based on hearsay evidence that would be admissible only if she had, in fact, killed him.

Another exception is "deathbed" confessions—statements made by a man who knows he's dying and speaks in anticipation of his imminent death.[56] The "science" behind this exception is the assumption that no person will lie if he knows he is about to meet his maker. But this too is junk science, since there is no real evidence to support the assumption. Moreover, there was no evidence (aside from the challenged statement itself) that Binion actually anticipated death or that he was a religious man who feared meeting his maker with a lie on his lips.

The final relevant exception is that an otherwise hearsay statement is admissible if it is relevant to the "then-existing state of mind" of the dead person.[57] For example, if Binion had told his lawyer that he was feeling depressed and was considering suicide, that statement could be heard by the jurors to help them decide whether his subsequent death was caused by his suicide rather than murder. The prosecution argued that Binion's "fear" of being murdered was evidence of his state of mind, and that his death was not caused by self-administered drugs. The problem with this argument was that Binion's statement was *also* evidence of Murphy's allegedly murderous state of mind, and the jurors would not be able to limit its consideration of this explosive statement only to Binion's state of mind. As lawyers like to argue: "When you throw a skunk in the jury box, you can't get rid of the smell even if you remove the skunk." This was especially true since the judge had failed to give the jury what is called a "limiting instruction," namely that "you can consider the statement *only* to prove what *Binion* was thinking and *not* what *Murphy* was thinking." (There is grave doubt whether jurors actually follow such limiting instructions, or whether they are more like the admonition "Don't think about the eight-hundred-pound gorilla in the room." In any event, the judge didn't give that instruction.)

Because of this serious and prejudicial error (as well as others), the Nevada Supreme Court reversed the murder convictions and ordered a new trial.[58]

The jury at the second trial, having heard our new scientific evidence, acquitted Murphy of murder.[59] They believed neither the burking nor the cocktail theory. The more likely cause of death, they apparently concluded, was a self-administered overdose of heroin. Murphy now lives in California, where she runs an art gallery. She recently had her second baby daughter.

ASSISTING MERCY SUICIDE: THE CASE OF DR. PETER ROSIER

Another highly emotional case in which science was used to establish the immediate cause of death involved the mercy killing by a doctor of his cancer-ridden wife. This case also raised profound and controversial moral, religious, and legal issues.

Although the media characterized Patricia Rosier's death as a "mercy killing,"[60] it is more aptly described as a "mercy suicide," because she alone made the decision to end her life. A mercy suicide, when committed by an adult of sound mind, is not a crime. (Although historically suicide was a crime, it obviously can't be prosecuted if it succeeds. Attempted suicides were sometimes prosecuted.)

Mercy killing—the taking of the life of another person who is suffering and usually no longer sentient—is different from mercy suicide in the eyes of the law. The letter of the law simply does not generally recognize mercy as a defense to murder: It regards all deliberate killings as murder, whether done in the name of love or hate. But suicide is not a crime, though in some religions it is still regarded as a sin, even when committed to relieve the pain accompanying an imminent death.[61]

Assisted suicide, on the other hand, remains a crime in most jurisdictions. In 2012, one of the most controversial referenda issues on the Massachusetts ballot was a proposal to authorize assisted suicide in a narrow range of cases. Following the expenditure of a considerable sum of money by opponents and strong opposition from the Catholic Church, it was narrowly defeated.[62]

The line between suicide and assisted suicide is not always clear. Sometimes it is simply a function of timing or happenstance. When what was originally intended as an unassisted mercy suicide cannot be completed without the help of others, it becomes, in the eyes of a prosecutor, a criminal mercy killing.[63]

What began as a clear case of mercy suicide by Patricia Rosier ended up with the trial of her husband, Peter, for first-degree murder and conspiracy to murder. The prosecutor sought the death penalty, analogizing the crime to "a serialized gang murder."

The basic facts were not much in dispute, but the legal consequences of those facts gave rise to one of the most contentious and emotional cases in Florida legal history.[64]

Dr. Peter Rosier, who was a pathologist, learned of his wife's cancer by examining X-rays. After being told she had incurable cancer and had only weeks to live in excruciating pain, Patricia made the fateful decision to pick the time and circumstances of her death, not wanting to leave it to the unpredictable clock of cancer. When she told her husband of her decision, Peter said that he would end his life with her. When the children learned of this, they pleaded with their father not to take his life. Peter relented. No one tried to talk Patricia out of her decision, for two reasons: First, she had made up her mind; second, it wasn't really suicide, since her act would only hasten her painful demise by a few weeks.

Patricia selected the time of her death and planned a farewell dinner for her family. Among those in attendance, in addition to her husband and children, were her stepfather and her two half brothers.

There was wine, and there were toasts. Patricia wore an elegant dress and had had her nails polished. After dinner they all watched the movie *Harold and Maude*, about an aging woman who commits suicide to prevent herself from "growing old."[65] When it was over, Peter and his wife retired to the bedroom and made love. After bidding farewell to family members, Patricia Rosier took twenty pills that she had selected. She quickly fell into a coma, from which she expected never to wake.

But the coma began to lighten. Peter didn't know what to do. Would she awaken or remain comatose? Would there be brain damage? Pain? Emotional turmoil? All Peter knew was that his wife did not want to awaken. What was his obligation to his comatose wife? Would he be breaking his final promise to her if he did not assist her in achieving her goal: a painless and dignified death? He could not ask her. The decision was his, but it was *her* decision—she had already made it and acted on it, albeit incompletely.

Peter administered morphine, but it was not enough. While Peter was outside the house, pacing and crying, Patricia's stepfather placed his hands over her nose and mouth. She died in her sleep.

The stepfather and brothers informed Peter that Patricia had died, without providing any more information. For nearly a year, the circumstances surrounding Patricia's death remained a secret. Then Peter decided to write a book about his wife's decision[66] and gave an interview to a local television reporter in which he related what he believed were the circumstances of his wife's death,[67] still unaware that her stepfather had administered the coup de grâce.

As soon as the interview was aired, the local prosecutor began a murder investigation. He wanted to interview Patricia's stepfather, but he demanded total immunity from prosecution for himself and his sons. That should have tipped off the authorities that he might have something to hide. But instead of asking for a "proffer"—a truthful outline of the facts—before deciding whether to grant immunity, the prosecutor agreed to his condition.

The stepfather then disclosed that it was he who had caused Patricia's death. The prosecutors had committed a blunder feared by every law-enforcement official: They'd given the wrong person immunity. But they could not back out of their deal. Now the only possible target was Peter.

Despite the certainty that Peter had not actually killed his wife, and that she wanted to take her own life, the prosecutor treated the loving husband as if he were the triggerman in a serialized gang murder. Peter was indicted on charges of first-degree murder and conspiracy to murder. The prosecution's theory was that the stepfather's ultimate act was merely the final stage in a family conspiracy of which Peter was the architect and participant. Under the same principle that had been used against Harry Reems and the Tison brothers, Peter would be deemed guilty of the stepfather's acts. Moreover, Patricia's death, according to the prosecutor, would never have occurred but for Peter's actions in helping her kill herself.

Suddenly Peter Rosier found himself in jail, facing a possible death sentence in a state that has one of the highest execution rates in the country. Right-wing commentators, such as Patrick Buchanan, absurdly compared what Peter had done to what the Nazis had done under Hitler.[68] Rosier called me from prison on the day of his arrest and asked me to help him. I worked with his local lawyer to get him out on bail and to formulate a trial strategy. In the event of his conviction, I was to be his appellate lawyer.

First we had to establish through scientific evidence that suffocation, rather than morphine, was the immediate cause of death, since Rosier did not suffocate Patricia. (Cancer was, of course, the real "but for" cause, in the sense that but for the cancer she would not have tried to commit suicide.) Second, we had to show that the stepfather's decision to suffocate his daughter was not part of any plan or conspiracy agreed to by Peter. And finally, we had to make the jurors wonder what *they* would have done under such circumstances and to conclude that the criminal law should not sit in judgment over loving family members who had to make a tragic choice between keeping a promise to a comatose loved one or abandoning her in a moment of crisis.

Peter's trial lawyer, Stanley Rosenblatt of Miami, did an excellent job persuading the jury that the murder statutes were put on the books not for loving husbands like Peter Rosier but for brutal killers like Charles Manson and Ted Bundy. He tried the case with emotion and empathy, inviting the jurors to put themselves in the unenviable situation Peter faced on that terrible night.[69] The prosecutor, on the defensive for having given Patricia's stepfather immunity before he knew the facts, played the avenging angel. He demanded that the jurors simply apply the law to the facts and not distinguish among murders on the basis of motive.

The jury understood—even if the prosecutors and Pat Buchanan did not—the differences between love and hate, between a self-willed, voluntary death and an involuntary death imposed by others. After weeks of trial, it took the jury only a few hours to acquit Peter Rosier of all criminal liability. The prosecution had lost all credibility by asking the jury to treat Dr. Rosier as if he were the functional equivalent of a gangland killer. Had the prosecution charged Dr. Rosier with assisting the suicide of another—which is a crime under Florida law[70]—it might have had a better shot at a conviction. But by *overcharging* him with first-degree murder, the prosecution made it difficult for the jury to take its case as anything but a vendetta. This practice of overcharging is common among some elected prosecutors.[71]

One important role the jury plays is to serve as the conscience of the community and as the commonsense moderator of harsh general statutes. This jury, which included several older people who themselves had living wills, decided that what Peter had done was not murder, even if the strict letter of the law did not authorize him to help his wife choose the time and manner of her imminent death.

THE SCIENCE OF ELICITING FALSE CONFESSIONS: THE CASE OF JONATHAN DOODY

Another notorious murder case involved the dark science of eliciting confessions from suspects.

In 1991, Jonathan Doody, the son of a Thai mother and an American soldier, was accused of the mass murder of nine Buddhist monks and nuns in Arizona. The victims were placed in a circle on the floor of a Buddhist shrine and systematically shot in the head, apparently by a group of armed robbers, who took several hundred dollars from their charity boxes. It was a horrendous crime, even worse than the multiple murders committed by Gary Tison and Randy Greenawalt in the same state thirteen years earlier. The difference was that everyone knew who murdered the Lyons family in cold blood, while the police were stymied as to the perpetrators of this mass murder. Originally, a motorcycle gang was suspected. After a lengthy interrogation, four of them confessed, but it soon became clear to the police that they had been pressured into making false confessions, and they were freed.

Doody, who was seventeen and in high school at the time, was then arrested and subjected to a thirteen-hour interrogation. The tactics used against Doody were eerily similar to those that had elicited the false confessions from the motorcycle gang members. The police began by giving Doody his Miranda warnings: You have the right to counsel; you have the right to remain silent; and anything you say can and will be used against you in the court.[72] They then proceeded, gradually, to "de-Mirandize" him, by taking back everything they had originally said! You have a right to an attorney "*if* you were involved in [the murders]"; anything you "tell us" is "gonna stay right here" and *not* be used "in court"; and "you just have to open up"—that is, confess—and we will keep you here until you do. Finally, the exhausted seventeen-year-old confessed to being involved *with* the motorcycle gang—which the police knew was untrue—and to participating in the killings. Based largely on this confession, he was convicted and sentenced to life imprisonment.

I was asked by a Buddhist monk to argue his appeal. He told me he was certain that Jonathan was not involved in the killing of his fellow monks. He gave me a tiny golden Buddha to keep with me when I worked on the appeal, assuring me that it would help render justice. I took the Buddha, but insisted on conducting an extensive investigation. The murder scene was near an air base, and I learned that Russia was selling some of the Soviet Union's old satellite photographs of the United States. I bought the photographs for the location of the murder, in the hope that perhaps they might show evidence that people other than Doody were responsible for the crime. Unfortunately, the sky had been overcast that day and the photographs were useless. We would have to limit ourselves to making arguments based on the record of the trial, with an emphasis on how the police had elicited the confession from Doody. I did extensive research on the "science"—or "art"—of eliciting confessions from reluctant suspects. I learned how interrogators place objects from the crime scene in view of the suspect, how they suggest answers, how they create an atmosphere of intimidation and omniscience, and how they contrive to turn the Miranda warnings to their own advantage.

I had long been interested in coercive interrogation, having written a paper on false confessions in law school. I had also drafted Justice Goldberg's majority opinion in the Escobedo case,[73] which had laid the foundation for the Miranda rule. And as a professor I had taught and written about self-incrimination, torture, and related subjects.[74] When I listened to the hours of the recorded interrogation, I immediately suspected that Doody's confession was false.

I argued the initial appeal, along with my brother Nathan's law firm, in 1996. The Arizona Supreme Court affirmed the conviction.[75] My brother's partner, Victoria Eiger, then took prime responsibility for preparing a federal writ of habeas corpus. My brother and I worked closely with her. I was convinced that the precedent established by allowing such a questionable confession to serve as the basis for a murder conviction was dangerous and inconsistent with the constitutional privilege against self-incrimination. I also believed that the decision upholding Doody's conviction was part of a larger trend attacking or ignoring the progress that had been made by the Warren court.[76] Among its most significant achievements were the rules limiting the power of rogue policemen to employ backroom tactics—including the notorious "third degree"—to elicit confessions. The lower court decisions in the Doody case threatened to legitimate such backroom tactics. It was important to challenge this trend. It was also crucial to leave no stone unturned in trying to secure Jonathan Doody's freedom.

We decided to appeal the denial of habeas corpus to a panel of the United States Court of Appeals for the Ninth Circuit, which reversed Doody's conviction in a decision that ruled his confession involuntary and ordered him to be freed, unless the state granted him a new trial.[77] The state then appealed the reversal to the entire Ninth Circuit, which set the case down for argument before twelve judges. They also ruled in Doody's favor, by a vote of 9–3.[78] Still the case was not over. The state sought a writ of certiorari from the Supreme Court, which remanded the case back to the Ninth Circuit for reconsideration in light of a recent Supreme Court decision.[79] The Ninth Circuit reconsidered and once again threw out Doody's conviction on the ground that the confession was involuntary.[80] Again the state sought review by the Supreme Court. This time their petition was denied,[81] and Doody's conviction was finally and definitively reversed, after almost twenty years of litigation. But the case was still not over.

The State of Arizona is now planning to retry him.[82] Bail has been set at $5 million,[83] which is, of course, impossible for the Doody family, which has no money, to raise.

If justice delayed is justice denied, then Jonathan Doody has surely been denied justice. He has been in prison for nearly twenty years. The thorough decisions of the United States Court of Appeals have all been in his favor, but he remains in jail for a horrible mass murder of which he is now presumed innocent and which he may not have committed.

If Doody is retried, his confession will not be admissible, because, thanks to the decisions rendered by the Ninth Circuit, the law now prohibits the kind of tactics used by the police. The dangerous trend reflected by the lower court decisions in this case has been halted, at least for now.

THE SUPPRESSION OF SCIENCE: THE CASE OF JEFFREY MACDONALD

A case in which science has not yet produced a victory—or, in my view, justice—is the forty-year-old whodunit involving the murder of the family of Jeffrey MacDonald. Science could perhaps provide a definitive answer to this highly publicized case, but so far the doors of the courtroom have been shut to newly discovered scientific evidence and evidence that was deliberately suppressed by the prosecution. The courts in this case have placed the alleged need for "finality" above the search for truth. But history and science know no finality. Nor should the law, especially when a possibly innocent defendant remains convicted of a crime that science could prove he may not have committed.

I had followed the Jeffrey MacDonald case in the media from its grisly inception on February 17, 1970, when the wounded Green Beret doctor told authorities that his pregnant wife, Colette, and his daughters, Kimberley, five, and Kristen, two, had been murdered by drug-crazed intruders. Like most Americans, I had my doubts about his story. It seemed conveniently modeled on the notorious Manson murders that had occurred just months earlier. I knew that the statistics showed that wives are more likely to be killed by husbands than by strangers. I wondered why, if there had been intruders, they had left behind no hard evidence—no fibers, hairs, or fingerprints. My doubts were confirmed by reading Joe McGinniss's bestseller *Fatal Vision*,[84] which concluded that MacDonald was indeed guilty, and by seeing the TV movie,[85] which was even more persuasive of his guilt.

While I was on a visit to Terminal Island Federal Prison in California to confer with another inmate, a graying prisoner introduced himself to me. He was Jeffrey MacDonald, and he asked if he could have five minutes of my time to show me some documents. I agreed. What I learned that day—and afterward—convinced me that I had to try to help him.

In one of the most dramatic scenes in the TV movie, investigators dig up the graves of the victims. The federal government's chief lawyer (played by Andy Griffith) explains to their grieving stepfather and their grandfather Freddy Kassab (played by Karl Malden) why the bodies must be exhumed:

> *We've got to know if the hair found in Colette's hand was her own, Jeff's, the kids' . . . [Freddie Kassab interjects] . . . or someone with a floppy hat.*[86]

At the trial, the prosecution's case relied heavily on the claim that the blond hair found in the murdered Colette MacDonald's hand was her own, and not that of an intruder with a floppy hat, who Jeffrey MacDonald claimed had been there that night. It had already been found not to match Jeffrey MacDonald's hair. Thus, if it *did not match* Colette's own hair or the hair of the children, that finding would lend support to MacDonald's claim that there had been intruders—including a woman with long, blond hair who was wearing a floppy hat and boots—in his home on the night of the attack. It would also indicate that at least one of these intruders had come in contact with Colette.

A woman named Helena Stoeckley had told police and others that she and three friends had been in the MacDonald house on the night of the murders and that her friends, and not Jeffrey, had committed the crimes. Though Stoeckley's word alone may not have been worth very much—she was a drug addict—she provided some details, which tended to corroborate her story and the story Jeffrey told. She described a broken rocking horse like one found in Kristen's bedroom. At the time of the crime, she had owned a floppy hat, black clothing, and a long blond wig, all of which corresponded with MacDonald's description. And a woman fitting that description had been seen by a military policeman near the MacDonald home shortly after the crime.

But the single hair in Colette's hand turned out to have come from her own head, thus undercutting MacDonald's intruder theory. The government investigators reported that they had found no other physical evidence—no hairs, no fibers, no skin, no blood—that could not be traced to the inhabitants of the MacDonald house.

The prosecution could therefore argue to the jury that Jeffrey MacDonald was lying—because if there had been intruders, they surely would have left some evidence behind. An old adage says that "absence of evidence is evidence of absence." Applied to this case, the prosecution argued that the absence of evidence left behind by intruders was evidence of the absence of intruders. It was a persuasive argument.

Moreover, at the trial Helena Stoeckley claimed to have amnesia as to her whereabouts on the night of the murders, despite her previously claimed recollection that she had been in the house. The defense was surprised by Stoeckley's sudden inability to remember what she had previously described in such detail, but they could not effectively challenge her claim of amnesia, because they had no basis for suggesting that she had been pressured to forget what she actually remembered having done—namely participating in the murder of the MacDonald family.

But then, in a shocking turn of events, Jeffrey MacDonald's legal team discovered that, before the trial, the government had in its possession handwritten lab notes indicating that investigators had discovered long, blond wig hairs at the scene of the crime that *did not match* anything in the MacDonald household. This evidence was already in the government's secret files before the graves of the victims were disturbed.

Nor was this all the prosecution had in its secret files. The handwritten lab notes confirmed the presence of black wool fibers on the murder weapon used against Colette, and around her mouth. These fibers did not match any clothing belonging to Jeffrey or to anyone else in the MacDonald household. (Helena Stoeckley often wore black clothing.)

In addition, in the bedclothes of each victim, government investigators found other human hairs that did not belong to any of the victims or to Jeffrey. But these hairs were never tested against Stoeckley or any members of her group.

These lab notes were powerful evidence that an intruder wearing a long blond wig and black wool clothing was at the murder scene on the night of the murders. They certainly undercut the prosecution's "absence of evidence" argument. But Jeffrey MacDonald's lawyers had not been aware of the notes. Had they been, the entire trial would have unfolded differently.

For example, Helena Stoeckley testified to the jury that she could not remember where she had been on the night of the murders. MacDonald's attorneys tried to introduce the testimony of six witnesses—including a police officer—to whom she had previously admitted that she was in the MacDonald house with her friends that night. Since testimony about Stoeckley's prior admissions would constitute "hearsay"—that is, testimony by one witness about what another witness had said outside the courtroom—the judge ruled that the jury could hear about Stoeckley's hearsay admissions only if corroborating evidence showed that they were trustworthy.

The judge—who was also unaware of the handwritten lab notes—ruled that there was no physical evidence that corroborated Stoeckley's admissions; therefore, they were not trustworthy. Had he been aware of this corroborating evidence, he would have been obligated to allow the hearsay admissions into evidence, and the jury would have heard that Stoeckley had confessed to the murder and that her confession was corroborated by hard, scientific evidence. But because this evidence was deliberately suppressed by prosecutors, the jury never was presented with this alternative answer to "who done it."

Moreover, in 2005, the former deputy marshal Jim Britt, who was in charge of escorting Helena Stoeckley to the courtroom, came forward and told MacDonald's lawyer the following:

> *That he personally witnessed Helena Stoeckley state to James Blackburn [the prosecutor] that she and others were present in the MacDonald home on the night of the MacDonald murders and that they had gone there to acquire drugs; Jim Britt further avers that he witnessed and heard James Blackburn, upon hearing this, directly threaten Helena Stoeckley, telling her that if she so testified in court he would indict her for first-degree murder.*

This threat caused Stoeckley to claim on the witness stand that she had amnesia as to her whereabouts from midnight until 5 A.M. the morning of the MacDonald murders—the precise time frame during which the crimes occurred. "James Blackburn never disclosed to the court or defense counsel what Helena Stoeckley had admitted to him in Jim Britt's presence. On the contrary, Blackburn, at a critical juncture in the trial, advised the court that Stoeckley, when he interviewed her, denied having any knowledge of the MacDonald family, the MacDonald home, or involvement in the MacDonald murders. Blackburn even went so far as to elicit from Stoeckley, through leading questions before the jury, testimony that was contrary to what she had told him during his interview of her the day before in the presence of Jim Britt."[87]

This was unethical behavior by a federal prosecutor, bordering on criminal, since it essentially suborned the witness (induced her to commit perjury). (Blackburn has since been disbarred for misconduct unrelated to this matter.)[88]

These dramatic revelations finally came to light because of Dr. Jeffrey MacDonald's search for evidence of his own innocence, which he has protested since the beginning of his case. Over many years, he and his lawyers filed requests under the Freedom of Information Act, seeking access to government documents on the case. Slowly, they pieced together the amazing scientific and evidentiary story that the prosecutor kept from the jury.

It is a story that raises the disturbing question of why the government would suppress such critical evidence. It is impossible to know the mindset of the prosecutors in the case, especially those whose responsibility was to see that the defense received any evidence in the government's file that could help MacDonald's case. We do, however, know that the chief prosecutor was aware of the contents of the lab notes, since he wrote a memo to a legal assistant asking him whether "the detailed data of a lab report; as distinguished from the conclusions of the report, [must] be disclosed [to the defense]."[89] This question is significant, because the "detailed data" refers to the blond wig hair, the black wool, and the human hairs, which were described in the handwritten lab notes but somehow not mentioned in the lab's final typed report.

Brian Murtagh, the chief prosecutor, has refused comment, except for a cryptic statement that "if there were fibers useful to the defense, MacDonald's original trial lawyers should have found them" among the crates of raw evidence to which they had access. Talk about needles in haystacks!

How much more exculpatory evidence may be hidden in some government file—or may have been destroyed or lost—we will probably never know. For example, a fragment of human skin was found under one of

Colette MacDonald's fingernails. Yet, unbelievable as it sounds, the government claims that it lost this singularly important item of evidence.[90] Prosecutors in several other cases in which I've been involved have mysteriously "lost" evidence that could have proved innocence.[91] If that skin fragment were available, it could prove conclusively—through DNA matching—whether or not Jeffrey MacDonald was the killer.

If the government suppressed these highly relevant lab notes, a new trial should certainly be granted. But several problems remain: First, most Americans who have read the book or seen the TV movie of *Fatal Vision* already "know" that Jeffrey MacDonald is guilty, because the Jeffrey MacDonald portrayed in those one-sided presentations was guilty. The evidence shown to the audience—like the evidence presented to the jury—did not include the physical evidence that corroborates the Stoeckley confessions. Nor did it include the evidence that the prosecutor pressured Stoeckley to lie about her memory.

The second problem is that current law makes it nearly impossible to reopen a closed case on a second or third writ of habeas corpus, since the "great writ" has been severely restricted by Congress, and even compelling evidence of innocence does not guarantee a new trial.[92] In fact, when I argued an appeal from the denial of a second petition for habeas corpus in the MacDonald case[93]—my only courtroom involvement to date in this long case—one of the judges warned me not to bring any further petitions.[94] I told him I would be obliged to bring a further petition if the evidence warranted it.

Such new evidence has now been found, and the court of appeals recently ordered the district court to consider all the new "evidence as a whole."[95] This includes testimony by a lawyer appointed to represent Stoeckley at the trial confirming the fact that Stoeckley remembered being in the MacDonald home on the night of the killing, and that she was pressured by prosecutors to "forget" the truth. Moreover, a new book has been written by a highly credible investigator, Errol Morris, which supports MacDonald's claims of innocence and the unfairness of his trial.[96] So the case is far from over. I continue to confer on it with Harvey Silverglate, who was my cocounsel in the earlier habeas corpus appeal.

Whatever happens, I believe that Jeffrey MacDonald has not yet received a fair trial. I believe he deserves one—and the American people deserve to know the full story, not the abbreviated one presented at the trial or the biased one presented in the book and the TV movie. One of the appellate judges who heard argument on the MacDonald case has publicly stated that "the case provokes a strong uneasiness in me."[97] As well it should, in light of the repeated efforts of prosecutors to suppress the truth and hide exculpatory evidence.

More important, I believe that courtrooms should never be closed to new credible evidence of innocence and that the "great writ," which goes back to the Magna Carta, should not become a barrier to truth, as it often does under current law, but should remain an open door to justice.

HOW SCIENCE HAS CHANGED HOMICIDE CASES OVER THE PAST HALF CENTURY

There are two discernible trends in regard to the use of science to solve homicide cases—and they point in opposite directions. Science is helping to solve cases that previously remained unsolved (cold cases) or that produced erroneous results. Innocent people who were wrongly convicted of murder have been exonerated by the new science of DNA, and some guilty murderers who had never been suspected have been successfully prosecuted.[98] There have been some cases in which the DNA of the killer has been found and analyzed but could not be matched—yet—with a specific person. In at least one case, an indictment has been issued against the unnamed person who matches the "guilty" DNA.[99] If the person who matches the sample is ever found, he could presumably be prosecuted under the indictment, even if the statute of limitations has expired. Recently, DNA evidence was used to establish the identity of the notorious "Boston Strangler," a case on which I had consulted nearly half a century ago.

Such is the progress of science, and it will play an even larger role in the future. I teach about these developments in the classroom. I write about them. And I try to bring my academic knowledge—whether it involves chemistry, psychiatry, politics, or any other discipline—into the courtroom.

At the same time that science is offering progress in criminal law, the law itself is regressing. It is becoming increasingly difficult to reopen "closed cases," even homicide cases that carry long prison sentences or the possibility of execution.

Over the past several decades, an increasingly conservative Supreme Court and a Congress that doesn't seem to care about wrongly accused defendants have shut the courtroom door to new evidence, including new scientific evidence, that might change the outcome of a case. Some judges and justices even believe that it is not unconstitutional for an innocent person to be executed or to remain in prison if his conviction was "otherwise" constitutional. The idea that a process resulting in the conviction of an innocent defendant could be "otherwise" constitutional reminds me of the apocryphal question put to Mary Todd Lincoln after Abraham Lincoln's assassination in Ford Theater: "Other than that, Mrs. Lincoln, how did you like the play?" If a defendant is factually innocent, there is no "other than that."

Here is Justice Antonin Scalia on this subject:

> *This court has* never *held that the Constitution forbids the execution of a convicted defendant who has had a full and fair trial but is later able to convince a habeas court that he is "actually" innocent. Quite to the contrary, we have repeatedly left that question unresolved, while expressing considerable doubt that any claim based on alleged "actual innocence" is constitutionally cognizable.*[100]

Let me be clear what this means. If a defendant were convicted, after a constitutionally unflawed trial, of murdering his wife, whose body was never found, and then came to the Supreme Court with his very much alive wife at his side and sought a new trial based on newly discovered evidence that his wife was alive, Justice Scalia, along with several other justices, would tell him, in effect: "Look, your wife may be alive *as a matter of science*, but *as a matter of constitutional law*, she's dead. And as for you, Mr. Innocent Defendant, you're dead too, since there is no constitutional right not to be executed merely because you're innocent." The same would be true if DNA evidence proved *another* person guilty of a murder for which an innocent person was about to be executed. According to Scalia's view of the Constitution, there would be nothing unconstitutional about executing the innocent man—and then trying, convicting, and executing the guilty man too. Such is the regress of law, and it may get worse if more justices with Scalia's anachronistic views are appointed to the courts.[101]

At the moment, the Supreme Court remains closely divided on the issue of innocence in the context of habeas corpus. On May 28, 2013, a 5 in 4 majority—with Scalia in dissent—ruled in a case called *McQuiggin v. Perkins* that "actual innocence, if proved," serves as "a gateway" through which a defendant may obtain relief even if he filed his petition beyond the allowable time. The majority cautioned, however, that "tenable actual gateway pleas are rare," because the defendant has to prove to a judge that "in light of the new evidence, no juror, acting reasonably, would have voted to find him guilty beyond a reasonable doubt." Under this daunting standard, the husband who produces his living wife would win, but MacDonald might not, because some reasonable juror somewhere might still find him guilty. Moreover, the court didn't adequately address the "chicken-egg" problem: How does a confined inmate with no money, no lawyer, and no investigator, "prove" his innocence *before* receiving a hearing with subpoena power.

Even with this new ruling, it is possible for actually innocent defendants to be imprisoned or executed because they can't meet the high threshold set by the Supreme Court to prove their innocence.

VIGNETTE

My Love-Hate Relationship with the Scalias

My first encounter with the Scalia family took place when I was president of the student government at Brooklyn College and Professor Eugene Scalia—Justice Antonin Scalia's father—was a professor of romance languages. It was the tail end of the McCarthy era and Brooklyn College had fired a colleague of Professor Scalia's named Harry Slochower, on the grounds that he had refused to testify in front of a congressional committee about his alleged Communist affiliations years earlier. I supported Professor Slochower's right to continue to teach, while Professor Scalia opposed it.

Years later, Professor Scalia's only child became a justice of the Supreme Court. Shortly after his appointment, the phone rang in my office. I picked it up and the voice on the other end said, "Hey Alan, it's Nino. I accept." I said, "Nino who?" He responded, "Justice Scalia, and I accept your challenge." I asked, "What challenge?" He said, "Oh, they didn't tell you?" "Who didn't tell me?" I asked. "Your first-year criminal law students."

Justice Scalia then explained that several students in my class had called him and said that I was critical of his opinions and asked if he would come to class and debate me about his legal philosophy. He was calling to accept the students' invitation, and I immediately accepted it as well. Several weeks later, he appeared in my class and a feisty debate ensued. I'm told a tape of our encounter exists in the Harvard archives but is not accessible to the public. I wish it were.

Our next encounter occurred after he granted a stay of the Florida recount, effectively ending the 2000 election, and handing it over to the candidate he voted for—George W. Bush. I wrote a book called *Supreme Injustice*, in which I singled out Justice Scalia for harsh criticism. Shortly thereafter, he came to Harvard to speak and I was invited to a lunch with him. He opened the floor to questions and I asked the first one. "Many people, including many sitting in this room, believe that if the shoe were on the other foot—that if Bush were seeking the recount—you would have voted for Bush. If that is true, haven't you violated your oath of office which requires that you will administer justice without respect to persons?" He responded angrily, "I don't like being accused of violating my oath of office." I quickly responded, "Then you shouldn't have violated it." He turned away angrily. He then answered several other questions and no other hands went up, so I raised my hand again. Dean Elena Kagan, now Justice Scalia's colleague on the Supreme Court, pretended not to see me, obviously trying to avoid further unpleasantries. But to his credit, Justice Scalia said, "I see Dershowitz's hand. I'm not afraid of him. What is your question?" I persisted in my line of aggressive questions and he persisted in his aggressive answers.

Shortly thereafter we met again when we were both visiting Israel and giving lectures. A similar confrontation occurred. Although many observers were unnerved by our aggressive back and forth, neither Justice Scalia nor I took it personally. This became evident when he wrote me a "Dear Alan" letter dated July 19, 2005.

He began by discussing his father, describing him correctly as "a man of unbending principle." He then went on to discuss my criticism of his role in *Bush v. Gore*:

> *If my joining the equal-protection opinion was a mistake, I will be delighted if it is the worst one I make in this job. After all, it determined neither my vote (I would have come out the same way on the other ground, which I preferred) nor the judgment of the Court (there were six votes for equal protection anyway). I have frankly not revisited the issue, or read the extensive commentary (mostly critical, I gather) concerning it. At the time, however, I thought that ground correct. Even if you think that was wrong, considering the severe time constraints, the pressure to come out with a near-unanimous opinion, and the fact that it did not determine my vote in the case, you should cut me some slack. As for the stay: I think*

I can persuade you it was proper. We will talk about it sometime—as you say, before senility.

He ended his letter with a backhanded compliment:

You are not as nasty a guy as my right-wing friends believe. Warm regards.

Sincerely,
Nino

This is not to suggest that innocent people are being routinely executed in the United States. There are other checks and balances, such as gubernatorial commutation.[102] (Though in some states, they are rarely, if ever, granted.) Moreover, the courts, even the Supreme Court, sometimes find other ways to free the obviously innocent.

The real problem is *how* to prove one's innocence when the courts deny *possibly* innocent defendants the tools necessary to prove the *certainty* of their innocence. The Jeffrey MacDonald case is a prime example of this problem.[103] The courts repeatedly shut the door on his serious claims that he could establish his innocence if he were to be given an opportunity to subpoena evidence and witnesses. In his case several crucial witnesses have died. These include Helena Stoeckley and her boyfriend, who may have been the actual killers, and Jim Britt, the deputy marshal who would have testified that the prosecutor improperly pressured Stoeckley to "forget" what she had seen—that is, to lie about her memory.

In the MacDonald case, justice delayed by the courts may actually result in justice being denied to an innocent man.

Nor is MacDonald alone in having the courthouse door shut on new scientific evidence that could acquit the innocent and convict the guilty. It is possible that several innocent people have been executed because the courts refused to consider the scientific evidence that could have proved that others committed the murders.[104]

One such case came to my attention too late for me to do anything to prevent a possible miscarriage of justice. A letter arrived at my office on a Monday. I opened it and read a poignant request from a condemned man to review his case. I receive many such requests, but this one was different. It began by informing me that by the time I read this letter, the writer might already have been executed. I checked, and sure enough, he had been executed a few days earlier. Nevertheless, he asked me to help clear his name posthumously, so that his family would know he was innocent. He had asked to have the blood on a towel tested for DNA, but his request had been denied. He believed that the DNA test would show that the killer was someone else. I immediately sought to have the blood tested at my own expense, but the authorities told me that the evidence had been destroyed as soon as the defendant was executed.

In other words it is entirely possible that an innocent man was executed while the guilty man remains at liberty, because the courtroom doors were shut to *gathering* and *testing* new scientific evidence that could have proved both innocence and guilt.

The prime lesson of the important scientific developments over the past half century is that the courthouse must always remain open to new evidence, even if such openness denies legal finality in criminal cases in which there is no scientific finality.

The current Supreme Court has expressly rejected this important lesson. The mind-set of the majority justices can be gleaned from a 2009 case[105] in which I was not involved. Justice Stevens, in dissent, aptly described the relatively simple issue before the court:

> *The State of Alaska possesses physical evidence that, if tested, will conclusively establish whether respondent William Osborne committed rape and attempted murder. If he did, justice has been served by his conviction and sentence. If not, Osborne has needlessly spent decades behind bars while the true culprit has not been brought to justice. The DNA test Osborne seeks is a simple one, its cost modest, and its results uniquely precise. Yet for reasons the State has been unable or unwilling to articulate, it refuses to allow Osborne to test the evidence at his own expense and to thereby ascertain the truth once and for all.*[106]

Osborne claimed a substantive due process right, among others, to test the evidence, pointing out that not only was his right to liberty at stake, but also that "in more than one third of all exonerations DNA testing identified the actual offender," who may still be at large.

The majority rejected Osborne's claim on the ground that "there is no *long history* of [any] right" to "apply new DNA testing technology that might prove his innocence." They quoted an earlier case that had ruled that the "mere novelty of such a claim is reason enough to doubt that 'substantive due process' sustains it."[107] In other words, the newness of the science itself is "reason enough" for the courtroom door to be slammed shut on it, even if that means an innocent person will remain behind bars.

This absurd legal rejection of "new" science was authoritatively answered by Oliver Wendell Holmes in 1897:

> *It is revolting to have no better reason for a rule of law than that it was laid down in the time of Henry IV. It is still more revolting if the grounds upon which it was laid down have vanished long since, and the rule simply persists through blind imitation of the past.*[108]

So it is with the anachronistic rules of finality that shut the courtroom doors to new scientific developments that can both free the wrongly convicted and apprehend the guilty who remain at large.

16

DEATH, POLITICS, RELIGION, AND INTERNATIONAL INTRIGUE

Sharansky, Kennedy, and the Former President of the Ukraine

While most of my death cases have involved science, others have concerned politics, religion, diplomacy, and international intrigue. Some prosecutions involving death have political implications. Defendants are targeted and falsely charged with capital crimes because of their political activities. Some prosecutions grow out of politically controversial activities, such as unpopular wars. Some politically popular defendants may benefit from a double standard, while other, less popular defendants may suffer from differential treatment. Some defendants try to raise political defenses to homicide charges, while others claim that the courts before which they are to be charged are themselves "political," rather than "judicial." I have been asked to become involved in many such cases, some of which I have accepted and others I have rejected. Here are their stories.

ANATOLY SHARANSKY: DEATH FOR SPYING FOR THE UNITED STATES

The client with whom I most closely identified personally was falsely charged with a capital crime because he was a political dissident in the Soviet Union who made repeated contact with American political and media figures. He was a Soviet Jew whom I never met during the years I was fighting to save his life. His name (at the time) was Anatoly (it's now Natan) Sharansky.

Sharansky was a prominent defender of human rights, not only of his fellow Soviet Jews but of all victims of Soviet oppression. He worked closely with Andrei Sakharov, the father of the Soviet nuclear weapons program who had become the leading voice for human rights in the Soviet Union.

Sharansky was arrested by the KGB in 1977 on charges of spying for the United States—a charge that carried the death penalty. I had previously represented two Jewish refuseniks who had tried to steal a small airplane in which to escape to Israel, via Sweden. They had been sentenced to death. Although we got their death sentences reversed and they were eventually allowed to emigrate to Israel,[1] there was no assurance that similar efforts would help Sharansky, who faced the more serious charge of spying for an enemy.

I had been asked, along with Canadian law professor Irwin Cotler, to represent Sharanksy. The request came from his wife, who was in Israel, and his mother, who lived in Moscow. They had no money to pay for a lawyer. We agreed to do what we could to save his life and, hopefully, secure his freedom.

Our first job was to try to get the espionage charge dropped, since that was the one that carried the death sentence. Because Sharanksy was accused of spying for the United States, I decided to go directly to the White House to try to persuade President Carter to issue a statement expressly denying the Soviet charge that Sharansky had been a CIA operative.[2] Carter faced great pressure from the CIA to continue the long-standing American policy of never affirming or denying anyone's alleged association with the agency. But after several requests, and pressure from his chief domestic policy advisor, Stuart Eizenstat, who had been my student, President Carter did issue the following statement:

I have inquired deeply within the State Department and within the CIA, as to whether or not Mr. Sharansky has ever had any known relationship in a subversive way, or otherwise, with the CIA. The answer is "no." We have double-checked this, and I have been hesitant to make that public announcement, but now I am completely convinced.

Shortly after President Carter made his unprecedented statement, the Soviet prosecutors dropped the espionage charge and took the death penalty off the table. But they were still determined to see Sharansky die in prison. The Soviets called it "special regime," consisting of a diet that no one could long survive on. The prisoners called it "death on the installment plan."

Sharansky's wife pleaded with me to get him out of prison before he starved to death and before she was too old to have children. We had saved him from execution; now we had to save him from starvation.

We decided that the best way to keep him alive was to personalize him to the world. If the world got to know Anatoly as a human being, rather than merely as another prisoner of conscience, it would become more costly, in terms of international reactions, to the Soviet Union to let him die in the Gulag. With this in mind, we set out to plaster his smiling face on every possible magazine cover, newspaper front page, and television show. I appeared on ABC News with Barbara Walters, published a mini-brief in *Newsweek* magazine, gave dozens of speeches, and testified on his behalf at many governmental and nongovernmental proceedings, as did Professor Cotler. We enlisted Sharansky's very beautiful, very photogenic, but very shy wife (Natasha, now Avital) in our campaign. Before long, Sharansky's name became a household word and his image became familiar around the world.[3] His wife's pleas to release him in time to father their children fell on receptive ears—at least outside of the Soviet Union.

At the same time, we filed legal briefs, lobbied for legislative action, and convened academic conferences.

Ultimately, after nine years of unremitting efforts, I traveled to Paris on Thanksgiving day to meet with an East German lawyer whose specialty was arranging spy swaps. We were able to arrange a prisoner exchange that resulted in the release of an East German spy, whom I had been asked to represent in Boston, and Sharansky, along with several others. Because Sharansky was not a spy, but a human rights activist, he refused to participate in any "spy swap." The compromise we reached resulted in Sharanksy walking alone, and not as part of any exchange, across the Glienicke Bridge in Berlin, his book of Psalms in his hand. We later learned that Mikhail Gorbachev had personally ordered Sharansky's release.

VIGNETTE

Mikhail Gorbachev

Shortly after Sharansky's release, I invited Soviet president Mikhail Gorbachev to join me at Rosh Hashanah services in Moscow, where I had been invited to the Kremlin to speak at a conference on law and bilateral economic relations in September 1990. It was a time of transition, but the Soviet Union was still in existence and Gorbachev was still running it.

Gorbachev attended the closing dinner, having just come from an emotional meeting of the Supreme Soviet at which he had sought emergency powers to confront the ongoing crisis. I introduced myself to him as he was eating dinner, and we had a lengthy conversation in which I asked him to come with me to the synagogue and denounce anti-Semitism as Pope John Paul II had done when he appeared at the Rome synagogue and deplored "the hatred, persecutions, and displays of anti-Semitism directed against the Jews at any time and by anyone."

Gorbachev smiled and asked me rhetorically, "Are you here to help bring down my government?" He said he could not go to the synagogue, but he promised me that he would condemn anti-Semitism. Shortly thereafter, he announced that "the Democratic Russian public denounces anti-Semitism and will do everything in its power to uproot the phenomenon from our society."

Sharanksy got out in time to father two beautiful daughters, whom I enjoy meeting when I visit Natan and his wife in their home in Jerusalem. The reason I so closely identify with Sharansky is that there, but for the grace of God and the luck of having grandparents and great-grandparents with the foresight to leave Eastern Europe, go I. If Sharansky's grandparents had come to America and mine had remained in Europe, our roles could easily have been reversed. That's why helping to save Sharansky's life was the case about which I had the most personal feelings. It was also the case that required the widest array of weapons—law, politics, diplomacy, media, economics, persistence, and luck—to win.

Natan Sharansky became a prominent political and moral leader who continues to serve the Jewish people and humanity.

DEFENDING THE FORMER PRESIDENT OF UKRAINE AGAINST MURDER CHARGES

An international client with whom I could not easily identify was the former president of Ukraine, Leonid Kuchma, who was facing an array of charges for having ordered the killing of a journalist. The lawyer who asked me to help the former president assured me that the case was politically motivated and the charges "trumped up."

In T. S. Eliot's famous play *Murder in the Cathedral*,[4] King Henry II is anxious to be rid of Thomas Becket, the archbishop of Canterbury. Unwilling to bloody his own hands, the king hints of his wishes to several loyal knights by issuing a rhetorical challenge: "Will no one rid me of this turbulent priest?" The knights, believing they are following the king's command, then murder the archbishop.

Lawyers and historians have long debated whether the king was legally, morally, or historically guilty of Becket's murder. Prosecutors believed that the Kuchma case was a modern-day variation on *Murder in the Cathedral*.

Ukrainian prosecutors were investigating Kuchma for ordering the murder of a journalist who was allegedly critical of the government. The journalist was murdered during President Kuchma's term in office, and the resulting scandal contributed to the ending of Kuchma's political career.

Over the next several years, there were investigations, but they all exculpated the former president. But now, a decade later, the prosecutors claimed they had a smoking gun: a surreptitiously recorded conversation involving President Kuchma in his "Oval Office" making statements about the murdered journalist akin to those made by King Henry II about the archbishop.[5]

The conversations were allegedly recorded on a small Toshiba digital recorder that had been secreted beneath a couch in the president's office. The voice on the recording was unmistakably that of Kuchma and the words—if he had indeed uttered them—were damning.

My brother and I were retained by a former student of mine, Doug Schoen, a brilliant political strategist who was counseling the former president's family. Our job was to advise the Ukrainian lawyers with regard to the recording and other legal and scientific issues.

I flew to Kiev to meet my client. It was an emotional trip for me, since my family—including many who were murdered during the Holocaust—

came from areas not too far from there. They would have been shocked to learn that their descendant was now representing the former president of a nation that was known to them primarily as a hotbed of anti-Semitism.

I went to Babi Yar, the site of one of the worst mass slaughters of Jewish residents of the area. I had been told that some members of my mother's family were almost certainly among the tens of thousands of victims of the Babi Yar massacres. I was shocked to see that there was hardly any memorial to the murdered Jews. A current resident of Kiev who visited the area, which is just outside the center of town, wouldn't even know that the Jewish residents of Kiev had been gathered in the area and systematically shot and thrown into pits. The tiny memorial has a faded plaque that is extremely vague about what happened. I knew that under the Soviet regime, there had been denial and silence. I knew that from the famous poem by the Soviet dissident poet Yevgeny Yevtushenko, which begins:

No monument stands over Babi Yar
A steep cliff only, like the rudist headstone
I am afraid.[6]

Now there is a monument, but it is unworthy of that term, and it is not as if the city of Kiev doesn't know how to build giant monuments. In the center of Kiev stands a monumental statue to Bohdan Khmelnitsky, who conducted pogroms in the seventeenth century that slaughtered tens of thousands of Ukrainian Jewish babies, women, and men.[7] To this day, Khmelnitsky's picture adorns Ukrainian currency. I found it much harder to identify with a leader of such a country than it had been to identify with a dissident like Anatoly Sharansky, whose family had come originally from the Ukraine.

The visit to Kiev wasn't easy for me, for my wife, or for my brother (who had made a separate visit with his late wife, Marilyn). It was especially difficult for Marilyn, my sister-in-law, whose father's entire family had lived in the Ukraine, where almost all of them were murdered during the Holocaust. The difficulty was exacerbated when one of the Ukrainian lawyers with whom I was working was found dead in his bed just after we completed an evening work session and hours before we were to resume our work in the morning. The official cause of death was ruled a heart attack, but the KGB—whose role in the case we were investigating—is expert at giving enemies "heart attacks." Nor was this the only mysterious death that occurred during the investigation. Earlier, the interior minister, on whose direct orders the man who killed the journalist had allegedly acted, was found dead just hours before he was scheduled to testify. The death was officially declared to be a "suicide," despite the fact that two bullets were found in his body. As the BBC put it: "Questions have been asked about how he managed to shoot himself twice in the head."[8] These questions have never been answered. But we were there to save the life and liberty of a Ukrainian political leader and we got down to work.

President Kuchma immediately told me that although it was his *voice* on the smoking gun recording, they were not his words, as least not in the sequence that appeared in the transcript. I listened to the recording but could not tell very much because the words were Russian and they were difficult to hear.

I told my client that I too had been the victim of a doctored recording in which my voice and words had been edited and resequenced to make it sound as if I had said the exact opposite of what I had actually said.[9] This fake recording had been made by a man named David Marriot, who had offered to be a witness in the Claus von Bülow case. He had asked me for money, and I told him it would be improper to pay him for his testimony and we wouldn't do it. He surreptitiously recorded our conversation on a tape and then simply cut and spliced the tape to make my refusal to pay him sound like a willingness to pay him. His splicing job was so amateur—he used Scotch tape—that our expert was able to demonstrate it without any question. Moreover, in an abundance of caution, I had recorded my side of one of the telephone conversations that he had spliced to change the meaning. My unspliced recording showed that I had categorically rejected his request for payment.[10]

But times had changed, and the recording at issue in the Kuchma case was digital. Changes on a digital recording are much more difficult to detect than on a tape recording. It was our job to demonstrate that the Kuchma recording, like mine, had been tampered with to change the meaning of his words. It would be a challenging scientific task in this new age of recording technology, but my team was up for it. We retained the most sophisticated audio scientists in the world, who were able to demonstrate that words could be digitally resequenced to alter the meaning of a conversation without the change being detectable.

We also established that the recording device and the recording had been removed from the chain of custody, thereby enabling the tampering to be accomplished. Finally, we proved that under Ukrainian law, the recordings had been made and handled unlawfully. The end result was that the court ruled that the recordings could not be used against President Kuchma in any criminal case and the prosecution was dropped.[11]

Once again science had come to the rescue, this time of a man who was being framed by his political enemies. Part of my fee for taking the case was a promise to try to get the picture of Khmelnitsky removed from the Ukrainian five-hryvnia bill. Unfortunately, it is still there, as is the statue of the mass-murdering anti-Semite in the center of Kiev. Science progresses, but some things never change.

THE CASE OF THE HEADLESS KIDNAPPERS

Following the breakup of the Soviet Union, many individuals took advantage of the emerging free market system to earn extraordinary amounts of money. Among them was a young doctor from Tiblisi, the capital of the Georgian Republic. He and his family moved to Russia and developed lucrative businesses.

In the meantime, criminals from the Georgian Republic, encouraged by some political leaders, figured out a way to relieve their nouveau riche former neighbors of part of their wealth: They would kidnap relatives and hold them for ransom. Kidnapping became a thriving business, and paying ransom an occupational hazard in the new Russian economy.

One day the young doctor's father was kidnapped and a multimillion-dollar ransom demanded. The doctor met with two of the kidnappers and negotiated his father's release. So far, business as usual. Then, several days later, the bodies of the two kidnappers were found in shallow graves, their heads severed from their torsos. The young doctor was arrested, and his family—including the father whom he had rescued—came to see me, imploring me to become involved in his defense.

The family reminded me of my own, a generation or two back, except that they were rich. They were close-knit, somewhat insular, and very warm. They were also very frightened. They assured me that the young doctor could not possibly have killed anyone, and especially not two professional and armed gangsters. But the Russian authorities needed a suspect, and the young doctor was an obvious target because he had a motive: revenge.

It seemed like a weak circumstantial case, but I knew enough about the Russian criminal justice system to understand that unless we could solve the crime—unless we could point to the real killers—the young doctor would languish in prison for years, even if he were ultimately acquitted following a long-delayed trial. Our burden was not only to prove our client innocent; we had to take on the role of Perry Mason—to find the guilty parties.

I agreed to help the doctor's Russian lawyers, both by becoming involved in the investigation and by trying to secure support from American and international human rights advocates.

I studied the history of kidnapping in the Georgian Republic and reviewed the sketchy evidence in this case. We followed the money and the forensics. Ultimately, we concluded that the kidnappers had been murdered by the crime bosses who had sent them on their mission. The motive was to silence them and cut off the chain of evidence—along with their heads—that might link them to their bosses if they were apprehended and tortured, or otherwise coerced, into implicating higher-ups. This, we discovered, was not an unusual consequence, especially if the kidnappers had a face-to-face meeting with the ransom-payer, who might then be able to lead the police to them.

Notwithstanding this compelling evidence that exculpated the doctor, and inculpated the real killers, the Russian authorities kept our client in prison, even while claiming to search for the real murderers. The family believed that some people in authority were trying to extort a second ransom from family members, this time for the release of the doctor, who had paid the first ransom to the kidnappers. I was asked to keep the outside pressure up, which I did. During a trip to Moscow, I met with several influential people and told them that the pressure would be maintained until justice was done.

After several more months of imprisonment, the doctor was finally released and allowed to join his family, who now live in Israel. I was invited to his birthday party and celebration of freedom in Israel as a guest of honor. I have remained close to him and his family ever since.

MY MOST UNGRATEFUL HOMICIDE CLIENT: ANGELA DAVIS

Another "political" defendant with whom I had a hard time identifying was Angela Davis, who was charged as an accessory to murder.

Clients whose cases I have helped to win generally respond in one of two ways: some express great, sometimes excessive, gratitude. Claus von Bülow, for example, frequently writes me from London thanking me for saving his life. These clients offer to do anything in exchange for you having saved their lives. Others behave as if the case never happened and you don't exist. Some, like O. J. Simpson, refuse to pay the fees they still owe. I have seen former clients purposely cross the street to avoid even "seeing" me. They don't want to be reminded of the dark period in their lives during which they required a criminal lawyer. In only one case, though, did a former client show absolute ungratefulness for my role in helping her avoid a murder conviction.

During the year that I was a visiting scholar at the Center for Advanced Study in Behavioral Science at Stanford, I was asked to consult on several aspects of the Angela Davis accessory to murder case. Davis, who was a leader of the American Communist Party, was accused in connection with a shoot-out at the Marin County Courthouse as part of an attempted escape of radical prisoners. Davis was accused of purchasing and providing the shotgun that was used. She was also suspected of having engineered the attempt to take hostages in order to barter them for the release of a prisoner she loved. Under legal principles similar to those at play in the Tison brothers case, Davis, if convicted, could expect to serve a very long prison term.

I worked on jury selection as well as on some constitutional issues. Davis was claiming that she could not get a fair trial in any American court because she was black, female, and a Communist. Part of the reason I took the case was to help assure that she did get a fair trial. After several grueling months, she was acquitted and set free.[12] I don't know whether she now believes she received a fair trial. I do know that she was subsequently hired to become a professor at the University of California in Santa Cruz.

Shortly thereafter, I learned that she was going to Moscow to receive the Lenin Peace Prize. She said that she was pleased to receive the prize and that she would spend the rest of her life helping to free political prisoners around the world. I called her office and gave them a list of prisoners of conscience in the Soviet Union—mostly Jews who had been imprisoned because they wanted to emigrate to Israel or to learn about their heritage. I asked if she would be willing to speak up on behalf of *these* political prisoners. Several days later, I received a call back from Ms. Davis's secretary informing me that Davis had looked into the people on my list and none of them were political prisoners. "They are all Zionist fascist opponents of socialism." Davis refused to speak up on behalf of the Soviet dissidents.[13]

Recently, I ran into an older Angela Davis on the porch of the Chilmark Store on Martha's Vineyard. She was wearing a bicycle outfit and was cycling around the island with some mutual friends, including her trial lawyer in the murder case, who had become a judge. It was a strange scene in this bastion of bourgeois affluence to see these former radicals enjoying the comforts of capitalism. I reminded Davis of my participation in her case, which she acknowledged. I also reminded her of her refusal to speak up on behalf of Soviet dissidents. In her mellow response, she said, "Well so many other people were speaking up for them that I didn't think it was necessary for me to add my voice." It's interesting how time changes people's memories. I did not press her as to whether she would today speak up on behalf of Cuban, Chinese, or Venezuelan dissidents, or other heroic people who stand up against what remains of Communist oppression.

Angela Davis is the best proof that in America, as distinguished from the countries she so admires, it is possible for a dissident to receive a fair trial. The key, of course, is for the trial to have the kind of high visibility and media attention hers received. There are still far too many obscure defendants, of all races, who do not receive fair trials or fair sentences. The struggle to achieve universal fairness and equal treatment is an ongoing one.

HARE KRISHNA MURDER

The most bizarre murder case I ever litigated involved both politics and religion. My client was a politically unpopular Hare Krishna leader in West Virginia, who was charged with a wide assortment of crimes, ranging from murder—to copyright infringement! My client's name was Keith Gordon Ham, but he had called himself Kirtanananda Swami when he founded a Krishna community in West Virginia, which he called New Vrindaban. He became the absolute ruler of this cultish community, whose members testified that he exercised total control over all aspects of community life. Vrindaban became a magnet for people who wanted to lose their identity beneath the saffron robes and changed names, including several with criminal records and violent backgrounds. The community expanded to three thousand acres, with five hundred "devotees" and profits from solicitations that reached $10 to $12 million. Much of this money was obtained by selling counterfeit copyrighted images of sports teams. Hence the copyright infringement charge.

The events that precipitated the murder prosecution were described by the court as follows:

The . . . incident involved the murder of devotee and community member Charles St. Denis on June 10, 1983. When community member Daniel Reid learned that St. Denis had raped Reid's wife, Reid decided to kill St. Denis. Before attempting to murder St. Denis, Reid consulted Swami. Swami instructed Reid that the killing was acceptable under Krishna scriptures, but that such action violated secular laws and that Reid might be caught and punished. Swami then directed Reid to talk to Thomas A. Drescher, a fellow devotee. When Reid approached Drescher and told him what Swami had said, Drescher testified he felt duty bound to help Reid kill St. Denis. The two then enticed St. Denis to Reid's house one night, shot and stabbed him several times, and then buried him in a pre-dug grave before he was dead.

[Another] incident likewise involved the murder of a devotee. In 1985, Steven Bryant, a former New Vrindaban devotee, began publishing statements accusing Swami of engaging in homosexual activity and permitting sexual molestation of children in the community. Around April of 1986, members of the Krishna community in Los Angeles notified Drescher that Bryant was in Los Angeles. Drescher received $2,500 from the New Vrindaban community, authorized by Swami, and flew to Los Angeles. He located Bryant and shot him twice in the head.[14]

Swami and several of his lieutenants were convicted and sentenced to long terms of imprisonment. My brother and I were asked to appeal Swami's conviction. We read the transcript of the trial and found it to be filled with prejudicial evidence that was irrelevant to whether Swami was responsible for the crimes of his followers. I took this case not because I approved of anything about Swami, but because I believe that if the most reviled defendants are not afforded a fair trial, there is grave risk to all defendants. Greta Van Susteren, then a lawyer, now a TV commentator, was retained by one of the lieutenants.

I argued that the prosecutors had deliberately "thrown a skunk into the jury box" when they introduced irrelevant evidence that Swami had engaged in a homosexual relationship with a follower. To a West Virginia jury back then, this could be massively prejudicial.

In addition, the prosecution introduced evidence that teachers at the community school had molested children and that Swami was aware of this but did nothing. Finally, they introduced

a videotape segment from [a] television program [that] showed a child of the New Vrindaban community stating that he prayed "to" Swami, a statement generally offensive to the religious sensitivities of typical jurors. More inflam-

matory was a statement by Swami comparing women to dogs and condoning lightly slapping one's wife for disciplinary reasons.[15]

In addition, the case raised the interesting question of whether a religious leader (even of a "cult") could be held criminally responsible for the actions of followers who had sought and then accepted his advice and guidance.[16]

I argued the appeal before a panel of the U.S. Court of Appeals for the Fourth Circuit consisting of three elderly conservative judges in Charleston, South Carolina. I could not imagine a group that would be less sympathetic to a Hare Krishna guru accused of the horrendous crimes of which my client stood convicted. I worried that they too might be prejudiced by the legally irrelevant evidence of his homosexuality, sexism, and bizarre religious views. But my wife's older cousin, the late Morris Rosen, an experienced lawyer from Charleston, cautioned me not to give up. "These old-line southerners care about justice, and they don't have ambitions beyond their current job. They'll give your client a fair shake as long as you don't overstate your case. Be straight with them and they'll be straight with you." He also suggested that their own somewhat narrow backgrounds might sensitize them to the prejudicial impact the government's evidence might have had on the jury. He cautioned me to be subtle when making this point.

My cousin, who was himself "a good ol' boy," was absolutely on target. He had taught me an important lesson. What Tip O'Neill had famously said about politics—"all politics is local"—was equally true of law. It was essential to understand the mores and traditions of the local bench and bar. I argued in a low-key manner, focusing on precedents from the court, and especially from the three judges. In their decision, they followed the law, concluding as follows:

We accept without need of extensive argument that implications of child molestation, homosexuality, and abuse of women unfairly prejudice a defendant. Indeed, no evidence could be more inflammatory or more prejudicial than allegations of child molestation. When evidence of a defendant's involvement in several of these activities is presented to the jury, the risk of unfair prejudice is compounded. In such a case, we fear that jurors will convict a defendant based on the jurors' disdain or their belief that the defendant's prior bad acts make guilt more likely. Furthermore, we are especially sensitive to prejudice in a trial where defendants are members of an unpopular religion.[17]

The court reversed the convictions. The rule of law prevailed over the political and religious prejudices of men and women.

Following the reversal of their convictions, the defendants entered into a plea bargain with the prosecutors and were sentenced to serve prison terms considerably shorter than those to which they had been sentenced previously.

THE CASE I STILL CAN'T TALK ABOUT: CHAPPAQUIDDICK

One homicide case tinged with politics in which some people believe the defendant was advantaged by his political popularity involved Senator Edward Kennedy. I am still not free to disclose everything I know about the case, even though all the principals are dead and the case is more than forty years old, because the lawyer-client privilege extends beyond the life of the client. I was one of the lawyers involved in the Chappaquiddick case—the investigation of Senator Edward Kennedy for driving his car off a bridge on the island of Chappaquiddick, resulting in the drowning death of Mary Jo Kopechne.

It was an eventful summer in 1969. My family and I were on Fire Island anticipating watching a man walk on the moon. I had no idea how much more exciting the summer would become.

I received a call from one of Senator Kennedy's aides, telling me that the senator had been involved in a fatal automobile accident and asking me to make my way to Martha's Vineyard—a place I had never visited. I was asked to become part of the legal team being assembled in anticipation of the upcoming criminal investigation. My primary job was to prepare a brief concerning the rights of the young women (they were referred to as the "boiler room girls" because they had worked on Kennedy campaigns from an office that had once served as a boiler room) who had been vacationing on Chappaquiddick along with Senator Kennedy and several of his friends. The women were being subpoenaed to testify at an "inquest" regarding the tragedy.

There was very little law on the rights of witnesses at this sort of hybrid hearing, which is neither a trial nor a grand jury proceeding. One important issue was whether or when their testimony, which might require them to divulge personal matters, would be made available to the media, which was seeking every possible tidbit of information—or gossip—about the events surrounding the tragedy. I worked with my colleague Professor Charles Fried, and we produced a brief that succeeded in keeping the testimony of the women confidential during the course of the criminal investigation.

I also consulted with, and did legal research for, the lawyers responsible for trying to prevent Senator Kennedy from being charged with vehicular homicide or some other serious crime. We succeeded, and the senator ultimately pleaded guilty to a relatively minor offense.

Although I am not free to disclose what I know, I am comfortable saying that if the full truth were ever to be disclosed, it would not tarnish the senator's well-deserved reputation as one of the great political figures of the last half century. Chappaquiddick was my first personal encounter with Senator Kennedy. We became much closer over the years. I remained close to the senator until his death. During his unsuccessful run for the Democratic presidential nomination against Jimmy Carter in 1980, I acted as a surrogate speaker for him and accompanied him to various events in California and other states. We worked especially closely on helping Soviet refuseniks emigrate to the United States. I vividly recall driving to Logan Airport with Senator Kennedy to greet a family that included a sick child whom he had helped bring to Boston. I consulted with him on numerous projects involving criminal law, constitutional law, judicial appointments, and human rights.

Ken Feinberg, who served as his chief of staff and in many other capacities, recently told me that before anything involving these issues left his office, Senator Kennedy would tell his staff members, "Check it with Alan." The senator told *Newsweek* that my "advice was invaluable" to him.[18] It was a high honor and privilege to assist so great a senator on so many occasions.

The last time I saw him was just months before his death, when he invited me to sit next to him for several innings during the opening game of the Red Sox season on April 7, 2009. He asked me about the Soviet refuseniks he had helped to bring to this country. When I told him how well so many of them were doing—they were professors, engineers, symphony players—he was pleased. He inquired specifically about the sick baby we had met at the airport, and I told him she was about to graduate from Brandeis University. He cared deeply about human rights, not only in the abstract, but as they related to real people. Though the events at Chappaquiddick may have prevented Ted Kennedy from becoming president, they did not stop him from becoming one of the greatest senators in American history.

DEFENDING SOLDIERS

Politically controversial wars need scapegoats, and soldiers often are placed into that unfortunate position. For that and other reasons, I have a policy of representing, without fee, soldiers who risk their lives for our liberties and are charged with killings growing out of their military service. I have helped to defend several soldiers, most prominently Colonel Michael Steele, the real-life hero of the tragic events in Mogadishu that gave rise to the film *Black Hawk Down*.[19] I have also helped to defend ordinary enlisted men accused of unlawful killings of noncombatants.

Several of Colonel Steele's enlisted men had killed "five unarmed Iraqis" following deadly attacks by Iraqi militants against U.S. soldiers.[20] Colonel Steele was being investigated for the instructions regarding the rules of engagement that he had given to his men prior to the killings. Some higher-ups believed that his "fiery rhetoric" had incited the killings, or at the very least had created an atmosphere in which such killings would be seen as acceptable. Colonel Steele adamantly denied any such responsibility and asked me to help his military lawyers prepare a defense to any such charge.

The rules of engagement with terrorist groups are confusing at best. The directive Colonel Steele had received granted him the authority to target "groups, cells and facilities belonging to terrorist groups." How to distinguish such groups from noncombatants in the fog of asymmetric warfare, in which terrorists blend into the civilian population, is one of the most daunting challenges of modern combat. After conducting extensive research on the applicable law and on what Colonel Steele had actually told his men, I was convinced that he had complied with both the letter and spirit of the laws of war, and that the soldiers who had killed civilians were not following his lawful directives. We prepared a brief arguing against any charges being brought against the colonel.

We showed that Colonel Steele's actions were motivated by an understandable need to protect his soldiers, and that he succeeded: Steele's Rakkasan unit suffered half as many losses as the units that had preceded and succeeded them.

In the end Colonel Steele was not charged with any crime. An investigation found that he "continually told soldiers they must be prepared to use deadly force without hesitation, within the boundaries of the law." And though it was "clearly possible that some soldiers, especially young, inexperienced ones, could misinterpret the message," Steele's leadership had not "encouraged illegal, wanton, or superfluous killing."[21]

Despite this finding, Colonel Steele was reprimanded by his superior, with whom he had been in continuous conflict.

A detailed article in the *New Yorker* made the case that the operation during which the killing took place

> *displayed more discipline than recklessness. During the three-day mission, hundreds of Iraqis were detained without incident, and when soldiers were presented with morally confusing situations, or the opportunity to do something that seemed unlawful, many of them either refused to kill or prevented others from acting wrongly. Quantifying the level of discipline in a unit as large as a brigade is not easy, but, according to Army data, the number of Rakkasan escalation-of-force incidents in 2006 was below the median for brigades in Iraq.*[22]

In appreciation for my work on his case, the colonel sent me an American flag that had been "flown for 9 minutes and 11 seconds over the 3rd Brigade Combat Team Head Quarters, Tikrit, Iraq" near a flag that was "hanging inside of Building #7 on the morning of 11 September 2011." In his letter accompanying the flag, Colonel Steele explained that a policeman ran into Building Seven right after the attack, to help get everyone out. On his way out, he saw the flag in the atrium and took it. "The building came down about ten minutes later." The policeman gave the colonel the flag to take with him into combat. Colonel Steele ended his letter with the following words: "My sincerest thanks, Alan, for all you have done for me and for the men of the Rakkasans." The flag stands in a place of honor in my home office, as a reminder of those who have risked their lives to defend our liberties.

The complex issues surrounding the war against terrorists play out not only on the battlefields of Iraq and Afghanistan, but in Israel and Gaza as well. I stand ready to defend Israeli soldiers and commanders who have been falsely accused of killing Palestinian civilians in their efforts to protect Israeli civilians from terrorist rocket attacks. In December 2011, I traveled to The Hague in an effort to persuade the prosecutor of the International Criminal Court not to bring charges based on the deeply flawed "Goldstone Report,"[23] the conclusions of which Richard Goldstone himself subsequently reconsidered.[24] The prosecutor decided that he lacked the jurisdiction to bring such charges and he thanked me for my input.

I have also represented the Mossad in its efforts to prevent prosecution of its agents by foreign governments. Several Mossad agents were captured on Cyprus and accused of spying for Turkey. It wasn't true. They were watching Palestinian terrorists who were planning an attack against Israeli civilians. I helped secure their release. Shortly thereafter, I received a hand-delivered letter of thanks from the head of that shadowy organization, which included the following:

> *I remember the energy you showed when we came to you seeking both advice and action. You threw yourself into the fray and showed every possible willingness to give us both your time and renowned counsel.*
>
> *As you know, there is no greater "Mitzva" in Judaism than "Pidyon Shevuyim"—prisoner release. And nevertheless, not every person would be prepared to be associated with "one of us." So be it you, for your part, acted in the best and noblest of our traditions.*
>
> *We wish you well; we thank you for what you did and what you were willing to do. May we all live to see the day when a profession such as mine gives way to more pleasant occupations. There is still some way to go before this comes about.*

Tragically, the world is still far from a time when those brave men and women who serve in the United States and Israeli armed forces and intelligence services can pursue "more pleasant occupations." Until that day arrives, I will always remain available to lend my time and counsel in support of their noble, risky, and controversial efforts to combat evil.

HELPING THE PROSECUTION KEEP AN FBI MURDERER IN PRISON

For much of my career at Harvard, the second most influential political family in Massachusetts (after the Kennedys) was the Bulger family. "Billy" Bulger was the president of the Massachusetts Senate, the president of the University of Massachusetts, and the leader of the state Democratic Party, to whom presidents, governors, and other movers and shakers paid homage. Billy presided over the annual Saint Patrick's Day Parade celebration, at which he roasted friends and enemies, and at which attendance was mandatory for local politicians, as was a phone-in from national leaders, including the President of the United States. Billy's older brother "Whitey" was the mass-murdering leader of the notorious "Irish mob" in the Boston area and was responsible for dozens of cold-blooded murders.

For years, the media portrayed the Bulger brothers as if they were stock characters in a B movie: the "good" brother, Billy, who could do no wrong, versus the "bad" brother, Whitey, who could do no right. I always wondered about this media-driven dichotomy. It made for a good story, but was it true? I began to research and write about the connection between the Brothers Bulger. What I discovered was a symbiotic, rather than an antagonistic, relationship between them.[25]

Neither brother would have succeeded without the other. Together they controlled Boston politics and crime—which became largely interchangeable—for decades. The conduit between them was a corrupt FBI agent who grew up in their "Southie" neighborhood, John Connolly, who was Billy's friend and protégé.

I first encountered the Bulger corruption when a client of mine was forced to make a quarter-million-dollar payment to Billy in order to get permission to build a high-rise structure in downtown Boston. When I wrote about this alleged extortion, I received a late-night phone call warning me that "an attack on Billy is an attack on Whitey so watch your back." It was widely understood that criticizing the "good" Bulger brother might provoke the wrath of the "bad" Bulger brother. Whitey was known to threaten Billy's political critics, as he did when he confronted one of Boston mayor Ray Flynn's political operatives with the following warning: "You've been running down my brother. I won't have that."[26] Whitey threatened to kill *Boston Herald* columnist Howie Carr, who, like me, exposed the connections between the Brothers Bulger.

Despite these threats, I continued to write and speak about the connection, thereby antagonizing much of the Boston establishment, which had a stake in perpetuating the myth of the good Bulger brother, with whom they had to work and to whom they had to show deference. This establishment included "good government" political figures, such as Governor Michael Dukakis, who should have known better. It also included several prominent prosecutors, who also should have known better.

It was widely known in political and law enforcement circles that those who helped Whitey evade justice were rewarded by Billy with jobs and other forms of political patronage, while those who went after Whitey were punished. Every effort to bring either Billy or Whitey to justice was thwarted by FBI agents who were on the take and prosecutors who feared retaliation.

Billy Bulger had managed to exploit the justice system to protect his brother. His influence extended to the highest levels of government, including the speaker of the house, John McCormack, the director of the

Bureau of Prisons, and several state and federal prosecutors and judges who helped Whitey get out of prison and stay out of prison.[27]

I'm a defense lawyer. Unlike many current defense lawyers, I never served as a prosecutor, though I advise my students who want to become defense attorneys to work in a good prosecutor's office for a few years. Also unlike some defense attorneys, I admire good prosecutors, who do their jobs ethically and professionally. The adversarial system of justice requires zealous prosecution as well as zealous defense. Good prosecutors are the "gatekeepers" of justice: They decide which of the many cases that come to them to prosecute, which not to prosecute, what charges to seek, when to plea-bargain, and how high a sentence to recommend. Bad prosecutors—those who base such critical decisions on political, personal, financial, or other corrupt considerations—can do enormous harm to our system of justice. I've been privileged over my career to know some extraordinary prosecutors. I've also been privileged to help expose some corrupt prosecutors, policemen, and FBI agents.

The case of John Connolly was an example of corruption in high places. In that highly charged case, which was the subject of the semifictional film *The Departed*,[28] I helped an excellent prosecutor keep the corrupt FBI agent in prison. The prosecutor who asked for my help is the state attorney of Dade County, Florida. Katherine Fernandez Rundle replaced Janet Reno in 1993, when President Clinton appointed Reno to serve as attorney general of the United States. She has been repeatedly reelected and served with distinction since.

John Connolly was a high-ranking FBI agent in Boston, who had grown up in the "Southie" neighborhood of Boston along with Whitey and Billy Bulger. Billy served as president of the Massachusetts Senate and then president of the University of Massachusetts before he was forced out of office by then governor Mitt Romney, who threatened to put me and Howie Carr on the board of the university unless Billy resigned, which he did.

During the reign of the Bulger brothers, Billy served as a sort of "godfather" and Whitey as the enforcer of a systematically corrupt political, economic, and legal system.[29] Nothing got done—no large buildings were constructed, no important jobs secured, no political appointments made—without "tribute" being paid to the godfather. If anyone crossed Billy, he had to worry about being literally killed by Whitey. If anyone crossed Whitey, he had to worry about suffering political or economic death at the hands of Billy. For example, when a state trooper stopped and searched Whitey at Logan Airport, finding a large bag filled with cash, the trooper found himself demoted, disgraced, and ultimately driven to suicide. And when Whitey was about to be indicted, Billy's protégé John Connolly tipped the gangster off, allowing him to escape and become a fugitive for sixteen years, during which time the "good" Bulgers—his brothers and sisters—communicated with him, moved money for him, and helped him to avoid capture. As Billy Bulger understated it: "I hope that I personally am not helpful to anyone against him." The "good" Bulger said this *after* knowing that his bad brother had murdered dozens of men and women in cold blood and was ready to murder many more to preserve his freedom. John Connolly also tipped off Billy—the good brother—to the details of an investigation that targeted him for extorting a quarter-of-a-million-dollar bribe from the Boston builder I had represented.

But these were not the only tip-offs John Connolly provided the Bulgers. He gave Whitey the names of "stool pigeons" who were about to inform or testify against him—in other words, those who had to be "silenced" to protect Whitey and his colleagues. Several people were murdered by Whitey as a direct result of Connolly's information.

In exchange, Connolly received bribes amounting to well over a quarter of a million dollars in cash, as well as many valuable gifts, plus a lucrative retirement package from brother Billy.[29] He claimed he also received information from Whitey about Whitey's competitors in crime—the Italian mob—but it is doubtful that law enforcement got much in return for giving Whitey not only a license to kill but a road map as to *whom* to kill. Central to this corrupt deal was the good brother. As Whitey's biographer put it:

> *Brother Bill had served as the enabler while Whitey was in prison, continually lobbying Congressman McCormack on Whitey's behalf. With the FBI, Bill Bulger was also a presence, seeming to hover over everything. He was a mentor to John Connolly, and Whitey's Winter Hill Gang certainly believed that the link with Bill Bulger was the very reason John Connolly had reached out to Whitey.*
>
> *The deal made sense. . . . Connolly brought something to the table that no other agent could—Southie . . . and a close relationship with brother Bill Bulger. Connolly adored Bill Bulger. His wife said that after they'd moved back to Boston in 1973 her husband John "frequently socialized" with Bill Bulger at a private club and also in Bulger's home. Marianne Connolly observed that Bill Bulger had had a "significant influence" on her husband.*[30]

That influence included making sure that Connolly always had Whitey's back, which included the leaking of secret information to Whitey about

FBI informers who needed to be killed.[31] One such murder was committed in the Miami area, and John Connolly was successfully prosecuted by the state for conspiring to commit it. The problem was that several years had passed between the murder and the prosecution, and Connolly had a plausible statute of limitations argument on appeal.

I was asked by State Attorney Rundle to consult with her appellate lawyers and to prepare them for what they expected would be a grueling argument. I worked with them, and with federal prosecutors in Boston, on the appellate brief. I also conducted a "moot court," in which I played judge and asked the hardest questions I could come up with. The prosecution won the appeal.[32] It was the first time I recall cheering when I heard that the prosecution had won and the conviction of the defendant had been affirmed.

There is nothing more corrosive to the administration of justice than corrupt law enforcement officials (except, perhaps, corrupt judges, several of whom Billy Bulger had appointed to "his" bench). The Bulger gang is now history. Whitey and Connolly are in prison, probably for the rest of their lives.[33] Billy is "retired" from politics but remains widely admired by some in Boston, who still can't face the reality that without the help of the "good" brother, there never would have been the mass-murdering bad brother—and without the complicity of some high-ranking and "good government" public officials, there never would have been a corrupt and corrupting good brother.[34]

DEFENDING A MAN WHO ADMITTED HIS GUILT

One murder case that involved international politics, diplomacy, and law required me to represent a defendant I knew for certain was guilty. The myth that guilty clients, even those who have committed murder, will confide their guilt to their trusted lawyer is widespread in literature and reflected in legal rules of confidentiality that encourage a relationship of trust between lawyer and client.[35] The reality is that guilty (as well as some innocent) clients don't trust lawyers with their dark secrets. Most believe that their lawyer will work harder for innocent defendants than for guilty ones, so they claim that they are the totally innocent victims of a horrible injustice. They admit nothing.

Only one client who was accused of a killing admitted to me that he was guilty. He really had no choice, since the very fact of his guilt was an essential element of his defense. This was the Jewish Defense League murder case discussed earlier. Not only was my client guilty of having participated in a crime that resulted in the death of a young woman, he also—it turned out—was a government informant who was providing information to the police as to what he and his group were doing.

When I first undertook the pro bono representation of Sheldon Siegel, he faced a possible death sentence for causing the death of Iris Kones by making the smoke bomb that killed her. He initially assured me he was innocent. I suspected that he had some involvement with the crime, but I had no idea that he was informing against the Jewish Defense League at the same time that he was making bombs for them.

Informers are a peculiar lot, often undecided about which side they are on—other than their own side. Siegel was committed to the ideology of the JDL, including their use of violence to make their point. But he was also desirous of protecting his own head and he knew he was vulnerable to prosecution for the bombs he had constructed that had been used against other Soviet targets. He hoped to avoid prosecution by providing the government with selective information about his JDL colleagues and their plans. He also hoped the JDL would never find out that he was playing both sides against the middle. He didn't even tell his own lawyers, until we figured it out. He then told us the whole story, including his role in the death of the victim. He also told us that in order to protect himself against being double-crossed by the police, he had surreptitiously recorded some of his conversations with them on a tape recorder hidden in his car, where they often talked. The tapes confirmed his claim that the police had made him certain promises, but they did not include the crucial promise that if he told them who planted the bomb that killed Iris Kones, they would never use him as a witness against his JDL colleagues. Siegel told us that this promise had been made while they were talking on the street, where he was unable to record it.

I devised a tactic designed to get the police officer—Sam Parola, who grew up in the same neighborhood Siegel and I did—to admit that he had made that promise. First I pretended we had no tapes, and the officer, confident he could lie without fear of recorded contradiction, denied making *any* promises.

> Q: Did you ever promise him that he would never have to be publicly revealed if he gave you the information in the Amtorg case?
>
> A: No, sir.

> Q: In regard to information that you were seeking from Mr. Siegel relative to a shooting into the Soviet Mission, did you at any point tell him that if he gave you information about that, that you would never call upon him to testify at any trial or ever reveal him as an informant?
>
> A: Oddly enough, Mr. Siegel volunteered that information to me.

Then I questioned him by reading from the actual transcript of the tapes, asking him whether he had ever had "the following conversation with Mr. Sheldon Seigel":

> Q: "You're not going to jail on either one of them, and if you ever say that I said it, I'm gonna deny it and I'm gonna meet you some fuckin' night, and I'm gonna run you over with a truck."

The police officer did not immediately understand what was happening.

> A: No, sir, I deny that.
>
> Q: You are certain that you never said anything about running him over with a truck?
>
> A: I never said anything like that.

I continued to press the witness. I asked him if he had made the following statement:

> Q: "You ever fuck me up like that when I tell you something, you ever rat on me, I will fuckin' brain you."

Parola became a little less certain about his answer:

> A: I don't believe I made that statement.

As I continued to read Parola's recorded words back to him, he began to realize that we might have him on tape, saying things he had sworn he didn't say. Parola's relaxed composure began to change. He asked for water. His face grew pale. His fingers trembled. He almost dropped the glass of water.

> A: The only thing I can say to that, Counsel, is that I would use that that type of language at times. . . .

The officer's self-confident denials gradually softened into evasiveness and forgetfulness: "I don't remember, but it sounds familiar"; "I possibly would say something like that"; "I would have said something like that in order to keep the rapport with the informer."

Now realizing that we definitely had him on tape, the officer began to vacillate and admit he had made *some* promises.

It was time to use the ploy we had devised to get him to tell the truth about the crucial promise not to use Siegel as a witness in the Hurok case. Pretending that we had *that* promise on tape, I read a "transcript" prepared by my client from memory. I began slowly asking the officer if he recalled having the following conversation with Sheldon Siegel:

> PAROLA: Hey, where you been?
>
> SIEGEL: What do you mean?
>
> PAROLA: I told you two o'clock, didn't I?
>
> SIEGEL: No. You told me between two and two-fifteen.
>
> PAROLA: Hey, don't get cute. Hey, look, you got to do us a favor. If you can help us on the Hurok thing I would appreciate it. I promise you, Shelley, just give us the names and leave the rest to us. If we can't prove it without ya, then we can't prove it.

I asked him, "Do you remember having that conversation in substance?"

Parola mumbled, "In substance, I could have had that conversation."

I continued reading from "the transcript."

> PAROLA: Once we know who did it, you don't think we can turn these guys? Are ya kidding? We'll get it out of them. I'm tellin' ya, we can do it.
>
> SIEGEL: What if someone finds out?
>
> PAROLA: No one's going to find out. You won't even have to go to the grand jury on this one. We can do this whole shmeer without even using you. Look, just tell me who did the Hurok thing. Just give their fucking names.

At this point the judge joined the questioning:

> THE COURT: In March of 1972 did you have such a conversation with Mr. Siegel?
>
> MR. PAROLA: Yes, I could have had that conversation relative to Hurok, Your Honor.

MR. DERSHOWITZ: [reading] "We will never use you as a witness, we will build the case around you. We will use your leads."

THE COURT: Did you say that to him in that conversation—and don't tell me you could or couldn't have—I want to know did you or didn't you?

MR. PAROLA: I believe I have testified on the record, Your Honor, that I did, in fact, say to Mr. Siegel that we could build a case around him.

The judge was now helping to conduct my cross-examination. I continued:

[reading] "We ain't going to use you. We just ain't going to, won't have to, we can make the case without you."

THE COURT: [voice rising] Did you say that?

MR. PAROLA: In those exact words, I don't recall, Your Honor.

MR. DERSHOWITZ: Did you give the substance of that statement to Mr. Siegel?

MR. PAROLA: In substance I would say yes.

THE COURT: Then it is a fact, isn't it, that at some point in time you said to Siegel: "We will never use you." Is that correct?

MR. PAROLA: My conversations, Your Honor, with Siegel: "We would never use you if we can build a case around you."

THE COURT: I didn't put that "if" part in. I am asking you whether you ever told it to him without the "if." Read that language, Professor, please. The last few lines of that.

MR. DERSHOWITZ: [reading] "We ain't going to use you. We just ain't. We won't have to. We can make the case without you."

THE COURT: Did you say that to him?

MR. PAROLA: That sounds familiar to me, Your Honor. I don't recall exactly if those words are the words.

THE COURT: [shouting in anger] Just don't interrupt me. I take it when you say "that sounds familiar," that that means that you recollect that in substance, if not in those words?

MR. PAROLA: In substance, si . . .

THE COURT: Yes.

Parola thus admitted that he had promised Siegel he would never be called as a witness in the Hurok case.

As a result of this controversial tactic and our other legal arguments, the court of appeals ruled that Sheldon could not be used as a witness and all the defendants went free.

I still use these recordings in my class to demonstrate the pressures employed by police to turn defendants into informants, and I use my cross-examination tactic to stimulate debate about the limits of what is appropriate cross-examination of a hostile police witness. I also use this case to try to make the students experience what it feels like to "win" for a client you know is guilty of complicity in the murder of an innocent young woman—who was their age and in the prime of her life. I have them read the words of the trial judge who was ordered to dismiss the case against the JDL killers:

> *Do you know who isn't in court today? Iris Kones. Someone has committed a dastardly, vicious, unforgiveable, unforgettable crime; someone is frustrating the administration of justice in a case that, in my mind, involves murder. People who deliberately do so will learn the power of the law even if there are those who have literally gotten away with murder.*

While enunciating these final words, Judge Bauman turned his eyes from the defendants and focused them on me, almost as if to say, "And you, Dershowitz, are the one responsible for frustrating justice and allowing guilty murderers to go free."

His look pained me, because he was right. In a sense I was responsible. Had I not devised novel legal arguments and an edgy cross-examination tactic—had my team and I not devoted days and nights to Siegel's defense—it is possible that the court of appeals might have ruled against him and the other JDL defendants.

I've thought of Iris Kones often, and of other victims of my clients who have gone free because of my legal arguments and my investigative work. I think especially of Iris Kones because she is the only homicide victim who was killed by someone I defended who I know for sure was guilty and went free. I suspect there were other such victims as well, but I can't be sure of any but Iris Kones, because my client in that case told me, and the world, that he was guilty.

I also think of Iris Kones because her family—who are active in both Jewish causes and Harvard University—constantly remind me, and all of our mutual friends and associates, of my role in freeing the murderers of their relative.

Although I don't believe in divine justice, it is true that Sheldon Siegel died at a very young age after an unsuccessful heart transplant. His premature death didn't make me feel any less responsible for the morally unjust, but legally proper, result I helped produce in his case.

THE KILLING OF JOHN LENNON

Another death for which I felt some responsibility was that of John Lennon, who was shot in front of his Manhattan home by Mark Chapman in 1980. Lennon was in the United States on that fateful day because I had helped him avoid deportation back to England in 1975. Had our legal team not been successful in stopping the Nixon administration's political efforts to deport Lennon on trumped-up allegations relating to his use of marijuana in England, Lennon would have been deported and banned from the United States. It is highly unlikely that Chapman would have stalked and shot him on the streets of London or Liverpool, as he did near his Central Park West apartment. This case thus combined elements of politics, psychiatry, and celebrity.

I had been retained by an excellent deportation lawyer named Leon Wildes to write a legal memorandum on the impropriety of the deportation and on several constitutional issues surrounding Lennon's earlier arrest on the marijuana charges that formed the basis for the deportation. (My fee was to be a record album signed by John Lennon: Lennon signed it; the lawyer lost it; and my children nearly killed me!) We won the case,[36] and Lennon continued to live in the Dakota for the several years before he was killed by Chapman.

His killer had no money to hire a lawyer, and so the court appointed a former student of mine, Jonathan Marks, to represent him. Marks is a brilliant and innovative lawyer who wanted to raise a defense based on Chapman's mental state. He asked me to consult with him, but I didn't feel comfortable helping a defendant who had killed my former client. So I declined. Marks put on a compelling case, but the jury rejected his insanity defense and convicted Chapman.

Several years later, I ran into Yoko Ono at an art auction. I told her how sad I was that we had won the deportation case, because if we had lost,

John would still be alive. She became angry: "Don't ever think that," she admonished me. "Those years we had together in New York were the happiest in his life and mine. He gave me Sean Ono. You did a good thing."

I'm not so sure.

POLITICAL MURDER CASES I DIDN'T TAKE

I have refused to take some cases because I did not believe in the "political" defense the client wanted me to raise.

For every client whose case I agree to take, I must, regretfully, turn down many. Every week, I receive dozens of calls, e-mails, and letters asking me to review cases. Many of them involve homicides, because some of my most highly publicized cases have involved clients accused of murder. Being a full-time professor makes my time for litigation limited. So I must choose only a handful each year among the many worthy cases. I have several criteria. I rarely turn down cases in which defendants face the prospect of the death penalty, and when I do, I try to get another lawyer, often a former student, to take the case. (The same is true for cases involving freedom of speech.)

I have explained why I defend the innocent and guilty alike, but there are certain categories of clients I will almost never accept. These include professional criminals who are in the business of doing illegal things and will almost certainly go back to that business if I get them off: drug dealers, Mafioso, terrorists, gang leaders. These professional criminals are entitled to counsel, but I do not want to become a consigliere to a crime family (remember Tom Hagen in *The Godfather*)[37] or an advisor to those who are in the ongoing business of committing crimes.

I also do not generally represent fugitives from justice while they are still "on the lam." A lawyer's job does not include helping a client illegally evade or escape from justice.

I try to take interesting cases that will have an impact on law, cases in which an injustice has been done, and cases involving my personal areas of expertise (science, constitutional law, psychology). I take about half of my cases on a pro bono basis and the other half on a fee basis. I use the fees to support the expenses of my pro bono cases.

Perhaps the most difficult case for me to turn down involved the Israeli student Yigal Amir, who was accused of assassinating the late Yitzhak Rabin, the prime minister of Israel. Several days after the crime that rocked the world, the family of the man accused of committing it came to my home and asked me to become his lawyer. I met with them, and they told me that Amir had in fact pulled the trigger, but that he was legally innocent, because the killing was justified under the Jewish law of *rodef*—a concept akin to preventive or anticipatory self-defense, or defense of others.[38] This concept, which derives from a biblical passage,[39] as interpreted by Jewish sages including Maimonides,[40] authorizes the killing of a person who is about to do great harm to the community. The man who killed Rabin believed that Rabin was about to make a peace with the Palestinians that involved giving back "sacred" land that had been captured by Israel during the Six Day War. He also believed that this would endanger the lives of Israelis, and so he set out to stop it by killing the *rodef* who was, in his view, endangering his land and people.[41]

The trial of Rabin's killer promised to be among the most interesting of my career and among the most important in the history of the Jewish state. Although the crime did not carry the death penalty (Israel has abolished the death penalty except for the Nazi genocide against the Jewish people, under which Adolf Eichmann was hanged),[42] the case fit many of the criteria I generally consider in taking a case. But I decided not to take it.

The reason was that it involved the kind of political defense that I abhor. If every citizen had the right to decide who was a *rodef* deserving of death, there would be anarchy. The "rule of personal politics" would replace the rule of law. The defense of *rodef* was not, in my view, a legitimate legal defense, and I, as a lawyer, was not obligated to present it.

I had a more personal reason as well for turning down this case. I deeply admired Rabin and I supported his efforts to make peace. We knew each other, though not well, and he had consulted with me regarding several issues, including the one that may have led to his death.

Eight days before Rabin was killed, Israel's ambassador to the United States had asked me to meet with the prime minister when he was scheduled to speak in Boston later that month. I asked the ambassador what the subject of the meeting would be, and he told me that the prime minister was deeply concerned about the increasingly virulent level of rhetoric in Israel and the fact that certain fringe religious and political figures were advocating violence against government officials. He wanted to discuss whether there were ways of constraining the level of vitriol without infringing on the right of free speech

I agreed to meet with Rabin and wrote the appointment in my calendar. I also did some research on Israeli law in preparation for the meeting. But it was not to be. Rabin was murdered a week before his scheduled trip to Boston. I could never erase the scheduled meeting from my appointment book or from my mind.

I declined the offer to represent Amir, and watched with interest as his lawyers tried to present the *rodef* defense to an appropriately unsympathetic judge. Amir was convicted and sentenced to life in prison.[43] He was married while in prison and allowed conjugal visits, during which he fathered a child.[44]

Other clients accused of "political" murders whose cases I rejected included Radovan Karadžić, the head of the Bosnian Serbs during the ethnic wars in the former Yugoslavia. Karadžić first called me to ask me to represent him while he was still a fugitive and while the killings were still ongoing. I told him of my policy of not representing fugitives or people involved in ongoing crimes. He asked if he could call me again if the circumstances changed. I did not say no.

Shortly after receiving this call, I had occasion to be at a dinner with then president Clinton and First Lady Hillary Clinton. My decision to turn down Karadžić had been reported in the press (he or someone close to him disclosed it) and it became the subject of discussion.[45] Mrs. Clinton was adamantly against my representation of this "butcher," but President Clinton said that if I could persuade him to turn himself in to the international tribunal in The Hague as a condition of my representing him, it would be a worthwhile trade-off. Karadžić did not turn himself in, and when he was finally caught many years later, he asked me to meet with him in his prison cell in The Hague. I met with him just days after his capture, and we discussed his case, as well as the cases of several of his former colleagues (one of which I was involved in).[46] In the end, I did not represent him. He is still on trial in The Hague.

During the "Arab Spring" of 2011, I received calls from individuals representing both deposed president Hosni Mubarak of Egypt and the then fugitive leader of Libya, Muammar Qaddafi, both of whom were being accused of killing innocent civilians.

A Norwegian human rights activist who was close to Mubarak asked me if I would be willing to go to Cairo as part of the Mubarak legal team. I raised the question of whether it would be wise for Mubarak to be represented by a Zionist Jew. He said that I would be part of a team of three lawyers, the other two to be selected by the Arab League. I doubted that the Arab League would agree to have me participate in such a team, but he assured me that he would try to obtain their consent. That was the last I heard.

I was less tempted by the offer made by Qaddafi's Libyan lawyer. The Qaddafi offer was firm, accompanied by a signed formal retainer letter and contract. I have the contract in front of me as I write these words. It begins "In the Name of G-d, the most gracious, the most merciful. In G-d we trust." In the end, I couldn't agree to what they wanted me to do, and the issue became moot with the fall of the Qaddafi government and the assassination of Qaddafi. I was later asked whether I would consider representing his son in the International Criminal Court, but that issue too became moot when the rebels decided to try him in Libya.

Another offer came from a deposed African head of state accused of mass murder, who offered to pay me with gold bricks he had stolen from his country. Needless to say, I declined his offer, since the gold was not his to give.

One American murder case I turned down grew out of a request from the author Norman Mailer that I represent Jack Henry Abbott. Mailer told me that he had urged the authorities to release Abbott, who was serving time for murder, because he had become a great writer while in prison. Abbott had written a memoir, called *In the Belly of the Beast*,[47] that had become a bestseller and had elicited excellent reviews. Mailer told me that he had succeeded in his efforts to have Abbott released, but that shortly after being set free, Abbott stabbed a waiter to death. The case then became a political hot potato, with everyone involved in releasing Abbott trying to shift the blame for his release to others.

Whoever was to blame, Abbott was now facing a murder charge, and if convicted he would never again experience freedom, regardless of his writing skills.[48]

I agreed to visit Abbott in jail, where he was being held pending trial. I was allowed to meet with him in a lawyer's conference room, with guards standing outside. We began to talk, and I became increasingly skeptical of the media story that Mailer had secured his release. I had his prison record in front of me, and as I perused it, the thought occurred to me that perhaps Abbott had earned his freedom by informing on other prisoners. I made the mistake of asking Abbott whether he was a "snitch." Upon hearing that word, he leaped over the table and grabbed me around the neck. The guards quickly rescued me from his clutches. The last words he heard me say as I left the room were "No way I'm becoming your lawyer."

Finally, I was asked to assist in the defense of George Zimmerman, the "neighborhood watchman" who was accused of murdering a black teenager named Trayvon Martin. The governor's political decision to appoint a special prosecutor well known for her sleazy tactics and excessive charging decisions turned this case from a fact-driven homicide investigation into a politicized, racially divisive prosecution. I decided not to become directly involved in Zimmerman's defense so that I could continue to provide expert commentary on the highly charged case. Following the jury's verdict of not guilty—which I had predicted from the time the charges were brought—I was interviewed by many media outlets around the world. I defended the verdict on the ground that the prosecution failed to meet its burden of proving beyond a reasonable doubt that Zimmerman did not kill in self-defense. I received many emails, some agreeing, and some disagreeing, with my assessment. The following email from a young man serving as a law clerk to a justice of the Tennessee Supreme Court was the most poignant:[49]

Dear Professor Dershowitz,

My name is Daniel Horwitz, and I'm a recent graduate of Vanderbilt Law School. We've never met, but you've been a personal hero of mine for as long as I can remember, and you are largely responsible for both my decision to go to law school at all and my desire to become a Public Defender after graduating. For your unapologetic commitment to due process, and for being—best I can tell—the only truly principled and uncompromising voice for the rights of the accused left in the world, I want to thank you.

In the wake of the George Zimmerman trial, I found myself more lost than I've been in a while. Seeing much of the political left—an ideology with which I have always associated—wholly abandon bedrock constitutional principles like the presumption of innocence and the accused's right to a fair trial was more disheartening than I can realistically explain. Just when I'd almost given up hope, however, hearing you condemn the state's abuse of its charging discretion, emphasize the need for a not guilty verdict given the state's clear inability to satisfy its burden of proof, and remind everyone what due process of law actually means, was all that it took to restore my faith.

I read "Letters to a Young Lawyer" both the day before I began law school and the day after I graduated, and I know that you counsel people like me to "expect to be disappointed" by our heroes. Much to my regret, that advice has already proven sound more times than I can count. That said, though, as someone who's deeply committed to the ethic of criminal defense, you have never once let me down, and for that I will always be grateful to you. For your unwavering commitment to principle, thank you so, so much.

All the best,
Daniel Horwitz

17

DEATH CASES FROM THE CLASSROOM TO THE COURTROOM AND FROM THE COURTROOM TO THE CLASSROOM

Shooting a Corpse and Crashing a Helicopter

I was one of the first full-time law professors at a major law school to represent criminal defendants on an ongoing basis. I have always believed that practicing law made me a more relevant teacher, because I could bring my courtroom experience in the classroom, and that teaching law made me a more effective lawyer, because I could bring my scholarship into the courtroom. In deciding which clients to accept, I have always looked for factual or legal issues I could bring into the classroom to benefit my students, and for cases that could bring my classroom experiences into the courtroom to benefit my clients. For me such cases present a win-win situation for students and clients alike.

The most intriguing of these "academic" cases involved a young man from Brooklyn who shot an acquaintance who he believed was alive but who was already dead at the moment he shot him. That case raised a classic legal conundrum that has been debated in classrooms throughout the world since the days of the Talmud: Is it murder, or attempted murder, to try to kill someone who, unbeknownst to you, is already dead? The Talmud gave the following theological response to that age-old question:

> *All agree that if one kills a person whose windpipe and larynx (gullet) are cut, or whose skull is fractured, he is free (for it is considered as if he had attacked a dead man). And they agree also that, if one killed a person who was struggling with death through sickness caused by Heaven, he is guilty of a capital crime.*[1]

Until my Brooklyn case, this conundrum had generally been presented to students as an abstract hypothetical, as in the Talmud, since no real case had actually presented such a factual situation to an appellate court. One such classroom "hypo" came from a Sherlock Holmes story in which Holmes is being stalked by Colonel Sebastian Moran, who is determined to kill the sleuth. In order to lure his pursuer, Holmes commissions a likeness of his own head. The "bait" is placed in the window of Holmes's house. Moran takes the bait and shoots "Sherlock Holmes" with his high-powered rifle. The bullet strikes the sculpture "plumb in the middle of the back of the head and smack through the 'brain.'" Moran is captured and admits his intent to murder Holmes. As the arresting officer is taking Moran away, Holmes asks, "What charge do you intend to prefer?" Inspector Lestrade replies, "Why, of course, the attempted murder of Mr. Sherlock Holmes." The great detective ponders for a moment and then shakes his head, suggesting that this would be a questionable application of the law. Neither the reader nor the students studying this hypothetical case can ascertain whether, under English law, a "killer" who shoots the "brains" out of a dummy, believing it to be a live human being, can be convicted of attempted murder. When an intended killer shoots the dummy, is he attempting to kill the dummy, which is both legally and factually impossible, or is he attempting to kill Holmes?

I had been fascinated by the law of attempts since my first year in law school. One of the earliest cases I studied involved a man who had placed a pistol to his wife's head and pulled the trigger.[2] But the gun did not fire, because he had forgotten to load it! Two police officers heard the man shout—after he had pulled the trigger—"It won't fire. It won't fire." (There was no evidence as to whether the exclamation was made in a tone of assurance, disappointment, surprise, or desperation.) He was convicted of attempted murder, and he appealed on the ground that it had been impossible to kill his wife with an unloaded gun. The court upheld the conviction, concluding that the fact that the gun was unloaded when the defendant pulled the trigger "did not absolve him of [attempted murder], if he actually thought at the time that it was loaded."[3]

Above: *Mike Tyson being led to jail. (Getty Images)*

Left: *Me arguing a legal issue in the 1994 O. J. Simpson case. (Getty Images)*

Below: *A courtroom sketch of me testifying in the Woody Allen–Mia Farrow custody case. (Jane Rosenberg, CBS News)*

The Washington Post

FINAL

Inside: Food, Classified

Wednesday, December 2, 1998

25¢

Both Sides Harden Impeachment Views

Alan Dershowitz testifies before the House Judiciary Committee, where he engaged Chairman Henry J. Hyde (R-Ill.) in a heated argument about whether the panel was singling out President Clinton regarding his alleged perjury.

Widening of Probe Irks Democrats

By Juliet Eilperin and Ruth Marcus
Washington Post Staff Writers

House Judiciary Committee Republicans yesterday opened a new front in their impeachment inquiry against President Clinton, voting in a rancorous session to examine allegations of Democratic fund-raising abuses even as Democrats assailed the move as an eleventh-hour "fishing expedition."

The campaign finance dispute was one of several signs of increasing intransigence on both sides. Republican House members privately discussed plans to block any vote on a Democratic alternative of censure that could undermine their impeachment drive, senior GOP sources said. White House officials, convinced that the Judiciary Committee had miscalculated, raised the possibility of declining to present any defense before the panel.

The public clash came over a party-line vote in the Judiciary Committee to compel testimony from FBI Director Louis J. Freeh and Charles G. LaBella, the former head of the Justice Department task force investigating the 1996 campaign. It also subpoenaed internal Justice documents generated by the probe, including the arguments by Freeh and LaBella to Attorney General Janet Reno about why she should recommend an independent counsel in the case. Lawyers for the panel later appeared in federal court seeking approval to obtain the memos.

The subpoenas interrupted what was supposed to be the day's main event, a nine-hour committee hearing on "the consequences of perjury" featuring two convicted perjurers that was meant to showcase what Republicans view as their strongest impeachment charge against Clinton: that he lied under oath to conceal his affair with Monica S. Lewinsky. The panel has been tentatively scheduled to vote on articles of impeachment related to the Lewinsky matter next week.

See IMPEACH, A20, Col. 1

Analysis

Republicans' Elusive Target: a Strategy

By Dan Balz and John F. Harris
Washington Post Staff Writers

If there is a strategy House Judiciary Committee Republicans are following in their impeachment inquiry against President Clinton, it is no longer evident—even to many of their GOP colleagues on Capitol Hill.

Yesterday's actions by the committee, particularly the decision to expand the inquiry into Democratic fund-raising practices in the 1996 presidential campaign—a subject already explored by two other congressional panels—underscored the feeling that a solemn constitutional process has begun to veer out of control.

"There's a major concern that we let it out of the box and we don't know how to get it back in, and it's blown up in our face," said Rep. Christopher Shays (R-Conn.), who does not serve on the committee.

At a time when the impeachment proceeding had appeared to be heading toward a conclusion—with most Democrats and some Republicans favoring censuring the president for his attempts to conceal his affair with Monica S. Lewinsky—yesterday's action raised the prospect that it could spill into 1999, a prospect favored by neither Republicans nor Democrats.

Both House Republicans and Clinton's advisers say they want the process over, but actions of recent days have shown that neither side is ready to take the steps necessary to bring that about. Clinton's legalistic answers last week to 81 questions from the committee infuriated Republicans and seemed to embolden commit-

See ANALYSIS, A19, Col. 1

Hyde told Dershowitz that two perjurers who testified had suffered "permanent damage" because they had lied about trivial matters and were victims of a "double standard." Story on Page A18.

Top: *Hillary and Bill Clinton at Rosh Hashanah services with me, my son, Elon, and my wife, Carolyn. (Courtesy of the White House)*

Above: *The* Washington Post *account of my testimony in Congress against President Clinton's impeachment. (Courtesy of the* Washington Post*)*

Right: *President Clinton with my daughter, Ella, and his daughter, Chelsea, on the beach at Martha's Vineyard. (From the author's collection)*

Top: *Debating with Noam Chomsky about the Middle East at Harvard's Kennedy School of Government. (MerlinONE)*

Left: *Fouling my brother during a one-on-one basketball game. (Harry Benson)*

Below: *Carolyn and me in our funky living room in Cambridge. (Getty Images)*

Host

ALAN DERSHOWITZ KASHAS IN ON HIS FAME AND OPENS A SLAW PRACTICE

When Alan Dershowitz was a student at New York's Yeshiva University High School, he was called in by the principal, a rabbi, and given some career counseling. "You have a good mouth on you, but no head," the rabbi said. "So you gotta do something that you need a good mouth for but no brains. Become a lawyer."

He did—and quite a successful, high-profile lawyer too, not to mention a professor at Harvard Law School. Dershowitz defended Claus von Bülow, he defended porn actor Harry Reems, and he defends the First Amendment wherever he believes it is threatened. But there was at least one thing he found indefensible: the criminal lack of a good kosher delicatessen in the predominantly white-bread environs of Cambridge, Mass., where you can get a B.A., an M.A. and an LL.D., but until recently, says Dershowitz, you

Deli partners Dershowitz, left, and Marcus Weiss get the approval of Rabbi Abraham Halbfinger.

Right: *My ill-fated Harvard Square deli, with co-founder Marcus Weiss. (Courtesy of* People *magazine)*

Below: *With former Harvard Law School student Chief Justice John Roberts. (From the author's collection)*

Top: *Preparing to teach a class at Harvard Law School with Stephen Jay Gould and Robert Nozick. (From the author's collection)*

Above: *With President Obama and his Middle East national security team at the White House, sharing a joke I told. (Courtesy of the White House)*

Left: *Being detained by Swiss security after confronting President Ahmadinejad in Geneva. (Haaretz)*

Top: *Israeli president Shimon Peres shows me his Nobel Peace Prize at his office in Jerusalem. (Courtesy of Thomas Ashe)*

Left: *With Palestinian National Authority president Mahmoud Abbas, signing a plan to restart Israeli-Palestinian peace negotiations. (Courtesy of the* Jerusalem Post*)*

Below: *With Israeli prime minister Benjamin Netanyahu at his home in Jerusalem. (Courtesy of the Prime Minister's office)*

membering three
ish artists
od — Matzoh Burn-Out
alth — Jamaican Journey
$1.25 April 25, 2008/ Nisan 20 5768
BALTIMORE
Jewish Times
efender
of
Israel
Alan Dershowitz comes to Baltimore as Israel turns 60.
jewishtimes.com

On the cover of the Baltimore Jewish Times, *in a familiar role as defender of Israel. (Courtesy of the* Baltimore Times*)*

Above: *My family at Martha's Vineyard in 2005: (Top row) My daughter, Ella, a graduate of Yale and an actor in New York; me; my wife, Carolyn; my younger son Jamin, chief counsel of the WNBA; my son Elon, a film producer. (Bottom row) My grandson, Lyle, now a freshman at Harvard; my granddaughter, Lori, now a junior at Harvard; and my daughter-in-law, Barbara, an emergency room doctor at New York– Presbyterian Hospital. (Peter Simon)*

Below, left: *At Fenway Park before throwing out the first pitch, eating a sandwich named after me on my seventieth birthday. (From the author's collection)*

Below, right: *Throwing out the first pitch—a strike to Kevin Youkilis—at Fenway park. (Courtesy of Thomas Ashe)*

I wrote a student article for the *Yale Law Journal* on this case[4] in which I analyzed the concept of "impossible attempts," using as my major "hypo" the "firing of a gun at an apparently sleeping man who had ultimately died of natural causes moments before the shooting."[5] I tried to distinguish between attempts that were impossible because of fortuitous factors that were beyond the control of the individual (such as the mechanical jamming of the gun as it was being fired) and attempts that failed because the individual exercised some control (such as a rapist who changed his mind when he discovered that his potential victim was pregnant).[6] Citing Sigmund Freud's studies of the unconscious, I speculated that the defendant's failure to load the pistol may have reflected unconscious ambivalence on his part about killing his wife.[7] My paper was sophomoric and fraught with all the pitfalls of armchair psychology, but it got me thinking about the law of attempts and the defense of impossibility. It also brought me to the attention of the Harvard Law School hiring committee.

When I began to teach Criminal Law several years later, I devoted a significant portion of the course to untangling the web of criminal attempts. Every year the class would divide into warring factions over the Sherlock Holmes story or the hypothetical case of the "killer" who shot his enemy believing him to be alive, only to be saved from a murder charge by his victim's fortuitous demise moments earlier.

By the time the class was over, many of the students had come to the conclusion that there really was no principled distinction between attempts that were impossible and those foiled by unanticipated circumstances. In each case, the defendant intended to kill and did everything in his power to bring about that result. I then pressed them to consider whether in a moral sense there was any valid distinction between the defendant who did everything within his power to kill but failed and the defendant who actually succeeded. Why, I asked, should the fortuity of success or failure determine the extent of a defendant's punishment?

The hypo I used to make this point involved two epileptic drivers who were both told by their doctors not to drive without taking their anticonvulsive medicine. They both disregarded this admonition and experienced seizures while driving through Harvard Square. They both crashed after blacking out: one killed a child crossing the street; the other pinned against a wall a bank robber escaping with a million dollars. At the moment before they blacked out, they were equally culpable, morally and legally. But following the crashes, their legal accountability would have been considerably different: The first would have been guilty of manslaughter for killing the child; the second might have been considered a hero eligible for a reward. The first would almost certainly have been sentenced to prison; the second—though perhaps guilty of reckless behavior—would likely have escaped punishment.

Why, I asked, is there such a considerable legal difference between these cases? They appear to be equally culpable from a moral point of view. The major difference—the death of the child versus the capture of the robber—was a fortuity that occurred *after* the two drivers were both unconscious and thus incapable of controlling their conduct. It is true that the first driver caused a death, while the second driver caused the capture of a robber, but why should legal consequences depend on the different fortuitous outcomes of morally comparable actions and intentions? Would the Angel Gabriel or God treat these equally culpable sinners differently in deciding whether to relegate them to hell, heaven, or somewhere in between? If not, then why should human law treat them so differently?

These were the kind of issues I loved to debate with my students, but there was always an air of unreality about the discussion of hypothetical corpses and car crashes. I looked for actual cases that added flesh and blood to the bones of these made-up cases.

I found one in a bizarre encounter between Melvin Dlugash and two friends in a Brooklyn basement in 1973.

An attorney I knew asked me whether I would be interested in arguing an appeal for the brother of a friend of his who had been convicted of murder for shooting a corpse.

"You've got to be kidding!" I exclaimed. "Cases like that don't really happen except in the warped minds of law professors and fiction writers."

He assured me that it had really happened. I told him that if the court record of the case actually presented that intriguing issue, I would definitely want to argue it. What an addition it would make to my Criminal Law course! I also told him that my academic background might help me win the case.

This is what the record showed: His friend's brother, Melvin Dlugash, came from a middle-class family in the Bensonhurst section of Brooklyn (the neighborhood adjoining Boro Park). Mel had had a troubled life since his adolescence and had begun to run with a tough crowd. (Law professors, in the excitement of a fascinating fact pattern, sometimes tend to forget the human tragedies that often underlie it.)

On Friday night, December 21, 1973, Melvin Dlugash and two of his friends, Mike Geller and Joe Bush, had gone out drinking. Mike lived in a basement apartment in the Flatbush section of Brooklyn; Joe had been staying with him and was supposed to be sharing the rent. Back at the apartment that night, Mike asked Joe several times for his share of the rent, and Joe responded angrily that he didn't owe anything. At about three o'clock, the argument between Joe and Mike escalated. Mike again demanded the rent money—$100—and Joe threatened to hurt him if he didn't lay off. Mike repeated his demand.

Suddenly Joe drew a .38-caliber revolver from his pocket and fired his pistol three times at Mike's heart. Mel watched as Mike fell to the floor, blood cascading from the wounds in his chest.

Joe then pointed his gun at Mel and said, "If you don't shoot him, I'll shoot you." Joe wanted it to appear that they were in it together, so that Mel would not be able to point an accusing finger at him, because under New York law the uncorroborated testimony of an "accomplice" is insufficient for a conviction.[8] After some hesitation, Mel walked over to Mike's prone and motionless body and pulled the trigger of his .22-caliber automatic pistol. Five bullets ripped into Mike's head several minutes after Joe's .38-caliber bullets had penetrated Mike's heart. Mel was convicted of murder. I agreed to handle his appeal.

I argued that the murder conviction must be reversed on the basis of scientific evidence that it was impossible to know whether the victim was alive or dead at the moment my client shot him in the head, since someone else had shot him in the heart just moments earlier.[9] I cited the scientific and medical literature relating to gunshot wounds in the heart and the time it takes for death to result. The court agreed with my scientific argument and ruled that the prosecution had not satisfied its burden of proving beyond a reasonable doubt that Mike was still alive when my client's bullet shattered his brain.[10] I also argued that my client could not be convicted of attempted murder, on the ground that since it is factually impossible to murder a corpse, it is also legally impossible to attempt to do that which it is factually impossible to do.[11] The court agreed with this argument as well and ordered my client to go free.

It was a total victory, but short-lived, because the state appealed the decision to New York's highest court. On the second appeal, which I argued in Albany, the court agreed that my client could not be convicted of murder because "man dies but once," but it concluded that he should be convicted of attempted murder.[12] Not willing to give up, I then brought a federal habeas corpus petition, and the federal court threw out the attempted murder conviction as well, on the ground that the intent requirement for proving attempted murder was higher than it was for a completed murder[13]—an academic argument if there ever was one! My experience in the classroom helped my client remain free.

This intriguing case[14] is taught today in many law schools as part of the standard course on criminal law.[15] The issue of whether it is legally possible to attempt to do what is factually impossible—namely, to kill a dead person—continues to confound new generations of law students.

Another attempted murder case presented a problem right out of the Bible. My client was accused of attempting to kill his sister's former boyfriend. The boyfriend was suspected of burning down the sister's house and causing painful burns from which she ultimately died. But while she was still alive, my client—her brother—went to her former boyfriend's home, held a knife over his chest, and said he would kill him unless he admitted his role in the fire. The police burst into the apartment and disarmed my client before he could stab the former boyfriend. My client was convicted of attempting to kill the former boyfriend, and I was retained to argue the appeal.

I analogized the situation to the one described in the book of Genesis when God told Abraham to sacrifice his son Isaac, and Abraham was standing, knife in hand, ready to inflict the fatal wound, when God's angel came down and told him to stop.[16] I argued that we can never know whether my client would actually have killed the boyfriend had the police not intervened, just as we can never know for sure whether Abraham would actually have complied with God's command. There were other issues in the case as well and we won the appeal.[17] The state declined to reprosecute and this client too went free. I use this case as well in my teaching in both Criminal Law and a seminar on the biblical sources of law.

A highly publicized case that raised issues similar to those discussed in the classroom grew out of the making of a major motion picture directed by Steven Spielberg, John Landis, and others. The film was *Twilight Zone: The Movie*,[18] based on the television series *The Twilight Zone*.[19] There were four segments to the film. John Landis, already famous for directing *Animal House*, *The Blues Brothers*, and other megahits, was directing a segment involving the Vietnam War.[20] The star of that segment was the veteran actor Vic Morrow. The scene at issue called for Morrow's character to be running through a rice paddy, in pitch darkness, carrying two children as helicopters fired at them.

Landis wanted to make the scene as realistic as possible, so he filmed it at night, with extensive pyrotechnics and a real helicopter flying low to the ground. Tragically, the helicopter crashed, and fell on Morrow and the children, killing them instantly. Landis was charged with involuntary manslaughter. He was the first film director in history to be criminally charged with causing the death of an actor.[21] The prosecutor was determined to see him imprisoned for many years.

The Landis case involved a variation of the classroom hypothetical involving the two cars crashing into a child and a bank robber. When the helicopter crashed to the ground, it could have fallen in one direction or another. If it had fallen in one direction, it might have killed Landis, but because it fell in the other direction, it killed the actors. Landis had no control over the direction the helicopter would travel as it crashed. In that sense, he was like the epileptic driver after he blacked out. Yet he was being criminally charged with manslaughter on the ground that his direction caused the deaths.

The Landis case also involved daunting issues of causation in science and law: Did Landis "cause" the death of the victims; or was the mechanical failure of the helicopter the actual cause? Those questions were starkly presented by the facts in the Landis case.

An important issue at the trial was whether the accident should have been foreseeable to Landis. If it was foreseeable to a reasonably prudent director that a helicopter, placed in the circumstances in which this one had been placed, might malfunction and crash, then the directorial decision to have the helicopter fly close to the pyrotechnics could satisfy the legal criteria for involuntary manslaughter. But if the crash could not reasonably have been anticipated, then it would have to be regarded as an accident, giving rise, perhaps, to civil liability, but not to a criminal charge. The stakes were high both for Landis and for the film industry.

John Landis came to my home in Cambridge to try to persuade me to become involved in his defense as a trial consultant and as his appellate lawyer if he was convicted. I told him that I had been teaching and writing about the issue of causation in criminal law for many years. I knew that whichever way this prosecution turned out, it would become a leading case and an excellent teaching tool. I thought that my academic interest in the issue could add a useful element to Landis's defense, and that my involvement in the Landis trial would add a useful element in my teaching.

I explained to John Landis that my interest in his case was, in part, academic and that I would like to use it in the classroom. He agreed, saying he would be getting free legal advice from some of the most brilliant law students in the world. My class discussed the case, and some useful legal and tactical insights emerged.

The prosecutor called seventy-one witnesses, many of whom offered scientific testimony about the cause of the crash and why it should have been anticipated. The defense summoned scientific witnesses who testified that an accident of this kind—the heat from pyrotechnics causing the tail rotor of the helicopter to delaminate—had never before occurred and could not have been anticipated. We pointed out that if Landis had any reason to fear the helicopter crashing, he surely wouldn't have put his own life at such great risk, as he did when the helicopter crashed very close to where he was standing.

The jury deliberated for nine days before finding Landis not guilty. There would be no appeal, but the trial became a staple of law school teaching, appearing in many legal casebooks.

Several years later, it appeared as if another director might be in trouble for the death of an actor, this time while filming *The Crow*.[22] The actor was Brandon Lee, the son of Bruce Lee, the famous martial arts actor, who himself died while filming *The Game of Death*.[23] Brandon Lee was killed by a projectile that was accidentally shot from a gun that was supposed to be firing blanks. A thin but lethal shard of metal penetrated Lee's heart, killing him.

A criminal investigation was opened and I was asked to consult with the lawyers for the production team. Eventually, the lawyers persuaded the authorities not to indict anyone for the tragic accident.[24]

The end result in both the Landis and Lee cases was that greater care is now being exercised during filming of sequences that pose significant risks to participants. Sometimes it takes tragedies to improve safety.

I use each of these cases in teaching my Criminal Law students about causation and the importance the law attributes to results, even if they are fortuitous and beyond the control of the defendant.

WAS JOHN DUPONT INSANE?

Another area of law about which I have long been teaching and writing is the relationship between law and psychiatry. My interest in this subject began when I was a law student studying with Professors Joseph Goldstein and Jay Katz, both of whom were trained in psychoanalytic theory.

It continued during my clerkship with Judge David Bazelon, who was the leading judicial authority on the insanity defense. I taught courses for several decades with Dr. Alan Stone on law and psychiatry and related subjects. So it was natural that when I began to litigate cases I would be attracted to alleged murders committed by mentally ill defendants. These cases also involved science—though a somewhat different kind of science than that involved in the biochemistry and DNA cases.

One of the most disturbing of these cases involved a wealthy and prominent sportsman who shot his best friend in cold blood for no apparent reason. John Du Pont, an heir to the famous chemical company, used his enormous wealth to create a training facility for Olympic wrestlers. World champion wrestler and gold medal winner David Schultz was his best friend. Yet on the afternoon of January 26, 1996, Du Pont drove up to Schultz's residence and, without any provocation, shot him three times with a .44 Magnum at point-blank range, killing him in front of his wife. He drove away, hid in his mansion, and refused to surrender to the police unless they notified the Bulgarian embassy, which he claimed would give him asylum.

As later emerged, Du Pont did not believe he was killing his best friend Schultz, but rather a Soviet agent who had taken over Schultz's body. Following his mother's death nearly a decade earlier, Du Pont had become a full-blown paranoid schizophrenic. He believed at different times that he was the Dalai Lama, Jesus, and a deposed Russian czar. And he was convinced that Soviet agents were determined to kill him.

If this case had arisen before John Hinckley's attempt to assassinate Ronald Reagan, it never would have come to trial. Everyone would have agreed that an insanity defense was appropriate, and Du Pont would have been committed to a mental hospital to receive treatment. But following Hinckley's insanity acquittal in 1982, several states, including Pennsylvania, where Du Pont shot Schultz, changed their insanity defense laws, introducing an intermediate concept called "guilty and mentally ill."[25] Given this alternative, most juries rendered that compromise verdict, rather than finding the defendant not guilty by reason of insanity. The defendant did, after all, kill the victim, the jury would reason, and therefore he was *guilty*, but he was *also* mentally ill. It was the perfect verdict for Du Pont's situation.

Accordingly, John Du Pont was found guilty of third-degree murder (without an intent to kill) but found to be mentally ill. He asked me to argue his appeal. I didn't think he was likely to win, given the climate of the times and the nature of his crime, but I agreed to participate in the appeal, along with his local Pennsylvania lawyers. I saw this case as a perfect vehicle for teaching my students about the changing nature of the insanity defense.

I visited Du Pont on several occasions in prison. He was extremely intelligent, well read, and polite. Our conversations would begin in a normal fashion, with him asking about developments in the news, particularly those regarding foreign affairs. Gradually his paranoid schizophrenia would emerge as he put himself more and more into the news accounts, especially those involving Russia, Bulgaria, China, and Tibet. By the end of the conversation, he was in a different world—the world he had obviously inhabited when he shot his friend. He was the czar whom the Russian agents were determined to kill in order to prevent him from regaining his throne, or he was the Dalai Lama whom Chinese agents were hunting, or he was Jesus, whom Pontius Pilate was seeking to crucify.

Under Pennsylvania's narrow insanity defense, every defendant is presumed sane, regardless of how bizarre his conduct or thought process. The defendant must prove his insanity by a preponderance of the evidence. Insanity is defined as an inability "to know the nature and quality of the act he was doing, or if he did know it, that he did not know he was doing what was wrong."[26] This "right and wrong test" goes back nearly two hundred years, to the English Common Law,[27] and is difficult to establish, especially if the jury has the option of finding the defendant "guilty" and "mentally ill."

No one disputed Du Pont's mental illness. But the prosecution contended that he had known the nature and quality of his act—namely that he was shooting a human being—and that he had known it was a legally wrong thing to do. Du Pont's "reality"—that he was shooting a Russian agent who had taken over the body of his friend—was legally irrelevant, because he knew he was shooting a person. The law of self-defense does not permit preventively killing someone who is planning to kill you unless he is in the act of trying to kill you. And neither Schultz nor "the Soviet agent" who had allegedly "taken over Schultz's body" was in the act of trying to kill Du Pont when Du Pont fired the fatal shots. Hence, in the eyes of the law Du Pont was guilty, even if severely mentally ill.

The appellate court agreed with that assessment and affirmed the jury verdict.[28] Remarkably, Du Pont was given no treatment, despite the finding of mental illness, and remained in a prison setting until he died in 2010,[29] shortly after his federal appeal was denied and before he could file a writ of certiorari in the Supreme Court. It is unlikely he would have prevailed in federal court, since it remains uncertain whether the Constitution requires a state to provide an insanity defense to crime. My students have debated this poignant case, with most believing that a person like John Du Pont should be found not guilty by reason of insanity and treated rather than punished.

DOES A BATTERED WOMAN HAVE THE RIGHT TO KILL HER BATTERER?

Yet another issue about which I have been teaching and writing for many years is the so-called battered woman syndrome. This syndrome is, in some respects, a variant on the insanity defense. Many women who have undergone years of physical assault by husbands or lovers are believed by some experts to suffer from a form of mental disturbance that denies them the power to escape from their batterers or even to reach out for help from law enforcement. This diagnosis is controversial,[30] but when a woman who had been convicted of murdering her husband, who she claimed had abused her, asked me to argue her appeal, I agreed, since her claim seemed compelling and her case would make for interesting classroom discussion.

Whenever I defend an accused killer, I'm asked how it feels to be up against the family of the victim. It's a hard question, even when asked in the abstract. In this case I was confronted directly by the mother of the victim.

My client was Lisa Rubin, who had admittedly shot and killed her husband. She claimed that he had abused her and that she killed him in self-defense. The problem was that the evidence showed that after she emptied her gun into his head, she reloaded and emptied it again into his body. She was found guilty of premeditated murder and asked me to try to get the conviction reversed or reduced to manslaughter.

I argued the appeal in the Maryland Court of Appeals.[31] I was satisfied that I had done the best I could with a difficult fact pattern. As I was leaving the courtroom, feeling pretty good about myself, an elderly woman approached me. "You did a fine job, sir," she began. I thanked her and started to walk away. "The man she murdered was my son," she politely continued, "and I want you to know that my son never abused or tried to kill her." She looked me straight in the eye and persisted: "He would never do such a thing. He was a fine young man. She was just trying to get rid of him because she had another man in her life. I want you to know the truth regardless of how the court decides the case." She showed me his picture: "Look at him. Look at his eyes and tell me whether you think he could try to kill her."

I looked at the picture and simply said, "I'm sorry for your loss." The woman began to cry as she walked away.

I couldn't sleep for several days, as the picture of the sobbing mother holding her dead son's photograph kept popping into my head. Maybe he hadn't abused her. Maybe he didn't try to kill her. Maybe my client made up the story to justify a cold-blooded murder. Maybe not. Nice-looking people often do not nice things. You can't tell a killer by his eyes—or by his mother. I could never know. All I could go on was the evidence that had been presented at the trial.

But the encounter with the victim's mother haunts me still, as do the other possible victims of what my clients may have done. Any defense lawyer who says he doesn't lose sleep over the moral ambiguity and complexity of his role is either lying or is unworthy of the responsibility of representing the possibly guilty in order to prevent the conviction of the possibly innocent.

The Rubin case was convoluted in the extreme. It actually involved several cases. Lisa Rubin claimed to have evidence that her estranged husband, whom she admitted shooting, had tried to poison her previous lover, who had tried to beat her up. Doubly abused, she then developed "a personal relationship" with one of her investigators and an unusual relationship with several of her trial lawyers. She later complained about those relationships as well. Eventually, after years and years of litigation, her conviction was reversed on the ground that several of her trial lawyers were guilty of a conflict of interest that denied her the effective assistance of counsel under the Sixth Amendment.[32] I still have no idea whether the victim's mother was correct in her assessment of her dead son. What I do know is that she honestly believed that her son was a victim, not a perpetrator, of violence.

In July 2011, my own family learned what it felt like to become the victim of a possible homicide. My brother's beloved wife, Marilyn, was killed while riding her bicycle on a New York City street. Marilyn was a brilliant lawyer who had just retired from being a judicial referee in the New York Matrimonial Court. Her sudden death was devastating to my brother, their children, and our entire family. She had been run down by a U.S. Postal Service truck. She was rushed to the hospital, where a team of doctors worked feverishly to try to save her life. But in the end they couldn't save her, and she died.

Because New York City, like many large urban areas, has security cameras on nearly every block, my nephew (who is an engineer) and I were able to view video footage of the event from several different angles. What we saw was a mail truck and an unidentified van barreling down a narrow street in what appeared to be a game of chicken. Neither would give the right of way to the other, so they both drove down the narrow street in tandem. The mail truck struck my sister-in-law. The driver then stopped his truck, appeared to look back, and then proceeded to drive away. The truck stopped again down the street and then made a sharp left turn into the basement of the mail building.

Upon viewing the video and talking to witnesses, we came to believe that Marilyn had been the victim of two crimes: negligent vehicular homicide and leaving the scene of an accident. Suddenly our family became the victims seeking justice from a reluctant prosecutor. It was a painful shifting of roles, as my brother demanded a thorough investigation and prosecution of the offending driver or drivers (the driver of the van was never identified or caught). We were now using technology and engineering science to try to prove criminal guilt on the part of the truck driver. In the end, the prosecutor charged the driver only with leaving the scene of an accident, but not with causing Marilyn's death. After several days of trial, the jury acquitted the driver. No one was ever brought to justice for her death. This tragedy made me better understand what it feels like to be the family of a homicide victim.

There is no crime as horrible, or as final, as homicide. There is no penalty as cruel, or as final, as death. Death really is different. The stakes are higher, the passions greater, and the costs of error unmatched. That is why I have devoted so much of my career—as a teacher, a writer, and a litigator—to the changing law and science of death cases. There are, however, other crimes as well that have experienced significant changes over the course of my career with regard to how the law treats them. While the crime of murder—as distinguished from the scientific evidence used to prove and disprove it—has remained essentially the same since the time of the Bible, the crime of rape has changed significantly over the course of my career. Indeed, it is fair to say that no crime has undergone a more significant change of attitude regarding both accusers and accused than the crime of rape.

18

THE CHANGING POLITICS OF RAPE

Mike Tyson, DSK, and Student Protestors

When I began teaching, there were enormous barriers to the successful prosecution of rapists. The testimony of the alleged victim had to be corroborated by external evidence, unlike other crimes, where the testimony of the victim is sufficient.[1] The alleged victim could be cross-examined about her entire sexual history, thus discouraging rape victims from coming forward. A husband could not be convicted of raping his wife, no matter how much force he used, because by law, "the husband and wife are one," and "he is the one."[2] Under this bizarre sexist metaphysic, a husband was deemed "incapable of raping himself."[3] Juries were reluctant to convict "upstanding" young men who were accused of raping "loose" women (often defined as unmarried nonvirgins).[4] Moreover, being "dressed for sex" was considered a form of consent by some courts,[5] and prostitutes could not be raped since they were in the "business" of consenting.[6] In some states, lack of consent alone wasn't enough to establish rape; the victim had to "resist" to the "utmost" even in the face of deadly threats.[7] Some commentators went so far as to suggest that it was physically impossible for a nonconsenting woman to be raped.[8] Date rape wasn't even considered a crime.[9] Instead it was deemed a manifestation of macho entitlement among certain groups, such as some college fraternities, soldiers, gangs, and athletic teams. Within some such groups, if one "brother" was accused of raping a woman, all the other brothers would say that they too had sex with the complainant.

The upshot was that many predatory males got away with rape, because victims were unlikely to complain, prosecutors were reluctant to bring charges, jurors were eager to acquit, and appellate courts were quick to throw out convictions.

As I taught my students, this male-centered attitude toward rape, and the special rules reflected by that attitude, go back millennia in time. The Bible, in which the Ten Commandments includes a prohibition against coveting one's neighbor's wife,[10] does not explicitly prohibit rape. In the Bible, there are permissible and impermissible sexual encounters, depending on the status of the man and woman.[11] A married woman is prohibited from having sex with anyone but her husband, while a married man is permitted to have sex with any unmarried or unspoken-for woman. If sex is permitted, it may be accomplished by force.[12] If a man rapes an unmarried girl who is still in her father's care, his "punishment" is to pay the father a specified amount for damaging his "property," and he must marry the girl and may not divorce her.[13] Who is punished more under this regime, the perpetrator or the victim? And who is the "victim," the girl or her father?[14] Similar rules prevailed in other religions and other cultures during biblical times and for centuries thereafter.[15]

The common law attitude, which governed American courts from the beginning of our history, was summarized by British lord chief justice Matthew Hale, who cautioned that rape was a charge "easily to be made and hard to be proved, and harder to be defended by the party accused, tho' never so innocent."[16]

Even as recently as the early twentieth century, the influential legal commentator John Wigmore absurdly proposed that women who accuse men of rape should be subjected to a psychiatric examination because "modern psychiatrists" have concluded that many "errant young girls" have psychic complexes that cause them to contrive false charges of rape:

> *The unchaste (let us call it) mentality finds . . . expression in the narration of imaginary sex incidents of which the narrator is the heroine or the victim. . . . The real victim, however, too often in such cases is the innocent man.*[17]

During the last quarter of the twentieth century, political and academic feminism began to focus attention on the gender inequalities implicit, and often explicit, in rape laws.[18] It began in the classrooms and academic journals and then moved swiftly into legislative halls and courtrooms. Within a short period of time, thousands of years of anachronistic rules governing the prosecution of rape cases were changed. The testimony of rape victims no longer had to be corroborated.[19] Rape shield laws prohibited defense attorneys from questioning alleged rape victims about their prior sexual history.[20] Husbands could be prosecuted for forcing their wives to have sex.[21] The force and resistance elements of rape were amended in most jurisdictions to require only a lack of consent.[22] Date rape was punished as seriously as stranger rape. Most important, attitudes changed, at least among some groups, which no longer treated predatory males as macho heroes and women who dressed provocatively as automatically consenting sex partners.

VIGNETTE

Jury Duty

In Massachusetts, everyone is called for jury duty, even current Supreme Court justice Stephen Breyer, when he was a court of appeals judge. I was called several years ago in a brutal child rape case. I was anxious to serve, both to learn what a jury trial was like from the inside and also to help render justice in an important case. I made it past the initial screening and was seated. The lawyers apparently didn't know who I was, but the judge did. She called both lawyers up to the bench and said, "Do you know who juror six is? Do you want to be in his next book? Will one of you please strike him?" The prosecution struck me. I followed the case closely and think I would have voted "guilty," but I never got the chance.

Nearly all of the rules that had made it difficult to prosecute rapists were amended within the course of little more than a decade, as the pendulum swung quite dramatically from a male-centered view of rape to a female-centered view. As with many wide swings of a pendulum, there was little effort to strike a carefully calibrated balance that represented our general approach to all crimes: Namely, that there must be a heavy burden of proof on the prosecution and that it is better for ten guilty rapists to go free than for even one innocent accused rapist to be wrongly convicted. Indeed even that salutary rule was challenged by some feminists in the context of rape.[23] One influential, if radical, scholar went so far as to suggest that all sexual intercourse is essentially rape[24] and that all men should be presumed guilty of this crime.[25] This led one of my colleagues to quip that "some feminists regard rape as so heinous a crime that even innocence should not be recognized as a defense."

For the most part, the changes in the laws governing rape prosecutions were for the better: Many more guilty rapists were successfully prosecuted, and the number of rapes went down perceptibly.[26] But these radical changes were not cost-free: More innocent defendants, or those against whom the evidence was doubtful, were also convicted. When it comes to changing the rules governing prosecution of crimes, there is rarely a free lunch. Virtually every change that makes it easier to convict the guilty also makes it somewhat more likely that some innocents will be convicted as well. The difficult question is whether, as to any particular crime or rule, the trade-off is worth it.

I have experienced and participated in the changing approaches to the prosecution and defense of rape cases, both in the courtroom and in the classroom. At the beginning of my career, when the rules were heavily skewed against women, I was reluctant to defend accused rapists, because I didn't want to cross-examine alleged victims about their sexual history. I regarded it as an unfair tactic designed not to probe their credibility as witnesses, but rather to discourage rape victims from bringing charges. Were I to have defended an accused rapist in those days, I would have had no choice other than to use every legally permissible tactic. As the rules changed, I began to defend accused rapists (as well as some rape and sexual harassment victims)—and to teach and write about rape—in order to help assure that an appropriate balance was maintained in the inevitable trade-off between the rights of the alleged victim and those of the accused defendant.

A revealing example of how this trade-off works in practice is provided by the controversial rape prosecution of Mike Tyson, in which I served as his appellate lawyer. Tyson was convicted of raping Desiree Washington, a young woman whom he met when she was a contestant in the Miss Black America pageant in Indianapolis and he was an invited celebrity. He called her at one-forty-five in the morning and invited her to his hotel room, where they engaged in sexual intercourse. She subsequently claimed that he had forced her. He said it was consensual. The jury believed her. Following his conviction, Don King—Tyson's promoter—asked if I would represent the former heavyweight champ on his appeal.

WAS MIKE TYSON THE VICTIM OF THE CHANGING POLITICS OF RAPE?

The first time I met Mike Tyson was the night before he was to be sentenced and sent to prison. Mike was deciding whether to accept Don King's recommendation that he hire me as his appellate lawyer. He was in a hotel room in Indianapolis, Indiana, with his entourage. After briefly discussing the case and the appeal, he turned to me and asked point-blank, "So, Professor, I have two questions. Do you believe I'm innocent and what do you think of me as a person?" I replied that I had no basis at that time to form a judgment about his guilt or innocence since I had not yet read the transcripts. He said, "OK, that's lawyers' talk. Now, man-to-man, what do you think of me?" I looked him straight in the eye and said: "If you're innocent, you're a schmuck." He looked back at me and said, "You calling me a schmuck?" I said, "Yes, if you're innocent, then you're a schmuck for going up to a hotel room at two o'clock in the morning with a woman who you didn't know, without any witnesses, thereby putting yourself in a position where she could accuse you of rape." He turned to his entourage and said, "This man's calling me a schmuck. He's right. I want to know why you guys didn't call me a schmuck. He's hired. I need somebody who's willing to call me a schmuck when I am a schmuck."

That was Mike Tyson—direct and to the point. While preparing his appeal, I went to visit him in prison several times. The prison rules required that we sit side by side, facing a camera. Whenever I would say something he agreed with, he would give me a gentle love tap on my arm or on my thigh. A love tap to him! When I got back to my hotel, I was black and blue.

One day I saw a guard taunt him mercilessly and watched him strain to control himself. He did hard time in prison. I sent him books to read—about subjects that interested him, such as ancient Egypt, the Roaring Twenties, and the history of boxing. When I would come to visit him, he would ask me to test him on his knowledge of the books. He passed with flying colors.

Mostly we talked about his appeal by phone. Mike would have to wait in line for hours to call me. Once, as I picked up the phone, he heard my baby daughter crying in the background. He told me to "take care of your kid" and he would call back later. He was always considerate.

Some people find it hard to believe, but Mike was a wonderful client, always polite, always honest, always honorable, and always thinking of others. He ran out of money during the appeal, and I continued to represent him without pay. I never thought I would see a penny of what he owed me, but several days after he fought his first fight upon being released, he sent checks to every one of his lawyers for the full amount that he owed.

Tyson's trial had been a disaster. His trial judge was determined to see him convicted, and his prominent white-collar trial lawyer had little experience in rape cases and didn't seem to like Tyson. He was ill-suited to the job of defending the controversial black boxer. Although he was assisted by several able younger lawyers, it was to no avail. The legal expert who reported on the trial for *USA Today* described the trial as "filled with mistakes, omissions and elementary errors" by Tyson's chief trial lawyer. I had followed the trial in the media, but I didn't realize what an unfair trial Tyson had had until I reviewed the transcript. After agreeing to do the appeal, I decided to start from scratch with a new investigation. My goal was to secure a new trial for the ex–heavyweight champ.

I assembled a superb team, which included my brother Nathan, my son Jamin, who had just completed a two-year stint with the New York Legal Aid Society following his graduation from Yale Law School and a clerkship with the chief judge of the federal district court in Massachusetts. The team also included my coclerk for Justice Goldberg, Lee McTurnan, who was a leading Indiana lawyer.

On the basis of our investigation and the new evidence we uncovered, I was convinced that Mike Tyson did not intend to rape Desiree Washington, and that he'd gotten a bum rap.

Several of the jurors agreed with me after learning some of the new evidence. One of them said: "We [the jurors] felt that a man raped a woman. . . . In hindsight, it [now] looks like a woman raped a man." Another told the media that Desiree Washington, the pageant contestant who accused Tyson of raping her, "has committed a crime."

In order to understand why these jurors had such dramatic second thoughts about their verdict, we must go back to the trial itself and see how Desiree Washington, the alleged victim, was portrayed. During the trial she did not allow her name or face to be revealed. She was presented as a shy, young, inexperienced, religious schoolgirl, who wanted nothing more than to put this whole unpleasant tragedy behind her.

Her family said they had hired a lawyer for the express purpose of "ward[ing] off the media," because she did not want publicity. She said she had no plans to sue Tyson and she had certainly not hired a lawyer for that purpose. When she and her family were asked whether they had a contingency-fee agreement with any lawyer—the kind of agreement traditionally made with lawyers who are contemplating a suit for money damages—they all claimed not even to know what that term meant. When Desiree's mother was asked whether there had ever been any discussions with lawyers about fees, she said no, and she swore that there were no "written documents relating to the relationship between [the family] and [the lawyer who was supposed to ward off the media]."

As one of the jurors later put it: "When she [Washington] said she wasn't looking to get any money," the juror believed her and "thought then that we made the right decision." Another juror agreed, saying that at the trial, "she was very, very credible," because she had no motive to lie, since she was not intending to collect any money, or to benefit in any way from Tyson's conviction. This was the centerpiece of the prosecution's presentation to the jury: that the victim was interested only in securing justice, not in receiving money.

Another key was that Desiree Washington was an inexperienced virgin before she met Tyson. She testified that she was "a good Christian girl," and the prosecutor told the jury that she expected to go home after her date with Tyson "the same girl" that she was before her date, a virgin. She was an "innocent, almost naive" girl, according to the prosecutor. She knew how to "handle the hometown boys" if they even dared to try to cop a "quick feel," thus suggesting that she did not even neck or pet. As a waitress in Washington's hometown put it: "America thought this girl was a blushing, virginal type." (Under the rape shield law, Tyson's lawyer could not counter this portrayal. The prosecution thus used the rape *shield* law as a *sword* to present a one-sided—and as it turned out totally false—picture of the alleged victim.)

The prosecutor also argued to the jurors a variation on the "dressed-for-sex" theory, telling them that Washington went to meet Tyson wearing "little pink polka-dot panties," rather than "Frederick's of Hollywood underwear," suggesting that she did not put on the kind of sexy underwear that women wear when they are out to have sex.

Finally, Desiree Washington solidified her image as a nonsexual platonic date who only wanted to go sightseeing with Tyson at two o'clock in the morning, by describing to the jury how she responded when Mike tried to kiss her as she entered his limousine for the ride to his hotel: "He went to kiss me and I just kind of jumped back."

In other words, the jurors were presented with the picture of a zealously religious, naive, "virginal type" girl, who did not kiss, neck, or wear sexy underwear, and for whom money or media attention were the farthest thing from her mind.

No wonder the jurors believed her testimony, in what was a classic "she said, he said" contest.

We discovered during our investigation that virtually everything "she said," her family corroborated, and the prosecution knowingly presented to the jury was highly questionable if not outright false. The Washington family did not hire a lawyer to "ward off the media" as they'd claimed, but rather to do precisely the opposite—namely to sell Desiree's story for huge sums of money. After the trial, Donald Washington, Desiree's father, publicly acknowledged that he discussed movie rights with the very lawyer whom he falsely told the jury he had hired solely to "ward off the media." In an interview he gave after the trial he admitted that "I expected to get money from movie rights, that's where the money is."

It also turned out that the trial testimony denying any contingency-fee agreement and any written document between the Washingtons and the lawyer concerning a planned damage suit against Tyson was perjurious. Immediately after Desiree Washington's sexual encounter with Mike Tyson, the Washington family went to see a high-powered money lawyer. The discussion turned to how the Washington family could parlay Desiree's date with Tyson into big bucks. They talked about movie rights, book deals, and multimillion-dollar lawsuits. The lawyer carefully explained what a contingency-fee agreement was, and the family agreed with this arrangement. Desiree signed a contingency-fee agreement, which her father and mother officially witnessed. The family was given a copy.

The prosecutor was fully aware of the contingency-fee arrangement and of his witness's perjury. Indeed, during the prosecutor's "rehearsal" cross-examination of Desiree Washington, the issue of the contingency-fee agreement was raised. Yet the prosecutor did everything in his power to keep the truth from coming out. He arranged for the Washington family to take the courtroom pass away from their lawyer, so that he could not attend the trial and feel ethically compelled to stand up and correct the Washingtons' testimony when they falsely denied any contingency-fee or written agreement with him. The prosecutor also had an ethical and legal obligation to correct the false testimony given by his witness. Indeed he had an even greater obligation, because he was the one who put on the testimony that he knew was false. Not only did he suborn the family, but by keeping Washington's lawyer out of the courtroom he actively encouraged them to perjure themselves.

The ploy worked—at least for a while. But the Rhode Island lawyer soon learned that his clients were not being straight with the jury. He began to worry that he might have an ethical obligation to blow the whistle, as lawyers do when their clients or witnesses are committing perjury. So the lawyer went to the Rhode Island Disciplinary Counsel—the attorney in charge of enforcing the ethical rules that govern lawyers—to obtain guidance. She referred the matter to the Rhode Island Supreme Court, which issued an unprecedented opinion concluding that "the attorney had an obligation to disclose the existence of his contingent fee agreement to the [Indiana] criminal trial court"[27] because the agreement's "existence might well have had a bearing upon the jury's determination."[28] He did so, but the Indiana authorities ignored this new information, despite the conclusion of the Rhode Island Supreme Court that it might have affected the jury's verdict. Indeed, what could be more important than the fact—unbeknownst to the jury—that Desiree Washington had millions of dollars riding on whether Mike Tyson was convicted or acquitted, since without a conviction, it would have been difficult for her to collect monetary damages or sell her story to the media? The only thing that might have been more important was that she—with the active assistance of the prosecution—had lied to the jury about her financial motive for accusing Tyson of rape. When jurors learn that a key prosecution witness has lied to them, the case generally collapses, especially if the prosecutor was complicit in the lie.

It also turned out that Desiree was hardly the naive virgin she pretended to be. Once her name was disclosed following the trial, numerous witnesses confirmed that Desiree Washington was a sexually active young woman who hung out in nightclubs. Indeed, her lawyer seems to have implied that Washington had been examined for venereal disease a month *before* she had sex with Tyson.

Nor had Desiree *chosen* to wear her "polka-dot panties," rather than "Frederick's of Hollywood underwear," when she met Tyson. The prosecutor knew, but withheld from the jury, that her sexy underwear had been washed and was still wet when Tyson called. Her only dry pair were the ones with the polka dots.

Not only was the jury misinformed about Desiree Washington's general sexual proclivities, they were also denied the most crucial eyewitness testimony of what she was doing just minutes before she went to Tyson's hotel room. She denied necking with Tyson in the limo on the way to the hotel. Indeed, she testified that she rebuffed his attempt to kiss her and "jumped back." Tyson's testimony was precisely the opposite. He swore that when he kissed her, "she kissed me," and that on the drive to his hotel, he and Washington were "kissing, touching." The jury obviously believed Desiree's testimony because Tyson's was uncorroborated and self-serving.

But it turns out that there were three eyewitnesses—disinterested outsiders who happened to be in front of the hotel when the limo pulled up—who saw what was going on inside and outside the limo just before Tyson and Washington left it to go to his hotel room. They saw them necking—"they were all over each other"—and holding hands on the way to the hotel. (Desiree denied both necking and holding hands.)

Of course, the fact that they were necking and holding hands doesn't preclude the possibility that Desiree may have said no when it came to intercourse. Nor does it mean that a woman who engages in sexual foreplay may not refuse further sex at any point. Of course she may, and if the man then forces her to have sex without her consent, it is rape. But the testimony of these eyewitnesses shows three important facts: that Washington was lying when she denied necking with Tyson; that Tyson was telling the truth when he testified that they were necking; and that just moments before the hotel door closed behind them, Washington was involved in sexual foreplay with Tyson.

Despite the importance of this eyewitness testimony by three disinterested witnesses in an otherwise uncorroborated "she said, he said" credibility contest, the trial judge adamantly refused to allow the jury to hear the evidence of the eyewitnesses. She ruled that the prosecution—which admitted that the testimony was "pivotal"—would have been "prejudiced" by its late disclosure. This was absurd: The three witnesses had come forward *before* the close of the prosecutor's case—after learning that Desiree Washington had denied necking with Tyson—and well *before* the defense case even began. There was plenty of time for the large team of prosecutors to prepare to cross-examine them, and if they needed more time, the judge could have briefly recessed the trial. Moreover, the defense had brought those new witnesses to the attention of the court as soon as they could check that the limo had windows that the witnesses could see through. In any event, surprise defense witnesses are common in criminal trials, and the Bill of Rights explicitly guarantees a criminal defendant the right to call "witnesses in his favor."[29] Despite this, the judge denied Tyson the right to call these three pivotal witnesses. So much for the "search for truth."

In all my years of practice and teaching criminal law, I had never heard of a case in which a judge refused to allow a criminal defendant the right to call eyewitnesses who could help establish his innocence. The law, including the law of Indiana, clearly supported Tyson's right to do so. It was a clear reversible error for the court to suppress these truthful witnesses.

It should come as no surprise, however, that this particular trial judge made such a bizarre and unprecedented ruling to exclude such relevant and exculpatory evidence. The trial judge, Patricia Gifford, who used to be a full-time professional rape prosecutor, had prosecuted more than fifty rape cases. She expressed extremely strong feelings about rape, especially what has come to be called "date rape." Indeed, she lectured the lawyers against even using the term "date rape" in her courtroom[30] and refused to give the traditional date rape instruction, which requires acquittal if the jury concludes that the defendant reasonably believed the woman had consented, even if she did not intend to consent.

After I had read the transcript, it became clear to me that Patricia Gifford did not see her role in rape cases as being a neutral judge, but rather as being another prosecutor, with a stake in the outcome. She wanted to see the most famous "rapist" in Indiana history convicted and put away. Judge Gifford made virtually every important ruling in the prosecutor's favor, including the exclusion of those three "pivotal" witnesses.

In light of Judge Gifford's attitudes and professional background in regard to rape, it might be wondered how the prosecution got so lucky as to have her as the judge in the Tyson case. Luck, however, played no part in the selection. Under Indianapolis law and practice, the prosecutor was able to pick the judge who would preside over the Tyson case. I am aware of no other place in the free world where a prosecutor gets to pick the judge. And the prosecutor picked wisely, if not fairly.

Several distinguished commentators—including Indiana's leading authority on criminal procedure—concluded that the trial judge committed a serious legal error by excluding those three crucial witnesses. Articles in the *American Lawyer* and the *New York Law Journal* reached the same conclusion, as did most of the lawyers and law professors with whom I conferred.

Despite the strong issues that she knew would be presented on appeal, Judge Gifford denied Tyson bail pending appeal, accepting the prosecutor's silly argument that this celebrity defendant would somehow sneak away and flee to a country with no extradition treaty. She also ruled that all the appellate issues would be "frivolous"—that is, so unlikely to prevail that it would be unethical for a lawyer even to present them! (We, of course, ignored this preposterous conclusion and presented these "frivolous" arguments, which several appellate judges found compelling.) Finally, as if to prove she was an advocate rather than a judge, she actively lobbied in the media against reversal of the conviction, convening a press conference and, according to news accounts, "express[ing] some worries about having her ruling overturned, especially in an internationally publicized case in which prosecution costs alone reached $150,000." She commented on "the enormousness of the reversal of a case that would have to be tried again like this." We were advised by several local lawyers that she also personally lobbied the appellate judges against reversing the conviction. These actions, if they occurred, would be unethical, and in violation of the Code of Judicial Conduct. They could have resulted in her being removed from the bench, but instead she was praised by the local media. Apparently lobbying by a judge is acceptable in Indiana, if the defendant is a despised out-of-stater.

The case was a close one at trial. Judge Gifford's one-sided rulings shifted the balance against Tyson in what was otherwise a difficult prosecution. Even without all this exculpatory evidence, the initial jury vote was six to six. Eventually, the six who voted for conviction were able to persuade the six who voted for acquittal that there was no reason to disbelieve Desiree Washington's account. But that account, especially when reviewed against the background of the information that was kept hidden and is now known, is extremely unconvincing.

What then was Desiree Washington's account of what happened that night?

Although Desiree Washington insisted she had no interest in having sex with Tyson, she acknowledged that she led him on and that she acted in the way a groupie would behave. The director of the Miss Black America Pageant, in which Desiree was a contestant, even criticized her for behaving like a "groupie." She sat in Tyson's lap and hugged him during the pageant rehearsal, when they first met. She showed him a picture of herself in a bathing suit, gave him her hotel room number, and agreed to go out with him. She took his call at one-forty-five in the morning and agreed to come down to meet him in his limo. She then went into her bathroom and put on a panty liner to keep her expensive borrowed dress from becoming stained by the beginning of her menstrual flow during the partying and sightseeing she said she expected to do over the next several hours. She willingly accompanied Tyson to his hotel room at two o'clock in the morning, sat with him on his bed, and then went into his bathroom and removed her panty liner without replacing it. How did she expect to prevent her borrowed $300 outfit from becoming stained over the next several hours of anticipated partying and sightseeing? The most plausible explanation for the removal and nonreplacement of the panty liner was that it was done in anticipation of consensual sex.

Moreover, if she did not want to have sex, she could easily have locked herself in the bathroom and called for help from the bathroom phone. The bathroom had a working lock and a phone. Instead, she willingly came out of the bathroom, passed a door leading to the outside corridor, and went back to Tyson's bedroom, where they had sex on the bed.

According to Washington's own testimony, Tyson asked her during their sexual encounter whether she wanted to "get on top" and she responded "yeah," and proceeded to get on top—not the usual position for a rape victim!

Mike Tyson had every reason to believe that Desiree was just another groupie looking for sex with a celebrity athlete. The "rules" of groupie sex are well known. The groupies want sex with superstars in exchange for bragging rights that they slept with the "high-scorer," the "champ," or the "star." Some, like Washington, hope that the star will fall for them and make them rich and famous. Indeed, several other contestants testified that after meeting Mike Tyson, Desiree bragged that she was going out with him because "this is Mike Tyson. He's got a lot of money. He's dumb. You see what Robin Givens got out of him." She told a friend that "Robin Givens had him. I can have him too. . . . He's dumb anyway." To her roommate, she said: "Mike doesn't have to know how to speak well. He'll make all the money and I'll do the talking."

Tyson testified that when he first asked her out—in front of a witness—Desiree suggested a movie or dinner. But he said no: "That's not what I [have] in mind. . . . I want you. I want to fuck you." A witness—Johnny Gill, a singer—confirmed under oath that Tyson said, "I want to fuck." Gill later asked Tyson how he could be so straightforward with women, and Tyson explained that he was used to saying what was on his mind.

Desiree Washington knew full well that Mike wanted to have sex when she went to his hotel room. Yet she testified that she had no idea that Tyson had any interest in having sex. How any rational person could believe that is mind-boggling. She may have been disappointed and hurt when he later treated her like a groupie rather than as a continuing romantic interest. She realized that she could not exploit his sexual interest in her the way Robin Givens had done, and she was afraid of the reaction of her family when it became known that she had indulged in a one-night stand with Tyson. A friend of hers told the press that Desiree "only cried rape" after her furious father found out she'd had sex with Tyson.

Our investigation revealed that she had previously engaged in consensual sex with the high school football hero, and when her father found out about it and threatened to beat her, she lied to her father and told him she had been raped, falsely accusing the football player.

Our investigation also uncovered that Desiree's father had a history of violence toward her. Her mother had had Desiree's father arrested and charged with assault and battery against Desiree. "In her account," reported in the media, "Desiree alleged to the police that her father 'hit me and pushed my head under the sink. . . . He continued slamming my head into the wall and the floor. I freed myself and reached for a knife to protect myself.'" A sworn statement by her mother reportedly said that her husband "flew off the handle" when Desiree told him "she had lost her virginity" well before she ever met Mike Tyson.

In order to avoid his fury once again, this time for having consensual sex with Tyson, Desiree apparently decided to cry rape once again. At first, she said that Tyson had "tried" to rape her. She initially denied having sex with him. Then she said they had sex "on the floor." She told the female chaplain at the hospital that there had been some "participation" and consensual physical involvement on her part before he forced her. Finally, she settled on the account she gave at trial: that he had raped her on the bed with no prior consensual involvement on her part.

No one except Tyson and Washington knows exactly what went on behind the closed doors of his hotel room. There was no videotape. Nor was there any physical evidence to corroborate Washington's story. Indeed, the available physical evidence completely undercut her story. She was wearing a sequin-studded outfit, which she claims Tyson "yanked" off her as he "slammed [her] down on the bed." If that had happened, there would have been sequins all over the hotel room. Indeed, at the trial, when the dress was gingerly introduced into evidence, sequins fell off in the courtroom. But only one sequin was found in Tyson's hotel room after the allegedly forcible rape.

Nor were any bruises—external or internal—found on Ms. Washington that were consistent with her account of how Tyson had "forced" her to have sex. She testified that Tyson got on top of her, held her down with his forearm across the chest, and forced himself inside her.[31]

Had the 230-pound, muscular Tyson done that to the 105-pound

Washington, there would have been bruises, welts, contusions, and even broken ribs. Yet there was not even the slightest bruise on Washington's body when she went to the hospital just hours after the sexual encounter. The doctors found only two tiny microscopic abrasions, which, according to leading experts, are perfectly consistent with consensual sex—especially if the man has a larger-than-average penis or the woman has a smaller-than-average vagina. Such tiny abrasions are also more likely when two people have consensual sex with each other for the first time and are not used to each other's sexual movements. Mike Tyson's account of what occurred, on the other hand, was entirely consistent with the physical evidence. And it would have been corroborated had the judge not excluded the three objective eyewitnesses who saw the couple necking and kissing just moments before they went to his hotel room.

Despite the absence of physical evidence to corroborate Desiree Washington's story, the jury eventually believed her because there was no compelling reason to disbelieve the testimony of a young, religious, sexually inexperienced girl who had no possible motive to put herself through the agony of a rape trial. But it turns out that there were very good reasons for not believing her. As one juror subsequently put it: "She was very, very credible [at the trial], but now she's not credible at all. Right now, I wouldn't believe anything she said. I would sign an affidavit that if we had known about the money, I couldn't have voted to convict him. Mike Tyson deserves a new trial."

In light of the numerous errors made by Judge Gifford at the trial, this should have been the easiest appeal I ever argued. The law, the new evidence, and the judicial and prosecutorial errors made at trial clearly required a reversal of the conviction and a new trial.

Legal experts who read our brief and heard the oral argument concluded that we should win the appeal. The law was on our side. The facts were on our side. And our briefs and arguments were much stronger than those of our opponents. As the legal expert who reported on the trial and appeal for *USA Today* put it after watching the appellate argument:

> *Mike Tyson had his best day in court Monday. . . . In spite of a trial record filled with mistakes, omissions and elementary errors by the fighter's ex-defense team, Dershowitz and colleagues argued that Tyson's conviction must be set aside. . . . Tyson got his money's worth Monday. . . . Reversal of a criminal conviction by a jury is rare, but Tyson's attorneys might have successfully pinpointed the crucial issues that will free him.*

I am convinced—and I think most observers were convinced—that if Tyson had gotten a second trial with all the new evidence before the jury, he would have quickly been acquitted. But this was Indiana. They had a trophy in Tyson. And they had a trial judge so determined to prevent a new trial that would have embarrassed her and freed Tyson that she unethically held a press conference and may have improperly lobbied the appellate judges.

The conviction was eventually affirmed on a 2–2 tie vote by the Indiana Supreme Court, with the chief justice disqualifying himself from participation in the decision on a phony pretext. He had sent his wife to speak to me during a Yale Law School reunion event. I was conversing with the president of George Washington University, when a woman came up to me and said, "Your New York style won't work in Indiana." I didn't know who she was, but as soon as she identified herself as the wife of the Indiana chief justice, I moved away, saying, "We can't talk." The chief justice subsequently used this contrived encounter as an excuse to disqualify himself.[32] At first he wouldn't admit it, but after I provided an affidavit from the president of George Washington University, the chief justice reluctantly acknowledged the ground on which he had recused himself. His recusal was particularly hypocritical in light of the fact that none of the judges who were allegedly lobbied by the trial judge to affirm the conviction recused themselves. I believe that the real reason the chief judge got out of the case was that his own previous decisions would have required him to vote for reversal, and if he did, the public would have been reminded that he himself had been accused by a fellow judge of sexual impropriety with a law clerk.

In my half century of practicing law throughout the world, I have never encountered a more thoroughly corrupt legal system than I did in 1992 in Indiana, and a less fair trial and appeal than those accorded Mike Tyson. If hard cases make bad law,[33] then the Tyson case proves that unpopular celebrity defendants often receive bad justice. If Mike Tyson had not been a world famous boxer, with a reputation for toughness, and if he had had a zealous trial lawyer experienced in rape cases, and a fair judge, he never would have been convicted of a rape he didn't commit. And if he had been convicted, his conviction would have been reversed. The deck was stacked against Tyson and he paid a heavy price—the loss of his career, and several years of hard prison time—for what I'm convinced was a consensual one-night stand with a young woman who apparently regretted giving her consent and then decided to exploit it for money. Eventually, she got her money—a large amount—despite her sworn testimony that she wasn't interested in receiving any payment.

My decision to represent Mike Tyson on appeal generated considerable controversy and some outright animosity. Rape is a highly emotional issue, which extremists see in black-and-white terms.

Some radical feminists, such as Judge Gifford, regard acquaintance rape, in which the man honestly but mistakenly believes his partner has consented, as indistinguishable from rape at the hands of a stranger at knifepoint. A letter to the editor critical of my views on date rape made the point as follows:

> *Dershowitz further endears himself by explaining that date rape and acquaintance rape is an area in which differing perceptions may produce inadvertently false testimony about actions that fall into a gray area. Let me explain something: No means no. There is no gray area.*

But in many date rape cases, the alleged victim didn't say no. Nor did she say yes. There *are* gray areas.

I received countless letters, phone calls, and personal attacks denouncing me for agreeing to represent Tyson on his appeal. Here are some excerpts:

> *It's too bad that a punk like Tyson can afford to pay for the top legal representation . . . but since you had the right to refuse to represent him, I fault you!*

> *When you choose to represent someone like Mike Tyson, you attach the Jewish community to your action. . . . I now find it hard to understand how you can mount a passionate defense for a convicted rapist.*

> *Shame on you, Alan Dershowitz, if you handle this appeal.*

The most surprising response came from some Harvard Law School students, who should have understood that our adversary system of justice requires that all convicted defendants be accorded a zealous appeal.

I don't know what took place in Mike Tyson's hotel room on that fateful night, but it may have fallen into the category of a gray area. He believed that Desiree Washington wanted to have sex with him. She may have been ambivalent or sending mixed signals (though I doubt it). It was a close case, and Tyson was entitled to have his defense presented vigorously.

Yet several of my students strongly objected to me, their teacher, representing "a convicted rapist." A couple of them even threatened to file "sexual harassment" charges against me because my representation of Tyson created a "hostile environment" for students who believed he was guilty.

The protest broadened to the way I discussed the crime of rape in class. In my Criminal Law class, I teach the law of rape as an example of a cutting-edge subject that often poses a sharp conflict between the rights of defendants and the rights of their accusers. As usual, I take a "devil's advocate" position on politically correct issues. For example, although I personally oppose capital punishment, I argue in favor of the death penalty and ask the students to come up with better arguments to oppose it. Unless they can, they will never be able to persuade the majority of Americans, including judges, who favor the death penalty.

Similarly, in the area of rape, I present positions that students are reluctant to defend, but which many Americans believe. I point out that according to FBI statistics, rape is both the most underreported and the most overreported crime of violence: For every reported rape there are an estimated ten that are not reported; but at the same time, a significant percentage of all reported rapes turn out to be unfounded, and this rate of false reports is higher than for other violent crimes.[34]

All in all, my classes on rape tend to be controversial and emotionally charged. The majority of students seem to love the exchanges. Some even change the opinions they brought to class.

But my devil's advocate views on rape are deemed politically incorrect by some students. Indeed that is precisely why I insist that they be expressed. The education of my students would be incomplete if they heard only the comfortably "correct" views. I tell my students that my job is not to make them feel good about their opinions, but rather to challenge every view. That is what the "Socratic method" of teaching law is all about. That is also what the real-life practice of law demands.

A small group of students complained about my teaching rape from a civil liberties perspective, by which they meant that I balanced the legitimate interests of alleged rape victims against the constitutional rights of accused defendants. I responded that it was important for the students to hear a variety of perspectives about rape, just as they hear, without objection, about other crimes. I reminded them that the majority of students who speak in class present the politically correct views. I also invite guest lecturers to present a feminist perspective on the subject. The answer to an offensive argument is not to censor it but rather to come up with a better argument. But these students don't want to hear, and don't want their fellow students to hear, any perspective but their own. They know "the Truth," and there's no reason to listen to offensive "Lies."

I was told that several radical feminist students had met and decided on a course of action in response to my decision to represent Mike Tyson: They would use the student evaluations at the end of the semester to send a message to professors who don't follow the "party line" in teaching about rape. I was warned that I should expect to be "savaged" in the semester's evaluations.

When the evaluations arrived, I realized how dangerous it would be for an untenured professor to incur the wrath of the political-correctness patrol. Most of the students appreciated the diversity of viewpoints in my classes ("willingness to broach sensitive subjects and take unpopular viewpoints," "very good at presenting alternative views," "helped me get a less dogmatic view of the law," "open to criticism," "fair in presenting sides that usually aren't raised," "the most engaging class on campus," "the most intellectually honest professor I've had"). But a small group of students used the power of their evaluations to exact their political revenge for my politically incorrect teaching. One student said that I did "not deserve to teach at Harvard" because of my "convoluted rape examples." Another argued that women be allowed an "option" not to take my class because I "spent two days talking about false reports of rape." Another demanded that my "teaching privileges" be suspended. (In classes I teach in which rape is not part of the syllabus, my student evaluations tend to be near perfect.)

I always try to learn from my evaluations, but I refused to be bullied into abandoning a teaching style that I believe is the best design to stimulate thinking. It takes no courage for me to exercise my academic freedom, since I have tenure. But would an untenured assistant professor have the courage to risk the wrath of the PC cops? Are other, less established, teachers being coerced into changing their teaching by the fear of negative evaluations (which can be fatal to tenure)? You bet they are. And it poses a real danger to academic freedom and good education. One Criminal Law professor told me that he searches for casebooks that don't cover rape: "If it's covered in the book and I skip it, I get criticized. And if I discuss it, I get criticized. This way I can blame it on the book." Talk about lack of courage!

I told the students who threatened to charge me with sexual harassment to go ahead—I would love to defend against such a charge, by demonstrating their misuse of the serious moral crime of real sexual harassment. I have represented women who have experienced real sexual harassment—including a graduate student who was told by her faculty advisor that the quality of her recommendation would depend on whether she slept with him. I understand the enormous pain it can cause. The student was devastated, her self-confidence shattered. She wanted justice, and to make sure that her career as an academic would not be hurt by her refusal to "go along" with the offer of a good recommendation.

That was real sexual harassment! Listening to differing views about rape isn't sexual harassment. It's education.

In the case of the sexually harassed graduate student, I advised her to file a complaint and bring a lawsuit, and explained to her what a complaint would entail. She said she understood and was prepared to endure the depositions, cross-examinations, and other attacks on her. But the next day she came to my office and told me she couldn't go through with it. She was terrified that it would destroy her prospects for an academic appointment to take on so influential and powerful an academic. But she was also afraid that if she did nothing, he would carry out his threat to write her a bad recommendation.

I suggested that she talk to the professor and tell him that she had consulted with me, but had decided not to file a complaint or lawsuit, and that she hoped that he would give her the recommendation she deserved. She did that, and eventually received a superb recommendation. She is now teaching at a fine university. So is he.

The students in my class never followed through on their threat.

SOME PEOPLE LIE, EXAGGERATE, OR MISREMEMBER

I continue to challenge my students by teaching both about rape cases in which guilty rapists are wrongly acquitted and cases in which innocent people have been falsely accused. The reality that rape is among the most underreported of serious crimes, and that many rapists still go free and repeat their crimes, should not blind us to the equally important reality that rape is also among the most falsely reported of crimes. I teach that when it comes to the serious crime of rape, it appears that both men and women lie, exaggerate, or misremember more often than with other, less emotionally charged, crimes. I learned this early in my career, from an alleged rape that took place in Provincetown, Massachusetts.

A young woman who was related to an associate of one of my legal colleagues was engaged to a man, and they were vacationing together in Provincetown. The man went out for a stroll and came back several hours later upset and disheveled. His fiancée asked him what had happened, and he told her that he was invited to go on a boat ride with a group of guys and one of them proceeded to rape him while the others did nothing to stop him. He described the rapist as a black man wearing a shark's tooth around his neck. At his fiancée's insistence, he reported the alleged rape to the police, who immediately issued an all-points bulletin describing the alleged rapist.

The young man's fiancée called my colleague and asked her to advise him. She sought my assistance. We went to the police station, where we observed the police interrogation of the young man. As experienced defense attorneys, we soon became suspicious of his story.

My colleague asked to be alone with her client and questioned him about the circumstances of the encounter. Eventually the young man broke down and admitted that he had consented to the sex. He confided to her that he was uncertain about his sexuality, that he was about to be married, and that he wanted to test his attraction to men. He was ashamed of what he had done and didn't want his fiancée to find out, because he was afraid it would end the engagement. My colleague told the young man he had a moral obligation to his fiancée and a legal obligation to the police to be truthful.

At first, the young man refused. After conferring with me, my colleague told him he really had no choice, because she would be obligated to report his continuing crime of making a false report—a crime that endangered the life and liberty of anyone fitting the description of the black man with the shark's tooth. (The young man hadn't wanted to get the man with whom he'd had consensual sex in trouble, so he'd invoked the stereotype of the "black man" rapist.) My colleague told him that she would try to make a deal with the police under which he wouldn't be charged with a crime in exchange for telling the truth.

The young man then told the police and his fiancée the truth. The police called off the all-points bulletin, and my colleague persuaded them not to press charges against the young man. I do not know how the engagement worked out, but I do know that I learned a great deal from this experience about the complexities of sexual encounters, and the need to subject claims of rape to the usual probing of the adversarial process.

Moreover, acquaintance or date rape is an area in which differing perceptions may produce inadvertently false testimony about actions that may well fall into the gray area between aggressive seduction and criminal sexual assault. When it comes to sexual encounters, both men and women often "remember" differently from what a videotape would show. As a British journalist, Angela Lambert, who analyzed several cases of falsely reported rapes, put it: There are "plenty of reasons why a woman might falsely accuse a man of rape." She went on to argue that "the belief that all women are truthful and all men are rapists does not prove us good feminists; quite the contrary. It reveals us as prejudiced, narrow-minded, and as bigoted as any racist."[35] The truth-testing mechanisms of our criminal justice system must not be compromised in the service of some politically correct notion that when it comes to rape only women tell the truth.

A highly publicized case in 2011 may well illustrate the reality that both men and women may lie, even when a rape has occurred. A cleaning woman in a fancy New York hotel accused Dominique Strauss-Kahn—then the head of the International Monetary Fund—of forcing her to have oral sex with him.[36] His lawyers first reportedly denied that there had been any encounter, claiming that he was having lunch with his daughter at the time.[37] When his DNA evidence was found on the cleaning woman's underwear and in the area of the room where she said he had ejaculated, his lawyers admitted the oral sex but insisted it was entirely consensual.[38] DSK, as he was known throughout the world, was indicted for sexual assault.[39]

Within days, the credibility of the alleged victim began to fall apart. She had made false statements on her application for asylum, including a claim that she had been gang-raped back in Guinea. A recorded phone conversation between her and a friend in prison also suggested, though her words (translated from a local African jargon) were ambiguous, that she may have had a financial interest in suing the wealthy man who she said assaulted her.[40]

Eventually, the Manhattan district attorney decided to drop the charges.[41] I thought that this was a perfect teaching vehicle, and I invited the lawyer for the alleged victim to join my Harvard class, to which I had assigned the DA's memorandum seeking dismissal. The following year I invited DSK's lawyer to present his perspective to the students. They were spirited classes, after which several students told me they had changed their minds—both ways. One student described the class as "*Rashomon*—first, I thought he was guilty, then not guilty, then guilty, and finally 'I'm not sure.'" I pressed the students on what the appropriate standard should be for a DA to drop a rape prosecution when he has doubts about the alleged victim's credibility. Some argued that as long as he believed the crime had occurred, he should let the jury decide, based on all the evidence, including the DNA and other circumstantial proof. Others argued that he should never bring a prosecution unless he has complete faith that the alleged victim is being truthful.

To put some flesh on the bones of these abstract arguments, I decided to role-play in front of the class a zealous prosecutor's hypothetical closing argument:

> *The alleged victim in this case says she was forced by DSK to give him oral sex. DSK's defense counsel have argued in the press, and in their briefs and in their opening statements, that the oral sex was entirely consensual.*
>
> *In deciding which version is true and which false, I want you to accept the fact that the alleged victim has told many lies in the past and can't be completely trusted. In other words, if there were no other evidence or arguments beyond the uncorroborated word of the victim, there would be reasonable doubt of DSK's guilt. But the totality of the evidence and arguments in this case establish that it is far more likely that the oral sex in this case was forced rather than consensual.*
>
> *First, I want you to look at the participants. She is an attractive young woman who was wearing two pair of panty hose and an additional undergarment. The defendant's DNA was found on the elastic of her undergarments, strongly suggesting that he was trying to pull them off.*
>
> *You have seen the photograph taken of the defendant, naked, following his arrest, when he was examined by doctors for bruises. Look at that photograph and imagine what the alleged victim in this case saw, when DSK walked out of the shower and into the bedroom naked, as his lawyers acknowledge he did.*
>
> *In order to accept the defense theory of consensual oral sex, this is what you have to believe:*
>
> *The alleged victim looked at this overweight, out-of-shape, sixty-two-year-old man and decided, without any words spoken, that she was so sexually attracted to him, that she simply had to give him seven minutes of oral gratification in the corner of the bedroom. What was in it for her? According to the defense theory, only the pleasure of giving a short, fat, old man oral sex.*
>
> *That, in essence, is the defense lawyers' version of what took place. Now, we all know that the burden of proof is on the prosecution to prove our case beyond a reasonable doubt, and that the defendant need not take the wit-*

ness stand nor offer any proof of innocence. But in this case, the defendant, because he is a public figure, has put forward a defense: that she wanted *to give him oral sex, that it was entirely consensual. If you believe that—or even if you have a reasonable belief that she might have offered him oral sex because she was so attracted to him—you should acquit. But if you believe, beyond a reasonable doubt, that the defense theory of consensual oral sex is utterly implausible, then you should look at the totality of the evidence corroborating the alleged victim's account—that he forced her to give him oral sex—and decide whether it establishes beyond a reasonable doubt that her account is true.*

This corroborative evidence includes the location of the DNA in the room and on her undergarments; the shoulder pain she reported to the doctors; the time sequence; the absence of evidence that she knew who DSK was at the time of the encounter; and a comparison between the two participants, in terms of their ages, appearances, status, and what each had to gain or lose by a consensual sexual encounter in that room.

When you consider the totality of the evidence and arguments offered in this case, I am confident that you will have no reasonable doubt that the oral sex in this case was not consensual.[42]

After hearing my "mock" argument, many of the students concluded that the DA acted hastily in dismissing the case. Most believed that this was a case in which *both* the woman and the man had lied, but that the man's lies were far more relevant than the woman's to the issue of consent.

It is possible, of course, that there was a third alternative: that DSK paid the alleged victim to give him oral sex. But there was no claim or evidence of any such payment—indeed DSK has publicly stated that he doesn't believe in paying for sex. And although the defense has no obligations to prove anything, a jury and prosecutors are supposed to base their decisions on evidence, not surmise. It is also possible, as DSK's lawyer suggested to the class, that the alleged victim willingly gave him oral sex in the *expectation* that he would pay her, and when he didn't, she decided to file a complaint so that he would be compelled to settle the matter financially, as he eventually did. This too is possible, but there is nothing but surmise—no evidence—to support this theory of a disappointed expectation of payment, or of an extortionate motive.

By any objective standard, the case against DSK was far stronger than the case against Mike Tyson, since there was far more corroborative evidence. Moreover, Tyson's alleged victim was caught in a series of lies that challenged her account of the alleged rape and her motive for bringing the charge.

Yet Tyson was convicted, and the case against DSK was dropped. Such are the vagaries of rape prosecutions, in which objective truth can rarely be established,[43] as evidenced by several other cases I have litigated or consulted on over the years.

RAPE AND EXTORTION

Rape is a crime that, because it is so heinous, sometimes lends itself to extortion. I've been involved in several cases over the course of my career in which my clients have been threatened with being falsely accused of rape unless they pay large amounts of money. In one such case, on which I consulted, the FBI managed to record the extortionate call, and the woman who made it went to prison. In another case, the man refused to pay the money and the extortionist didn't carry out the threat. In yet another case, the man paid the money and the extortionist kept her word to remain silent.

It is possible, of course, for a guilty rapist to be extorted. This is what the Brooklyn district attorney's office claims occurred in a case that took place in Boro Park, the neighborhood in which I grew up. That's why he prosecuted both the accused extortionist and the accused rapist.

My client was an elderly Chassidic man with a wealthy son. A twenty-something man accused him of having improperly touched him years earlier, just before his seventeenth birthday (seventeen being the age of consent in New York). The accuser was a heavy drug addict who paid for his expensive habit by breaking into synagogues and stealing money from charity boxes. He also, according to acquaintances, received drug money from clients in exchange for sex. The young man claimed that my client had allowed him to drive his car and had engaged in oral sex with him on several occasions. A jury believed him and a judge sentenced the defendant to up to thirty-four years in prison—for him a life sentence.

The defendant's son asked me to prepare and argue his appeal. He told me that before the trial, he had been approached by another Chassid who told him he could make the case "go away for several hundred thousand dollars." He also played us a tape, surreptitiously recorded by an acquaintance of the alleged victim, in which the alleged victim admitted that the only reason the defendant was in prison was because he wouldn't pay the money. I agreed to investigate the matter and argue the appeal.

We uncovered a massive extortion mechanism that exploited the sad reality of sexual abuse among some Chassidim. As with other religious (and secular) groups, there was pressure within the community not to "wash our dirty laundry in public" by reporting sexual abuse to law enforcement authorities. Knowing of this dual phenomenon—abuse, coupled with pressure to keep it secret from law enforcement—an extortion industry developed, focusing on respected Chassidim who were vulnerable to accusations of sexual misconduct and who had the resources to pay hush money.

We provided the results of our investigation to the prosecutor, and a grand jury indicted two of the alleged extortionists. Nevertheless, the prosecutor insisted that my client—the victim of the extortion—was guilty, despite the fact that his accuser was apparently part of the extortion plot and was offered money to testify against my client, and despite the fact that our investigation established that the "victim" was not even in Boro Park when the events about which he testified allegedly occurred.

We won the appeal on the ground of police suppression of favorable evidence—including evidence of extortion.[44]

RAPE BY COCAINE?

Is it possible for a man to rape a woman even if he uses no force and she offers no resistance and appears to consent? The answer is yes. Under the law, the sexual partner's consent must be freely given and not the product of drugs, alcohol, or other factors that may negate voluntary consent. This is especially so if the drug was administered to her without her knowledge.[45] This is a serious problem not only when date rape drugs are slipped into an unsuspecting woman's drink, but also when men deliberately get their dates drunk in order to lower their resistance. In the former situation the law is clear: The use of drugs to lower a woman's defenses is not only rape; it is also a separate crime to drug a person against her will. In the case of a man plying a date with alcohol, the law is less clear: A woman is generally deemed responsible for her own decisions—to drink, to get drunk, to agree to sex. But if a man takes unfair advantage of a woman's drunkenness, he may cross the line into rape. It's very much a matter of degree.

Several years ago, I worked on a case raising a number of these difficult issues. My client was an accountant in a western state, who had an unsavory reputation for seducing female secretaries who worked for him.[46]

Seduction, of course, is not a crime, although it may constitute sexual harassment if the seducee works for the seducer. In this case, the accountant's office was set up more for seduction than for work. It was light on books and heavy on thick, plush rugs, couches, pillows, and a fully stocked bar. On the evening at issue, a secretary who worked in the office stayed late after work and had dinner and several drinks with her boss and a few of his friends. When the other guests left, she and her boss remained behind. He walked her into his office. She lay down on the rug. He undressed her, performed oral sex on her, and then engaged in sexual intercourse. She did not object, and she appeared to be consenting—as others had apparently done in that office.

During the sexual encounter he asked her if she was using birth control. She said no, and as a result, he did not ejaculate in her. Afterward, she dressed, he walked her to the parking lot, kissed her, and she drove home.

The problem was that she was married. When she got home, her husband sensed that something was amiss. After he pressed her, she acknowledged having sex with her boss and said she must have been "drugged." They went to the police, claiming that her boss had given her a "Mickey," which had denied her the ability to object. She told the police that she couldn't say no even though she didn't want to have sex. (She did, however, say no when her alleged rapist asked her if she was on birth control.) She also told the police, and subsequently testified before the grand jury, that she had taken no cocaine prior to the night at issue. When a test turned up positive for cocaine the police believed that the drug she had been given on that night was cocaine.

The police decided to outfit the woman with a wire and have her try to get her boss to admit that he had used cocaine to seduce her—that is, to rape her. The wired conversation consisted mostly of the accountant bantering with the secretary while trying to persuade her to continue to have a relationship with him. She repeatedly asked him whether he had given her cocaine, and he said no.

The accountant was prosecuted for rape. The case was essentially a "he said, she suspected" contest, and there was some forensic evidence—the cocaine in her system—to corroborate her suspicions. But the value of the forensic evidence depended entirely on whether she was telling the truth about not having used cocaine prior to the alleged rape. If she *had* used cocaine in the days or weeks prior to the sexual encounter, then the test would not establish that her boss had given her the drug.

We came up with the idea of testing her hair for traces of cocaine residue. Based on previous research, I knew that the past use of cocaine could be determined by a test of the hair. Indeed, the location of the cocaine residue in the hair could establish the approximate time frame of the cocaine use if the hair was long enough, since hair grows at a fairly consistent rate. The secretary had long hair.

Accordingly, we subpoenaed her hair samples. Immediately upon receiving the subpoena, she rushed to the nearest barbershop—that cut men's hair—and got a very short haircut, leaving an insufficient amount of hair to be tested. We tried, unsuccessfully, to find the barbershop and collect her hair. But her efforts to destroy the evidence upon receiving the subpoena suggested that she had not been truthful about her cocaine use.

In the end, the jury, after hearing the evidence, concluded that there was a reasonable doubt about whether the accountant had placed cocaine in her drink, or whether she alone was responsible for her decision to drink alcohol and then engage in relatively consensual sex with her boss.

The acquittal certainly did not signify approval of the accountant's behavior. But in a courtroom, proof of rape, like proof in every other serious crime, must be beyond a reasonable doubt. And in the event of there being reasonable doubt, the case must be resolved in favor of the defendant, regardless of what the jurors might think of the aleged perpetrator's morality.

RASHOMON RAPE CASES

In the great Japanese film *Rashomon*,[47] a horrible crime is presented through the very different perspectives of several participants. In some rape cases, a similar *Rashomon* scenario is sometimes at work. In the Mike Tyson case, for example, it is possible (though unlikely in my view) that Desiree Washington did not intend to consent to sex but that Mike Tyson reasonably believed—based on her groupie-like actions and statements—that she did. What should the law be in such situations?

Under American law, if a person makes a reasonable mistake of fact which leads to the commission of a crime, he is generally not guilty. For example, if a person walking down the street sees another person coming at him with a gun about to pull the trigger, and he shoots first and kills his assailant, he is not guilty, even if the "assailant" turns out to be an actor in a movie holding a gun that shoots blanks. Since the defendant reasonably, though mistakenly, believed that his life was in danger, his reasonable mistake of fact constitutes a defense to a murder charge. A crime requires both a criminal act and a criminal intent, and if the defendant reasonably believes that facts, as he saw them, made what he was doing permissible under the law, then he does not have a guilty mind. A mistake about law, on the other hand, is not a defense, since everybody is presumed to know the law. (This led an English wag to comment that "everybody is presumed to know the law except His Majesty's judges, who have a Court of Appeal set over them to put them right.")[48]

In recent years, however, there has been a movement to deny defendants in rape cases the right to raise the defense of reasonable mistake of fact, especially when it comes to whether the woman consented. No means no, and no man should be allowed to believe that no might mean yes or even maybe.

The law is correct in demanding that a man understand no to mean no. He may *subjectively* believe that no means maybe *when it comes to him*, but such a belief should be deemed unreasonable as a matter of law. In some situations, however, the woman does not say no. Nor does she say yes. Nor does she even say maybe. (There was a song made famous by Ella Fitzgerald entitled "She Didn't Say Yes": "She didn't say yes, she didn't say no. / She didn't say stay, she didn't say go.")[49] In real life, women (and men) often convey their intentions via ambiguous cues. In such situations, it is morally wrong, in my view, for a man to assume consent, but it may also be legally wrong for the law to consider it rape to engage in such immoral behavior. There are clearly gray areas in which the *man* ought to resolve doubts in favor of not acting, and where the *law* ought to resolve doubts in favor of not convicting.

I have represented several clients who fit this situation. One such case was a highly publicized prosecution of three prominent doctors at one of Boston's leading hospitals.

One of the doctors had a party at his house for some of the hospital staff. During the party, a nurse danced with several of the doctors, and two of them "fooled around" with her in the bathroom. As the party was ending, the three doctors invited the nurse to join them for a drive to Rockport, where one of the doctors had a vacation home. She went along with them because, in her words, she thought they were just "horsing around."

When they arrived at the Rockport home, two of the doctors smoked marijuana and began to disrobe. The nurse testified that she protested and told them to stop when the doctors began to undress her. Each of the defendants had sex with the nurse in the bedroom. She said that she felt numbed and could not resist.

Sometime later, they drove back to Boston and stopped to view the beach, to have breakfast, and fill the car up with gasoline. One of the doctors gave the nurse his card and said he would be interested in hooking up with her again.

The defendants each testified that the sexual intercourse was consensual, that the nurse never said no, that it was she who took her dress off and that she appeared at all times to be a willing participant.

The issue in the case was what the jury should do if they believed that *both* the nurse *and* the doctors were truthfully recounting their perceptions—that is, if they thought that the nurse did not want to have sex with the three doctors, but that the doctors believed she was a willing participant.

In the trial against the doctors, the jury convicted the defendants, and the judge sentenced them to six months' imprisonment; the leniency of the sentence suggests that he had some doubts about the sufficiency of the case. I was asked to consult on the appeal. I accepted the assignment because I wanted to preserve the mistake-of-fact defense in the face of efforts to abolish it in rape cases.

Unfortunately for these defendants, their trial lawyers had not appropriately raised the issue of reasonable mistake of fact. They asked for an instruction that might have invited the jury to acquit even if the mistake had been unreasonable—that is, even if the doctors believed that no meant yes. The appellate court ruled, therefore, "We need not reach the issue whether a reasonable and honest mistake to the fact of consent would be a defense, for even if we assume it to be so, the defendants did not request a jury instruction based on a reasonable mistake of fact. We are aware of no American court of last resort that recognizes mistake of fact, without consideration of its reasonableness."[50] The conviction, therefore, was affirmed.

In a subsequent case, in which I was not involved, a Massachusetts appeals court ruled that even a reasonable mistake of fact is not a defense when it comes to consent or lack of consent in the context of a rape prosecution.[51]

To me, this decision, disallowing even the most reasonable mistakes of fact in rape cases, opens up the possibility of some very unjust results. To illustrate this, let's go back to the filming of the movie *Deep Throat.*

Harry Reems had sex on camera with Linda Lovelace. Anyone watching the film[52] can see that she is consenting, both verbally and by her unambiguous actions. But according to a book she wrote, her apparent consent wasn't real; she was compelled to pretend she was consenting, by her husband's threats to kill her unless she went forward with her role. Under the extreme view expressed by some radical feminists and accepted by the Massachusetts appeals court, Reems could be guilty of rape, even though she said yes and his mistake of fact about her consent was entirely reasonable.

Or consider the following case[53] that I discuss in class. Among the group of American in California who come from the Hmong tribes in the mountains of Cambodia there is a traditional wedding ceremony for arranged marriages. The groom is supposed to go to the home of the bride, where the father of the bride greets him at the door. The groom pushes the father aside, finds the bride, and carries her, screaming and yelling, from her parents' abode. He is supposed to act like a warrior, and she is supposed to act like a virgin who wants to retain her status. It's all playacting, and part of the traditional wedding ceremony. In the case I teach, the young woman didn't actually want to go through with the marriage, and her resistance was not playacting; it was real. But there was no reason for the groom to know this. He took the bride home to his house, and over her "resistance," which he believed was feigned, he consummated the arranged marriage. She then ran away and reported the rape to the police, who arrested the young man. I ask my students how a case like this should be decided.

The class is generally divided. Some argue that no always means no, even in the context of a traditional marriage ritual in which no is supposed to mean yes. Others argue that it would be unfair to impose our values on a minority that has its own culture and traditions.

THE HEAVY COST OF CHANGING THE LAW—AND THE EVEN HEAVIER COST OF NOT CHANGING IT

A motto that hangs on many courthouses reads: "The known certainty of law is the safety of all."[54] But for the law to be absolutely certain, it must remain static, and static law quickly becomes anachronistic. Law is always changing to adapt to current realities. Even constitutional originalists, like Justice Scalia, who believe that the Constitution means today what it meant when it was enacted, acknowledge the need for statutory and common law change.[55] No legal concept has changed more fundamentally during my career than the law of rape. This change has produced much good, not only for the victims of that horrible crime, and all women, but for our legal system in general. No should mean no, and a maybe should not be taken as yes. The changes in the laws of rape are an example of how empowering a previously disempowered group—in this case, women—can bring about improvements in the law, in policy, and in attitudes. But there are always costs attached to legal change, especially during the period of transition, when changes in the law may run ahead of changes in attitude.

These costs can be high for defendants who honestly believed they were acting lawfully, but whose actions ran afoul of the newly imposed demands of the changing legal landscape. Such is the price of progress. It may be difficult to live with—yet it would be even more difficult to live without. My role, as a defense lawyer, as a teacher, and as a writer, is to try to maintain a proper balance between the need for progress and the imperative of fairness and due process.[56]

19

THE CHANGING IMPACT OF THE MEDIA ON THE LAW

Bill Clinton and Woody Allen

Criminal trials involving life and death, such as the O. J. Simpson and Claus von Bülow cases, or rape, such as the Mike Tyson and DSK cases, always generate massive media coverage, especially when famous people are in the dock. Certain kinds of civil trials, especially those with allegations of sexual misconduct, are also widely covered. Here, I focus on two such cases—both quasi-criminal in nature, both involving allegations of improper sexual relations—that reflect the changing impact of the media on our legal process and remind us that the law does not operate in a vacuum. I also discuss my involvement in other cases in which celebrities and public figures have become the focus of media attention.

In the days before radio and television, trials were covered primarily by the print media. Newspapers wrote articles about notorious cases. Pamphlets were issued containing excerpts from the transcripts. A few great lawyers became famous even without the benefit of the electronic media: Daniel Webster, Abraham Lincoln, William Jennings Bryant, and Clarence Darrow were all household names.

The advent of gavel-to-gavel television coverage has changed the way in which the public views the law and the way in which the law operates. It has turned lawyers into celebrities and clients into household names. Today, everyone has an opinion on the high-profile cases of the day, and these opinions have an impact not only in the court of public opinion but in the courthouse as well. No lawyer, especially one who practices criminal or constitutional law, can afford to ignore the impact of this phenomenon on tactics and strategy. Cases can be won or lost on the courthouse steps.

I have played a role in the ongoing debate regarding the manner by which trials are covered, most particularly whether they should be televised. (I think generally they should be and have advocated that view in debates, on television, and in articles.)[1] Several of my cases were among the first and most widely televised trials in our history. In others, I have served (and I continue to serve) as a commentator for network television and Court TV.[2]

Throughout my career, I have tried to use the media to the advantage of my clients, and the media has tried to use me and my clients in an effort to sell ads. Sometimes the relationship is symbiotic. More often it is antagonistic. It is rarely neutral. This is especially the case when celebrities are involved.

Although the majority of my clients have been obscure and often penurious, the media often portrays me as a "celebrity" or "high-profile" lawyer. I don't like those characterizations of my lifework, but there is some truth in it, because many of my cases have been extensively covered by the media. That is in the nature of a criminal or constitutional lawyer, since cases involving my specialties tend to raise issues of public interest. It is also true that because I have become well known as a result of these cases, I receive calls from famous people seeking my advice or representation. I don't like the term "celebrity lawyer" because it suggests that I select my cases on the basis of the status of the client, rather than the nature of the case or cause. I turn down most celebrity requests, and cases involving celebrity clients have formed a tiny fraction of my practice over the years. But the few that I do take garner far more publicity than do the many cases involving unknown clients.

VIGNETTE

Turning Down Bobby Fischer

One celebrity whose case I turned down was Bobby Fischer, who was training for his world championship chess match at Grossinger's, where my family and I were spending Passover. I received a note from Fischer asking me to meet with him. Since he grew up in Brooklyn and went to high school right next to the yeshiva I attended, I was anxious to meet him. He told me that he had heard that I was a good lawyer, and he wanted to ask my advice about an issue relating to whether he could copyright or trademark his chess moves. It was an intriguing question, and one that I would have been happy to research.

I told him that I would be willing to provide a legal memorandum to him on the subject, and he asked me whether I would be willing to do it without charge to him. I said, "Sure, I will provide you legal advice for free, if you would do me the favor of playing one quick chess match with my son Elon." He looked at me sternly and said, "I'm not a circus performer. I don't perform for children."

I looked him straight in the eye and said, "I'm not a circus performer either. I don't perform free legal services for ingrates who refuse to do a small favor for a young child who is learning how to play chess. Find another lawyer and pay him the going rate." He walked away. I never saw him again.

My own "celebrity" status among lawyers has been a decidedly mixed blessing. It has brought me some cases and clients I would not otherwise have gotten, and it has made me relatively wealthy, at least compared to other less well known law professors. This has caused some resentment and jealousy and has painted a target on my back at which ambitious journalists have repeatedly fired. It has also intruded on my privacy and that of my family. Once at a talk, a woman asked my wife, Carolyn, "So what is it like to sleep with Alan Dershowitz?" But the reality is that my "celebrity" is largely derivative: It derives from the famous and infamous clients I have *represented* over the years.

Most people see celebrities at a distance—on the screen, stage, television, or athletic field. They see them at their best—acting, posing, playing, speaking, being interviewed, or participating in charitable causes.

I see celebrities close up and at their worst. They come to me when they are in trouble, often deep trouble. Their celebrity is no longer a shield protecting them from the ordinary tribulations that befall most people on a daily basis. When they come to me, their celebrity has been turned into a sword being wielded against them. Celebrities generally live by publicity. When they come to me, they are dying from the publicity and want privacy and anonymity. But they can't have it, because the very celebrity that brought them fame and fortune now threatens to magnify their problems.

I have represented, advised, and consulted with dozens of celebrities, ranging from presidents and prime ministers to world famous athletes, actors, writers, and financiers. Most have gotten into trouble for one overarching reason: because they were willing to risk what they had *limited* amounts of in order to obtain more of what they had *unlimited* amounts of.

This may sound self-defeating, if not bizarre—so let me explain. Celebrities share several common characteristics. They have more of something than ordinary people have: great athletes have extraordinary physical skills; good actors have unusual thespian skills; successful politicians have a special charisma; financiers have money and the ability to make more. These special characteristics generally give celebrities access to certain desiderata of life: lots of money and the things money and fame can buy, and the benefits that come with these commodities, such as access to numerous sexual partners—if they choose to use their celebrity to obtain such access (and excess!).

Many of my celebrity clients, who have unlimited amounts of money or access to sex, have sacrificed what they have limited amounts of—freedom, career, time with loved ones, health—in order to obtain even more money or sex. Let me provide a few examples of such bizarre risk-taking in cases that are a matter of public record. (I could provide many more examples if I were free—which I am not—to disclose confidential information given to me by celebrity clients.)[3]

Leona Helmsley, the celebrity hotel "queen," had more than a billion dollars in the bank when, according to the government, she whited-out the words "stereo system" on a bill for services and changed them to "security system" in order to have her accountant deduct the system's cost from her taxes.[4] She also, according to the government, evaded sales taxes on expensive jewelry in New York (which had a sales tax) by having the jeweler send empty boxes to Florida (which had no sales tax).[5] As a result, she may have saved several thousand dollars, but she spent more than a year in prison, when she had only a few years left to live and even less time to spend with her dying husband. By any rational calculus, this was crazy behavior.

VIGNETTE

The Queen of Mean

Leona Helmsley was boring and rather stupid. She was called the queen of mean, and I can only disclose incidents that occurred in public. Here's one that shows how she earned her title. We were having breakfast in the dining room of her hotel when a waiter brought me a cup of tea. She noticed that a little bit of the tea had dripped onto the saucer. She grabbed the cup and saucer and threw them on the floor in the direction of the waiter, shattering them, and screamed at the waiter, "Now clean it up and beg me for your job." I walked away, not wanting to be associated with that kind of public rudeness.

When my daughter was born, Leona had her private jet fly a large stuffed bear to Boston, where it was placed in a limo and brought to our home. My daughter loved the bear and several years later had an opportunity to thank Leona for sending it. Leona replied: "It's stolen merchandise. I stole it from Donald Trump." She then explained how she had sold a hotel to Trump that included a pastry restaurant called Rumplemyer's, which was decorated with large stuffed animals. The sale included the stuffed animals, but Leona took the bear, which belonged to Trump, and sent it to my daughter. I told Leona that I would either have to return the stolen bear or get Trump's permission to keep it. She said, "Tell the Donald I stole it from him. See what he says." I told Trump. He laughed and said, "I'm not surprised. Let your daughter enjoy the bear."

One day my brother, who was another of Leona's lawyers, was invited to a birthday party at her house. He brought my mother along. Leona knew that my mother did not want to be confronted with the reality that my brother is not kosher outside of his house. My brother, sensitive to this, always ate only kosher food in her presence. He was at the buffet with my mother, choosing among the smoked salmon and vegetables, when Leona came over and in her booming voice yelled, "In front of your mother you eat salmon. In front of me you eat lobster. Ha ha ha." It was entirely gratuitous, hurtful, and all too typical.

Mike Tyson, as the world's greatest boxer, had a limited career ahead of him but virtually unlimited access to sex. As with many famous athletes, women were falling all over him, sending him "audition" tapes, waiting for him wherever he appeared, and begging to have sex with him. Yet he agreed to be alone in a hotel room with a young woman he had just met and to risk being falsely accused of rape—which, in my view, he was—in order to get even more sex. The result was that he was sentenced to several years in prison near the end of his short career and lost almost everything he had worked so hard to acquire. Even he later acknowledged to me that he was a "schmuck" for risking so much for so little.

In both of these cases, celebrities risked what they had limited amounts of—in Helmsley's situation, the few remaining years of her life and time with her husband; in Tyson's situation, the few remaining years of his career—in order to obtain more of what they had unlimited amounts of: money and sex. Of course, they didn't expect to be convicted for what they did, but they both engaged in behavior that carried the risk that they would be deprived of what they had only limited amounts of. No rationally calculating person, weighing the costs and benefits of taking such risky actions, would do so. But these celebrities—and many others who have consulted me—did just that.

Some of my celebrity clients have also gotten into trouble because they needed, or felt entitled to, immediate gratification without sufficiently considering the longer-term implications of their conduct, not only to themselves and their careers but to their loved ones, friends, and associates. They believed that when the future finally arrived, there would be new quick fixes. And often they were right. Someone generally managed to clean up the mess they left behind. It requires a combination of unlikely factors and some bad luck to produce their particular brand of disaster, since most successful people are good at making problems go away. But even celebrities are subject to the law of probabilities, and eventually—if they persist in their reckless behavior—the statistics will likely catch up with them.

Why do so many celebrities—even relatively intelligent ones—act so recklessly? Is there something special about being a celebrity that makes one feel invulnerable to ordinary risks? Are they so accustomed to "getting away with it" that they weigh costs and benefits differently from ordinary people? Is there a sense of entitlement? Are there expectations that the rules don't apply to them? Do they feel guilty about their "undeserved" success and unconsciously want to be caught? Do they surround themselves with groupies who encourage bad behavior and refuse to be truthful with them about the risks? Are temptations placed so readily before them that they become difficult to resist?

One answer may well be that some of them have been doing it all their lives, starting well before they were rich and famous. People often have a hard time changing old habits. I know that no matter how much money I now have, I cannot throw away a tea bag after using it only once. It drives my family crazy to see a soggy tea bag in a cup waiting to be reused, but I simply can't "waste" a good tea bag that has at least one more cup in it. I'm not suggesting that reusing tea bags is in any way analogous to cheating on one's taxes or committing other financial or sexual crimes, but I am suggesting that people who have earned their money or fame by illegally cutting corners will sometimes continue to do so, even though there is no longer a financial or other rational need to do so. Old habits die hard, but they can also kill or at least wound those who can't break the illegal ones. This is not in any way to justify such continuing misconduct. Indeed, quite the opposite, it is to condemn it—because celebrities have few excuses for their misconduct—while at the same time trying to explain why it persists among some celebrities.

I have thought a great deal about what motivates famous and powerful people to act so self-destructively. The celebrities whom I have represented and advised have faced a wide array of problems, ranging from criminal charges, to loss of careers, to public humiliation, to custody fights, to defamations, to physical threats. Some of the most fascinating stories I can never tell, because I learned them in confidence and helped to resolve them so that they would never become public. Most have become matters of public record, and I am free to write about those stories and to offer my insights about the famous people I advised over the years and the problems they faced.

The question I am asked most frequently about this is: Does being famous help a celebrity who gets in trouble with the law? Or does it hurt? My answer is yes. Sometimes it helps. Sometimes it hurts. Always it matters. One of the most important jobs a lawyer who represents famous people has is to figure out how to turn that celebrity into an advantage rather than a disadvantage, or at the very least to neutralize it (which is a near impossibility in our celebrity-driven world). I recall Claus von Bülow once telling me that in England it's all about "class and breeding," while in America it's all about "fame and celebrity." Before he became famous for being accused of trying to kill his wife, von Bülow couldn't get a good table at certain posh restaurants despite his wealth and social status, but when his name and face began to appear in every newspaper—as a high-profile defendant—he got the best table in every restaurant.[6]

VIGNETTE

It's All in the Name

A wealthy friend invited me to a party filled with financial celebrities. "Say hello to Donald." It was Trump. "To Ron." It was Perlman. "To Mort." It was Zuckerman. Then he introduced me to a man wearing a sweatshirt. "Say hello to Andy." I asked Andy what he did: "Are you one of these financial guys?" He replied, "No, I work for my mum." "Does she run a company?" I inquired. "I guess you could say so," he replied. "Would I have heard of the company she runs?" I wondered. "Most definitely," he said with a smile. "What is it?" I asked. "It's Great Britain," he replied. "My mum's the Queen." I had been conversing with Prince Andrew.

During the conversation, he asked whether he could attend one of my classes. I invited him to a class during which we were discussing the use of deadly force. Being a member of the British military, he joined the class discussion. He then wrote me a letter describing his experiences:

> Dear Alan,
>
> Thank you for a most intellectual experience, it was a fascinating insight into the law and the very serious subjects and dilemmas you face. Your generous offer of attending one of your lectures was a true revelation in thought provocation.
>
> My mind . . . has not been educated in the way you and your class thinks but I managed to keep up for most of the time and find where you were off to with your hypotheticals. As you know I made the decision to attend the university of life rather than the academic variety at an early stage in my life and until now I would not change that in any way. You have managed to awaken an interest which I didn't realise had lain dormant. Perhaps, when I leave the Royal Navy to rejoin the real world, I will get the chance to conduct further academic studies. But in the meantime, the opportunity to be a student for just one lecture was an expanding experience and I cannot begin to thank you enough for your kindness.

I look forward to continuing my intellectual challenge with you . . . in the coming months. Thank you again for a fantastic experience.

Yours sincerely,
Prince Andrew

The most frequent misconception about celebrities is that they must be "so fascinating." The opposite is often the case. Most of my famous clients, with some important exceptions, have been uninteresting. Some have been outright boring. We tend to confuse their public persona and surroundings, which fascinate us, with their private personalities, which are often banal, mundane, and self-centered. Many of them have no ideas, no insights, and little to say about matters outside the narrow spheres of their professional lives. Yet we listen to their often uninformed opinions on important issues of the day affecting the world, just because they have a handsome face, strong muscles, or other talents or attributes that are irrelevant to their presumed credibility on the matters about which they are opining. Celebrities may seem fascinating from a distance, but the reality, viewed close-up, is often very different.

Their cases and controversies may be fascinating in part because of who they are, in part because of what they are accused of doing, and in part because the public obsesses over celebrity.

VIGNETTE

Brando

I have a small apartment in New York, which my wife and I use on weekends. On this particular weekend, I lent it out to my doctor, who called me from the apartment and said that while he was out, a message was left on the machine from a guy who did a pretty good imitation of Marlon Brando. He told me that the caller had criticized my diction on the outgoing message. I called my machine. It *was* Marlon Brando. I called him back, and he asked me if I would help get his son out of jail.

Christian Brando was originally charged with murder, after he shot his half-sister Cheyenne's boyfriend, claiming that the boyfriend had physically abused her. Christian claimed that he confronted the boyfriend and they struggled over his gun, which fired accidentally. The prosecution claimed that it was a cold-blooded murder fueled by Christian's drunken state.

Marlon Brando asked me to work with Robert Shapiro to get his son out of prison. Brando blamed himself for his family problems and wanted to help as much as he could. He said he heard that I "could perform miracles," and he wanted my input. I tried to disabuse him of the notion that I could free his son immediately, but I promised to work as hard as I could with Shapiro. Eventually a plea bargain was struck and Christian pleaded guilty to manslaughter. He was released from prison after serving only five years, much to the chagrin of many in the public and the media. The story did not, however, have a happy ending. Cheyenne committed suicide in 1995 at age twenty-five and Christian died of pneumonia in 2008 at age forty-nine.

Marlon Brando, whose stage and screen presence was electric, was boring and predictable when I encountered him. He had stereotypically "Hollywood" political views, conventional ideas, and no sense of humor. He was accustomed to yes-men agreeing with his every idea and didn't take criticism or disagreement easily. He loved his children but didn't seem to have any notion of how to relate to them. All in all he struck me as a rather pathetic figure, totally at odds with his public persona.

The two cases I will now discuss received enormous media coverage. Both, not surprisingly, involve sex. Both involve world-famous people who were accused of having inappropriate sexual contact with inappropriate young women. Unlike most celebrities, both of these were fascinating people.

The paradigm of a famous person being tried under the klieg lights of worldwide media coverage was, of course, the impeachment of President William Jefferson Clinton, in which I played several roles: lawyer, witness, political advocate, television commentator, book author, and friend.

PRESIDENT BILL CLINTON

I first met President and Mrs. Clinton on Rosh Hashanah in 1993. We shared mutual friends and teachers from Yale Law School, but we had never actually met before I invited the President and the First Lady, who were vacationing on Martha's Vineyard, to join my family for Rosh Hashanah services. When I learned that the Clintons were living near us on the Vineyard, I had the following letter delivered by a mutual friend:

> Dear Mr. President:
>
> It is my honor to invite you on behalf of the Martha's Vineyard Hebrew Center to attend our Rosh Hashanah services. It is a part of the Jewish tradition for the congregation to bless the President and the great nation that has given us the freedom to practice our religion without prejudice or discrimination. Our congregation would love to extend that blessing personally to you and to invite you to respond with your own New Year's greeting or to accept our good wishes silently.
>
> In years gone by, Jews in different countries lived in fear that government officials would enter their religious sanctuaries. Such visits were often prelude to crusades, inquisitions, pogrom, and—eventually—the Holocaust. The lyrics of the Broadway hit "Fiddler on the Roof" include the following mock prayer for the Russian Czar. "May the good Lord bless and keep the Czar—far away from us." In contemporary America, the attitude of the Jewish community is quite different: We welcome our president with open arms, [along with] your family and staff members (Jewish or non-Jewish).

The President accepted, thus becoming the first sitting American president ever to attend a Jewish High Holiday service. I sat next to him during the service and shared a *mahzor* (Holiday prayer book) with him for most of the davening, pointing out the prayers and whispering explanations of such concepts as the *talit* ("prayer shawl") and *mitzvot* ("good deeds"). We used a prayer book in which the Hebrew was transliterated for the parts that are chanted, and the President and Mrs. Clinton sang along in Hebrew. Then the President spoke, declaring his role in the Mideast peace process "one of the most rewarding things I've done" and wishing the Jewish people a "*Shana Tova.*" He wore a white *kippah* my wife and I gave him from our wedding. He and Hillary signed it. We have kept it as a treasured reminder of that historic night.

As I watched the President davening in his yarmulke, I thought of Jules Feiffer's quip: "The time is at hand when the wearing of prayer shawl and skullcap will not bar a man from the White House—unless, of course, the man is Jewish!"[7]

Following the service, the Clintons invited us to join them for dinner at the Savoir Fare restaurant in Edgartown. At a relaxed dinner, the President discussed movies with my son, who is a producer, while my wife and I discussed health care policy with Hillary.[8] At the end of the evening, the President lifted a glass of champagne to toast the Jewish New Year. As I touched my glass to his, I gave the traditional Jewish toast, *"L'Chaim"*—"To Life."

During subsequent summers, the Clintons vacationed in Martha's Vineyard and lived near us. We frequently dined, partied, and even square-danced with them, and became friends. We were invited to the White House on several occasions and to Bill's birthday parties on the Vineyard. The President sought my advice from time to time.

Sometimes, I offered unsolicited advice, such as when I urged him to commute to time served the life sentence of Jonathan Pollard, who had pled guilty to passing classified information to Israel while working as an American intelligence analyst. The President wanted to commute the sentence, but he got push-back not only from the intelligence community but also from several Jewish senators. He asked me: If he couldn't even get the Jewish senators to support commutation, how could he justify it to the intelligence community, which was adamantly opposed to it?

Another issue on which I initially offered my unsolicited advice involved the Monica Lewinsky scandal. As I watched the drama unfold, I saw a familiar pattern that had gotten other celebrities in trouble: opting for short-term gratification without considering the longer-term consequences.

At every decision point, it seemed to me, the President and his advisors opted for a political tactic that helped them get good headlines and poll results in the short term, rather than focusing on the longer-term strategy that might have prevented an entirely lawful sexual indiscretion from turning into a possible crime.

The first point was, of course, the President's decision to engage in a sexual relationship with a White House intern in the first place, especially at a time when he knew he was under intense investigation by Kenneth Starr, a somewhat puritanical prosecutor.

If there was a "vast right-wing conspiracy" out there waiting to "get" the President, as Hillary Clinton had alleged, it is difficult to imagine any action more reckless than Oval Office sex with a young blabbermouth whose goal was probably as much to brag about her conquest of the President as to engage in an intimate relationship. She really did want *oral* sex: She wanted to *talk* about it. And she did—to more than a dozen people. The President achieved immediate gratification, while risking long-term consequences to his marriage, his presidency, and, above all, the nation's stability.

At the time he began his encounter with Lewinsky, Clinton knew that he might have to testify about his sex life. He knew that his enemies had the powerful weapon of subpoena power aimed directly at his presidency. That is probably why he was reluctant to engage in sexual intercourse. He wanted sex with deniability. What he got was unsatisfying sex with unconvincing deniability. Or, as Maureen Dowd put it:

> *Mr. Clinton's habit, with language and behavior, has been to try to incorporate his alibi into his sin. The result is more twisted than titillating.*[9]

This was not the first time Bill Clinton put his future at risk for immediate sexual gratification. But in every other instance he had been able to avoid the long-term consequences. I am certain that he believed that this pattern of short-term risk-taking and subsequent avoidance of long-term consequences would be repeated. I doubt he believed, at the moment that he first allowed Lewinsky to touch him in a sexual manner, that this action would eventually lead to possible removal from office. He would not have consciously taken such a known risk. But when people have succeeded so often in the past in achieving both immediate gratification and avoidance of long-term consequences, they miscalculate the odds and act as if they can have their cake and eat it too.

The history of many of my own celebrity clients is largely a history of defendants who for years—sometimes decades—have risked their careers, family lives, fortunes, and freedom for some form of immediate gratification. Finally, when they are caught, everyone asks: "How could they have risked so much for so little?" What people fail to understand is that the "little" thing for which they were caught was usually only the tip of a large iceberg of misconduct that they had gotten away with for years. In their minds, therefore, they were risking very little (the unlikelihood that *this time* they would get caught) for a great deal (a lifetime of small, short-term gratifications, which add up to something for which it is worth taking small risks).

In retrospect, we consider such actions reckless because we are running the video backwards: We know he was caught. But at the time Clinton made the decision, he probably did not regard it as any more reckless than the similar decisions he had previously made, when it seemed from the results that he had not risked his career. He had probably played the same sexual-verbal game before: limiting his sexual contact so that he could plausibly deny that he engaged in "sexual relationships" outside of his marriage.[10] But he never before had to testify under oath about these relationships. What he failed to appreciate was how much the risks had increased as the result of the legal proceedings then in place—the Paula Jones case, in which a former Arkansas state employee was suing Clinton for sexual harassment—and the Kenneth Starr investigation. These legal proceedings escalated the stakes by turning a private sexual encounter into the subject of sworn testimony and investigation by an independent counsel.

It is unlikely that Bill Clinton confided the truth of his relationship with Monica Lewinsky to his lawyers, because his principal lawyer was representing both him and his wife. Thus if he didn't want his wife to find out about Lewinsky, he could not tell his lawyer about her. But it is likely that his lawyers suspected that there was some truth to the rumors that something untoward had occurred between Clinton and Lewinsky. After all, Clinton did testify that he had engaged in adulterous sex with Gennifer Flowers, despite his previous public denial. Moreover his reputation was well known. Any lawyer worth his salt should have based decisions regarding the President's testimony on the assumption that he *may* have engaged in a sexual relationship with Monica Lewinsky. A good lawyer should also have assumed that a twenty-two-year-old intern who had engaged in a sexual relationship with the President would talk about it.

President Clinton's lawyer in the Paula Jones case, Robert Bennett, was on notice that the President was going to be asked about Lewinsky. If he had conducted any investigation to determine the nature of their relationship, he would have uncovered the widespread concern around the White House over Lewinsky's unusual access to the President. He would also have learned of the dozens of logged meetings between the President and a young government employee. This should have alerted Bennett to probe more deeply. At the very least he should have interviewed Lewinsky, confronted her with the concerns, and asked her direct questions. He should also have interviewed those White House officials who had expressed concern. Yet on the basis of little more than an assurance from the President, he allowed an affidavit to be submitted by Lewinsky denying any sexual relationship.

Putting aside the ethical issues arising from relying on an affidavit that he was on notice might be false, and having his client testify to facts that he had to suspect might be false, it is difficult to understand the tactical considerations that led the President's lawyers to allow him to testify about his sex life.

It is not as if Bennett had not been cautioned about the risks of having the President testify about his sex life at the Jones deposition. On May 27, 1997, six months before President Clinton testified at a deposition in the Paula Jones lawsuit, as a guest expert on *The Geraldo Rivera Show,* I offered the following advice:

> *This case never should have gotten this far. It should have been settled early when he could have settled it easily. He must settle the case. . . .*
>
> *Remember, depositions are very broad in latitude. He could be asked questions about adultery. He could be asked questions about his prior sexual life. There are no relevancy objections that are generally sustained to depositions. . . .*
>
> *I think the President could win if it actually went to trial, but it won't go to trial. What I would do if I were his lawyer is to say, "Look, the dignity of the office precludes the President from answering any of these questions. We realize that as a result of not answering these questions, we will reluctantly, without admitting anything, have to be sanctioned by having the verdict directed against us on the merits. We accept that because we can't answer the questions and preserve the dignity. And now let's move on to the damages, where the focus is not on the President but on Paula Jones." And in that way, he can, in effect, settle the case, even if the other side doesn't settle because the damages will be very low, there won't be an apology. There'll be a judgment against him, but the judgment will be explained on the basis of the dignity of the presidency. So if the settlement talks fail, that's what I would recommend that his lawyers think about.*

I went on to suggest that the President had to start asking himself, "Is he well advised here?"[11]

To my mind, the President had three options. But he was aware of only two of them. He knew that he could litigate and try to win—as he ended up doing. He also knew that he could try to settle the case, which would have avoided the necessity of testifying at the deposition or trial. A settlement requires both sides to agree. In the Jones case, the President reportedly offered to pay Jones $700,000 in order to settle the case. Jones insisted on an apology[12] and the settlement talks broke down.

The third option, *of which the president was unaware*, was to default the Jones case. Every litigant in a civil case has the right to default—which means, essentially, to settle the case unilaterally by simply refusing to contest the allegations in the complaint. Consider, for example, the following hypothetical: A fired employee of a high-tech business sues for $10,000 in back pay. The business realizes that in order to defend its actions, it would have to reveal commercial secrets valued at $1 million and take the time of executives which it estimates at being worth $200,000. It offers to settle the case for the $10,000 the employee is demanding, but the angry employee prefers a trial at which he will be publicly vindicated. The company has the right simply to default, have the judgment entered against it, and have the court order it to pay the damages sought by the employee. Defaulting a case does not necessarily entail an admission of liability. It represents a practical assessment of the costs and benefits of litigating and not litigating.

Robert Bennett never told President Clinton that he could have defaulted and paid Jones without making any apology. Perhaps the Lewinsky story would have leaked, but the President would not have had to dignify a rumor with a response. It was the entirely avoidable decision to have him testify under oath—not once, but twice—that turned a sex rumor into a possibly impeachable offense.

How do I know that Robert Bennett never told President Clinton of the default option? Because both men personally told me.[13] Here is the story:

On January 17, 1997, President Clinton was deposed in the Paula Jones lawsuit. In the course of the deposition, he was asked questions about his relationship with Monica Lewinsky, including "Did you have an extramarital sexual affair with Monica Lewinsky?"

The judge defined the term "sexual relations" as follows:

For the purpose of this deposition, a person engages in "sexual relations" when the person knowingly engages in or causes

1. *contact with the genitalia, anus, groin, breast, inner thigh, or buttocks of any person with an intent to arouse or gratify the sexual desire of any person.*
   Contact means intentional touching, either directly or through clothing.

Clinton answered:

I have never had sexual relations with Monica Lewinsky. I've never had an affair with her.

Under the judge's definition, oral sex does, of course, constitute sexual relations. After the Jones lawyers completed their questioning, the President's lawyer, Robert Bennett, asked the following question:

In paragraph eight of her affidavit, [Monica Lewinsky] says this, "I have never had a sexual relationship with the President, he did not propose that we have a sexual relationship."

Is that a true and accurate statement?

The President responded: "That is absolutely true."

Shortly thereafter, reports began to appear of tape-recorded conversations between Linda Tripp and Monica Lewinsky suggesting that there had been a sexual relationship of some kind between the President and Lewinsky.

On January 23, 1998, I appeared on MSNBC and criticized Bennett for allowing the President to walk into a perjury trap. I recommended that the President "get a new lawyer, tell him the truth, sit down with your new lawyer . . . and [have him give you] the straight poop." The lawyer has to be someone "who doesn't care what the President thinks of him. His obligation is to tell the President what he doesn't want to hear."

Several days later, Robert Bennett called me to complain about what I had said on television. Bennett kept me on the phone for nearly half an hour telling me that I did not understand his "strategy" in the case, accusing me of "Monday morning quarterbacking" his decisions.

So I asked Bennett: "Did you ever advise the President that in addition to the option of settling the Jones case, he could simply default on the liability phase of the case?"

Bennett replied that defaulting would have been "ridiculous" and "a stupid idea" and that he would never recommend it.

So I asked Bennett what kind of an investigation he had conducted of the Lewinsky matter before he allowed the President to be deposed. He admitted that he'd simply accepted the President's word, since it was supported by Lewinsky's affidavit. When I asked him whether he had ever questioned Lewinsky, he gave a vague response. He said he was surprised about the questions asked concerning Lewinsky at the deposition.

I told Bennett that I strongly believed he had made a mistake by walking his client into a perjury trap. He assured me that he knew what he was doing. I told him I hoped he was right, but that I still thought he had made a mistake.

A lawyer owes his client the duty to explain all available legal options, even if he believes that the client will probably reject a given option. Bennett failed in this duty. He argued, in his own defense, that if Clinton had defaulted the Jones case, many more litigants would have "come out of the woodwork" and sued Clinton in the hope that he would default. To me, this is a fallacious argument for several reasons. First, the statute of limitations would have passed on virtually all allegations arising—as the Jones case did—before Clinton became president. Even more important, the moment it became public—which it quickly did—that the President previously had offered a $700,000 settlement to Jones, there was more than enough incentive for gold diggers to come forward and sue. If Clinton was prepared to pay $700,000 to settle a suit he regarded as utterly frivolous and untrue, no greater incentive would have been added if he defaulted and paid.

The sad reality is that Robert Bennett, perhaps in his zeal to chalk up a high-visibility win, failed or neglected to tell the President that this was one case that was better for the client to *lose* and avoid testifying rather than to win and risk testifying falsely.

Defaulting the Jones case would have resulted in bad headlines the next day—and perhaps for an additional week. But testifying about his sex life resulted in a dangerous threat to the Clinton presidency—a threat that would not materialize for several months. It was another instance of the President making a decision that helped him in the short run—by avoiding the negative headlines of a settlement or default—but hurt him in the long run. And it was a pattern that would persist.

On January 26, 1998, President Clinton, with the assistance of Hollywood producer Harry Thomason, decided to make a public statement denying a sexual relationship with Monica Lewinsky. Pointing his finger at the TV camera for emphasis, he said:

"I want you to listen to me. I'm going to say this again. I did not have sexual relations with that woman, Miss Lewinsky. I never told anybody to lie, not a single time—never. These allegations are false. And I need to go back to work for the American people."

This statement, made directly to the American public and not under oath, came back to haunt Clinton. Why did he make it? He was under no legal obligation to make any statement. He could easily have said, as so many others have said, "Since the matter is now the subject of a legal proceeding, my lawyers have advised me to make no public comment about it. I'm sure you understand."

Instead, he issued a firm denial of what he would later have to admit was essentially true: Namely, that he did, in fact, have a sexual encounter with "that woman."

Once again, the President and his advisors opted for the quick fix. They felt that it was necessary to put out the political brushfire. By issuing a firm denial, the President could postpone—perhaps forever—the longer-term consequences of his improper sex and his misleading testimony. At the time he made the statement, the President likely was not aware that Lewinsky had saved the semen-stained dress that would eventually force him to change his story. Without the dress, it would always be a "she said, he said" conflict between the President and a woman who acknowledged on the Tripp tapes that she frequently lied, and whose own lawyer said was an impressionable woman who sometimes fantasized.

Ultimately, the disclosure of the semen-stained dress made it undeniable that there had been sexual activity between them. President Clinton had to appear on television and acknowledge that he had behaved "inappropriately" with Monica Lewinsky. It was a low point both in his presidency and in his personal life.

A few days later, President Clinton publicly acknowledged that he had behaved "inappropriately"; he flew to the Vineyard. The next day, we were at dinner together. The President gathered a small group—including several lawyers—around him and began to discuss the case. He said that following the unanimous Supreme Court decision refusing to postpone the lawsuit brought against him by Paula Jones,[14] he'd had no choice but to submit to a deposition about his sex life, because Jones refused to settle the case. At that point, I told him he *had* had an alternative, and explained to him that he could have ended the lawsuit by simply defaulting and paying the damages that Paula Jones had sought. The President looked surprised: "Nobody ever told me I could have had the case dismissed if I had paid the money. [My lawyer] told me I had to be deposed."

Shortly thereafter, Bob Bennett was no longer representing President Clinton, and Clinton was seeking my legal advice, as his problems—all of which derived from the deposition he didn't have to give—multiplied. He came close to being indicted. He was impeached by the House of Representatives (and eventually acquitted by an evenly divided Republican Senate) and disbarred.

During the course of these proceedings I conferred with the President, provided legal memoranda to him and his lawyers, and discussed his case in the court of public opinion.

I also testified on the President's behalf as an expert witness on the law of perjury before the congressional committee that was considering whether to impeach him for the "high crime" of perjury.[15] The chairman of the committee was Republican congressman Henry Hyde. Hyde and I repeatedly clashed. The front page of the *Washington Post* featured photographs the next morning of the two of us angrily pointing accusatory fingers at each other.[16]

The source of our conflict was the selective outrage directed by Congressman Hyde and other Republican lawmakers at President Clinton's alleged perjury. I began my testimony by putting President Clinton's false statements into a broader historical context:

> *For nearly a quarter of a century I have been teaching, lecturing, and writing about the corrosive influences of perjury on our legal system—especially when committed by those whose job it is to enforce the law. . . .*
>
> *On the basis of my experience, I believe that no felony is committed more frequently in this country than perjury and false statement crimes. Perjury during civil depositions and trials is so endemic that a respected appellate judge once observed that, quote, "experienced lawyers say that in large cities scarcely a trial occurs in which some witness does not lie." Police perjury in criminal cases, particularly in the context of searches and other exclusionary rule issues, is so pervasive that the former police chief of San Jose and Kansas City has estimated that hundreds of thousands of law enforcement officials commit felony perjury every year testifying about drug arrests alone. But in comparison with their frequency, perjury crimes are among the most under-prosecuted in this country.*

I then went on to distinguish among various types of perjury—ranging from bearing false witness against a defendant facing the death penalty to being evasive about embarrassing sexual misconduct—and tried to place Clinton's false statements in their proper place along this continuum.[17]

> *I think it is clear that the false statements of which President Clinton is accused fall at the most marginal end of the least culpable genre of this continuum of offenses, and would never even be considered for prosecution in the routine cases involving an ordinary defendant.*

I went on to blast the committee for having never conducted hearings on the corrosive problems of police perjury—"testilying."

I warned that

> *history will not be kind to this committee. History will not be kind to this Congress. I think this committee and this Congress will go down in history along with the Congress that improperly impeached Andrew Johnson for political reasons.*

Congressmen Hyde and Conyers then continued the questioning:

> REP. HYDE: I thank you, Professor Dershowitz. I don't thank you for criticizing the motives, saying that we're out to get the President. You haven't the slightest idea of the agony that many of us go through over this question.
>
> We are concerned about the double standard. That may mean nothing to you, . . .
>
> MR. DERSHOWITZ: It means a great deal to me. [applause] When is the last time this committee has expressed concern about the rights of criminal defendants— [a chorus of "regular order" from committee members]. . . . It's a sham.

Then Congressman Hyde angrily began to lecture me about the rule of law:

> *Does the rule of law— Have you been to Auschwitz? Do you see what happens when the rule of law doesn't prevail?*
>
> *Now, I don't leap from the Oval Office on a Saturday afternoon to Auschwitz, but there are similarities when the rule of law doesn't obtain, or where you have one law for the powerful and one for the nonaristocratic.*

He did not give me an opportunity to respond to his absurd invocation of Auschwitz. But I did insist on responding when Congressman Barr contrasted me with the "real America" and how "the real America views these matters."

> MR. DERSHOWITZ: Can I respond, thirty seconds, to what I perceive to have been a personal attack? First of all, whenever I hear the word "real Americans," that sounds to me like a code word for racism—a code word for bigotry, a code word—
>
> REP. BARR: That's absurd, Professor, you ought to be ashamed. That is the silliest thing I have ever heard—

MR. DERSHOWITZ: When I hear you describe me as something other than a real American—shame on you. We may have a disagreement about the merits of these issues, but I would no more impugn your Americanism than you should impugn mine, sir.

Not all the congressmen were angered by my aggressive testimony. Congressman Rogan summarized his views this way:

I know that you raised a few hackles here with some of my colleagues with controversial comments, but I want you to know I personally found them to be very therapeutic, because up till now the only excuse I had for not having attended Harvard Law School was my grade point average. [laughter] So you've given me a little different perspective.

Following my testimony before the congressional committee, I worked closely with the President's legal team both on the impeachment and on the Starr investigation.

One summer day, during the impeachment crisis, the White House switchboard tried unsuccessfully to reach me. (The White House has an unparalleled capacity to reach people. Once when I was flying on a commercial flight, the pilot came out and whispered in my ear, "The President is on the radio-phone." I took the call in the cockpit.) I was on a beach, which had no cell phone service. When I got back to my house, there were seven frantic messages that the President needed to see me right away. He was staying a couple of miles away from our house, at the home of Dick Friedman in Edgartown. I jumped into my old Volvo and drove straight to Friedman's house. The Secret Service man told me that the President was expecting me, but they had to search under the hood of my car. I started looking for the mechanism to open the hood. After a few minutes, the Secret Service man smiled and said, "Professor, you don't know how to open up the hood on your own car, do you?" I responded by telling him the Jackie Mason joke about how when a non-Jew hears knocking under the hood of his car, he fixes and fixes. But when a Jew hears knocking under the hood of his car, he immediately trades it in for a new one.[18] He laughed, and showed me where the lever was. I then drove down the road a short distance to where the President was waiting for me, having heard that I didn't know how to open up the hood of my own car and laughingly wondering whether he should be seeking advice from such a klutz. But he continued to seek my advice until the matter was resolved.

Shortly afterward, John Kennedy, Jr.—now the late son of the former president—called and asked me if I would contribute an article to his magazine, *George*. He asked me if I would describe the ten greatest legal blunders of the twentieth century. Here is what I described as the number one and two greatest blunders:

> *By far the greatest legal blunder of the 20th Century was committed by President Clinton's lawyer in the Paula Jones case, Robert Bennett.*[19]

I went on to describe that Bennett had never presented the President with the option of defaulting.

The second greatest blunder was also committed by Bennett:

> *After walking his client into the perjury trap, Bennett himself helped to spring it. Not content to let the President answer the opposing lawyers' questions, Bennett did the unthinkable: he asked the President to affirm, under oath, the truth of Monica Lewinsky's affidavit without having asked Lewinsky what she meant when she said she had not engaged in sexual relations with Clinton. Then, Bennett mischaracterized the affidavit by saying that the affidavit indicated that "there is absolutely no sex of any kind in any manner, shape or form." Finally, in a "cover your ass" letter to the court, Bennett implicitly blamed his client for misleading the court, instead of forthrightly acknowledging his own failure to find out what Lewinsky meant by sexual relations. These blunders [to me] give Bennett almost unique bragging rights as the only lawyer in American history who has helped his client get impeached.*[20]

At the very beginning of the Lewinsky matter, I had received a call from someone close to the White House giving me the phone number for where Monica was staying and urging me to call her. Perceiving a possible conflict of interest, I didn't call. Several years later, I was approached by Monica's mother at a Jewish event. She said, "I wish you had called Monica." I often wonder, would the case have turned out differently if I had called and agreed to represent her?

Remarkably, I have remained on friendly terms with both Bill Clinton and Kenneth Starr, despite criticizing the former's sexual behavior and the latter's prosecutorial tactics. Most celebrities I have encountered have extremely thin skins. They never forgive even small slights because they are accustomed to being universally adored. Both Clinton and Starr have thick skin. They accept criticism, especially when they know it is well intentioned. The same cannot be said about the next celebrity (and his lawyers) in whose case I played a major role.

WOODY ALLEN VS. MIA FARROW

In my article on the ten greatest legal blunders of the twentieth century,[21] I also included the decision by Woody Allen's lawyers to sue Mia Farrow for custody of several of her adopted children and the child they conceived together. I played an unusual role in that lawsuit. Both sides were focused heavily on the media: Woody was concerned that negative coverage, particularly of allegations involving sexual improprieties with a young girl, might ruin his career; Mia was concerned that any coverage might hurt her children. Every legal maneuver in the case was made with an eye (sometimes two) on the media.

I first met Woody Allen when he was filming *Manhattan*.[22] My introduction to him was a birthday present from a group of friends, one of whom knew Woody from his earlier film *The Front*.[23] Woody agreed to meet me for lunch; he didn't know he was my birthday present. When I told him, he immediately began to speculate as to whom he would want as a present: "Louis Armstrong," he said, would be his first choice.

"He's dead," I reminded him.

"Exactly," he replied. "Jimmy Hoffa would be my second choice."

"He's missing," I said.

"Exactly," he repeated.

He then asked me which dead person I would have wanted to represent as a criminal lawyer. I immediately replied, "Jesus."

"Do you think you could have won?" he asked.

"In front of a Jewish jury, maybe."

"Those biblical Jews were tough. They didn't tolerate troublemakers like Jesus. They probably wouldn't have liked Jews like us from Brooklyn," Woody mused.

"Yeah, but imagine how different history would be if a Jewish lawyer saved Jesus. They couldn't accuse us of killing their Lord."

"But he wouldn't have been their Lord, if you had won. He wouldn't have been crucified. And without crucifixion, there's no Christianity, so if you had won they'd be blaming the Jews for destroying Christianity."

"But there wouldn't be any 'they' to blame us," I replied.

"There's always a 'they,'" Woody said, smiling.

Woody reminded me of the riff that got Lenny Bruce into trouble. Bruce quipped that if the Romans had electrocuted rather than crucified their enemies, millions of Christians would be walking around wearing tiny electric chairs around their necks.

We discussed blacklisting, McCarthyism, and other subjects in which we shared a common interest. It was a wonderful birthday present.

Several years later Woody and his then girlfriend, Mia Farrow, came to hear me speak in New York about the Rosenberg trial. I had written a positive review for the *New York Times* about a book that had concluded that Julius Rosenberg had indeed been a Soviet spy.[24]

Woody and Mia both insisted that the Rosenbergs were innocent, and I promised to send them the evidence that Julius was a spy and Ethel a collaborator if not a conspirator.

Over the next several years I saw Woody and Mia on a few occasions. Mia called me a few times to discuss political issues, and Woody and I wrote to each other.[25]

Then everything changed. Early one morning, Mia called. We exchanged pleasantries and I asked her how Woody was. "He's abusing my children," she said. I replied, "Don't even joke about that, it's not funny." She said, "No, really. He's been sleeping with one of my daughters and acting inappropriately with another one." I again asked her if she was serious, since the allegations seemed so out of character. She told me she was dead serious and asked if I could drive down to her house in Connecticut and meet with her. I told her I would, and that I would bring my wife, who is a PhD psychologist with extensive experience in such matters.

We drove to Mia's house in Connecticut and she greeted us. She was fixing a leaky roof while trying to take care of her numerous children, including a blind girl and a crack baby, both of whom she had adopted. She told me that Woody had started an affair with her adopted Korean daughter, Soon-Yi. When I asked her how old Soon-Yi was, she told me nobody knew for sure because she was adopted when she was a baby; she could be anywhere from seventeen to nineteen. She then told me that Woody had been seen by one of the nannies touching her daughter, Dylan, in an inappropriate way. Dylan had told her that Woody had taken her up to an attic crawl space, where he had touched her. Mia showed me the crawl space. She also showed me naked Polaroids that Woody had taken of Soon-Yi, which she had found in Woody's apartment, along with a naked photo of Dylan. My wife then had a conversation with Dylan about her relationship with Woody.

I was shocked and asked how I could help. Here was yet another example of a celebrity putting his own desire for immediate gratification above the needs of his longtime lover and her family. Even if only the allegations regarding Mia's adopted daughter Soon-Yi were true, Woody's actions would demonstrate extreme insensitivity to Mia's family. Here is how the appellate court ultimately characterized Woody's behavior:

> *In January of 1992, Mr. Allen took the photographs of [Soon-Yi]. Mr. Allen [testified] that he took the photos at [Soon-Yi's] suggestion and that he considered them erotic and not pornographic. . . . We do not share Mr. Allen's characterization of them. We find the fact that Mr. Allen took them at a time when he was formally assuming a legal responsibility for two of Ms. [Soon-Yi's] siblings to be totally unacceptable. The distinction Mr. Allen makes between [Soon-Yi and] Ms. Farrow's other children . . . is lost on this Court. The children themselves do not draw the same distinction that Mr. Allen does. This is sadly demonstrated by the profound effect his relationship with [Soon-Yi] has had on the entire family. Allen's testimony that the photographs ". . . were taken . . . between two consenting adults wanting to do this . . ." demonstrates a chosen ignorance of his and [Soon-Yi's] relationships to Ms. Farrow, his three children and [Soon-Yi's] other siblings. His continuation of the relationship . . . shows a distinct absence of judgment. It demonstrates . . . Mr. Allen's tendency to place inappropriate emphasis on his own wants and needs and to minimize and even ignore those of his children. At the very minimum, it demonstrates an absence of any parenting skills.*[26]

On that day we met at her house Mia asked me to call Woody and tell him to stop doing what he was doing. She told me that Woody admired me and that he kept a copy of my book *Chutzpah*[27] on his bedside table.

I asked Mia to have Woody call me. When he didn't, I decided to write him a letter, which I asked his lawyer to give him. In the letter, I urged Woody to try to resolve the matter privately:

> *I still believe that matter can be resolved without even more escalation and damage to all parties. As you and Mia both know, I am a great admirer of your work, and I do not want to see your career and your life destroyed. Right now you are on that road and something must be done to head it off, not only for your sake, but for the sake of the children and for Mia.*

I don't know whether he ever got the letter. I received no reply. Mia then asked me to contact his lawyers to see if the matter could be resolved without any public disclosure. I called his lawyers and they agreed to a meeting in New York. I brought with me to the meeting a law school classmate, David Levett, who was a leading lawyer in Connecticut and was knowledgeable about Connecticut law relating to such issues. Our goal, and Mia's, was to bring about some resolution of this troubling matter without any publicity, which she felt would be harmful to her children.

In the middle of the meeting, we received notice that Woody's lawyers, the very lawyers we were discreetly negotiating with, had publicly filed a lawsuit against Mia, and that Woody was about to hold a press conference in which he was going to accuse Mia of making up stories about him.

I was shocked at this duplicity—I'm not used to dealing with lawyers who mislead their opponents in this way.

Woody Allen's suit sought custody of several of the children Mia had originally adopted, as well as the biological child they had conceived together. It was an extraordinarily stupid move on the part of Allen's lawyers, because at the time he filed the custody suit, Woody Allen barely knew the children and their siblings, had no idea who their friends were, did not know the names of their pediatricians, and had virtually nothing to do with their upbringing. Mia Farrow, on the other hand, was a hands-on mother who was deeply involved in every aspect of her children's lives.

At the trial, Woody's lawyers pulled off an even more boneheaded maneuver. They claimed that Levett and I, by seeking to resolve the matter quietly, were "blackmailing" Woody into settling the case favorably to Mia. This was a ridiculous claim, as the judge found, since Mia was focused on the welfare of her children, not on money. Courtroom observers could not believe that Woody's lawyers would force me to appear as a witness, knowing that I would surely side with Mia in her efforts to maintain custody of her children. But having been falsely accused of trying to blackmail Woody, I had no choice but to testify as to precisely what had transpired. It was entirely predictable that I would testify, especially since Woody Allen's lawyers made certain that their accusations against me were given to the media. No one could understand why Woody's lawyers had decided on a tactic that would make me a witness. But I knew something others didn't know, which led me to conclude that the lawyers had put me in this position not out of a desire to help Woody, since there was no way my testimony could in any way support his claim. They had accused me of blackmail in an effort to hurt *me*.

Why would they want to hurt me rather than help their own client? Because the senior partner of the law firm representing Woody, a former prosecutor named Robert Morvillo, was seeking revenge against me for my having prevented him from becoming the United States attorney for the Eastern District of New York. It was his dream job, and he had been about to get it when I exposed his prosecutorial misconduct in a case I was litigating. He had essentially bribed a key government witness with money that was owed to the creditors of a bankrupt corporation. He had arranged for the witness to obtain the bankrupt funds, which he knew had been secreted in a Caribbean account. In doing so, Morvillo had committed two serious crimes: bribing a witness and facilitating the stealing of bankrupt funds. The federal district judge who presided over the case wrote a scathing opinion condemning Morvillo's actions. That opinion appeared as a front page story in the *Village Voice* (under the title "Prosecutor Beyond the Law?"),[28] thus scuttling any chance Morvillo had of receiving a federal appointment. Morvillo was so angry that he told the *Village Voice* that if he ever saw me again, he would "deck" me.[29] He never had a chance to throw a punch at me, and so he decided, in my opinion, to use the Woody Allen lawsuit as a way to deck me. I'll bet that he never told Woody of his hidden agenda.[30]

As any decent lawyer would expect, the ploy backfired. My letter to Woody, coupled with the testimony of other lawyers who were involved in the negotiations, proved that my interest was in protecting the children, not in blackmailing Woody. I testified that I was seeking "to have a preliminary discussion which might eventuate in saving the children from the kind of atmosphere that they have tragically been placed in as a result of Woody Allen's lawyers."

My testimony, in sum, was very supportive of Mia's efforts to retain custody of her children and highly critical of Woody's attempt to portray her in a negative light.

The judge credited my testimony and ruled against Woody Allen in every respect, denying him not only the custody of the children, but even the right to see his own biological son without severe restrictions. As far as I know, Woody Allen has not seen his biological son since, who has grown into quite an adult, having won a Rhodes Scholarship for his work on human rights.[31] To this day, I doubt that Woody knows how Robert Morvillo tried to use *his* case to settle a score with *me*.

Shortly after it was publicly announced that I would be helping to defend Mia Farrow against the lawsuit brought by Woody Allen, I got a phone call. When I picked up, the voice on the other end said, "Hey Alan, this is Frank."

I asked, "Frank who?"

The voice on the other end sounded surprised by the question. "Frank Sinatra."

Sinatra had previously called me when Kitty Kelley's notorious biography about him[32] was about to be published. He had asked if I was interested in representing him in a lawsuit against Kelley for defamation. I had described what effect the lawsuit would have on the quality of his life and told him that I thought it would be a bad idea to bring one.

"Nice to talk to you, Mr. Sinatra," I responded.

He immediately got down to business. "I love Mia. We were married, you know. She's a great girl. Woody's trying to bully her. He can't be allowed to get away with that. What can I do to help?"

I told Mr. Sinatra that I appreciated the call, but that the legal case was under control.

He quickly responded, "Well, beyond the legal case, what can I do to call Woody off?"

Aware of Sinatra's reputation as a tough guy, I nervously told him to leave it to the lawyers, and that any approach to Woody Allen would be used against Mia and would likely backfire.

Several months later, during the summer, André Previn—another of Mia's former husbands—was performing on Martha's Vineyard. My wife and I attended his concert and then went to a reception that followed. Previn, like Sinatra, told me how much he loved Mia.

He continued, "I feel like marching up to Woody's apartment, knocking on the door, and punching him in the face."

Recalling the Sinatra call, I let out an uncontrollable laugh. "If I wanted any of Mia's former husbands to put the fear of God in Woody Allen, I'd pick Frank Sinatra over you, Mr. Previn." He laughed in agreement.

I continue to have a good relationship with Mia. Woody Allen eventually married Soon-Yi, and they have adopted children. Their marriage seems to be working.

Surprisingly, the massive publicity generated by Woody Allen's foolish lawsuit did not hurt his career. Nor does it seem to have had a negative impact on the quality of his life. During the trial itself, the publicity was brutal, but when it was over, both Allen and Farrow managed to restart their lives.

I try to learn something from every case. The Woody Allen–Mia Farrow and the Clinton-Lewinsky cases taught me how perilous it can be to litigate instead of settling cases involving high-profile clients.

You don't learn how to manage such cases in law school. There are no rule books. Experience is the only teacher. After years of working on dozens of high-profile cases, I now try to teach my students how to avoid, or at least minimize, inevitable mistakes. Here are some of the rules I've come up with for handling high-profile cases:

1. Never take a case just because the client is a celebrity, or because the case is "high profile." Make sure the issues in the case are within your area of expertise.
2. If you do take the case, don't socialize with the celebrity. Never assume the celebrity is your friend. You have a professional relationship. Charge your usual fee. No discount, and no price gouging.
3. Settle the case quietly if at all possible. Don't let the good publicity *you* might get from trying the case influence your judgment if trying the case may cause *bad* publicity or other negatives for your client.
4. Never say anything about the client or the case to anyone unless you are prepared to see it printed in the *New York Times*, the *National Enquirer*, or the *Huffington Post*. Remember that judges, jurors, and prosecutors, their family members, their friends and colleagues all watch television and read the papers. The media environment may have an impact on their decisions.
5. Every time you meet the client, be prepared to be fired for telling him what he doesn't want to hear. Famous people often get bad medical treatment and bad legal advice for the same reason: The doctor and lawyer don't want to offend or upset them. They care more about holding on to the patient or client than telling him the painful truth.
6. Don't pretend your celebrity or high-profile case is just like every other case. The media is watching your every move, and every move you make should take into account the anticipated media coverage. This doesn't mean you should make or refrain from making the right move because of the coverage, but rather you should consider what the right move is.
7. High-profile and celebrity cases tend to distort the legal system, because the law treats famous people differently—sometimes better, sometimes worse. It has been said that hard cases make bad law. So, often, do high-profile cases.

8. Celebrities will almost always disappoint you. Most are boring, banal, and self-centered. Working on a high-profile case is a decidedly mixed bag. If you never have a celebrity case during your career, you haven't missed anything.

9. Clients, whether civil or criminal, are increasingly brought to trial not only before a judge in robes and a jury of peers, but also in the "court of public opinion," where every citizen gets to cast a vote on the legal and moral aspects of the case. For some clients in the public eye, the "verdict" rendered by the court of public opinion may be as important as the verdict of the jury. A lawyer must be prepared to face the media, where the usual rules of evidence do not prevail. A lawyer must learn the different "rules" of the court of public opinion and must develop the skills with which to win in that important forum as well.

10. Despite the often distorting effect of the media on the administration of justice, the press can serve as an important check and balance on judges, prosecutors, and defense lawyers. The First Amendment, which guarantees freedom of the press, may sometimes be in conflict with other amendments designed to guarantee a fair trial. An appropriate balance, difficult as it is to achieve, is essential to democratic governance.

VIGNETTE

My Seventy-Fifth Birthday Party

During the summer of 2013, my family was planning a party on Martha's Vineyard to celebrate my seventy-fifth birthday. President Obama and his family were planning to vacation in the house right next to ours during that period, and I agreed to allow some unused land near my home to be used for a communication truck. When the workers began to install the communication equipment, one of them mentioned my birthday party. When I asked how he knew about the party, he said, "The code name for the presidential visit is: 'Alan Dershowitz's birthday party.'"

PART IV

THE NEVER-ENDING QUEST FOR EQUALITY AND JUSTICE

20

THE CHANGING FACE OF RACE

From Color Blindness to Race-Specific Remedies

When I was growing up in the pre–*Brown v. Board of Education* era of legally mandated segregation, the goal of all decent people was the same: color blindness. As Martin Luther King was to put it so eloquently several years later:

> *I have a dream that my four little children will one day live in a nation where they will not be judged by the color of their skin but by the content of their character.*[1]

Among my friends and family, we all shared that dream of a color-blind America, where success would be based on merit, not race, religion, gender, national origin, ethnicity, class, sexual orientation (this came a bit later), or any other irrelevant or invidious characteristic.

Our neighborhood idol was Jackie Robinson, who by his skill, speed, grace, and character broke down the color barrier and who became the best player on my beloved Brooklyn Dodgers, leading his team to several pennants and its sole World Series championship (only to be unceremoniously traded to the hated New York Giants at the end of his career, a trade Robinson rejected by retiring with dignity).

At college my hero was Professor John Hope Franklin, the first African-American to chair an academic department at a college that had not been historically black.

At law school, two of my classmates were African-American twins, one of whom went on to become a judge on New York's highest court, the other of whom became a professor.

All that these and other heroes needed in order to achieve great success was the elimination of racial barriers—color blindness. That had been the case for Jews: As soon as religious barriers were dropped, Jews raced to the top of the legal, medical, and academic professions.[2] I believed that the same would be true of all victims of racial and other forms of discrimination. All they needed was equal opportunity and equal access to achieve equal outcomes. I believed it because I saw it with my own eyes—at least with regard to my heroes.

I lived through the civil rights movement, at first vicariously and then more directly. When I was fifteen, the Supreme Court decided *Brown v. Board of Education*, mandating desegregation of public schools. I recall reading the decision and applauding both its conclusion and its social science methodology. It was an important first step toward making Martin Luther King's dream of equality a reality.

During the 1950s and '60s, there was little talk of race-specific affirmative action—of having positive, rather than negative, decisions based on the race of the person. It was enough, we believed, to *eliminate* race from decision making. The result, we believed, would be equal opportunity and success, as it had been for Jackie Robinson, John Hope Franklin, and my law school classmates.

We were unaware of the pervasive poverty and deprivations—educational, economic, medical, nutritional—that would make real equality impossible, at least in the near term, for so many black people, even if legal inequalities were eliminated.

I should have known better, especially after I twice traveled to the Deep South on occasions during the turbulent years of the civil rights movement. My first trip was in the early 1960s, as part of a student group that was trained at the Howard Law School to be "observers" of the civil rights struggle. During that short visit I had little direct contact with local black residents. I did meet several black lawyers and civil rights workers, but they were generally from similar backgrounds to my own. On my second trip, by myself in the early summer of 1965, Harvard Law School sent me to several historically black colleges in an effort to recruit students for a special program we had instituted to help prepare minority students for law school. I traveled and lived on the campuses of predominantly black colleges for several days. I met students and professors, many of whom came from middle-class homes.

I also spent time at several southwestern colleges and met with Native American and Hispanic students. I had insisted that our recruitment efforts not be limited to African-American students. Even back then, I felt uncomfortable having any decisions, even affirmative ones, based on race alone. I believed then, and I believe now, that the ideal goal of affirmative action is to level the playing field by providing a *current* advantage to individuals who were subject to *past* disadvantages, in order to assure *future* equality. That is the theoretical ideal—individual justice to assure that people are judged by the quality of their character and other meritocratic criteria. But I soon learned that in practice other factors inevitably come into play. The real issue is how to strike the appropriate balance between the theoretical ideal and the practical necessities.

This issue came to the fore in a series of controversial Supreme Court decisions in which I played different roles. The first was the DeFunis case in 1974,[3] brought by a white applicant named Marco DeFunis, who had been rejected by the University of Washington Law School. He claimed that if he had been black, he would have been admitted under the school's affirmative action program. The school did not dispute this claim, but argued that it had the right to try to achieve "a reasonable representation" of minority students.

The lower court ruled in favor of DeFunis and ordered his admission. By the time the case reached the Supreme Court, he had nearly graduated, and the school told the justices that he would be allowed to graduate even if the court ruled against him. For that reason, the high court dismissed the case as moot, thus postponing the decision as to whether it would uphold race-specific affirmative action programs. But Justice William O. Douglas, probably the court's most liberal member at the time, and a man who had grown up in the state of Washington, wanted to decide the issue. He wrote a dissenting opinion that represented the conventional liberal view with which I, and many in my generation, had been brought up. He argued that the equal protection clause does not prohibit law schools from evaluating an applicant's prior achievements in light of the barriers that he had to overcome.

> *A black applicant who pulled himself out of the ghetto into a junior college may thereby demonstrate a level of motivation, perseverance, and ability that would lead a fair-minded admissions committee to conclude that he shows more promise for law study than the son of a rich alumnus who achieved better grades at Harvard. That applicant would be offered admission not*

> *because he is black, but because as an individual he has shown he has the potential, while the Harvard man may have taken less advantage of the vastly superior opportunities offered him. Because of the weight of the prior handicaps, that black applicant may not realize his full potential in the first year of law school, or even in the full three years, but in the long pull of a legal career his achievements may far outstrip those of his classmates whose earlier records appeared superior by conventional criteria.*[4]

Douglas acknowledged that black applicants might, in practice, be "the principal beneficiaries" of such a race-neutral admissions policy, but he opined that "a poor Appalachian white, or a second generation Chinese in San Francisco, or some other American whose lineage is so diverse as to defy ethnic labels, may demonstrate similar potential and thus be accorded favorable consideration by the Committee."[5]

Justice Douglas was, in fact, describing his own background in Washington State.[6] His autobiography was informing his constitutional ideology,[7] as is often the case.[8] He went on to distinguish the approach he described from the one employed by the University of Washington Law School, which made its admissions decision solely on the basis of race.

He concluded that since the "clear and central purpose" of the equal protection clause was to "eliminate all official sources of racial discrimination in the states," it follows that each applicant must be evaluated in "a racially neutral way."[9] Douglas thus rejected the school's efforts to achieve "representation" of minorities:

> *The purpose of the University of Washington cannot be to produce black lawyers for blacks, Polish lawyers for Poles, Jewish lawyers for Jews, Irish lawyers for Irish. It should be to produce good lawyers for Americans.*[10]

Justice Douglas's dissenting views quickly became the standard approach of liberals, like me and many of my friends (though always, in the back of my head, I remembered Douglas's membership in a discriminatory club and his argument with Judge Bazelon).

I became an active advocate for an aggressive affirmative action program at Harvard based on nonracial criteria. I participated in numerous campus and faculty meeting debates, believing that I was on the side of the angels, favoring a system that would produce real diversity without violating the racial equality mandate of the Constitution.

But not every liberal accepted Justice Douglas's race-neutral approach. Many black leaders saw the issue not as one of *individual* rights, but rather as one of *group* aspirations. Blacks had a collective right, under this view, to "reasonable representation" in the student bodies of universities and other institutions, both public and private. Some went so far as to argue for "proportional representation." This raised the specter of quotas, which might limit the number of those accepted or hired to their proportion of the population.

The fear of quotas or proportional representation increased as schools throughout the country adopted affirmative action programs with numerical elements. Some contained "targets" for the number of admitted blacks. Other had "floors." Nonblack students who were denied admission to schools with such programs began to file lawsuits.

As these cases made their way through the courts, a conflict arose between some leaders of the African-American and Jewish communities.[11] Most (but not all) African-American leaders were deeply committed to race-specific affirmative action programs that gave advantages to *all* black applicants, regardless of their *individual* backgrounds. Most colleges preferred this group approach as well, since it was simpler and they preferred to admit wealthy, well-educated, and privileged black candidates over poorer, less well-educated, and more "difficult" inner-city blacks. Derek Bok, first the dean of Harvard Law School and then the president of Harvard University, candidly acknowledged that it was far easier to integrate African-American graduates of Groton, Fieldston, and St. Paul's into Harvard than it would be to integrate inner-city public school graduates.[12]

Many (though not all) Jewish leaders were worried that the hard-earned access of Jews to elite schools would be endangered by what they regarded as "racial quotas."[13] They recalled, with bitterness, the "quotas" that had limited Jewish applicants to single-digit "Jewish places" in college and university admissions.[14] There is, of course, a difference between "floor quotas" and "ceiling quotas." Blacks were seeking a floor on the number of affirmative action admittees: *no less* than 10 or 15 percent. Jews had been subjected to "ceilings": *no more* than 7 to 8 percent. (When I started Yale Law School in 1959, I noticed that the university's motto was written in Hebrew—the biblical words *Urim V'Tumim*. When I asked a friend who had graduated Yale College why Yale's motto was in Hebrew, he replied: "It's a test—if you can read it, you can't go here!") But in a zero-sum game—which admissions surely are—floors can impose ceilings, especially if the black percentage is *taken from* the Jewish percentage, as Jewish leaders feared was happening. This reality led to the famous "bagel" exchange:

Dr. Chase N. Peterson, dean of admissions at Harvard, recently addressed a group of Jewish faculty members suspicious that Harvard had decided to reduce the number of Jews it would admit. Peterson averred that there is no particular "docket" or area of the country whose quota of admissions has been reduced. Rather, he said, it is "the doughnuts around the big cities," which are not as successful with the Harvard Admissions Committee as they used to be. . . . "But now we have to be terribly hard on people with good grades from the good suburban high schools, good, solid clean-nosed kids who really don't have enough else going for them." The doughnuts, said Peterson, included such areas as Westchester County and Long Island, New York, suburban New Jersey, and Shaker Heights, Ohio. When he described these areas to the Jewish faculty members, the Crimson *reports, one stood up and said, "Dr. Peterson, those aren't doughnuts, they're bagels."*[15]

After the account of this exchange appeared, I received dozens of letters and calls from indignant alumni and parents of applicants concerned that Harvard was returning to a quota system.

These concerns increased when the Bakke case came to the Supreme Court, in 1977,[16] and Harvard took the lead in defending race-specific affirmative action programs, such as the one it had adopted. My brother, Nathan, was then working as the top lawyer for the American Jewish Congress, a generally progressive social action organization. He asked me to help draft an amicus brief in the Bakke case that presented the views of Jews who supported civil rights but who were concerned about the impact of race-specific affirmative action programs on Jewish applicants. It was a daunting task, requiring an exquisite balance.

The Bakke case involved a white applicant to the medical school at the University of California at Davis. Allan Bakke had been denied admission, he claimed, based on his race. This time there could be no claim of mootness—Bakke had not been admitted to medical school. The court would have to confront directly the divisive issues of race-specific affirmative action.

Our brief strongly supported affirmative action as a mechanism for remedying past "educational handicaps" and for assuring diversity among the student body. But we opposed the concept that every racial, religious, or ethnic group was entitled to proportional representation—or quotas:

A society permeated by racial, ethnic, religious, and sexual proportional representation would be something quite different from the America we have known. . . . Racial and ethnic classifications would be officially sanctioned and recognized in all walks of life; each professional or office holder would be regarded, and would regard himself, as a representative of the group from whose quota he comes. . . . Individual aspiration would be limited by the proportionate size of the group to which the individual belongs.[17]

We argued in favor of individualized preferences based on actual experiences:

If individual blacks applying to Davis Medical School have suffered economic hardship because they encountered discrimination, attended segregated schools or lived in segregated neighborhoods, these facts could be brought to the attention of the Admission Committee and their records evaluated accordingly. Any other system of preferences based on mere membership in a group which, because of its color or physiognomy, has suffered discrimination can only result in a society in which race consciousness and partisanship become the significant operative forces and race prejudice, rather than being minimized, is legitimated.[18]

We quoted black leaders, such as Roy Wilkins, who opposed proportional representation:

No person of ability wants to be limited in his horizons by an arbitrary quota or wants to endure unqualified people in positions that they fill only because of a numerical racial quota. . . .

God knows it is true that the cards have been deliberately stacked against blacks. Every feasible step, even those costing extra money, should be taken to correct this racialism.

But there must not be a lowering of standards.[19]

We urged the court to require the medical school to develop an affirmative action program that was compatible with the dream of a colorblind America:

Schools may, and we think should, evaluate both grades and test scores in the light of a candidate's background; whether he or she came from a culturally impoverished home; the nature and quality of the schools he attended; whether family circumstances required him to work while attending school; whether he chose to participate in athletics, the orchestra, school newspaper, literary magazine, campus government; whether he had demonstrated a concern and interest in the broader community by political activity or volunteer work among the sick or underprivileged; and whether he had manifested leadership, industry, perseverance, self-discipline and intense motivation.[20]

Moreover, we argued, if the petitioner were to conclude that the medical profession as presently composed fails to serve the disadvantaged elements in society, "it could expressly offer special consideration in the admissions process to those who enter into a binding commitment to serve for a specified period in an urban ghetto, barrio or Indian reservation."[21]

Our point was that these remedies would accord greater educational opportunities to *all* "economically and culturally deprived" applicants without running afoul of the equal protection clause of the Constitution.[22]

The Supreme Court's decision in *Bakke* accepted our argument against the sort of racial quotas employed by Davis Medical School. But it approved affirmative action programs, such as the one used by Harvard College, that vested enormous discretion in the admissions committee. A five-person majority ruled that the type of admissions program used by Davis did not pass constitutional muster, while the type used by Harvard College did. Justice Powell, whose opinion contained the judgment of the court, expressly singled out Harvard College for approval.[23] He quoted extensively from the description of the Harvard program contained in the amicus curiae brief submitted by Harvard, Columbia, Stanford, and Pennsylvania Universities.[24] Powell apparently found it easier to point to an existing system than to define the factors that would satisfy the constitutional and statutory standard.

I felt that Powell's selection of Harvard *College* as a model for Davis *Medical School* was inapt, both because medical school admission is different from college admission[25] and because Harvard, with its vast applicant pool, is vastly different from Davis.[26] But Powell had a good reason for pointing to the Harvard undergraduate admissions program: It was so vague and discretionary as to defy description. It reposed all decision making with a group of Platonic guardians whose task was to shape an entering class so as to maximize its diversity in unspecified ways. A Harvard admissions officer might be unable to define the factors that make a good candidate for admission, but was supposed to know a Harvard man or woman when he saw one.

The *Bakke* decision was, in my view, a triumph of ambiguity and discretion over clarity and candor. Powell condemned Davis Medical School for reserving a discrete number of places in each class for disadvantaged members of specified minority groups, but he applauded Harvard College for employing a process that eschews "target-quotas for the number of blacks" but allows "the race of an applicant [to] tip the balance in his favor just as geographic origin or a life spent on a farm tip the balance in other candidates' cases."[27]

At bottom, Powell's opinion said little about affirmative action as such. It simply delegated to universities the discretionary power to decide on the degree and definition of the diversity—including or excluding racial factors—that they felt enhanced the educational experiences of their students.

The Harvard College description failed to disclose the enormous efforts that Harvard undertook to assure a certain kind of uniformity in its student body over time. Harvard (like other Ivy League colleges) always has given great weight to genealogy—whether the applicant's parents or other family members attended Harvard. Since Harvard's past students were anything but diverse, this "grandfather policy" guarantees a good deal of homogeneity over the generations of Harvard College classes, as well as homogeneity in a large part of any given class.[28]

Justice Blackmun doubted there was much difference between the Davis and Harvard programs, commenting that the "cynical" may say that "under a program such as Harvard's one may accomplish covertly what Davis concedes it does openly."[29] Justice Powell did not dispute this. His answer seemed to be that even if both programs produce the same result, the Davis program—because of its explicit acknowledgment of racial quotas—"will be viewed as inherently unfair by the public generally as well as by applicants for admission,"[30] whereas the Harvard program—with its vague consideration of many unquantified factors—will not be as grating to the public or to its unsuccessful applicants.

But there is one way in which the Harvard system was, perhaps, less fair than the Davis one. In order to receive special consideration under the discredited Davis program, an applicant had to be *both* individually disadvantaged *and* a member of a specified racial minority. Under the approved Harvard program, the applicant's race alone "may tip the balance" in his favor even if he is the scion of a wealthy and powerful family who attended the best schools and personally experienced almost none of the trauma of racial discrimination.[31] (Indeed, some applicants seek a double preference: as a disadvantaged black and as an advantaged offspring of a Harvard alumnus.) The Harvard program approved by Justice Powell had the effect of preferring the wealthy and black applicant, for example, over the poor and disadvantaged black or white applicant. In practice, Harvard probably made more turn on race alone than did Davis. But it did it with typical Harvard class: low-key, muted, and without displaying too much exposed skin. Moreover, the history of Harvard's use of "geographic distribution" as a subterfuge for religious quotas[32] left lingering doubts about the bona fides of its alleged quest for diversity[33]—at least at the time of the *Bakke* decision.

Once the Supreme Court decided to leave admissions decisions largely to the discretion of university committees, the role of the courts began to diminish considerably. Indeed, it is not even clear how much impact Supreme Court decisions have ever actually had on admissions practices. Just as the life of the law has been experience rather than logic,[34] so too has the life of universities been influenced far more by experience than by legal logic. Experience has demonstrated that race-specific affirmative action has worked. It has made classrooms more diverse, class discussions more interesting, and graduates more representative of the population at large. It has accomplished these positive results at a cost—namely, the postponement of fulfilling Martin Luther King's dream of a color-blind society. Race consciousness in affirmative action has made a difference in our society.[35] As with so many other important issues, there is no free lunch.

VIGNETTE

Turning the Ben Shahn Lithograph

During the height of the civil rights movement, I bought a Ben Shahn lithograph showing a white hand lifting up a black hand, with the Hebrew and English words for "Do not stand idly by the blood of your neighbor." It hung in our home for many years, until one day my son Jamin turned it on its side, so it showed the two hands, side by side, helping each other equally.

It has been suggested by several justices, judges, academics, and commentators that the constitutional permissibility of taking race into account in admissions decisions should be limited to a certain number of years—say twenty-five. It should be regarded as a temporary, emergency measure, and not become a fixed part of our constitutional jurisprudence.[36] As I write these words, the Supreme Court has ruled that for a race-specific affirmative action program to pass constitutional muster, the state university must show "that its plan is narrowly tailored to achieve" the kind of diversity that encompasses a "broad array of qualifications and characteristics of which racial or ethnic origin is but a single though important element." The High Court thus left open the broad issue of how much weight a state university may accord race in its admission process. Whichever way the Supreme Court ultimately decides this issue, the die has been cast. As with other areas of the law, experience will prevail, affirmative action will continue, race will remain a significant factor, and the issue will continue to divide people of goodwill.

The ironic reality is that affirmative action, even with race consciousness, has moved us closer to a color-blind society in which the race of a candidate, an applicant, or even a spouse matters less today than it ever did before. I think Martin Luther King would approve of the direction in which our society is moving, though we have long, long roads still to travel.

21

THE CRUMBLING WALL BETWEEN CHURCH AND STATE

Attempts to Christianize America

The "equal protection clause" of our Constitution[1] is not the sole mechanism to secure equality. The clauses that require separation of church and state were designed, at least in part, to assure religious equality. History has demonstrated that when one religion is the officially established one—or when religious tests are required for office-holders—adherents to other faiths or to no faith become second-class citizens. The United States was the first nation in history to prohibit the establishment of religion or religious tests. It is no accident that it was also the first nation in which Jews were regarded, in theory if not always in practice, as first-class citizens.

My first memory of being aware of the separation of church and state goes back to the 1950s, when the words "under God" were being added to the Pledge of Allegiance.[2] The yeshiva teachers I studied under were very patriotic. We recited the pledge at assemblies, and some teachers made us say it every day in class.

Most kids hate change, so when the two words "under God" were added to the pledge, there was some grumbling—not because of the content of the words, but just because it was different from the way we always had done it.

I remember thinking about the meaning of the two new words. Under *which* God? Under *whose* God? Is there only one God that all Americans can pledge allegiance to, or are there different gods that different religions worship? What about the Trinity? Is Jesus God? And what is that thing the Catholic kids call "the Holy Ghost"? Are Jews even supposed to say the word "God" (we were always taught to spell it G-d)? Is Allah the same god as Elohim?[3] What about Jehovah—the name we were absolutely prohibited from pronouncing?

These were precisely the sort of theological questions we were not supposed to be thinking about. We were supposed to *do* and *not do*—go to shul, don't eat shrimp—and to ask our rabbi what to think about such esoteric issues. He knew the religiously correct answer. Yet the addition of the two words to the pledge forced me not only to think about them, but to try to place them in the context of my own role as a young Orthodox Jewish skeptic in a largely Christian America. Our school taught us that even though America was a majority Christian country, George Washington, in his famous letter to the congregants of the Touro Synagogue in Newport, had assured Jewish Americans that in this new republic "it is now no more that toleration is spoken of, as if it was by the indulgence of one class of people that another enjoyed the exercise of their inherent natural rights."[4] Here, all Americans "possess alike liberty of conscience and immunities of citizenship" because our government "gives to bigotry no sanction, to persecution no assistance."[5]

These powerful words, written by the father of our country, were displayed on the bulletin board of our yeshiva as if they constituted the Magna Carta for American Jews.[6]

Yet we saw bigotry all around us. We knew that no Jew had ever been elected president of the country. At the time, no Jew had ever been the head of a major corporation[7] or university.[8] We knew that there were quotas limiting the number of Jews at most Ivy League colleges.[9] Still, we believed that this was a land of opportunity and that we could do anything, within certain limits, and that even these limits were narrowing, though not yet disappearing.

I knew that our Constitution said some things about religion. In our yeshiva we learned mostly about the First Amendment's protection of freedom of religion. But when I started to read a little more about the Constitution, I quickly learned that there were three references to religion. The first, in the body of the Constitution, declared that "no religious test shall ever be required" for holding office in the United States.[10] I wondered then, why hasn't there been a Jewish president? And why was there only one "Jewish seat" on the Supreme Court? It sure seemed to me as if religious tests *were* being applied, which made me think about the difference between the law as written and as practiced.

I also discovered that the First Amendment, in addition to guaranteeing freedom of religion, had an awkwardly phrased guarantee: "Congress shall make no law respecting an establishment of religion."[11] At the time there were two words I didn't understand. What did "respecting" mean in this instance? I had always used it to suggest a positive attitude—respect—toward others. Clearly it had a different meaning in the First Amendment, something more akin to "regarding." Second, what did the word "establishment" mean? I had no idea, and so I began to do some research, which led me to discover the longest word in the English language—antidisestablishmentarianism. This referred to those who were against the disestablishment of the Church of England as the official national church. But I was still unclear exactly what it meant to "establish" a religion. The answer was anything but simple—the meaning of the term is still not completely clear to me after sixty years of thinking, writing, and teaching about it.[12]

So there was an upside for me in the words "under God" being added to the Pledge of Allegiance. It not only got me thinking; it got me arguing with my friends and even with some of my teachers, an argument that goes on to this day.

The downside, which was evident to me even back then, was that whatever the words prohibiting an "establishment of religion" meant, they seemed incompatible with compelling every schoolboy and -girl to declare his or her belief in God inserted into the pledge by Congress. So, although I believed in God (or more likely never thought about any alternative), I decided never to say the words. I continued to recite the old pledge, confident that it was I, and not those who amended the pledge, who was being patriotic and faithful to the meaning of the Constitution. I guess I was an early Originalist in that regard, since my reading suggested to me that Jefferson and Madison would not have approved of making young kids declare a belief in God.[13]

Flashing forward a generation, my oldest son, Elon, had a similar epiphany in 1971, when my family moved to California for a year. We enrolled our kids in a Palo Alto public school and ten-year-old Elon got into trouble for refusing to recite the words "under God." When he came home from school, I asked him how come he had just noticed the words, since his elementary school in Cambridge required periodic recitations of the pledge. He told me that we were at war in Vietnam and he thought the words—

pronounced with a Boston accent—were "under guard." It was only a California teacher writing the words on the blackboard that revealed to him that he was being required to take a pledge that included God. By this time the Supreme Court had ruled that a religious objector could not be required to recite the pledge, because, as the justices put it:

> *If there is any fixed star in our constitutional constellation, it is that no official, high or petty, can . . . force citizens to confess by word or act their faith.*[14]

Elon was excused from saying the words for the remainder of the year.

Elon suffered no adverse consequences from his religious dissent, but the same cannot be said for Susan Shapiro, a seventeen-year-old high school senior in the Boston area. When she exercised her right not to participate in the pledge, her teacher said it was as if someone had spit on the Star of David. She was called names by fellow students and told to "go back to Israel." (She was born in America).[15] I agreed to represent her, and after we threatened to bring a lawsuit,[16] we got the school to permit her not to participate in the pledge and to inform the students that she was within her rights.[17]

A few years later I became involved in a highly publicized case involving the right of a criminal defendant not to be discriminated against on account of his religion, even though he himself was accused of using his religion to defraud coreligionists. The case involved television evangelist Jim Bakker, who was married to Tammy Faye Bakker. I was retained to argue his sentencing appeal, following his conviction for defrauding PTL ("Praise the Lord" and "People That Love") Club Lifetime Partners who had paid for homes in Heritage U.S.A.—a Christian family retreat—but were never able to live in them. The government had accused Bakker of overselling thousands of "partnerships" and using the millions of dollars he raised "to support a lavish lifestyle." The result was that "the overwhelming majority of the partners never received the lodging benefits Bakker promised them."[18]

After a lengthy and emotional trial, Bakker was convicted by a jury. The judge sentenced him to forty-five years in prison. In imposing that lengthy sentence, the judge—the Honorable Robert Potter, known around the courthouse as "Maximum Bob"—made an invidious comparison between Bakker and himself in terms of their "religion": "Those of us who do have a religion are ridiculed as being saps from money-grubbing preachers or priests."[19]

Bakker wrote me a long handwritten letter from prison imploring me to join his appellate team and save him from a lifetime of imprisonment. There was not enough time before the appellate brief had to be filed for me to take over the entire appeal, but I was particularly appalled by the length of the sentence and the religious basis the judge seemed to give for imposing it. I agreed therefore to brief and argue the sentencing issue on the appeal (a team of Texas lawyers had been retained long before to argue against the conviction) and the *New York Times* reported:

> *He was to handle only a small part of Mr. Bakker's appeal, concerning the 45-year sentence meted out by Judge Robert D. Potter. Mr. Dershowitz insisted he would remain in the background.*
>
> *But that, it turned out, was a bit like George Steinbrenner's saying "Yogi Berra is my manager for the rest of the year." In October, when the Bakker appeal was argued, it was around Mr. Dershowitz that everyone clustered. . . .*
>
> *Even his co-counsel, two Texans schooled in a tradition of great oratory, were dazzled by what they saw in court. "It was kind of like watching a terrific maestro in front of an orchestra," Mr. Ervin said. Mr. Wice called the performance "mesmerizing" and added: "He looks like a schlep, wearing suits he could have bought in Filene's Basement. . . . But the judges hung on every word he had to say and bought what he was selling."*

We waited several months for the decision. When it was finally released, the court of appeals ruled that the conviction was valid but the forty-five-year sentence was not. In vacating the sentence, the court established a powerful precedent against a judge using his own religious beliefs as a factor in determining the degree of punishment:

> *Courts . . . cannot sanction sentencing procedures that create the perception of the bench as a pulpit from which judges announce their personal sense of religiosity and simultaneously punish defendants for offending it.*[20]

They remanded the sentencing to a "different district judge to ensure that the ends of due process are achieved."[21]

This was precisely the result we had asked for: resentencing by a judge other than Maximum Bob, who surely would have imposed the same sentence again, this time without referring to his religion. The new judge eventually reduced the sentence to eight years, and Bakker was released after serving a bit more than four years—quite a reduction from the forty-five years originally imposed by Maximum Bob.[22]

Following our victory, Tammy Faye Bakker gushed that I had singlehandedly restored her faith in lawyers, and she declared the judicial ruling "a great victory for Christianity." I responded that "the fact that a Jewish lawyer helped bring that about must show that it was a great victory for all Americans." She said that one of her "biggest desires now is to meet [Alan]. . . . He's our kind of people."[23]

Eventually, I did meet her. She kissed and hugged me and repeatedly blessed me in the name of Jesus, in the process transferring so much of her makeup to my face that it took me several minutes and some hard scrubbing to remove it.

Several weeks later, I received a gift in the mail from Tammy Faye. It was a Passover Haggadah—the prayer book that is read at the Seder. We have a large collection of Haggadahs, some dating back hundreds of years, many with beautiful illustrations of the Passover story. At our ecumenical Seder, which usually includes several dozen guests of all religions, we distribute the different Haggadahs among the participants, and each one reads a passage in the English translation. I try to make the passage selected relevant to each guest's background. I purposely gave the Bakker Haggadah to a friend who reads very expressively and who focuses more on his delivery than on the content. He began to read about the reasons we eat matzo on Passover.

> *This is the bread of affliction that the people of Israel had to eat when they fled from Egypt.*

So far so good. But then, it went on to describe why matzo has small holes:

> *The holes in the matzo represent the wounds on the body of our Savior, Jesus Christ, who in his body was punctured during his crucifixion.*

Not in the traditional Jewish Haggadah! Tammy Faye had sent me a Christian Evangelical knockoff of the Haggadah designed for use at Seders conducted by Jews for Jesus. I had perused it before distributing it to my friend to recite, so I knew what it contained. We all had a great chuckle.

VIGNETTE

Camelia Sadat

A guest at our Seder brought with him Camelia Sadat, the daughter of the late Egyptian leader Anwar Sadat. She had never before been to a

Seder, and I was concerned that she might be offended by the story of how the Jews defeated the Egyptians and their leader Pharaoh. I took her aside before we began to recite the Haggadah, summarized the story, and told her that I hoped it wouldn't upset her. "Why should it upset me?" she wondered. "Because you're Egyptian," I replied. "But now we are Muslims," she said, "and as such are on the side of Moses and against the Pagan ruler Pharaoh." She joined enthusiastically in the reading of the Haggadah.

These stories and cases highlight one of the great ironies of the American experiment with separation of church and state. And it was surely an experiment. Ours was the first nation in the history of the world to separate religion and government, at least in theory.[24] Our constitutional provisions remain among the strongest in the world. Yet we are the most religious democracy on the face of the earth. More Americans believe in God and go to houses of worship than people in any other democracy. (Even among the 20 percent or so of Americans who do not believe in God, church and synagogue attendance on important religious holidays is common.) Indeed, in order to get elected, a candidate must loudly and repeatedly proclaim a deep belief in God and a strong commitment to "faith" (which has become the new political buzzword).[25]

Is this an irony, or is there a causal connection between our constitutional separation of church and state and the high level of religiosity among our people? I believe the latter is the case.

The original theory behind the metaphor of "the wall of separation" was to protect the holiness of the church from the corrupting influences of the secular state. Roger Williams, who is credited with coining the metaphor, was a seventeenth-century Baptist minister in Providence, Rhode Island. He insisted that a "hedge or wall of separation between the garden of the church and the wilderness of the world"[26] was necessary to protect religion, as well as to assure freedom of conscience. And this wall has helped to do both.[27]

Churches are thriving in America, unlike in most European countries that have long traditions of established churches. When the state supports churches, resentment against government, which is inevitable, spills over to religion. In the United States, on the other hand, resentment against the government (Congress's approval rating is always quite low) does not translate into resentment against the churches. To the contrary, cynicism about politics may well drive some people *toward* greater commitment to their churches.

I believe, therefore, that perhaps the single most important guarantee in our Constitution is one that is not explicitly enumerated: the separation of church and state. Although those words do not appear in either the body of the Constitution or in the First Amendment, there can be no doubt that the founding fathers constructed a system of checks and balances that required such separation. Without it, the church (representing organized religion) could not serve as an effective check on the secular excesses of the state; nor could the state, through its courts, serve as an effective check on the excessive involvement of the church in the business of governance and in the rights of religious and nonreligious dissenters. The marvel of our unique system of checks and balances is that it does not simply involve each branch of government—executive, legislative, and judicial—checking on the others; it also encourages—through the freedoms guaranteed by the First Amendment—other institutions to serve as checks on the government. In addition to the churches (broadly defined to include all religious institutions), these include the media, the academy, the business community, and especially the "people," who have the right to vote, to assemble, and to petition for a redress of grievances.

Just before the fiftieth anniversary of the Declaration of Independence—the day on which two of its primary authors, Jefferson and Adams, both died—Jefferson wrote the following about the purpose of the Declaration:

> *May it be to the world the signal of arousing men to burst the chains under which monkish ignorance and superstition had persuaded them to bind themselves, and to assume the blessing and security of self-government. That form which we have substituted, restores the free right to the unbound exercise of reason and freedom of opinion. All eyes are opened, or opening, to the rights of man. The general spread of the light of science has already laid open to every view the palpable truth, that the mass of mankind has not been born with saddles on their backs, nor a favored few booted and spurred, ready to ride them legitimately, by the grace of God.*[28]

While president, Jefferson—who believed in the nonbiblical God of Deism—had written to the Danbury Baptist Association, describing the "act of the whole American people which declared their legislature should 'make no law respecting an establishment of religion, or prohibiting the free exercise thereof,' *thus* building a wall of separation between church and state."[29]

Even earlier, while Adams was president and Jefferson secretary of state, they jointly signed a treaty, ratified by the Senate, with the Barbary regime in Tripoli that stated unequivocally that "the government of the United States is not *in any sense* founded on the Christian religion" (emphasis added).

It is difficult, therefore, for any reasonable person, especially anyone who gives weight to the original understanding of the Constitution, to dispute Jefferson's conclusion that the First Amendment built a wall of separation between church and state and that our state is not based on the Christian religion.

Despite this history, there are those who continue to insist that the United States is a Christian nation, as a matter of law. I became personally involved in this divisive controversy in 1988, when the Republican Party of Arizona proposed the enactment of a resolution declaring the United States to be "a Christian nation . . . based on the absolutes of the Bible."[30]

The leader of the group (characterized by the late Arizona senator Barry Goldwater as a "bunch of kooks")[31] wrote to Justice Sandra Day O'Connor on the United States Supreme Court asking her to support their efforts:

> *Republicans are making some interesting advances in this heavily controlled Democratic area. Some of us are proposing a resolution which acknowledges that the Supreme Court ruled in 1892 that this is a Christian nation. It would be beneficial and interesting to have a letter from you.*[32]

Despite the crass partisan objective of the undertaking and its utter incompatibility with the Constitution O'Connor had sworn to uphold, she agreed to help, writing the following letter on Supreme Court stationery for circulation by the Republican Party of Arizona:

> *You wrote me recently to inquire about any holdings of this Court to the effect that this is a Christian nation. There are statements to such effect in the following opinions: Church of the Holy Trinity vs. United States; Zorach vs. Clauson; McGowan vs. Maryland.*[33]

Not only was O'Connor wrong to write *any* letter in support of this unconstitutional, partisan, kooky proposal, she was wrong on the law, wrong on the facts, and wrong on her history.[34] First of all, if this were a "Christian" nation, its form of Christianity would be decidedly Protestant. Catholics would be second-class citizens. Indeed the Declaration of Independence was designed, at least in part, to protect Americans from the influence of the Catholic Church, which was reviled by many of our founding fathers, including Adams and Jefferson. ("Monkish ignorance" was a clear reference to the Catholic Church.)[35] Second, there are no such "holdings." Third, the first case she cited (which had long ago been discarded, if not discredited) contained—in dictum—some of the most bigoted language in Supreme Court history by one of the most religiously bigoted justices in its history, David Brewer.

Brewer's dictum, in an obscure immigration case, declared "Mahomet" and "the Grand Lama" to be "imposters."[36] In his other writings and speeches, he decried the evil of Mormonism and other non-Christian faiths. He was anti-Catholic and anti-Jewish. He believed that we were a Protestant nation, and he smuggled the concept of a "Christian nation" into dictum in a case that did not even raise the issue.[37]

When, in 1892, Brewer wrote the bigoted opinion cited by O'Connor, the United States was, demographically, a white Protestant Christian nation. The nation's demography changed dramatically in the nearly a century between that decision and O'Connor's letter. And the law reflected that change.

Since 1892, the court has not referred to this nation as "Christian" or "Protestant." Indeed, the justices have gone out of their way to be inclusive. For example, when Justice William O. Douglas sustained a New York program permitting public school students to be released for an hour each week for religious instruction, he specifically gave as an example of religious accommodations "a Jewish student [asking] his teacher for permission to be excused for Yom Kippur."[38] Yet this was one of the decisions miscited by Justice O'Connor as containing statements to the effect that this is a Christian nation.[39]

When her letter was disclosed, Justice O'Connor issued a statement regretting that it had been "used in a political debate," and the Supreme Court media office said that O'Connor "had no idea" that the letter would be used politically.[40] But that simply isn't true, since the request to Justice O'Connor—stating that it would be "beneficial" to have a letter from her as part of a Republican proposal to enact a Christian Nation resolution—made it clear that she was being asked to write her letter specifically for use in a political campaign to make Republican "advances in this heavily controlled Democratic area."

When I got wind of Justice O'Connor's letter, I wrote a scathing op-ed for the *New York Times* criticizing her judicial ethics as well as her miscitation of the law. It accused her of giving

> *aid and comfort to partisan Republican causes. Her regrets came too late and only after public criticism. She has . . . allowed her name and judicial office to be used improperly. She has . . . violated the Code of Judicial Conduct, which unambiguously directs sitting judges to refrain from political activity. . . . A seat on the Supreme Court does not exempt a Justice from complying with the rules of the profession. Justice O'Connor must remember that her allegiances are no longer to a particular wing of the Arizona Republican Party but to all Americans, regardless of party affiliation, region or religion.*[41]

I was told by several law clerks that after my op-ed appeared, Justice O'Connor was deeply embarrassed by what she had done, and she did not repeat her error during her subsequent years of service on the court.

Justice O'Connor was not, of course, the first (or the last) in public office to use Christianity in support of partisan politics. The issue got so bad during the 1984 presidential race that Walter Mondale found it necessary to remind Ronald Reagan that in the United States the president, unlike the queen of England, is "not the defender of the faith" but rather the "defender of the Constitution."[42]

In 2012, a Republican candidate for president, Rick Santorum, said that the concept of an absolute separation of church and state, as articulated by John Kennedy when he was running for president, "makes me want to throw up."[43] Other candidates, though expressing themselves less graphically, have also railed against the separation of church and state. "Faith" has become synonymous with "values" in the minds of many, although there is absolutely no correlation. Indeed, the "values" espoused by some of the people who would impose their faith on others are highly questionable. They include denying gays the equal protection of the law; denying women (and young girls) the right to choose abortion, and sometimes contraception, even in compelling cases; and, often, other conservative political "values" that have nothing to do with religion, such as low taxes, the right to bear arms, the death penalty, and widespread censorship.[44] The debates over these issues, especially gay rights and the right to choose abortion, have become wedge controversies that are unduly influenced by the churches in violation of the spirit, if not the letter, of our Constitution.

THE RIGHTS OF GAYS TO ABSOLUTE EQUALITY

When I was growing up, it was impermissible to use any words that were demeaning to African-Americans (whom we called Negroes or colored), to other religions or ethnic minorities (except for the Germans and the Japanese during World War II), or to women. But insulting gay boys (we had no idea there even were lesbians) was perfectly acceptable. Indeed, we commonly used the "F" word to insult nonathletic classmates or effeminate-looking boys. We never actually met a real live homosexual (at least to our knowledge), but we knew there was "something wrong" with anybody who was sexually attracted to people of the same gender.

Our bigotry was not religiously based, though we knew that the Bible prohibited sex between men[45] (perhaps the Bible's authors, like us, had no idea there were lesbians). We just didn't like "homos." It was as simple as that. You really do have to be taught to hate,[46] and we were taught to treat all people, except gays, equally.

It's very different among today's youth, at least in the parts of the world that I frequent. Most young people I encounter can't understand why anyone would discriminate against someone based on his or her sexual orientation or preference.

Today, the discrimination against gay people does seem religiously based, at least to a significant degree. The Bible is frequently cited as the authoritative source for condemning homosexuality, and the sanctity (a religious term) of marriage between a man and a woman serves as the primary basis for opposition to gay marriage.

Since my youth, the movement toward full equality for gays has made great strides, despite continuing religious objection from some church groups and some Orthodox Jews. The fact that many churches, as well as Conservative and Reform Judaism, support equality has muted the impact of the religious right somewhat on this issue. Before long, I predict, it will not be an issue for most Americans.

VIGNETTE

Walking Out on the Chief Justice

In 1986, the Supreme Court upheld a Georgia statute criminalizing homosexual acts between consenting adults.[47] In his concurring opinion, Chief Justice Warren Burger went out of his way to demonize homosexuality by quoting, with approval, William Blackstone's characterization of homosexuality as "the infamous crime against nature," an offense of deeper malignity than rape, and "a crime not fit to be named."[48] Shortly after this decision was rendered, I attended a meeting of the American Bar Association at which the Chief Justice was to speak. When he was introduced, I stood up and led a quiet walkout in protest of his bigoted opinion.

In 2003, during the beginning of the 2004 presidential election season, the Supreme Judicial Court of Massachusetts rendered the first-in-the-nation decision declaring it unconstitutional to limit marriage to heterosexual couples.[49] This decision was truly a knife that cut both ways: It was a Magna Carta for gay and lesbian couples, but it was also a boon to social conservative candidates who could use it as an important part of their appeal to the majority of Americans who then believed that marriage should be reserved for heterosexual couples.

I decided to write an op-ed that would seek to eliminate gay marriage as "a wedge issue" in the upcoming political campaign.[50] I argued that if marriage is indeed a blessed sacrament between man and woman as ordained in the Bible, it would follow that the entire institution of marriage has no place in our civil society, which recognizes the separation between the sacred and the secular, between church and state. Just as the state has no role in baptisms, circumcisions, or other religious rituals, it should play no role in sacred marriages.

The state is, of course, legitimately concerned with the secular rights and responsibilities currently associated with the sacrament of marriage: the financial consequences of divorce, the custody of children, Social Security and hospital benefits, and so forth.

The solution I proposed was to unlink the religious institution of marriage—as distinguished from the secular institution of civil union—from the state. Under this proposal, any couple, regardless of gender, could register for civil union, recognized by the state, with all its rights and responsibilities.

Religious couples could then go to the church, synagogue, mosque, or other sacred institution of their choice in order to be married. These religious institutions would have total decision-making authority over which marriages to recognize. Catholic churches would not have to perform gay marriages. Orthodox Jewish synagogues would not perform a marriage between a Jew and a non-Jew who did not convert to Judaism. And those religious institutions that chose to perform gay marriages could do so. It would be a religious decision beyond the scope of the state.

Under this arrangement, marriage would remain a sacrament, as ordained by the Bible and as interpreted by each individual church, and gay couples would win exactly the same civil rights as heterosexual couples in relationship to the state. They would still have to persuade individual churches of their point of view, but that is not the concern of the secular state.

Not only would this solution be good for gays and for those who oppose gay marriage on religious grounds, it would also strengthen the wall of separation between church and state by placing a sacred institution entirely in the hands of the church while placing a secular institution under state control.

My column generated considerable debate. I was invited to appear on television and radio shows, where extremists on both sides pilloried me: gay activists for not going far enough; religious antigay activists for going too far.

Shortly after my column appeared, I received a phone call from the then governor of Massachusetts, Mitt Romney, who told me that he found my idea interesting and asked me to draft legislation that he might consider proposing in order to break the deadlock. I drafted the legislation but never heard back from the governor, who by the time I submitted it had decided to run for president. He was almost certainly fearful of the pushback he would get from the religious right—whose votes he needed to be nominated—if he were seen as favoring anything that even resembled gay marriage.

Since that time, several states have adopted gay marriage or civil unions, and the trend is clearly in the direction of full equality for gay men and women. I predict, based on the reaction of my current students to this issue, that the next generation will not even understand why earlier generations took so long to recognize equality for gays. On June 26, 2013, the Supreme Court rendered two important decisions regarding gay marriage. While neither expressly recognized a constitutional right to gay marriage, both signaled a growing acceptance of equality based on sexual orientation. Once again, the public acceptance of equality for gays will be more important than Supreme Court decisions regarding gay rights.

A WOMAN'S RIGHT TO CHOOSE ABORTION

As easy as the resolution of the gay marriage issue should be, both politically and constitutionally—full equality either in marriage or civil unions for all—that's how difficult it is to resolve the issue of abortion as a matter of constitutional law. Politically I have always supported a woman's right to choose abortion, since I do not regard an early-term fetus as a human being when a woman decides that she doesn't wish to carry it to term.[51] For me the decision to abort is very much a matter of degree, and the woman carrying the child should have primary responsibility to make that decision. But as a matter of constitutional law, I find little basis in either the right of privacy or the right to equal protection to grant a woman the right to terminate her pregnancy, particularly as the fetus comes closer to viability. Most legal systems establish exit from the birth canal as the moment of humanity, but a nine-month-old fetus in the womb is biologically indistinguishable from a fetus that has just exited the womb. (Indeed when kangaroos exit the womb, it is only a temporary condition and the joey returns periodically to the mother's external womb for nourishment.) A fetus is as viable at nine months as at nine and a half, but distinctions must be made by the law.

The religious component in the abortion debate is quite pronounced. For a believing Catholic, and for some Protestants, life begins at conception. If I believed, as some do, that abortion is the killing of a human being with a soul, I would probably be marching in front of abortion clinics to stop the murder of innocent babies. The fact that I don't believe this is largely a matter of my religious upbringing. Some scholars believe that they can demonstrate, as a matter of philosophical "truth," that the Catholic position is wrong. I think that this is the height of arrogance.[52] Nor am I convinced by the faulty argument, offered by some, that if Catholics and others really believed that fetuses were human beings, they would punish abortion by the death penalty, and the fact that they don't proves that they don't really believe that fetuses are human beings. This argument is wrong for several reasons. First, some religious extremists do believe that abortion should be punished by death. Indeed, they have killed abortion doctors. Second, some Catholics are opposed to the death penalty even for murder. Indeed, that is the official position of the Vatican.[53] Third, one can believe that abortion is murder and yet understand that there may be mitigating factors.

Following the infamous Supreme Court decision in *Bush v. Gore*,[54] I wrote a book[55] in which I argued that "the seeds" of *Bush v. Gore* "were planted by the campaign to constitutionalize a woman's right to choose abortion."[56]

I argued that the abortion issue is quintessentially political. It involves a clash of ideologies, even worldviews. Unlike issues of equality, the controversy over abortion has no absolute right and wrong side, either morally or constitutionally.[57] Virtually everyone today acknowledges that segregation was both immoral and unconstitutional. All it took was a strong push by a unanimous Supreme Court to set in motion a process that was ongoing in most other democracies throughout the world, but that had gotten stuck in the United States because the channels of democracy had been blocked by malapportioned legislatures and other perversions of the democratic process. Over a period of years, the Supreme Court placed its moral imprimatur on desegregation and eventually unblocked these channels of democracy. It worked—not perfectly, but perfection is rarely possible in a heterogeneous and divided democracy. And congressional legislation regulating voting, housing, education, and other matters followed. A similar process is today under way with regard to equality for gays.

Abortion is different. The Supreme Court's decision,[58] now more than forty years old, changed few minds on this issue, because those who believe that abortion is tantamount to murder are not like those who believed that segregation was right. The former believe that they occupy the moral high ground. And they *do, if* their underlying premise—that a fetus is a human being—is correct. No rational argument, whether made by philosophers or Supreme Court justices, will ever disprove the truth of that a priori premise. Nor will experience alter it, unlike views concerning segregation or gay rights, which have been markedly changed by experience.

Moreover, the nation was—and remains—closely divided about the morality of abortion, both in the abstract and under various circumstances. Advocates of a woman's right to choose abortion could have organized politically to win that right (at least for most women under most circumstances) in the elected branches of government. According to the ACLU,

> *between 1967 and 1971, under mounting pressure from the women's rights movement, 17 states decriminalized abortion. Public opinion also shifted during this period. In 1968, only 15 percent of Americans favored legal abor-*

> *tions; by 1972, 64 percent did. When the Court announced its landmark 1973 ruling legalizing abortion in* Roe v. Wade, *it was marching in step with public opinion.*[59]

But it is the proper role of the elected legislative and executive branches, not the appointed Supreme Court, to march "in step" with public opinion. Instead of devoting all their resources to continuing the legislative and public opinion battle, the pro-choice movement devoted much of its resources to the litigation option, whose goal it was to get the Supreme Court to constitutionalize a woman's right to choose abortion. It worked as planned, thus sparing the pro-choice movement the difficult political task of organizing and fund-raising on a state-by-state basis. The justices did the work for them, by simply striking down most abortion laws in one fell swoop.

The short-term consequences of constitutionalizing the abortion issue were powerful and positive for the choice movement. I would argue that the long-term consequences, however, were disastrous. *Roe v. Wade* provided the religious right and the conservative wing of the Republican Party one of the best organizing tools and rallying cries imaginable. The right-to-life movement was energized by this decision and became one of the most potent political forces both nationally and in a large number of states. At the same time, the pro-choice movement became lethargic, celebrating its great judicial victory and neglecting the hard work of organizing and fund-raising—at least in the beginning. As the ACLU has put it:

> *The backlash was swift and fierce. Anti-choice forces quickly mobilized, dedicating themselves to reversing* Roe. *In 1974, the ACLU established its Reproductive Freedom Project to advance a broad spectrum of reproductive rights.*[60]

Litigation continued to be the weapon of choice in the battle to defend a woman's right to an abortion.

I would argue that *Roe v. Wade* helped secure the presidency for Ronald Reagan, by giving him a "free" issue. It was free because he—and other "pro-life" Republicans—could strongly oppose all abortion, without alienating moderate Republican women and men who favored a woman's right to choose but felt secure in the knowledge that the Supreme Court would continue to protect that right, regardless of what Reagan and others said or did. Abortion became an important election issue for right-wing religious zealots, and a marginal issue for moderate Republicans who favored a woman's right to choose but who also supported the Republican economic and other programs. *Roe v. Wade* thus contributed to the demise of the moderate wing of the Republican Party (the so-called Rockefeller Republicans) and drove former moderates such as the elder George Bush to the right. (He started as a pro-choice Republican and ended up as a pro-life Republican whose hands were tied by the Supreme Court.)[61]

At bottom, *Roe v. Wade* and *Bush v. Gore* represent opposite sides of the same currency of judicial activism in areas more appropriately left to the political processes. Courts ought not to jump into controversies that are political in nature and are capable of being resolved—even if not smoothly or expeditiously—by the popular branches of government. Judges have no special competence, qualifications, or mandate to decide between equally compelling moral claims (as in the abortion controversy) or equally compelling political claims (counting ballots by hand or stopping the recount because the standard is ambiguous). Absent clear governing constitutional principles (which are not present in either case), these are precisely the sorts of issues that should be left to the rough-and-tumble of politics rather than the ipse dixit of five justices.[62]

There are, of course, considerable differences between *Roe v. Wade* and *Bush v. Gore*. No matter how critical one may be of *Roe*, no one can accuse the justices who voted for it of having been politically partisan, which was not the case with the five Republican justices in *Bush v. Gore* who voted to stop the recount and hand the election to the candidate and party for whom they had voted on election day.[63]

The right of a woman to choose abortion and the right of gay couples to marry are the prime wedge issues that today divide the religious right from the rest of the country. But there are other issues that also divide the country along religious lines. Some involve religion directly, such as the effort to permit prayer in the public schools, and the right of religious groups and persons to be exempted from laws of general application, and religious discrimination—in law or in fact—against atheists, agnostics, or members of unpopular religions or "cults."

The difficult question of how to balance freedom of religion with the equally important freedom from religion—the two sides of the First Amendment coin—is never going to be neatly resolved in a pluralistic democracy. It is an ongoing tightrope walk that requires sensitivity from all sides. It also requires a Supreme Court willing to buck popular pressures in this highly sensitive area that the framers of our Constitution deliberately removed from majoritarian politics. Most importantly, it requires a collective decision by public officials of all political stripes to agree to stop running as defenders of the faith, and to end the contest over who is more religious or committed to "faith." Religion and faith, as Jefferson recognized, are private matters, and no one should be judged based on their "religious opinions, any more than [their] opinions in physics or geometry."[64] With this in mind, let me end this chapter with my own "Ten Commendments" (a commendment is a cross between a "commandment" and an "amendment" that I would "commend" candidates for following):

1. Do not claim God as a member of your party, or claim that God is on your side of an issue.
2. Do not publicly proclaim your religious devotion, affiliation, or practices, or attack those of your opponents.
3. Do not denounce as antireligious or intolerant of religion those who differ with you about the proper role of religion in public life.
4. Do not surround your political campaign with religious trappings or symbols.
5. Honor and respect the diversity of this country, recalling that many Americans came to these shores to escape the tyranny of enforced religious uniformity and, more recently, enforced antireligious uniformity.
6. Do not seek the support of religious leaders who impose on members of their faith religious obligations to support or oppose particular candidates.
7. Do not accuse of immorality those who reject formal religion. Recall that some of our nation's greatest leaders did not accept formal or even informal religion.
8. Do not equate morality and religion. Although some great moral teachers were religious, some great moral sinners also acted in the name of religion.
9. When there are political as well as religious dimensions to an issue, focus on the political ones during the campaign.
10. Remember that every belief is in a minority somewhere, and act as if your belief were the least popular.

22

FROM HUMAN RIGHTS TO HUMAN WRONGS

How the Hard Left Hijacked the Human Rights Agenda

The United States Constitution guarantees equality under American law, but the vast majority of the world's population has no such legal protection. *Human* rights should not be limited by geographic or political borders. They should apply to all human beings, regardless of nationality, race, or religion. I have devoted much of my life to trying to turn this theory into reality on an international scale.

I was brought up in the golden age of human rights. Our heroes were Eleanor Roosevelt, René Cassin, and Albert Schweitzer. Our great hope was the United Nations, with its Universal Declaration of Human Rights.[1] Our mantra was FDR's "Four Freedoms": freedom of speech and expression; freedom of worship; freedom from want; freedom from fear.[2] (I also have an apartment in New York directly across the river from the Four Freedoms Park.)

The enemies of human rights were also clear: fascism, communism, racism, religious discrimination, McCarthyism, authoritarianism, slavery, apartheid, and other forms of oppression emanating from both the extreme right and the extreme left.

All good liberals—and my friends, neighbors, and coreligionists were almost all good liberals—were knee-jerk supporters of the human rights agenda. And why not? How could any decent person be opposed to the Four Freedoms and other universal human rights, such as racial and religious equality, the ability to travel freely, the right to a fair trial, and the ability of workers to join unions and collectively bargain for fair wages and working conditions?

We all admired the United Nations and looked to it as a guarantor of peace and a protector of human rights. And again, why not? It had been founded in the wake of the Allied victory over Nazism by nations—mostly democracies—that had been on the right side of the war against Germany, Japan, and other members of the fascist Axis. One of the UN's first actions was to divide the British mandate over Palestine into two states—one for Jews, the other for Arabs—thereby creating the conditions that led to the establishment of Israel. I vividly recall watching the UN vote with my father on a small black-and-white television and cheering when the deciding vote was cast in favor of the two-state solution (which Israel accepted and the Arab states and Palestinian Arabs rejected).[3] In those golden years, there was no conflict between supporting the UN and supporting the United States and its democratic ally, Israel.

MY FIRST CONFRONTATION WITH THE UNITED NATIONS

My earliest experiences in human rights (other than signing the petition to save the Rosenbergs, which earned me both the respect and the concern of my frightened parents, and my act of civil disobedience against the slave-owning king of Saudi Arabia, which nearly got me arrested) involved the United Nations.

When I was a junior in high school, the United Nations came up with the idea of a universal calendar that would introduce a "bland day at the end of each year [that] would disrupt the 7 day Sabbatical cycle."[4]

The Orthodox Jewish community was in an uproar about this well-intentioned proposal, because it would change the natural order of when the Jewish Sabbath fell. Under the conventional calendar, the Sabbath corresponded with Saturday. Under the brave new world proposal, the Jewish Sabbath could fall on any day of the week. Jews (and Seventh-day Adventists) had fought hard to recognize Saturday as a day off from most jobs and school activities. The UN proposal would require Sabbath-observers to be absent from such activities when the Sabbath fell on a weekday.

At the time I was president of the "Inter-Yeshiva High School Council"—a group I had formed after the principal of my high school banned me from running for the presidency of my own school's student body. I used the newly formed organization as the nerve center for the campaign to stop the universal calendar. We did not consider the proposal to be anti-Semitic; it was motivated by benign universalistic aspirations. We regarded it as insensitive to the religious concerns of certain groups.

In an effort to broaden the opposition, I reached out to Seventh-day Adventists (who joined our efforts), Muslims (who seemed less concerned about whether their day of rest corresponded with the UN's "Friday"), and other religious groups. The result was a postcard campaign (I still have the postcard) in which we sent thousands of printed cards with the following message to the UN:

> Ambassador Henry Cabot Lodge
> United States Delegation
> United Nations, N.Y.
>
> Dear Sir:
>
> As a student of a Hebrew parochial high school in New York, I wish to express my opposition to the World Calendar Reform proposal soon to come before the United Nations. This proposal, which would move the Jewish Sabbath to other days of the week, would have disastrous effects on Jewish religious life, thus impairing the freedom of religion which we so cherish.
>
> Respectfully yours,
> Under Auspices of the Inter-Yeshiva High School Student Council

It was a modest effort by later standards: no marches, sit-ins, or lawsuits. But it succeeded. The UN dropped the proposal, and our small group got credit in the media. Here is how the *New York Post*—my community's "newspaper of record" in those days—reported our success, beneath the headline CALENDAR REFORM TOPS FORMOSA ISSUE IN LETTERS TO U.N.:

> *World Calendar reform, not Formosa, is the topic provoking most of the letters being received at the U.N. These [209 letters] were the result of a postcard campaign instituted by the Inter-Yeshiva HS Council. The opposition of religious groups to calendar reform—and it came from all faiths—prevailed. The U.S. informed Secretary General Hammarskjold that it did not favor any action by the U.N. to revise the present calendar. "Large numbers of the U.S. citizens oppose the plan," the U.S. note said.*[5]

We were thrilled that our campaign—involving not quite the "large numbers" reported—had succeeded. We regarded it as a victory for religious freedom. It persuaded me that even small efforts could have an impact on large organizations—a lesson that has stayed with me over my career. And it enhanced my admiration for the UN, which had shown sensitivity to religious minorities.

During my high school years, my class made several visits to the UN, where we watched the General Assembly in action. We debated whether "Red China should be admitted to the UN." (I took the affirmative side.) Several of us joined the "United Nations Association," and we participated in "model UN" sessions, each playing the role of a representative from a particular country. No one could have predicted, in those days, how the UN would soon become an organization that stood idly by and even facilitated genocide, terrorism, and other human wrongs by so many of its own member states.

WHAT ARE HUMAN RIGHTS?

During my college and law school years, most of my focus was on domestic civil rights.

After I became a teacher and a lawyer, my involvement in the human rights movement broadened, both academically and politically. I taught courses at Harvard Law School on human rights with Professors Telford Taylor and Irwin Cotler and wrote numerous articles on various aspects of the subject.

In my academic work, I began to explore the meaning of the term "*human* rights," as contrasted with "*civil* rights," "civil *liberties*," and "*political* rights."[6] To be an advocate of *human* rights meant to me going beyond one's particular group. A Jew who fights only against anti-Semitism is an advocate for *particular* rights, as is an African-American who struggles only against racism, a woman who only opposes sexism, a gay person who fights only homophobia, or a person of the left who supports only left-wing causes. These are commendable activities, but they do not qualify as advocacy of *human* rights.[7] Just as joining the "First Amendment Club" requires the active defense of expression one deplores,[8] so too, joining the "Human Rights Club" requires an active commitment to the universal rights of *all* people, even those you disagree with or despise. The membership roles of both "clubs" are, tragically, quite small under these criteria, though many claim their honorific mantles.

Being a member of the Human Rights Club does not require abstaining from advocacy for one's own group (however defined). But it does require more universal advocacy as well. The motto for the club might well be the famous dictum of the Jewish sage Hillel: "If I am not for myself, who will be for me, but if I am for myself alone, what am I? And if not now, when?"[9] I have tried hard to live by these words—which hang on the wall in my office—and to maintain my membership in the Human Rights Club, although my priorities have changed with shifting threats to particular groups over time.

As a young lawyer, I witnessed little threat to the Jewish community in America, despite lingering anti-Semitism in law firms, social clubs, and some universities and neighborhoods. I fought against these remnants of bigotry, but it was clear that the trend was in the right direction: top-down anti-Semitism and elite discrimination against Jews were on the way out. Jews, I felt, did not need my help. Certainly not as much as other groups.

THE VIETNAM WAR

During the height of the conflict over the Vietnam War, I represented numerous defendants, protestors, and civil disobedients. I also advised lawyers who were suing the government in an effort to stop what they believed was an illegal war. The faculty of Harvard Law School was divided over the morality, legality, and effectiveness of the war, and there were interesting discussions in the faculty lunchroom involving such luminaries as Archibald Cox, Erwin Griswold, Abram Chayes, and Paul Freund. I decided that these discussions should be shared with our students, and so I organized the first law school course on the Vietnam War. I felt the debate over the war was a teaching moment and we had to take advantage of it. I prepared a set of legal materials and invited professors with different views to share their perspectives with the students. The course was a remarkable success. Students attended in droves, and the media covered the lectures. The *New York Times* story was headlined 400 ENROLL IN A HARVARD COURSE ON "LAW AND THE LAWYER" IN THE VIETNAM WAR:

> *More than a dozen professors have volunteered as teachers, including Prof. Derek C. Bok, the dean-designate of the law school.*
>
> *Professor Dershowitz said that the participating professors "reflect every view." . . . The course would be the first of its kind offered in any law school in the United States. "It is our hope," he said, "that this will be a pilot and a model for other law schools throughout the country." . . .*
>
> *He said the course would not be "biased or political," but would "look at these issues in a detached, lawyer-like, scholarly way."*[10]

Time magazine also ran a story:

> *Harvard Professor Alan Dershowitz had just finished giving the first class in a brand-new, ten-week Harvard course entitled "The Role of the Law and the Lawyer in the Viet Nam Conflict." It has no exam or grades, offers no credit, and involves a good deal of reading over and above the students' already heavy regular work load. But it has a record enrollment of more than 400—one-quarter of the student body—and is one of the most popular courses in the 150-year history of the school.*[11]

Lawyers who were contemplating legal action against the war sat in on the class, as well as several faculty members. I received dozens of requests for copies of the materials from professors at other schools who wanted to offer the course to their students. For me, it was the beginning of a practice that I have followed throughout my teaching career: offering courses about highly relevant contemporaneous issues that respond to interesting teaching moments. Over the half century of my teaching at Harvard Law School, I have offered a new course just about every year, many of them dealing with pressing issues of human rights generated by the conflicts of the day.

In addition to teaching courses, I wrote articles on human rights and brought lawsuits challenging human rights abuses. And I participated in political campaigns to end apartheid, the war in Vietnam, and other human wrongs. My early work on human rights won me a coveted Guggenheim Fellowship and other honors. It also earned me the media title "Global Watchdog."[12] In an article by that name, a reporter interviewed me about the core concept of human rights. I said:

> *Everyone should be free to express opinions and views, to read what one chooses, to have some influence in the process of government, to leave one's country. One should be free from arbitrary arrest and trial, torture and execution.*[13]

I told the reporter that

> *I try hard to balance my attack, right and left—for every attack on . . . a right-wing repressive government, there should be an attack on a left-wing repressive government.*[14]

I also explained that

> *in practice you can do a lot to implement human rights in this generation but in teaching you can both help this generation and help plant the seeds for progress later on.*[15]

Despite my deep involvement in human rights work, I wondered whether I was really having a discernible impact on the problems of the world. Unlike litigation in American courts, where the results are immediately evident, the impact on foreign countries of petitions, op-ed articles, congressional resolutions, and other conventional human rights activities tends to be less visible or immediate.

I will never forget one encounter that made it all seem worth the apparently unrewarded efforts. I attended a concert by the great Russian cellist Mstislav Rostropovich, several years after he left the Soviet Union. Since he had been a sometimes threatened advocate of human rights in Moscow, I wanted to meet him. So I stood in line waiting to shake his hand after the performance. When I introduced myself, he grabbed me in a long bear hug. "You gave us hope," he told me. "We knew you were out there fighting for our rights, even though we couldn't contact you. You made us feel safer."

I had no idea that Rostropovich, or any of the other artists or dissidents whose rights we advocated, had ever heard of us, or had any idea of what we were doing on their behalf. Rostropovich's hug, and what he said, was more than enough compensation for all the pro bono work we had done on behalf of dissidents and artists around the world.

BEING MENTORED BY ELIE WIESEL

I had become interested in the defense of Soviet dissidents after reading Elie Wiesel's book *The Jews of Silence*,[16] which first alerted me to the plight of Soviet Jewish and non-Jewish dissidents. It was an eye-opening book that contributed to changing the direction of my life, both professionally and personally, in several different ways. It bought home to me the need to reprioritize my human rights focus. It made me feel guilty for largely ignoring the plight of my own coreligionists in a distant land that continued to repress them. Wiesel made me realize that, perhaps in an overreaction to my Jewish background, I was following Hillel's second admonition ("If I am for myself alone what am I?") more than his first ("If I am not for myself who will be for me?"). I decided that I had to become involved in what was then an emerging human rights struggle. (I was influenced as well by my representation of Sheldon Siegel in the Jewish Defense League murder case, discussed earlier.)

Reading Wiesel's slim volume also provided the incentive for me to try to meet the world's most influential Holocaust survivor. I had read his accounts of life during and after his confinement at Auschwitz-Birkenau, but I could not personally identify with that dark period of his tragic life. Now he was writing about a current crisis that my generation of Jews could do something about. A mutual friend—Bernard Fishman, a great New York lawyer—arranged a meeting, and since that time Elie has served as a guide, mentor, and friend. I have sought his advice on many issues, and he has sought mine. We have worked together, commiserated about the state of human rights, and have tried, along with others, to repair the world.

As a professor of Public Law, I get to nominate candidates for the Nobel Peace Prize. In 1986, I nominated Elie Wiesel. In my letter of nomination, I wrote the following:

> *No one in the world today deserves the Nobel Peace Prize more than Elie Wiesel.*
>
> *To understand Professor Wiesel's unique and immeasurable contribution to peace, one must only imagine how it might have been without a Wiesel.*
>
> *There are many excellent reasons for recognizing Professor Wiesel. But none is more important than for his role in teaching survivors and their children how to respond in constructive peace and justice to a worldwide conspiracy of genocide, whose complicitous components included mass killing, mass silence, and mass indifference. Professor Wiesel has devoted his life to teaching the survivors of a conspiracy which excluded so few, to reenter and adjust in peace to an alien world that deserved little forgiveness. He has also taught the rest of the world the injustice of silence in the face of genocide. Wiesel's life work merits the highest degree of recognition—especially from representatives of the world that stood silently by.*

Many others wrote on his behalf as well, and Wiesel was awarded the prize.

Several years later, I urged the Nobel committee to use Elie Wiesel as its model for selecting future Nobel Prize winners because

> *many of the Nobel Peace Prize winners [worked only] on behalf of their own people, but Elie Wiesel's work is far more universal. . . . Wiesel makes no distinctions based on religion, race, creed or even enmity against his own people. He will bear witness, even at the risk of his life, to the suffering of any human beings, so long as they are not the aggressors. And for Elie Wiesel, tomorrow is never an excuse for not acting today.*[17]

Over the years, Elie and I have worked closely together on issues relating to Soviet dissidents, the Armenian genocide, the massacres in Rwanda and Darfur, efforts to delegitimate Israel, and other human rights concerns.

VIGNETTE

Mitterand's Joke

Elie and his wife, Marianne, invited me to their home in New York for an intimate dinner with French president François Mitterrand. Elie and his wife speak fluent French, but I do not, and neither did the two other couples at the dinner. Mitterrand spoke passable English, but he insisted on conducting the entire conversation in French, with a British translator at his side. At one point, Mitterrand told a joke in French. None of the French-speaking people at the table laughed. His translator then repeated it in English, and everyone laughed hysterically. I asked Elie whether the joke was funnier in English than in French, and he replied, "No, but Mitterrand doesn't know how to tell a joke; his translator does."

In 1982, Elie was asked to present me with the William O. Douglas Award by the Anti-Defamation League. In presenting the award, he paid me the highest compliment: "If there had been a few people like Alan Dershowitz during the 1930s and 1940s, the history of European Jewry might have been different." Although I have always believed that these words were exaggerated—no one could have stopped Hitler's maniacal determination to kill the Jews of Europe—I have tried to hold myself up to his expectations. I recall his words every time I think of slowing down or doing less to protect the victims of human rights abuses.

Recently, Elie had quintuple bypass surgery. I had lunch with him shortly thereafter, and all he could talk about was the future and how important it was to keep up the struggle for human rights. We also discussed teaching a joint seminar with my Harvard and his Boston University students. Elie Wiesel is truly one of the great men of the twenty-first century. When I think of how close he came to not surviving, and when I think of how many other Elie Wiesels were lost in the flames of Auschwitz, I begin to understand the full horrors of the Holocaust.

VIGNETTE

How Many of You Have Suffered from the Holocaust?

During a talk to the lawyers of Hamburg, I asked audience members, "How many of you have suffered from the Holocaust?" A few hands of elderly lawyers were raised. I then asked, "How many of you or your family members have had cancer, coronary problems, diabetes, or a stroke?" Nearly every hand went up. I paused and then asked, "How can you be sure that the cures for those diseases did not go up in the smoke at Auschwitz or Treblinka?" There was a stunned silence. Following my talk, dozens of the German lawyers came up to me and said, "We too have suffered from the Holocaust."

In 1973, Elie urged me to travel to the Soviet Union to provide legal services to Jewish refuseniks and others who faced imprisonment for their advocacy of human rights. I went there on several occasions during the 1970s and '80s and filed briefs on behalf of dissidents refuseniks and others. I have written extensively about this aspect of my human rights work elsewhere[18] and will not repeat it here. Suffice it to say that my unwillingness to limit my advocacy only to Jewish refuseniks in the Soviet bloc—I also worked on behalf of non-Jewish dissidents, such as Andrei Sakharov and Václav Havel—caused a rift with some Jewish and Israeli organizations, but I insisted that human rights must extend to all who are oppressed.

One of my Soviet clients was Sylva Zalmanson, who after several years of confinement was released from the Soviet Gulag. When she finally came to America, I, along with her other American lawyers, arranged to meet her over lunch at Lou Siegel's, a kosher restaurant in Manhattan. It would be our first "reunion"—hopefully the first of many—with the clients we had never met. Our encounter was emotional. Knowing of Sylva's love for all things Jewish, we decided to order a real old-fashioned Jewish meal for our Friday lunch. The first dish was *cholent*, a delicious concoction of beans, potatoes, barley, and a small amount of beef, cooked for hours in a savory sauce. When the *cholent* came, I turned to Sylva and explained that it was a traditional dish served in Jewish homes on the Sabbath. She took one taste of it, and her face turned sad—and then she burst out laughing as she exclaimed, "Traditional Jewish food? This is Russian prison food! I've just been through eating food like this for four years!"

Only then did we realize that the old-fashioned food, which was such a treat for us, was peasant food, designed to use the least amount of meat possible. The same economics that dictated the diets of our peasant forebears now determined the menus prepared by the prison authorities. We all had a good laugh, and I ordered a slice of rare roast beef for our guest.

During one of my trips to Moscow, I met a young man who had been a dissident and refusenik but who had been drafted into the army because of his activities. He wanted to smuggle a message out in his own voice, using his broken English, to seek support from human rights organizations throughout the world. Tape recorders were not permitted in the Soviet Union at that time, and it was illegal to smuggle out tapes. But he had managed to get his hand on a primitive cassette recorder and he brought me a copy of a Tchaikovsky tape that was being sold in the Soviet Union. In order to prevent rerecording over the tape, certain changes had been made in the cassette. My Soviet client knew how to override those changes, and he managed to record his statement in lieu of the third movement of Tchaikovsky's Fifth. He told me that it was always wise to have the recorded statement in the middle of the music, because Soviet authorities tend to listen to the beginning and end of any music tape to ensure that it does not contain forbidden material. I managed to get his statement back to the United States. Shortly thereafter he was released and came to live in my home while he was trying to get into school here.

Although my interest in the Soviet Jewry movement was stimulated by Elie Wiesel's book, a more personal encounter got me interested in a case involving one particular Romanian family. In 1971, during my fellowship at the Center for Advanced Study in the Behavioral Sciences on the Stanford campus in Palo Alto, California, I met a fellow who had been invited from Communist Romania, Michael Cernea. He was chairman of the Department of Sociology and Anthropology at the University of Bucharest and an active member of the Romanian Communist Party. On the day before Rosh Hashanah, he invited me to take a walk with him through the woods. When we were away from any possibility of surveillance, he told me that his original name was Moishe Catz, that he was a committed Jew, and that he desperately wanted to defect along with his family from Communist Romania and move either to the United States or Israel. He swore me to secrecy and asked if I would become his pro bono lawyer in what would surely be a long-term activity, since his family was being held hostage in Romania. I immediately agreed and invited him for dinner that night at my home, where we stayed up until dawn, listening to Jewish cantorial music, which he had not heard since his youth some thirty years earlier. Tears flowed freely from his eyes.

Several years later, we were able to arrange for him and his wife to be out of the country at the same time. Both were attending academic conferences. I arranged for them to obtain political asylum at the American embassies in the countries they were visiting. They both defected at the same moment. But they had to leave their two children and Michael's elderly mother behind. We worked tirelessly to get them out, petitioning members of Congress, the State Department, and the White House. Finally after a year of being left alone in Bucharest, the rest of the family was permitted to leave. Senator Ted Kennedy played a key role in their release. The daughter, then of college age, moved in with my family, and I helped her to be admitted to Brandeis University. She is now a medical doctor. We have all remained close friends since that time.

Another close friend who started out as a client is Natan Sharansky, now a prominent Israeli public figure. I have already recounted the story of my representation of him, but it is interesting to note, especially in light of Sharansky's high position in the Israeli government, that when Sharansky was first arrested, the Israeli government wanted to have nothing to do with his case, since they regarded him as a human rights dissident rather than as a Prisoner of Zion. He was, of course, both. When he was finally released, some of the very same people who had fought hardest against Israel doing anything on his behalf were among the first to claim credit for his release.

I will never forget how I watched my client walk—really bounce—across the Glienicke Bridge and into the safety of the West. I knew he was well even while watching him on television. Shortly thereafter I met him in person for the first time. He threw his arms around me and whispered in my ear, "*Baruch matir asurim*," which means, "Blessed be those who help free the imprisoned." Several years later I was being interviewed on a television show and the host asked me what my biggest fee had been. He thought I would mention the Michael Milken or Leona Helmsley cases, but instead I said it was in the Sharansky case. He expressed surprise, saying that he didn't know Sharansky had any money. I said he did not, but that when he put his arms around me and gave me that hug and whispered those words, that was the biggest fee I ever earned.

Another "payment" for my work was the opportunity to speak in Carnegie Hall on behalf of Václav Havel and other dissident artists in 1991.[19]

Several Americans who had fought for the human rights of censored artists were invited to read from and discuss works banned by repressive regimes. I had been part of a team of lawyers assembled to help Havel and other Czech dissidents get out of prison in the 1970s. The readers included Garrison Keillor, Marvin Hamlisch, Peter Ustinov, William Warfield, Martin Garbus, and Maurice Sendak. I was honored to be included among them. My mother loved showing her friends the Carnegie Hall program, with my name listed as a "performer." She would tell them a variation of the old joke: A man asks a musician carrying a violin case, "How do you get to Carnegie Hall?" My mother's answer: "Practice, practice, practice law, like my son."

The next time I saw Havel was in Jerusalem during the celebration of Israel's sixtieth birthday.[20] Havel, Sharansky, and I were on a panel together discussing human rights. When it was over, we got onto the same elevator with Mikhail Gorbachev. (It sounds like the beginning of a bad joke: "Havel, Sharansky, Gorbachev, and Dershowitz get into an elevator . . .") Gorbachev turned to me and said, "You're the big shot lawyer who tried to get these people out of prison. You did a good job, but I did a better job. I'm the one who got them out." We all laughed. Then Havel turned to Gorbachev and asked, "Why didn't you get us out sooner?" Gorbachev replied, "I'm not that good."

THE STRUGGLE AGAINST REAL APARTHEID

My interest in South Africa apartheid began while I was editor in chief of the *Yale Law Journal* in 1961. An article was submitted on the legal structure of the apartheid system.[21] At that time little was known about the legal aspects of this highly regulated practice, and this lengthy draft laid it out. It was my job to edit it so as to make it comprehensible to an American audience. It was shocking to me that only a few decades after the Nuremburg Laws in Nazi Germany, a "civilized" country, with a British and Dutch heritage, could construct a system of laws based on overt discrimination, under which a small white minority controlled a nation with a large black majority, and under which racial classifications determined who could vote, hold office, live in certain areas, be treated in good hospitals, attend public events, and enroll in schools. I was determined to help dismantle this system, and I actively joined in the campaign against it. But I was not willing to support the "blacklisting" of artists who had performed in

South Africa. To me, this constituted reverse McCarthyism, even if it was in the interest of a just cause.

As I wrote in a 1985 article:

> *"The Register of Entertainers" to be shunned is officially published by the United Nations [and lists] the names of entertainers and actors who have performed in South Africa since 1981. Anyone whose name appears on the list is prohibited from performing at any function sponsored by the United Nations. Other organizations also use the U.N. blacklist to screen politically unacceptable artists. . . .*
>
> *Among those . . . on the blacklist are Ray Charles, Linda Ronstadt, Frank Sinatra, the Beach Boys, Cher, Goldie Hawn, Sha Na Na, Ernest Borgnine, and the British rock group Queen.*
>
> *Among those volunteering to perform [at a concert for African famine relief] was the rock group Chicago. But Chicago was on the blacklist. And because of the absolute prohibition against using blacklisted artists at U.N.-sponsored events, plans for the concert had to be postponed. It is ironic that some black African children may die of hunger because of the U.N. blacklist.*[22]

VIGNETTE

Woody Allen on Blacklisting

I sent a copy of my article to Woody Allen, with whom I was then on friendly terms. He was a strong opponent of both apartheid and blacklisting.[23] He wrote back, saying that

> *on the face of it the issue certainly seems to me like blacklisting. I'm sure they make good arguments for it on the basis that a legitimate tactic of the United Nations is boycotting, but still I'm sure that if I examined it as closely as you have, I would find there would be no excuse for it. Thanks for keeping me informed. Best, Woody*

During the apartheid regime, I was invited to speak at the University of the Witwatersrand in Johannesburg. Many in that university had been on the forefront of opposing apartheid, and I was anxious to lend support to these efforts by delivering a strong human rights message. When I appeared at the South African consulate in Boston to receive my visa, the consul general had the *Yale Law Journal* article I had edited. He wanted to see a copy of my proposed speech. I refused, and my visa was denied. My first visit to South Africa came after the end of apartheid.

I had hoped to try to get to Robben Island to meet with the imprisoned Nelson Mandela. I was working with Professor Irwin Cotler, with whom I had taught human rights at Harvard Law School, on a complicated legal plan to free Mandela.

Our plan began following the arrest of an East German professor in Boston on charges of spying. I received a call from an East German lawyer asking if I could represent him. The East German lawyer—who was a well-known and trusted "spy swapper"—told me that he might be willing to arrange a "spy swap" for my client Anatoly Sharanksy. I told him that my client wasn't a spy, so a "spy swap" was off the table. He then proposed a possible "prisoner exchange, including prisoners who were accused of spying but were innocent."

I called Irwin Cotler, who was working on both the Sharansky and the Mandela case. He suggested that we inquire whether there were any South African spies in Soviet bloc prisons, and whether South Africa might be willing to release Mandela as part of a prisoner exchange.

In the end, Anatoly Sharansky was exchanged for an East German professor (who was represented by other lawyers), but we learned from the African National Congress lawyers that Mandela refused to participate in any prisoner exchange. He wanted to be released on his own terms, even though his decision would require him to remain imprisoned until his own terms were accepted by the South Africa government (which they finally were in 1990).

My negotiations with the East German lawyer were shrouded in secrecy and included elements right out of a John Le Carré novel. We used code words over the phone and met in out-of-the-way places at unusal times. He was a man of his word and could always be counted on to honor his commitments. After the fall of the Berlin Wall, he was indicted on an assortment of concocted charges, and he sought my help, which I was pleased to give. Eventually, he was cleared of all charges.

HUMAN RIGHTS IN ISRAEL

A human rights case that tested my commitment to universal rights involved an Israeli Arab who was accused by Israel of assisting terrorism. He was being held in administrative detention, instead of being formally charged with a crime. I was in Israel at the time writing a long article on administrative detention[24] (or as the United States government calls it, "preventive detention"). I was critical of the practice, though I understood why some Israelis believed it was necessary to combat terrorism. After meeting the Israeli Arab in the detention center and reviewing his case, I concluded that his detention was unjustified. I met with Israeli officials and urged them to reconsider his case. They did, and they released him. He moved to Lebanon, where he became an active member of the more moderate wing of the Palestine Liberation Organization. To my knowledge, he has never engaged in any acts of terrorism.

I helped several other Palestinian prisoners and detainees as well. I also wrote critically of and litigated against several Israeli policies, including the use of unacceptable interrogation methods, the overuse of wiretaps, religious discrimination against women, and de facto discrimination against Israeli Arabs. Since the early 1970s, I have been a vocal and persistent opponent of Israeli settlements in the West Bank and Gaza.[25] And after the war in Lebanon, I protested the overuse of cluster bombs that, though lawful, unduly endanger the lives of civilians.[26] I have never believed that my strong, general support of Israel is in any way inconsistent with my opposition to, and criticism of, specific Israeli policies that violate neutral principles of human rights.

VIGNETTE

Netanyahu's Question

Among the public figures I have counseled is Israel's prime minister Benjamin Netanyahu. I had met Bibi when he was an MIT student in Cambridge in the early 1970s. We got to know each other when he served in New York as Israel's representative to the United Nations. He has been to our home for dinner, and we have been at his. Over the years, he has sought my advice on legal and governmental matters, but not on Israeli domestic politics, which he knows I stay out of.

Shortly after he first became prime minister, he invited me to his office on a Friday afternoon. My wife, our daughter, and I stood outside of the King David Hotel trying to hail a cab, but all the cabdrivers were heading home for the weekend. It looked like we might be late for our appointment with the prime minister. Suddenly a car pulled up. It was the mayor of Jerusalem, Ehud Olmert, saying, "Alan, you'll never get a cab on a Friday afternoon. Where do you need to go?" I told him, and he agreed to drive us there. As I got into his car, a cab-driver pulled over, shouting, "I don't try to run Jerusalem, why are you trying to be a cabdriver? Stop taking business from me."

When I got to the prime minister's office, Bibi invited me to his secure private office. "There's been something I have been waiting to ask you," he said. I expected him to ask my advice on some critical security issue. He put his arm around me and whispered in my ear, "So, did O.J. do it?" I was taken aback, but I quickly responded, "So, Mr. Prime Minister, does Israel have nuclear weapons?" Bibi looked at me sternly and said, "You know I can't answer that question." I looked back at him and said, "Aha!" Bibi understood and we both laughed.

HUMAN RIGHTS IN CHINA

In 1979, Senator Edward Kennedy asked me to travel to China and report to him on the condition of human rights. The Cultural Revolution was just ending, and the first sparks of freedom were being ignited at a place in Beijing called "Democracy Wall," where dissidents gathered and posted anonymous notes. I was to be one of the first human rights advocates allowed into what had long been a closed society. Senator Kennedy, with whom I worked on numerous human rights issues, was the key to why I was invited, not only to visit prisoners and courtrooms, but also to lecture on criminal law in several of China's most important universities. Although I was invited to lecture exclusively on technical aspects of criminal law, in order to help China develop a modern penal code, I managed to smuggle some discussion of human rights into my lectures.

During my visit to several prisons, I learned about a practice that seemed unique to China. When the sentence of death was imposed for certain types of crimes, the condemned prisoner was sent to a particular institution to await execution. After about a year, half of the condemned would actually be executed, while the other half would be spared. All the condemned were competing against one another in a zero-sum game, in which the stakes were life and death. The "winners" were selected not only on the basis of good behavior—needless to say, everyone in this high-stakes game was on his best behavior—but also on their commitment to Maoism and their "worthiness" to live.

I've been to many prisons and on numerous death rows, but I've never experienced so grim a place as this "life-or-death row," where every inmate saw every other inmate as a competitor in the quest to remain alive.

The warden invited me to play basketball with the inmates. No one fouled me, trash-talked me, or in any way misbehaved, as the warden watched, notepad in hand. I was conscious that anything a player did or didn't do could become part of his score of death—or life. I tried hard to make everyone look good in the eyes of the warden.

When I returned to the United States, I tried to find out which inmates I'd met had been executed and which spared. I could learn nothing. I reported my findings to Senator Kennedy, and he made inquiries about the life-or-death-row prisons. He too hit a brick wall. The Chinese government has clamped down about its policies regarding the death penalty, especially in light of subsequent charges that they harvested organs from executed prisoners.

When I returned to China on a lecture tour many years later, I asked to revisit the life-or-death-row prison. My hosts denied the existence of any such institution and assured me that the organs of executed prisoners were not being harvested.

THE CHANGING CONSENSUS REGARDING HUMAN RIGHTS

By the mid-1970s, the consensus regarding human rights was beginning to change—at least for many on the extreme left. Although the Soviet Union had long used the language of "human rights" (as well as the language of "civil rights") as a club against Western democracies, few serious people gave this hypocritical ploy any credence when Soviet diplomats at the United Nations postured against the imperfections of the United States, even as their Communist masters locked up dissidents, made a mockery of justice,[27] and kept entire nations in subjugation behind an iron curtain.

But Soviet criticisms were beginning to be expropriated by the extreme left in the United States and Europe. Radical professors such as Professors Noam Chomsky of MIT and Richard Falk of Princeton claimed that the United States was the worst human rights violator in the world.[28] (Falk later joined with conspiracy nuts who blamed 9/11 and the Boston Marathon bombing on the United States and Israel.) Extreme left lawyers such as William Kunstler refused to say anything critical of the human rights records of the Soviet Union, China, Cuba, or other "socialist" countries, while railing against the human rights violations of the United States and its allies.

VIGNETTE

Abbie Hoffman on "Jew Lawyers"!

I was part of the legal team in the Chicago Seven case, which grew out of demonstrations during the Democratic National Convention of 1968. My client Abbie Hoffman, who was one of the defendants, had allegedly made some crude remarks about how his "Jew lawyers" cared more about Israel than America. When I called him out on his comments, he responded with an angry handwritten two-page letter that included the following:

> *I never made a remark about my "Jewish Lawyers." I might have spoken more positively about the PLO but I would never make an anti-Semitic juxtaposition such as you think you heard. If you read my current autobiography you will see I flaunt my "Jewishness" at every turn of the road.*

At the time Hoffman penned these words, the PLO was a terrorist organization that was hijacking airplanes, murdering civilians, and blowing up synagogues. Israel had not yet established any settlements in occupied areas.

Father Daniel Berrigan, a Catholic priest who had become the darling of the extreme left as the result of his anti–Vietnam War activities, began to call both the United States and Israel "criminal" entities.[29] Chomsky defended the ruthless Cambodian dictator Pol Pot against charges of genocide, insisting that Western media reports of millions of dead Cambodians were exaggerations falsely attributed to Communist regimes.[30] The National Lawyers Guild dismissed accusations against Communist regimes as "red baiting." They also became the legal arm of anti-Israel extremists, including terrorists. They did not support these clients on grounds of human rights principles, but rather because they *agreed* with their politics. By the late 1970s, I broke with the National Lawyers Guild, with which I had worked closely when it had been a neutral human rights organization. In a widely read article in *The American Lawyer*,[31] I told the sad story of the transformation of the National Lawyers Guild from a genuine human rights organization into an advocate for some of the worst human wrongs on the planet.

The National Lawyers Guild was established in 1937 as a counter to the American Bar Association, which was then fighting the New Deal, excluding black lawyers from membership, and opposing the labor movement. The original guild strongly supported Israel's struggle for independence. The guild accomplished much good on the domestic front and had an excellent record of providing legal assistance to the civil rights, labor, and antiwar movements. In the early 1970s, at the height of the antiwar movement, the guild began to be taken over by younger, more militant lawyers from the New Left.[32] Law students and other "legal workers" were admitted, strengthening the hold of the young radicals but reducing the percentage of actual lawyers in the guild to less than half.

In a highly publicized speech delivered on October 19, 1973[33] (just after Israel had barely survived a surprise military attack from Egypt and Syria) the Reverend Daniel Berrigan described Israel as "a criminal Jewish community" that had committed "crimes against humanity," had "created slaves," and had espoused a "racist ideology" reminiscent of the Nazis, aimed at proving its "racial superiority to the people it has crushed." Recall that this was *before* Israel allowed civilian settlements in the West Bank and Gaza Strip, and *before* the Israeli right began to win elections. It was an attack not against Israeli policies, but rather against the very concept of Israel as the nation-state for the Jewish people. Berrigan also chastised "the Jewish people" around the world for giving "their acquiescence or their support to the Nixon ethos" that had led to the death, maiming, and displacement of "some six million Southeast Asians." Berrigan referred to the iconic figure of six million as "one of those peculiar facts which we called free floating."[34] The truth was that "Jewish people" were among the leaders of the anti-war movement and voted disproportionately against President Nixon, but Berrigan ignored these facts in his anti-Semitic diatribe against "the Jewish people" and the Jewish nation.

Reaction to Berrigan's polemic was swift and sharp, especially among lawyers who had represented left-wing causes and individuals. Battle lines were quickly drawn. Some, like William Kunstler, supported Berrigan. Others—among them lawyers who had represented Berrigan and Kunstler—were appalled at Berrigan's anti-Jewish screed. Berrigan became the guru of the National Lawyers Guild, which soon agreed to commit "the resources of the organization to continuing and expanding our internal political education on the Palestinian question."[35] (They expressed no interest in the "Cuban Question," the "Tibet Question," or the "Soviet dissidents question.")

As part of this educational process, the guild sent a delegation to the Middle East, which was funded by the Palestine Liberation Organization. The grateful delegation showed its appreciation by beginning its fact-finding mission in PLO camps and, according to one member of the delegation, limiting its interviews almost exclusively to PLO-approved Palestinians and Israeli anti-Zionists. The resulting report contained few surprises: It caricatured Israel as a repressive totalitarian society. Nowhere in its 127 pages was there any discussion of the PLO terrorism that plagued the civilian population of Israel and the West Bank. Indeed, the single mention of terrorism in the report was a reference to "acts of terrorism" by Israeli authorities against the peaceful Arab occupants of the West Bank.

The resulting one-sided "report" became a litmus test: "Basically . . . you had a situation where a bunch of Third World types wanted to ensure that the Jews in the guild—and the Jews were almost certainly a majority—would be forced to eat crow, to choose sides."[36]

I decided to devise a litmus test of my own to challenge the bona fides of the guild's claim that it was still a neutral human rights organization. I requested that the guild send an observer to the Soviet trial of Anatoly Sharansky. The national vice president of the guild told me that he doubted the guild would be willing to send an observer to a Soviet trial, since the "reality" of the situation is that a considerable number of the guild members approved of the Soviet Union and would not want to criticize a Soviet judicial proceeding:

> *The problem is that we do not approach matters such as this purely from a human-rights perspective. We regard it as well from the standpoint of the importance of focusing attention on human-rights violations in a particular country. With respect to the U.S.S.R., we have not had discussion or come to any decision about the appropriateness of focusing on human-rights issues there.*

In my article I put the choice to the guild:

> *If the guild decides to continue its foray into international politics, it will have to make a choice: either to perpetuate its double standard on human*

> *rights, which will surely alienate much of its support here at home for its domestic programs; or to report honestly on human rights throughout the world, which will surely alienate the PLO and the Soviet Union.*[37]

The guild decided to abandon any pretense of reporting neutrally on human rights. And as a result, it lost all its credibility as a human rights organization.

Nor was the guild alone. Other organizations that were founded on the principles of neutral human rights, such as Human Rights Watch,[38] the Carter Center, and Amnesty International,[39] were hijacked by radical ideologues who focused disproportionate attention on imperfect democracies at the expense of victims of far more serious human rights abuses by tyrannical regimes.

In my view, the worst offender in this inversion of "human rights" and "human wrongs" has been the UN. When my mentor Arthur Goldberg was appointed as United States ambassador to the UN in 1965, he asked me to help him in an informal capacity as an advisor on human rights and matters of international law.

I worked closely with him on a number of such issues, meeting with him regularly in New York. In 1967, following Israel's victory in the Six Day War, Goldberg asked me to consult with him on the drafting of Security Council Resolution 242, which sought to provide a framework for peace in that troubled part of the world. The resolution, which was carefully crafted in diplomatic language, called for Israel to return "territories" (not *all* territories or even *the* territories captured in the defensive war) in exchange for recognition by the Arab state and secure borders.[40] This formulation was intended to allow Israel to make border adjustments it deemed necessary to its security.[41] Israel accepted 242, but the Arab nations held a conference in Khartoum, where they issued their three infamous "no's." "No peace. No negotiation. No recognition."[42] Israel's UN representative, Abba Eban, quipped that "[this was] the first war in history that on the morrow the victors sued for peace and the vanquished called for unconditional surrender."[43]

From that point on, the UN (most particularly the General Assembly, the Human Rights Council, UNESCO, and several other agencies) began its downhill spiral away from neutrality and toward becoming an organization focused almost exclusively on the imperfections of democracies such as the United States and Israel, while ignoring genocides and repressions by nondemocratic nations.

While Pol Pot was murdering millions, the UN did nothing. Its major bodies refused even to condemn the genocide until after the killing was over and millions lay dead. The General Assembly did not mention Cambodia in a single resolution until November 1979—nearly a year after the genocide's end.[44] Even then the resolution was framed in terms of sovereignty and did not mention specific human rights violations, let alone genocide.[45]

Just a few months after the Cambodian atrocities began, the General Assembly adopted the most infamous resolution in its history, resolution 3379, declaring that "Zionism is a form of racism and racial discrimination."[46] Seventy-two countries voted in favor, including, ironically, Cambodia. Thirty-five voted against and thirty-two abstained. This and other similar actions by the General Assembly led Abba Eban to proclaim that if Algeria offered a resolution than the earth was flat and Israel flattened it, it would pass 164 to 13, with 26 abstentions.[47] The United States representative to the United Nations, Daniel Patrick Moynihan, fumed, saying that "the United States rises to declare before the General Assembly of the United Nations and before the world that it does not acknowledge, it will not abide by, it will never acquiesce in this infamous act."[48]

The result of this resolution was that "Zionists" were blacklisted and banned from speaking at several colleges and universities that had "anti-racist" speaking policies. In a world where genocide, slavery, disappearances, torture, systematic rape, murder of dissidents, and other grave violations of human rights were being routinely perpetrated by its member nations, Zionism and Israel became the number one enemy of the UN, with more resolutions condemning Israel than all the other member nations combined.

The Zionism-racism resolution was ultimately rescinded in 1991 by a vote of the General Assembly,[49] but it continued to animate UN actions, especially by the "Human Rights Council" of the UN (previously known as the UN Commission on Human Rights). In 2001, the council convened the first of several "Durban Conferences" against "racism, racial discrimination, xenophobia and related intolerance."[50] Its primary focus was on Israel. It ignored racial genocides, slavery, and other obvious manifestations of racism and discrimination. The final preparatory session was held in Tehran. Israeli and Jewish NGOs were excluded.

According to Irwin Cotler, who attended the Durban Conference, the air was filled with hate speech, such as "too bad the Holocaust was not completed." The conference became a "festival of hate such that we had not experienced anywhere at any time before." To Cotler, it was "the most dangerous form of anti-Semitism that we are witnessing in the 21st Century."[51] And all of this was done under the aegis of the UN.[52]

The late congressman Tom Lantos, from California, observed:

> *Whenever the word "Holocaust" was read during the plenary review of the combined text, one of the Islamic delegates—usually Egypt—intervened to change "Holocaust" to "holocausts." Adding insult to injury, the same delegates requested that the phrase "and the ethnic cleansing of the Arab population in historic Palestine" be inserted after the appearance of "holocausts."*[53]

A second "Durban Conference" was held in Geneva in 2009. Although the United States, Canada, Italy, and several other countries boycotted what it had become clear by this time would be another hate conference, I decided to travel to Geneva in an effort to restore the human rights agenda to its proper priorities, or if that wasn't possible, to expose the UN Human Rights Council for what it had become—an enemy of neutral and universal human rights. It would be an uphill fight because the primary speaker invited to address the second Durban Conference was Mahmoud Ahmadinejad, the Holocaust-denying president of Iran.

I worked with several genuine human rights organizations in an effort to shame the Human Rights Council into broadening its agenda to include the genocides in Africa and other serious human rights abuses around the globe. We brought real victims of human rights abuses from Rwanda, Darfur, and other locations where genocides had been ignored by the UN. We conducted a parallel human rights conference in which we took testimony from these victims and witnesses, to whom the UN had refused to listen. I also delivered an address on the inversion of "human rights" and "human wrongs."

I was staying in the same hotel as Ahmadinejad. My wife and I were having a drink in the lobby bar when Ahmadinejad and his entourage paraded through the lobby. He looked at us and smiled. I approached one of his handlers, introduced myself, and told him that I challenged the president to a debate about the Holocaust. His handler asked, "Where, at Harvard?" Ahmadinejad had previously spoken at Columbia University, and I suspected that he might have welcomed an invitation from Harvard. I replied, "No, the debate should be at Auschwitz; that's where the evidence is." He said he would communicate my offer to the president, who, he told me, was on the way to a press conference. I went and tried to ask Ahmadinejad directly whether he would debate me at Auschwitz. I was immediately hauled off by the Swiss police, removed from the hotel, and told I would not be allowed to return "for security reasons." I insisted that "security reasons" did not justify protecting the president from a hostile question. They told me that my belongings would be removed from my room and my key changed. I immediately called someone I knew in the Obama administration, who phoned the U.S. consulate in Geneva, and I was allowed back into the hotel with an apology. The photograph of me being forcibly removed from the hotel was flashed around the world, with the following caption:

> *Harvard Law professor Alan Dershowitz is led away after declaring he planned to challenge Iranian President Mahmoud Ahmadinejad about his views on the Holocaust and Israel minutes before the meeting between Swiss President Hans-Rudolf Merz and the Iranian president in Geneva, Switzerland, on April 19, 2009.*[54]

The next day, Ahmadinejad was scheduled to give his address. We were not allowed into the chamber but were told to go to a special room where we could watch and listen to his talk. We assembled and watched as Ahmadinejad was greeted with applause by many of the delegates. When he began to speak, we discovered that his words, delivered in Farsi, were not being translated to our room, but only to the assembly chamber. So I led a march into the chamber. Several delegations were absent, and we took their seats. As soon as Ahmadinejad denied the Holocaust, which he did near the beginning of his speech, I stood up and shouted "Shame!" and walked out, passing directly in front of his lectern. Many others walked out as well, including several European delegations. Ahmadinejad's talk was a fiasco, and was so reported by the media. He had made a fool of himself—with our help.

The following year, the Durban Conference on human rights was convened in New York. Once again, we convened parallel conferences. In my address, I made the following point:

> *One important reason why there is no peace in the Middle East can be summarized tragically in two letters, UN. That building dedicated in theory to peace has facilitated terrorism, stood idly by genocide, given a platform to Holocaust deniers, and disincentivized the Palestinians from negotiating a reasonable two-state solution. . . .*
>
> *How dare states such as Saudi Arabia, Cuba, Venezuela, Zimbabwe, Iran, Bahrain, Syria, Belarus, and other tyrannies too numerous to mention . . .*

> *lecture Israel about human rights? How dare states such as Turkey, that have attacked their own Kurdish minorities and Armenian minorities, and Russia, which has attacked its own Chechnyan minority . . . lecture Israel about peace?*
>
> *Is there no sense of shame . . . ? Has the word "hypocrisy" lost all meaning . . . ? Does no one recognize the need for a single, neutral standard of human rights? Have human rights now become the permanent weapon of choice for those who practice human wrongs? For shame. For shame.*[55]

THE WORST FIRST

If an organization—governmental or nongovernmental—is to remain true to a genuine commitment to universal and neutral human rights, it must prioritize the use of its resources. "The worst first" must be its governing criteria. The "worst" has two major components.

First and foremost is the nature and scope of the human wrongs: genocide, mass murder, widespread torture and mutilation of dissidents, rape as a policy, slavery, genuine apartheid, pervasive sexism,[56] and other comparable abuses. Second is the inability of victims to secure relief from their own judiciary, from human rights groups, from the media, and from other domestic sources. Failure to prioritize is a sure sign of bias and lack of neutrality. Today's UN and most "human rights" NGOs fail this test.[57]

My defense of Western democracies, and most particularly Israel, against deliberately exaggerated charges regarding human rights led to an offer that presented me with an existential challenge to my dual identity as an American and a Jew. In 2010, the prime minister of Israel, Benjamin Netanyahu, urged me to accept the position of Israel's ambassador to the UN. He told me that in order to serve in that capacity, I would have to become an Israeli citizen, though I could also retain my American citizenship. I realized immediately that I could not accept the offer, despite the reality that I would have enjoyed the job immensely. The idea of standing up against the hypocrisy and double standard of the UN appealed to me. But I am an American, not an Israeli. For me to switch sides—even to a nation that is so close an ally to my own nation—would raise the specter of dual loyalty that has been directed at Jews since biblical times, when they lived as minorities in the lands of Egypt and Persia.[58]

After much discussion, I persuaded Netanyahu that if I accepted the position, it might be good for me, but it would not be good for American

Jews or for Israel. So I declined, after promising the prime minister that I would be available, as an international lawyer and an American, to help defend Israel against unjust charges brought by international bodies such as the International Criminal Court, the International Court of Justice, and various UN agencies. But because I am a private citizen, I can also continue to criticize Israel's human rights record when criticism based on a single universal standard is warranted by its actions.

THE SECOND SIX MILLION

The sad reality is that the inversion of the human rights agenda, especially at the UN, has needlessly cost many innocent lives. Since the time the world promised "never again" at the end of World War II and built a structure and jurisprudence designed to fulfill that important promise, another six million innocent victims of preventable genocides have been slaughtered while the world once again stood silent.

Cambodia, Rwanda, and Darfur are just the beginning of the story. The UN has also failed to help desperate civilians in Burundi, the former Yugoslavia, Syria, and other countries. While ignoring the gruesome killings by the member states in its midst, the United Nations has focused its time and attention on a single country—Israel. Its constituent bodies—especially the General Assembly and the Human Rights Council—have condemned Israel more frequently and more harshly than all the other nations of the world combined.

The UN's obsession with Israel is not necessarily the only cause of its inaction on genocide, but it is certainly a contributing factor. Like all institutions, the United Nations has limited resources. When it dedicates so many of those resources to criticizing Israel, it decreases its ability to respond effectively to genocide. It is important to realize that the sheer amount of time the UN spends chastising Israel in one-sided and repetitive resolutions is also time *not* spent on preventing or at least condemning genocide.[59]

What might have been if, *during* the Cambodian genocide, the General Assembly had passed a single resolution on the atrocities instead of wasting time debating whether Zionism was racism? How would the situation in Darfur have changed if during its 2006–2007 sessions, the General Assembly had once condemned the genocide in Sudan instead of passing nearly two dozen resolutions condemning Israel?

One might dismiss the UN's obsession with Israel, if the body's failure to stop suffering was not so serious. The UN could have intervened more quickly and vigorously and saved millions of lives during ongoing genocides. It is a broken institution. Until it ends its obsession with Israel, the UN cannot be fixed. Even some of its top officials recognize this reality, but their hands are tied, because anti-Israel (and anti-American) countries constitute a majority of the UN membership, thus giving anti-Israel resolutions an automatic majority.

The UN will remain a key facilitator—through its actions and inactions—of the tragic inversion of human rights that has characterized its work over the past forty years.

The real victims of this inversion have not been Israel and other Western democracies that have been the specific focus of the UN condemnations. The real victims have been those willfully ignored by the UN, which has used its focus on Israel and other democracies as an excuse—a cover—for its malignant inaction against horrible human wrongs committed by the tyrannical regimes that control much of the UN agenda and give themselves exculpatory immunity from any UN condemnations or intervention. "Never again" has been turned into "Again and again and again." The label of "human rights" has been used to promote human wrongs. Our heroes—Eleanor Roosevelt, René Cassin, Albert Schweitzer—should be turning over in their graves, as the shields they constructed to protect the helpless from oppression and genocide have been beaten into swords to be used to facilitate these human wrongs.

Tragically, many, if not most, organizations that currently claim the mantle of "human rights" are part of the problem, not part of the solution. I refuse to allow these human rights pretenders to hijack and invert the honorable agenda of neutral and universal human rights. I will keep struggling until my dying day to return human rights to its proper place in the international community.

CONCLUSION

Closing Argument

As I begin my second half century of law practice and teaching, I look back with nostalgia and a heavy dose of surprise at my life and career, even as I look forward to my remaining years. I try to prepare my students to be lawyers over their entire careers. And since the career of a lawyer now extends to a full half century, I must always think ahead to what our legal system will look like when my current students end their careers, around the year 2065, when they will reach the age I am at now. Some of my former students are now in the prime of their careers, and have many more productive years ahead. One example is Elena Kagan, who may still be serving as a justice of the Supreme Court close to the middle of the twenty-first century.

I could not have asked for better from my first half century. I have accomplished far more than I could ever have anticipated, and I have had a more interesting life than I could ever have imagined, growing up as I did in an insular working-class neighborhood of Brooklyn. Like many children and grandchildren of hardworking immigrants, I have lived the American dream and experienced the passion of my times. I've been very lucky, at least so far. (I don't want to give myself a *kneina hura*.)[1] Like the fictional Zelig in Woody Allen's great film of that name,[2] I was privileged to have been present at many of the most important legal and political events that transpired during my adult life. For some I volunteered, for others I was solicited. Sometimes I was a direct participant, other times an active observer and reporter. I will try to summarize my role in the important legal and political developments in which I participated, and speculate about what the future may hold for our system of laws and justice.

Oliver Wendell Holmes, Jr., viewed the role of the lawyer as a predictor of future legal decisions and trends.[3] But the Talmud cautioned that prophecy ended with the destruction of the second temple and that he who tries to prophesy the future is either a fool or a knave.[4] Or as a contemporary sage, Yogi Berra, put it: "Prediction is very hard, especially about the future."[5] I agree that prognosticating the future is a daunting challenge, but lawyers and law professors must confront it, because one of the most important jobs we have is to identify trends and to anticipate significant developments. I will try, therefore, with these cautions in mind, to extrapolate from the past what a lawyer writing fifty years from now might look back on.

MY CURRENT LIFE

Before I summarize my past and speculate about the future, let me say a word about my present life. I remain extremely active in every phase of my career. Here is a summary of the week during which I first wrote these words:

On Sunday morning I was picked up by a limo and taken to the Bedford airport, where I boarded a private 747 jet owned by Sheldon Adelson, reputed to be one of the richest Jews in history and among the handful of wealthiest Americans. Although we could not be further apart politically—he is a conservative Republican who contributed tens of millions of dollars to the campaigns of Newt Gingrich and Mitt Ronney, while I am a liberal Democrat who campaigned for Barack Obama—we share a common interest regarding many Jewish matters, especially education. The son of a Boston cabdriver, Adelson has accumulated billions of dollars by building and running casinos in Las Vegas, Macao, and Singapore and has contributed much of his wealth to worthy charities. His jet, which was once owned by the sultan of Brunei, is a flying mansion, equipped with a bedroom, sitting rooms, a chef, and other appurtenances of wealth and glamour. I spent much of the trip conferring with Sheldon and his wife, Dr. Miriam Adelson, who is an expert in addiction and the psychological problems associated with drug dependency. As we were about to land, I was invited into the cockpit, where I saw the Hoover Dam and other sights on the approach to Las Vegas. Upon arriving I was taken to the Dr. Miriam and Sheldon G. Adelson Educational Campus and shown around. Then I was picked up by Larry Ruvo, who wanted me to see the brain institute that architect Frank Gehry had built in his father's memory. Ruvo credits me with helping to get this project done, after the local university ran out of money and broke its agreement with him. I wrote a strong letter on his behalf, and the result was an arrangement with the Cleveland Clinic, one of the great medical institutions in the world. After touring the facility, I went to the Venetian Hotel, where I spoke on behalf of the Adelson Day School and was honored with a beautiful plaque made from Jerusalem stone. The students of the school presented me with a book of drawings that they had done in my honor, representing their views of justice. (Later that week, I passed the book around to the college students in my seminar on morality.) At 10 P.M., I was taken to the airport, where a smaller jet—a Gulfstream—was waiting to fly me back to New York, where I arrived at 5:30 A.M.

Following a few hours of sleep in my New York apartment, I was picked up by a paralegal and driven to the women's jail on Rikers Island, where I spent the morning conferring with my client Gigi Jordan, who is accused of murder. She killed her autistic son and tried to kill herself after learning that her child had been repeatedly abused, both sexually and physically, by his biological father, and after unsuccessfully seeking help from numerous government and social service agencies.

After returning from Rikers Island, I was driven to Brooklyn College, where my legal and personal papers—more than a million of them in sixteen hundred boxes—were being opened for public viewing. I am contributing all of my papers to my alma mater. I made a talk about the papers and my experiences at Brooklyn College to a crowd that included my wife and sons, old friends, classmates, current and former faculty members, and current students. It was a thrilling experience for me to go back more than half a century to the college that meant so much to me and to express my appreciation to people who so influenced my life.

On Tuesday I appeared in New York State Supreme Court on behalf of my client Gigi Jordan and made arguments in preparation for her trial. Following that court appearance, I boarded the Acela train and went home for a good long night's sleep.

On Wednesday morning I met with the chief prosecutor of the International Criminal Court, Luis Moreno Ocampo, for breakfast. He had invited me to discuss with him the then-pending application of the Palestinian Authority to be recognized as a state by the International Criminal Court, in order to bring charges against Israel for the war in Gaza and for building settlements in the West Bank. We had a long and fruitful discussion.

I then went back to the law school, where I prepared for my first class of the day—a Legal Ethics course from 1 to 3 P.M. Before class I had a short lunch in the faculty dining room, where I sat with an old friend, Michael Boudin, who is a judge on the U.S. Court of Appeals for the First Circuit and an adjunct member of our faculty. The first half of the Legal Ethics class was devoted to discussing the difficult problem of what a lawyer should do when a client gives him physical evidence the possession of which itself might be a crime. Such evidence might include videos of child pornography, stolen goods, or other contraband. We considered a case where a legal aid lawyer had been told where his client buried the body of a college student he had murdered, and the murder was not known to her parents or to the police. We also discussed the Joe Paterno case, which was then in the news and which raised questions regarding obligations to report serious misconduct.[6] During the second hour, Prosecutor Ocampo made a brief appearance in the classroom to discuss ethical problems faced by international prosecutors. The class ended with a discussion about the scope of confidentiality and what a lawyer should do if his client claims innocence and would like to testify as to his innocence, but the lawyer firmly believes that he is guilty.

Following that class I spent an hour preparing for my next seminar, which was for a class of freshmen at Harvard College. The subject was "Where Does Your Morality Come From?" and we discussed the moral limits on spying and other forms of subterfuge directed against enemy countries.

Straight from class I went to the Huntington Theater, where I had been asked to comment on a play about the capture of Adolf Eichmann.[7] I spent about an hour on the stage speaking and responding to questions from the director and the audience about the legal issues growing out of the capture and trial by Israel.

Thursday was essentially my day of rest. I spent the day writing several short articles and doing research and writing on several pending projects, including this book. Thursday night was my only night of the week at home with my wife, and we spent it watching a silly but entertaining movie called *Crazy, Stupid, Love.*[8]

Friday began with my annual checkup at my doctor's office, followed by lunch with Peter Norton, developer of the Norton antivirus software. I met him and his wife, Gwen, for lunch at the Harvest, where we discussed, among other things, the use of computer viruses against the Iranian nuclear threat. After lunch, I received an e-mail from a lawyer representing Seif Qaddafi, who had just been apprehended by the Libyans. He wanted me to represent Qaddafi in the International Criminal Court and to negotiate for him to be tried in The Hague rather than in Tripoli. I asked for more information before making a decision. I spent the rest of the afternoon working on writing projects and then went back to the law school at 6:30 P.M. for a Shabbos dinner sponsored by Chabad and the Jewish Law Students Association. I am faculty advisor to both of those organizations, and I gave a brief talk at the beginning of the dinner. My wife and I then attended a concert at Sanders Theater.

The next morning, I flew to Washington, D.C., to be a keynote speaker at an event sponsored by Iranian dissidents. The other speakers included former secretary of homeland security Tom Ridge, former chairman of the Democratic National Committee Howard Dean, former congressman Patrick Kennedy, and several other former and current government officials. I then took the train back to New York, where I was hoping to attend the Metropolitan Opera. But I was too tired, and I went back to my apartment and ended the week by falling asleep at about 10 P.M. My wife was proud of me for acknowledging my limitations, saying that five years earlier, I never would have been willing to miss anything because of being tired. A friend, who is a psychoanalyst, has labeled my affliction "FOMS"—"fear of missing something." I plead guilty to that diagnosis.

Nor was this event-filled week unusual. Two weeks later, my wife and I were off to Israel, where I received the Begin Prize for my "contributions to the Jewish people" and gave several lectures in Jerusalem and Tel Aviv. During my visit to Israel, I flew to Paris for a talk and to The Hague on a human rights matter. Then I went back to Israel for a conference and meetings with the prime minister and other government officials. I spoke at an economic conference, and was followed by Netanyahu, who began his speech with the following words: "First off, I would like to congratulate the Globes Conference for its foresight in inviting Alan Dershowitz, and I would like to say to Alan: Israel has no greater champion and the truth has no greater defender than Alan Dershowitz." Shortly after those words were broadcast on Israeli television, President Obama called me on my cell phone, and we had a substantive discussion regarding Iran's efforts to develop nuclear weapons. He invited me to continue our discussion at the White House, which I did several weeks later.

Following my visit to Israel, my granddaughter joined us in Vienna for a few days of opera and strudel, followed by a visit to Prague as guests of the U.S. ambassador, a speech at a Czech university, a tearful visit to the church in which the body of Václav Havel, who had just died, was lying in state, and the lighting of Chanukah candles at the U.S. embassy.

I don't know how long I will be able to keep up this pace. I am now teaching only in the fall semester at Harvard Law School, though I generally squeeze four or five separate courses into that one semester. During the semester in which I am writing these words, I am teaching a large course, Professional Responsibility: Tactics and Ethics in Criminal Cases; a seminar with Dr. Alan Stone on "Justice and Morality in the Tragedies of Shakespeare"; a seminar with Larry Lucchino on "The Law of Baseball"; a freshman seminar at Harvard College on "Where Does Your Morality Come From?"; and a reading group on "Writing for the General Public About Legal Issues." At the end of the fall semester in December, we move to South Beach, where I write, lecture, and consult on cases. I am trying to accept fewer commitments, but I find it hard to say no to interesting offers (FOMS?). I also cannot remain passive in the face of injustice and bigotry, which appear to be on the increase. I still love a tough challenge and welcome a good fight. I hate to lose and I never give up.

If past is prologue,[9] my approach to life—living the passion of the times—will not change. But nature has its claim, and physical energy inevitably abates and requires choices and priorities. My priorities will continue to be determined by the seriousness of the wrongs that need to be challenged by rights.

Since the theme of this book is change—change in the freedom of expression, change in the way homicides and rapes are prosecuted and defended, change in the nature of media coverage of high-profile cases, change in attitudes toward race, change in the relationship between religion and government, change in the uses and misuses of "human rights," and change in the way law is taught and learned—it is appropriate to end with changes I have experienced in my own personal and professional life over the years and changes I expect to experience in the years to come.

MY EVER-CHANGING LIFE

The questions I am most often asked by others—and sometimes by myself—are about significant changes in my life and *why* they occurred. Going back to my teen years, why did I change, within a few short months, from a C and D student in high school to an A+ student in college and law school? The change was dramatic and sudden—literally over the summer of 1955, between high school and college, between the ages of sixteen and a half and seventeen. What happened in those few months to change me from being last, or close to last, in a class of 50, to being at the top of a highly competitive college class of 2,000, and then first in a class of 170 even more competitive students at Yale Law School? Was it me who changed, or was it the schools?

It was both. I think I had begun to change during my last year in high school, but my reputation among the faculty was so firmly established and so negative that teachers simply couldn't see past it. Even when I got A grades on the statewide Regents exams, the teachers gave me Cs and Ds as semester grades. My occasionally intelligent classroom comments were taken as "wiseass" remarks. Some of my teachers even thought I must have cheated whenever I got a good grade on a test. So I doubt it was possible for me ever to shine in a high school where my favorite teacher insisted that I was "a 75 student" and would always be "a 75 student." (I didn't quite live up to his expectations, graduating with an average below 75.)

Moreover, my high school was a yeshiva—a "parochial school"—and I am not a parochial person. I did not respect most of my teachers, and the feeling was obviously mutual. Creativity was frowned upon. Rote memorization was rewarded. And "respect" for "authority" was not only demanded, it was actually graded—I got a U, for unsatisfactory. Had I attended Yeshiva University, as my mother had hoped, my high school reputation might have followed me. Moreover, although Yeshiva University was considerably less parochial than its high school, it was still a religious institution, with limits on completely free inquiry. When I got to Brooklyn College, I found a place where creativity was rewarded, rote memorization frowned upon, and respect was something to be earned, not merely accorded by the title of rabbi. The same kind of creative and challenging answers that got me Cs and Ds in Yeshiva earned me As in college and law school.

But there was more at work than a change of schools. I changed over that summer as well. I went as an assistant counselor to a new summer camp, Maple Lake, where I excelled and received praise for my creativity as a songwriter for "color war" and for my leadership skills. I had always been a leader, even during my darkest days in high school, but the school rejected my leadership, fearful that other students would follow me in my heretical ways. I always had an abundance of energy, but it was—in the views of my high school teachers—misdirected.

That summer at Camp Maple Lake, I received confirmation of my talents, and the result was heightened self-confidence.

I also met a young woman and began my first serious romantic relationship, which culminated four years later in my first marriage. Suddenly, I was "talented," "attractive," and "accepted." It was a great send-off to college.

I also had a bit of a chip on my shoulder and an "I'll show them" attitude toward my high school teachers, who told me I'd never amount to anything, and my principal, who persuaded Yeshiva College not to admit me. I was motivated and raring to go.

In college, although I succeeded beyond my wildest imagination, I also had deep-seated doubts about whether I was really as good as my grades. I had recurrent nightmares about failing exams and being exposed as a "phony." I also wondered whether Brooklyn College was easier than Yeshiva, because half the day was not devoted to religious studies. But I didn't let these doubts get in the way of my success. I loved Brooklyn College, and Brooklyn College loved—and still loves—me.[10] (Yeshiva *now* loves me as well, bestowing on me an "Alumni of the Year" award and an honorary doctorate, reflecting some selective amnesia about our past unhappy relationship.)

Moving from my teens to my twenties, I find that another question about change arises: Why did I change—again dramatically and precipitously—from a strictly observant Jew into a mostly nonobservant secular Jew? Within a brief period of time, I transformed myself from an Orthodox Jew who put on tefillin and davened every day and *never ate* anything—even a Nabisco cookie—that didn't have the magical U, into a secular Jew who went to synagogue only a dozen or so times a year and who did not keep kosher (except in my home, so my parents could eat there).

These changes occurred in my middle to late twenties and did not reflect any theological epiphany, but rather a rational decision to become my own person, rather than a follower of my parents' lifestyle. It would have been easy for me to remain observant. By the time I was making the decision, my career was well established. I had been hired by Harvard as an observant Jew, and I could have remained observant with no adverse consequences (other than some silly questions from the dean). Indeed, from a career perspective, there would have been a distinct advantage in remaining part of the Orthodox community. I would have been among the most successful Orthodox lawyers and professors in the world. Having given up Orthodoxy, I was just one among the thousands of highly successful Jewish lawyers and professors.

I often think about what my life, and that of my family, would have been like had I remained a member of "the club" of Modern Orthodox Jews. The "road not taken" often appears less bumpy than the road actually traveled. But I have no regrets.

Many of my friends who have remained Orthodox do not understand my decision. They, like me, are skeptics and agnostics, but that has not stopped them from remaining observant. As one old friend put it: "The older I get, the less I believe, but the more I observe." They love the community of Orthodox observers and want to remain part of it. That requires complying with a set of rules, not believing a set of beliefs. Since I am very rule-abiding in my secular and professional life, following the religious rules would have been easy for me, but I chose the road less traveled, at least in comparison to the friends with whom I grew up. And that has made all the difference, both for me and for my children—for better or worse. I simply did not want to impose my *parents'* rules on my *children*. My parents imposed their rules on me and my brother, and I wanted my children to be free to choose a lifestyle for themselves. Of course no one is entirely free from parental influences, and choice is always a matter of degree.

In my thirties, I made another significant choice. Having spent my first five or six years at Harvard as a pure scholar, writing dozens of law review articles, two casebooks, and hundreds of academic lectures, I was becoming restless. I wanted more action. "I *think*, therefore I am"[11] (even if Descartes got the order right) was not enough. I wanted to *do*. "I do, therefore I am" is more consistent with my personality and energy level. But I also loved teaching. I didn't want to stop being a professor.

I also have always hated to choose among good things. My choice has always been to do everything—not to miss anything. ("FOMS" again! I am terminal!) My wife always reminds me of the wonderful Yiddish expression "With one *tuchis* [rear end] you cannot dance at two weddings." Maybe not, but there's no harm in trying. And why only two, if there are three? (My son Elon, a filmmaker, recently made a clever, short cartoon video showing me breaking the Martha's Vineyard record by attending five parties in one night!)

And so, consistent with my lifelong aversion to choosing, I chose not to choose. I decided to remain a professor while also arguing cases and becoming deeply involved in causes.

Once having dipped my toe in the water of practice, I wouldn't stop. I loved the challenge of the courtroom and took to it quite naturally. I've never looked back. Practice has made me a better teacher, and teaching has made me a better practitioner.

In my forties, I made another career change. I stopped writing law review articles and started to write books about law for a general audience. My first book, written in my early forties, was *The Best Defense*,[12] which became a national bestseller and is still in print. It has been followed by twenty-eight additional books, six of which became bestsellers. My books have been translated into more than a dozen languages, and well over a million of them have been sold throughout the world. One of them, *Chutzpah*, was the number one bestseller on the *New York Times* and other lists. My career as a popular writer of nonfiction and fiction has been gratifying, especially when readers tell me that my books have influenced their thinking and their lives. I think of my book writing as part of my job as a teacher, both of my Harvard law students and of my readers.

In my forties, I also became a regular presence on national television, explaining the law and advocating civil liberties positions. I appeared frequently with Ted Koppel, Larry King, Barbara Walters, and on other widely watched shows. As a result, I became something of a public figure, for better or worse. I also met my second wife, Carolyn Cohen, and began to live a more stable and rewarding home life.

In my fifties, my life changed again. Because of my success as a lawyer, my media visibility, and my books, I began to attract world famous people as clients. The nature of my practice changed considerably, and although I still took half of my cases without fee, the fees for my paying cases went up dramatically, and for the first time in my life I was relatively wealthy. My wife and I—by this time we had our daughter, Ella—bought a beautiful home in Cambridge and a vacation home on Martha's Vineyard. We began to collect art and to open our home to students and charity events. Shortly thereafter, my son Jamin married my daughter-in-law Barbara and had two children, Lori and Lyle, making me a relatively young grandfather.

Clients, including several billionaires, were flocking to me, and I had my choice of cases. I tried to strike a balance among the ones I took, but the media focused only on my rich and famous clients. Suddenly I was a celebrity lawyer. I hated that designation, and it didn't accurately reflect my day-to-day work, but it stuck, and my obituary will probably use the term, no matter when it is published.

VIGNETTE

Shooting Foul Shots at Boston Garden and Throwing the First Pitch at Fenway

Some of my most gratifying performances occurred *on*, rather than *in*, court. I was a varsity basketball player but never started in high school. I even played for two minutes in Madison Square Garden. So when the great sports lawyer Bob Wolfe challenged me to a foul-shooting contest at halftime at a Boston Celtics basketball game in the old Boston Garden, I couldn't refuse, even though he had been a starting guard on a very good Boston College team. It was for charity, and I had always been a good foul shooter.

My sons helped prepare me for the shootout. Jamin kept warning me that it doesn't matter if you win or lose, as long as "you don't shoot an air ball on your first shot, because everyone will laugh at you." I practiced shooting off the backboard to avoid the humiliation of an air ball.

We were allowed to practice a couple of hours before the game. We were each assigned a "coach." Bob got Larry Bird, because he was Bird's agent. I got Kevin McHale, a really nice guy.

The Garden was packed for an important, nationally televised Sunday afternoon game, and I was more nervous than I ever get in court.

Sure enough, my first shot was an air ball. Sure enough, everyone laughed at me.

Bob's first shot was a swish. All net. My sons were sure I would be humiliated.

But I thrive on challenge. So I got down to business, and hit thirteen of the next nineteen shots (we each had twenty shots in two minutes). Bob hit only six. I was cheered and given a check for my favorite charity.

A few weeks later, we invited Bob and his wife to our Seder. Before we began, he said he wanted to show a short video of our shootout. OK! He had doctored the video to show twenty swishes by him and twenty air balls by me. He said he had made it for his grandchildren!

Years later, my son Elon arranged for me to throw the first ball at Fenway Park to celebrate my seventieth birthday. Again, I trained. Again, I was nervous. This time there would be no second chance.

Only one pitch. My friend David Ginsberg, who owns a small share of the Red Sox, gave me some advice: "You're not used to throwing from a mound, so it is natural that your pitch will bounce in front of the plate. You have to compensate. Throw high."

I followed his advice, and threw a strike to Kevin Youkalis. I have an undoctored photo to prove it.

My birthday was complete when the Bleacher Bar, located under the centerfield stands, named a New York pastrami sandwich "the Dersh" in my honor. I get a big kick out of quietly ordering "the Dersh" whenever I go there before a game.

My next career change took place in my sixties, when I began to devote considerable time and energy to the defense of Israel against efforts to demonize and delegitimize the Jewish state. As I entered my seventh decade and looked back on my life's work, I saw most trends in the law moving in a positive direction: Freedom of expression, though never secure, was expanding; science was playing more of a role in solving homicides than ever before, though the courts were not keeping pace with technological developments; racial, gender, religious, and even sexual orientation equality, though far from complete, was much closer to reality than when I was growing up. There was, however, one important issue that was moving in the wrong direction: the campaign to demonize Israel, being conducted by the strangest of bedfellows, the hard ideological left and the hard Islamic right. Israel's imperfections (and what nation is anything but imperfect?) were becoming the newest excuse for legitimizing the oldest of bigotries. The line from anti-Zionism to anti-Semitism—a line Martin Luther King warned about shortly before his death—to me was being crossed. For the first time in my adult life, I was seeing an increase in the hatred of Jews, especially Jews who supported Israel.

Moreover, the fervor against Israel could not be explained in rational policy terms. Israel, the "Jew Among Nations," was being treated by many on the extreme left and on the Islamic right in the way the Jewish people had been treated for millennia—with irrational hatred often coupled with incitement to violence. This change took me by surprise.

In the conclusion to my 1991 book, *Chutzpah*,[13] I predicted the end of mainstream, top-down anti-Semitism in America, and its replacement by anti-Zionism. I also predicted "a sharp decline in support for Israel among college and university students," those who would be tomorrow's leaders.[14]

I did not anticipate that the new anti-Zionism would, at least for some, morph into anti-Semitism. I should have, because hatred of Israel was so irrational, so extreme, that it could be explained only by a hatred for Israel's Jewishness. A confrontation I experienced in 2004 was all too typical.

It took place in front of Faneuil Hall, the birthplace of American independence and liberty.[15] I was receiving a justice award and delivering from the podium of that historic hall a talk on civil liberties in the age of terrorism. When I left, award in hand, I was accosted by a group of screaming, angry young men and women carrying virulently anti-Israel signs. The sign carriers were shouting epithets at me that crossed the line from civility to bigotry. "Dershowitz and Hitler, just the same, the only difference is the name." The sin that, in the opinion of the screamers, warranted this comparison between me and the man who murdered dozens of my family members was my support for Israel.

It was irrelevant to these chanters that I also support a Palestinian state, the end of the Israeli occupation, and the dismantling of most of the settlements. The protestors went on to shout, "Dershowitz and Gibbels [*sic*], just the same, the only difference is the name"—without even knowing how to pronounce the name of the anti-Semitic Nazi butcher.

One sign carrier shouted that Jews who support Israel were worse than Nazis. Another demanded that I be tortured and killed. It was not only their words; it was the hatred in their eyes. If a dozen Boston police had not been protecting me, I'm afraid I might have been physically attacked. The protestors' eyes were ablaze with fanatical zeal.

The feminist writer Phyllis Chesler aptly describes the hatred some young people direct against Israel and supporters of the Jewish state as "eroticized."[16] That is what I saw: passionate hatred, ecstatic and orgasmic. It was beyond mere differences of opinion.

To be sure, these protestors' verbal attack on me was constitutionally protected speech, as was the Nazi march through Skokie. But the shouting was plainly calculated to intimidate.

When I turned to answer one of the bigoted chants, as I always do in these situations, the police officer in charge gently but firmly insisted that I walk directly to my car and not engage the protestors. It was an order, reasonably calculated to assure my safety, and it was right.

The officer climbed into my car with me and got out only when we were beyond the range of the protest. The intimidation had succeeded. I had been silenced. The false and horrible message had gone unanswered in the plaza near Faneuil Hall.

I have experienced similar hatred around the world: in California, Toronto, Trondheim, Cape Town, London, and Paris. I needed police protection—sometimes with shields and bulletproof vests—when I spoke about Israel.

The most bizarre aspect of this old/new hatred I began to experience was that some of it was coming from people who identified themselves as Jews or Israelis (or former Jews or former Israelis). A few even sought to burnish their credentials by identifying themselves as the children or grandchildren of Holocaust victims or survivors. This occurred on the University of Massachusetts Boston campus, where a group of anti-Israel students, led by a Jewish professor who identified herself as a child of Holocaust survivors, tried to prevent me from speaking by shouting me down. They succeeded in stopping the event before its scheduled ending time.

I could not remain silent in the face of this dangerous phenomenon. I decided therefore to give priority to my legal and human rights work in defense of Israel and the Jewish community as long as this threat persisted.

I had wanted to write a book called *The Case for Peace*, in which I criticized both sides of the Arab-Israeli conflict for not doing enough to bring about a compromise peace. Instead, I decided to write *The Case for Israel*, in 2003,[17] in order to provide students with a factual basis for responding to the untruths that are rampant on campuses. (I did subsequently write *The Case for Peace*.) *The Case for Israel* became an instant bestseller, both on campuses and around the world, where it was published in many languages and made into a documentary film. I believe it helped change the terms of the debate on many campuses and changed the minds of many people. One example is particularly gratifying. An Arab man named Kassim Hafeez wrote an article in April 2012 entitled "From Anti-Semite to Zionist."[18] In it, he described his journey as follows:

> *Growing up in a Muslim community in the UK I was exposed to materials condemning Israel, painting Jews as usurpers and murderers. . . .*
>
> *There was also constant, casual antisemitism around me. My father would boast of how Adolf Hitler was a hero, his only failing being that he didn't kill enough Jews.*
>
> *What changed? In Waterstones one day I found myself in the Israel and Palestine section. To this day I don't know why I actually pulled it off the shelf, but I picked up a copy of Alan Dershowitz's* The Case for Israel.
>
> *In my world view the Jews and the Americans controlled the media, so after a brief look at the back, I scoffed, thinking "vile Zionist propaganda."*

But I decided to buy it, eagerly awaiting the chance to deconstruct it so I could show why Israel had no case and claim my findings as a personal victory for the Palestinian cause.

As I read Dershowitz's systematic deconstruction of the lies I had been told, I felt a real crisis of conscience. I couldn't disprove his arguments or find facts to respond to them with. I didn't know what to believe. I'd blindly followed for so long, yet here I was questioning whether I had been wrong?

I decided to visit Israel to find the truth. I was confronted by synagogues, mosques and churches, by Jews and Arabs living together, by minorities playing huge parts in all areas of Israeli life, from the military to the judiciary. It was shocking and eye-opening. This wasn't the evil Zionist Israel that I had been told about.

After much soul searching, I knew what I had once believed was wrong. I had to stand with Israel, with this tiny nation, free, democratic, making huge strides in medicine, research and development, yet the victim of the same lies and hatred that nearly consumed me.[19]

Not all people were so positively influenced. A woman in England asked the manager of a large bookstore for a copy of *The Case for Israel*. He responded, "There is no case for Israel."[20]

I have devoted much of my seventh decade to the defense of Israel (while continuing to criticize many of its policies, especially regarding settlements). This has earned me the titles "the Jewish State's lead attorney in the court of public opinion"[21] and "America's most public Jewish defender."[22] It has also earned me the titles "Ziofascist," "Jewish Nazi," "Tool of the Likud," and "Israel Firster."[23]

It is these latter titles that have brought about the most recent change in my life, during my eighth decade. Until recently, I was always known as a liberal Democrat, aligned politically with the likes of Senator Ted Kennedy, President Bill Clinton, Secretary of State Hillary Clinton, Senator Hubert Humphrey, Justices Arthur Goldberg and William Brennan, the Reverend Martin Luther King, and Judge David Bazelon. The organization with which I have been most closely associated has been the American Civil Liberties Union, on whose national and local boards I have served. The causes with which I have been most often associated were freedom of speech; opposition to the death penalty; due process for criminal suspects and defendants; the separation of church and state; racial, gender, religious, economic, and sexual orientation equality; and political accountability. Indeed, when my name has been mentioned for judgeships and other government positions requiring Senate confirmation, I have been generally regarded as "too liberal" to be confirmed.

Today, my views on the above subjects remain essentially the same, but because of my support, critical as it may be, for Israel, I am now widely regarded as a "conservative," a "right winger," a Republican, a "sell-out," even a fascist. Many college and university students have no idea of my views on the core issues that separate liberals from conservatives (inexact as those categories are). All they know is that I defend Israel, and that is enough for them to brand me as "politically incorrect" and worse. This is the way MJ Rosenberg, an anti-Israel blogger who used to work for Media Matters, a Democratic think tank, put it:

> *Dershowitz is not a Democrat. The only issue he cares about—and the only issue he ever spouts off about—is Israel. Unlike most Americans, say 99%, Dershowitz has no particular opinion on any issue that does not relate to Israel.*

Rosenberg's obsession over Israel's imperfections has blinded him, and others of his ilk, to the fact that the vast majority of my books, op-eds, cases, and causes relate to civil liberties and criminal and constitutional law. Despite this reality, and because of my support for Israel, Noam Chomsky has absurdly called me "a passionate opponent of civil liberties."[24] And despite my longtime opposition to Israeli civilian settlements and to the "greater Israel" movement, Andrew Sullivan has mendaciously characterized me as a "greater Israel fanatic."[25] Whether these lies are a result of ignorance, willful blindness, or malice, they have spread widely across the Internet and have changed my image among some thoughtless Israel haters.

My centrist views regarding Israel have also resulted in calumny from the pro-Israel hard right, many of whose adherents are appalled at my support for a two-state solution and my opposition to some Israeli settlement policies. I have been called a "traitor to the Jewish people," a "vapid, doctrinaire leftist," a "willfully blind hypocrite," "a liberal first, a Zionist second," and someone who "would never offer an opinion which could remotely be perceived as politically incorrect."[26]

This last change—the effort by the hard left to erase my long history and continued espousal of liberal policies coupled with the effort by the hard right to erase my long history and current espousal of centrist Zionism and support for Israel—is not one that I have brought about by changing *my* views or actions, as was the case with the earlier changes. I have done nothing different. My views about Israel, the two-state solution, and the settlements have remained relatively constant over the past forty-five years. It is the world around me that has changed with regard to Israel, and attitudes toward me have changed because of this. I will continue to live by my principles. I'm probably too old and too set in my ways to change even if I wanted to, which I don't. I will not adapt my principles to changing attitudes, when I believe that these changing attitudes are wrong and bigoted. But I must recognize that the perception *of me* by many others has changed. So be it.

THE CHANGING LAW

How will our legal system change over the next half century? I began my career during the golden age of law. The Supreme Court was the most respected, indeed revered, institution of government, at least among my peers, teachers, and family members.[27] The justices had ended segregation, helped to constrain McCarthyism, kept high the wall of separation between church and state, protected the rights of those accused of crime, and applied the rule of law fairly, without taint of partisanship.

The United Nations was viewed as the protector of universal human rights. It was going to replace war with law.

Young people were flocking to law school in order to do good and repair the world. The legal profession was respected.

Of course this idealized image was, in reality, far from perfect. Law firms remained largely segregated. Judicial corruption was rampant in many parts of the country. The remnants of McCarthyism still constrained freedom of expression. Racism, sexism, and homophobia were still common among lawyers in many places. And human rights were absent throughout most of the world. But the important trends were all pointing in the right direction—toward equality, justice, and the rule of law.

In which direction are today's trends pointing? What do they tell us about the rule of law over the coming half century?

These questions do not allow for simple, single directional answers, but some disturbing trends are discernible.

THE AUTHORITY OF THE SUPREME COURT WILL DIMINISH OVER TIME

The Supreme Court was never intended, by our framers, to have the power it has assumed since the ratification of our Constitution.[28] The judiciary was expected, according to the Federalist Papers, to be "the least dangerous" branch of our government, because it lacks "the sword" of the executive and "the purse" of the legislative branches. "It may truly be said to have neither force nor will, but merely judgment."[29] In other words, whatever authority the Supreme Court is to enjoy must be earned by the soundness of its "judgment" and the public's perception of the justices as fair and above the partisan politics expected of the "popular"—that is elected—branches of government.

This authority was—with some striking exceptions—well earned from the time of Chief Justice John Marshall through the end of the twentieth century. It was never without controversy, whether in the years leading up to the Civil War, to the New Deal, or to the "activist" Warren court. But never before the beginning of this century have the justices been accused of playing partisan politics—of engineering outcomes that favor their own political parties and candidates. Yet that is precisely what many, if not most, Americans believe the Supreme Court did in *Bush v. Gore,*[30] and in the Citizens United case.[31] In *Bush v. Gore*, as I wrote in my book *Supreme Injustice*, the five Republican justices voted inconsistently with their *own* prior decisions to assure that a Republican was elected president. In *Citizens United*, they did much the same thing. According to reporting by Jeffrey Toobin in the *New Yorker*, Chief Justice John Roberts, in deciding how to resolve the complex and contentious issues raised by the Citizens United case, had a single criterion: What would be best for the Republican Party? If this is true, it reminds me of my grandmother's single-mindedness. When I came home from a Brooklyn Dodgers game and reported that the home team had won, my grandmother asked, "Yeah, but is it good or bad for the Jews?" The difference is that my grandmother was not the chief justice of the United States, whose job description includes a commitment to be nonpartisan when deciding cases.[32]

In previous eras of controversy, the divisions among the justices were less along partisan and more along ideological lines. The New Deal was opposed by justices appointed by both parties. Earl Warren (a liberal Republican) and William Brennan (a liberal Democrat), who generally voted for liberal outcomes, were appointed by a Republican president.

It is inevitable that an activist Supreme Court—whether activist on behalf of the left or the right—will eventually lead to a more partisan judiciary. When courts limit themselves to deciding narrow legal issues that affect only the particular litigants before them, the general public is less interested in who serves as judges. But when the courts become involved in highly controversial political issues that affect everyone—abortion, presidential elections, gay rights, and so forth—then the general public begins to care who is deciding their fate. The nomination and confirmation of judges become more contentious and partisan. Politicians do not want to buy "a pig in a poke." They want to be sure they know what they are getting, and they want judges who will vote their political preferences. This change has occurred all over the world, beginning with the United States.

Even before the Supreme Court's self-inflicted wounds cut into its credibility, the power of the justices was somewhat overstated by many academics, media analysts, and members of the public. The Supreme Court is, after all, *just a court*. It decides only issues presented to it by litigants in actual cases. It does not *initiate* policy changes. It is a reactive, rather than proactive, institution—even when it is in an "activist" mode. Justices such as Arthur Goldberg, William O. Douglas, Warren Burger, and Antonin Scalia may have brought proactive agendas with them to the high court, but they soon came to realize how difficult it is to implement those agendas through an institution that has neither "sword" nor "purse" nor the ability to ensure that its policy preferences are carried out by the other branches.

Nor are the justices all paragons of virtue. Some are petty, others bigoted, and still others not particularly learned in the law. As Justice Jackson eloquently put it: "We are not final because we are infallible, but we are infallible only because we are final."[33]

As I demonstrated in Chapter 6, the Supreme Court adamantly rejected my approach to "vicarious offensiveness"—people being offended by the mere knowledge that *others* might be viewing pornography—as a matter of constitutional law. But the public accepted that approach, which has now become the law in action throughout the nation. The same can be said about the death penalty, which—if one were to read only Supreme Court decisions—should be increasing in its application. But the law in action has reduced the frequency of executions dramatically since the justices restored the death penalty, as a matter of constitutional law, in 1976. This phenomenon may also be in evidence with regard to race-specific affirmative action, which will likely continue to matter, no matter what the justices say. It may also be in evidence in cases in which the Supreme Court upholds the wall of separation between church and state only to see it eroded in practice by school administrators and other bureaucrats who believe that a little religion never hurt anyone. Nor could the high court reverse the trend toward equality for gays, regardless of how it decides particular cases.

On the basis of what I have observed over the past fifty years, I predict that the Supreme Court's moral authority will be further diminished over the next fifty years. The golden age of the rule of law has become tarnished by the partisan politicization of law, especially by the Supreme Court in *Bush v. Gore*, a decision that administered a self-inflicted wound on our judiciary.

At the same time, the power of the legislature will continue to diminish and the authority of the executive continues to expand. The imperial presidency has taken on new powers as the perceived need for quick and efficient action has increased The result is a weakening in our system of checks and balances as process becomes subordinated to outcome, and outcome becomes more dependent on money.

THE AUTHORITY OF THE UNITED NATIONS WILL DIMINISH OVER TIME

A similarly destructive process has diminished the moral authority of the United Nations and its constituent bodies, most especially the Human Rights Council and the International Court of Justice. This process will continue unless the United Nations makes considerable structural changes, which is highly improbable. The diminishing credibility of the UN will also affect nongovernmental "human rights" organizations, especially those that are seen as biased either against or in favor of the West. The International Criminal Court, which has up to now resisted any show of bias, will be tested over the coming years. Human rights around the world will continue to suffer, as organizations refuse to follow the correct priority of dealing with the worst first.

THE FUTURE OF ISRAEL

The nation-state of the Jewish people will remain an endangered democracy. It is the only nation in the world today whose very existence is challenged by other nations and by hundreds of millions of people. Since much of the hatred directed against Israel is religious, irrational, and deep-seated, the usual rules of deterrence that maintained a cold peace between the United States and the Soviet Union and between Israel and secular Arab regimes, such as Mubarak's Egypt and Assad's Syria, are not as effective and do not guarantee rational decision making. The unpredictable outcome of the Arab Spring, Iran's quest for nuclear weapons, Turkey's movement away from secularism, and the thus far unsuccessful efforts to resolve the Israeli-Palestinian conflict make predictions even more daunting. But the likelihood of Israel becoming a "normalized" Middle Eastern country, accepted by its neighbors, is slight. Nonetheless, Israel will continue to thrive scientifically, economically, militarily, and in every other way that depends on its own human capital and innovative character.

Anti-Semitism, often disguised as anti-Zionism, will increase in Europe and other parts of the world as the Holocaust fades from memory. It will soon return to pre-Holocaust levels among many Europeans, even if Israel makes peace with the Palestinians.

INTERNATIONAL LAW WILL BE LARGELY REPLACED BY TRANSNATIONAL LAW

International law—that is, law applied by international bodies such as the International Court of Justice—is on life support and may be headed toward an unceremonious death. Transnational law—that is, the law applied by domestic courts to crimes and transactions that cross national borders—is thriving, and may well replace much of what has traditionally been called international law. The reasons for the likely demise of international law is similar to the reasons why the United States Supreme Court and the United Nations will likely suffer a decline in authority. The institutions that apply international law have become partisan and biased. Moreover, because there is no international "legislature" (aside from the United Nations), academics have played a disproportionate role in defining the substance of international law. This too has resulted in ideological bias against Western nations. As a result, international law itself, to the extent that law is defined by the precedents of the courts and the writings of academics, has been skewed by partisan and ideological considerations. Most reasonable people do not take seriously the pronouncements of courts or other institutions associated with the United Nations. They also recognize the bias of the academy. They do take seriously the pronouncements of credible domestic courts or arbitration boards in resolving disputes that are multinational in nature.

An exception to this trend may be the International Criminal Court, which is not a creature of the United Nations but rather of a multinational treaty. Its credibility will depend on whether or not it succumbs to pressures from its constituent governments and ideological staff members, or whether it can administer justice in an independent and neutral manner.

THE FUTURE OF FREE SPEECH: MORE SPEECH AND MORE CENSORSHIP

There will be both more and freer speech throughout the world, but at the same time there will be more attempts to regulate speech, especially on the international level. Every new technology—from the printing press to the Internet—has made the job of the censor both more challenging and, in the eyes of the establishment, more important. From the time humans were first able to communicate with one another, the establishment—whether it be tribal leaders, religious leaders, or the state—has tried to limit their speech through censorship. In the beginning, the censorship was ad hoc and somewhat informal, but as the threats to the establishment became greater through the democratization of speech, censorship became more formalized and structured. Before the advent of the moveable-type printing press, which made the mass production of books more easily accessible, censorship was not deemed as essential to the survival of powerful institutions like the Church, the monarchy, and the state, because only the educated and affluent elite had access to the printed word, and most such establishment figures (with some striking exceptions, such as Martin Luther and Erasmus) sought to preserve the status quo.

The democratization of the written word raised the specter of democratic challenge and change, hence the need, as Hobbes put it, for the Leviathan to have the power to decide what the people would be allowed and not allowed to read. All governments, even our own, seek to control what the public can see and hear, but our First Amendment places considerable barriers in the way of government censorship. So does quickly changing technology that makes it considerably harder to censor.

The further democratization of the written and spoken word, by means of the Internet and other ever-changing technologies, has produced contemporary demands to control what is read and heard. The United Nations has been debating a universal speech code that would protect sensitive religious and ethnic groups from being offended. Some demands for selective control over the dissemination of information—for example, the need to prevent the outing of spies, the disclosure of military plans and weapons development, or other legitimate state, business, or personal secrets—are reasonable, if often overstated. Others—such as protecting religious sensibilities from being offended—are entirely unreasonable, though aggressively sought by some from the United Nations and other international bodies. The tension between full freedom of expression and the desire of establishments to control expression will continue on the battlefields of both technology and law. In the end, technology will prevail over law.

THE FUTURE OF CONFLICT RESOLUTION

The conflicts between religious dogma and reason will sharpen as traditional societies challenge modernity with new weapons, particularly terrorism. This will bring about a weakening of the distinction between combatants and civilians during asymmetrical warfare, in which combatants use civilians as both shields and swords. It will also make it more difficult to arrive at any consensus regarding grievances and resolutions of conflict, as demands and agreements that seem rational to one side seem entirely irrational to the other. The "age of reason" is being challenged by both religious dogma from the hard right and ideological dogma from the hard left.

THE FUTURE OF PRIVACY

Personal privacy will diminish as a value. The pervasiveness of social media, especially among the young, is a harbinger of changing values: Community is regarded as more important than privacy among many. Some young celebrities have even allowed themselves to be videotaped engaging in the most private of sexual activities and then have these videotapes posted on the Internet for all to see. Even for those who crave more privacy, technology is making it more difficult to achieve. The omnipresent street camera, the GPS on cell phones, the depositing of samples in DNA banks, are on the tip of a very deep, and largely invisible, iceberg of intrusion, both by governments and industry. The law will respond to this new reality by reducing the "expectation of privacy" that is the hallmark of our Fourth Amendment.

THE FUTURE OF THE LEGAL PROFESSION

The legal profession has suffered a diminution in moral authority and status over the past several decades. Law used to be regarded as a "learned profession." Today it is rightly seen as a bottom-line business that generates enormous earnings for successful law firms and for some personal injury lawyers who advertise widely. This diminution, though understandable, is not entirely justified. In fact, the practice of law has improved by almost every relevant measure since I began to practice it. Law firms are much fairer in their hiring and promotion policies. They service the poor better—though not nearly well enough. There is less corruption in the practice of law—from outright bribery of judges to the "old boys network"—than there used to be. There is greater transparency and accountability throughout the legal profession, though still more is needed. All in all, the legal profession is in better shape today than it was fifty years ago, and most trends are in the right direction.

Why then has there been a diminution in the moral authority and status of lawyers? The answer is simple: money. Lawyers—at least those at the top of their profession—not only make more money than ever before but their earnings are now a matter of public record, published by media such as the *American Lawyer* and on blogs. When I began to practice, a lawyer's earnings were like his sex life—never to be discussed. Today *both* are discussed, even bragged about.

Law firms openly compete with one another for business and for "rainmakers." They merge with other firms at the suggestion of investment bankers and business advisors. They file for bankruptcy to achieve tactical and strategic advantages.[34]

They look like, behave like, and do business like other commercial ventures that sell soap, furniture, and underwear.

Their main function, like that of hedge fund managers, is to help make the superwealthy even wealthier and to pay less taxes; to circumvent environmental, health, and welfare regulations; and to increase the bottom line.

It should not be surprising therefore that the public views lawyers in much the same way they view other businesses. The difference is that many lawyers really do good: They represent the poor without fee; they challenge the government to comply with the Constitution; they help to preserve and expand liberty; they labor for the underprivileged in the trenches and "emergency wards" of our broken legal system.

The law, as an institution, has had a decidedly mixed history over the past half century; although its virtues have been greater than its vices, its vices have been more visible. Hence, the increasingly negative public trust in lawyers and in the law.

The leaders of the legal profession understand that the practice of law must change if the profession is to maintain its comparatively high status among other professions and among the legal professions of other countries. I predict therefore that we will see dramatic changes in the practice of law over the next half century. Many lawyers will be replaced by less expensive paraprofessionals, research specialists, computers, and forms. Arbitration and other alternative mechanisms for dispute resolution will replace expensive and time-consuming trials. Law will become more streamlined, efficient, and accessible. Most lawyers will make less money than they now do.

THE FUTURE OF LEGAL EDUCATION

If the practice of law is to change over the next half century, as it must, will law schools be equipped to prepare their students for their new careers? Not unless law schools better adapt to the emerging realities of legal practice. Many of today's law schools are teaching their students to be yesterday's lawyers, instead of tomorrow's. They are using pedagogic methods developed in the mid-nineteenth century to teach students who will be practicing in the mid-twenty-first century.

Criminal Law, for example, is taught largely through the vehicle of analyzing appellate cases decided years ago or studying the Model Penal Code, drafted near the beginning of my career by academics with little practical experience. Courses based on these anachronistic materials do not prepare students to confront the realities of current practice, in which trials are rare and bargaining is the central role of the lawyer, whether prosecutor or defense attorney. The few trials that do take place tend not to revolve around what is commonly taught in class—elements of traditional crimes, such as homicide and theft; theories of causation; common law defenses like duress, self-defense, and insanity—but rather on cutting-edge issues, such as computer fraud, insider trading, RICO, esoteric conspiracies, and novel defenses. Many current crimes involve transnational or multistate components, since so many of today's criminal activities cross federal and state lines. Evidence is presented by experts in DNA analysis, blood splatter, and other modern forensic and scientific developments.

Prosecutors conduct searches of computers, servers, clouds, satellite and drone images, medical and credit card records—in addition to the conventional searches of homes, offices, and pockets. Sentencing is based on sophisticated guideline calculations, rather than on the whims of judges.

To prepare a student effectively to represent clients in the future will require professors with real-world and real-time experience. But the trend is away from hiring such professors—at least at the most elite law schools, where PhDs in philosophy, economics, and history are preferred over practical work experience. A balance must be struck between the theoretical and practical in both the hiring and the teaching processes.

Moreover, law schools and law firms must learn what some consumers already know: that many of the routine tasks that lawyers are paid exorbitant legal fees to perform—such as drafting simple wills, contracts, divorce papers, and tax forms, or conducting elementary research—can be done more expeditiously and inexpensively by paralegals, outsourced research firms, computers, and standardized forms.[35] This has resulted in the loss of many legal jobs (along with jobs in other "knowledge-based professions") that can be done at lower cost over the Internet and by paraprofessionals. Law has become far too expensive and inaccessible for the average person, and even for many businesses. Moreover, the cost of attending law school has skyrocketed—it is more than twenty-five times higher today (about $50,000 a year for Harvard and Yale) than it was when I was a student (about $1,500 a year).[36] At the same time that the cost has gone up, the benefits have gone down, as more and more law graduates are not getting the jobs they want or any jobs at all. Law schools and law firms must figure out ways to contain the cost of attending law school as well as the costs of obtaining legal advice.

In light of these trends, it should come as no surprise that applications to law school are drastically down over the past several years. (According to the *New York Times*, there were 100,000 applicants in 2004 and 54,000 for the 2013 class, with only about 38,000 expected to matriculate.)[37] Many college graduates do not regard the six-figure expense of a law school education and degree as a worthwhile investment. They are pursuing other options, particularly in the business world. As the dean of one law school put it: "Students are doing the math. . . . Most law schools are too expensive, the debt coming out is too high and the prospect of attaining a six-figure-income job is limited."[38]

Years ago I proposed a change in the structure of law school education whereby the academic portion would be completed in two years, and the third year would be focused specifically on the student's career choice. For those who want to become professors, the third year would consist of a mini-PhD program, with an emphasis on research, writing, and teaching; for those interested in government work, a supervised internship with a local, state, federal, or international organization; for those interested in practice, clinical training in the relevant areas of specialization. During this year away from conventional teaching, the students would remain connected to their teachers through interactive electronic communication. At the end of the third year, everyone would return to the classroom for a monthlong series of lectures and seminars designed to bring together the academic lessons of the first two years and the practical experiences of the third year.

Variations of this "two-year-plus" law degree are now being considered by some law schools and legal educators.[39] The law school of tomorrow will have to be a different place than the law school of yesterday and today if legal education is to prepare the next generation of lawyers for a quickly changing profession and world.

Education in general will change, as most learning will be done outside the formal classroom, on computers, at home, in the workplace, and while commuting. Admissions criteria will also change, with less emphasis on race and gender, and more on class.

MY FUTURE

Of course, the only future about which we can be absolutely certain is our death. We cannot even be sure how, or even if, we will be remembered after we shuffle off our mortal coil. As Erich Segal once put it, "Fear of death is universal. But what lies beneath that fear is the terror of insignificance. Of not being remembered, not counting."[40] May I add: No one should live life so as to assure a positive obituary, any more than a writer should write plays or books to garner positive reviews. But it blinks reality to deny that public figures think about their obituaries as they approach the final years of life: They worry that they will be remembered for insignificant matters, or not remembered for significant ones.

When I helped win the Claus von Bülow, O. J. Simpson, and other high-profile cases, I thought that my celebrity clients would be the focus of my obituary. Now I think it will also be my defense of Israel. Since I'm never satisfied unless I get the last word, I penned the following letter to the editor to be sent following my death:

Dear Editor:

I don't want you to think that I don't appreciate some of the kind words written about me in your obituary, but I had a policy throughout my life of setting the record straight with regard to things written about me, and I see no reason to allow my untimely death to change that. Your understandable emphasis on my high-profile cases distorts my record by downplaying the numerous pro bono cases I handled on behalf of obscure and indigent clients. I made it a policy throughout my life to devote at least half of my professional time to nonpaying cases and causes.

One such cause was the defense of Israel against unfair attacks. But I was not an uncritical advocate for the nation-state of the Jewish people. To the contrary, I was critical when criticism was warranted, as with regard to Israel's settlement policy. I supported Israel not despite my liberalism, but because of it—and because I have always defended just causes against unjust attacks.

I tried to live my life based on principles and consistency. This was not always understood by those who disagreed with where my principles sometimes took me and whom they led me to represent. That is why I have made it a policy to correct the record. I admit that I have always tried to get the last word. Hence this posthumous letter to the editor, which I promise *is* my last word.

Alan Dershowitz
From I don't know where

I hope this posthumous letter to the editor isn't published for a while, but I suspect it will be relevant whenever my obituary appears. That's OK—as long as I get to take the stand one last time in my own defense.

ACKNOWLEDGMENTS

When a witness takes the stand, he needs to be prepared by a team of lawyers, paralegals, and assistants. The same is true of an autobiographer. In undertaking this endeavor, I have been greatly assisted by Aaron Voloj Dessauer, a brilliant young lawyer who helped me with the research and the source notes. Others helped as well, including Mitch Webber, Aaron Rabinowitz, and the staff at the Brooklyn College Archives, who made my life easier by having catalogued all of my papers very thoroughly.

My assistant, Sarah Neely, performed so many invaluable roles from typing the manuscript, arranging the credits for the photographs, conducting Google searches, managing my schedule, and dealing with the thousands of people who call and write me.

Several relatives and friends read portions of the manuscript and gave me useful suggestions. These included my wife, Carolyn Cohen, my children Elon, Jamin, and Ella, my brother, Nathan, and my friends Michael Miller, Rollie Savage, Alex MacDonald, Tom Ashe, Ken Sweder, and Merle Berger.

Finally, my appreciation goes to all those, too numerous to mention, who helped me do the things that are the subject of this memoir.

NOTES

Introduction

1 Alexis de Tocqueville, *Democracy in America* 357 (1862) ("Scarcely any political question arises in the United States which is not resolved, sooner or later, into a judicial question").

2 Frank Lloyd Wright said he had to "choose between honest arrogance and hypocritical humility." He chose the former. Meryle Secrest, *Frank Lloyd Wright: A Biography* 159 (1998). Lord Chesterfield perceptively quipped that "modesty is the only sure bait when you angle for praise." *The Beauties of Chesterfield* (Alfred Howard, ed.) 249 (1828).

3 *Reversal of Fortune*, Warner Bros. (1990).

4 The "Johnson brothers" of the film were a play on the "Tison brothers" in real life. See infra in Chapter 14.

5 Alan M. Dershowitz, *The Best Defense* (1983).

6 Alan M. Dershowitz, *Reversal of Fortune* (1985).

7 Alan M. Dershowitz, *Reasonable Doubts* (1997).

8 Alan M. Dershowitz, *Chutzpah* (1991).

9 Some overlap is, of course, inevitable. I discussed some of my most significant earlier cases, though in different contexts, in previous books.

10 Rene Descartes, *Principles of Philosophy* (1644), part 1, art. 7. Half a millennium earlier, Augustine expressed a similar view, focusing on "doubt." Augustine, *City of God* (Penguin Classics) 460 (2003).

11 The ability to think is inborn—a biological and genetic endowment. The content of one's thinking—the nature and quality of our ideas—is more nurture than nature. Without human experiences there could be no well-formed ideology, merely simple inborn reflexes based on instinct and genetics. There is no gene, or combination of genes, that ordains the content of our views regarding politics, law, morality, or religion. Biology gives us the mechanisms with which to organize our experiences into coherent theories of life, but without these experiences—which begin in the womb and may actually alter the physical structures of our brain over time—all we would have would be the mechanics of thought and the potential for formulating complex ideas and ideologies.

12 Perhaps, of course, had my forbears remained in Poland, my father might not have met my mother (although their families lived in neighboring shtetels). Accident, timing, and luck determine virtually everything relating to birth.

13 In 1999, I wrote a novel, *Just Revenge*, that reflected my deep feelings about the unavenged murders of so many of my relatives.

14 My mother's father did travel by boat to Palestine in the 1930s, hoping to move there, but after a few weeks, he determined that he couldn't make a living there and he returned to Brooklyn.

15 In a recent documentary about American Jews, Justice Ginsburg asks and answers the following question: "What is the difference between a bookkeeper in the garment district and a Supreme Court justice? One generation." *The Jewish Americans: A Series by David Grubin*, PBS (2008).

16 French politician François Guizot remarked, "Not to be a republican at twenty is proof of want of heart; to be one at thirty is proof of want of head." John Adams expressed a similar idea. In a 1799 journal entry, Thomas Jefferson quotes Adams as having quipped, "A boy at 15 who is not a democrat is not good for nothing, and he is no better who is a democrat at 20." Fred Shapiro, *John Adams Said It First*, August 25, 2001, http://www.freakonomics.com/2011/08/25/john-adams-said-it-first/.

17 *People v. Dlugash*, 51 A.D.2d 974, 380 N.Y.S.2d 315 (1976). For a discussion, see infra at pp. 311–313.

18 *United States v. Sabhnani*, 599 F.3d 215 (2d Cir. 2010).

19 Matter of Baby Boy C., 84 N.Y.2d 91 (1994).

20 *Lucido v. Cravath, Swaine & Moore*, 425 F. Supp. 123 (S.D.N.Y. 1977).

21 See infra at pp. 172–175.

22 Transcript for John A. Farrell, *Clarence Darrow: Attorney for the Damned*, http://thedianerehmshow.org/shows/2011-06-16/john-farrell-clarence-darrow-attorney-damned/transcript. Farrell also mentioned my friend and colleague Roy Black. The comparison to Darrow, while flattering, is also

troubling, since it is likely that Darrow bribed jurors, witnesses, and judges in an era when this was all too common. See Alan M. Dershowitz, *America on Trial*, 213–17, 260–61 (2004). *The Boston Phoenix* described me as "probably America's most famous attorney" (Scott Kearnan, "At Home with Alan Dershowitz," October 31, 2012); and Nabeal Twereet said I was "the best known criminal lawyer in the world" (Nabeal Twereet, LawCrossing, available at http://www.lawcrossing.com/article/900005794/Alan-Dershowitz-Is-the-Best-Known-Criminal-Lawyer-in-the-World/#).

23 More than one hundred of my submissions have been published by the *New York Times* since 1969. More than one thousand have been published by other media. See *Albany Law Review* 71, pp. 794–859 for a list through 2008.

24 These include *Sports Illustrated, TV Guide, Good Housekeeping, Penthouse, Parade, New Women, American Film, Newsweek,* the *New York Review of Books,* the *Saturday Review,* the *Atlantic,* the *Daily Beast,* the *Huffington Post,* and *Harpers.*

25 See Alan M. Dershowitz, "Lox on Both Their Houses," *New York Times,* August 18, 1988.

26 "Activism," *Forward,* November 14, 2003.

27 *Jewish Daily Forward* 50, 2007, available at http://forward.com/forward-50-2007/.

28 Steve Linde, "World's 50 Most Influential Jews," *Jerusalem Post,* May 21, 2010.

29 Oliver Wendell Holmes, Address delivered for Memorial Day, May 30, 1884, at Keene, New Hampshire.

Part I
From Brooklyn to Cambridge

Chapter 1
Born and Religiously Educated in Brooklyn

1 My great-grandfather "Zecharja Derschowitz," who was born in Pilsno in 1859, was a tailor who sewed small coin purses. He emigrated to the United States in 1888. His wife, Lea, and their four children, including my grandfather Leib (Louis) followed in 1891. My maternal grandparents arrived during the first decade of the twentieth century.

2 My paternal grandfather is credited with having been the cofounder of Torah V'Daas.

3 My uncle Morris Ringel moved to California to work in the aeronautics industry. In 1951, he wrote the family a letter in which he said that he was being hounded by the House Un-American Activities Committee, who wanted to question him about possible Communist associations. He asked that no one try to contact him. He was never seen or heard from again. In 1971, when I lived in California for a year, I tried to locate him, but without success.

4 The origin of the name Dershowitz is unclear. According to my uncle Zecharia, the only living member of my father's generation:

> *The name "Derschowitz" or "Deresiewicz" is reported to be a derivative of Derzow or Derzowci (a powerful Jewish leaseholder in Galicia). "Dereszewicz," "Dershovitz," or "Derschovitz" are also reported to be derivatives of* deresz *(a roan—a reddish-gray horse). Finally, "Derschowitz" is also reported to derive from the town Derschowitz in Moravia. It was also the name of a Polish patriot in the 17th Century.*

Family legend also relates our name to the Hebrew words *drash, doresh,* and *darshan,* which mean "interpretation" or "interpreter," particularly of the Bible. There is also a town near the Polish-German border called Dershov, from which it could derive. My great-grandfather's original name, Derschowitz, lost the "c" somewhere along the way, either by design or by a transcription error at Ellis Island.

5 And another (sung to the melody of "My Country, 'Tis of Thee"):

My country, 'tis of thee
Sweet land of Germany
My name is Fritz
My father was a spy
Caught by the FBI
Tomorrow he must die
My name is Fritz.

6 For my seventieth birthday, my brother found a card that commemorated the superhero phase of my life; it showed an elderly Superman standing on a ledge, ready to fly, but wondering, "Now, where is it I'm supposed to be flying?"

7 My Grandmother Ringel, who was recovering from a heart attack, took me to a rehabilitation home in Lakewood, New Jersey, where several wounded or shell-shocked soldiers were also being rehabilitated.

8 A few weeks earlier, we had cried over Roosevelt's passing, which I heard of while listening to the radio, and broke the news to my grandmother Ringel, who was taking care of me. She refused to believe it, until she herself heard it on the radio. Then she cried. Roosevelt (which she pronounced like "Rosenfeld") was the hero of our neighborhood (and other Jewish neighborhoods).

9 With regard to this cultural stereotype, Steven Pinker writes:

> *It cannot be taken for granted that Jewish culture favors achievement in physics, philosophy, or chess. In his autobiography, the eminent social psychologist Stanley Schachter wrote that "I went to Yale much against my father's wishes. He couldn't have cared less about higher education and wanted me to go to a one-year laundry college (no kidding) out in the Midwest and join him then in the family business. I never have understood what this intellectually driven Jewish immigrant business is all about. It wasn't true of my family, and I know very few families for which it was true. . . . To me, Jewish love of learning has always seemed a myth perpetrated by a few rabbis' sons who weren't good at anything much but going to school and then spending the rest of their lives writing novels about it. (Steven Pinker, "The Lessons of the Ashkenazim: Groups and Genes,"* New Republic, *June 26, 2006)*

10 Decades later, I saw my FBI file. It was quite thick, but there was no reference to the Rosenberg petition.

11 For a fuller account of my collection, see Alan Dershowitz, *Finding Jefferson* 3–25 (2007).

12 Stephen Jay Gould, "Nonoverlapping Magisteria," *Natural History*, March 1997.

13 Half a century later, my daughter, Ella, was graded down by her teacher at Milton Academy for raising her hand too frequently in class.

14 One of my jokes did get chosen recently for the online version of *Old Jews Telling Jokes*. It can be accessed at www.gocomics.com, dated January 6, 2013.

15 To David Snir, November 10, 1963, translated from the Hebrew.

16 For a fuller account of this episode, see Alan M. Dershowitz, *The Best Defense* 12 (1983).

17 The classic Jewish joke reflecting this xenophobia is about Moishe, who says to his wife, "It's too hard to be a Jew. I'm converting to Christianity." He goes to church, converts, and goes home to sleep. Next morning his wife wakes up and sees Moishe wearing his *talit* (Jewish prayer shawl) while davening (praying in Hebrew). "What are you doing, Moishe?" she asks. "You're a Christian." Moishe replies, "I forgot! Goyisher Kup."

18 Joshua Prager, "For Branca, an Asterisk of a Different Kind," *New York Times*, August 14, 2011.

19 Alan M. Dershowitz, *The Genesis of Justice* (2001).

20 I'm reminded of the joke about the pollster who approaches four random people in Times Square and says, "Excuse me, I'd like your opinion on the meat shortage." The first one, an Ethiopian replies, "There's a word I don't understand. What 'meat' is?" The second, an American, also says there's a word he doesn't understand: "What's 'shortage'?" The third, from China, also doesn't understand something: "What's 'opinion'?" Finally, the Israeli too says there's something he doesn't understand: "What's 'excuse me'?"

We never said "excuse me." Conventional politeness was not part of our language. Nor was rudeness. We simply didn't regard interrupting someone as rude, as long as everyone eventually got to say what he wanted.

21 I still have the letter from Production Services Company at 667 Madison Avenue informing me that the results of my written examination "are gratifying" and inviting me for the personal interview I failed.

22 Shoftim, Deuteronomy 16:18–21:9.

23 Similar differentials are still at work today, but they operate beneath the radar screen, under the rubric of "diversity" and "discretion." An admissions officer at an elite college told me that he turns down many students with perfect SAT scores. When I asked him who these rejected students were, he acknowledged that they were almost exclusively of Asian and Jewish background: "If we took everybody with perfect SAT scores, there would be little diversity," he explained. He too apparently believed in the "*Yiddisher* (and Asian) *kop*" theory. According to a recent study examining more than nine thousand students applying to selective universities, white students were three times more likely to be admitted than Asian students with the same academic record. See Carolyn Chen, "Are Asians Too Smart for Their Own Good?" *New York Times*, December 20, 2012.

24 Alan Dershowitz, "Collectible Adolescence," *New York Times*, May 31, 1987.

Chapter 2
My Secular Education

1 Larry Ruttman, *American Jews and America's Game* (2013).

2 For years, I had been telling people that the flights were canceled, but a couple of summers ago I was at a party with a man (now married to a prominent public figure) who was at Brooklyn College with me. He and several of his friends were also going to Havana for the same reason. "I made it to Havana," he boasted. "But the flights were canceled," I replied. "No, they weren't. The State Department just issued a warning that it was a little bit dangerous." I guess he was more determined to lose it than I was. His wife, who was then his college girlfriend, said that she didn't "touch him for a year after that."

3 In my application, I wrote the following:

> *I believe that my college career has been a period of moral and intellectual growth throughout which time I have felt an increasing responsibility to my conscience in matters of self improvement. I felt this personal responsibility so strongly in college because I had almost completely neglected it throughout high school. A firm determination to show myself, as well as my high school contemporaries, that I could become an outstanding student in college has been a most potent motivating force.*

I also listed my academic, political, and athletic achievements, and promised that if admitted to Oxford

> *I would read for the Oxford B.A. in the Honor School of Jurisprudence and then enter Law School in the United States.*

4 Brooklyn College received its first Rhodes Scholarship in 1991. See James Barron, "Brooklyn College Firsts: Marshall and Rhodes," *New York Times*, December 12, 1991.

5 One of the reasons I chose Yale was that I was thinking—even back then—of becoming a professor. An article in the Brooklyn College paper about my tenure as president of the student council included the following:

> *Alan's leisure time has somehow stretched to include pitching for Knight House's baseball team, listening to music (his tastes run to early Classical, late Baroque, choral music), watching wrestling on television, teaching a Sunday school class, contributing to the activities of the Young Israel of Borough Park and commuting between New York and Bayonne, New Jersey, where his fiancée, Sue Barlack, is a Rutgers sophomore.*
>
> *His future plans are almost as impressive as his past activities. He plans to become a professor of law.*

6 The Finzi-Continis were a wealthy Jewish-Italian family whose destruction was immortalized in the Giorgio Bassani novel *The Garden of the Finzi-Continis* (1962) and the Oscar-winning movie of the same name (1970).

7 The current chairman of Sullivan & Cromwell is an ordained Orthodox rabbi. Cyrus Sanati, "For Law Firm's New Chief, Challenges Abound," DealBook, *New York Times*, January 4, 2010.

8 *Lucido v. Cravath, Swaine & Moore*, 425 F. Supp. 123 (S.D.N.Y. 1977). For a full account, see Alan M. Dershowitz, *Chutzpah* 54–55 (1991).

9 Alan Dershowitz, *A Pragmatic Approach to the Effect of the 5th Amendment upon Administration of Justice*, Political Science 34, Prof. Wilson (Brooklyn College, New York, 16 May 1958). From the Brooklyn College Archive.

10 Alan M. Dershowitz, *Is There a Right to Remain Silent?* (2008).

11 Alan M. Dershowitz, "Why Do Criminal Attempts Fail? A New Defense," 70 *Yale Law Journal* 160 (1960).

12 Alan M. Dershowitz, "Increasing Community Control over Corporate Crime—A Problem in the Law of Sanctions," 71 *Yale Law Journal* 280 (1961).

13 See Alan M. Dershowitz, *Chutzpah* 166–70 (1991).

14 Guido Calabresi, "Some Thoughts on Risk Distribution and the Law of Torts," 70 *Yale Law Journal* 499 (1961).

15 Joseph Goldstein and Jay Katz, "Dangerousness and Mental Illness: Some Observations on the Decision to Release Persons Acquitted by Reason of Insanity," 70 *Yale Law Journal* 225 (1960).

16 Jay Katz, Joseph Goldstein, and Alan M. Dershowitz, *Psychoanalysis, Psychiatry, and the Law* (1967).

17 See Telford Taylor, *Courts of Terror: Soviet Criminal Justice and Jewish Emigration* (1976) (with Alan Dershowitz, George Fletcher, Leon Lipson, and Melvin Stein).

18 John F. Kennedy, Yale University Commencement, New Haven, Connecticut, June 11, 1962.

Chapter 3
My Clerkships

1 David Lat, "The Supreme Court's Bonus Babies," *New York Times*, June 18, 2007; Adam Liptak, "San Francisco Led in Fighting Marriage Ban," *New York Times*, March 19, 2013, 1, 12 ("Signing bonuses are now in the neighborhood of $280,000.00.")

2 Mory's did not allow women until 1972, three years after Yale College had became coeducational. See http://www.morys1849.org/Home/test.aspx. Eventually (and resentfully), Rodell moved his seminar to a classroom after several women complained.

3 For my views on Bickel's constitutional jurisprudence, see my review of his *The Morality of Consent, New York Times Book Review*, September 21, 1975, 1–2.

4 See Noah Feldman, *Scorpions: The Battles and Triumphs of FDR's Great Supreme Court Justice* 430 (2010).

5 The Harvard Club of New York started to accept women in 1973. Jeffrey R. Toobin, "The New York Harvard Club: Changing Traditions on West 44th," *Harvard Crimson*, January 3, 1979.

6 A variation on this story was told by Judge Learned Hand: "I remember once I was with [Justice Holmes]; it was a Saturday when the Court was to confer. It was before we had a motor car, and we jogged along in an old coupé. When we got down to the Capitol, I wanted to provoke a response, so as he walked off, I said to him: 'Well, sir, goodbye. Do justice!' He turned quite sharply and he said: 'Come here. Come here.' I answered: 'Oh, I know, I know.' He replied: 'That is not my job. My job is to play the game according to the rules.'" Judge Learned Hand, "A Personal Confession," in *The Spirit of Liberty* 302, 306–7 (Irving Dilliard, ed., 3d ed., 1960).

7 Deuteronomy 16:20. The traditional translation "pursue" doesn't quite capture the essence of the Hebrew words "*Tzedek, Tzedek, Tirdof*," since *Tirdof* comes from the root that means "to run or chase after."

8 Sanhedrin 32b.

9 *Durham v. United States*, 214 F.2d 862, 875 (D.C. Cir. 1954) abrogated by *United States v. Brawner*, 471 F.2d 969 (D.C. Cir. 1972).

10 As I wrote these words, I was working on a pro bono case with Judge Bazelon's granddaughter, Lara Bazelon, a clinical law professor at Loyola Law School. I told her about her grandfather's demanding approach and promised not to replicate it with her.

11 The Bazelon Center, *He the Pebble, We the Ripples on the Pond: Reminiscences About Judge David L. Bazelon by 58 of His Clerks, Colleagues and Friends, Written for the Center's 1993 Rededication to Honor His Pioneering Role in Mental Health Law* (1993).

12 This changed with the District of Columbia Court Reform and Criminal Procedure Act of 1970 (84 Stat. 473). See Federal Judicial Center, Federal Courts of the District of Columbia, http://www.fjc.gov/history/home.nsf/page/courts_special_dc.html.

13 309 F.2d 234 (1962).

14 372 U.S. 335 (1963).

15 For an account of Ely's involvement in the case, see Anthony Lewis, *Gideon's Trumpet* 122–29 (1964).

16 *Miller v. United States*, 320 F2d 767 (1963).

17 Ibid. 768.

18 Ibid. 776.

19 Jay Katz, Joseph Goldstein, and Alan M. Dershowitz, *Psychoanalysis, Psychiatry, and the Law* (1967).

20 Ibid. 771 (quoting *Wigmore on Evidence* 173 [1940]).

21 Ibid. 772 (quoting Sigmund Freud, "Psychoanalysis and the Ascertaining of Truth in Courts of Law" [1906]), in *Collected Papers* (1959), vol. 2, p. 13.

22 Ibid. 772 n.10. Centuries earlier, the Jewish scholar Maimonides had provided an even more nuanced psychological insight. "The Sanhedrin . . . is not empowered to inflict the penalty of death or of flagellation on the admission of the accused. For it is possible that he was confused in mind when he made the confession. Perhaps he was one of those who are in misery, bitter in soul, who long for death, thrust the sword in their bellies, or cast themselves down from the roofs. Perhaps this was the reason that prompted him to confess to a crime he had not committed, in order that he might be put to death." Maimonides, *The Book of Judges* 53 (1949).

23 Ibid. 775.

24 See Alan M. Dershowitz, *Reasonable Doubts* 58 (1997); Alan M. Dershowitz, *The Best Defense* 51 (1983).

25 *Mapp v. Ohio*, 367 U.S. 643 (1961).

26 Alan M. Dershowitz, *The Best Defense* xxi–xxii (1983).

27 Alan Dershowitz, "A Judicial Hero Retires," *Gainesville Sun*, May 31, 1985.

28 A popular column in the *New York Post, The Lyons Den*, made my family heroes in the Jewish community by reporting that Justice Goldberg and I

> *met when Dershowitz came to be interviewed for the coveted job of law clerk to Goldberg, then on the Supreme Court. All went well, and Dershowitz said he felt compelled to add one vital fact, that he's Orthodox.*
>
> *This meant he couldn't work on Saturdays, not even answer a phone. Goldberg had him meet the young man who'd be the other law clerk, Lee McTiernan. The Justice told them: "Lee can work on Saturdays, Alan on Sundays, giving me a functioning staff seven days a week." (Leonard Lyons,* The Lyons Den, New York Post, *September* 5, 1969, *p.* 47.*)*

29 *Youngstown Sheet & Tube Co. v. Sawyer,* 343 U.S. 579 (1952).

30 See, e.g., David Stebenne, *Arthur Goldberg: New Deal Liberal* 277, 354 (1996).

31 Quoted in Potter Stewart, *Reflections on the Supreme Court, Litigation* 8, 9 (1981–1982).

32 See Jeffrey Toobin, *The Nine: Inside the Secret World of the Supreme Court* 57 (2008).

33 Alexander M. Bickel, *The Least Dangerous Branch* 111 (1986, 2d ed.)

34 S.C. Res. 242, U.N. SCOR, 22d Sess., 1382d mtg. at 8, U.N. Doc. S/INF/22/Rev.2 (1967).

35 The French movie *Les Amants (The Lovers)* was the matter of dispute in *Jacobellis v. Ohio,* 378 U.S. 184 (1964).

36 John Cleland, *The Life and Adventures of Miss Fanny Hill* (1748). The Supreme Court discussed the redeeming social value of this book a few years later in *Memoirs v. Massachusetts,* 383 U.S. 413 (1966).

37 For a detailed account, see Laura Kalman, *Abe Fortas: A Biography* 322 (1990).

38 Cert. granted on January 7, 1963, 371 U.S. 946 (1963).

39 Hats are still not permitted in the courtroom. Supreme Court of the United States, *Guide for Counsel in Cases to Be Argued Before the United States Supreme Court,* October Term 2011 19, available at http://www.supremecourt.gov/oral_arguments/guideforcounsel.pdf.

40 Numbers 5:18. For a discussion of the Talmudic codification of this rule, see Rabbi Mayer Schiller, "The Obligation of Married Women to Cover Their Hair" 30 *Journal of Halacha* 81 (1995).

41 Today, the Supreme Court will not hear any oral arguments on Yom Kippur, even if it coincides with the first Monday of October, the legally mandated beginning of the new term. For a history of this recent tradition, see Tony Mauro, "Glasnost at the Supreme Court," in *A Year at the Supreme Court* (Neil Devins and Davison M. Douglas, eds.) 204–5 (2004).

42 This principle is known in Jewish law as *Pikuach nefesh*. See Alan M. Dershowitz, *The Genesis of Justice* ii (2000).

43 See, e.g., Paul C. Bartholomew, "The Supreme Court of the United States, 1963–1964," 17 *Western Political Quarterly* 595 (December 1964) ("With a consistency that seems to know no bounds, the Supreme Court during the recent term continued the history-making course it has been following for some time. Seldom has the Court caused as much controversy as in recent years, and perhaps never have the matters in controversy covered such a broad field of legal issues."); Philip B. Kurland, "The Supreme Court, 1963 Term," 78 Harvard Law Review 143, 160 (1964) ("In his sophomore year on the Court he [Goldberg] gave ample evidence that he would run second to none in effectuating reforms in our body politic").

44 *Escobedo v. Illinois,* 378 U.S. 478 (1964).

45 *Miranda v. Arizona,* 384 U.S. 436 (1966).

46 *Escobedo v. Illinois* 490.

47 See Alan Dershowitz, "Visibility, Accountability and Discourse as Essential to Democracy," 71 *Albany Law Review* 731 (2008).

48 This story has been corroborated by Goldberg's biographer. David Stebenne, *Arthur J. Goldberg: New Deal Liberal* 108.

49 That was later confirmed by the CBS News producer Fred Friendly. When he asked President Eisenhower whether appointing Warren was *one* of the mistakes he had made during his tenure, Eisenhower reportedly put up two fingers and said, "Two. They're both sitting on the Supreme Court: Earl Warren and William Brennan. Brennan is just as bad. Those two were very important jobs and I didn't do a good job with them." Seth Stern and Stephen Wermiel, *Justice Brennan: Liberal Champion* 139.

Chapter 4
Beginning My Life as an Academic

1 Thomas S. Johnson, "The Psyche and the Law: The Twain Do Meet," *Harvard Law Record*, October 22, 1964, 3.

2 In addition to first-year students, there were graduate students, Neiman Fellows, and other auditors.

3 Joseph Goldstein, Alan M. Dershowitz, and Richard D. Schwartz, *Criminal Law: Theory and Process* (1974).

4 Once I was teaching about a criminal concept that required the prosecution to build a wall separating information obtained under grant of immunity from information independently secured through investigation. The courts described this as a "Chinese Wall" because it had to be impenetrable. I was raising the possibility that one prosecutor may have improperly leaked information to another, and I described it as follows: "There may have been a chink in the Chinese Wall." A Chinese-American student in the class immediately took offense, erroneously believing that I was referring to Chinese people with that racial epithet. The thought had never occurred to me, but I never used that particular phraseology again.

5 *Annie Hall* (United Artists 1977) in Woody Allen, *Four Films of Woody Allen* 16 (2003).

6 For a picture of the lithograph, see Alan Dershowitz, *Finding Jefferson* 10 (2007).

7 My mother loved to write me letters at Harvard, and she would always address me as "Ass Prof," the abbreviation for assistant professor. Naturally, a student came upon one of the envelopes, and the word got around that my mother was calling me "the Ass Professor." My grandmother couldn't get the pronunciation right, calling me the "Profresser" (in Yiddish, *fresser* means "overeater").

8 Thomas S. Johnson, "The Psyche and the Law: The Twain Do Meet," *Harvard Law Record*, October 22, 1964, 3–4.

9 Ibid. 3.

10 Ibid.

11 Ibid.

12 Ibid. 4.

13 Arthur Auslander, "Course Termed 'Unreal,'" *Harvard Law Record*, November 5, 1964, 16.

14 Arthur J. Goldberg, "Dershowitz Defended," *Harvard Law Record*, November 19, 1964, 15.

15 Victor S. Navasky, "The Yales vs. The Harvards," *New York Times Magazine*, September 11, 1966.

16 *Malcolm X: Speeches at Harvard* (Archie Epps, ed.) (1968).

17 See infra at pp. 195–197, 296–302.

18 Women were first admitted in 1950, as members of the class of 1953. See Paul Massari, "HLS Fetes 50 Years of Women Graduates," *Harvard Gazette*, May 8, 2003.

19 Alan M. Dershowitz, "Psychiatry and the Law: A Knife That Cuts Both Ways," 51 *Judicature* 370 (1968).

20 Thomas Paine, *Dissertation on the First Principles of Government* (1795).

21 Among my early articles on prevention were the following: "Psychiatry and the Legal Process: A Knife That Cuts Both Ways," 51 *Judicature* 370 (1968); "The Law of Dangerousness," 23 *Journal of Legal Education* (1970); "Pretrial Preventive Detention, Legal Thought in the United States of America Under Contemporary Pressures: Reports," for *Am. Assn. for the Comp. Study of L* (1970); "The Law of Dangerousness: Some Fictions About Predictions," 23 *Journal of Legal Education* 24 (1971); "Imprisonment by Judicial Hunch," *ABAJ* (1970); "Preventive Detention of Citizens During a National Emergency: A Comparison Between Israel and the United States," 1 *Israel Yearbook of Human Rights* 295 (1971); "Preventive Disbarment: The Numbers Are Against It," *American Bar Association Journal*, August 1972 815; "The Role of Law During Times of Crisis," *Civil Disorder and Violence* (1972); "Could It Happen Here? Civil Liberties in a National Emergency," in *The Seventies* (Howe, ed.) (1972); "Abolishing the Insanity Defense: The Most Significant Feature of the Administration's Proposed Criminal Code—An Essay," *Criminal Law Bulletin*, January 1973, 434; "Constitutional Dimensions of Civil Commitment," 6 *Drug Use in America: Problem in Perspective*, Appendix (1973) (technical papers on the Second Report of the National Commission on Marijuana and Drug Abuse); "Preventive Confinement: A Suggested Framework for Constitutional Analysis," 51 *Texas Law Review* 1277 (1973); "Towards a Jurisprudence of Harm Prevention," in XV *The Limits of Law, Nomos* 135 (1974); "Dangerous as a Criterion for Confinement," *Bulletin of the American Academy of Psychiatry and the Law*, September 1974; "Indeterminate Sentencing as a Mechanism of Preventive Confinement," *Report to the Ninth Congress of the International Academy of Comparative Law* (1974); "The Origins of Preventive Confinement in Anglo-American Law," 43 *University of Cincinnati Law Review* (1974) (parts I and II); "Indeterminate Confinement: Letting the Therapy Fit the Crime," 123 *University of Pennsylvania Law Review* (1975); "Karyotype, Predictability and Culpability," *Genetics and Law* 63 (1976); "Criminal Sentencing in the United States: An Historical and

Conceptual Overview," *Annals*, American Academy of Political and Social Science, January 1976, 117. For a complete list of my scholarly publications, see "Symposium: Conference Honoring the Scholarship and Work of Alan M. Dershowitz," *Albany Law Review* 788–94, vol. 71, no. 3 (2008). (Hereinafter, "Symposium.")

22 In 1960, 1,887,000 residents of the United States were classified as inmates of institutions. Of these, only 346,000 were incarcerated in correctional institutions, while fully 630,000 resided in mental hospitals. U.S. Bureau of the Census, *Statistical Abstract of the United States: 1971*, Table 52 (1971) 41.

23 Alan Dershowitz, "The Origins of Preventive Confinement in Anglo-American Law—Part I: The English Experience," 43 *University of Cincinnati Law Review* 1 (1974); Alan Dershowitz, "The Origins of Preventive Confinement in Anglo-American Law—Part II: The American Experience," 43 *University of Cincinnati Law Review* 781 (1974).

24 Ibid. 59.

25 Ibid.

26 Ibid. In recent years, thousands of alleged sexual recidivists have been held in a form of preventive detention following completion of their prison sentences. They are held until they can demonstrate they no longer pose a risk. This constitutes, in practice, indeterminate confinement based on questionable predictions. The Supreme Court upheld the constitutionality of these practices: see *Kansas v. Hendricks*, 521 U.S. 346 (1997); *Kansas v. Crane* 534 U.S. 407 (2002).

27 Ibid.

Part II
The Changing Sound of Freedom of Speech

Chapter 5
The Evolution of the First Amendment

1 Congress originally voted to submit twelve amendments to be ratified by the states. (I own an original copy of the *Congressional Record* containing the Bill of Rights as proposed by Congress.) The First and Second—which dealt with the size of Congress and the compensation of senators and congressmen—were not ratified and the Third Amendment became the First. See, e.g., Akhil R. Amar, "The Bill of Rights as a Constitution," 100 *Yale Law Journal* 1131, 1137 (1991).

2 Charlton Heston, "The Second Amendment: America's First Freedom," speech to the National Press Club, Washington, D.C., September 17, 1997, available at http://www.c-spanvideo.org/program/90857-1.

3 Quoted in *Critical Essays on H. L. Mencken* (Douglas C. Stenerson, ed.) 37 (1987).

4 See, e.g., Lauren A. E. Schuker, "Dershowitz Accused of Plagiarism," September 29, 2003. For a rebuttal of these phony charges, see Alan Dershowitz, *The Case for Peace* 180–87 (2005).

5 Michele Steinberg, "Professor Francis Boyle: Israel Is Committing Genocide," February 2, 2010, available at http://www.scoop.co.nz/stories/HL1002/S00026.htm. See also Alan Dershowitz, "The Brooklyn College BDS Debate and Me: The Critics' Real Agenda," *Guardian*, February 8, 2013.

6 For a full account, see Alan Dershowitz, *Finding Jefferson* 135 (2007).

7 For more on my views on the "marketplace of ideas" justification for freedom of speech, see Alan Dershowitz, *Finding Jefferson* 127 (2007).

8 Thomas Hobbes, *Leviathan Book II (of Common Wealth)* (1651), chapter 18.

9 See Alan Dershowitz, *Rights from Wrongs* 108 (2005).

10 The rarely invoked Tenth Amendment makes this clear: "The powers not delegated to the United States by the Constitution, nor prohibited by it to the States, are reserved to the States respectively, or to the people." U.S. Constitution Amendment X. For a concise overview of the creation and ratification of the Constitution, see Erwin Chemerinsky, *Constitutional Law: Principles and Policies* 9 (2006).

11 Richard H. Fallon, Jr., *The Dynamic Constitution* 32 (2005).

12 Noah Feldman, *Divided by God* 31–32, 47 (2006).

13 See, e.g., Akhil R. Amar, "Did the Fourteenth Amendment Incorporate the Bill of Rights Against States?" 19 *Harvard Journal of Law and Public Policy* 443, 447 (1995–1996).

14 U.S. Constitution, Amendment XIV, section 1.

15 The Third Amendment is only incorporated in the Second Circuit, *Engblom v. Carey*, 677 F.2d 957 (2d Cir. 1982). The Sixth Amendment's right to a jury selected from residents of the state where the crime occurred, the Seventh Amendment's right to a jury trial in civil cases, and the Eighth Amendment's protections against excessive fines have all been held not to be incorporated by the Fourteenth Amendment. The Ninth Amendment has not been incorporated since it is not a separate source of individual rights. See Laurence H. Tribe, *American Constitutional Law* 776, n.14 (1998).

16 For a discussion on how the First Amendment has become applicable to the states through the Fourteenth Amendment, see Jerold H. Israel, "Selective Incorporation Revisited," 71 *Georgetown Law Journal* 253, 305 (Dec. 1982).

17 403 U.S. 15 (1971).

18 Ibid. 27.

19 Bob Woodward and Scott Armstrong, *The Brethren* 156 (Simon & Schuster paperback 2005).

20 Ibid. 170

21 Ibid.

22 Theodore White, *In Search of History: A Personal Adventure* 119–20 (1978).

23 *Miller v. California*, 413 U.S. 15 (1973), affirming *Roth v. United States*, 354 U.S. 476 (1957).

24 Cohen v. California, 403 U.S. 15 (1971).

25 I wrote about originalism in *Rights from Wrongs* 224 and *Is There a Right to Remain Silent?* 129.

26 *Schenck v. United States*, 249 U.S. 47, 52 (1919).

27 An additional, quite controversial, mechanism involves the financing of political campaigns. See *Citizens United v. Federal Election Commission*, 558 U.S. 50 (2010). Some critics argue that allowing unlimited corporate contributions to political campaigns drowns out the voices of those who cannot begin to match these contributions. See, e.g., "When Other Voices Are Drowned Out," *New York Times*, March 25, 2012. Civil libertarians are divided over this issue. Compare Ronald Dworkin, "The Decision That Threatens Democracy," *New York Review of Books*, May 13, 2010, with Floyd Abrams, "Citizens United and Its Critics," 120 *Yale Law Journal Online* 77 (2010), available at http://yalelawjournal.org/2010/9/29/abrams.html. I have not yet litigated cases in this area, though I have participated in several controversies growing out of it. After David Harris, the president of the National Jewish Democratic Council (NJDC), called on Jewish Democrats to sign a petition demanding that Mitt Romney stop taking campaign contributions from Sheldon Adelson on unfounded allegations that Adelson's money was "tainted," I yelled foul and wrote an op-ed in Adelson's defense. Alan M. Dershowitz, "NJDC Doesn't Speak for Me on Adelson," *Huffington Post*, July 6, 2012. The NJDC subsequently removed the petition from its website. However, it would not apologize for deliberately spreading lies regarding Adelson's business practices. Adelson brought a defamation lawsuit against the NJDC in the Southern District of New York, on which I have consulted. Nicholas Confessore, "Adelson Libel Lawsuit Seeks $60 Million," *New York Times*, August 9, 2012.

28 Tom Stoppard, *Rosencrantz and Guildenstern Are Dead* 60 (1966).

29 Richard Polenberg, *Fighting Faiths: The Abrams Case, the Supreme Court and Free Speech* 213 (1987).

30 Thomas Healy, *The Great Dissent* 91, 97 (2013).

31 *Schenck v. United States*, 249 U.S. 47 (1919).

32 The core analogy is the nonverbal alarm, and the derivative example is the verbal shout. By cleverly substituting the derivative shout for the core alarm, Holmes made it possible to analogize one set of words to another—as he could not have done if he had begun with the self-evident proposition that setting off an alarm bell is not free speech.

33 *Gertz v. Robert Welch, Inc.*, 418 U.S. 323, 339 (1974).

34 See infra at pp. 184–187.

35 Lewis M. Steel, "Where Rocker's Rights End," *New York Times*, February 12, 2000.

36 See Alan M. Dershowitz, "Baseball's Speech Police," *New York Times*, February 2, 2000.

37 *Smith v. Collin*, 439 U.S. 916, 919 (1978) (J. Blackmun dissenting). Outside court the analogies become even more absurdly stretched. A spokesperson for the New Jersey Sports and Exposition Authority complained that newspaper reports to the effect that a large number of football players had contracted cancer after playing in the Meadowlands—a stadium built atop a landfill—were the "journalistic equivalent of shouting fire in a crowded theater." An insect researcher acknowledged that his prediction that a certain amusement park might become roach-infested "may be tantamount to shouting fire in a crowded theater." The philosopher Sidney Hook, in a letter to the *New York Times* bemoaning a Supreme Court decision that required a plaintiff in a defamation action to prove that the offending statement was actually false, argued that the First Amendment does not give the press carte blanche to accuse innocent persons "any more than the First Amendment protects the right of someone falsely to shout fire in a crowded theater." Quoted in Alan M. Dershowitz, "Shouting 'Fire!'" 263 *Atlantic Monthly*, January 1989.

38 In one case in which the fire analogy was directly to the point, a creative defendant tried to get around it. The case involved a man who calmly advised an airline clerk that he was "only here to hijack the plane." He was charged, in effect, with shouting fire in a crowded theater, and his rejected defense—as quoted by the court—was as follows: "If we built fire-proof theaters and let people know about this, then the shouting of 'Fire!' would not cause panic." *Bauge v. Jernigan*, 671 F. Supp. 709, 711 (D. Colo. 1987).

39 Abbie Hoffman, *The Best of Abbie Hoffman* 196 (1993).

40 Alan M. Dershowitz, "Shouting 'Fire!'" 263 *Atlantic Monthly*, January 1989.

Chapter 6
Direct and Vicarious "Offensiveness" of Obscenity

1 At common law, truth was not a defense to defamation, because a "truthful defamation was deemed more harmful than a false one." See Alan Dershowitz, *Finding Jefferson* 104–5 (2007).

2 There is a strong case for some restrictions on the use of such epithets by some people in some contexts—such as a teacher calling a student by such names. See 184–187 infra. Alan M. Dershowitz, "Visibility, Accountability and Discourse as Essential to Democracy," 71 *Albany Law Review* 731, 758 (2008).

3 *F.C.C. v. Pacifica Found.*, 438 U.S. 726 (1978). The issue of whether the FCC can regulate "indecency" as defined in the *Pacifico* decision was recently addressed by the court. *F.C.C. v. Fox Television Stations, Inc.*, 556 U.S. 502 (2009).

4 The exposure of such material to children raises separate issues, but the Supreme Court has ruled that the potential exposure of children does not by itself justify censoring adults. See *Butler v. Michigan*, 352 U.S. 380 (1957).

5 See Alan M. Dershowitz, *The Best Defense*, chapter 5 (1983).

6 *Williams v. Hathaway*, 400 F. Supp. 122 (D. Mass. 1975).

7 See Nikki Craft, "Alan Dershowitz, Joseph Mengele and Me," 1987.

8 The issue is somewhat complicated, because it may be true that certain kinds of violent pornography (as well as violent nonpornography) are contributing factors in certain people's decision or propensity to rape, just as alcohol or other drugs may be contributing factors. What is undeniably clear is that only a minuscule fraction of men who view pornography go on to rape or commit violence, and that a great many rapists do not view pornography. See Alan M. Dershowitz, "Why Pornography?" in *Shouting Fire* 1630–75 (2002).

9 The young girl who played the lead role, and later appeared in an Ingmar Bergman film *Autumn Sonata* (1978), recently died at the age of sixty-six, thus bringing home to me how much time had passed. Dennis Hevesi, "Lena Nyman, Star of 'I Am Curious' Films, Is Dead at 66," *New York Times*, February 5, 2011.

10 354 U.S. 476 (1954).

11 394 U.S. 557 (1969).

12 For an elaboration of the argument in my appellate brief, see *Byrne v. Karalexis*, 1970 WL 136414 (U.S.) (U.S., 2004).

13 28 U.S.C.A. § 1253.

14 The prologue read as follows:

> *There are a number of scenes which show the young girl and her lover nude. Several scenes depict sexual intercourse under various circumstances, some of them quite unusual. If you believe that you would be offended or embarrassed by the showing of such scenes, you are invited at this time to obtain a refund of your admission at the box office.*

15 *Griswold v. Connecticut*, 381 U.S. 479 (1965).

16 *Byrne v. Karalexis*, 306 F. Supp. 1363, 1365 (D. Mass. 1969).

17 Ibid. 1366. The court continued:

> *The question is, how far does* Stanley *go. Is the decision to be limited to the precise problem of "mere private possession of obscene material," is it the high water mark of a past flood, or is it the precursor of a new one? Defendant points to the fact that the court in* Stanley *stated that* Roth v. United States *was "not impaired by today's holding" and in the course of its opinion recognized the state's interest there upheld in prohibiting public distribution of obscenity. Yet, with due respect,* Roth *cannot remain intact, for the Court there had announced that "obscenity is not within the area of constitutionally protected speech or press," whereas it held that Stanley's interest was protected by the First Amendment, and that the fact that the film was "devoid of any ideological content" was irrelevant.*

18 Ibid.

19 Ibid.

20 Ibid. 1367.

21 *Byrne v. Karalexis*, 401 U.S. 216 (1971).

22 413 U.S. 15 (1973).

23 *Paris Adult Theatre I v. Slaton*, 413 U.S. 49 (1973).

24 *Paris Adult Theatre I v. Slaton*, 413 U.S. 49, 57.

25 Ibid. 57–58.

26 As my colleague Richard Fallon has observed: "*Miller* has done little to stem a mounting flood of sexually explicit materials into American popular culture. The Court's conservative stand against

sexually licentious material thus appears to have little practical significance." Richard H. Fallon, *The Dynamic Constitution* 48 (2005).

27 Nor would this be my last encounter with Chief Justice Burger. See infra at 409.

28 See Alan M. Dershowitz, *The Best Defense* 174–78 (1983).

29 I was also involved—either as a defense lawyer, consultant, or commentator—in the defense of several magazines and books. See, e.g., Alan M. Dershowitz, *Shouting Fire*, chapters 18–20 (2002).

30 During a preview of a film about the *Deep Throat* controversy—*Inside Deep Throat* (Universal Pictures, 2005)—I saw some soft-core excerpts. They were awful.

31 Tom Goldstein, "Notables Aid Convicted 'Deep Throat' Star," *New York Times*, June 29, 1976.

32 Nat Hentoff, "How to Make the First Amendment Obscene," *Village Voice*, June 28, 1976. A follow-up story appeared in the next issue: Nat Hentoff, "But What If the Supreme Court Won't Listen?" *Village Voice*, July 5, 1976, 36.

33 It also generated numerous other stories presenting our side of the case. The headlines include the following:

KING OF THE PORNO ACTORS FINDS HIMSELF IN DEEP THROES
IN TROUBLE UP TO HIS THROAT
HOW HARRY GOT REAMED
DEEP THREAT
PORN'S DEEP GOAT
REEMS SHAFTED IN BIBLE BELT

34 The *New York Times* described a joint appearance at the Harvard Law Forum:

> *Harry stood with a portrait of Supreme Court Justice Felix Frankfurter beaming down on him. Beside him sat Alan Dershowitz, looking like a tweedy Marx Brother with his wild nimbus of ash-blond hair, saying that he felt Harry Reems' trial was the most significant First Amendment conspiracy case since Dr. Spock. (Tom Goldstein, "Notables Aid Convicted 'Deep Throat' Star,"* New York Times, *June 29, 1976)*

> *Dershowitz acted as a sort of kibitzer for Harry. He noted that the crew of the Glomar Explorer, [which] had been shown a videotape of* Deep Throat, *had more to do with transporting obscene material in interstate commerce than Harry Reems did. Would Larry Parrish prosecute them? When I asked Parrish, he said: "They're not insulated against prosecution." (Ted Morgan, "United States Versus the Princes of Porn,"* New York Times, *March 6, 1977)*

35 Mike Royko, "Free Speech Costs Plenty But the Price Can Get Too High," Chicago Daily News Service, August 3, 1976.

36 I relate the other legal theories on which we might have won the case in *The Best Defense* 155–74 (1983).

37 Margalit Fox, "Harry Reems, Star of 'Deep Throat' Film, Dies at 65," *New York Times*, March 20, 2013.

38 Lisa J. Goodall, "A Younger Dershowitz Argues Porn Case," *Harvard Crimson*, December 5, 1987.

39 Gloria Steinem, "Linda Lovelace's Ordeal,'" *Ms.*, May 1980.

40 Linda Lovelace (with Mike McGrady), *Ordeal* (1980).

41 *Lovelace* (Millenium Films 2013)

42 "200 Protest Film Screening, Citing Sexism and Violence," *Harvard Crimson*, May 17, 1980.

43 "Two Arrested for Showing Deep Throat," *Harvard Crimson*, May 17, 1980.

44 *Miller v. California*, 413 U.S. 15 (1973).

45 *Paris Adult Theatre I v. Slaton*, 413 U.S. 49, 57 (1973).

46 *Brown v. Entertainment Merchants Association*, 131 S. Ct, 2729 (2011).

47 François de La Rouchefoucauld, *Collected Maxims and Other Reflections*, vol. 218 (Oxford's World Classics) 63 (2008).

48 Thomas Babington Macaulay, 1 *History of England from the Accession of James the Second*, chapter 2, 159 (1849).

49 Even if there were evidence that it harmed the viewer, that would not be a good enough reason for banning it, so long as there was no evidence it harmed others.

50 Indeed, since my last obscenity cases, there have been very few successful prosecutions and even fewer appellate affirmances of obscenity convictions.

51 Alan M. Dershowitz, "Why Pornography?" reprinted in *Shouting Fire* 163–75 (2002).

52 Ibid.

53 Ibid.

54 Ibid.

55 James Madison to William T. Barry, August 4, 1822, in James Madison, *Writings 1772–1836* (Library of America) 790 (1999).

Chapter 7
Disclosure of Secrets

1 This phrase is attributed to Oliver Wendell Holmes. See, e.g., Oliver Wendell Holmes, Jr., *The Path of the Law and the Common Law* (foreword by J. Craig Williams, Esq.) vii (2009).

2 For an account of how small groups, like NGOs and media watchdogs, serve as a check on executive secrecy, see Jack Goldsmith, *Power and Constraint* (2012).

3 *Kennedy v. Mendoza-Martinez,* 372 U.S. 144, 160 (1963).

4 Gertrude Samuels, "The Fight for Civil Liberties Never Stays Won," *New York Times,* June 19, 1966.

5 Deuteronomy 16:18–20.

6 Thomas Paine, *The American Crisis, Number IV: Philadelphia, September 12* (1777).

7 See Alan M. Dershowitz, "Stretch Points of Liberty," *Nation,* March 15, 1971.

8 Alan Dershowitz, "They Were Virtual Strangers, Yet the Government Charged Them with Conspiracy," *New York Times,* September 14, 1969.

9 Frank Snepp, *Decent Interval* (1977).

10 *Snepp v. United States,* 444 U.S. 507 (1980).

11 I discuss the Snepp case in *The Best Defense* 225–40 (1983).

12 Mike Gravel, *The Pentagon Papers* (1971).

13 *Gravel v. United States,* 408 U.S. 606 (1972).

14 *New York Times Co. v. United States,* 403 U.S. 713 (1971).

15 Transcript of oral argument in *New York Times v. United States* (Pentagon Papers (case)), available at the Oyez Project at IIT Chicago-Kent College of Law, http://www.oyez.org/cases/1970-1979/1970/1970_1873.

16 Erwin N. Griswold, "Secrets Not Worth Keeping," *Washington Post,* February 15, 1989.

17 See Gabriel Shoenfeld, *Necessary Secrets* 271–72 (2010).

18 See Alan Dershowitz, "The Trouble with Rape Prosecutions," *Daily Beast,* July 1, 2011.

19 The checks don't always work, as evidenced by the Murdoch scandals.

20 See, e.g., Geoffrey Stone, *Perilous Times,* chapter 1 (2004).

21 Ibid.

22 I can only disclose material that is in the public record or that he has given me permission to disclose.

23 Erwin N. Griswold, "Secrets Not Worth Keeping," *Washington Post,* February 15, 1989.

24 Charlie Savage, "Soldier Admits Providing Files to WikiLeaks," *New York Times,* March 1, 2013.

25 Ibid.

26 See Joachim Hermann, "The Rule of Compulsory Prosecution and the Scope of Prosecutorial Discretion in Germany," 41 *Univeristy of Chicago Law Review* 468 (1974); John H. Langbein, "Controlling Prosecutorial Discretion in Germany," 41 *University of Chicago Law Review* 439 (1974).

27 See, e.g., Steven D. Clymer, "Unequal Justice: The Federalization of Criminal Law," 70 *Southern California Law Review* 643, 713, 713 n. 300 (1997).

28 The Supreme Court has recognized, in the context of the First Amendment, that a law purporting to regulate speech or press, in order to survive the "strict scrutiny" standard of review required by the First Amendment, must not be overinclusive or underinclusive. See *Brown v. Entertainment Merchants Assn.,* 131 S. Ct. 2729, 2740–42 (2011).

29 *New York Times Co. v. Sullivan,* 376 U.S. 254, 276 (1964).

30 See Alan Dershowitz, "Who Needs to Know," *New York Times,* May 28, 2010. See also debate available at http://www.npr.org/2011/06/13/137086637/does-freedom-of-the-press-extend-to-state-secrets.

31 Alan Dershowitz, *Finding Jefferson,* 30–31 (2007).

32 As I wrote in *Shouting Fire*:

> *Though [students who seek to censor "offensive" speech] insist on being governed by the laws of the outside world when it comes to their personal lives, railing against visitor rules and curfews, they want their universities to adopt rules that restrict their First Amendment rights of free speech in order to shield them from the ugly realities of prejudice.* (Alan M. Dershowitz, *Shouting Fire* 192–93 [2002]).

33 See Alan M. Dershowitz, "Visibility, Accountability and Disclosure as Essential to Democracy," 71 *Albany Law Review* 731, 757 (2008).

34 Randall Kennedy, *Nigger: The Strange Career of a Troublesome Word* (2003).

35 In 2007, I taught a university-wide course with Professor Steven Pinker on the issue of taboo. The question was whether there are issues that are so delicate, sensitive, controversial, or disgusting that they should be treated as "taboos," even on a university campus. The idea for the class was stimulated by the forced resignation of Harvard president Lawrence Summers for having

suggested that women may be less suited by their biology to excellence in certain demanding intellectual pursuits.

We searched for a *theory* of taboo—a description or prescription of genres of expression that lie outside the presumption of discussability and are, or should be, subject to suppression, censorship, or tabooization. Professor Pinker presented evolutionary and psychological arguments for the existence and utility of some taboos. I discussed the legal and moral arguments for and against any exceptions to the general presumption of free expression. In the end, there was little agreement, except that there is and should be a difference between societal taboos, enforceable by social sanction, and official governmental censorship, enforceable by the power of the state. We also agreed that notwithstanding the clear words of the First Amendment, Congress *must* have the power to make *some* laws banning the disclosure of *some* secrets for *some* time.

Chapter 8
Expressions That Incite Violence and Disrupt Speakers

1 The leading case here is *Chaplinsky v. State of New Hampshire,* 315 U.S. 568 (1942) (stating that "there are certain well-defined and narrowly limited classes of speech, the prevention and punishment of which has never been thought to raise any Constitutional problem. These include . . . the insulting or 'fighting' words—those which by their very utterance inflict injury or tend to incite an immediate breach of the peace. It has been well observed that such utterances are no essential part of any exposition of ideas, and are of such slight social value as a step to truth that any benefit that may be derived from them is clearly outweighed by the social interest in order and morality" (Ibid. 571–72). Although the court continued to uphold the doctrine, it substantially narrowed the grounds on which fighting words are thought to apply, as evidenced by the recent Westboro Baptist church case, *Snyder v. Phelps,* 562 U.S. 131 S. Ct. 1207 (2011).

2 The "clear and present danger test" was penned by Oliver Wendell Holmes in a case we encountered earlier: *Schenck v. United States,* 249 U.S. 47 (1919). ("The question in every case is whether the words used are used in such circumstances and are of such a nature as to create a clear and present danger that they will bring about the substantive evils that Congress has a right to prevent." Ibid. 52.) Although *Schenck* was never formally overturned, the court later articulated a new test, the "imminent lawless action test," which remains the law today. *Brandenburg v. Ohio* 395 U.S. 444 (1969).

3 As I note elsewhere, how the balance between the right of the speaker and the right of the potential victim should be struck is context-specific and may differ from one democracy to another: "Modern-day Germany has criminalized Holocaust denial, as have several other democracies. The United States is the exception to the rule of placing any restraints on specific genres of dangerous hate speech. I would not want to see the United States change . . . but what is right for the United States—especially near the edges of absolute freedoms—may not necessarily be right for every democracy facing different problems" (Alan Dershowitz, *The Case for Peace* 85 [2005]).

4 The law regarding the "heckler's veto" is not entirely clear. The Supreme Court repeatedly held that a speaker cannot be preemptively stopped because of fear of a heckler's veto, but in the immediate face of violence, the police may ask the speaker to cease his action to satisfy the hecklers, provided the police are motivated not by a desire to silence the speaker but rather by a concern for the preservation of order. *Feiner v. New York,* 340 U.S. 315 (1951). However, the court criticized this approach in later cases, finding "governmental grants of power to private actors" to be "constitutionally problematic" in cases where "regulations allowed a single, private actor to unilaterally silence a speaker even as to willing listeners." *Hill v. Colorado,* 530 U.S. 703, 735 (2000).

5 Erwin Chemerinsky, "Criminal Charges Against Hecklers Go Too Far," *Orange County Register,* February 8, 2011.

6 Available online at http://www.youtube.com/watch?v=7w96UR79TBw.

7 "In Defense of UCI Muslim Student Union," open letter to O.C. district attorney Tony Rackauckas from the Council on American-Islamic Relations, Greater Los Angeles Area, available at http://www.baitcal.com/UCIMuslimStudentUnion.html. The letter was also signed by Chuck Anderson, president of the ACLU chapter, Orange County, and Hector Villagra, the incoming executive director of the ACLU of Southern California.

8 Ibid.

9 For a more detailed discussion, see my letter to the editor, "Lawyer Alan Dershowitz Decries ACLU Support of UCI Muslim Students," *Orange County Register,* May 12, 2011.

10 Erwin Chemerinsky, "Criminal Charges Against Hecklers Go Too Far," *Orange County Register,* February 8, 2011.

11 Hamed Aleaziz, "Should Heckling Be Illegal?" *Mother Jones,* September 26, 2011, available at http://www.motherjones.com/mojo/2011/09/should-heckling-be-illegal.

12 Had the school administered appropriate discipline, I could understand an argument against

piling on with a misdemeanor prosecution, but "the red badge of courage"—the minor discipline—given to them by the college only served to encourage repetition of their censorial conduct.

13 Vik Jolly and Larry Welborn, "UC Muslim Students Get Probation, Fines," *Orange County Register*, September 23, 2011.

14 Alan M. Dershowitz, "'Irvine 10' Conviction Constitutionally Sound," *Orange County Register*, September 27, 2011.

Chapter 9
The Right to Falsify History and Science

1 StGB§ 130 Public Incitement (1985, Revised 1992, 2002, 2005). ("(4) Whoever publicly or in a meeting disturbs the public peace in a manner that assaults the human dignity of the victims by approving of, denying or rendering harmless the violent and arbitrary National Socialist rule shall be punished with imprisonment for not more than three years or a fine.")

2 National Socialism Prohibition Law (1947, amendments of 1992). ("§ 3g. He who operates in a manner characterized other than that in § § 3a–3f will be punished (revitalizing of the NSDAP or identification with), with imprisonment from one to up to ten years, and in cases of particularly dangerous suspects or activity, be punished with up to twenty years imprisonment. § 3h. As an amendment to § 3 g., whoever denies, grossly plays down, approves or tries to excuse the National Socialist genocide or other National Socialist crimes against humanity in a print publication, in broadcast or other media.")

3 Law No 90-615 of July 13, 1990, *Journal Officiel de la République Française* [J.O.] [Official Gazette of France]. (" . . . to repress acts of racism, anti-semitism and xenophobia (1990) Art 9. ('Art. 24 (a): those who have disputed the existence of one or more crimes against humanity such as they are defined by Article 6 of the statute of the international tribunal military annexed in the agreement of London of August 8, 1945 and which were a carried out either by the members of an organization declared criminal pursuant to Article 9 of the aforementioned statute, or by a person found guilty such crimes by a French or international jurisdiction shall be punished by one month to one years imprisonment or a fine.")

4 Turkish Penal Code, Article 301, which makes it a crime "to publicly denigrate Turkishness." In January 2012, France enacted a law that makes it a crime to *deny* the Armenian genocide.

5 For examples of Faurisson's stances, see Robert Faurisson, "The Leaders of the Arab States Should Quit Their Silence on the Importance of the Holocaust," Institute for Historical Review Beirut Conference, March 22, 2001, accessible at http://www.ihr.org/conference/beirutconf/010331faurisson.html; and Robert Faurisson, "The Diary of Anne Frank: Is it Genuine?" *Journal of Historical Review* 19, no. 6, http://www.ihr.org/jhr/v19/v19n6p-2_Faurisson.html.

6 For example, Faurisson relies on an entry, dated October 18, 1942, from the diary of SS doctor Johann-Paul Kremer written during the three months he spent at Auschwitz in 1942. An eminent scholar checked Faurisson's use of the entry and demonstrated that Faurisson's "research" was fraudulent. The diary entry read: "This Sunday morning in cold and humid weather I was present at the 11th special action (Dutch). Atrocious scenes with three women who begged us to let them live."

Faurisson concludes that this passage proves (1) that a "special action" was nothing more than the sorting out by doctors of the sick from the healthy during a typhus epidemic; (2) that the "atrocious scenes" were "executions of persons who had been condemned to death, executions for which the doctor was obliged to be present"; and (3) that "among the condemned were three women who had come in a convoy since the women were shot and not gassed."

Faurisson, who said he had researched the trial, knew that his own source, Dr. Kremer, had testified that the gas chambers did exist. Yet he deliberately omitted that crucial item from his book, while including the fact that the women were shot. Faurisson also knew that the three women were "in good health." Yet he led his readers to believe that Dr. Kremer had said they were selected on medical grounds during an epidemic. Finally, Faurisson states that those who were shot had been "condemned to death." Yet he knew they were shot by the SS for refusing to enter the gas chambers.

A French scholar named George Wellers analyzed this diary entry and the surrounding documentation for *Le Monde*. He did *actual* historical research, checking the Auschwitz record for October 18, 1942. His research disclosed that 1,710 Dutch Jews arrived that day. Of these, 1,594 were sent immediately to the gas chambers. The remaining 116 people, all women, were brought into the camp; the three women who were the subject of the Kremer diary must have been among them. The three women were, in fact, shot—as Faurisson concludes. But that fact appears nowhere in Kremer's diary. How then did Faurisson learn it? Professor Wellers was able to find the answer with some simple research. He checked Dr. Kremer's testimony at a Polish war crimes trial. This is what Kremer said at the trial: "Three Dutch women did not want to go *into the gas chamber* and begged to have their lives spared. They were young women, *in good health*, but in spite of that their prayer was not granted and the SS who were participating in the action shot them on the spot" [emphasis added].

This type of pseudo-history is typical of Faurisson in particular, and of Holocaust denial "research" in general. Yet Chomsky was prepared to lend his academic legitimacy to Faurisson's "extensive historical research."

7 Robert Faurisson, *Mémoire en Défense* (1989), préface de Noam Chomsky.

8 Scot Lehigh, "Men of Letters," *Boston Phoenix*, June 16–22, 1989, 30.

9 Alan M. Dershowitz, "Chomsky Defends Vicious Lie as Free Speech," *Boston Globe*, June 13, 1989.

10 *Today Show* with Katie Couric, NBC Universal, February 10, 1999.

11 In re Hale, Comm. of Character & Fitness (Ill. App. Ct. 1998) reprinted in Geoffrey C. Hazard et al., *The Law and Ethics of Lawyering* 875 (1999).

12 Jodi Wilgoren, "40-Year Term for Supremacist in Plot on Judge," *New York Times*, April 7, 2005.

13 In a debate in Canada on laws criminalizing Holocaust denial, I took my usual position in favor of freedom of speech:

> *I regret to say this, but I think that Holocaust denial speech is not even a close question. There is no persuasive argument that I can think of in logic, in law, in constitutionality, in policy, or in education, which should deny [anyone] who chooses to the right to take whatever position he wants on the Holocaust. The existence of the Holocaust, its extent, its fault, its ramifications, its political use are fair subjects for debate. I think it is despicable for anybody to deny the existence of the Holocaust. But I cannot sit in judgment over the level of despicability of anybody's exercise of freedom of speech.*
>
> *Of course I agree that sticks and stones can break your bones, and words can harm you and maim you. That's the price we pay for living in a democracy. It's not that speech doesn't matter. If speech didn't matter, I wouldn't devote my life to defending it. Speech matters. Speech can hurt. That's not why those of us who defend free speech, particularly free speech of this kind, do it. We do it because we don't trust government. (International Human Rights Conference, Panel IV: "Words That Maim—Freedom of Expression, Freedom from Expression," McGill University, Montreal, November 3–4, 1987.)*

My remarks can be found in *Nuremberg Forty Years Later: The Struggle Against Injustice in Our Times* (Erwin Cutler, ed.) 131 (1995).

In response, a prominent Canadian judge, Maxwell Cohen, said that anyone who holds such views "ought not to be a law teacher." I disagree. Professors must defend the right of those they disagree with to express wrongheaded views, while insisting on their own right—indeed obligation—to express disagreement with such views.

14 Alan Dershowitz, *The Case for Peace* 29 (2005).

15 Even university professors seem to misunderstand this important distinction. I encountered this intellectual muddleheadedness in 2010 when I received an honorary doctorate from Tel Aviv University and was asked to deliver a talk on behalf of the honorees. In my talk, I defended the right of professors at the University of Tel Aviv to call for boycotts against Israeli universities. This is part of what I said:

> *Israeli academics are free to challenge not only the legitimacy of the Jewish state but even, as one professor at this university has done, the authenticity of the Jewish people. Israeli academics are free to distort the truth, construct false analogies, and teach their students theories akin to the earth being flat—and they do so with relish and with the shield of academic freedom. So long as these professors do not violate the rules of the academy, they have the precious right to be wrong, because we have learned the lesson of history that no one has a monopoly on truth and that the never-ending search for truth requires, to quote the title of one of Israel's founders' autobiographies, "trial and error." The answer to falsehood is not censorship; it is truth. The answer to bad ideas is not firing the teacher, but articulating better ideas which prevail in the marketplace. The academic freedom of the faculty is central to the mission of the university.*

After defending their right to freedom of expression, I exercised my own right to express my own views about the merits and demerits of their ideas:

> *But academic freedom is not the province of the hard left alone. Academic freedom includes the right to agree with the government, to defend the government, and to work for the government. Some of the same hard leftists who demand academic freedom for themselves and their ideological colleagues were among the leaders of those seeking to deny academic freedom to a distinguished law professor who had worked for the military advocate general and whose views they disagreed with. To its credit, Tel Aviv University rejected this attempt to limit academic freedom to those who criticized the government.*
>
> *Rules of academic freedom for professors must be neutral, applicable equally to right and left. Free speech for me but not for thee is the beginning of the road to tyranny.*

Following my talk a group of Tel Aviv professors accused me of McCarthyism and of advocating censorship. *The Chronicle of Higher Education* "reported" that I was pressuring the university to take action against professors who support boycotts against Israeli universities. I responded: "I continue to oppose any efforts by any university to punish academics for expressing anti-government views. But I insist on my right to criticize those with whom I disagree. Surely that is the true meaning of academic freedom. I urge your readers to read the full text of my controversial talk at Tel Aviv University." (May 12, 2010. The full text of the speech is available at http://www.haaretz.com/full-text-of-alan-dershowitz-s-tel-aviv-speech-1.289841).

16 John E. Mack, *Abduction: Human Encounters with Aliens* (1994).

17 Ibid. at 417.

18 Alan M. Dershowitz, "Defining Academic Freedom," *Harvard Crimson*, June 30, 1995.

19 Ibid.

20 Christopher B. Daly, "Harvard Clears Abduction Researcher John Mack," *Washington Post*, August 4, 1995, 1.

Chapter 10
Defamation and Privacy

1 William Shakespeare, *Othello*, Act 3, Scene 3.

2 Although some scholars have advocated group libel laws. See, e.g., Dan Kahan, "A Communitarian Defense of Group Libel Laws," 101 *Harvard Law Review* 682 (1988); Jeremy Waldron, *The Harm in Hate Speech* (2012).

3 In fact, a midlevel appeals court recently decided that it is no longer slander per se in New York to falsely say that someone is gay. The New York court overturned decades of previous cases, which were "based on a false premise that it is shameful and disgraceful to be described as lesbian, gay or bisexual." "Label of Gay Is No Longer Defamatory, Court Rules," *New York Times*, May 31, 2012.

4 See Alan Dershowitz, *Finding Jefferson* 104 (2007).

5 *New York Times v. Sullivan*, 376 U.S. 254, 280 (1964).

6 Ibid. 298–99.

7 In a 1990 column, Mike Barnicle wrote that in 1983, I had said to him: "I love Asian women, don't you? They're . . . they're so submissive." Barnicle simply fabricated this quote, as well as the meeting during which the statement was allegedly made. Alan M. Dershowitz, "There Was No Discussion of Asian Women," *Boston Globe*, December 13, 1990.

8 I discuss this story in Alan Dershowitz, *Finding Jefferson* 135 (2007).

9 Maurizio Molinarí, "*È la Magna Charta del terrorismo*," *La Stampa*, January 27, 2005.

10 Ibid.

11 *Hustler Magazine v. Falwell*, 485 U.S. 46, 54–55 (1988).

12 *Bowman v. Heller*, 420 Mass. 517, 520 (1995).

13 Ibid. 525.

14 When my book *The Case for Israel* hit the *New York Times* bestseller list, Noam Chomsky asked Finkelstein to savage it. Finkelstein then accused me of plagiarism for quoting a frequently used paragraph by Mark Twain and citing it to *Twain*, rather than to the secondary source in which he erroneously claimed I had originally found it. His charge was preposterous on its face and so found after I asked Harvard to investigate it. I recount this episode in *The Case for Peace*, chapter 16 (2005). Shortly after Finkelstein falsely accused me of plagiarism, he came up for tenure at DePaul University, and the former chairman of his department invited me to catalogue "the most egregious instances of [his] dishonesty." I did so. I also wrote an op-ed for the *Wall Street Journal* (Alan M. Dershowitz, "Finkelstein's Bigotry," *Wall Street Journal*, May 4, 2007). He was denied tenure.

15 Norman Finkelstein, "Should Alan Dershowitz Target Himself for Assassination?" *Counterpunch*, August 12–14, 2006.

16 The cartoon is still widely available on the Internet, for instance on the flickr-website of the cartoon "artist." http://www.flickr.com/photos/96755483@N00/222216939/.

17 Samuel D. Warren and Louis D. Brandeis, "The Right to Privacy," 4 *Harvard Law Review* 193 (1890).

18 Ibid. 193.

19 *Shields by Shields v. Gross*, 563 F. Supp. 1253, 1256–1257 (S.D.N.Y. 1983).

20 *Florida Star v. B. J. F.*, 491 U.S. 524 (1989).

Chapter 11
Speech That "Supports" Terrorist Groups

1 18 U. S. C. §2339B.

2 My talk continued:

> *Fulfillment of contractual obligation was deemed so important by the framers of our Constitution that they prohibited the states from "impairing the obligation of contracts," and required the government to satisfy all debts "contracted and engagements entered into" even before our Constitution. These provisions were referring to contracts involving money and property. How much more sacred is a contract involving life. Our Constitution places life before property in ordering our rights.*
>
> *Our Constitution empowers Congress "to make all laws which shall be necessary and proper for carrying into execution" the power vested in the government or its officers. You have the power to make our government keep its promise—satisfy its contractual obligations—to the residents.*
>
> *The President must enforce the laws and obligations of the United States.*
>
> *And the judiciary is the ultimate guarantor that the government complies with the due process of law and other constitutional provisions.*
>
> *As you may know, there is now a case pending before the courts of this district mandamusing the government, particularly the secretary of state, to delist the organization with which the residents of Ashraf are associated.*
>
> *I have the high honor of representing a group of distinguished Americans who have asked me to file a friend of the court brief supporting delisting. This group includes the former attorney general of the United States, the former head of the FBI, the former secretary of Homeland Security, and numerous generals, admirals, and others who have not only served our country with distinction, but at the risk of their lives.*
>
> *We place our sacred honor at risk by supporting this humanitarian cause—the saving of innocent lives, and the obligation of our government to keep its commitments. But we have little choice because we love our country, we love liberty (not Camp Liberty but real liberty), and we believe that promises made by our government must be kept.*
>
> *As a constitutional lawyer, I am confident that we are on the right side of this lawsuit, even though some of my dear friends are on the other side. We hope and expect that the courts will demand that our government provide due process and apply the law, which demand quick action in responding to a petition to delist.*
>
> *As soon as delisting occurs, the free nations of the world—which do not include Iran or, tragically, Iraq, which is now under the sway of Iran—will be willing to accept the residents of Ashraf as refugees.* (Alan Dershowitz, Washington, D.C., April 6, 2012)

"Senate Briefing: Iran's Nuclear Threat: Impact of Sanctions & Policy Options," May 15, 2012, 10–12, available at http://www.iaca-mo.org/senate.pdf.

3 Scott Shane, "Iranian Dissidents Convince U.S. to Drop Terror Label," September 21, 2012.

4 This quotation is attributed to Voltaire but its original source is unknown. It first appeared in Evelyn Beatrice Hall, *The Friends of Voltaire* 199 (1906). Voltaire did apparently write the following: "I detest what you write, but I would give my life to make it possible for you to continue to write."

5 The opposite side of the private self-censorship coin is the private circumvention of governmental censorship. Private hacking groups such as Anonymous will do everything in their power to thwart governmental censorship of any kind, including the use of unlawful means, even violence, to subvert or retaliate for legitimate restrictions on publication. This means that the future battles for freedom of speech are likely to be fought on private as well as governmental battlefields and may well involve violent actions on all sides. William J. Bennett and Alan M. Dershowitz, "A Failure of the Press," *Washington Post*, February 23, 2006.

6 See Nina Shea, "A Perverse Process," *New York Post*, December 16, 2011.

Chapter 12
Life Intrudes on Law

1 The original quotation, according to Boswell's famous biography, is as follows: "When a man knows he is to be hanged in a fortnight, it concentrates his mind wonderfully." James Boswell, *The Life of Samuel Johnson* 612 (Penguin Classics, 2008).

2 Alan M. Dershowitz, *The Best Defense*, chapter 1 (1983).

3 See Alan M. Dershowitz, *The Best Defense*, chapter 7 (1983); Alan M. Dershowtiz, *Chutzpah*, chapter 8 (1991); Telford Taylor (with Alan Dershowitz, George Fletcher, Leon Lipson, and Melvin Stein), *Courts of Terror* (1976).

Part III
Criminal Justice

Chapter 13
"Death Is Different"

1 *Gregg v. Georgia*, 428 U.S. 153, 188 (1976).

2 I have litigated or consulted on more than three dozen cases involving the death or intended death of human beings. These cases fall into three categories: (1) cases in which the defendant faced the death penalty; (2) cases in which the defendant was charged with killing someone; and (3) cases in which the defendant was accused of attempting, intending, or conspiring to kill.

3 The Tison brothers case was made into the movie *A Killer in the Family* (Warner Bros., 1983); the Claus von Bülow case was the basis for my book *Reversal of Fortune* (1985) and the film of the same name (Warner Bros., 1990); the O. J. Simpson case was the subject of many documentaries and books, including my own *Reasonable Doubts* (1997); the Jeffrey MacDonald case was made into an award-winning TV miniseries, *Fatal Vision* (1984), named after the bestselling book by Joe McGinniss (1983); the Sybers case was featured on the A&E TV show *Cold Case Files* (episode: "The Perfect Murder," season 4, episode 29, first aired April, 2, 2000); the Borukova case was the subject of Janet Malcolm, *Iphigenia in Forest Hills* (2011); the Sandy Murphy case was featured in several books and movies, including the TV movie *Sex and Lies in the City* (Lifetime, 2008), starring Mena Suvari; the John Connolly case inspired the Academy Award–winning movie *The Departed* (2006); the Angela Davis case was the subject of Bettina Aptheker's *The Morning Breaks* (1975); the murder of John Lennon was the subject of numerous books and movies, including *The Killing of John Lennon* (2006) and Jack Jones, *Let Me Take You Down* (1992); the murder case of Dr. Peter Rosier was the subject of Stanley Rosenblatt's *Murder of Mercy* (1992); the Chappaquiddick incident was also subject to many scandalous treatments, including A&E's *Investigative Report—Chappaquiddick* (2008), Leo Damore's *Senatorial Privilege* (1995), Jerry Shaffer and Leslie H. Leland's *Left to Die* (2010), and Richard and Thomas Tedrow's *Death at Chappaquiddick* (1980); the JDL murder case was the subject of several books and documentaries, including my own *The Best Defense*, chapter 1 (1983); the Lucille Miller case inspired the essay "Some Dreamers of the Golden Dream" (1966), in Joan Didion, *Slouching Toward Bethlehem* 3–28 (2008).

4 *Rudolph v. Alabama*, 375 U.S. 889 (1963).

5 Evan J. Mandery, *A Wild Justice: The Death and Resurrection of Capital Punishment in America* (2013).

6 For the original understanding of the Eighth Amendment, see John D. Bessler, *Cruel and Unusual: The American Death Penalty and the Founder's Eighth Amendment* 171 (2012).

7 Other misspellings on the debate card included "clen" for "clean" and "of" for "off."

8 Evan J. Mandery, *A Wild Justice: The Death and Resurrection of Capital Punishment in America*, 16 (2013).

9 "Judaism was the starting point, but the core of the true force of their bond was a shared intellectual commitment to civil liberties and tolerance. They worked together through scholarship and advocacy against the death penalty for the remainder of Goldberg's life. It is difficult to imagine that Goldberg could have found a more willing and able confederate than Alan Dershowitz." Evan J. Mandery, *A Wild Justice: The Death and Resurrection of Capital Punishment in America* 21 (2013).

10 *Trop v. Dulles*, 356 U.S. 86, 99 (1958).

11 I published my draft, decades later, in Alan M. Dershowitz, *Shouting Fire* 279–89 (2002).

12 *Weems v. United States*, 217 U.S. 349 (1910).

13 *Rudolph v. Alabama*, 375 U.S. 889 (1963).

14 Ibid. 889–91.

15 "U.S. Supreme Court Trio Encourages Rape," *New Hampshire Union Leader*, In Chambers: *Stories of Supreme Court Law Clerks and Their Justices* (2012).

16 *Sims v. Balkcom*, 220 Ga. 7, 11–12 (1964).

17 Ibid. 11.

18 Herbert L. Packer, "Making the Punishment Fit the Crime," 77 *Harvard Law Review* 1071, 1081–82 (1964).

19 Michael Meltsner, *Cruel and Unusual: The Supreme Court and Capital Punishment* (1973).

20 *McGautha v. California*, 402 U.S. 183, 185 (1971).

21 *People v. Anderson*, 6 Cal. 3d 628, 633, 493 P.2d 880, 882 (1972).

22 408 U.S. 238 (1972).

23 Ibid. 375 (Burger, C.J., dissenting).

24 See, e.g., Arthur J. Goldberg and Alan M. Dershowitz, "An End to the Death Penalty," *New York Times*, June 6, 1971; Arthur J. Goldberg and Alan M. Dershowitz, "Declaring the Death Penalty Unconstitutional," 83 *Harvard Law Review* 1773 (1970).

25 Alan M. Dershowitz, *Jerusalem Post*, 1987.

26 Ibid.

27 Alan Dershowitz, *The Guardian*, April 22, 2013.

28 Chris Hedges, "Acquittal in Jerusalem; Israel Courts Sets Demjanjuk Free, But He Is Now Without a Country," *New York Times*, July 30, 1993.

29 "Munich: Demjanjuk Found Guilty of Helping Kill 27,900 Jews," *Jerusalem Post*, December 5, 2011.

30 Robert D. McFadden, "John Demjanjuk, 91, Dogged by Charges of Atrocities as Nazi Camp Guard, Dies," *New York Times*, March 17, 2011.

Chapter 14
The Death Penalty for Those Who Don't Kill

1 I previously wrote about an early aspect of the case in my book *The Best Defense*, chapter 9 (1983). A variation on the facts of the case was featured as a subplot in the film *Reversal of Fortune* (Warner Bros., 1990).

2 Under the so-called Pinkerton rule: "So long as the partnership in crime continues, the partners act for each other in carrying it forward. . . . An overt act of one partner may be the act of all without any new agreement specifically directed to that act." *Pinkerton v. United States*, 328 U.S. 640, 646–47 (1946).

3 The felony-murder doctrine can be traced back to English common law, but England, as well as other common law countries, abolished the doctrine some time ago. Civil law countries do not have such a doctrine. As the comparative law scholar James Whitman put it: "The view in Europe is that we hold people responsible for their own acts and not the acts of others." Quoted in Adam Liptak, "Serving for Providing Car to Killers," *New York Times*, December 4, 2007. For this reason, criminal conspiracies are also not part of the civil law tradition, but there is an emerging concept of group crime in some jurisdictions, growing in part out of the fear of terrorist organizations.

4 408 U.S. 238 (1972).

5 *A Killer in the Family* (Warner Bros., 1983).

6 458 U.S. 782 (1982).

7 Ibid. 799.

8 Only four votes are needed for the court to grant a writ of certiorari, but five votes are needed to reverse a conviction.

9 The oral argument in this case can be accessed at the website of the Oyez Project at IIT Chicago–Kent College of Law, http://www.oyez.org/cases/1980-1989/1986/1986_84_6075.

10 *Tison v. Arizona*, 481 U.S. 137, 150 (1987).

11 Ibid. 157.

12 Ibid. 157–58.

13 The majority sloppily used two different formulations: "reckless *disregard*" and "reckless *indifference*," the former sounding as if it required a more affirmative finding of evil intent than the latter.

14 Another one of my clients, a far more sophisticated one, did convert to Judaism—on a weekly basis. He discovered that all the Jews in a particular federal prison were taken out every Friday night to have Shabbos dinner in the homes of local Jews, where they were treated to wonderful home-cooked meals. He told me that since he had become a Jew, he had gotten to love "those balls made out of fish and the other balls that they put in the chicken soup." I reminded him that he had always been a very religious Catholic, and he said, "Oh, I'm still a religious Catholic. My priest has given me permission to be a Jew on Friday night as long as I go back to being a Catholic for Sunday morning."

Chapter 15
Using Science, Law, Logic, and Experience to Disprove Murder

1 Oliver Wendell Holmes, *The Common Law*, Lecture I: "Early Forms of Liability" 1 (1881). Whether he knew it or not, Holmes was echoing the views of the fifteenth-century Jewish sage Isaac Abravanal, who observed that "experience is more authoritative than logic." *Don Isaac Abravanel: Statesman and Philosopher* (Benzion Netanyaha, ed.) 174 (1998).

2 Genesis 4:3–17. I discuss this story in Alan M. Dershowitz, *The Genesis of Justice*, chapter 2 (2001).

3 Genesis 4:9.

4 William Shakespeare, *Hamlet*, Act 1, Scene V.

5 Genesis 39:7–20. For my interpretation of the story, see *The Genesis of Justice*, chapter 10 (2001).

6 William Shakespeare, *Othello*, Act 2, Scene 1.

7 Fyodor Dostoyevsky, *Crime and Punishment*, part 6, chapter 8 (1866).

8 In nineteenth-century America, sheriffs would tell uneducated suspects that if the corpse bled in their presence, it proved their guilt. See George and Ira Gershwin, *Porgy and Bess*, Act 3, Scene 2 (1935).

9 Henry J. Friendly, "Is Innocence Irrelevant? Collateral Attack on Criminal Judgments," 38 *University of Chicago Law Review* 142 (1970). Judge Friendly starts his lecture by quoting Justice Black's statement that "the defendant's guilt or innocence is at least one of the vital considerations in determining whether collateral relief should be available to a convicted defendant." *Kaufman v. United States*, 394 U.S. 217, 235–36 (1969) (Black, J., dissenting).

10 Federal Rules of Evidence 103(a). ("A party may claim error in a ruling to admit or exclude evidence only if the error affects a substantial right of the party."); Federal Rules of Criminal Procedure 52(a). ("Any error, defect, irregularity or variance which does not affect substantial rights shall be disregarded.").

11 See the Jewish Defense League case, *U.S. v. Huss*, 482 F.2d 38 (1973).

12 In one case, a client who was acquitted of murder was subsequently convicted of an entirely different type of crime. I did not represent him the second time. He was convicted.

13 In some jurisdictions the defendant is given no opportunity to present exculpatory evidence to the grand jury. See also *United States v. Williams*, 504 U.S. 36 (1992) (holding that a district court may not dismiss an indictment because the prosecution failed to disclose "substantial exculpatory evidence" in its possession).

14 *Missouri v. Frye*, 566 U.S. __ (2012).

15 U.S. Department of Justice, *United States Attorneys' Annual Statistic Report, Fiscal Year 2010*. For state prosecutions, the conviction rate is similarly high.

16 Annual Report of the Administrative Office of the U.S. Courts. For the twelve months that ended March 31, the reversal rate for 2012 was 6.4 percent, for 2011 it was 5.6 percent, and for 2010 it was 5.8 percent.

17 According to the Court Statistics Project of the National Center for State Courts (NCSC), the reversal rate in state courts ranges from 1 percent in New York to 9 percent in Wyoming.

18 When Justice Ruth Bader Ginsburg was a civil liberties lawyer with a special interest in promoting feminist causes, she often took cases involving male clients whose cases would establish precedents favorable to women.

19 Joseph Stropnicky, 19 M.D.L.R. 39, 41 (1997).

20 See *The Best Defense* 413–14 (1983). For a more recent account of lawyers being underzealous, see Adam Liptak, "Lawyers Stumble, and Clients Take Fall," *New York Times*, January 7, 2013.

21 See Alan M. Dershowitz, *The Genesis of Justice* 85–92 (2001).

22 Lally Weymouth, "Von Bulow's Appeal Strategy," *New York*, May 10, 1982, 9.

23 Stephen Bello, "How Can You Sleep at Night," *Esquire*, 1983, vol. 99.

24 William Wright, *The Von Bülow Affair* 330 (1984).

25 Alan M. Dershowitz, *Reversal of Fortune* (1985); Alan M. Dershowitz, *Reasonable Doubts* (1997).

26 Alan M. Dershowitz, *Reasonable Doubts* 24–25 (1997).

27 *Miller v. California*, 389 U.S. 968 (1967).

28 At a panel in New York, Darden suggested that Johnnie Cochran may have tampered with the glove before O.J. was asked to try it on, but no one on the defense team had access to the glove until after O.J. tried it on. See, e.g., Clayton Sandell, "O.J. Simpson Trial Prosecutor Accuses Johnnie Cochran of Tampering with Evidence," ABC News, September 9, 2012.

29 *State v. von Bülow*, 475 A.2d 995 (R.I. 1984).

30 I was a major character in a novel called *Hope: A Tragedy* by Shalom Auslander (2012).

31 The case made local headlines for years.

32 *Sybers v. State*, 841 So. 2d 532, 541 (Fla. Dist. Ct. App. 2003) (quoting the *Frye* standard governing the admissibility of scientific evidence in Florida).

33 Ibid. (internal quotations omitted).

34 Ibid. (internal quotations omitted).

35 Ibid. 532.

36 The Rules of Professional Conduct prohibit a lawyer from offering evidence that he reasonably believes to be false. *Model Rules of Professional Conduct* (2004), Rule 3.3: Candor Toward the Tribunal (3)(a).

37 "Governor Won't Investigate Prosecutor," *Miami Herald*, November 15, 2003.

38 Paul Pinkham, "Won't Be U.S. Attorney," *Florida Times Union*, June 9, 2010.

39 "Facing Retrial, State Drops Murder Case," *Herald Tribune*, March 13, 2003.

40 Robert Louis Stevenson, "The Body Snatchers" (1884).

41 *The Body Snatcher* (RKO Radio Pictures, 1945).

42 *Burke and Hare* (Ealing Studios, 2010).

43 Glen Puit, "Doctor: Marks Prove Binion Murdered," *Las Vegas Review-Journal*, October 27, 2004.

44 Angie Wagner, "Ted Binion Overdosed on Sedatives, Authorities Believe," *Las Vegas Sun*, September 19, 1998.

45 "Autopsy: Binion May Have Had Fatal Cocktail," *Las Vegas Sun*, July 16, 1999.

46 Angie Wagner, "Binion Feared Girlfriend Would Kill Him, Attorney Testifies," *Las Vegas Sun*, August 27, 1999.

47 I had used this phrase before in describing the prosecutors' tactic in the von Bülow case. See Alan M. Dershowitz, *Reversal of Fortune* 213 (1985).

48 Peter O'Connell, "Guilty All Counts," *Las Vegas Review-Journal*, May 20, 2000.

49 The same was true with regard to the "cocktail of death" theory, since no one could know which theory formed the basis for the conviction, or if some jurors found the first, while others found the second. If either theory failed, there would have to be a new trial.

50 Glen Puit, "Binion Forensic Evidence Crucial," *Las Vegas Review-Journal*, November 27, 2004.

51 Ibid.

52 William Shakespeare, *Hamlet*, Act 1, Scene 5.

53 Federal Rules of Evidence 801.

54 The Sixth Amendment provides that "in all criminal prosecutions, the accused shall enjoy the right . . . to be confronted with the witnesses against him." U.S. Constitution, amend. XI.

55 Federal Rules of Evidence 804(b)(6). ("Not excluded by the rule against hearsay [is] . . . [a] statement offered against a party that wrongfully caused—or acquiesced in wrongfully causing—the declarant's unavailability as a witness, and did so intending that result.")

56 Federal Rules of Evidence 804(b)(2). ("Not excluded by the rule against hearsay [is] . . . a statement that the declarant, while believing the declarant's death to be imminent, made about its cause or circumstances.")

57 Federal Rules of Evidence 803 (3). ("Not excluded by the rule against hearsay [is] . . . [a] statement of the declarant's then-existing state of mind.")

58 This is what the court ruled:

> *Assuming that the statement was relevant to rebut the defense theories, we conclude that the district court abused its discretion under* Shults *in admitting the statement without an appropriate limiting instruction. The prejudicial impact was great: the statement strongly implied Murphy killed Binion. Moreover, the relevance of the statement was equivocal, even though there was little other evidence of Binion's state of mind before his death. But if the statement was relevant to show Binion's state of mind at the time he made the statement, the exception still does not allow the statement to be used as evidence of the intent or conduct of anyone else—in this case, Murphy. The district court did not give a limiting instruction advising the jury that the statement was only admissible for the limited purpose of showing Binion's state of mind.*

Tabish v. State, 119 Nev. 293, 310–11 (2003).

59 Glen Puit, "Reversal of Fortunes: Jurors Acquit Tabish, Murphy of Murder," *Las Vegas Review-Journal*, November 24, 2004.

60 See, e.g., "Doctor Freed in Mercy Killing of Ailing Wife," *Los Angeles Times*, December 1, 1988.

61 Christianity views suicide as a grave sin against God. Since one's life belongs to God, suicide amounts to asserting dominion over what is God's property. Another line of reasoning is that committing suicide is a violation of the Sixth Commandment, "Though shalt not kill." See, e.g., *The Catechism of the Catholic Church* 2281 and 2325. Judaism also condemns suicide—unless it is committed as an act of religious martyrdom. See, e.g., Sidney Goldstein, *Suicide in Rabbinic Literature* (1989). Islam, the youngest monotheistic religion, prohibits suicide as well. As the Quran instructs, "And do not kill yourselves, surely God is most Merciful to you." Quran, Sura 4:29. Some imams obviously believe that suicide bombing of any enemy is not only not forbidden, it is to be praised and rewarded in paradise. For a nuanced account of the theological justifications for jihad advanced in the name of Islam, see Noah Feldman, "Islam, Terror and the Second Nuclear Age," *New York Times*, October 29, 2006.

62 "Backers of Mass. Assisted Suicide Measure Concede," *Boston Globe*, November 7, 2012.

63 There is a third category that combines mercy killings with mercy suicides. In another one of my cases, a mother was accused of engaging in the combined act of trying to kill her autistic and sexually abused son and trying to kill herself. She succeeded in the former and failed in the latter. She reasonably believed that the child's biological father was repeatedly abusing the eight-year-old autistic boy and that her former husband was planning to kill her, which would leave the child in the hands of his father. This phenomenon too has a name: altruistic filicide-suicide. We are raising a defense based on necessity (choice of evils), justification (killing to protect her son), and duress (killing under fear of death). That case is pending as I write these words.

64 See, e.g., "When Is Death a Matter of Mercy?" *Miami Herald*, December 17, 1988; "A Conflict That Won't Rest Easy, Rosier Case Stirs Up Old Debate on Mercy Killing," *Orlando Sentinel*, December

5, 1988; "Acquittal Renews Euthanasia Debate," *Miami Herald,* December 3, 1988; "Doctor Freed in Wife's Death," *New York Times,* December 2, 1988; "Was His Act of Mercy Also Murder?" *New York Times,* November 7, 1988; "Euthanasia an Issue as Jurors Picked in Doctor's Murder Trial," *Orlando Sentinel,* November 2, 1988.

65 *Harold and Maude* (Paramount Pictures, 1971).

66 Peter Rosier, *The Lady.*

67 In the interview with the local WBBH-TV, he admitted: "I administered something to terminate her life." "Man's TV Admission He Killed Wife Spurs Probe," *Miami News,* November 14, 1986.

68 A strange analogy for Buchanan, who has expressed admiration for Hitler and doubt that the Nazis gassed Jews during the Holocaust. See Alan M. Dershowitz, *Chutzpah* 162–64 (1991).

69 Rosenblatt subsequently wrote a book about the case. Stanley M. Rosenblatt, *Murder of Mercy: Euthanasia on Trial* (1992).

70 Fla. Stat. Ann. § 782.08. ("Every person deliberately assisting another in the commission of self-murder shall be guilty of manslaughter, a felony of the second degree.") The Supreme Court left this issue to the state after holding that there is no right to physician-assisted suicide in the Constitution. *Washington v. Glucksberg,* 521 U.S. 702 (1997); *Vacco v. Quill,* 521 U.S. 793 (1997).

71 See, e.g., Jeff Weiner, "State Attorney Candidates Slug It Out in Debate," *Orlando Sentinel,* July 25, 2012 (quoting a veteran state attorney in central Florida as having served in an office "where prosecutors feel pressure to overcharge cases and take weak ones to trial").

72 *Miranda v. Arizona,* 384 U.S. 436 (1966).

73 *Escobedo v. Illinois,* 378 U.S. 478 (1964).

74 I subsequently wrote *Is There a Right to Remain Silent?* (2008).

75 *State v. Doody,* 187 Ariz. 363, 930 P.2d 440 (Ct. App. 1996).

76 Chief Justice Earl Warren had presided over the high court from 1953 to 1969, and his court had handed down many important decisions expanding civil rights, civil liberties, defendant's rights, freedom of speech and press, and other rights.

77 *Doody v. Schriro,* 548 F.3d 847 (9th Cir. 2008).

78 *Doody v. Schriro,* 596 F.3d 620 (9th Cir. 2010).

79 *Ryan v. Doody,* 131 S. Ct. 456 (2010).

80 *Doody v. Ryan,* 649 F.3d 986 (9th Cir. 2011).

81 *Ryan v. Doody,* 132 S. Ct. 414 (2011)

82 "Buddhist Temple Killing Retrial Begins," CBS 5 KPHO, January 25, 2012.

83 "$5 Million Bond Set in Temple Killings Case," CBS 5 KPHO, February 15, 2012.

84 Joe McGinniss, *Fatal Vision* (1983).

85 *Fatal Vision* (NBC, 1984).

86 Ibid.

87 *United States v. MacDonald,* 641 F.3d 596, 604–605 (4th Cir. 2011).

88 *In re Blackburn,* 174 N.J. 380 (2002).

89 Ross Gelbspan, "New Allegations in MacDonald Case," *Boston Globe,* October 20, 1990.

90 Memorandum from Thomas McNamara (U.S. attorney) to Carl W. Belcher (Crime Division, Department of Justice), re: Captain Jeffrey MacDonald Murder Case, June 26, 1973. ("Colette's right ring finger when examined for fingernail scrapings, revealed the presence of human skin. However, this skin was apparently lost.")

91 In another case, in which I am currently involved, the government lost crucial blood evidence that could establish whether my client tried to commit suicide after killing her son. See, e.g., Colin Moynihan, "Evidence Lost in Murder Case," *New York Times,* August 1, 2011.

92 Most notably, in 1996 Congress passed the Anti-Terrorism and Effective Death Penalty Act (AEDPA) (28 U.S.C. 2254), which imposes significant restrictions on the ability of federal courts to grant relief to state prison inmates. It is therefore not surprising that, just a year later, in 1997, the Court of Appeals for the Fourth Circuit refused to grant MacDonald's habeas review. See Harvey Silverglate, "Jeffrey MacDonald, Innocence, and the Future of Habeas Corpus," Forbes.com, October 18, 2012. But even before the enactment of the AEDPA, the chances of obtaining relief in state criminal proceedings were slim. As my colleague Daniel Meltzer put it, three years before Congress passed the AEDPA: "Of every 100,000 persons committed to state custody, no more than about 30 obtain federal habeas relief." Daniel J. Meltzer, "Habeas Corpus Jurisdiction: The Limits of Models," *66 Southern California Law Review* 2507, 2523–24 (1993).

93 *United States v. MacDonald,* 966 F.2d 854 (4th Cir. 1992).

94 See Harvey Silverglate, "Jeffrey MacDonald, Innocence, and the Future of Habeas Corpus," Forbes.com, October 18, 2012.

95 *United States v. MacDonald,* 641 F.3d 596, 599 (4th Cir. 2011).

96 Errol Morris, *A Wilderness of Error: The Trials of Jeffrey MacDonald* (2012).

97 *U.S. v. MacDonald,* 688 F.2d 224, 236 (1982).

98 According to the Innocence Project, which was founded by my cocounsels in the O. J. Simpson case Barry Scheck and Peter Neufeld, in almost 50 percent of postconviction DNA testing exonerations, the actual perpetrators have been identified through DNA testing as well. Innocence Project, Innocence Project Case Profiles, available at http://www.innocenceproject.org/know/.

99 *Com. v. Dixon*, 458 Mass. 446 (2010). See also Jonathan Saltzman, "SJC Ruling Extends Reach of DNA Cases," *Boston Globe*, December 10, 2010.

100 *In re Davis*, 130 S. Ct. 1 (2009) (Scalia, J., dissenting).

101 In 2009, I challenged Justice Scalia, who has written that he would have to leave the Supreme Court if his constitutional views conflicted with his obligation to the Catholic Church, to debate this issue:

> *I hereby challenge Justice Scalia to a debate on whether Catholic doctrine permits the execution of a factually innocent person who has been tried, without constitutional flaw, but whose innocence is clearly established by new and indisputable evidence. Although I am neither a rabbi nor a priest, I am confident that I am right and he is wrong under Catholic Doctrine. Perhaps it takes chutzpah to challenge a practicing Catholic on the teachings of his own faith, but that is a quality we share.*
>
> *I invite him to participate in the debate at Harvard Law School, at Georgetown Law School, or anywhere else of his choosing. The stakes are high, because if he loses—if it is clear that his constitutional views permitting the execution of factually innocent defendants are inconsistent with the teachings of the Catholic Church—then, pursuant to his own published writings, he would have no choice but to conform his constitutional views to the teachings of the Catholic Church or to resign from the Supreme Court (Alan M. Dershowitz, "Scalia's Catholic Betrayal,"* Daily Beast, *August 18, 2009).*

Scalia did not take up my challenge.

102 Most prominently, Governors George Ryan of Illinois, Winthrop Rockefeller of Arkansas, and Toney Anaya of New Mexico granted blanket commutations to all death-row inmates before leaving office. See, e.g., Jodi Wilgoren, "Citing Issue of Fairness, Governor Clears Out Death Row in Illinois," *New York Times*, January 12, 2003.

103 This is what the Court of Appeals for the Fourth Circuit said in the Jeffrey MacDonald case:

> *We acknowledge that MacDonald has a daunting burden ahead in seeking to establish that he is eligible for habeas corpus relief solely because of his "actual innocence." The Supreme Court has only "assume[d], for the sake of argument . . . that in a capital case a truly persuasive demonstration of 'actual innocence' made after trial would render the execution of a defendant unconstitutional."* Herrera v. Collins, 506 U.S. 390, 417, 113 S. Ct. 853, 122 L. Ed. 2d 203 (1993). *The Court has yet to come across any prisoner who could make the "extraordinarily high" threshold showing for such an assumed right. Ibid.;* see Dist. Attorney's Office v. Osborne, 129 S. Ct. 2308, 2321, 174 L. Ed. 2d 38 (2009). *("Whether [a federal constitutional right to be released upon proof of 'actual innocence'] exists is an open question. We have struggled with it over the years, in some cases assuming, arguendo, that it exists while also noting the difficult questions such a right would pose and the high standard any claimant would have to meet.")*

United States v. MacDonald, 641 F.3d 596, 616–617 (4th Cir. 2011).

104 See, e.g., David Grann, "Trial by Fire: Did Texas Execute an Innocent Man?" *New Yorker*, September 7, 2009.

105 *Dist. Attorney's Office for Third Judicial Dist. v. Osborne*, 557 U.S. 52.

106 Ibid. 88 (2009) (Stevens, J., dissenting).

107 *Dist. Attorney's Office for Third Judicial Dist. v. Osborne*, 557 U.S. 52, 72 (2009), quoting *Reno v. Flores*, 507 U.S. 292, 303 (1993).

108 Oliver Wendell Holmes, "The Path of the Law," 10 *Harvard Law Review* 457, 469 (1897)

Chapter 16
Death, Politics, Religion, and International Intrigue

1 Those were the original Prisoners of Zion: Mark Dymshitz and Eduard Kuznetsov. I discuss their case in Alan M. Dershowitz, *The Best Defense* 238 (1983).

2 I used to view President Carter as a man of integrity and principle, and even campaigned for him. But recent disclosures of Carter's extensive financial connections to Arab oil money and his bias regarding the Middle East have deeply shaken my belief in his integrity. See Alan Dershowitz, *The Case Against Israel's Enemies* 17–19 (2008).

3 On July 24, 1978, he appeared on the cover of both *Newsweek* and *Time*.

4 T. S. Eliot, *Murder in the Cathedral* (1935).

5 Michael Schwirtz, "Ex-President of Ukraine Is Implicated in Journalist's Death," *New York Times*, March 22, 2011.

6 Yevgeny Yevtushenko, *Selected Poems* 82 (2008).

7 Orest Subtelny, *Ukraine: A History* 127–28 (2000).

8 Irena Taranyuk, "Ukraine Gongadze Case: Court Convicts Journalist's Killer," *BBC News Europe*, January 29, 2013.

9 In another situation, a television ad by the organization J Street showed a video of my lips moving and a voice—not mine—saying words that I didn't say.

10 Alan M. Dershowitz, *Reversal of Fortune* 149 (1985).

11 Glenn Kates, "Former Ukrainian President's Murder Charge Is Dismissed," *New York Times*, December 14, 2011.

12 Earl Caldwell, "Angela Davis Acquitted on All Charges," *New York Times*, June 5, 1972.

13 See also Alan M. Dershowitz, *Chutzpah* 81–82.

14 *United States v. Ham*, 998 F.2d 1247, 1250–51 (4th Cir. 1993).

15 Ibid. 1252.

16 See Alan Dershowitz, *Finding Jefferson* 34–37 (2007).

17 Ibid. 1252–53.

18 February 20, 1978, p. 76.

19 *Black Hawk Down* (Columbia Pictures, 2001).

20 The story first appeared in the *New Yorker*. Raffi Khatchadourian, "The Kill Company: Did a Colonel's Fiery Rhetoric Set the Conditions for a Massacre?" *New Yorker*, July 6, 2009.

21 Raffi Khatchadourian, "The Kill Company: Did a Colonel's Fiery Rhetoric Set the Conditions for a Massacre?," *New Yorker*, July 6, 13, 2009, pp. 40–59.

22 Ibid.

23 U.N. Human Rights Council, *Fact-Finding Mission on the Gaza Conflict, Human Rights in Palestine and Other Occupied Arab Territories* 1884, 1895, U.N. Doc. A/HRC/12/48 (September 25, 2009). For my critique of the Goldstone Report, see Alan Dershowitz, "The Case Against the Goldstone Report," *Huffington Post*, February 1, 2010. A longer version of my critique is available at http://www.alandershowitz.com/goldstone.pdf.

24 Richard Goldstone, "Reconsidering the Goldstone Report on Israel and War Crimes," *Washington Post*, April 1, 2011.

25 See Alan M. Dershowitz, "Blood Brothers," *Boston* magazine, June 2000. I also wrote a few shorter follow-ups to this: Alan M. Dershowitz, "With Bulger Brothers, the Cover-up Continues," *Boston Daily*, July 8, 2001; Alan M. Dershowitz, "Oh, Brothers," *Boston* magazine, July 2002.

26 Dick Lehr and Gerald O'Neill, *Whitey* 217–18 (2013).

27 Ibid. 201

28 *The Departed* (Warner Bros., 2006).

29 When Connolly retired from the FBI, Billy arranged for him to get a high-paying job that included lobbying Billy at the State House.

30 Dick Lehr and Gerard O'Neill, *Whitey* 200, 201 (2013).

31 Ibid.

32 *State v. Connolly*, 2006 WL 6164733.

33 "Ex-FBI Agent John Connolly Sentenced to 40 Years," *Boston Herald*, January 16, 2009. Whitey Bulger was arrested in June 2011. Adam Nagourney and Ian Lovett, "Whitey Bulger Is Arrested in California," *New York Times*, June 23, 2011.

34 This was not the only time I offered to help prosecutors fight against evils. On September 12, 2001, I wrote a letter to the attorney general of the United States, offering to work—for a dollar a year—on the prosecution of terrorists, such as the ones who perpetrated the 9/11 attack against the United States. In my letter, I explained that as an experienced defense attorney, who had helped to defend several accused terrorists (including members of the Jewish Defense League), I knew all the tricks of the defense trade and how to combat them in the interests of justice. I received no reply to my letter.

35 ABA Model Rules of Professional Conduct 1.6 (b)(1)-(3). I discuss the lawyer-client relationship in my first novel, *The Advocate's Devil* (1995).

36 *Lennon v. Immigration Serv.*, 527 F. 2d 187 (2d Cir. 1975).

37 *The Godfather* (Paramount Pictures, 1972); *The Godfather Part II* (Paramount Pictures, 1974).

38 Babylonian Talmud, Sanhedrin 73a.

39 Leviticus 19:16.

40 Maimonides, Mishneh Tora, Hilkhot Rotze'ah U-Shmirat Nefesh I:9.

41 I am comfortable describing this "defense," since it was made public by him and his family. See, e.g., Jessica Stern, *Terror in the Name of God* 91 (2003).

42 See, e.g., William A. Schabas, *The Abolition of the Death Penalty in International Law* 65 (3d ed. 2002).

43 Excerpts of the sentencing decision from March 27, 1996, are available at http://www.mfa.gov.il/MFA/MFAArchive/1990_1999/1996/3/Excerpts+of+Yigal+Amir+Sentencing+Decision+-+March.htm?WBCMODE=PresentationUnp?.

44 Jonathan Lis, "Wife of Jailed Rabin Assassin Yigal Amir Gives Birth to Son," *Haaretz*, October 28, 2007.

45 "Defense Lawyer Alan Dershowitz May Defend Serb Leader Radovan Karadzic According to Harvard Crimson," PR Newswire, May 8, 1998.

46 I wrote a brief on joint criminal enterprise in the Momčilo Krajišnik case. *Prosecutor v. Momčilo Krajišnik*, IT-00-39-A, Appeal Judgement (March 17, 2009).

47 Jack Henry Abbott, *In the Belly of the Beast: Letters from Prison* (1981).

48 Mailer later expressed remorse over having secured Abbott's release. See, e.g., Claudia Wolffs and Dean Brelis, "In the Belly of the Beast," *Time*, August 3, 1981.

49 For some of my views on this case, see Alan M. Dershowitz, "Zimmerman Prosecutor Threatening to Sue Harvard for My Criticism," Newsmax.com, June 5, 2012; Alan Dershowitz, "New Forensic Evidence Is Consistent with Zimmerman's Self-Defense Claim," *Huffington Post*, May 21, 2012; Alan M. Dershowitz, "Drop Zimmerman's Murder Charge," *New York Daily News*, May 18, 2012; Alan Dershowitz, "The 'Rorschach' Facts in the Killing of Trayvon Martin," *Huffington Post*, April 11, 2012; Alan M. Dershowitz, "Prosecutor's Quandary: Zimmerman May Be Indicted, Then Acquitted," CNN, April, 10, 2012.

Chapter 17
Death Cases from the Classroom to the Courtroom and from the Courtroom to the Classroom

1 New Edition of the Babylonian Talmud (Section Jurisprudence—Damages) (Michael L. Rodkinson, ed.), Tract Sanhedrin, chapter IX, 229 (1903).

2 *State v. Damms*, 100 N.W.2d 592 (Wis. 1960).

3 Ibid. 597.

4 Alan Dershowitz, "Why Criminal Attempts Fail? A New Defense," 70 *Yale Law Journal* 160 (1960).

5 Ibid. 163.

6 Ibid. 164.

7 Ibid., citing Sigmund Freud, *A General Introduction to Psychoanalysis* 48 (Permabook ed., 1958).

8 N.Y. Crim. Proc. Law § 60.22 (McKinney).

9 *People v. Dlugash*, 51 A.D.2d 974, 380 N.Y.S.2d 315 (1976) aff'd as modified, 41 N.Y.2d 725, 363 N.E.2d 1155 (1977).

10 Ibid. 317.

11 Ibid.

12 *People v. Dlugash*, 59 A.D.2d 745, 398 N.Y.S.2d 560 (1977).

13 *Dlugash v. People of State of N.Y.*, 476 F. Supp. 921 (E.D.N.Y. 1979).

14 I wrote about this case in far more detail in Alan M. Dershowitz, *The Best Defense*, chapter 2 (1983).

15 Virtually every standard criminal law casebook discusses the case. See, e.g., Sanford H. Kadish, Stephen J. Schulhofer, and Carol Steiker, *Criminal Law and Its Processes: Cases and Materials* 587 (8th ed., 2007); Wayne R. LaFave, *Modern Criminal Law: Cases, Comments and Questions* 296 (3d ed., 2000); Russell L. Weaver, Leslie W. Abramson, and John M. Burkoff, *Criminal Law: Cases, Comments, and Questions* 249 (3d ed., 2008); John Kaplan, Robert Weisberg, and Guyora Binder, *Criminal Law: Cases and Materials* 678 (5th ed., 2004).

16 Genesis 22:1–12. For my interpretation of this story, see Alan M. Dershowitz, *The Genesis of Justice*, chapter 6 (2001).

17 *State v. Eldridge*, 951 S.W.2d 775 (Tenn. Crim. App. 1997).

18 *Twilight Zone: The Movie* (Warner Bros., 1983).

19 *The Twilight Zone* (CBS, 1959–1964).

20 First Segment ("Time Out").

21 See, e.g., Paul Feldman, "John Landis Not Guilty in 3 'Twilight Zone' Deaths: Jury Also Exonerate Four Others," *Los Angeles Times*, May 29, 1987.

22 *The Crow* (Miramax, 1994).

23 *The Game of Death* (Golden Harvest, 1972).

24 See, e.g., Terry Pristin, "Brandon Lee's Mother Claims Negligence Caused His Death," *Los Angeles Times*, August 11, 1993.

25 18 Pa. Cons. Stat. Ann. § 314 (West).

26 Id.

27 M'Naughten Case UKHL J16 (June 19, 1843).

28 *Com. v. duPont,* 1999 PA Super 88, 730 A. 2d 970 (Pa. Super. Ct. 1999).

29 Jeré Longman, John E. du Pont, Heir Who Killed an Olympian, Dies at 72, *New York Times,* December 9. 2010.

30 I have written critically about its occasional misuse. See Alan M. Dershowitz, *The Abuse Excuse* (1993).

31 *Rubin v. State,* 325 Md. 552, 555, 602 A.2d 677, 678 (1992).

32 *Rubin v. Gee,* 292 F.3d 396, 398 (4th Cir. 2002). Another murder-abuse case that I was involved in and that was eventually overturned was *DeLuca v. Lord,* 77 F.3d 578 (1996).

Chapter 18
The Changing Politics of Rape

1 One critic summed up the resulting injustice in a poignant headline: Martha Weinman Lear, "Q. If You Rape a Woman and Steal Her TV, What Can They Get You For in New York? A. Stealing Her TV," *New York Times,* January 30, 1972.

2 Blackstone articulated this so-called unity of person principle in his *Commentaries*: "The very being or legal existence of the woman is suspended during the marriage, or at least is incorporated and consolidated into that of the husband: under whose wing, protection and [cover] she performs everything." William Blackstone, *1 Commentaries on the Laws of England* 430 (1765).

For a history of the marital immunity doctrine, see Jill Elaine Hasday, "Contest and Consent: A Legal History of Marital Rape," 88 *Cal L. Rev.* 1373, 1392–406 (2000).

3 In his legal treatise *The History of the Pleas of the Crown*, Sir Matthew Hale reasoned that "the husband cannot be guilty of a rape committed by himself upon his lawful wife, for by their mutual matrimonial consent and contract the wife hath given up herself in this kind unto her husband, which she cannot retract." Matthew Hale, *1 Historia Placitorum Coronae: The History of the Pleas of the Crown* 628 (1778).

4 As Harry Kelven and Hans Zeisel observed, jurors were led to believe that the rape victim assumed some risk for what they deemed her "contributory fault" and thus often acquitted the defendant. Harry Kelven and Hans Zeisel, *The American Jury* 249–54 (1966).

5 As New York's highest court once put it: "Will you not more readily infer assent in the practiced Messina, in loose attire, than in the reserved and virtuous Lucretia?" *People v. Abbot,* 1838 WL 2949 (N.Y. Sup. Ct. 1838).

6 As one Tennessee court observed, "It would be absurd and shock all sense of truth for any man to affirm that there was not a much greater probability in favor of the proposition that a common prostitute had yielded her assent to sexual intercourse, than in the case of a virgin of uncontaminated purity; that all would readily assent to the proposition that she who follows prostitution as a trade would not be so likely to depart from her degraded habit and resist an offer for indulgence of illicit vice as would the woman of perfect purity." 140 A.L.R. 364 (originally published in 1942).

7 Susan Estrich, "Rape," 95 *Yale Law Journal* 1087, 1099 (1986). One court put it this way: "If the carnal knowledge was with the consent of the woman, no matter how tardily given, or how much force had therefore been employed, it is no rape." *Reynolds v. Nebraska,* 27 Neb. 90 (1889).

8 In the Talmud, one commentator suggested that some women may enjoy being raped: In Sotah 4:5, 19d, "A woman came to Rabbi Yohanan and said to him: I was raped. He said to her: And did you not enjoy it in the end? She said to him: If a man dips his finger in honey and puts it in his mouth on Yom Kippur, is it not bad for him, and yet he does enjoy it? And he accepted her argument." Quoted in 3 *The Talmud Yerushalmi and Graeco-Roman Culture* 209 (Peter Schaefer, ed.) (2002).

9 Those are the kinds of cases that Susan Estrich famously called "simple rape"—where the victim knows the rapist and violence is not necessarily involved. Susan Estrich, *Real Rape,* supra n. 582, at 1092 (1988).

10 Deuteronomy 5:21.

11 *Compare* the story of a concubine who is gang-raped and subsequently cut into twelve parts by her husband (Judges 19) with the story of Dina, one of the matriarchs of the Israelites, whose rape was avenged by her brothers (Gen. 34). For my interpretation of that story, see Alan M. Dershowitz, *The Genesis of Justice,* chapter 8 (2001).

12 The corollary is that if a sexual encounter is prohibited—such as between an unmarried man and a woman engaged to another—mutual consent is no defense.

13 Deuteronomy 22:29. For a general overview of the issue of rape in Jewish law, see Beth C. Miller, "A Comparison of American and Jewish Legal Views on Rape," 5 *Columbia Journal of Gender and Law* 182 (1996).

14 Alan M. Dershowitz, *The Genesis of Justice* 157 (2001).

15 See Susanne Scholz, "Religion," in *Encyclopedia of Rape* 206–9 (Merril D. Smith, ed.) (2004).

16 Matthew Hale, *1 Historia Placitorum Coronae* 635 (1778).

17 John Wigmore, 3 *A Treatise on the Anglo-American System of Evidence in Trial at Common Law* § 924a at 736 (1970). There is no scientific basis for this sort of psychobabble.

18 See, e.g., Susan Brownmiller, *Against Our Will* (1975); Susan Estrich, "Rape," 95 *Yale Law Journal* 1087 (1986).

19 Three states—New York, Ohio, and Texas—still impose the corroboration requirement for certain sexual offenses. N.Y. Penal Law § 130.16 (McKinney); Ohio Rev. Code Ann. § 2907.06 (West); Tx Crim Pro, Art. 38.07. For a discussion of the legacy of the corroboration requirement, as well as other rules that made successful rape prosecutions so difficult, see Michelle J. Anderson, "Legacy of the Prompt Complaint Requirement, Corroboration Requirement, and Cautionary Instructions on Campus Sexual Assault," 84 *Boston University Law Review* 945, 968–69 (2004).

20 For a current list of such statutes, see http://www.ndaa.org/pdf/NCPCA%20Rape%20Shield%202011.pdf.

21 There are spousal rape laws in all states and in Washington, D.C. New York is the only state that still has a complete marital exemption on the books, but the court of appeals declared this exemption unconstitutional, finding "no rational basis for distinguishing between marital and nonmarital rape." *People v. Liberta*, 64 N.Y.2d 152, 163 (1984).

22 A few states still have resistance requirements written into their criminal codes. See Michelle J. Anderson, "Reviving Resistance in Rape Law," 1998 *University of Illinois Law Review* 953, 954 n.12 (1998). Some scholars observe that, despite this legislative change, some courts still inquire about the victim's resistance to establish nonconsent. Susan Estrich, "Rape," 95 *Yale Law Journal* 1123–24 (1986).

23 Catherine MacKinnon, "Palm Beach Hanging," *New York Times*, December 15, 1991

24 Catherine MacKinnon, *Professing Feminism* (Daphne Patai and Noretta Koertge, eds.) 129 (1994). ("In a patriarchal society all heterosexual intercourse is rape because women, as a group, are not strong enough to give meaningful consent.") Andrea Dworkin, *Intercourse* 154 (1997).

25 Andrea Dworkin, *Letters from a War Zone* 142 (1993). ("All men benefit from rape, because all men benefit from the fact that women are not free in this society; that women cower; that women are afraid; that women cannot assert the rights that we have, limited as those rights are, because of the ubiquitous presence of rape.")

26 The dramatic reduction in rapes coincided with an equally dramatic increase in the easy availability of pornography, thus disproving the causation claim made by some radical feminists: that pornography causes rape. See Alan M. Dershowitz, *Shouting Fire*, chapter 19 (2002).

27 *In re Request for Instructions from Disciplinary Counsel*, 610 A.2d 115, 117 (R.I. 1992).

28 Ibid.

29 U.S. Const., amend. VI.

30 "Drop Term Date Rape, Sentencing Judge Says," *Ludington Daily News*, March 28, 1992.

31 The quotations above are from the record of the case and the briefs.

32 *Tyson v. State*, 622 N.E.2d 457 (Ind. 1993).

33 *N. Sec. Co. v. United States*, 193 U.S. 197 (1904) (Holmes, J., dissenting).

34 For a summary of these reports, see Stuart Taylor and K.C. Johnson, *Until Proven Innocent*, 373–76 (2007).

35 Angela Lambert, "No Smoke Without Fire: The Case of Rape," *Ottawa Citizen*, February 16, 1992.

36 Al Baker and Steven Erlanger, "I.M.F. Chief, Apprehended at Airport, Is Accused of Sexual Attack," *New York Times*, May 14, 2011.

37 "Strauss-Kahn Lawyers See Alibi in Sex Case," Reuters, May 16, 2011.

38 William K. Rashbaum, "Strauss-Kahn May Claim Consensual Sex as Defense," May 17, 2011.

39 John Eligon, "Strauss-Kahn Is Indicted and Will Soon Leave Jail," *New York Times*, May 19, 2011.

40 Jim Dwyer, "Housekeeper's False Tale About Gang Rape, Strauss-Kahn Case Crumbles," *New York Times*, August 23, 2011.

41 John Eligon, "Strauss-Kahn Drama Ends with Short Final Scene," *New York Times*, August 23, 2011.

42 See John Solomon, "Alan Dershowitz Convicts DSK," *Daily Beast*, March 5, 2012.

43 Several years ago, I gathered a series of cases that seemed to be based on truthful accounts that turned out to be false. Here are some of them:

> *A Dedham, Massachusetts, woman accused four men of rape. Several days later the charges were dropped because the accuser recanted when approached by the district attorney with inconsistent forensic evidence along with information that she had falsely accused other men.*
>
> *St. Paul, Minnesota, police determined that within one week, two reported rapes were false. In the first case, a woman reported being abducted and raped by a man who hid in her car as she*

gave a talk to a chemical dependency treatment group at a local high school. When police checked the story, they found that the treatment group had never heard of her and that she didn't have a car. In the second case, a sixteen-year-old girl claimed to have been abducted at a downtown bus stop, imprisoned in a closet, and sexually assaulted by a man and his son over a thirty-three-hour period. In reality, the woman had been seen with her boyfriend several times over that thirty-three-hour period and had apparently been bruised by him. In both cases the women gave police detailed descriptions of their attackers and in both case the alleged assailants were black.

A seventeen-year-old girl from Washington State accused three twenty-year-old men of holding her down and raping her. Several days after the men were arrested, the woman recanted, saying she had made the whole thing up out of spite.

In Rhode Island, a college student reported that her former boyfriend raped her at gunpoint. She admitted that she made up the entire story after learning that the man she accused was fifteen hundred miles away at the time.

In New York, a woman who claimed she was raped at gunpoint in Central Park was arrested after it was discovered that she had filed eleven false reports of rape.

In Nebraska, a woman was required to broadcast an apology to a man she had falsely accused of raping her in order to "get the attention of her husband."

In Great Britain, a nineteen-year-old woman from Lincolnshire accused her former boyfriend of raping her after she spent the night with a different man. A jilted nurse falsely accused her former lover of beating her and also falsely accused his best friend of raping her.

These are among the cases some radical students complained about being discussed in class. We also discussed cases in which guilty rapists were wrongly acquitted or not prosecuted.

In recent years numerous inmates serving time for rape based on eyewitness identification have been exonerated by DNA. In these cases, the rapes occurred, but the victim misidentified the rapist. Many of these cases involved black defendants misidentified by white victims. See Alan M. Dershowitz, "When Women Don't Tell The Truth," *The Bryan Times*, May 19, 1992.

44 *People v. Lebovits*, 94 A.D. 3d 1146, 942 N.Y.S. 2d 638 (2012).

45 Under the Model Penal Code, which many states have adopted, a man is guilty of rape if he has sexual intercourse with a woman who is not his wife and "has substantially impaired her power to appraise or control her conduct by administering or employing without her knowledge drugs, intoxicants or other means for the purpose of preventing resistance." MPC §213.1(b).

46 I have changed some identifying features of this case, but not the essential facts, at the request of my former client.

47 *Rashomon* (RKO Radio Pictures, 1951).

48 Glanville Llewelyn Williams, *Criminal Law, The General Part* 386 (1953), attributes this statement to Judge Maule.

49 *Ella Fitzgerald Sings the Jerome Kern Song Book* (Verve 1963).

50 *Com. v. Sherry*, 386 Mass. 682, 697 (1982).

51 *Com. v. Simcock*, 31 Mass. App. Ct. 184, 192 (1991) (holding that defendants were not entitled to instruction on reasonable mistake).

52 I have never seen the entire film (see pp. 130–131 supra), but during the preview of a documentary about the film, I saw excerpts from it.

53 *People v. Moua*, No. 315972 (Fresno Super. Ct. 1985).

54 Sir Edward Coke, *Systematic Arrangement of Lord Coke's First Institute of the Laws of England* (1644), Vol. III, Epilogue 574 (J. H. Thomas, ed.) (1836).

55 Antonin Scalia, "Common-Law Courts in a Civil-Law System: The Role of the United States Federal Courts in Interpreting the Constitution and Laws," in Antonin Scalia and Amy Gutmann (eds.), *A Matter of Interpretation: Federal Courts and the Law* 3–47 (1997).

56 Once I take a case, however, my role changes: I become a single-minded advocate for my client, whether he or she is an accused or an accuser.

Chapter 19
The Changing Impact of the Media on the Law

1 Alan M. Dershowitz, "Court TV: Are We Being Fed a Steady Diet of Tabloid Television? Yes . . . ," *American Bar Association Journal* 46 (May 1994).

2 In 2013, I argued against televising a civil trial in which Sheldon Adelson was a witness. His security consultant, a former deputy director of the U.S. Secret Service, testified that televising his testimony would constitute a security threat to him and his family. The court allowed his testimony to be televised.

3 See Larry David's "Mister Softee" episode on *Curb Your Enthusiasm*, where a psychiatrist tells Larry about his celebrity patients, without disclosing the names, while identifying them by unique characteristics: e.g., "a well-known film director who directed *Star Wars*." *Curb Your Enthusiasm*, season 8, episode 9, see http://www.hbo.com/curb-your-enthusiasm/episodes/8/79-mister-softee/synopsis.html.

4 *United States v. Helmsley*, 941 F.2d 71, 77 (2d Cir. 1991).

5 Ibid. 79.

6 This conversation suggests an important distinction between different types of celebrities and their relationship to the legal process.

The first type consists of individuals who were already very famous before they got into trouble or before they needed my legal advice. The second are those who were not well known to the public but whose alleged crimes made them famous.

A third category would include people who were somewhat well known, but whose trial brought them considerably more fame and/or infamy.

A final category includes very famous celebrities who have hired me to keep their name and alleged wrongs out of the media. I have had several such cases, and for obvious reasons, I cannot disclose the names of these celebrity clients. Nor can I disclose the names of clients who have successfully used their celebrity to avoid the consequences of their actions.

7 Wallace Markfield, *You Could Live If They Let You* 87 (1974).

8 The President told a joke that wasn't particularly funny. My family has very high standards of humor, so we didn't laugh. The President, apparently thinking we didn't hear or get the punch line, repeated it. This time, we laughed—a bit. When the dessert was brought, the waiter put a large chocolate bombe in front of the President. My son thought it was large enough to be shared by the table and so he raised his spoon to take a piece. The President stared him down, saying with his eyes, "That's all mine!" Elon dropped the spoon and the President consumed the entire bombe. (Today, Bill Clinton is a vegan—no more bombes for him!)

9 Maureen Dowd, "Maladroit Du Siegneur," *New York Times*, September 30, 1998. ("He would be laughed out of any locker room in the country.")

10 Prior to the Lewinsky matter becoming public, there were widespread reports that the President limited his extramarital sex to oral gratification since he believed that it did not constitute biblical adultery and it gave him verbal deniability regarding sexual relations. This history actually strengthens his legal claim that he did not commit perjury when he denied having what *he regarded* as sexual relations with Lewinsky. A twenty-eight-year-old waitress was quoted by *Newsweek* as saying that as Clinton continues to define sex more and more narrowly, she begins to think of herself as a virgin! Quoted in Alan M. Dershowitz, *Sexual McCarthyism* 269 (1998).

11 *The Geraldo Rivera Show*, May 27, 1997, quoted in Alan M. Dershowitz, *Sexual McCarthyism* 14 (1998).

12 Paula Jones's lawyers have subsequently revealed that the Jones lawsuit could have been settled at one point for no money, with just a simple apology from President Clinton that made it clear that Paula Jones did not do anything wrong in the hotel room.

13 For a full account, see my *Sexual McCarthyism* 17 (1998).

14 *Clinton v. Jones*, 520 U.S. 681 (1997).

15 *Testimony Before the Judiciary Committee's Impeachment Hearings*, December 1, 1998.

16 Juliet Eilperin, "Both Sides Harden Impeachment Views; Widening of Probe Irks Democrats," *Washington Post*, December 2, 1998.

17 "Historically I think we can all agree that false statements have considerable variation and degree. The core concept of perjury grows out of the Ten Commandments, 'bearing false witness,' a term that consisted in accusing another falsely of a crime. Clearly the most heinous brand of lying is the giving of false testimony that results in the imprisonment of somebody who is innocent. Less egregious, but still quite serious, is false testimony that results in the conviction of a person who may be guilty, but whose rights were violated in a manner that would preclude conviction if the police testified truthfully. . . . The least culpable genre of false testimony are those that deny embarrassing personal conduct of marginal relevance to the matter at issue in the legal proceeding."

18 Quoted in Joseph Telushkin, *Jewish Humor: What the Best Jewish Jokes Say About the Jews* 21 (1992).

19 Alan M. Dershowitz, "Top 10 Legal Blunders," *George*, April 1999, 56.

20 Ibid.

21 Ibid.

22 *Manhattan* (United Artists, 1979).

23 *The Front* (Columbia Pictures, 1976).

24 "Were Julius and Ethel Rosenberg guilty of transmitting American atomic secrets to the Soviet Union in the 1940's, or were they scapegoats of the cold war whose execution was a grave miscarriage of justice? That both are true is the intriguing argument of [the new book.]" Alan M. Dershowitz, "Spies & Scapegoats," *New York Times Book Review*, August 14, 1983.

25 See infra p. 430.

26 *Allen v. Farrow*, 197 A.D.2d 327, 331 (1994).

27 Alan M. Dershowitz, *Chutzpah* (1991).

28 Timothy Crouse, "Prosecutor Beyond the Law? Morvillo: His Informant Raided a Bankrupt Firm," *Village Voice*, May 15, 1978.

29 I recount this instance of prosecutorial misconduct more fully in *The Best Defense* 377 (1983).

30 I wrote these words while Morvillo was alive. He has since died.

31 "Ronan Farrow, Son of Mia and Woody, Lands Rhodes Scholarship," *Washington Post*, November 21, 2011.

32 Kitty Kelley, *His Way: An Unauthorized Biography of Frank Sinatra* (1987).

Part IV
The Never-Ending Quest for Equality and Justice

Chapter 20
The Changing Face of Race

1 Martin Luther King, Jr., "I Have a Dream (Washington, D.C., August 28, 1963)," in Martin Luther King, Jr., *A Testament of Hope: The Essential Writings and Speeches of Martin Luther King, Jr.* (James M. Washington, ed.) 219 (1990).

2 After President Eliot diminished Harvard's religious traditions, making Harvard "undenominational," and introduced College Entrance Examination Board exams in 1905 to attract a geographically more diverse student population, Jewish enrollment skyrocketed. By 1922, Jews made up more than 20 percent of the incoming freshman class. The same was true for other Ivy League schools, such as Princeton and Yale. Columbia University even had a 40 percent Jewish enrollment. This soon changed under President Lowell, who imposed anti-Jewish quotas. Jerome Karabel, *The Chosen: The Hidden History of Admission and Exclusion at Harvard, Yale and Princeton* 119 (2005).

3 *DeFunis v. Odegaard*, 416 U.S. 312 (1974).

4 Ibid 331–32 (Douglas, J., dissenting).

5 Ibid.

6 As a legal historian described it: "'The future justice attended Whitman College in Washington and not a more prestigious institution because only Whitman offered him a scholarship; when he left for Columbia University Law School, he traveled part of the way on a freight car, alongside sheep. "In a real sense Marco DeFunis . . . was William O. Douglas, many years earlier, waiting on tables and carrying two other jobs in Walla Walla stores to put himself through school and supported his widowed mother."' Dennis Deslippe, *Protesting Affirmative Action: The Struggle over Equality After the Civil Rights Revolution* 140 (2012).

7 For this view, see Noah Feldman, *Scorpions* 322 (2010) (arguing that Justice Douglas developed a jurisprudence of individual rights as a reaction to his tumultuous personal life).

8 This is, of course, not only true for liberal judges. When Justice Alito was asked at his 2006 confirmation hearings about how his Italian immigrant roots influence his judging in immigration cases, he openly admitted, "I do say to myself, 'You know, this could be your grandfather, this could be your grandmother.' "

Confirmation Hearing on the Nomination of Samuel A. Alito, Jr. to Be an Associate Justice of the Supreme Court of the United States: Hearing Before the Senate Committee. on the Judiciary, S. Hrg. No. 109–277, at 475 (2006).

9 *DeFunis v. Odegaard*, 416 U.S. 337 (1974).

10 Ibid. 342.

11 Paul Finkelman (ed.), 1 *Encyclopedia of African American History, 1896 to the Present: From the Age of Segregation to the Twenty-First Century* 207 (2009) (noting that "in the 1974 and 1978 affirmative action

cases, black and Jewish organizations had for the first time taken opposite positions regarding a civil rights issue").

12 William Bowen and Derek Bok, former presidents of Princeton and Harvard, respectively, found that 80 percent of black students who entered Ivy League colleges in 1989 came from middle- or high-income families, compared to 49 percent of black college-age students nationwide. William Bowen and Derek Bok, *The Shape of the River: Long-Term Consequences of Considering Race in College and University Admission* (1998).

13 DeFunis received amicus briefs support from four Jewish organizations: the Jewish Rights Council, the American Jewish Congress, the Anti-Defamation League, and the American Jewish Committee.

14 "Jews have deserted the civil rights coalition," wrote Nina Tottenberg, "because they see the DeFunis case as a matter of quotas, and quotas are anathema to Jews because they have been used for so many centuries to keep Jews out of universities."' Dennis Deslippe, *Protesting Affirmative Action: The Struggle over Equality After the Civil Rights Revolution* 127 (2012) (quoting Nina Totenberg, "Discriminating to End Discrimination," *New York Times*, April 14, 1974).

15 See Alan Dershowitz and Laura Hanft, "Affirmative Action and the Harvard College Diversity-Discretion Model, Paradigm or Pretext?," 1 *Cardozo Law Review* 379, 414 (1979) (quoting Michael E. Kinsley, "Admissions Policy: From Dollars to Doughnuts," *Harvard Crimson*, January 27, 1971).

16 *Regents of the University of California v. Bakke*, 438 U.S. 265 (1978).

17 1977 WL 188015 (U.S.) (Appellate Brief) 35–36.

18 Ibid. 37.

19 Ibid. 44.

20 Ibid. 56–57.

21 Ibid.

22 Ibid.

23 *Regents of the University of California v. Bakke*, 438 U.S. 265, 316 (1978).

24 Ibid. 316–17; 321–24 (appendix to Justice Powell's opinion).

25 See Alan Dershowitz and Laura Hanft, "Affirmative Action and the Harvard College Diversity-Discretion Model, Paradigm or Pretext?," 1 *Cardozo Law Review* 384, n.15 (1979).

26 Furthermore, the policies and actions of Harvard, a private university, are not considered "state action" and therefore not subject to constitutional scrutiny. Ibid. 385 n.17 (citing *Krohn v. Harvard Law School*, 552 F.2d 21, 25, 1st Cir. 1977).

27 *Regents of the University of Southern California v. Bakke*, 438 U.S. 265, 316 (1978).

28 According to its dean of admissions, Harvard's admission rate for legacy children is around 30 percecnt—more than four times the regular admissions rate. Justin Worland, "Legacy Admit Rate at 30 Percent," *Harvard Crimson*, May 11, 2011. For a critique of this legacy boost, see Daniel Golden, *The Price of Admissions* 21–48 (2006).

29 *Regents of the University of Southern California v. Bakke* 438 U.S. 265, 406 (Blackmun, J., concurring in part).

30 Ibid. 318, n. 53.

31 As my colleagues Henry Louis Gates and Lani Guinier point out: While 8 percent, or 530, of Harvard's college student body is black, two-thirds of them are children of West Indian immigrants or children of biracial couples rather than African-Americans—i.e., descendants of slaves whose families have been historically disadvantaged by the legacy of Jim Crow laws, segregation, poverty, and inferior schools. By contrast, students of West Indian descent are a "highly motivated, self-selected group"—they often come from wealthy areas, went to private schools, have more highly educated and more affluent parents, and, having encountered less discrimination in their upbringing, they are psychologically less disadvantaged by the stigma of race. As Professor Waters, a sociologist at Harvard, observed: "You need a philosophical discussion about what are the aims of affirmative action. . . . If it's about getting black faces at Harvard, then you're doing fine. If it's about making up for 200 to 500 years of slavery in this country and its aftermath, then you're not doing well. And if it's about having diversity that includes African-Americans from the South or from inner-city high schools, then you're not doing well, either." Sara Rimer and Karen W. Arenson, "Top Colleges Take More Blacks, But Which Ones?," *New York Times*, June 24, 2004.

32 For a detailed account how Harvard's quota system was used to exclude Jewish applicants, see Alan Dershowitz and Laura Hanft, "Affirmative Action and the Harvard College Diversity-Discretion Model, Paradigm or Pretext?" 1 *Cardozo Law Review* 387 (1979).

33 The current dean of admissions at Harvard College, William Fitzsimmons, genuinely seeks diversity and has worked hard to recruit inner-city blacks. But at the time of the *Bakke* decision this was not nearly as true.

34 Oliver Wendell Holmes, *The Common Law*, Lecture I: "Early Forms of Liability" (1881).

35 For my evolving views on affirmative action, see also Alan Dershowitz, "Visibility, Accountability, and Discourse as Essential to Democracy," *Albany Law Review* 784–87 (2008).

36 *Grutter v. Bollinger,* 539 U.S. 306, 343 (2003). ("We expect that 25 years from now, the use of racial preferences will no longer be necessary to further the interest approved today.")

37 *Fisher v. University of Texas,* 570 U.S. _ (June 24, 2013). (slip opinion, p. 16).

Chapter 21
The Crumbling Wall Between Church and State

1 U.S. Const., amend. XIV, sec. 1

2 Congress added the words in 1954. Pub.L. 83-396, Chap. 297, 68 Stat. 249, H.J.Res. 243, enacted June 14, 1954.

3 In a public high school in Colorado, some Muslim students substituted the words "one nation under Allah" in the pledge they recited over the loudspeaker. http://www.dailymail.co.uk/news/article-2270944/Rocky-Mountain-High-School-Outrage-high-school-recites-Pledge-Arabic-saying-One-Nation-Under-Allah.html

4 George Washington, *Letter to the Hebrew Congregation in Newport, Rhode Island,* August 1790.

5 Ibid.

6 Most of the words were borrowed by Washington from the letter written to him by the rabbi of the Touro Synagogue. Moses Seixas, *Address to the President from the Hebrew Congregation,* August 17, 1790.

7 According to one historian, the big breakthrough for American Jews came in 1973, when Irving Presser, the son of a Lithuanian-born pants presser, became the chairman and CEO of Du Pont Corporation, then America's largest chemical company and the nation's oldest corporation. Edward S. Shapiro, *A Time for Healing: American Jewry Since World War II* 115 (1995).

8 A turning point came in 1968, with the election of Edward H. Levi, the grandson of rabbis, as the president of the University of Chicago. Edward S. Shapiro, "The Friendly University: Jews in Academia Since World War II," *Judaism: A Quarterly Journal of Jewish Life and Thought* (Summer 1997).

9 See supra, ch. 20.

10 U.S. Const., Art. VI, par. 3.

11 U.S. Const., amend. I. The third reference to religion in the Constitution can be found in the free exercise clause of the First Amendment. Ibid.

12 When these words were written, they had a clear meaning: The *federal* government could not make any particular religion the official national one, though states were free to establish a particular church, as several did. The "incorporation" of the First Amendment to the states via the Fourteenth Amendment applied the establishment clause to the states as well.

13 Alan M. Dershowitz, *America Declares Independence,* 82–84 (2003). Nor would the composer of the original pledge, who was an early socialist. See Greg Beato, "Face the Flag: The Surprising History of the Pledge of Alliance," *Reason,* December 16, 2010.

14 *West Virginia State Board of Education v. Barnette,* 319 U.S. 624, 642 (1943).

15 Chris Chunland, "For Shapiro, Sitting Was an Act of Defiance," *Boston Globe,* December 6, 1984.

16 "Randolph Student Wants Court to Affirm Her Right Not to Join in Allegiance Pledge," *Boston Globe,* April 6, 1985.

17 "Girl Who Wouldn't Stand for Salute Gets Apology," *New York Times,* June 15, 1985.

18 *Teague v. Bakker,* 35 F.3d 978, 982 (4th Cir. 1994).

19 Quoted in *United States v. Bakker,* 925 F.2d 728, 740 (4th Cir. 1991).

20 *United States v. Bakker,* 925 F.2d 728, 740–741 (4th Cir. 1991).

21 Ibid.

22 "Jim Bakker Freed from Jail to Stay in a Halfway House," *New York Times,* July 2, 1994.

23 David Margolick, "At the Bar: Dershowitz Wows 'Em Again! (Is There No Escaping This Guy?)" *New York Times,* February 15, 1991.

24 See, e.g., Noah Feldman, *Divided by God* 22 (2005).

25 According to a 2011 Gallup poll, 49 percent of Americans said that they would not vote for an atheist. Lydia Saad, "In U.S., 22% Are Hesitant to Support a Mormon in 2012," June 20, 2011, available at http://www.gallup.com/poll/148100/Hesitant-Support-Mormon-2012.aspx.

26 Roger Williams, "Mr. Cotton's Letter Lately Printed, Examined and Answered" (1644), in *The Complete Writings of Roger Williams* (Samuel L. Caldwell, ed.) 392 (1963).

27 The irony is that the wall was essentially a contribution made by Baptists to America but is now being attacked by many Baptists.

28 Thomas Jefferson to Roger C. Weightman, June 24, 1826, in *The Life and Selected Writings of Thomas Jefferson* (Adrienne Koch and William Peden, eds.) 666 (1998).

29 Thomas Jefferson, Reply to Danbury Baptist Association, January 1, 1802, in ibid. 307 (emphasis added).

30 T. R. Reid, "Republicans Rue Mecham's Return; Arizonan's Maneuvers Embarrassing National Party Leaders," *Washington Post*, March 14, 1989.

31 Ibid.

32 Quoted in Alan M. Dershowitz, "Justice O'Connor's Second Indiscretion," *New York Times*, April 2, 1989.

33 Ibid.

34 See Alan M. Dershowitz, *Supreme Injustice*, 246 n. 67 (2001). See also Eric M. Yoder, Jr., "Justice O'Connor's Unfortunate Letter," *Washington Post*, March 19, 1989.

35 For such an interpretation of Jefferson's letter, see, e.g., Allen Jayne, *Jefferson's Declaration of Independence: Origins, Philosophy, and Theology* 173 (1998).

36 *Holy Trinity Church v. United States*, 143 U.S. 457, 471 (1892).

37 Actually, recent scholarship suggests that Brewer was not an across-the-board bigot. Some scholars point out that he was involved in the antislavery movement and quite sympathetic to women. See, e.g., J. Gordon Hylton, "The Judge Who Abstained in Plessy v. Ferguson: Justice Brewer and the Problem of Race," 61 *Mississippi Law Journal* 315 (1999).

38 *Zorach v. Clauson*, 343 U.S. 306, 313 (1952).

39 In at least one case, Justice Sutherland said—in passing—that "we are a Christian *people*." But he then quickly added in the same sentence that we are a people who accord "to one another the equal right of religious freedom" (emphasis added). *United States v. Macintosh*, 283 U.S. 605, 625 (1931). Justices Holmes, Brandeis, Stone, and Hughes dissented. Justice O'Connor failed to mention this case.

40 "Justice Regrets Her Letter's Use in 'Christian Nation' Debate," *St. Louis Post-Dispatch*, March 16, 1989.

41 Alan M. Dershowitz, "Justice O'Connor's Second Indiscretion," *New York Times*, April 2, 1989.

42 Walter Mondale, address to B'nai B'rith, Washington, D.C., September 6, 1984.

43 Rick Santorum on ABC's *This Week*, February 26, 2012.

44 Even the term "value voters" used during the last few presidential campaigns suggests that nonreligious or secular voters do not have strong moral values. The fact that this derogatory term is uncritically used not only by the religious right but also by the mainstream media shows how successful those in the religious right have become in turning "secularism" and "humanism" into dirty words. Alan Dershowitz, *Blasphemy* 116–17 (2007).

45 See, e.g., Leviticus 18:22. Interestingly enough, the story of Sodom and Gomorrah, though in many aspects the most obvious passage dealing with homosexuality, has not been interpreted by Jewish and Christian theologians as being about sexual sins but rather as being about inhospitality. John Boswell, *Christianity, Social Tolerance, and Homosexuality* 93 (2005).

46 The phrase is from the song "Carefully Taught," in Richard Rodgers, Oscar Hammerstein, Joshua Logan, and James Albert Michener, *Rodgers and Hammerstein's South Pacific* 77 (1956).

47 *Bowers v. Hardwick*, 478 U.S. 186 (1986).

48 Id, at 197.

49 *Goodridge v. Dep't of Pub. Health*, 440 Mass. 309 (2003).

50 Alan M. Dershowitz, "To Fix Gay Dilemma, Government Should Quit the Marriage Business," *Los Angeles Times*, December 3, 2003.

51 If a woman wants to carry her fetus to term, and someone deliberately aborts it, say by kicking her in the stomach, that should be a serious crime akin to murder.

52 Alan Dershowitz, *Rights from Wrongs* 169–70 (2005).

53 *Catechism of the Catholic Church*, 2265–67 (1997).

54 531 U.S. 98 (2000).

55 Alan M. Dershowitz, *Supreme Injustice* (2001).

56 Ibid. 191.

57 Ibid. 194.

58 *Roe v. Wade*, 410 U.S. 113 (1973).

59 ACLU Position Paper, *The Right to Choose: A Fundamental Liberty* (fall 2000), available at http://www.aclu.org/FilesPDFs/ACF4E49.pdf.

60 Ibid.

61 See, e.g., David Lauter and Douglas Jehl, "Parties Seek Abortion Issue's Middle Ground," *Los Angeles Times*, July 26, 1992, stating that Bush was pro-choice until 1980, when he switched sides and became Reagan's running mate.

62 Whether the same is true of the debate over capital punishment is a more complex issue, because of the unfairness and inequality in administering the death penalty. See supra, chapter 13.

63 Alan M. Dershowitz, *Supreme Injustice* 192–95 (2001).

64 Thomas Jefferson, The Virginia Act for Establishing Religious Freedom (1786).

Chapter 22
From Human Rights to Human Wrongs

1 *The Universal Declaration of Human Rights* (1948).

2 Franklin D. Roosevelt, "State of the Union (Four Freedoms), January 6, 1941," in *FDR: Selected Speeches of President D. Roosevelt* 135 (2010).

3 U.N. General Assembly Resolution 181 (II), A/RES/181(II), Nov. 27, 1947.

4 Joseph P. Lash, "Calendar Reform Tops Formosa Issue in Letter to U.N.," *New York Post*, April 21, 1955, p. 34, quoting a U.S. note to Secretary General Dag Hammarskjöld.

5 Ibid.

6 I also explored the concept of animal rights. See Alan Dershowitz, *Rights from Wrongs* 193–99 (2005).

7 Alan M. Dershowitz, *Chutzpah* 231 (1991).

8 See supra p. 187.

9 Pirkei Avot 1:14.

10 "400 Enroll in a Harvard Course on 'Law and the Lawyer' in the Vietnam War," *New York Times*, February 18, 1968.

11 "Student Lawyers & Viet Nam," *Time*, March 1, 1968.

12 Ellen J. Miller, "Global Watchdog," *Harvard Law School Bulletin*, summer 1978, 24–28.

13 Ibid. 24–25.

14 Ibid. 26.

15 Ibid., at 28.

16 Elie Wiesel, *The Jews of Silence* (1966).

17 Alan M. Dershowitz, "Nobel Laureate Works for Peace," *Boston Herald*, December 8, 1992.

18 See *The Best Defense*, chapter 7 (1983); *Chutzpah*, chapter 8 (1991); Telford Taylor (with Alan Dershowitz, George Fletcher, Leon Lipson, and Melvin Stein), *Courts of Terror* (1976).

19 American Booksellers Foundation for Free Expression, *Performers, Artists and Authors for Free Expression*, Carnegie Hall, New York, May 31, 1991.

20 Tomorrow: The Israel Presidential Conference 2008, ICC International Convention Center, Jerusalem, May 13–15, 2008.

21 Elizabeth S. Landis, "South African Apartheid Legislation I: Fundamental Structure," 71 *Yale Law Journal* 1 (1961); Elizabeth S. Landis, "South African Apartheid Legislation II: Extension, Enforcement and Perpetuation," 71 *Yale Law Journal* 437 (1962).

22 Alan M. Dershowitz, "Look Who's Blacklisting Now," February 22, 1985, reprinted in Alan M. Dershowitz, *Taking Liberties* 94–96 (1988).

23 Allen's film *The Front* (Columbia Pictures, 1976) dealt critically with blacklisting.

24 Alan M. Dershowitz, "Preventive Detention of Citizens During a National Emergency: A Comparison Between Israel and the United States," 1 *Israel Yearbook of Human Rights* 295 (1971).

25 For my early criticism of the settlements, see, e.g., "Dershowitz Calls for Mideast Peace: 'Israel Should Give Up Arab Land,'" *Harvard Crimson*, March 20, 1974.

26 See, e.g., Jennifer Mishory, "Dershowitz Shifts Focus to World Outside Israel," *Daily Bruin*, November 8, 2006.

27 An old Soviet dissident joke went this way: The leader of Czechoslovakia asked his Soviet masters for money for a Department of the Navy. The Soviet replied, "But you're a landlocked country and don't need a Department of the Navy." The Czech leader replied: "Well, you have a Department of Justice."

28 See, e.g., Noam Chomsky, "If Nuremberg Laws Were Applied" (delivered around 1990), available at http://www.chomsky.info/talks/1990----.htm

29 Daniel Berrigan, *Address to the Association of Arab-American University Graduates*, Washington, D.C., October 19, 1973.

30 See, e.g., Edward S. Herman and Noam Chomsky, *After the Cataclysm* 138–39 (1979). In his unmatched hatred against America and his penchant to defend the most violent dictators, Chomsky also asserted that "it seems fair to describe the responsibility of the United States and Pol Pot for atrocities during the 'decade of genocide' as being roughly in the same range." Edward S. Herman and Noam Chomsky, *Manufacturing Consent* 264–65 (1994). Along similar lines, Chomsky praised the Khmer Rouge regime by asserting that "at the end of 1978 Cambodia [under the Khmer Rouge] was the only country in Indochina that had succeeded at all in overcoming the agricultural crisis that was left by the American destruction." Noam Chomsky, *Language and Politics* 245–46 (2004). Edward S. Herman and Noam Chomsky, *After the Cataclysm* 160 (1979).

31 Alan Dershowitz, "Can the Guild Survive Its Hypocrisy?," *American Lawyer*, August 11, 1978.

32 As George Conk, an admiring guild historian and a former editor of the monthly *Guild Notes*, described it: "At the Boulder [Colorado] convention in 1971, the young veterans of the antiwar move-

ment found they had the Guild in their own hands, and many older members withdrew from active membership."

33 Daniel Berrigan, *Address to the Association of Arab-American University Graduates,* Washington, D.C. October 19, 1973.

34 Ibid.

35 "Special Report, The Malpractice of the National Lawyers Guild," 2 *Moment* 10, 10 (October 1, 1977).

36 Ibid.

37 Alan M. Dershowitz, "Can the Guild Survive Its Hypocrisy?," *American Lawyer,* August 11, 1978.

38 Alan M. Dershowitz, "What Are They Watching?," *New York Sun,* August 23, 2006. See also Robert L. Bernstein, "Rights Watchdog, Lost in the Mideast," *New York Times,* October 20, 2009.

39 See, e.g., Alan M. Dershowitz, "Amnesty International's Biased Definition of War Crimes: Whatever Israel Does to Defend Its Citizens," *Huffington Post,* August 29, 2006; Alan M. Dershowitz, "The 'Human Rights Watch' Watch, Installment 1," *Huffington Post,* August 21, 2006; Alan M. Dershowitz, *The Case Against Israel's Eemies* 33–34 (2008).

40 United Nations Security Council Resolution 242 (S/RES/242).

41 As the historian Benny Morris explained, this formulation was intended "to convert [Israel's] stunning military victory into a political achievement: the conquered territories could be traded for peace." Benny Morris, *Righteous Victims* 328 (2001).

42 Fourth Arab Summit Conference, *The Khartoum Resolutions,* September 1, 1967.

43 Abba Eban, "Israel's Dilemmas: An Opportunity Squandered," in Stephen J. Roth (ed.), *The Impact of the Six-Day War: A Twenty-Year Assessment* 25 (1988). See also Alan M. Dershowitz, *The Case for Israel* 205 (2004).

44 Tvuia Saa, "An Ignored Country," *New York Times,* December 1, 1977.

45 The record of the UN Commission on Human Rights (UNCHR) on the matter is much the same. In March 1978 the United Kingdom petitioned the UNCHR to appoint a special rappourteur for human rights in Cambodia. Syria, the Soviet Union, and Yugoslavia blocked the move. Instead of appointing a rappourteur, the commission invited comment by the Khmer Rouge, referred the matter to a subcommittee, and (despite the ongoing genocide) delayed consideration of the matter until 1979. By the 1979 meeting of the commission, Vietnam had already invaded Cambodia and effectively ended the killings. Yet again, however, the commission delayed consideration of the Cambodia matter. Only in 1980, nearly five years after the atrocities began, did the UNCHR finally pass a resolution condemning the genocide.

46 A/RES/337 Elements of All Forms of Racial Discrimination (Nov. 10, 1975).

47 Quoted in Alan M. Dershowitz, *Chutzpah* 224 (1991).

48 Quoted in Paul Hofmann, "U.N. Votes 72–35, to Term Zionism Form of Racism," *New York Times,* November 11, 1975.

49 A/RES/46/86 (Dec. 16, 1991).

50 The conference was authorized by UN Resolution A/RES/52/111 (Feb. 18, 1998).

51 The United States Holocaust Memorial Museum, *Voices on Anti-Semitism* podcast series, June 5, 2008, transcript available at http://www.ushmm.org/museum/exhibit/focus/antisemitism/voices/transcript/?content=20080605.

52 Even the UN high commissioner for human rights—Mary Robinson, no friend of Israel—was appalled at what she was witnessing. The Arab Lawyers Union distributed a booklet of anti-Semitic cartoons that could have been published by *Der Stürmer.* The *Jerusalem Post* reported Robinson's reaction:

> *Waving a book of anti-Semitic cartoons distributed at the anti-racism conference in Durban, UN High Commissioner Mary Robinson—in a dramatic act of identification with the Jews vilified in the pamphlet—declared "I am a Jew" at an NGO dinner there Wednesday night. (Herb Keinon and Janine Zacharia, "Robinson in Durban: I Am a Jew,"* Jerusalem Post, *August* 30, 2001.*)*

53 Tom Lantos, "The Durban Debacle: An Insider's View of the UN World Conference Against Racism," 26 *Fletcher Forum of World Affairs* 1, 7 (winter/spring 2002).

54 AFP News Agency, April 20, 2009.

55 *The Perils of Global Intolerance: The United Nations and Durban III,* New York, September 22, 2011. A video of my speech is available at http://www.pjtv.com/?cmd=mpg&mpid=457&load=6057.

56 In March 2013, the Muslim Brotherhood issued a statement in which it ordered women "to be confined within a framework that is controlled by the man of the house." It forbade married women to "file legal complaints against their husbands for rape" and "required the husband's consent in matters such as travel, work or contraception." David Kirkpatrick and Mayy El Sheikh, "Muslim Brotherhood Statement on Women Stirs Liberals' Fear," *New York Times,* March 14, 2013. Such sexism is pervasive in

numerous Muslim countries, like Saudi Arabia, Egypt, the Gaza Strip, and Iran. Yet at the same time, "the U.N.'s top women's rights body [condemned] only one state for violating the rights of women anywhere in the world"—Israel. Anne Bayefsky, "'Human Rights' Are a Weapon in the Political Arsenal of Israel's Enemies," *Human Rights Voices*, March 18, 2013.

57 I've elaborated on the "worst first principle" before in the context of the International Criminal Court, which, to its credit, has not failed this test yet. See Alan M. Dershowitz, "For the International Criminal Court to Work, the Worst Must Come First," *Huffington Post*, February 10, 2009.

58 Exodus 1:8–10. ("Then a new king, to whom Joseph meant nothing, came to power in Egypt. 'Look,' he said to his people, 'the Israelites have become far too numerous for us. Come, we must deal shrewdly with them or they will become even more numerous and, if war breaks out, will join our enemies, fight against us and leave the country.'") Book of Esther.

59 *UN Watch Report: UN, Israel & Anti-Semitism*, available at http://www.unwatch.org/site/c.bdKKISNqEmG/b.1359197/k.6748/UN_Israel__AntiSemitism.htm.

Conclusion

1 Yiddish corruption of the Hebrew for "evil eye."

2 *Zelig* (Orion Pictures, Warner Bros., 1983).

3 Oliver Wendell Holmes, "The Path of the Law," 10 *Harvard Law Review* 457 (1897).

4 Babylonian Talmud: Tractate Baba Bathra, 12b.

5 It is not clear who [actually] coined this bon mot. Besides Berra, the physicist Niels Bohr is often credited with it, as are Samuel Goldwyn and Mark Twain. See David Katzenberg, *All Things Considered*, National Public Radio, April 7, 2000.

6 As is frequently the case, the discussion in class inspired me to write an article. Alan M. Dershowitz, "Is Paterno Getting a Bum Rap?" *Huffington Post*, November 18, 2011, http://www.huffingtonpost.com/alan-dershowitz/is-paterno-getting-a-bum-_b_1101933.html.

7 Evan M. Wiener, *Captors* (2011).

8 *Crazy, Stupid, Love* (Warner Bros., 2011).

9 William Shakespeare, *The Tempest*, Act 2, Scene 1.

10 Though not the Political Science Department, in which I majored. See Alan M. Dershowitz, "Brooklyn College Political Science Department's Israel Problem," *Huffington Post*, January 30, 2013; Alan M. Dershowitz, "Does Brooklyn College Pass the Shoe on the Other Foot Test?" *Huffington Post*, February 1, 2013; Alan M. Dershowitz, "Did Brooklyn College's Political Science Department Violate the First Amendment?" *Huffington Post*, February 12, 2013.

11 René Descartes, *Principles of Philosophy*, Part 1, Art. 7 (1644).

12 Alan M. Dershowitz, *The Best Defense* (1983).

13 Alan M. Dershowitz, *Chutzpah* (1991).

14 Ibid. 353.

15 I wrote about this ugly encounter in Alan M. Dershowitz, "Hatred at Faneuil Hall," *Jerusalem Post*, March 21, 2004.

16 Phyllis Chesler and Nancy Kobrin, "Psychological Roots of Islamic Rage," *Jewish Press*, August 9, 2006.

17 Alan Dershowitz, *The Case for Israel* (2003). I eventually wrote *The Case for Peace* in 2005.

18 Kasim Hafeez, "From Antisemite to Zionist," *Jewish Chronicle*, October 7, 2011.

19 Ibid.

20 Jenni Frazer, "Fertile Mind," interview with Dame Ruth Deech, *Jewish Chronicle*, April 22, 2005.

21 *Jewish Daily Forward* 50, 2007, available at http://forward.com/forward-50-2007/.

22 "Activism," *Jewish Daily Forward*, November 14, 2003.

23 See Alan M. Dershowitz, "The Brooklyn College BDS Debate and Me: The Critics' Real Agenda," *Guardian*, February 8, 2013.

24 Democracy Now, April 17, 2007.

25 "How Obama Legitimated Torture," February 19, 2013, blog.

26 See, e.g., Andrew G. Bostom, "The Unbearable Lightness of Alan Dershowitz," *The American Thinker*, May 1, 2013; Alan M. Dershowitz, "Jews Who Boo Efforts to Make Peace," *Jerusalem Post*, May 5, 2013.

27 Today, the approval rating of the high court is at the lowest in decades. Adam Liptak and Allison Kopicki, "Approval Rating for Supreme Court Hits Just 44% in Poll," *New York Times*, June 7, 2012.

28 For the original understanding of the court's authority, see, e.g., Akhil Reed Amar, *America's Constitution: A Biography* 209 (2005).

29 *The Federalist Papers* 78 (A. Hamilton) 464 (C. Rossiter, ed., 2003).

30 531 U.S. 98 (2000).

31 *Citizens United v. Federal Election Commission,* 558 U.S. 50 (2010). For an excellent discussion of the behind-the-scenes struggles among the justices leading up to the Citizens United decision, see Jeffrey Toobin, "How John Roberts Orchestrated Citizens United," *New Yorker,* May 21, 2012. Three of the four dissenters in *Bush v. Gore* were appointed by Democratic presidents. The fourth, Justice Stevens, was appointed by a moderate Republican, Gerald Ford, at the recommendation of his Democratic attorney general, Edward Levy.

32 See also Ronald Dworkin, *The Supreme Court Phalanx* (2008). In his decision upholding the Obama health care law, Chief Justice Roberts sought to balance a desire to preserve the integrity of the high court against his views regarding the commerce and taxing clauses of the Constitution. See Alan M. Dershowitz, "The Health Care Decision Is Good in the Short Term, Questionable in the Long Term," *Newsmax,* June, 28, 2012.

33 *Brown v. Allen,* 344 U.S. 443, 540 (1953).

34 As the *New York Times* reports, several former partners of the now defunct firm of Dewey & LeBoeuf have asked a judge to reject the bankruptcy plan that the firm had proposed on the grounds that the plan "was designed and conceived to perpetrate a fraud on the firm's former partners." The article also cites a former partner who claims that the firm, which at one time employed more than fourteen hundred lawyers in twenty-six offices worldwide, owed him $38 million in compensation. Peter Lattman, "Several Former Partners Ask Judge to Overturn Dewey's Bankruptcy Plan," *New York Times,* February 16, 2013.

See also Peter Lattman, "With a Judge's Decision, Dewey Is Officially Dissoved," *New York Times,* February 28, 2013

35 As I write these words, the *New York Times* reports that the American Bar Association's Task Force on the Future of Legal Education is considering the establishment of the legal equivalent of nurse practitioners. Ethan Bronner, "Lawyers Call for Drastic Changes in Educating New Lawyers," *New York Times,* February 10, 2013.

36 As Professor Tamanaha notes in a recent blog spot, "From 1985 through 2009, resident tuition at public law schools increased by a staggering 820 percent—from $2,006 to $18,472 (non-resident tuition increased by 543 percent, from $4,724 to $30,413)—while tuition at private law schools went up by 375 percent—from $7,526 to $35,743. These increases far outstripped the rate of inflation. Had tuition merely kept pace with inflation, average resident tuition at public law schools today would be $3,945, less than a fourth of what it is, and average private school tuition would be $14,800, less than half of what it is. Law school would still be affordable if law schools had not extracted such a large premium over inflation." Professor Tamanaha goes on to examine the tuition fees at Yale Law School, which are roughly the same as Harvard's: "Tuition at Yale Law School was $12,450 in 1987; in 1999 it was $26,950; in 2011 it was $50,750—an increase of nearly $24,000 in just the last dozen years. Factoring in projected living expenses ($18,900), Yale students without scholarships (half of the class) who commenced their legal studies in 2010 will pay more than $200,000 to obtain their law degree. If the recent rate of increase continues, ten years hence tuition at Yale Law School will exceed $70,000 annually. That might sound impossible, but ten years ago many would have scoffed at the suggestion that the tuition at Yale would be $50,000 today." Brian Tamanaha, "The Responsibility of Yale Law School for the Rise of Tuition Nationwide—And What to Do to Help," *Balkanization,* November 21, 2011, available at http://balkin.blogspot.com/2011/11/responsibility-of-yale-law-school-for.html.

37 Ethan Bronner, "Law Schools' Applications Fall as Costs Rise and Jobs Are Cut," *New York Times,* January 30, 2013.

38 Ibid.

39 Peter Lattman, "N.Y.U. Law Plans Overhaul of Students' Third Year," *New York Times,* October 17, 2012. The article also states correctly that the "traditional third year of study is largely filled by elective courses. While classes like 'Nietzsche and the Law' and 'Voting, Game Theory and the Law' might be intellectually broadening, law schools and their students are beginning to question whether, at $51,150 a year, a hodgepodge of electives provides sufficient value."

40 Erich Segal, *The Class* 513 (1986)

INDEX